Regency Edition

JOE M. PULLIS, Ed.D.

Professor, Department of Office Administration
and Business Communication
College of Administration and Business
Louisiana Tech University

GLENCOE PUBLISHING COMPANY
Mission Hills, California

*Speedwriting Shorthand
Dictation and Transcription

Linda Bippen
Lesson/Exercise Writer

Cheryl D. Pullis, M. Ed.
System Consultant

Jordan Hale
Betty White
Contributors

Calligraphy: Juana Silcox
Cover and interior design: Harkavy Publishing Services/Levavi & Levavi
System editors: Karl C. Illg, Jr., and John Gastineau
Typesetter: Compolith Graphics
Printer: R. R. Donnelley and Sons Company

Send all inquiries to:
Glencoe Publishing Company
15319 Chatsworth Street
Mission Hills, CA 91345

Printed in the United States of America

Library of Congress Cataloging in Publication Data

Pullis, Joe M.
Speedwriting shorthand dictation and transcription
1. Shorthand—Speedwriting. I. Title.
Z56.2.S6P845 1984 653'.2 84-6414
ISBN 0-02-679590-6

3 4 5 6 90 89 88 87

CONTENTS

SETTING YOUR GOALS

Now that you have completed your study of the *Principles of Speedwriting Shorthand, Regency Edition,* you are ready to continue developing your shorthand skills. Before beginning the study of *Speedwriting Shorthand Dictation and Transcription,* ask yourself these questions. What do I expect from this course? How can I improve my skills?

You should establish meaningful goals for yourself. Although speed building is excellent training, recording dictation is only one part of the shorthand process. Refining your English usage skills and knowing how to keyboard, spell, and punctuate correctly are also important. Remember that the primary purpose of dictation is to generate top-quality correspondence. Once a letter has been dictated to you, it is up to you to convert your notes into an impressive, mailable transcript that reflects well on you and your employer.

Guidelines for using the text are presented in this introduction. By using proper study habits from the beginning, you will be able to develop various skills simultaneously. This text is designed to help you

1. increase your shorthand writing speed
2. improve your transcribing efficiency
3. increase your shorthand vocabulary
4. increase your knowledge of business terms
5. improve your spelling ability
6. improve your punctuation skills
7. increase your knowledge of keyboarding and formatting techniques
8. increase your knowledge of office procedures

Knowing the Structure of the Text

The text is divided into 12 units. The dictation material in each unit concerns a specific field, such as "Information Processing" or "Real Estate." The subject matter will help broaden your knowledge of terms and procedures related to these 12 areas. The five lessons in each unit represent a combination of skill-building information and exercises.

Each unit begins with a review of one or more *Speedwriting Shorthand* principles. Shorthand vocabulary words that illustrate the principle or principles are selected from the letters and memos presented in the unit. Also, in the opening section of each unit, punctuation rules are given and are illustrated with example sentences. Punctuation usage is reinforced in the letters and memos that follow, and frequently used rules of punctuation are highlighted in the reading and writing exercises.

Speedwriting Shorthand principles and specific applications of the system are reviewed in each lesson, as follows:

Theory Review. The first lesson of each unit contains a brief form and phrase review; the second lesson, an abbreviation review; the third and fourth lessons, a shorthand vocabulary review; and the fifth lesson, word development.

Transcription Aids. Transcription aids such as English usage and formatting procedures, similar words, and spelling are provided in the second, third, and fourth lessons, respectively, in each unit.

Your Business Vocabulary. Business terms that appear in the dictation material are defined and illustrated with example sentences.

Reading and Writing Exercises. A combination of five letters and memos is presented in each lesson. The fifth letter or memo of each lesson includes a punctuation exercise in which you will provide commas that have been omitted from the shorthand copy in the text. Numbers indicating the typing words for each line of shorthand have been provided for determining your transcription speed.

Beginning in Lesson 52, the fourth letter in each lesson includes an exercise in supplying missing shorthand outlines. You will be asked to provide an acceptable word for each of the two outlines that have been omitted from the shorthand copy.

Using Your Text

Prepare for each lesson carefully:

1. Read and write the example outlines in the *Shorthand Vocabulary Review* sections.
2. Study the concepts presented in the *Transcription Aids* and *Your Business Vocabulary* sections.
3. Study the punctuation drills. Think about each rule and how it is applied in the letters and memos that follow.
4. Read all shorthand (aloud, if possible) before writing it. If you cannot identify a particular outline, sound-spell the outline. If the translation is not readily apparent, continue reading to the end of the sentence. If the context of the sentence does not help you to read the outline, turn to the printed key at the end of the lesson.
5. Now write your shorthand copy as rapidly as possible, being careful to write correctly. Speed is important, but legibility is essential.
6. Read your notes aloud. If you are called upon later to read your notes in class, your reading fluency will be enhanced by your previous practice.

Reviewing Punctuation Rules

In *Principles of Speedwriting Shorthand, Regency Edition,* you studied eight rules of punctuation commonly used in business correspondence. These rules are also highlighted in the reading and writing exercises presented in *Speedwriting Shorthand Dictation and Transcription.* Review these rules thoroughly before proceeding.

Use commas between three or more words in a series. The last word in a series will be preceded by either of these two words: *and, or.* In this text, we will always place a comma before *and* and *or* in a series. Some offices, however, may prefer that this comma be omitted. Use the style preferred in your office.

An agenda will be written, typed, and distributed in advance of the meeting.
Would you prefer to pay the bill with cash, with a check, or with a credit card?

Use commas after introductory dependent clauses. An introductory dependent clause is a group of words containing a subject and a verb that occurs at the beginning of a sentence. However, this clause is not a complete thought and cannot stand alone. It requires a main (independent) clause to make the sentence complete.

Introductory dependent clauses usually begin with recognizable words. The most common words are *when, as,* and *if.* Other common examples are *although, though, unless, since, while, until, before, whether,* and *because.*

When the contract arrives, I will sign and return your copy immediately.
As Cynthia read the revised report, she noted the recent modifications.
If you mail the forms today, Mr. Harris should receive them by Friday.

Use commas with nouns of direct address. A direct address is a specific reference to a person's name, title, and/or other designation. When the direct address occurs in the middle of the sentence, place a comma before and after it. If the direct address occurs at the beginning or at the end of the sentence, use only one comma.

I would be delighted, Senator Walker, to join your committee.
We would greatly appreciate your help, Mrs. Cunningham.

Use commas with appositives. An appositive is a word or group of words that explains, renames, or identifies someone or something that immediately precedes it in the sentence. Appositives are usually set off by commas from the rest of the sentence.

My assistant, Allen Colvin, will meet you at the airport.
I enjoyed reading Mrs. Cooper's new book, *Today's Office.*

Use commas with parenthetical expressions. A parenthetical expression is a word or group of words that interrupts the natural flow of the sentence. These expressions are often used to add emphasis or show contrast, but when removed from the sentence, they do not change the meaning of the sentence.

When a parenthetical expression occurs in the middle of the sentence, place a comma before and after it. If the expression occurs at the beginning or the end of the sentence, use only one comma. Some common examples of parenthetical expressions are *for example, therefore, however, furthermore, of course,* and *in fact.*

We did, in fact, ship the order as requested.
Furthermore, Mr. Morrison did not indicate the time of his arrival.

Use a comma to set off dates in sentences. When naming a day of the week, followed by the date, place a comma after the day of the week and the date. If the date falls at the end of the sentence, place a comma only after the day of the week.

I will arrive on Tuesday, March 7, at approximately 10 a.m.
Please return the enclosed form by Friday, July 1.

Use a comma before coordinate conjunctions. When two complete thoughts are connected by the conjunction *and, or, but, for,* or *nor,* place a comma before the conjunction. Make certain that the conjunction is connecting two complete thoughts—that is, either thought can stand alone without the rest of the sentence.

The order was placed on Thursday afternoon, and the shipment left our warehouse on the following afternoon.
We received your check, but the order form was not enclosed in your letter.

Use commas with introductory phrases. Place a comma after an introductory infinitive phrase (a verb preceded by *to*).

To ensure completion of the project, we are reassigning responsibilities.

Place a comma after an introductory participial phrase (a verb form used as an adjective).

Taking care to avoid errors, we will produce the report as quickly as possible.

Place a comma after an introductory prepositional phrase consisting of five or more words, after introductory phrases containing more than one preposition, or after an introductory prepositional phrase containing a verb form.

In agreement with the terms of the contract, we will deliver the first shipment at no additional charge.

After talking with Mrs. Irwin, I am convinced that we should proceed with our plan.

unl 1

pm*

Shorthand Vocabulary Review

The following words will occur in the letters and memos in this unit. Read the principles and practice the words before beginning your study of this unit.

1. Write B for the word endings *bil, ble* (bul), or *bly*.

capable	cpB	comfortable	kflB
available	avlB	dependable	dpNB
possible	psB	eligible	eljB
responsible	rspB	favorable	fvrB
responsibility	rspBL	reliable	rliB

*Unit One
Employment

2. Write  for the sound of *st* (pronounced *est*).

best		tests	
justify		store	
outstanding		assistance	
Boston		finest	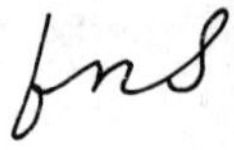
staff		request	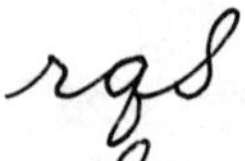
understand		system	

LESSON 1

Brief Forms and Derivatives

Brief forms and abbreviations are used to develop hundreds of new words called **derivatives**. Review the examples below before beginning the reading and writing exercises.

1. *v d · z l u p bs*
2. *O L du la f o kp ks*
3. *apo δι ap- prs rfN ogsl*

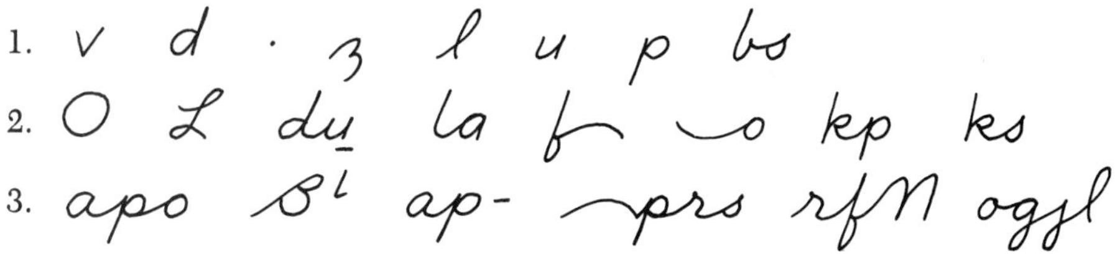

Key

1. of/have/very, would, a/an, as/was, will/well, your, please/up, business
2. over, letter, during, that, from, work/world, complete, consider
3. appropriate, ability, appreciated, employers, reference, organizational

Phrase Review

1. *ɩd ɩvh ɩ ɩhp ɩblv ɩcb*
2. *er ev edlc el ec*
3. *ur uc ul Lrc f ʌ*

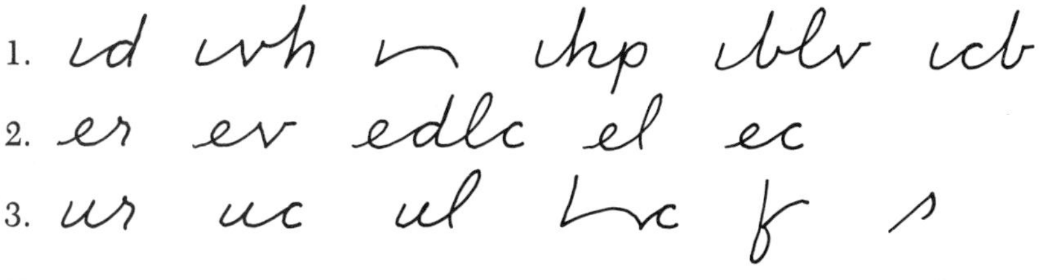

Key

1. I would, I have had, I am, I hope, I believe, I can be
2. we are, we have, we would like, we will, we can
3. you are, you can, you will, to make, for the, it is

Reading and Writing Exercises

The following letters contain many brief forms and commonly used business words. Before beginning each letter, practice the preview words. Then see how quickly you can read and write the letter.

---------------------------- **1** ----------------------------

Preview Words

resumé *rz⁀a*   career *crs*

helpful *hlpf*   interest *NS*

guidance *gdN*   education *ejcj*

justify *jSf*   forward *fw*

d⁀rs rjrs rsNl	*rcmy f⁀ u db v*
ι kp‐ ⁀u crss n	*hlpf n fM ⁀u*
bs ejcj + ⁀ no	*frS jb, ⁀a ιp*
lc fw ι· crs	*lS u m⁀z· rfN*
n ofs ⁀o, ι ⁀+	*o ⁀u rz⁀a×› w*
ι Uι u laι esp	*ap‐ u gdN O⁀lS*
njy‐ u crss n	*2 yrs⦾ + yfl la* [Conj]
lp + srlhN⦾ + [Conj]	*⁀ l Ppr‐ l ac*
ι lrn‐ ⁀C f⁀	*· pzj z sec‚ ιl*
⁀ clss u U› bcz	*du ⁀ι bS l jSf*
⁀S v ⁀u ofs lrn	*⁀ NS uv Sn n*
hs ocr‐ U u dry⦾· [Intro DC]	*⁀e, s*

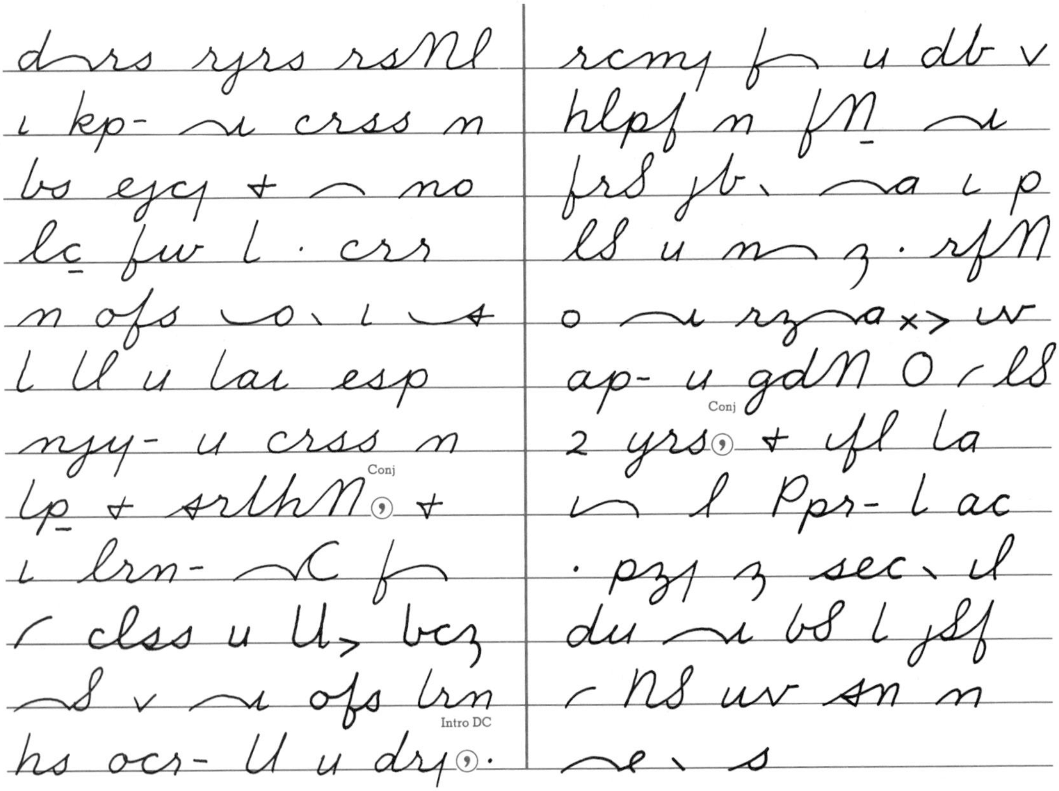

2

Preview Words

West	W	inquiry	nqe
routine	rln	interview	Nvu
answers	asrs	therefore	lrf
Jennifer	jnfr	willingness	l'

d—rs ryrs er ks
l vu SdNs, jnfr
W, f pzj v cor
sec, se rsv—.
hi rq o bo (
srlhN + lp lls,
+ se Aso —d.
fvrB —pzj du
hr Nvu, (Psn e
hr —S Pds. lrj
vol v cor dl, n
. fu css, ls Psn

l Aso b rspB f
ri asrs l rln
Ls v nqe, lrf,
er lc f . Psn hu
, dpNB, uzs q
jym, + sos . l'
l as— rspB',
d u rcm jnfr f
. pzj rq lz ql ls x>
edap rsv u rpli
—n l —c n od
Lc r dsj, vlu

3

Preview Words

result	rzlt	accounting	ak
data	dla	appointment	apym
described	dS-	expansion	vpnj
placement	plsm	extensive	xNv

d r Jsn lqf L
v aplcj, ev A
ncrj- (plsm ofs
vu clj l rf q SdNs
l s, z . rzlt, (Paren) ev
me fn pes f u
scl> z pl vr crN
vpnj, (Intro P) el sn opn .
nu Sr donton, /
la L el vr sNrl
ofss l la lcj, ev
plns l ncrs Psnl
n sv dpls, bcz
vu xNv bcgroN n
dla Pss + ak, (Intro P) u
u qlf f s v
nu pzjs er dv,
(o vp dS- n u
L u Aso b apo
f r cr dpl> u sug
lae Dcs lz opls
n Psn, if ud cl
u ofs f . apym, (Intro DC)
ucd ar l e u
1 d nx c, uvl

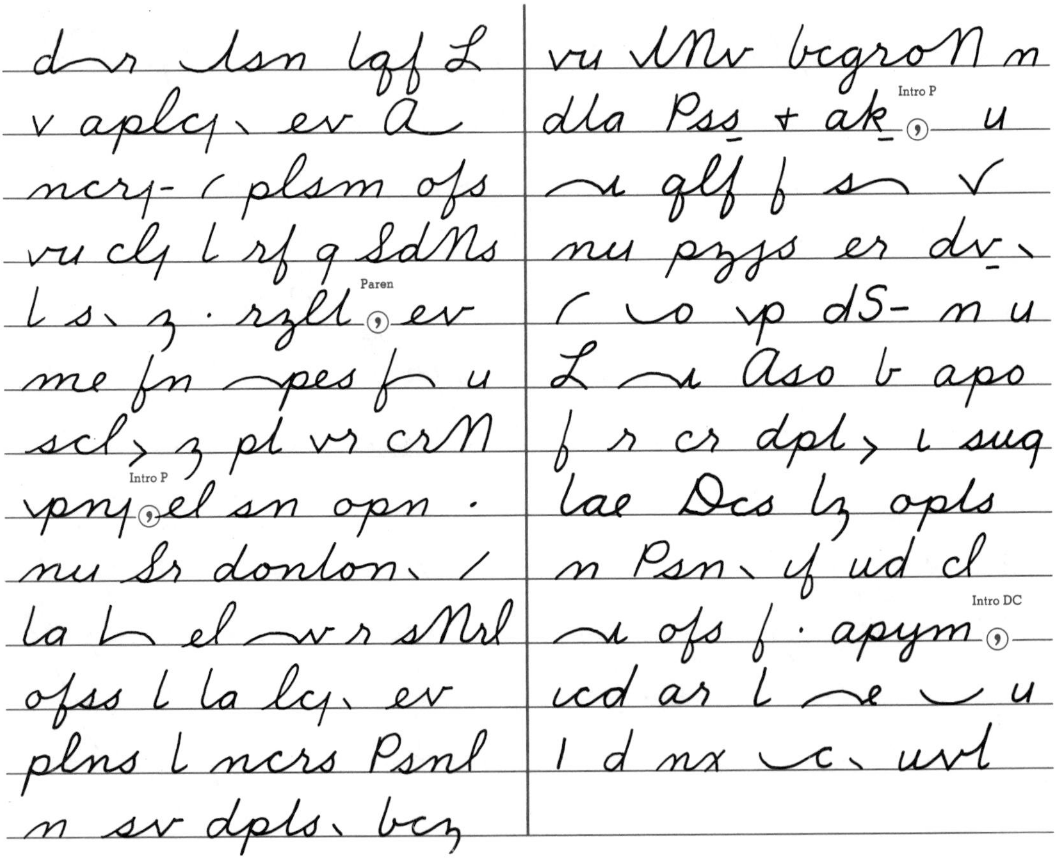

4

Preview Words

minds	ms	Jerry	jre
reward	rw	pleasure	plzr
Fields	flds	exceptional	vpjl
quickly	gcl	independently	NpNNl

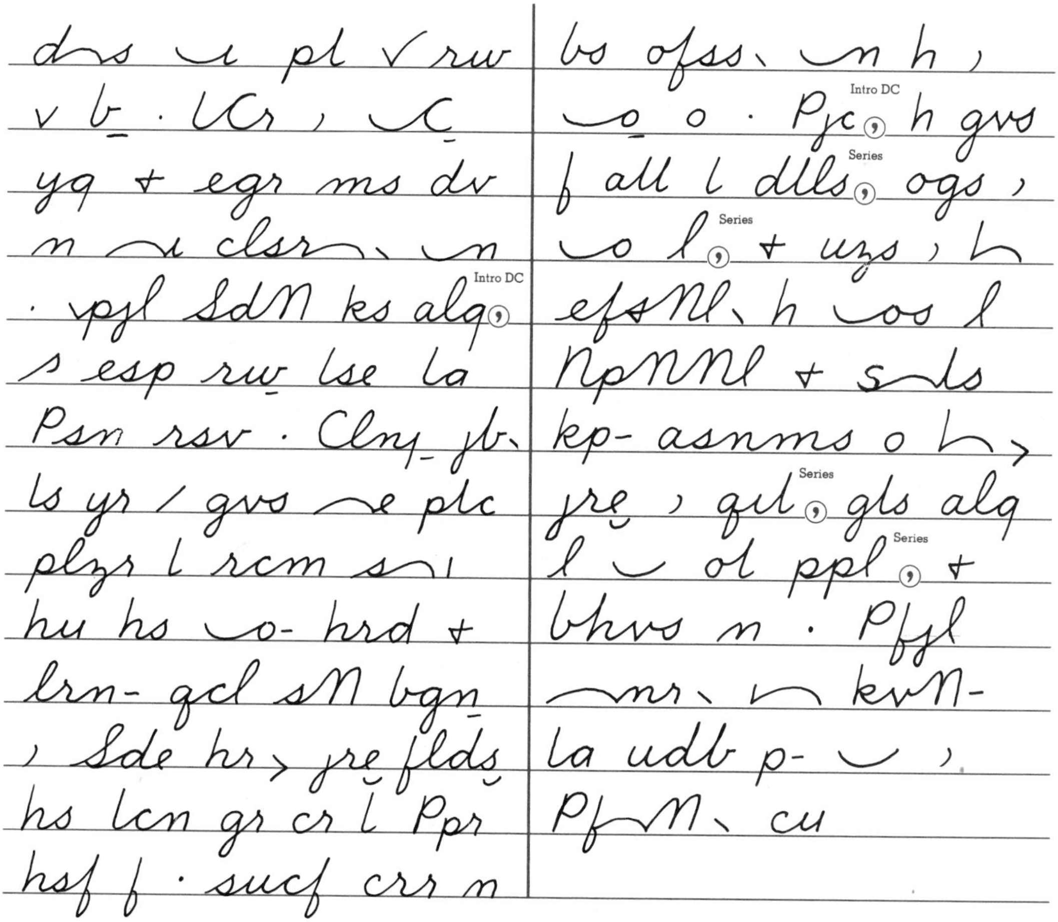

5

Punctuation Study

Four commas are missing from the following letter. Read the letter for meaning, then place a comma after the two introductory dependent clauses and after the words in a series.

Preview Words

image	document
things	academic
succeed	attractive
logical	dependability

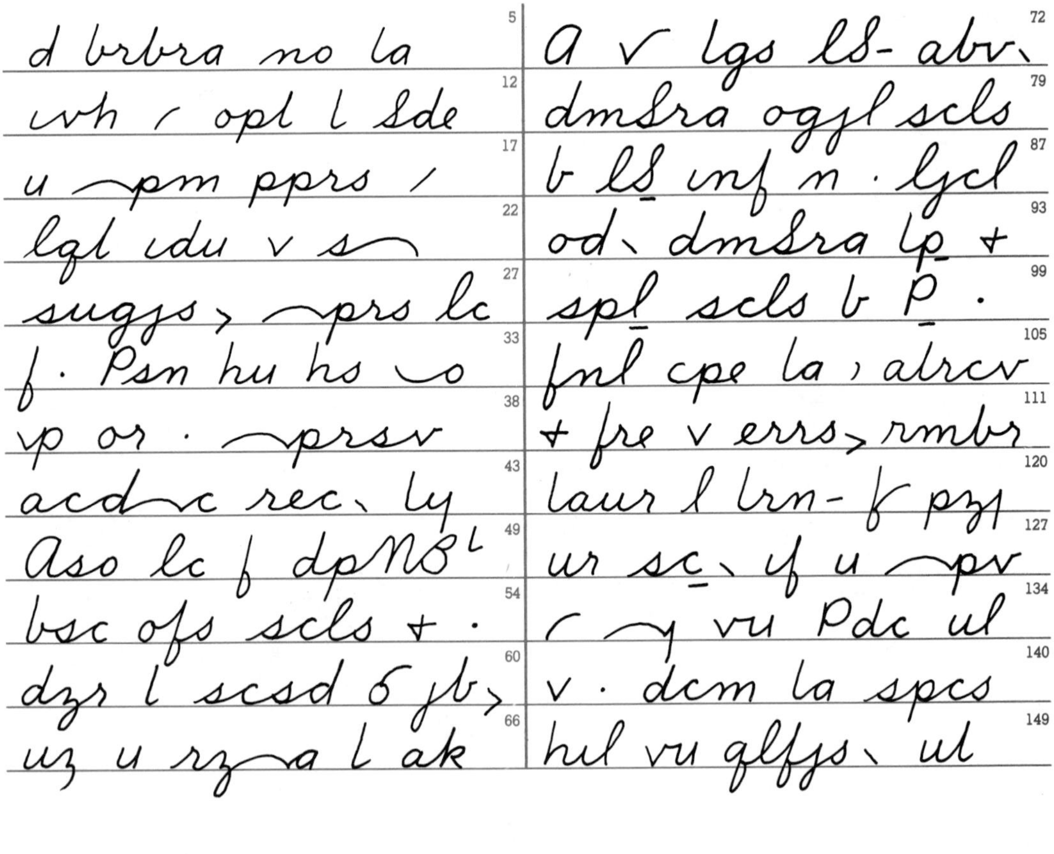

Key

1

Dear Mrs. Rogers:

Recently I completed my courses in business education and am now looking forward[1] to a career in office work. I wish to tell you that I especially enjoyed your courses in typing[2] and shorthand, and I learned much from the classes you taught.

Because most of my office training has occurred under your[3] direction, a recommendation from you would be very helpful in finding my first job. May I please list your[4] name as a reference on my resumé?

I have appreciated your guidance over the last two years, and[5] I feel that I am well prepared to accept a position as secretary. I will do my best to justify[6] the interest you have shown in me.

Sincerely, (129)

2

Dear Mrs. Rogers:

We are considering one of your students, Jennifer West, for the position of correspondence[1] secretary. She received a high rating on both the shorthand and the typing tests, and she also made[2] a favorable impression during her interview.

The person we hire must produce a large volume of[3] correspondence daily. In a few cases, this person will also be responsible for writing answers to[4] routine letters of inquiry.

Therefore, we are looking for a person who is dependable, uses good judgment,[5] and shows a willingness to assume responsibility. Would you recommend Jennifer for a position[6] requiring these qualities?

We would appreciate receiving your reply within one week in order to make[7] our decision.

Very truly yours, (146)

3

Dear Mr. Watson:

Thank you for your letter of application. We have always encouraged the placement office[1] of your college to refer good students to us. As a result, we have many fine employees from your school.

As[2] part of our current expansion, we will soon open a new store downtown. At that time we will move our central[3] offices to that location. We have plans to increase personnel in several departments. Because of your[4] extensive background in data processing and accounting, you might qualify for some of the new positions[5] we are developing. The work experience described in your letter might also be appropriate for our[6] credit department.

I suggest that we discuss these oppportunities in person. If you would call my office[7] for an appointment, I could arrange to meet with you one day next week.

Yours very truly, (155)

4

Dear Ms. White:

Part of the reward of being a teacher is watching young and eager minds develop in my classroom.[1] When an exceptional student comes along, it is especially rewarding to see that person receive[2] a challenging job. This year it gives me particular pleasure to recommend someone who has worked hard and learned[3] quickly since beginning his study here.

Jerry Fields has taken great care to prepare himself for a successful[4] career in business offices. When he is working on a project, he gives full attention to details, organizes[5] his work well, and uses his time efficiently. He works well independently and submits completed[6] assignments on time.

Jerry is quiet, gets along well with other people, and behaves in a professional[7] manner. I am convinced that you would be pleased with his performance.

Cordially yours, (154)

5

Dear Barbara:

Now that I have had the opportunity to study your employment papers at length, I do[1] have some suggestions.

Employers look for a person who has work experience or an impressive academic[2] record. They also look for dependability, basic office skills, and a desire to succeed on the[3] job.

Use your resumé to accomplish all of the things listed above. Demonstrate organizational skills[4] by listing information in a logical order. Demonstrate typing and spelling skills by presenting a[5] final copy that is attractive and free of errors.

Remember that you are well trained for the position you[6] are seeking. If you improve the image of your product, you will have a document that speaks highly of your[7] qualifications.

Yours truly, (145)

LESSON 2

Abbreviations and Derivatives

1. co q dpl mo att
2. rec enc inf + av

Key

1. company, question, department, month, attention
2. record, enclose/enclosure, information, and, advertising

Transcription Aids: Typing/Keyboarding Materials

The following items are essential for good transcription practices.

1. Dictionary: Use it for correct spelling, definitions, and pronunciations.
2. Zip code directory: Use correct zip codes to speed mail delivery.
3. Address file: Keep a file for frequently used addresses and phone numbers.
4. Secretarial handbook: Use it for preparing written communications; for supplying postal, telephone, and telegraphic information; and for assisting in other office activities.
5. English usage manual: Use it for punctuation, grammar, and other related information.
6. Supplies: Use items such as paper clips, staplers, rubber bands, and colored pens to organize your materials for transcription.

Your Business Vocabulary

confirm kfr — To verify or make certain of.

This letter is to confirm your reservations for September 23.

public relations pb rlys — Methods used to build goodwill with the public.

We are interviewing applicants who have a strong background in public relations.

Reading and Writing Exercises

1

Preview Words

useful	usf	creative	crav
public	pb	impression	pry
overlook	Olc	frequently	frqNl
unusual	uuz	intelligent	nllyN

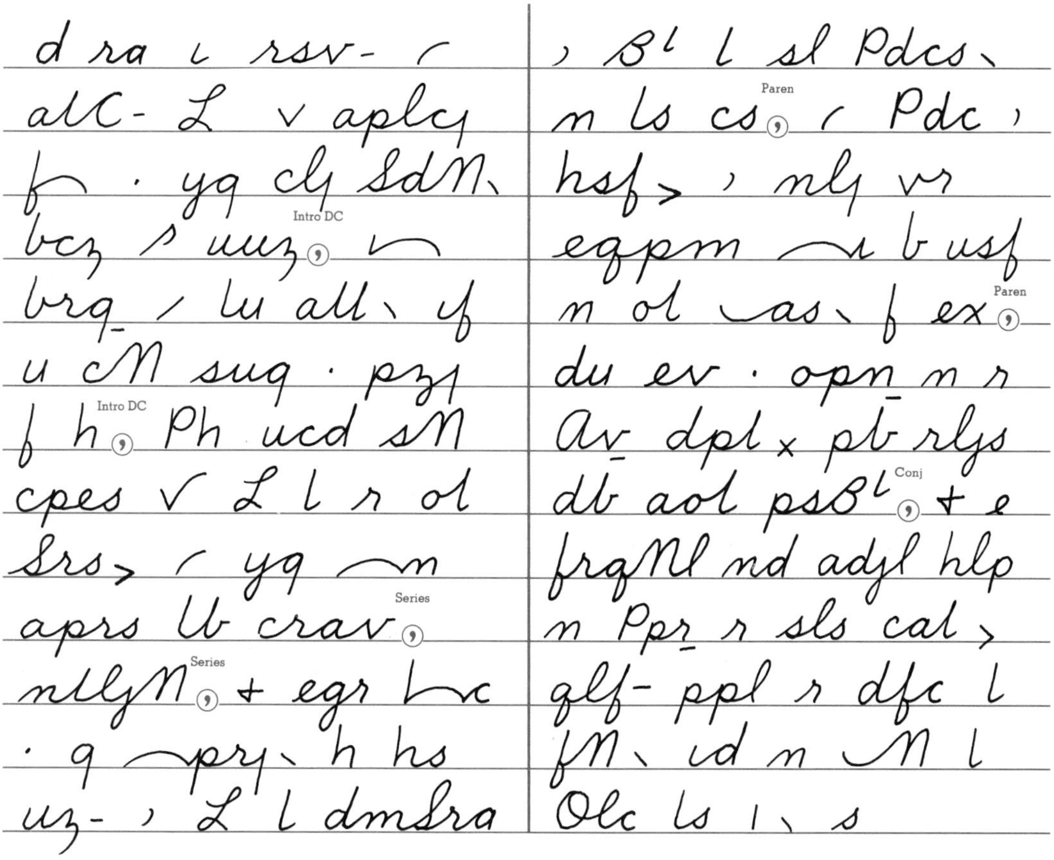

——————————— 2 ———————————

Preview Words

Jordan *jrdn̲*

computer *kpur*

automation *aty*

language *lgy*

subscribe *s S*

ordinary *ord*

appreciation *apy*

relationship *rljp*

[shorthand passage]

dr jrdn n L
l fr8 kpur (Intro DC)
L nu ls z no ord
rljp zz L lrn-l
spc 8 lgy (Intro DC) uz p8
(py v no rel L
fl n lv drn
aty L sl spN
l lf n co v
kpur8 = A lps (Series)
sz8 (Series) + prs rnjs
L gr8 hp l ps

apy o l Ks hu
r lc f gdN n b
+ op br o egpm
r jrdn (Dir Ad) chp ul
ks ef sls pzy
n u Sr nly
lNr + crN
mbr v 2 kpur
clb8 (Conj) + L sS L c
ld gyns p ll
e no y uc uz
8ls vlu

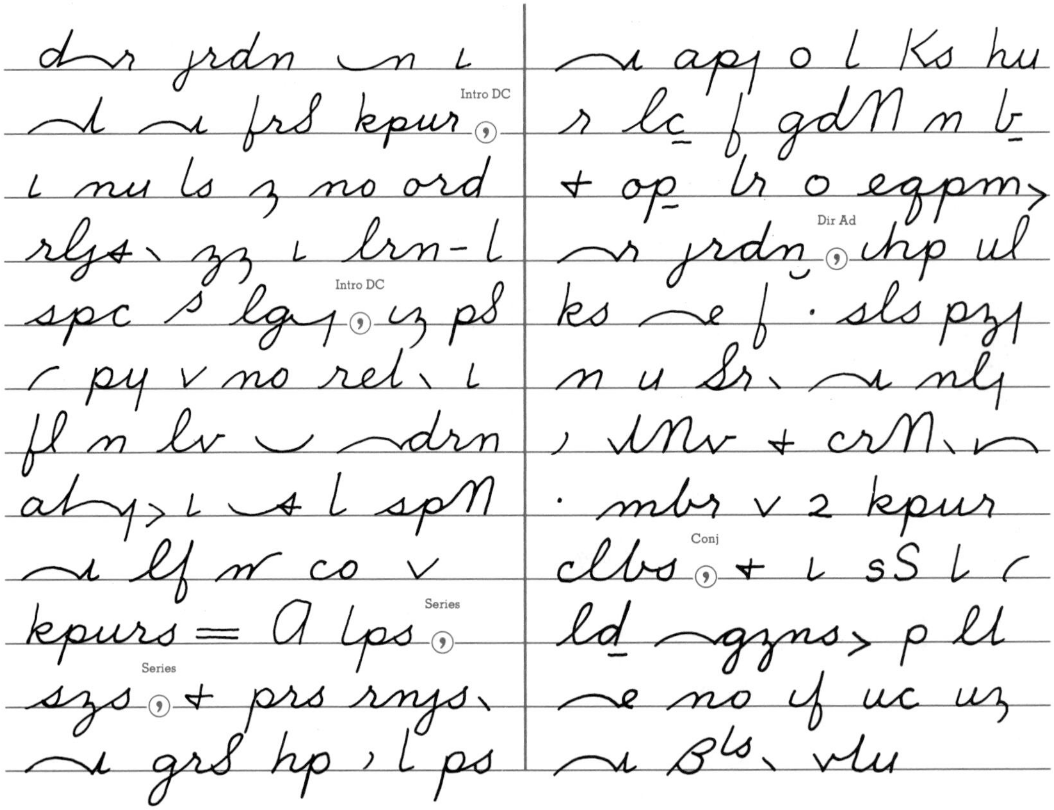

3

Preview Words

Webb   _b_

Janet   _jnt_

further   _frlr_

fashion   _bf_

firm   _fr_

graduating   _grja_

advancement   _AvNm_

outstanding   _olSN_

---

d M dyl ⌒ p- l
rcm lu fr · Psn
hu hsb · olSN
⌒pe n r dpl Sr ⟍
jnt b hs ⌒o-hr
sN grja f clf ⟍
se hsb P⌒o- l
dpl ⟋yr + z b
ks- f frlr AvNm
⌒n se nf⌒- s
la Psnl Sks d
⌒c / nes f hr l
⟍v lu sle ⟍ se
hs · ⌒prsv nlf

v ff ⟍ + r Ks v lrn-
l lr8 hr jm ⟍ n
adj l hr rglr
dles ⟍ se hs oq- lrn
sfs f nu ⌒pes +
hlp- pln sv sls
P⌒ys ⟍ blv la jnt
⟍ · cpB Psn f
pzf u dS- + l kb
grl l ⌒ suc vu
rll bs ⟍ p ll ⌒e
no f ub v frlr
asSN ⟍ su

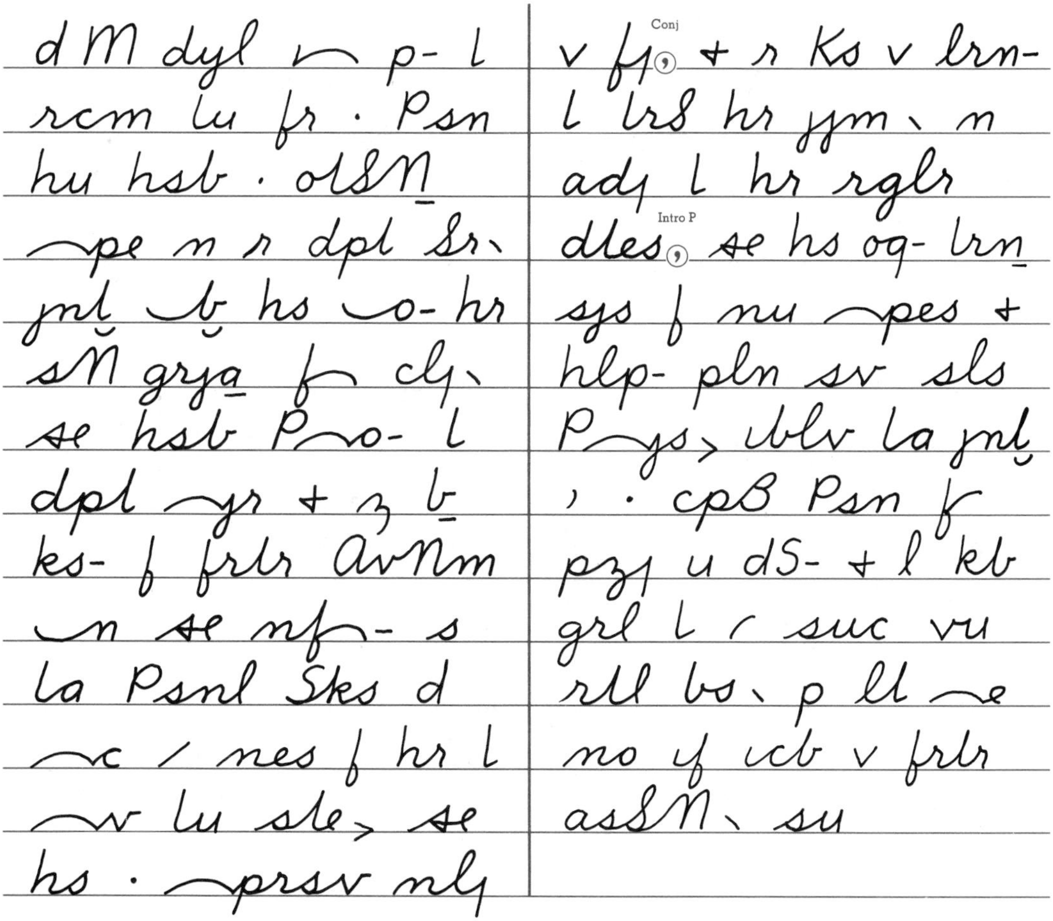

4

Preview Words

assume *as*

contract *kc*

Boston *bSn*

brochure *brsr*

excellent *eN*

comfortable *kflB*

relocating *rlca*

transportation *Tply*

[Shorthand text]

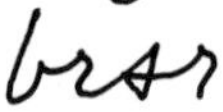

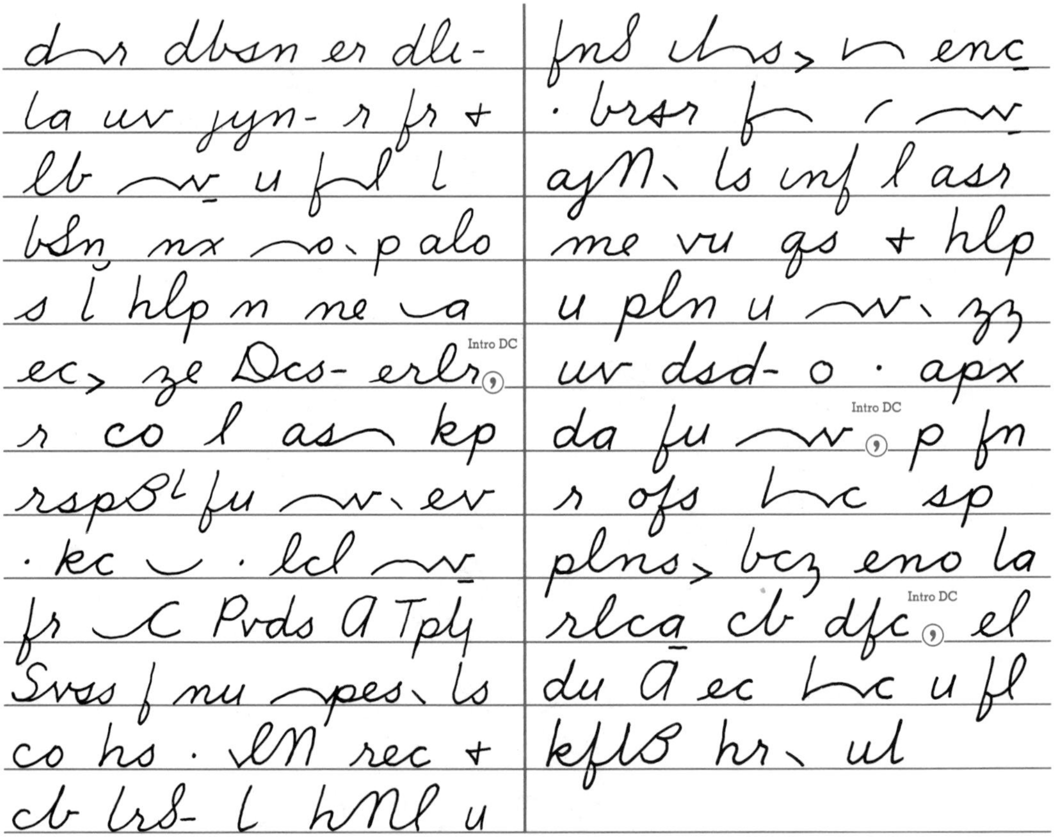

5

Punctuation Study

Five commas are missing from the following letter. Place one after each of the three introductory dependent clauses, after the parenthetical expression, and before the conjunction.

Preview Words

extra	X	Thursday	Th
confirm	kfr	register	rjSr
direct	dr	understand	USN
middle	mdl	supervisor	Svzr

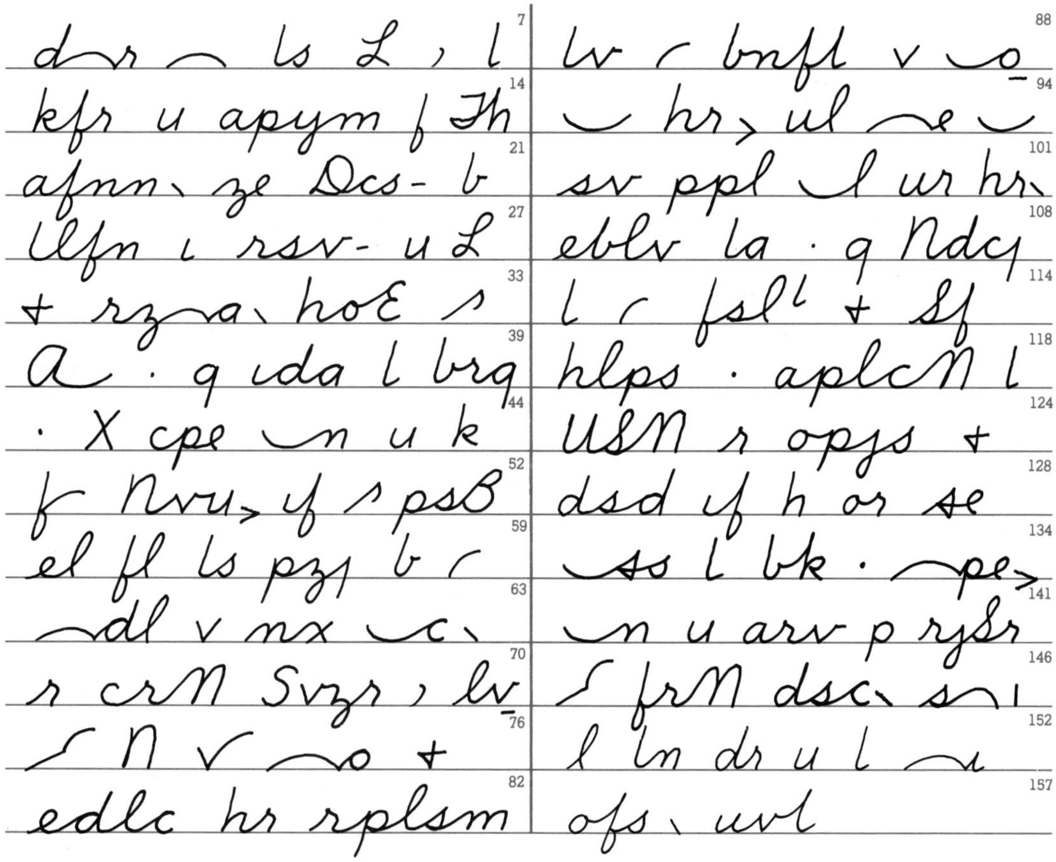

Key

1

Dear Ray:

I received the attached letter of application from a young college student. Because it is unusual,[1] I am bringing it to your attention. If you can't suggest a position for him, perhaps you could send[2] copies of the letter to our other stores.

The young man appears to be creative, intelligent, and eager[3] to make a good impression. He has used his letter to demonstrate his ability to sell products. In this[4] case, the product is himself.

His knowledge of our equipment might be useful in other ways. For example, do[5] we have an opening in our advertising department? Public relations would be another possibility,[6] and we frequently need additional help in preparing our sales catalog.

Qualified people are[7] difficult to find. I would not want to overlook this one.

Sincerely, (153)

2

Dear Mr. Jordan:

When I met my first computer, I knew this was no ordinary relationship. As soon[1] as I learned to speak its language, I was past the point of no return. I fell in love with modern automation.[2]

I wish to spend my life in the company of computers—all types, sizes, and price ranges. My greatest hope is[3] to pass my appreciation on to customers who are looking for guidance in buying and operating[4] their own equipment.

Mr. Jordan, I hope you will consider me for a sales position in your store. My[5] knowledge is extensive and current. I am a member of two computer clubs, and I subscribe to the leading[6] magazines.

Please let me know if you can use my abilities.

Very truly yours, (134)

3

Dear Miss Doyle:

I am pleased to recommend to your firm a person who has been an outstanding employee in our[1] department store. Janet Webb has worked here since graduating from college. She has been promoted to department[2] manager and was being considered for further advancement when she informed us that personal circumstances[3] would make it necessary for her to move to your city.

She has an impressive knowledge of fashion, and[4] our customers have learned to trust her judgment. In addition to her regular duties, she has organized training[5] sessions for new employees and helped plan several sales promotions.

I believe that Janet is a capable[6] person for the position you described and will contribute greatly to the success of your retail business.[7] Please let me know if I can be of further assistance.

Sincerely yours, (153)

4

Dear Mr. Dobson:

We are delighted that you have joined our firm and will be moving your family to Boston[1] next month. Please allow us to help in any way we can.

As we discussed earlier, our company will assume[2] complete responsibility for your move. We have a contract with a local moving firm which provides all[3] transportation services for new employees. This company has an excellent record and can be trusted to[4] handle your finest items.

I am enclosing a brochure from the moving agent. This information will[5] answer many of your questions and help you plan your move. As soon as you have decided on an approximate date[6] for your move, please phone our office to make specific plans.

Because we know that relocating can be difficult,[7] we will do all we can to make you feel comfortable here.

Yours truly, (153)

5

Dear Mr. Moore:

This letter is to confirm your appointment for Thursday afternoon. As we discussed by telephone,[1] I received your letter and resumé. However, it is always a good idea to bring an extra[2] copy when you come for the interview.

If it is possible, we will fill this position by the middle of[3] next week. Our current supervisor is leaving at the end of the month, and we would like her replacement to have[4] the benefit of working with her.

You will meet with several people while you are here. We believe that a good[5] introduction to the facility and staff helps an applicant to understand our operations and[6] decide if he or she wishes to become an employee.

When you arrive, please register at the front desk. Someone[7] will then direct you to my office.

Yours very truly, (150)

LESSON 3

Shorthand Vocabulary Review

Write the months of the year as follows:

January	Ja	July	Jl
February	Fb	August	Ag
March	Mr	September	Sp
April	Ap	October	Oc
May	Ma	November	Nv
June	Jn	December	Dc

Transcription Aids: Similar Words

weather  The condition of our atmosphere.

The weather today is mild and sunny.

whether  Used in an indirect question to indicate an alternative.

Please let me know whether or not you plan to attend.

Your Business Vocabulary

priority  Precedence; having a high ranking in order of importance.

Answering the telephone should take priority over all other duties.

anticipate alspa Expect to happen.

We anticipate having the report finished ahead of time.

Reading and Writing Exercises

---------------------------------- 1 ----------------------------------

Preview Words

claims *c͟ʮ*

contact *klc*

previous *Pves*

expansion *ʋpnʝ*

priority *prʋrᴸ*

inquiring *nʠ͟*

notation *nlʝ*

performance *Pf͟ʮ*

[shorthand text — two columns of handwritten shorthand notes]

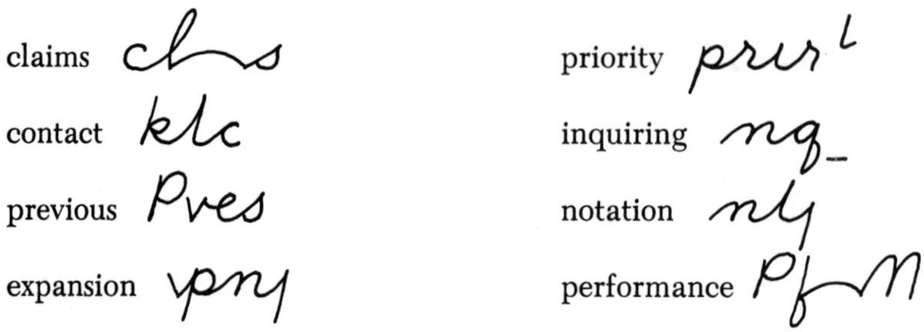

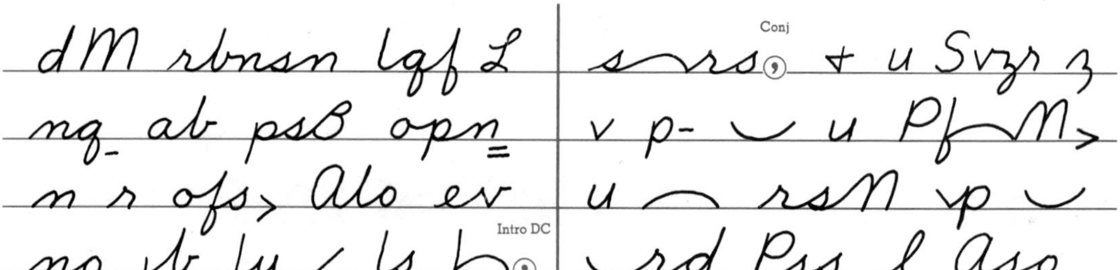

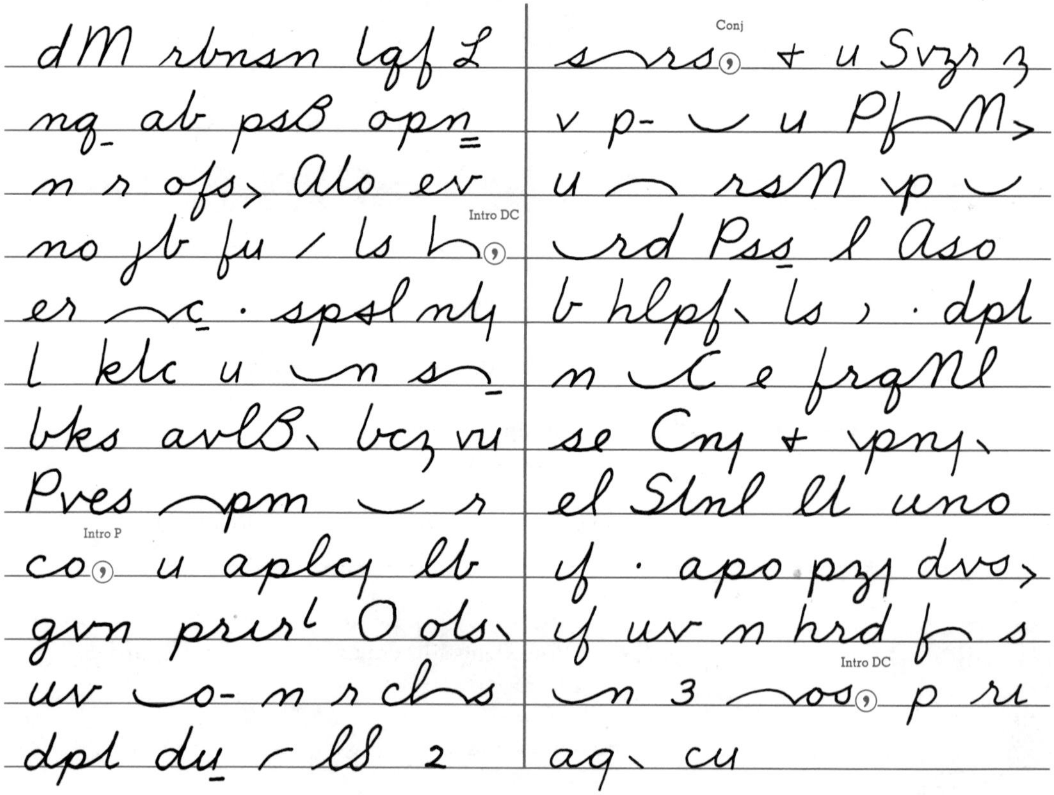

2

Preview Words

weather *Lr*

transfer *Tfr*

thought *U*

positive *pzv*

Denver *dnvr*

materials *Lrels*

physician *bzy*

controlling *kl*

mo l erc hMr
af gv ⌐ ⟋ U l
⌐ Lr , ⌐ rg8
. Tfr l · ofs lca-
n r Wrn dvy, L
aprⳇ ls rg8 ⌣
⌐x- fl, w nyy-
⌣o n ls knl v
⌐⟋, hoⳇ , ⌐ U
⌐ cr v · bzy hu
fls la ⌐ Lr n
dnvr d v · pzv
efc o ⌐ hll,

chp ⌐ co l ks ⌐
Pves rec n ⌐c s
dsy, rsN akms
I dv nu Lrels
f Pss f l8 ⌐ans,
L Aso dzn- · ⌐
efsN ss f kl
yl flo, lc fw l
⌐ fⳇr ⌣ ls co,
id no lc ⌐ opl
Lrc lz s cNs
v kbys N dnvr
ofs,

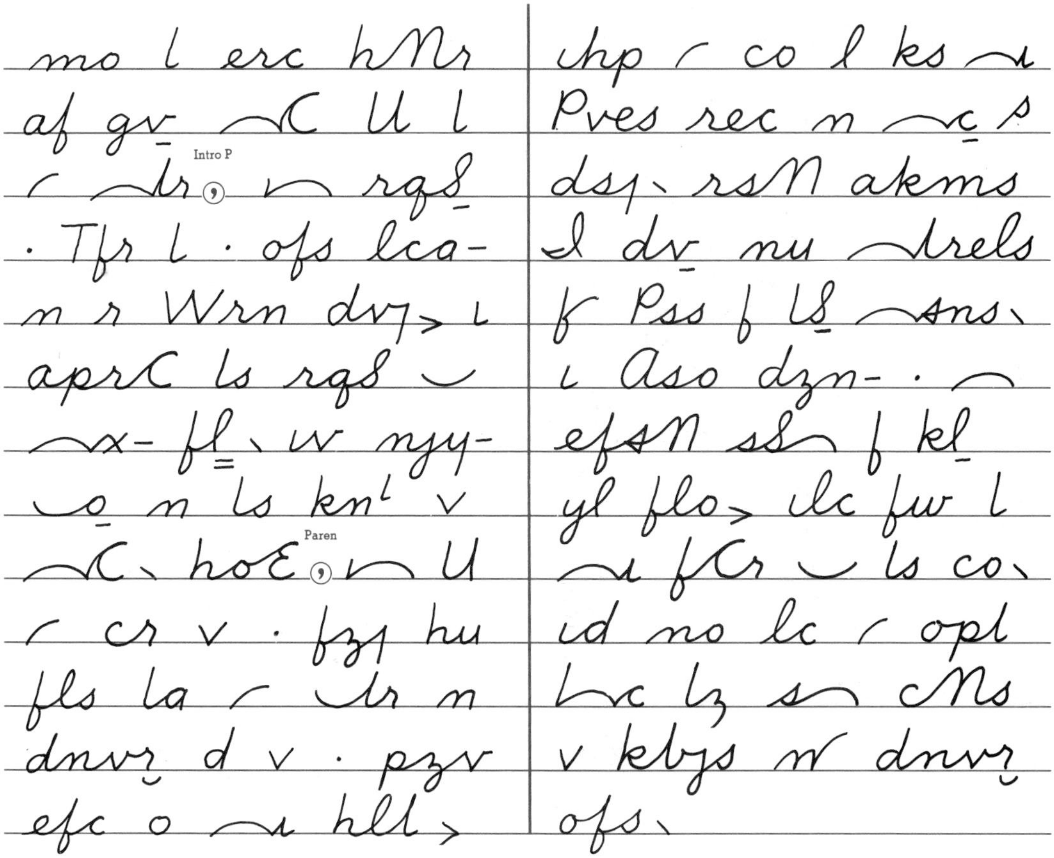

3

Preview Words

resign

exciting

refuse

include

National

Publications

departure

conventions

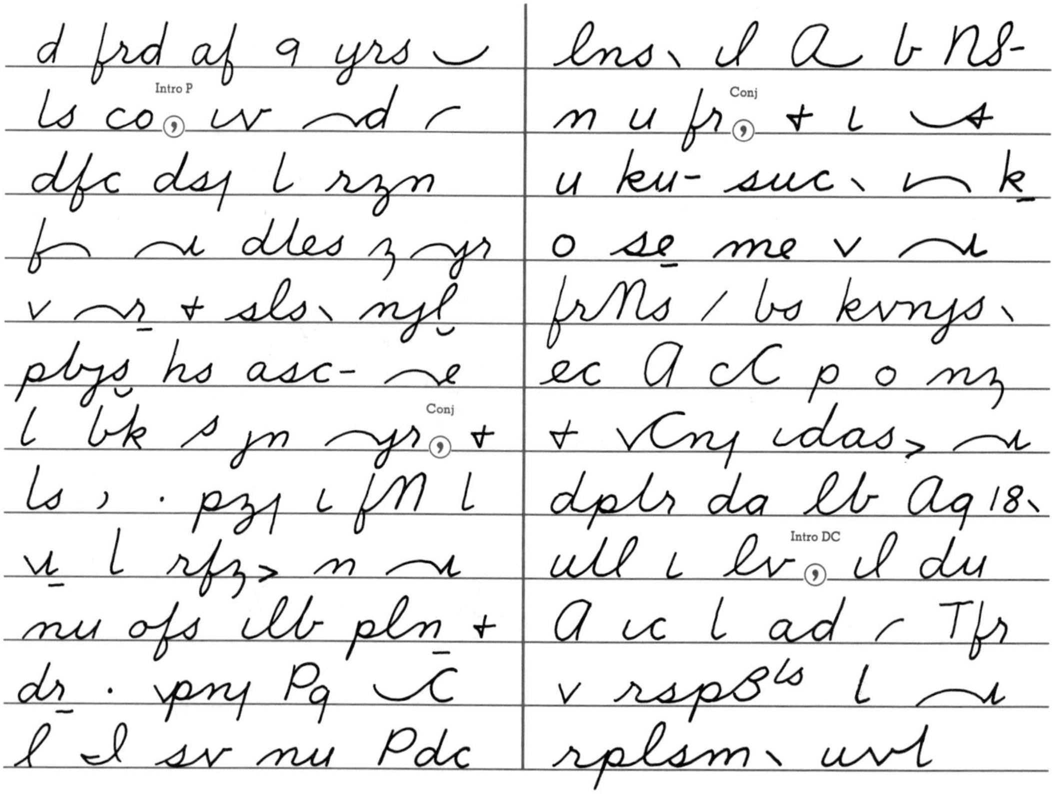

4

Preview Words

second	specific
network	assistant
directly	international
whether	immediately

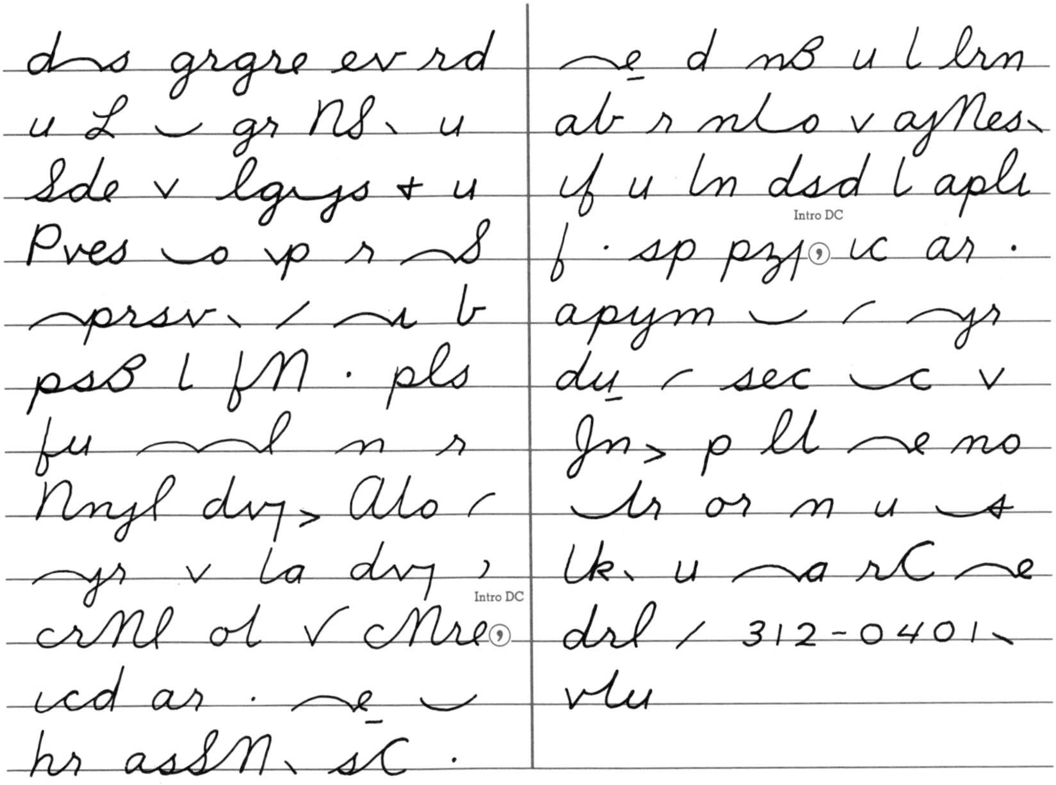

5

Punctuation Study

Six commas are missing from the following letter. Use commas to set off the two conjunctions, the introductory dependent clause, the parenthetical expression, and the introductory phrase.

Preview Words

branch	brnC	yesterday	ySrd
select	slc	candidate	cddl
equally	eqll	anticipate	alspa
excellent	xlN	continuing	ku̲

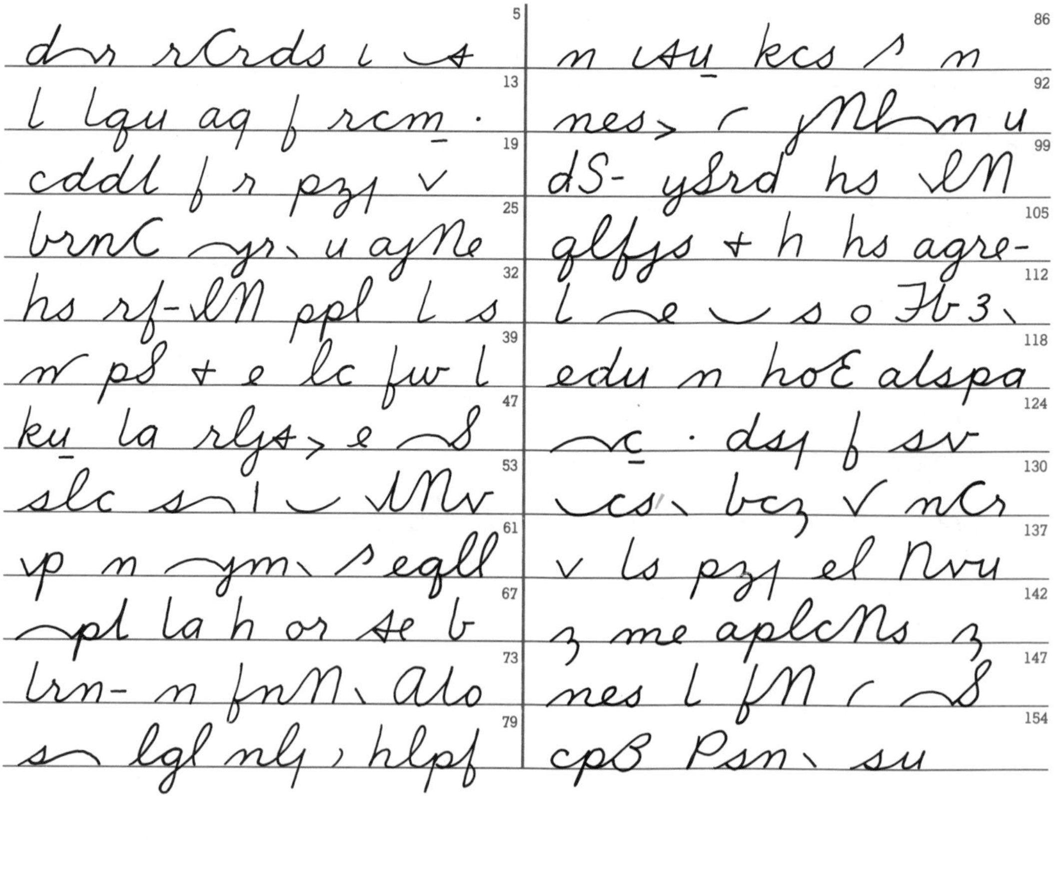

Key

1

Dear Miss Robinson:

Thank you for your letter inquiring about possible openings in our office.

Although[1] we have no job for you at this time, we are making a special notation to contact you when something becomes[2] available. Because of your previous employment with our company, your application will be given[3] priority over others. You have worked in our claims department during the last two summers, and your supervisor[4] was very pleased with your performance.

Your more recent experience with word processing will also be[5] helpful. This is a department in which we frequently see change and expansion. We will certainly let you know[6] if an appropriate position develops.

If you have not heard from us within three months, please write again.[7]

Cordially yours, (142)

2

MEMO TO: Eric Hunter

After giving much thought to the matter, I am requesting a transfer to an office[1] located in our western division.

I approach this request with mixed feelings. I have enjoyed working in[2] this community very much. However, I am under the care of a physician who feels that the weather[3] in Denver would have a positive effect on my health.

I hope the company will consider my previous[4] record in making its decision. Recent accomplishments include developing new materials for the[5] process for testing machines. I also designed a more efficient system for controlling oil flow.

I look forward[6] to my future with this company. I would now like the opportunity to make these same kinds of contributions[7] in the Denver office. (146)

3

Dear Fred:

After nine years with this company, I have made the difficult decision to resign from my duties[1] as manager of marketing and sales. National Publications has asked me to become its general[2] manager, and this is a position I find too exciting to refuse.

In my new office I will be planning[3] and directing an expansion program which will include several new product lines. I will always be interested[4] in your firm, and I wish you continued success. I am counting on seeing many of my friends at business[5] conventions. We can all catch up on news and exchange ideas.

My departure date will be August 18.[6] Until I leave, I will do all I can to aid the transfer of responsibilities to my replacement.

Yours[7] very truly, (143)

4

Dear Ms. Gregory:

We have read your letter with great interest. Your study of languages and your previous[1] work experience are most impressive. It might be possible to find a place for you immediately in[2] our international division.

Although the manager of that division is currently out of the country,[3] I could arrange a meeting with her assistant. Such a meeting would enable you to learn about our network[4] of agencies. If you then decide to apply for a specific position, I can arrange an appointment[5] with the manager during the second week of June.

Please let me know whether or not you wish to come. You may[6] reach me directly at 312-0401.

Very truly yours, (133)

5

Dear Mr. Richards:

I wish to thank you again for recommending a candidate for our position of branch[1] manager. Your agency has referred excellent people to us in the past, and we look forward to continuing[2] that relationship.

We must select someone with extensive experience in management. It is equally[3] important that he or she be trained in finance. Although some legal knowledge is helpful in issuing contracts,[4] it is not necessary.

The gentleman you described yesterday has excellent qualifications, and[5] he has agreed to meet with us on February 3. We do not, however, anticipate making a[6] decision for several weeks. Because of the nature of this position, we will interview as many[7] applicants as necessary to find the most capable person.

Sincerely yours, (154)

LESSON 4

Shorthand Vocabulary Review

Write O for the sound of *ow* (ou). This special sound is called a **diphthong.** Always write the sound of *ow* in an outline.

background	bcgroN	proud	prod
now	no	out	ol
however	hoE	sound	soN

Transcription Aids: Spelling

Many words contain similar sounds. The word endings *able* and *ible* sound alike. Learn the correct spelling of the following words which commonly occur in business correspondence. When you are in doubt about the spelling of a word, **look it up in the dictionary.** Your employer will count on you to spell correctly.

Words ending in *able*		**Words ending in *ible***	
dependable	dpNB	responsible	rspB
capable	cpB	possible	psB
valuable	vluB	flexible	flxB
payable	paB	eligible	eljB
available	avlB	deductible	ddcB

Your Business Vocabulary	data *dla*	Information that has been sequenced and organized for analysis.

We will make our decision based upon the data that we have available.

supportive *splv* To provide strength or assistance for; to boost morale.

The employees have indicated that they will be supportive of company policy.

Reading and Writing Exercises

--- 1 ---

Preview Words

science *suN*

projects *Pjcs*

shortly *srll*

worthwhile *rll*

reports *rpls*

electronics *elncs*

settled *sll-*

contributions *kbjs*

ddr hrpr u acN	*arv, n od lgv*
v ls pzf k z	*u bcgroN inf o*
Nrf nz, u p	*⌐ Intro P ⌐ enc 2*
n elncs + kpur	*rpls fu l rd no,*
suN lb v gr vlu	*ino laur v bze*
L s, lr r 2 v	*⌐v prprys Conj b yf*
pl Pjcs C l	*Sln la ⌐ L spN*
bgn srll af u	*o lz rpls l pv v*

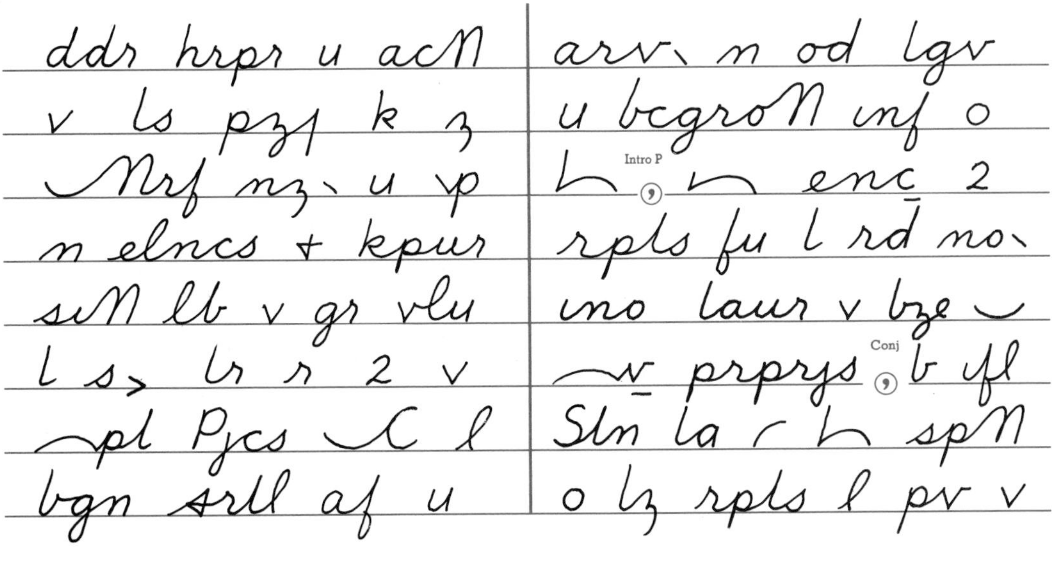

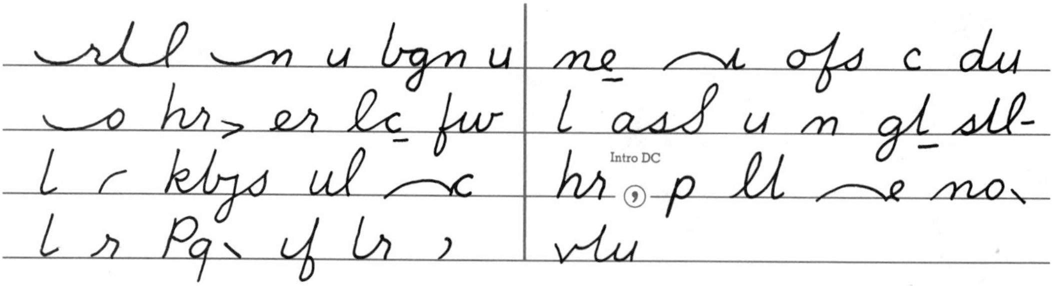

2

Preview Words

- data 
- thorough 
- once 
- possible 
- reliable 
- bookkeeping 
- resource 
- qualifications 

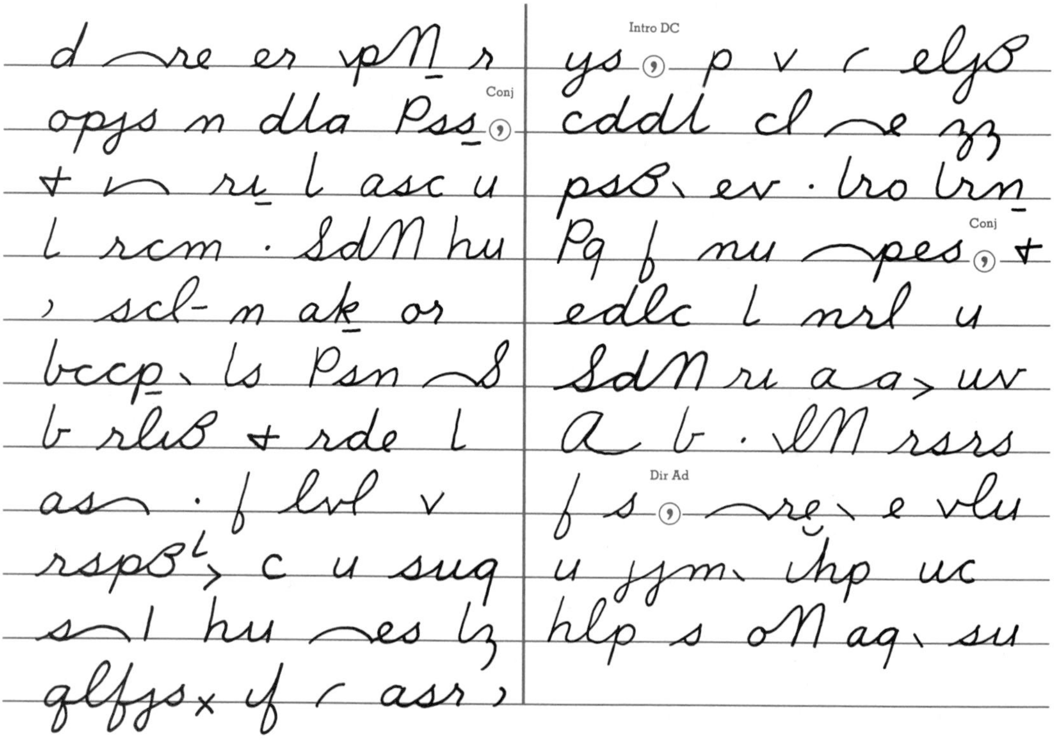

3

Preview Words

staff

advantage

educational

situation

college

confidence

generous

scholarship

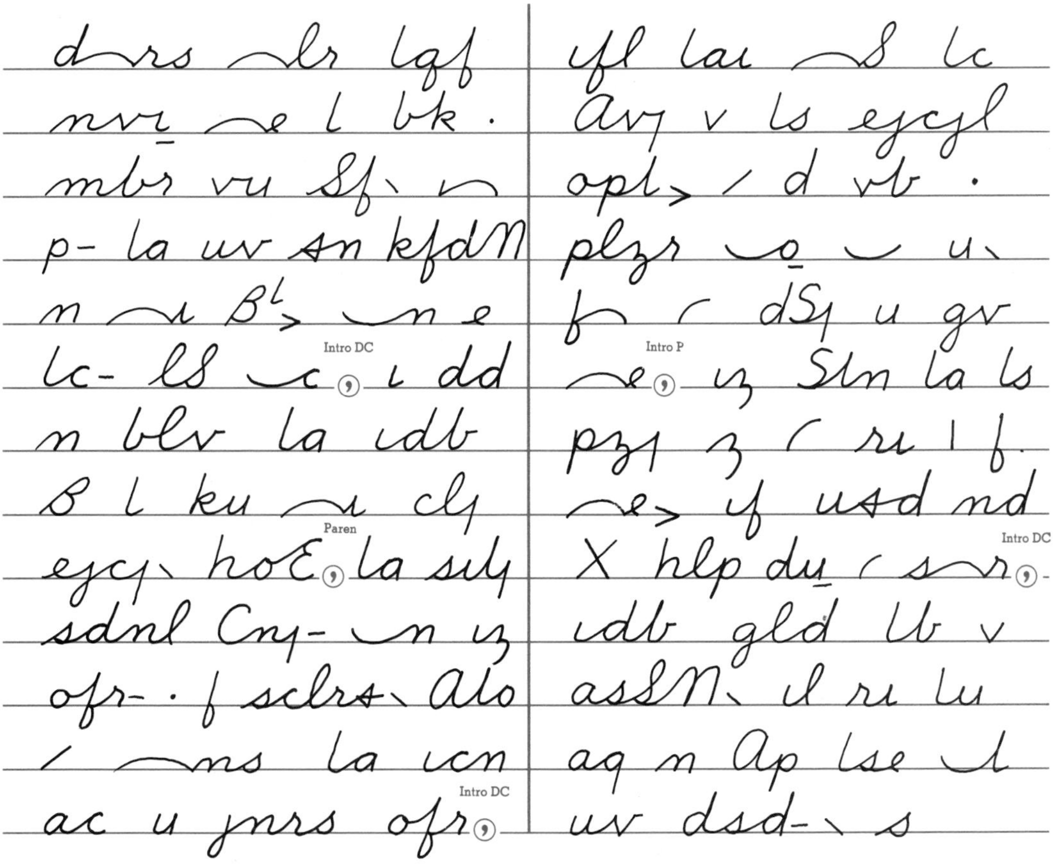

4

Preview Words

Olson	olsn	answer	asr
American		dedication	ddcj
regard	re	apparent	aprN
conditions	kdjs	supportive	splv

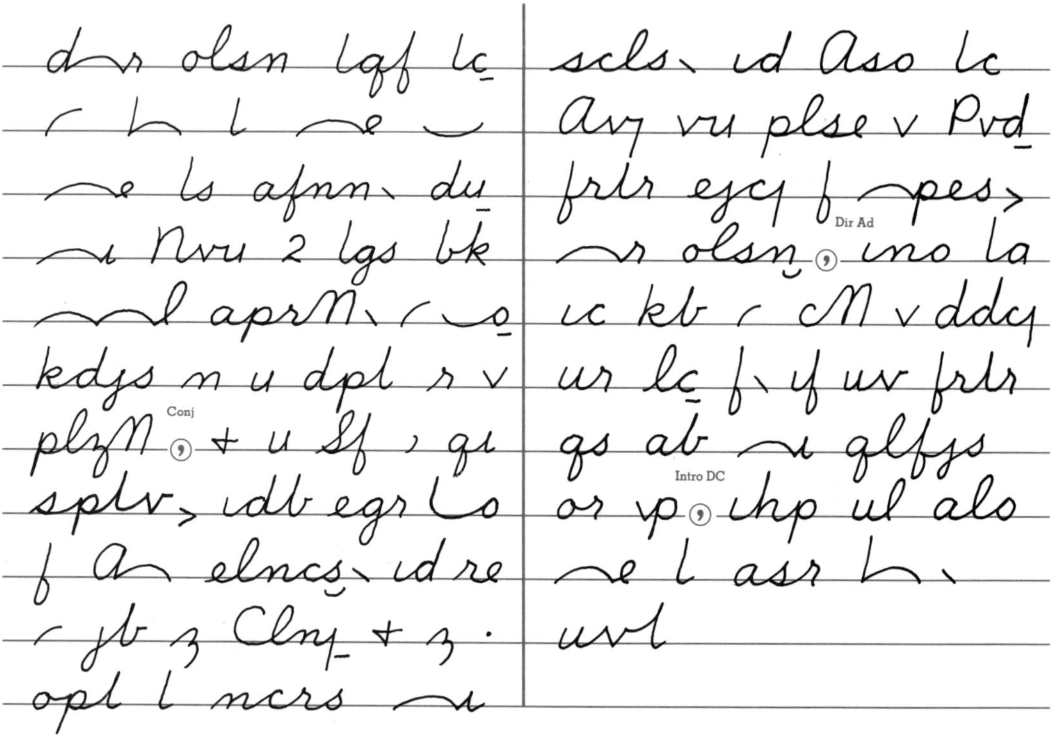

5

Punctuation Study

Place commas in the letter below. Use commas to set off the introductory phrase, two conjunctions, and two parenthetical expressions.

Preview Words

rarely		effective	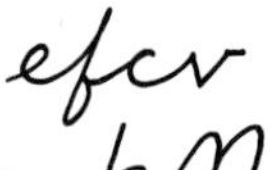
someday		commented	
varied		demanding	
favorable		workload	

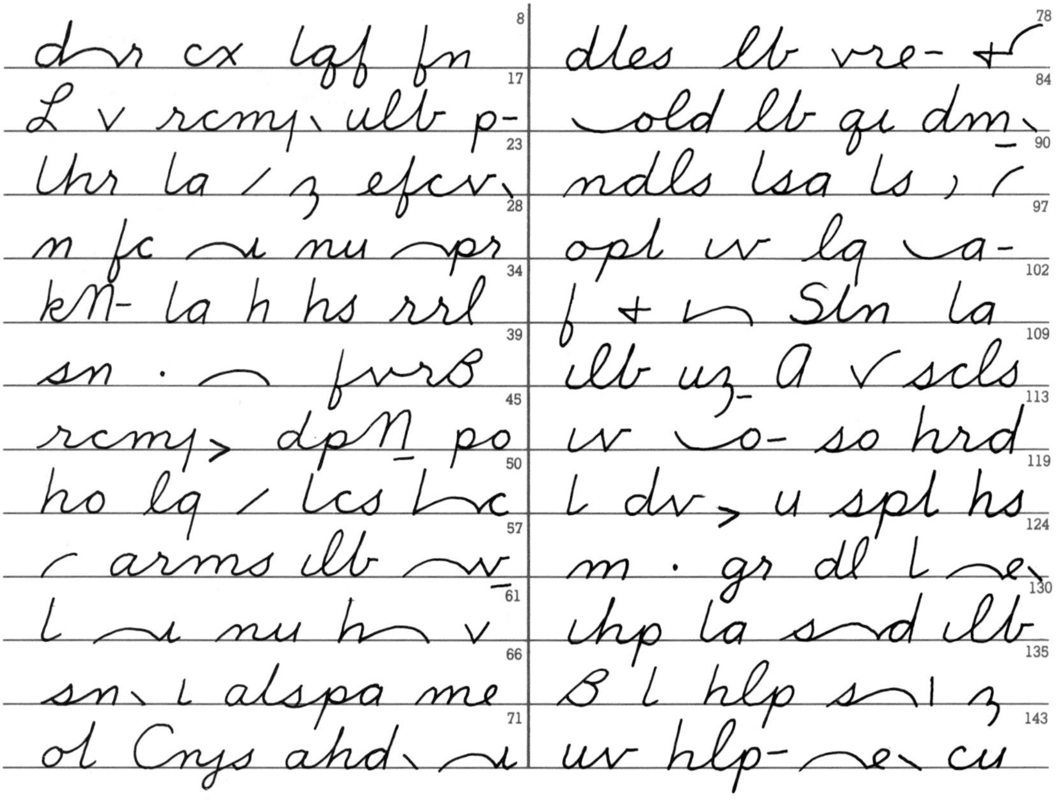

Key

1

Dear Dr. Harper:

Your acceptance of this position came as wonderful news. Your experience in electronics[1] and computer science will be of great value to us.

There are two very important projects which will[2] begin shortly after you arrive. In order to give you background information on them, I am enclosing[3] two reports for you to read now. I know that you are very busy with moving preparations, but I feel[4] certain that the time spent on these reports will prove very worthwhile when you begin your work here.

We are looking forward[5] to the contributions you will make to our program. If there is anything my office can do to assist you[6] in getting settled here, please let me know.

Very truly yours, (131)

2

Dear Mary:

We are expanding our operations in data processing, and I am writing to ask you to[1] recommend a student who is skilled in accounting or bookkeeping. This person must be reliable and ready[2] to assume a full level of responsibility.

Can you suggest someone who meets these qualifications?[3] If the answer is yes, please have the eligible candidate call me as soon as possible. We have a[4] thorough training program for new employees, and we would like to enroll your student right away.

You have always[5] been an excellent resource for us, Mary. We value your judgment. I hope you can help us once again.

Sincerely[6] yours, (121)

3

Dear Mrs. Miller:

Thank you for inviting me to become a member of your staff. I am pleased that you have shown[1] confidence in my ability.

When we talked last week, I did not believe that I would be able to continue[2] my college education. However, that situation suddenly changed when I was offered a full[3] scholarship. Although it means that I cannot accept your generous offer, I feel that I must take advantage[4] of this educational opportunity.

It would have been a pleasure working with you. From the description[5] you gave me, I was certain that this position was the right one for me.

If you should need extra help during the[6] summer, I would be glad to be of assistance. I will write to you again in April to see what you have[7] decided.

Sincerely, (143)

4

Dear Mr. Olson:

Thank you for taking the time to meet with me this afternoon. During my interview two things[1] became immediately apparent. The working conditions in your department are very pleasant, and your[2] staff is quite supportive.

I would be eager to work for American Electronics. I would regard the job[3] as challenging and as an opportunity to increase my skills. I would also take advantage of your[4] policy of providing further education for employees.

Mr. Olson, I know that I can contribute[5] the kind of dedication you are looking for. If you have further questions about my qualifications or[6] experience, I hope you will allow me to answer them.

Yours very truly, (134)

5

Dear Mr. Cox:

Thank you for your fine letter of recommendation. You will be pleased to hear that it was effective.[1] In fact, my new employer commented that he has rarely seen a more favorable recommendation.[2]

Depending upon how long it takes to make the arrangements, I will be moving to my new home very soon. I[3] anticipate many other changes ahead. My duties will be varied, and the workload will be quite demanding.[4] Needless to say, this is the opportunity I have long waited for, and I am certain that I will be[5] using all of the skills I have worked so hard to develop.

Your support has meant a great deal to me. I hope that[6] someday I will be able to help someone as you have helped me.

Cordially yours, (134)

LESSON 5

Word Development

Build new words using the following brief forms:

after

aftermath	af—d
afternoon	afnn
afterward	afw
hereafter	hraf

by

bylaws	blas
bypass	bps
thereby	trb
nearby	nrb

be

becoming	bk_
before	bf
maybe	—ab
became	bk

can

candy	cde
cancellation	csly
cannot	cn
candid	cdd

business

businessman	bs—n
businessmen	bsm
businesswomen	bs—m
businesslike	bslc

come

income	nk
welcome	lk
unwelcome	ulk
forthcoming	flk_

Reading and Writing Exercises

1

Preview Words

later *lar*

remaining *r‾m‾*

schedule *scjl*

standards *Sds*

candidates *cddls*

references *rfNs*

assistant *assN*

administrative *Amv*

---

d sle i no v r
fls f hf v ppl hu
apli- f pzj v Amv
assN, enc-, · ls
v r‾m‾ aplcNs,
cd u rd bru br
rz as bf re
re lar ls c, x,>
p slc r 5 aplcNs
hu r S lcl l re
r Sds, c u dsj

o bss v scls +
vp ls- o br pm
pprs, il asc v
sec l klc r fnl
cddls + ar f Psnl
Nvus, el ln ru Ls
l r rfNs + c
r fnl dsj, n
hpf la el v ls
pzj fl- o scjl s

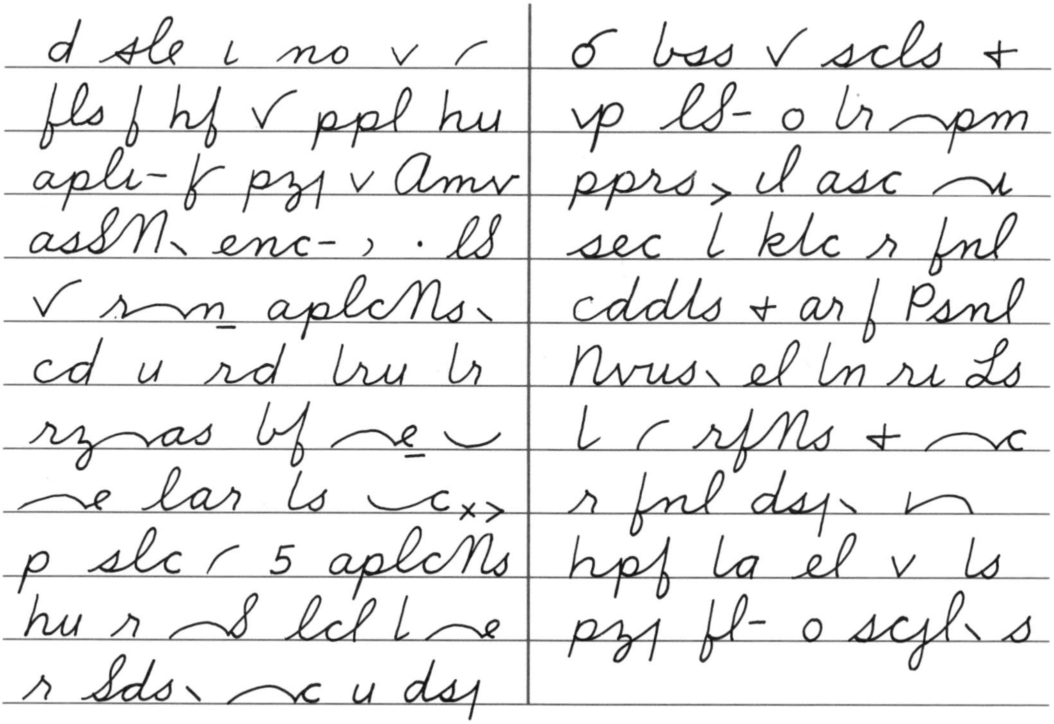

2

Preview Words

Tampa	Lpa	relocate	rlca
permanent	PmN	headquarters	hdqtrs
exactly	vcl	always	a
leadership	ldrs	establishment	eslm

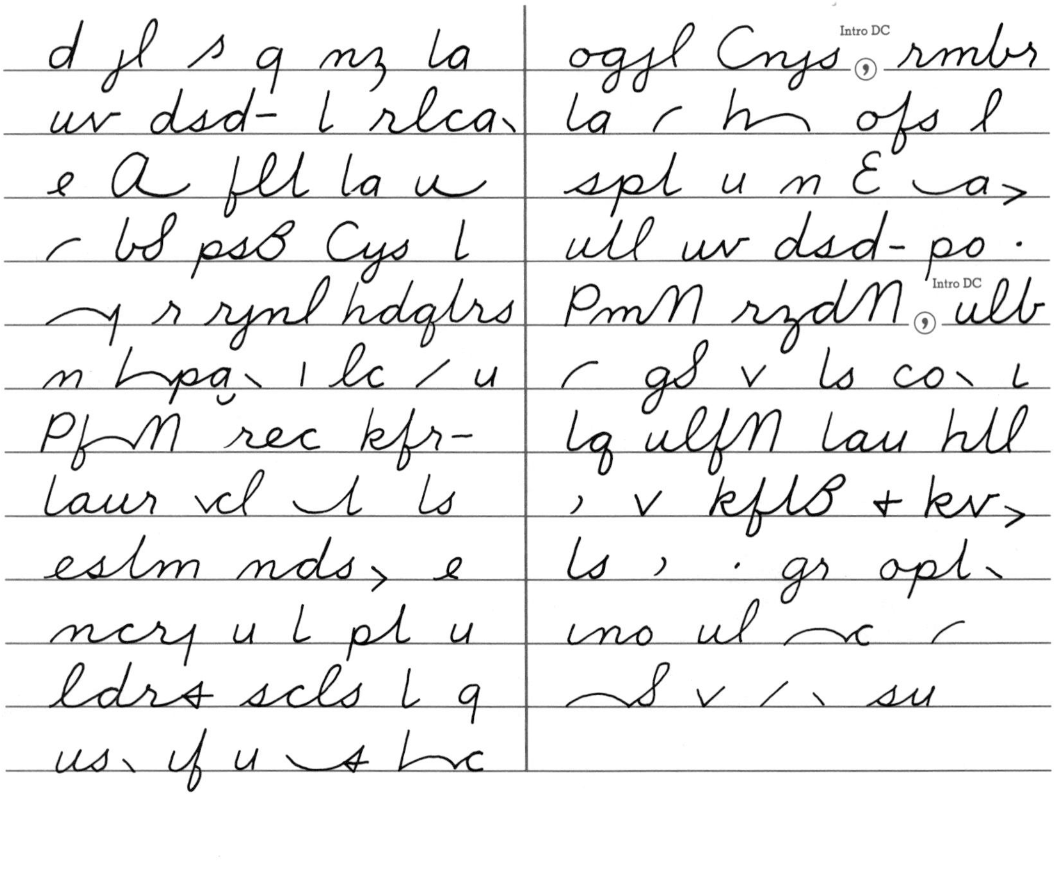

3

Preview Words

- Best
- welcome
- option
- carefully
- layout
- Industries
- initial
- hospitalization

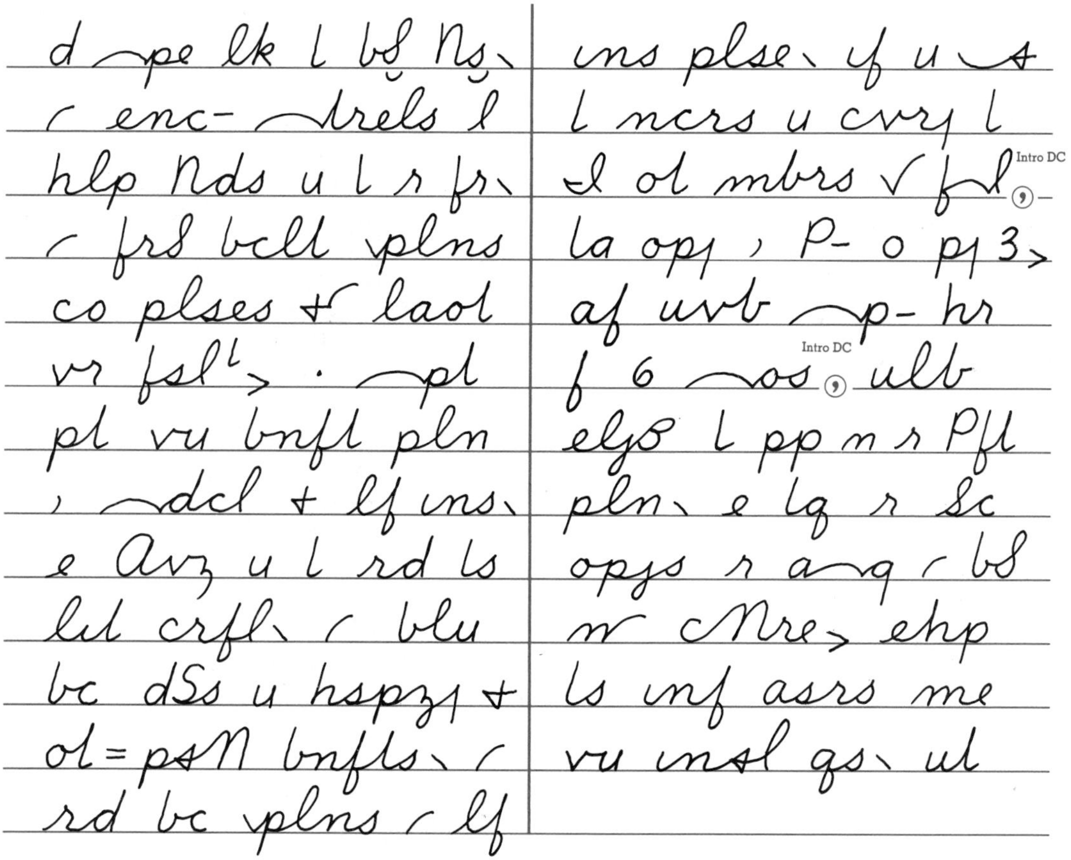

4

Preview Words

world _⁀o_

overseas _Oses_

travel _lrvl_

languages _lgɥs_

abroad _abrd_

procedures _Psyrs_

although _Alo_

communications _kncɥs_

---

d ⁀r le u sug-
_l ⁀e ɜ s | hu_
d v inf o apli f .
apym Oses. ⁀
alC̱ . Psnl dla
se dS̱ ⁀ɩ acd ⁀c
lrṉ ɬ ⁀o p. ɜ
uc se f ⁀ɩ rec ⁽Intro DC⁾
ɩv Sde- 2 ol lgɥs.
id Stnl b ḻ l lrn
adɥl |s, n̄ adɥ l

_lp_ ɬ srlhM_ ⁽Intro P⁾ _ɩv_
scls n ofs Psyrs
ɬ ⁀rd Pss. Alo
_ɩv A b NS- n_
pb rlɥs ɬ kncɥs ⁽Intro DC⁾
_id n ⁀M l bl_
⁀ɩ Cyss l loɜ
aras ol, ι nyy
⁀o lrvl ɬ d lk
⁀r p v lv̱ abrd.
_cu_

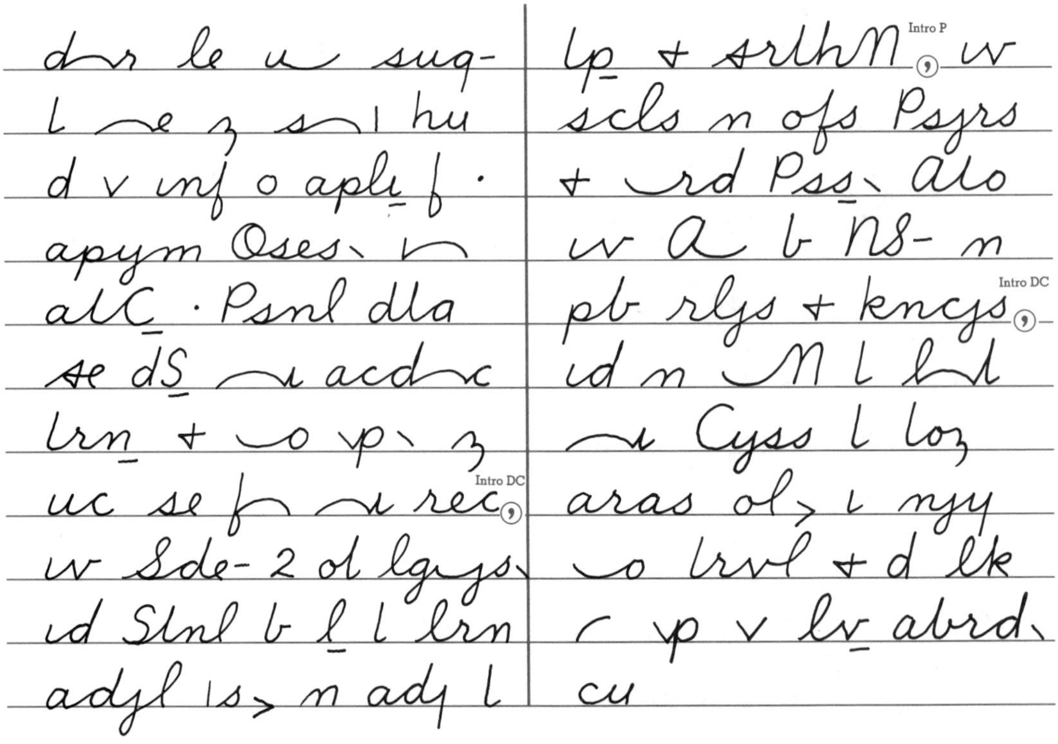

5

Punctuation Study

Punctuate the following letter by adding commas to three introductory dependent clauses and one parenthetical expression.

Preview Words

comfortable 

situated 

introduction 

paperwork 

already 

associates 

facility 

conversation 

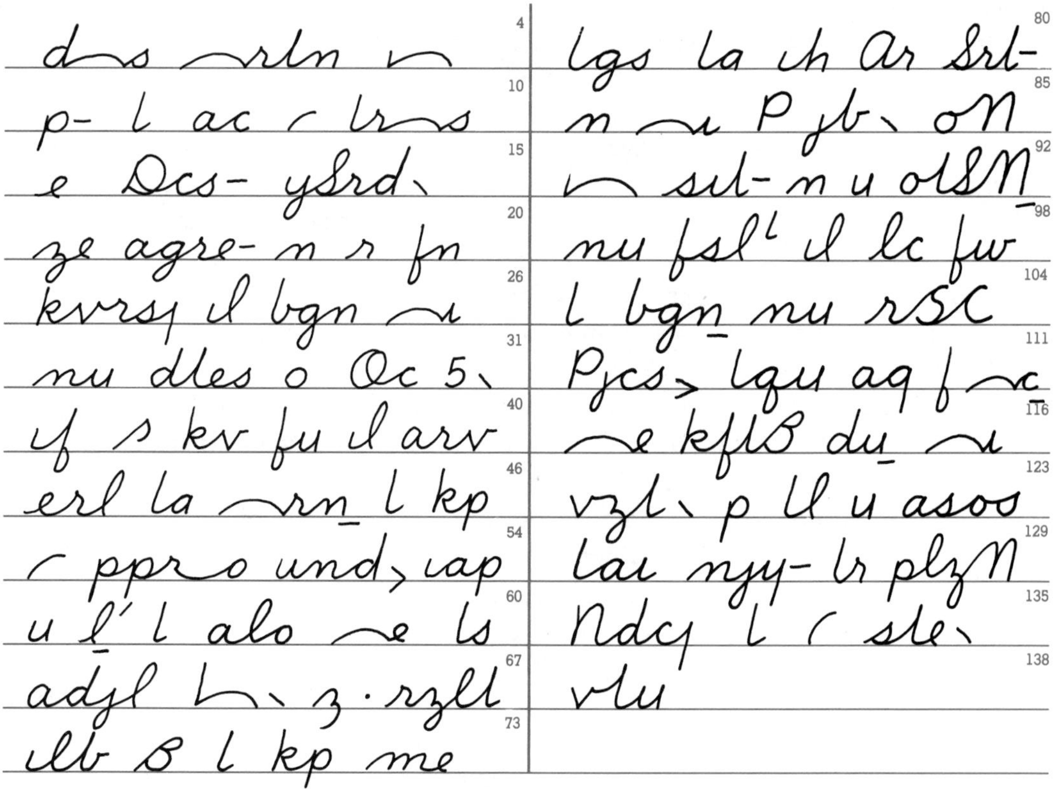

Key

1

Dear Shelley:

I now have the files for half of the people who applied for the position of administrative[1] assistant. Enclosed is a list of the remaining applicants. Could you read through their resumés before meeting[2] with me later this week?

Please select the five applicants who are most likely to meet our standards. Make your decision[3] on the basis of the skills and experience listed on their employment papers.

I will ask my secretary[4] to contact our final candidates and arrange for personal interviews. We will then write letters to[5] the references and make our final decision. I am hopeful that we will have this position filled on[6] schedule.

Sincerely, (123)

2

Dear Jill:

It is good news that you have decided to relocate. We always felt that you were the best possible[1] choice to manage our regional headquarters in Tampa. One look at your performance record confirmed that you are[2] exactly what this establishment needs.

We encourage you to put your leadership skills to good use. If you wish[3] to make organizational changes, remember that the home office will support you in every way.

Until[4] you have decided upon a permanent residence, you will be the guest of this company. I think you will[5] find that your hotel is very comfortable and convenient.

This is a great opportunity. I know you[6] will make the most of it.

Sincerely yours, (127)

3

Dear Employee:

Welcome to Best Industries. The enclosed materials will help introduce you to our firm. The[1] first booklet explains company policies and the layout of our facility.

An important part of your[2] benefit plan is medical and life insurance. We advise you to read this literature carefully. The[3] blue book describes your hospitalization and out-patient benefits. The red book explains the life insurance[4] policy. If you wish to increase your coverage to include other members of the family, that option[5] is presented on page 3.

After you have been employed here for six months, you will be eligible to participate[6] in our profit plan. We think our stock options are among the best in the country.

We hope this information[7] answers many of your initial questions.

Yours truly, (151)

4

Dear Mr. Lee:

You were suggested to me as someone who would have information on applying for an[1] appointment overseas. I am attaching a personal data sheet describing my academic training and[2] work experience. As you can see from my record, I have studied two other languages. I would certainly[3] be willing to learn additional ones.

In addition to typing and shorthand, I have skills in office procedures[4] and word processing. Although I have always been interested in public relations and communications,[5] I would not want to limit my choices to those areas only.

I enjoy world travel and would welcome[6] the experience of living abroad.

Cordially yours, (130)

5

Dear Ms. Martin:

I am pleased to accept the terms we discussed yesterday. As we agreed in our phone conversation,[1] I will begin my new duties on October 5. If it is convenient for you, I will arrive early that[2] morning to complete the paperwork you need.

I appreciate your willingness to allow me this additional[3] time. As a result, I will be able to complete many things that I had already started in my present[4] job. Once I am situated in your outstanding new facility, I will look forward to beginning[5] new research projects.

Thank you again for making me comfortable during my visit. Please tell your associates[6] that I enjoyed their pleasant introduction to the city.

Very truly yours, (136)

unl 2
Psnl*

Shorthand Vocabulary Review

Study the following principles and the words that illustrate them. Each word will occur in the letters and memos in this unit.

1. Write \ for words beginning with the sound of any vowel + x *(aks, eks, iks, oks, uks,* or *eggs).*

Write x for the medial and final sound of x.

exact	vc	exciting	vl_
expect	vpc	expansion	vpnj
explains	vplns	exercise	vrsz
flexible	flxB	accidents	vdNs

***Unit Two**
Personnel*

2. When a word contains two medial (middle) vowels that are pronounced consecutively, write the first vowel.

dial	dil	science	sN
radius	rdes	Miami	⌒me
period	pred	material	⌒trel
various	vres	manual	⌒nul
annual	aul	tuition	luj
realize	relz	Seattle	sell

3. When a word ends in two vowel sounds that are pronounced consecutively, write only the last vowel.

idea	ida	create	cra
area	ara	media	⌒da
radio	rdo	evaluate	evla
Gloria	glra	cafeteria	cftra

LESSON 6

Brief Forms and Derivatives

1. *plc Avn ku pl sug*
2. *sal sv bo k nkv arms*

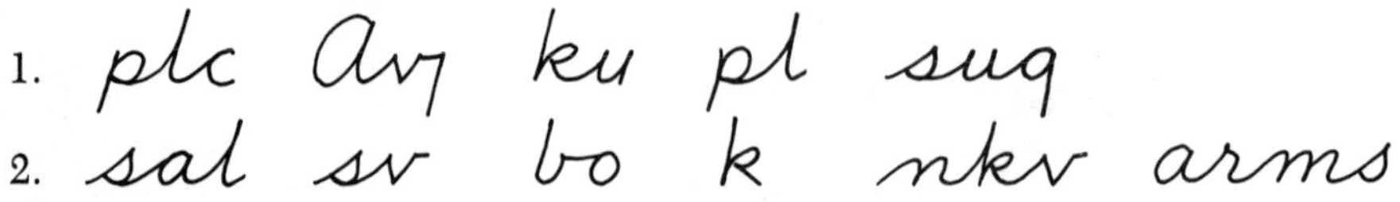

Key

1. particular, advantage, continue, part/port, suggest
2. satisfy/satisfactory, several, both, came/come/committee, inconvenience, arrangements

Phrase Review

1. *il iv ivt eblv ehp*
2. *uv ulb udb Ub lgv*
3. *S cb vn ✓ lb db*

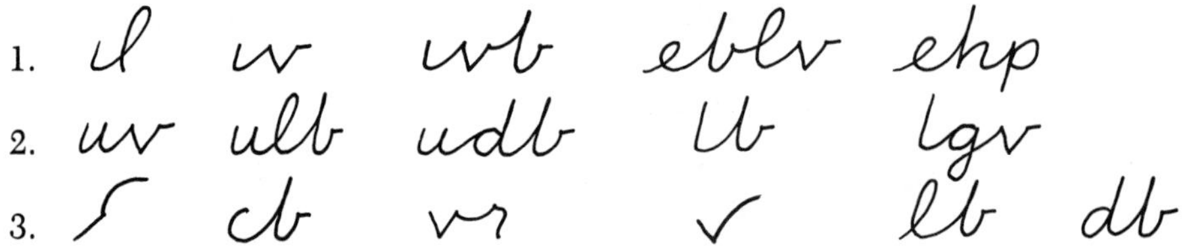

Key

1. I will, I have, I have been, we believe, we hope
2. you have, you will be, you would be, to be, to give
3. at the, can be, of our, of the, will be, would be

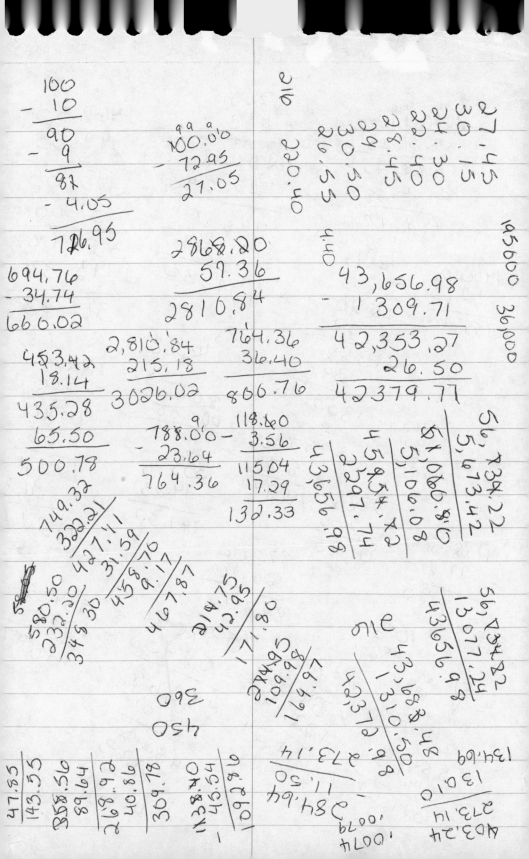

100
- 10
90
- 9
87
- 4.05
726.95

100.00
- 72.95
27.05

694.76
- 34.74
660.02

2868.20
57.36
2810.84

43,656.98
- 1 309.71
42,353.27
26.50
42379.77

453.42
18.14
435.28
65.50
500.78

2,810.84
215.18
3026.02

764.36
36.40
800.76

788.00
- 23.64
764.36

118.60
- 3.56
115.04
17.29
132.33

750.00
251.25
498.75
9.58
489.17

1,264
- 463.2
1200.8
- 60.04
1140.76
11.41
1129.35

462.50
92.50
370.00
37.00
333.00
13.32
319.68

1400.10
- 42.00
1358.10

1600
- 80
1520
152
1368
34.20
1333.80

16000
.05
800.00
00000

2200
- 880
1320
66
1254
31.3
1222.

840
- 84
756

87.60
8.76
78.84

355.75
14.23
341.52

277.50
- 5.55
271.95

276.80
- 27.63
248.85

870.00
- 26.10
843.90

534.08
- 123.11
410.97

10%
9%

23%

534.08
53.40
480.68
48.06
432.62
21.63
410.99

81
- 4

81
- 4
77

534.08
122.84
411.24

534.08
- 144.47
389.61

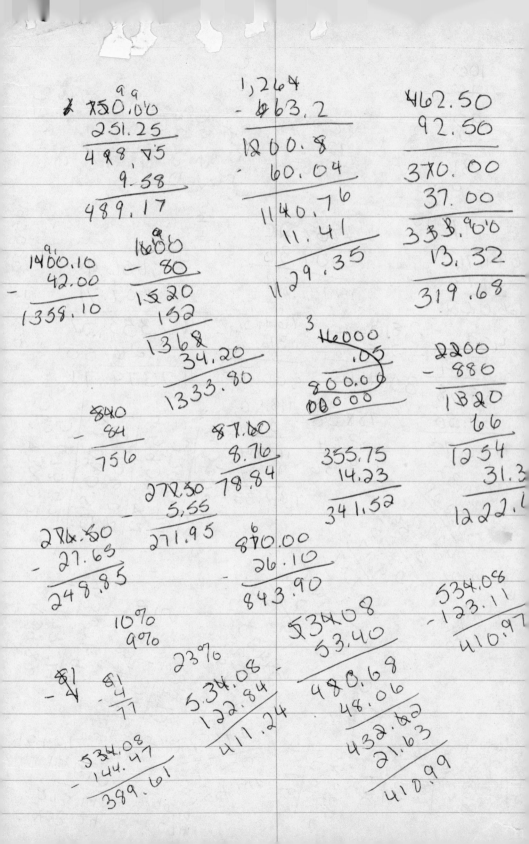

Reading and Writing Exercises

1

Preview Words

space	sps	cafeteria	cftra
entire	ntr	flexible	flxB
larger	lrjr	schedule	scjl
Christmas	X–s	satisfactory	sal

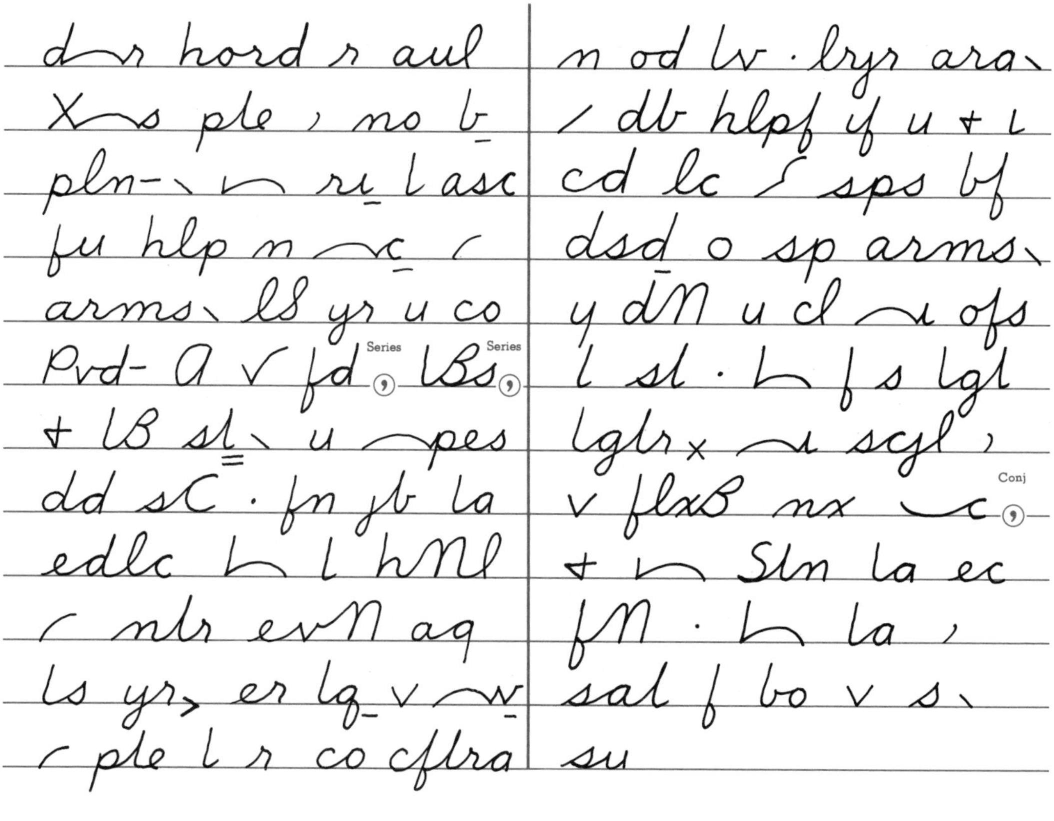

2

Preview Words

- careers
- science
- entrance
- 9 o'clock
- technical
- particular
- definitely
- engineering

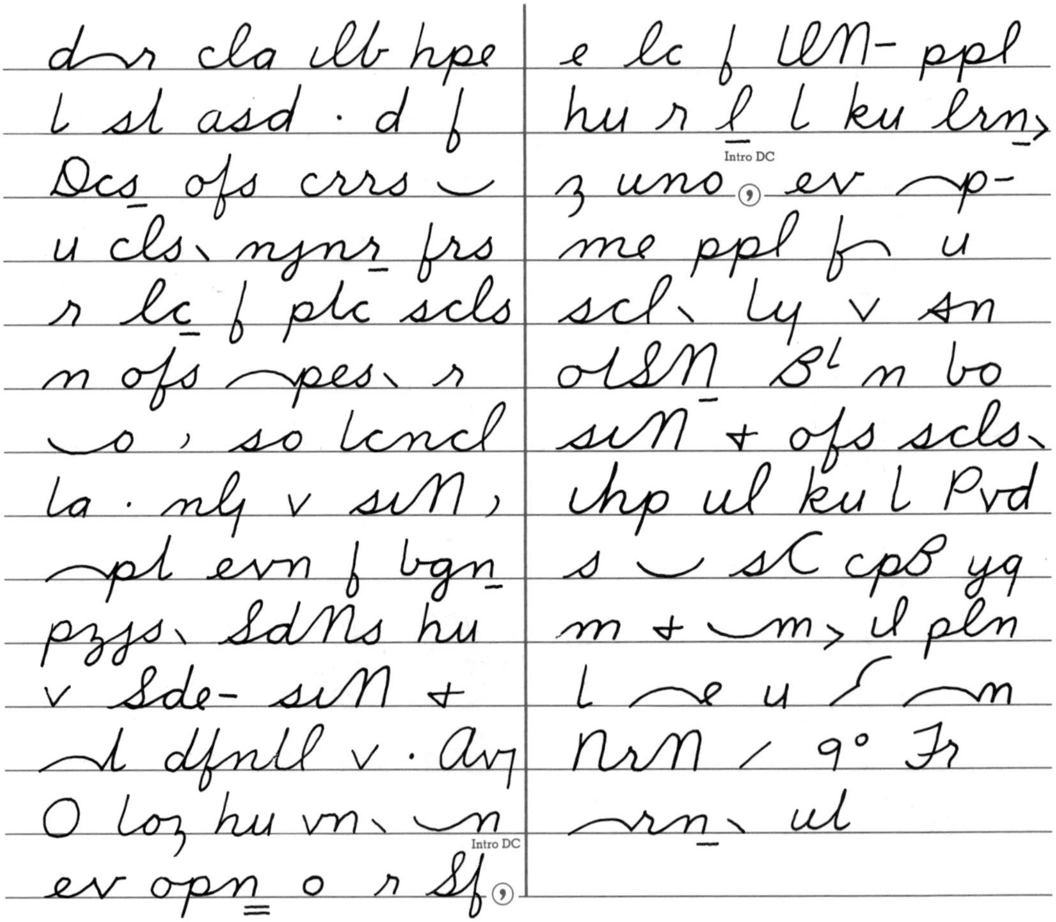

3

Preview Words

Miami

sponsor

thought

Florida

charter

reduced

weekend

practical

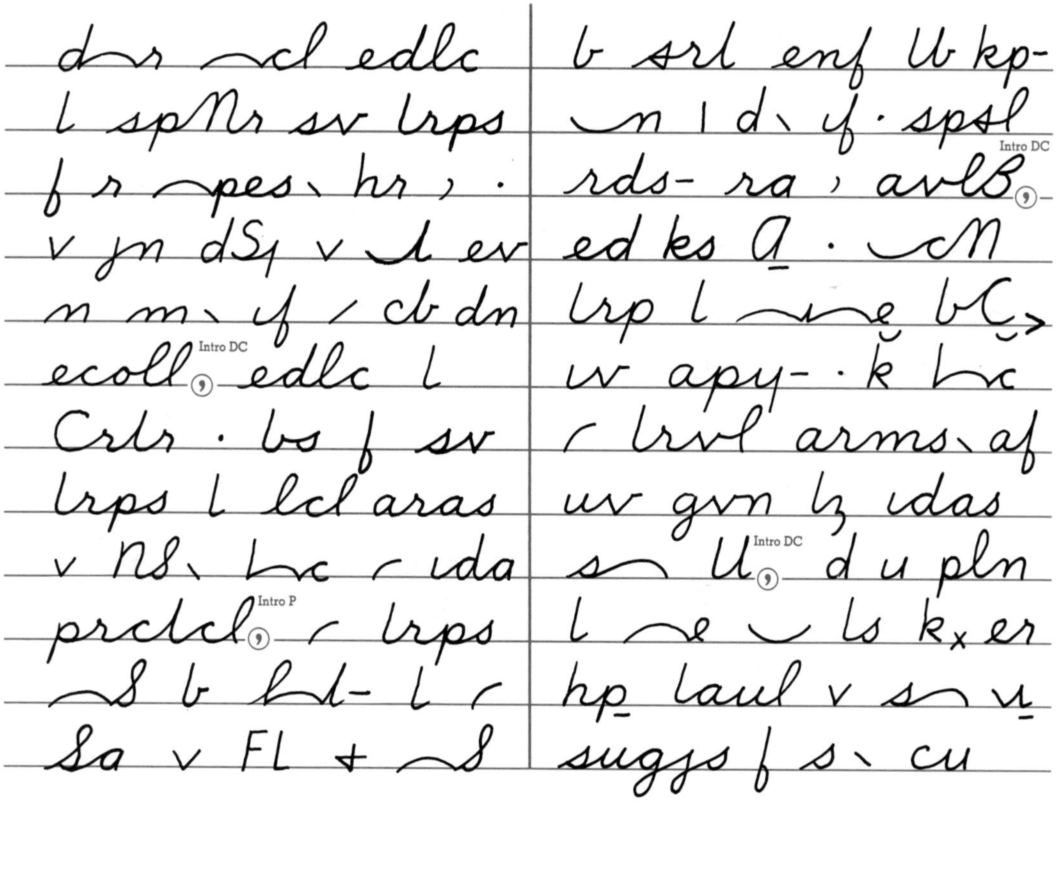

4

Preview Words

limit	lmt	sections	scjs
courtesy	crtse	unavailable	uavlB
confine	kfn	painters	pNrs
patience	psN	inconvenience	nkv

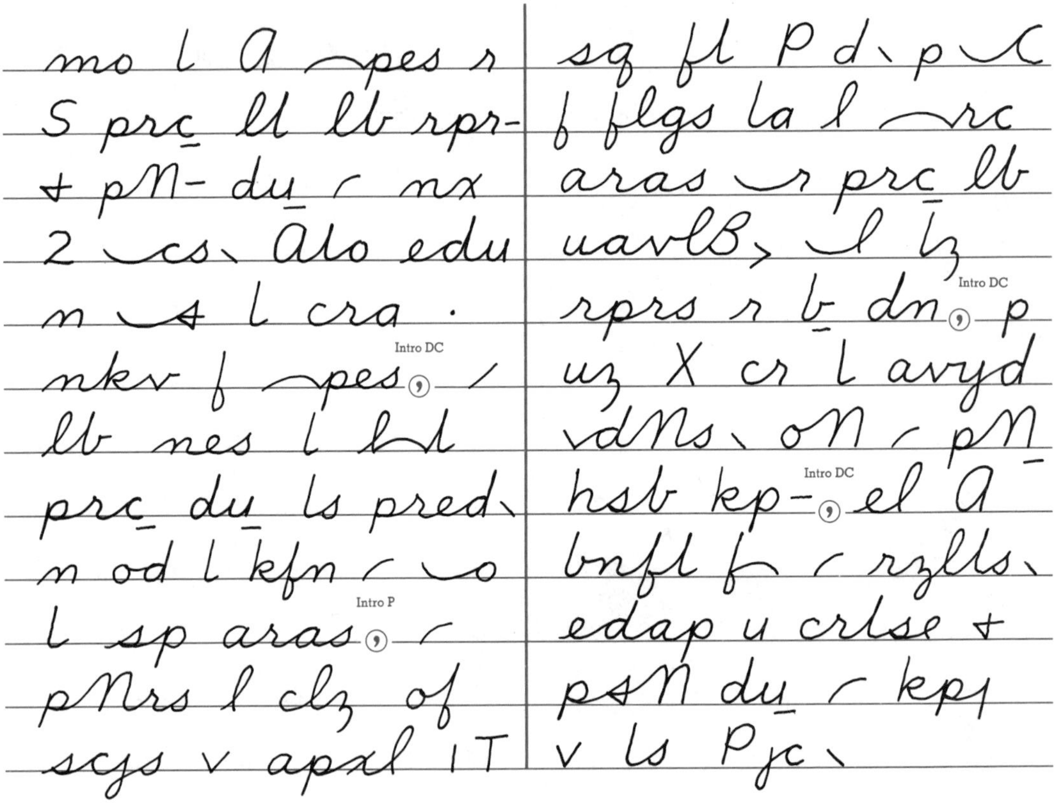

5

Punctuation Study

Punctuate the following letter. Add commas to set off one introductory phrase, two conjunctions, and one introductory dependent clause.

Preview Words

exact	vc	outside	olsd
consult	ksll	accordance	acrdN
agency	ajNe	specified	sp-
contacts	klcs	representatives	reps

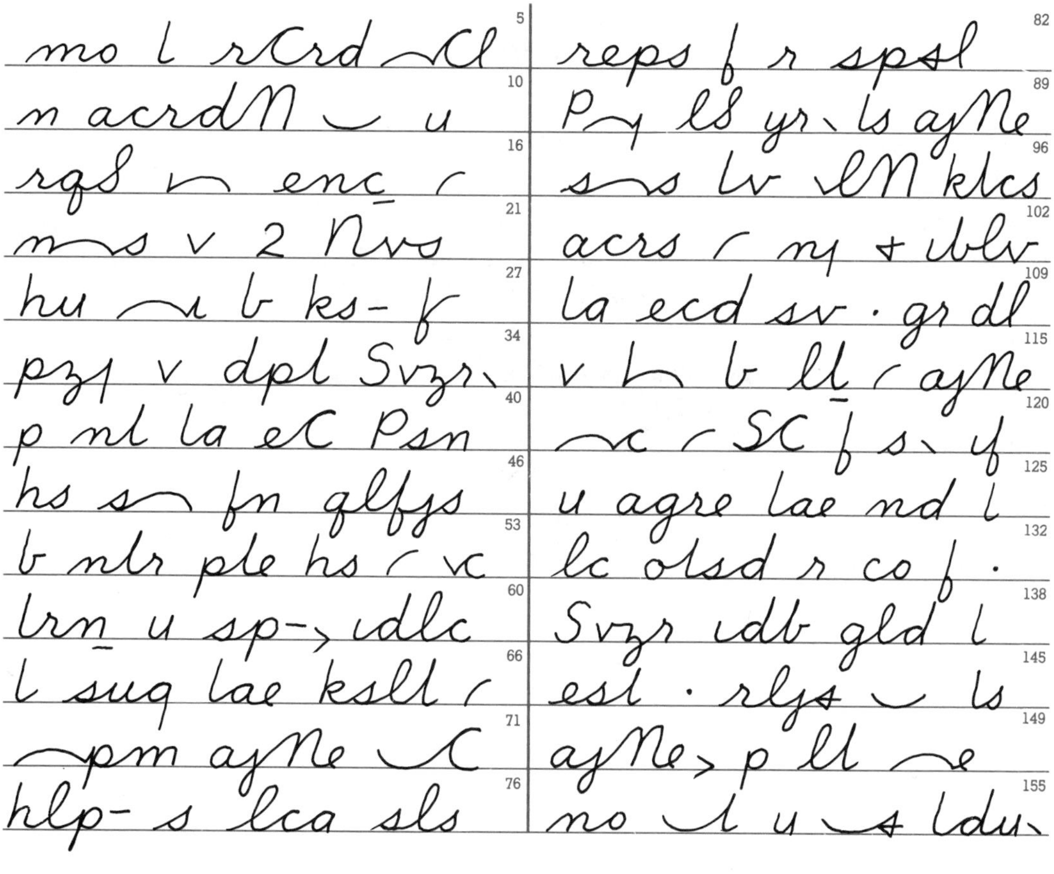

Key

1

Dear Mr. Howard:

Our annual Christmas party is now being planned. I am writing to ask for your help in[1] making the arrangements. Last year your company provided all of the food, tables, and table settings. Your[2] employees did such a fine job that we would like them to handle the entire event again this year.

We are thinking[3] of moving the party to our company cafeteria in order to have a larger area. It[4] would be helpful if you and I could look at the space before deciding on specific arrangements. Why don't you[5] call my office to set a time for us to get together? My schedule is very flexible next week, and I[6] am certain that we can find a time that is satisfactory for both of us.

Sincerely yours, (137)

2

Dear Mr. Clay:

I will be happy to set aside a day for discussing office careers with your class. Engineering[1] firms are looking for particular skills in office employees. Our work is so technical that a knowledge[2] of science is important even for beginning positions. Students who have studied science and math definitely[3] have an advantage over those who have not. When we have openings on our staff, we look for talented[4] people who are willing to continue learning.

As you know, we have employed many people from your school. They have[5] shown outstanding ability in both science and office skills. I hope you will continue to provide us[6] with such capable young men and women.

I will plan to meet you at the main entrance at 9 o'clock Friday[7] morning.

Yours truly, (143)

3

Dear Mr. Michael:

We would like to sponsor several trips for our employees. Here is a very general[1] description of what we have in mind. If it can be done economically, we would like to charter a bus[2] for several trips to local areas of interest. To make the idea practical, the trips must be[3] limited to the state of Florida and must be short enough to be completed within one day. If a special[4] reduced rate is available, we would consider adding a weekend trip to Miami Beach.

I have appointed[5] a committee to make the travel arrangements. After you have given these ideas some thought, would you plan[6] to meet with this committee? We are hoping that you will have some exciting suggestions for us.

Cordially yours,[7] (140)

4

MEMO TO: All Employees

Our south parking lot will be repaired and painted during the next two weeks. Although[1] we do not wish to create an inconvenience for employees, it will be necessary to limit parking during[2] this period. In order to confine the work to specific areas, the painters will close off sections[3] of approximately 1,000 square feet per day. Please watch for flags that will mark areas where parking will be[4] unavailable.

While these repairs are being done, please use extra care to avoid accidents. Once the painting[5] has been completed, we will all benefit from the results. We would appreciate your courtesy and patience[6] during the completion of this project. (127)

5

MEMO TO: Richard Mitchell

In accordance with your request, I am enclosing the names of two individuals[1] who might be considered for the position of department supervisor. Please note that each person has some[2] fine qualifications, but neither party has the exact training you specified.

I would like to suggest that[3] we consult the employment agency which helped us locate sales representatives for our special promotion[4] last year. This agency seems to have excellent contacts across the nation, and I believe that we could save a[5] great deal of time by letting the agency make the search for us. If you agree that we need to look outside our[6] company for a supervisor, I would be glad to establish a relationship with this agency.

Please[7] let me know what you wish to do. (146)

LESSON 7

Abbreviations and Derivatives

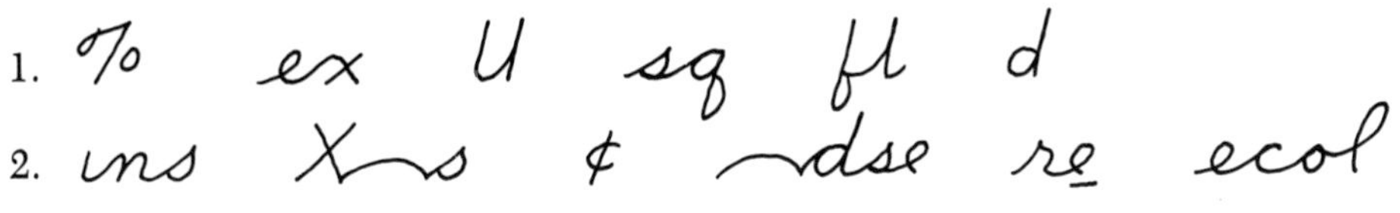

Key

1. percent, executive/example, university, square, feet, day
2. insurance, Christmas, cent/cents, merchandise, regarding, economical

Transcription Aids: Typing Numbers

1. In your transcribed copy, spell out numbers from one through ten in regular prose material. Use figures for 11 and higher.

   We have three new branch offices.

   Please send me 15 copies of your report.

2. When numbers below ten appear in the same sentence with related numbers above ten, use figures for both.

   Jane ordered 6 copies for Bill, 12 copies for Mark, and 16 copies for me.

3. Always use figures to show percentages. Spell out the word *percent* in contextual material.

   You will receive a discount of 10 percent on all merchandise.

Your Business Vocabulary		
guidelines	*gdlns*	A statement of policy or specific instructions regarding an activity.

Please follow the guidelines presented in the company manual.

| timely | *Ll* | Well timed; of current interest or an appropriate occurrence. |

I enjoyed hearing your timely remarks.

Reading and Writing Exercises

1

Preview Words

timely	*Ll*	handbook	*hNbc*
extremely	*Xl*	adjustments	*ajSms*
update	*pda*	participants	*ppNs*
workload	*old*	secretarial	*secl*

mo l hln rsl
me vr ofs Psnl
r sa la r secl
hNbc, ol v da,
d ub l l Cr · k
l pda r hNbc ×
u vp z · ex sec
db Xl vluB, ι

Aso no laur ·
mbr v sv ogjs
f secs. Ph lz ogjs
cd kb Ll inf Ub
I- n r pby, ι relz
la ls rspȝl , · bq
adj lu old ₉ b
e l b B hc

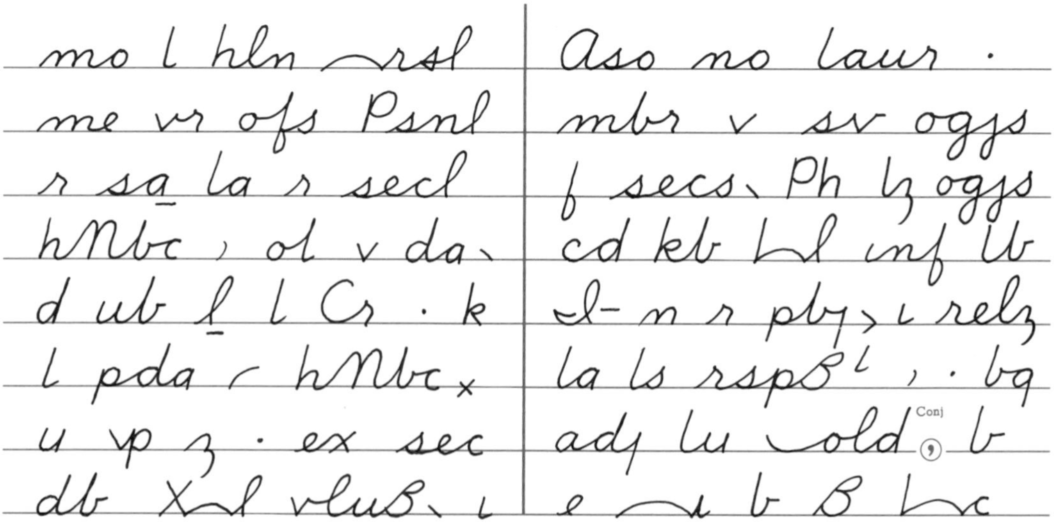

[shorthand outlines]

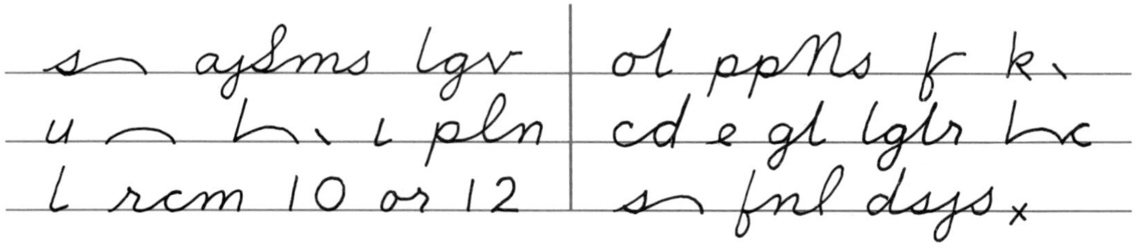

—— 2 ——

Preview Words

Davis	*dvs*	retirement	*rtrm*
health	*hlt*	dedicated	*ddca-*
total	*tol*	guidelines	*gdlns*
earliest	*erls*	Electronics	*elncs*

[shorthand outlines]

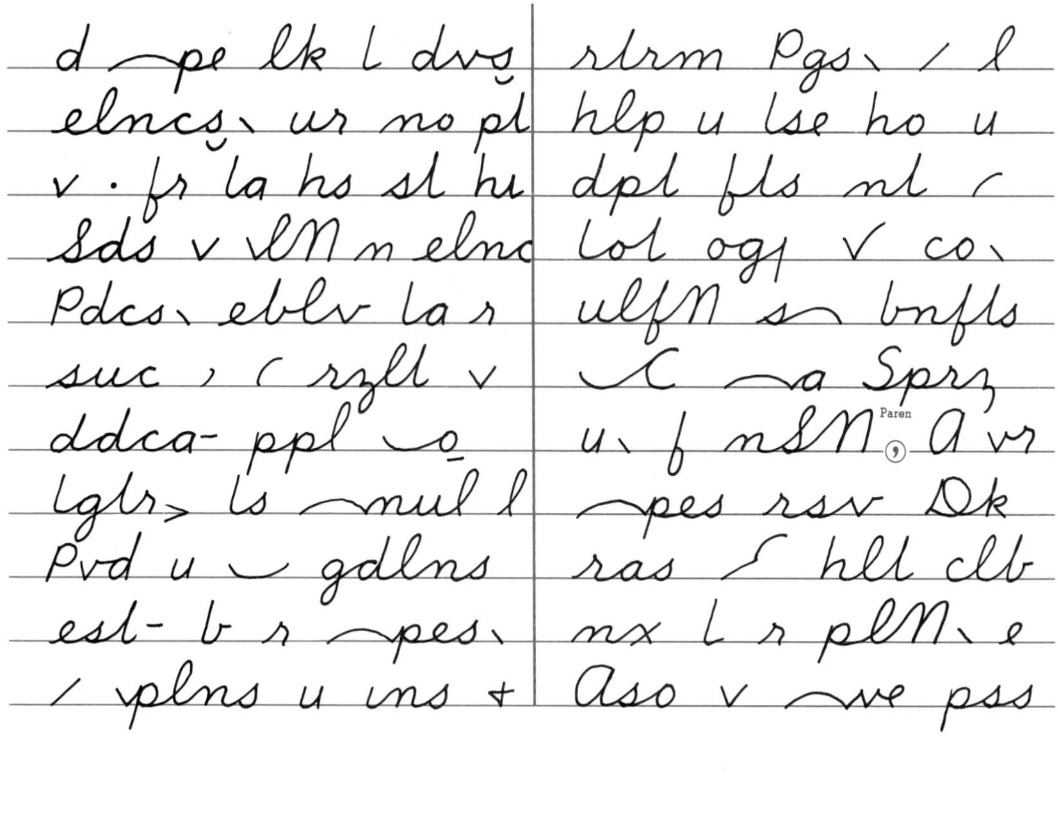

[shorthand]

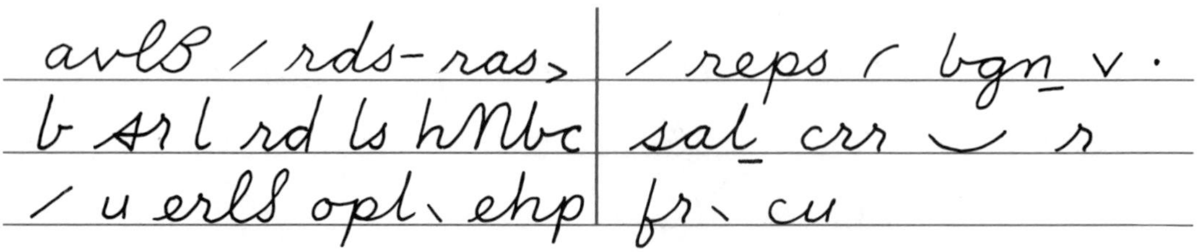

3

Preview Words

toy	_ly_	holiday	_hld_
retail	_rll_	merchandise	_dse_
small	_sl_	appliances	_aplNs_
feature	_fCr_	possibilities	_psB⁴s_

[shorthand passage]

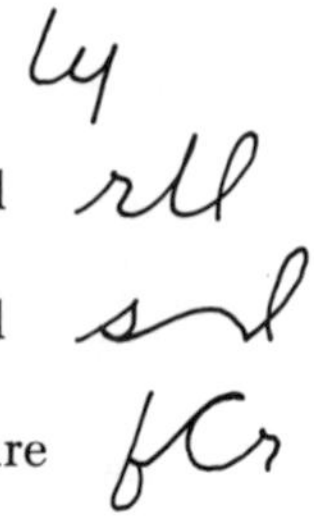

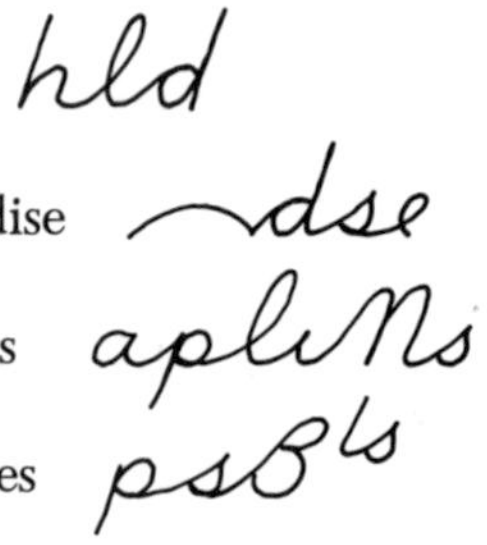

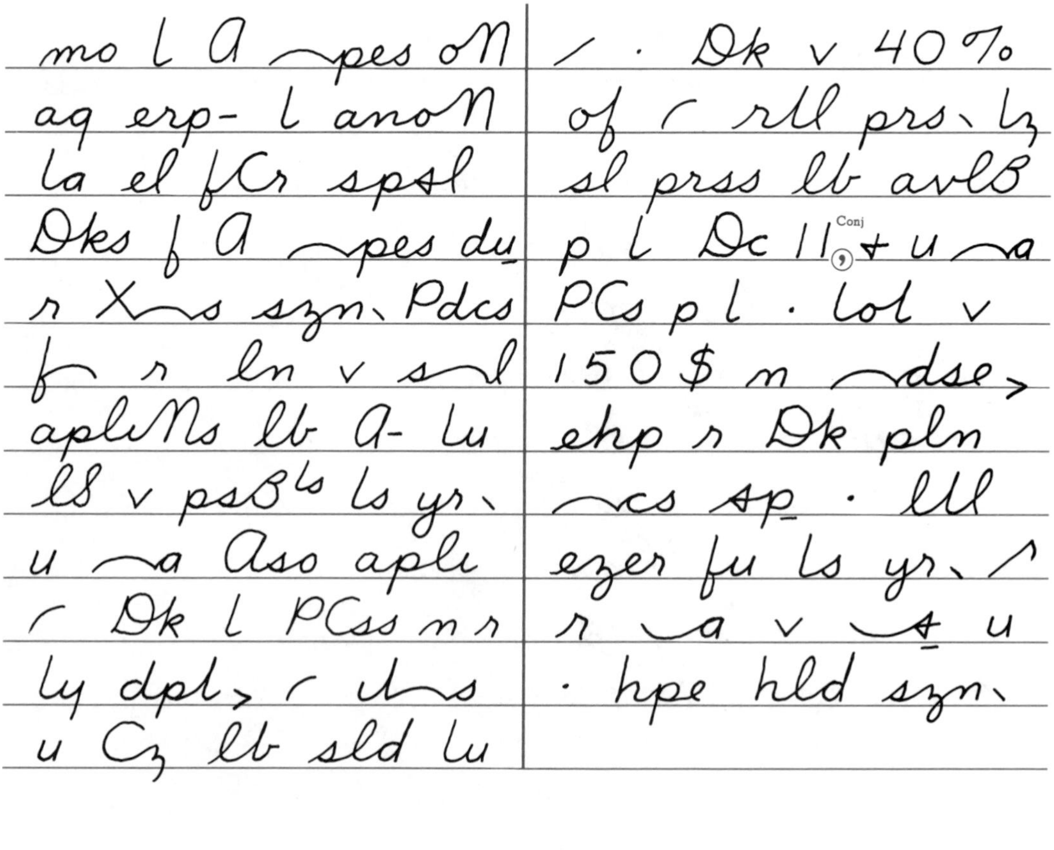

4

Preview Words

ours
hire
edit
pages
artwork
newsletter
periodical
photographs

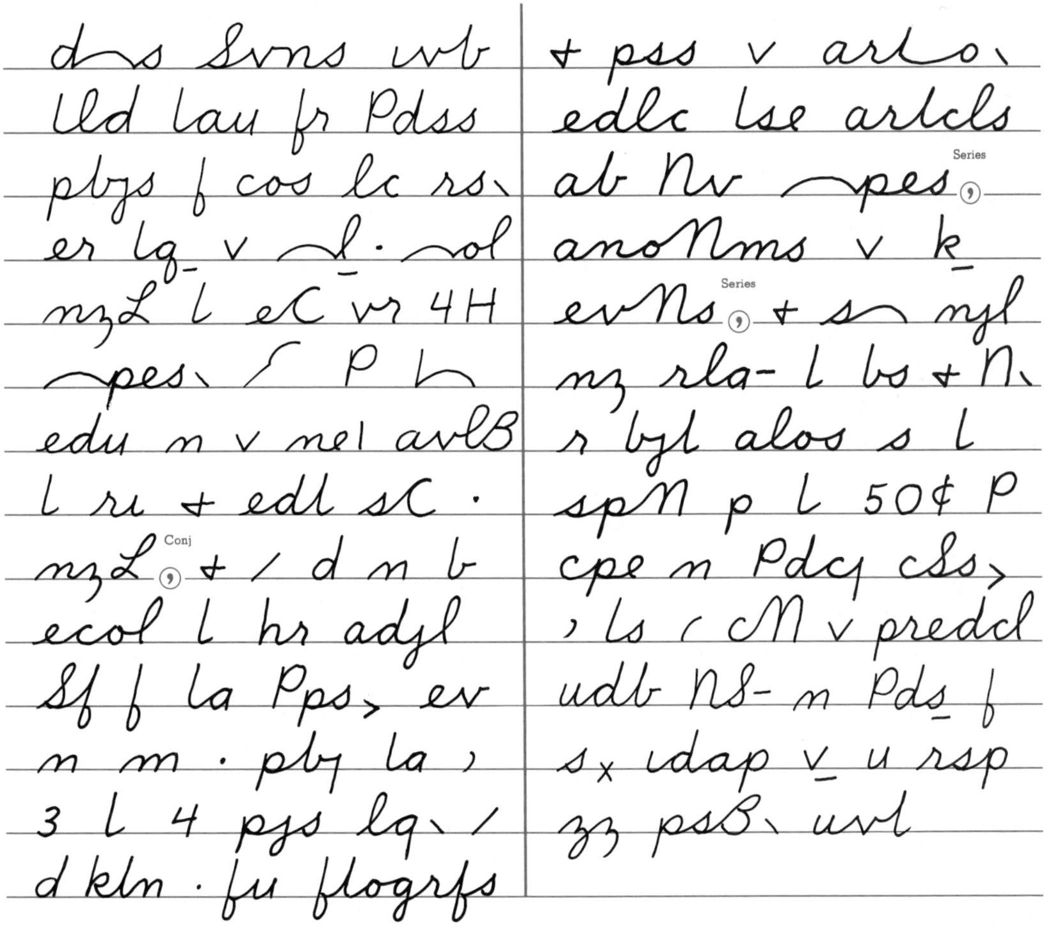

5

Punctuation Study

Add commas to show one introductory phrase and four introductory dependent clauses.

Preview Words

a.m.		clarify	
cancel		differently	
weather		snowstorm	
station		accumulation	

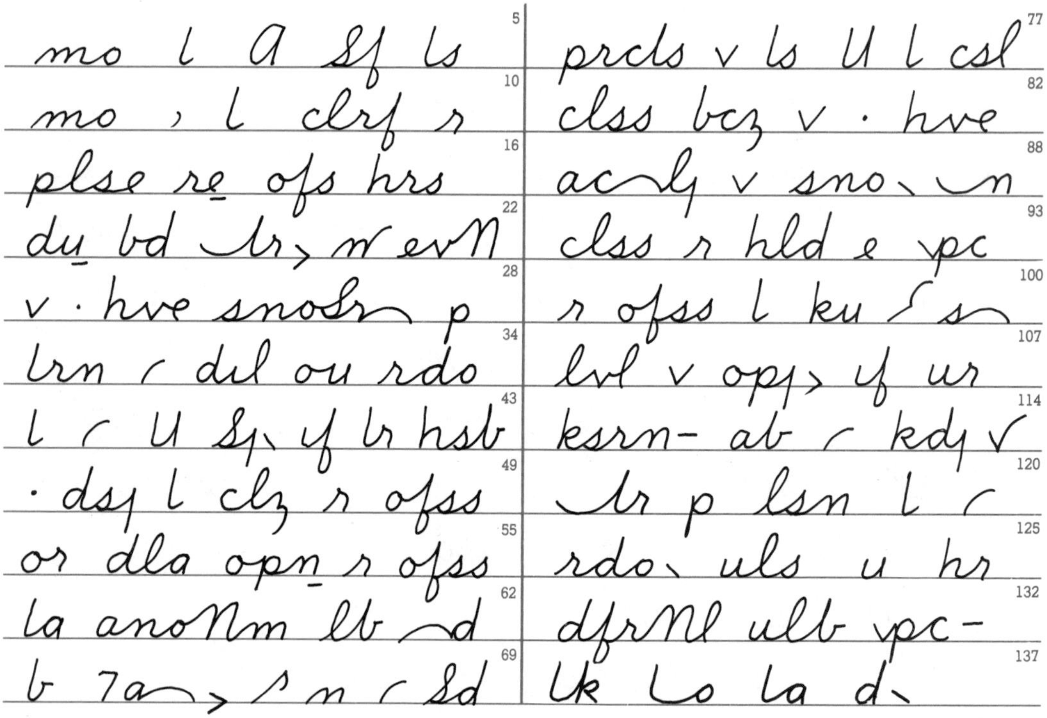

Key

1

MEMO TO: Helen Marshall

Many of our office personnel are saying that our secretarial handbook[1] is out of date. Would you be willing to chair a committee to update the handbook? Your experience as an[2] executive secretary would be extremely valuable. I also know that you are a member of several organizations for[3] secretaries. Perhaps these organizations could contribute timely information to be included in our[4] publication.

I realize that this responsibility is a big addition to your workload, but we[5] might be able to make some adjustments to give you more time. I plan to recommend 10 or 12 other participants[6] for the committee. Could we get together to make some final decisions? (135)

2

Dear Employee:

Welcome to Davis Electronics. You are now part of a firm that has set high standards of[1] excellence in electronic products. We believe that our success is the result of dedicated people[2] working together.

This manual will provide you with guidelines established by our employees. It explains your[3] insurance and retirement programs. It will help you to see how your department fits into the total[4] organization of the company. You will find some benefits which may surprise you. For instance, all of our[5] employees receive discount rates at the health club next to our plant. We also have movie passes available at[6] reduced rates.

Be sure to read this handbook at your earliest opportunity. We hope it represents the beginning[7] of a satisfying career with our firm.

Cordially yours, (151)

3

MEMO TO: All Employees

Once again we are pleased to announce that we will feature special discounts for all[1] employees during our Christmas season. Products from our line of small appliances will be added to your list of[2] possibilities this year. You may also apply the discount to purchases in our toy department.

The items[3] you choose will be sold to you at a discount of 40 percent off the retail price. These sale prices will be[4] available up to December 11, and you may purchase up to a total of $150[5] in merchandise.

We hope our discount plan makes shopping a little easier for you this year. It is our[6] way of wishing you a happy holiday season. (129)

4

Dear Ms. Stevens:

I have been told that your firm produces publications for companies like ours. We are thinking[1] of mailing a monthly newsletter to each of our 400 employees. At the present time we do not have[2] anyone available to write and edit such a newsletter, and it would not be economical to[3] hire additional staff for that purpose.

We have in mind a publication that is three to four pages long. It[4] would contain a few photographs and pieces of artwork. We would like to see articles about individual[5] employees, announcements of coming events, and some national news related to business and industry.[6] Our budget allows us to spend up to 50 cents per copy in production costs.

Is this the kind of[7] periodical you would be interested in producing for us? I would appreciate having your response[8] as soon as possible.

Yours very truly, (167)

5

MEMO TO: All Staff

This memo is to clarify our policy regarding office hours during bad weather.[1]

In the event of a heavy snowstorm, please turn the dial on your radio to the university[2] station. If there has been a decision to close our offices or delay opening our offices, that[3] announcement will be made by 7 a.m.

It is not the standard practice of this university to cancel[4] classes because of a heavy accumulation of snow. When classes are held, we expect our offices to[5] continue at the same level of operation.

If you are concerned about the condition of the weather,[6] please listen to the radio. Unless you hear differently, you will be expected to come to work that day.[7] (140)

LESSON 8

Theory Review

Indicate time in the following ways:

two o'clock	2°	7:30 a.m.	7 ^{30}a
12 noon	12 nn	11:45 p.m.	11 ^{45}p

Transcription Aids: Similar Words

adapt adpl To adjust to a situation.

You can adapt this software program for your business use.

adopt adpl To take a course of action.

Our personnel division will adopt a new policy.

Your Business Vocabulary

fiscal year fscl yr A 12-month period used by organizations for financial planning.

The fiscal year for our corporation begins July 1.

workshop ⌣osp A scheduled educational meeting or training session for a group of people in a specialized field.

The conference will include many workshops and lectures.

Reading and Writing Exercises

--- 1 ---

Preview Words

fiscal *fscl*

quality *qlʼ*

growth *grl*

promised *P—s-*

taught *U*

understaff *USf*

mistake *Mlc*

substitute *sSlu*

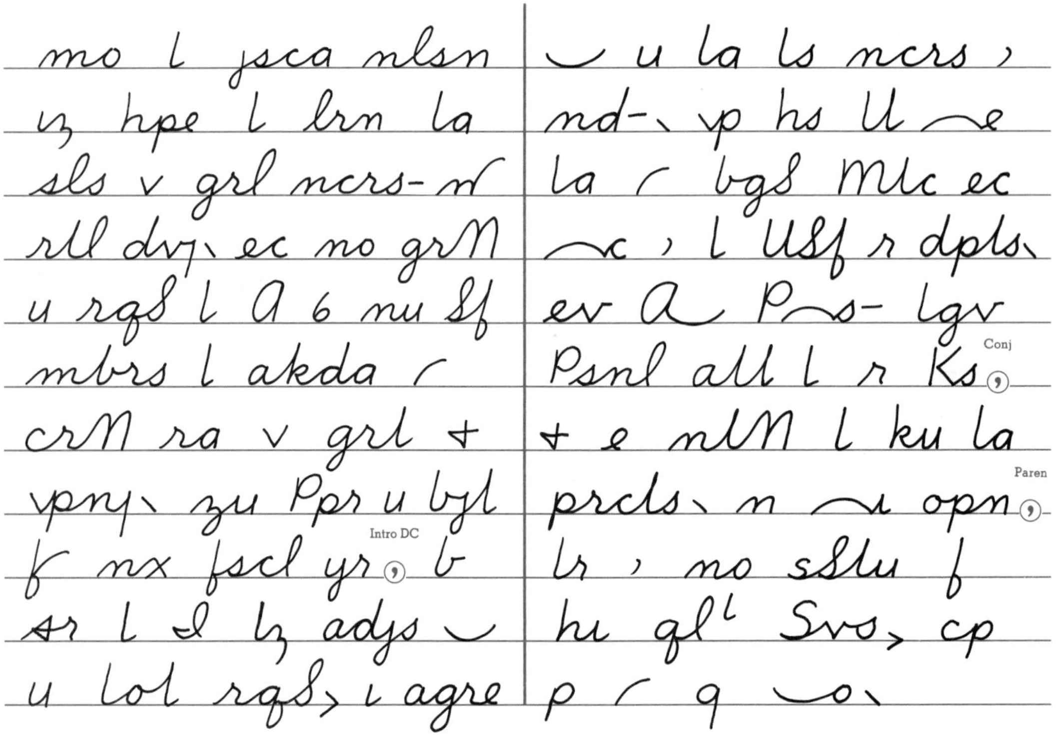

2

Preview Words

adults   *adlts*

Miami   *~ e*

outing   *ot_*

positive   *pzv*

length   *lqt*

pleasure   *plzr*

coupon   *cpn*

children   *Cldrn*

mo l A Sf r Psnl
dvy , ofr_ s_ nu
fu plzr. ev ~d
arms f . No v lrps
f ~pes + lr f~ls.
z uc se f r alC-
scyl , eC lrp , ab Intro DC
l d n lqt , y e
rsv . pzv rsp
l lz lrps , el ku Intro DC
lofr l., e ncy
u l s~l u o lrvl
cdas, cd u suq

s~ alrcys ~n
150 ~ls vr plN,.
er Aso ks_ . ~cM
lrp l ~ e bC,
p se r enc- lS
v hlls + prss. y
ur NS- ~r ✓M-
lrp , p rel r cpn. Intro DC
e Sl nd ldl y ls
ot_ sdb ar- f adlls
of or y Cldrn r
lb Jl-, ehp u fM
lz plns z v_ z edu.

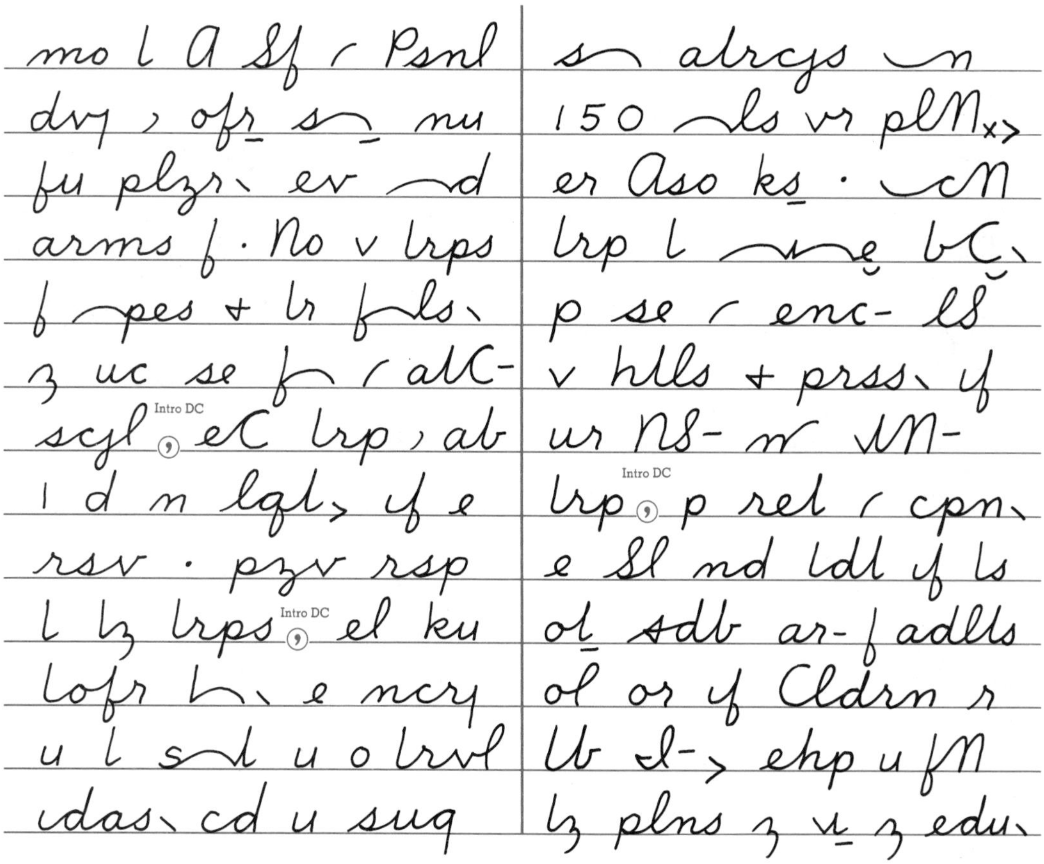

3

Preview Words

adopt	already
flexible	efficiency
permit	concept
decreased	encountered

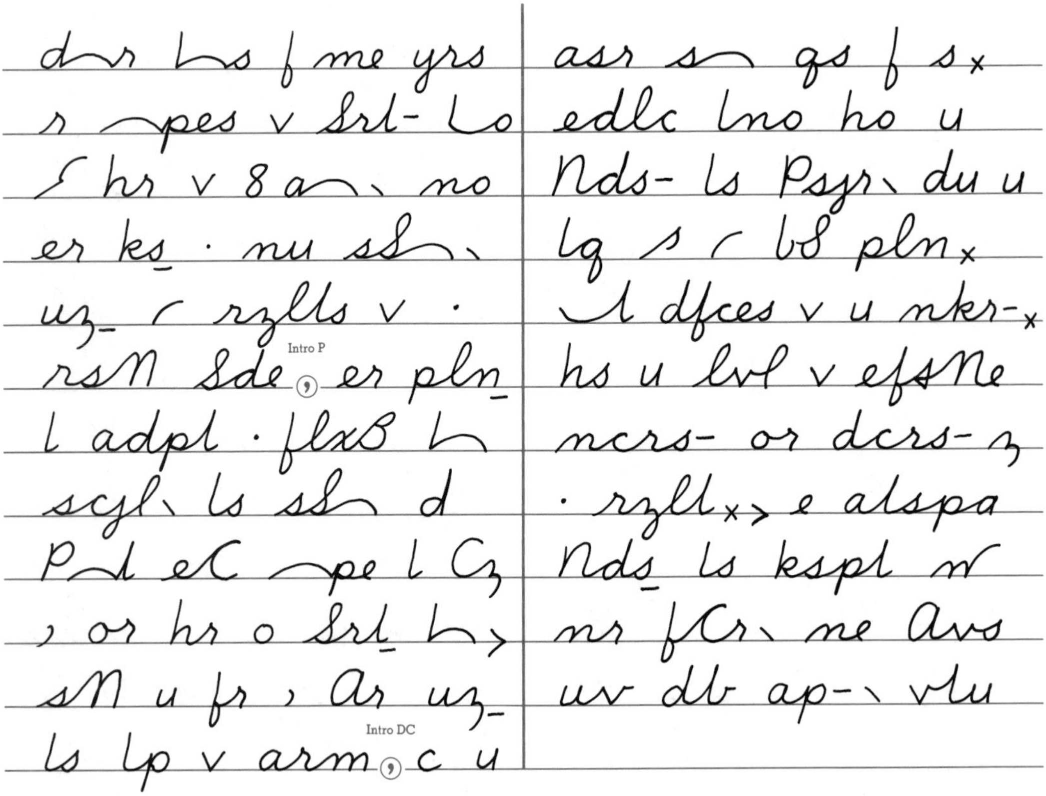

4

Preview Words

1:30 p.m.		exercise	
sessions		promotion	
workshops		evaluate	
evaluations		performance	

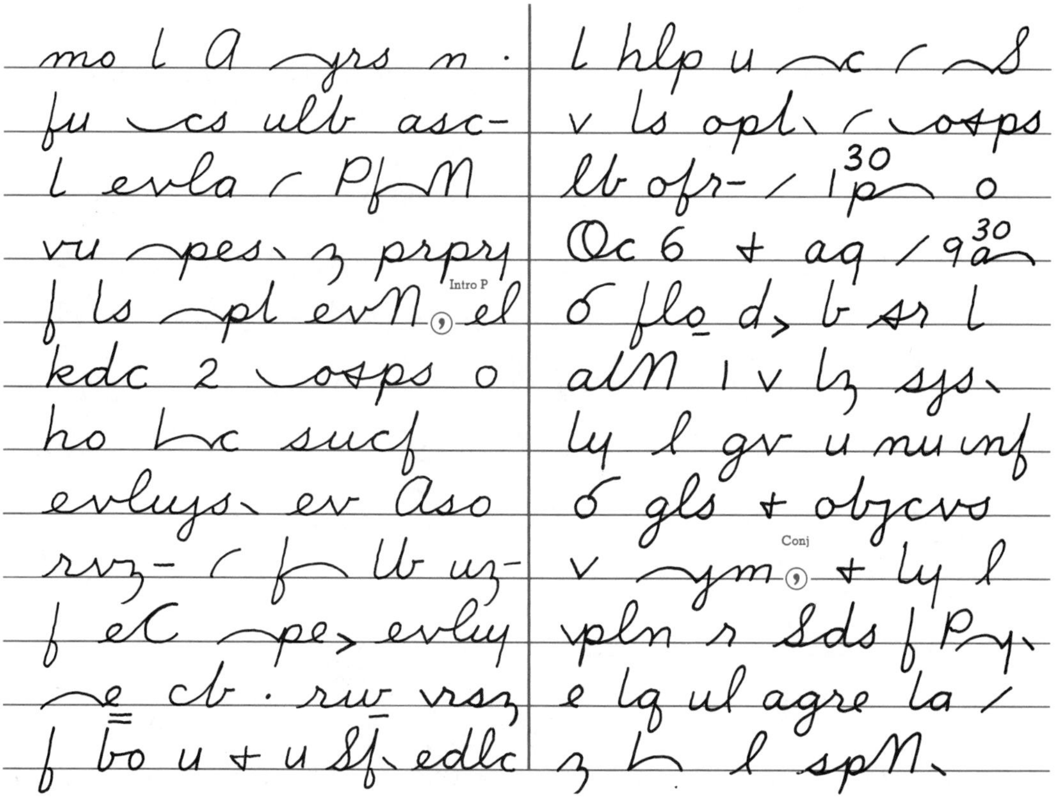

5

Punctuation Study

Add commas to the following letter to show two conjunctions, two introductory dependent clauses, and one introductory phrase.

Preview Words

maximum

adapt

unless

workday

active

obligation

volunteer

involvement

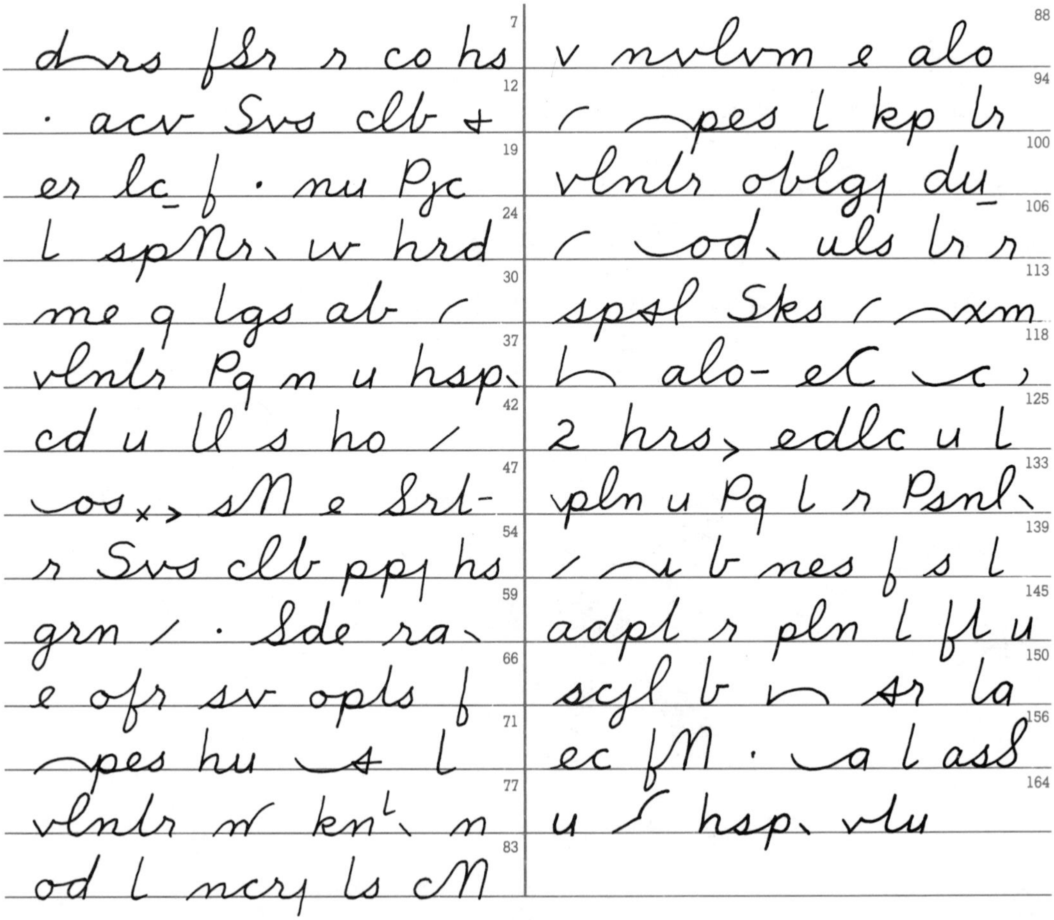

Key

1

MEMO TO: Jessica Nelson

I was happy to learn that sales have greatly increased in the retail division.[1] We can now grant your request to add six new staff members to accommodate the current rate of growth and expansion.[2] As you prepare your budget for the next fiscal year, be sure to include these additions with your total request.[3]

I agree with you that this increase is needed. Experience has taught me that the biggest mistake we can[4] make is to understaff our departments. We have always promised to give personal attention to our customers,[5] and we intend to continue that practice. In my opinion, there is no substitute for high quality[6] service.

Keep up the good work. (125)

2

MEMO TO: All Staff

The personnel division is offering something new for your pleasure. We have made arrangements[1] for a number of trips for employees and their families. As you can see from the attached schedule, each trip[2] is about one day in length.

If we receive a positive response to these trips, we will continue to offer[3] them. We encourage you to submit your own travel ideas. Could you suggest some attractions within[4] 150 miles of our plant?

We are also considering a weekend trip to Miami Beach. Please see the[5] enclosed list of hotels and prices. If you are interested in the extended trip, please return the coupon. We[6] still need to determine if this outing should be arranged for adults only or if children are to be included.[7]

We hope you find these plans as exciting as we do. (150)

3

Dear Mr. Thomas:

For many years our employees have started to work at the hour of 8 a.m. Now we are[1] considering a new system. Using the results of a recent study, we are planning to adopt a[2] flexible time schedule. This system would permit each employee to choose his or her own starting time.

Since your firm[3] is already using this type of arrangement, can you answer some questions for us? We would like to know how you[4] introduced this procedure. Do you think it is the best plan? What difficulties have you encountered? Has your level[5] of efficiency increased or decreased as a result?

We anticipate introducing this concept in the[6] near future. Any advice you have would be appreciated.

Very truly yours, (135)

4

MEMO TO: All Managers

In a few weeks you will be asked to evaluate the performance of your employees.[1] As preparation for this important event, we will conduct two workshops on how to make successful[2] evaluations. We have also revised the form to be used for each employee.

Evaluation meetings can[3] be a rewarding exercise for both you and your staff. We would like to help you make the most of this opportunity.[4] The workshops will be offered at 1:30 p.m. on October 6 and again at 9:30 a.m.[5] on the following day.

Be sure to attend one of these sessions. They will give you new information on the[6] goals and objectives of management, and they will explain our standards for promotion. We think you will agree that[7] it was time well spent. (144)

5

Dear Mrs. Foster:

Our company has an active service club, and we are looking for a new project to sponsor.[1] I have heard many good things about the volunteer program in your hospital. Could you tell us how it works?[2]

Since we started our service club, participation has grown at a steady rate. We offer several[3] opportunities for employees who wish to volunteer in the community. In order to encourage this[4] kind of involvement, we allow the employees to complete their volunteer obligation during the workday.[5] Unless there are special circumstances, the maximum time allowed each week is two hours.

We would like you to explain[6] your program to our personnel. It might be necessary for us to adapt our plan to fit your schedule, but[7] I am sure that we can find a way to assist you at the hospital.

Very truly yours, (156)

LESSON 9

Shorthand Vocabulary Review

Write 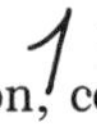 for the word ending *tion* (pronounced *shun*, *zhun*, or *chun*: sion, cian, shion, cean, cion) or for a vowel + *tion* (a-tion, e-tion, i-tion or ish-un, o-tion, u-tion).

national 

invitation 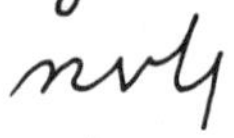

conservation 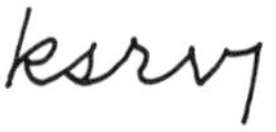

transition 

construction 

occasion 

reception 

reservation 

possession 

traditional 

Transcription Aids: Spelling

Omit the final *e* when adding *ing* to most words:

handl*e*, handl*ing*

mov*e*, mov*ing*

leav*e*, leav*ing*

hav*e*, hav*ing*

retir*e*, retir*ing*

solv*e*, solv*ing*

schedul*e*, schedul*ing*

stimulat*e*, stimulat*ing*

congratulat*e*, congratulat*ing*

distribut*e*, distribut*ing*

issu*e*, issu*ing*

mak*e*, mak*ing*

Your Business Vocabulary	radius	*rdes*	A measure of a circular area.

The broadcast will be carried within a radius of 42 miles.

evaluate *evla* To examine and judge.

A committee was appointed to evaluate the findings.

Reading and Writing Exercises

--- 1 ---

Preview Words

bring *brq*

awards *aws*

banquet *bnql*

conference *kfrN*

extremely *X-l*

invitation *nvly*

stimulating *S-la*

reservation *rzrvy*

d—s flds lqf ac
r nvly, er X—l
p— la uv agre—lb
r gS spcr / r aws
bnql, chp laul I
s—— v —trel u P—
l r Psnl —yrs lS
—o, af i hrd u
r—rcs S nyl

kfrN ,⑨ vz dt—l brq
u bf r o grp,
ev —d r trvl
arms fu vzl, r
arln lcl , enc—⑨.
+ u hll rzrvy hsb
kfr— b r co, il —e
u S arpl + drv
u l r hll, ul v

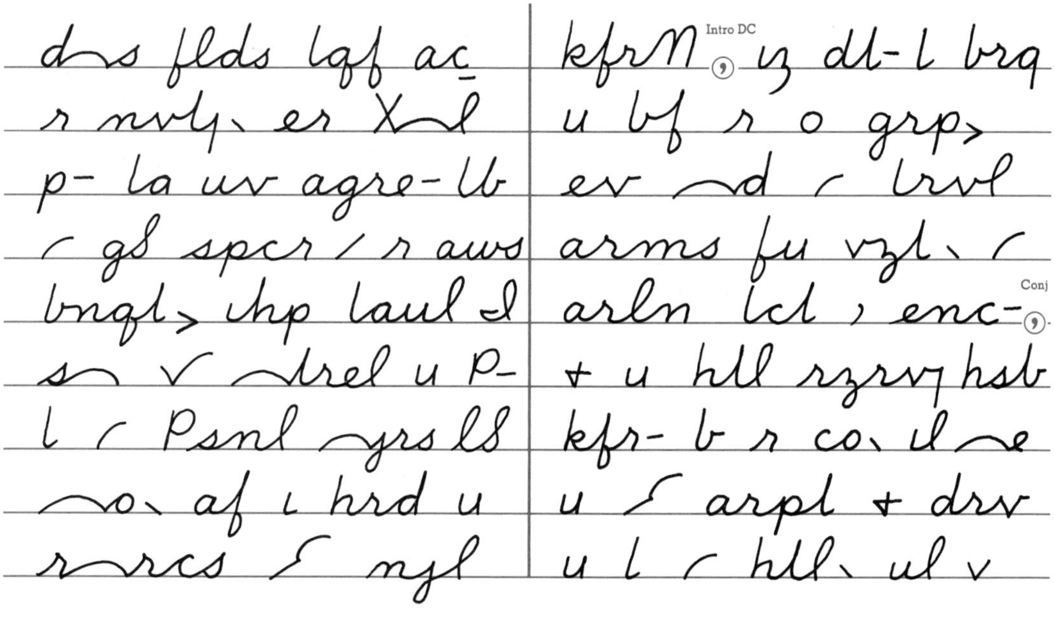

sv hrs l r8 bf
alN (dnr, uno
lau ~sj lb bo
hlpf + Sla, p ll

~e no if ic as8
u n ne ol ~a,
uvl

2

Preview Words

radius	rdes	evaluate	evla
separate	sprl	excessive	vsv
energy	nrje	electricity	els'
analysis	anlss	superintendent	S

dr clrc i USN
la uv kdc- ~C
rSC n nrje
ksrvj, w Aso hrd
lau vm rzdNs +
bss ldl ho efsNl
ly op, cd u k l r
bld l evla r lvl
v efsNex, sN bld
r plN 9 yrs aq
ev rpls- r he +
cl ss~ ~ 2 sprl

Intro P

unls, eC z dzn-
l akda · rdes v
6T sq fl, no er
ksrn- lae ~a b
uz · vsv a~l v
els', ublv la · kp
anlss , n od, p
cl ~ ofs l ar ·
d fu vzl, il asc
(S vr bld l sl
asd (nlr d fu, cu

3

Preview Words

create	cra	Debbie	dbe
expense	vpN	collecting	clc
badges	bjs	security	scrl
supervise	Svz	identification	idNf

mo l dbe lnrd
er w Pss v dzn
nu idNf bjs f
vzlrs n r bld, ul
sn rsv . bx v
idNf bjs lb uz- n
pls v m lgs la
ev uz- w ps, p
gv X all l D +
clc r bjs, lz ins
r f PmN us , + (Conj)
edu n s l cra

. unes vpN b v l
rpls ls bjs> ino
lau Svz sv ppl
hu lc O r rspf
dsc n ur a-a,
d u p se la eC
vu asSNs USNs r
Psjr f isu bjs x>
Ppr idNf, pl l
r scrl vr co, ino
la ec k ou spl , dbe, (Dir Ad)

---------------- **4** ----------------

Preview Words

Gloria *glrą*

generous *jnrs*

along *alq*

occasion *ocj*

gather *glr*

luncheon *lnCn*

Hastings *hS*

fortunately *fCntl*

mo l K Svs reps
me vu Ar no la
glrą hS lb rlz S
N v ls ⌒o, p jyn
s o Jn 30 f · lnCn
n onr v hr rlrm,
⌒ lnCn l bgn /
11 a^30 w brd r⌐,
ndls lsa ⑼ ls frN
+ aso lb N– b El
n r dpl, loz v s
hu vh ⌒ plzs v ⌒o

⌣ hr no la se hs
· spsl scl f slv
dfc Pbls, fCnll ⑼^Paren
se hsb v jnrs n ps
hr nlf alq l ⌒ ppl
⌣o ⌣ hr, yf u s
l alN ⌒ lnCn ⑼^Intro DC p
kp + rel ⌒ enc–
f⌐, ehp laul glr
⌣ s f ls v spsl
ocj⌐

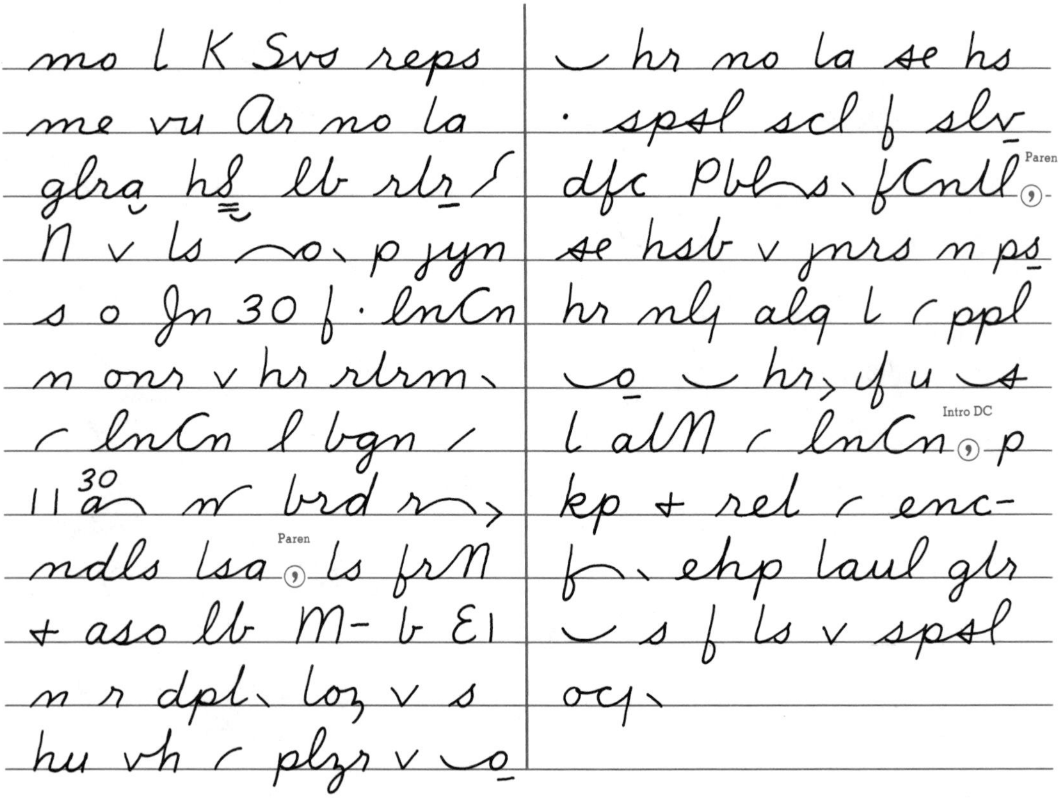

5

Punctuation Study

To the following letter, add commas to show two conjunctions, one introductory phrase, and two parenthetical expressions.

Preview Words

site	si	evidently	evdNl
install	nSl	transition	T1
doubts	dols	possession	pz1
wiring		construction	kSrc1

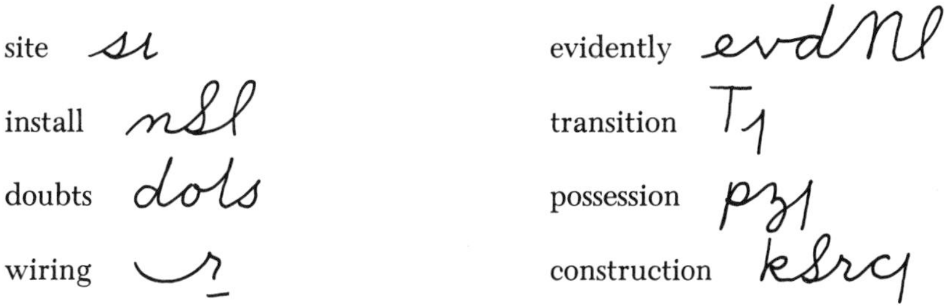

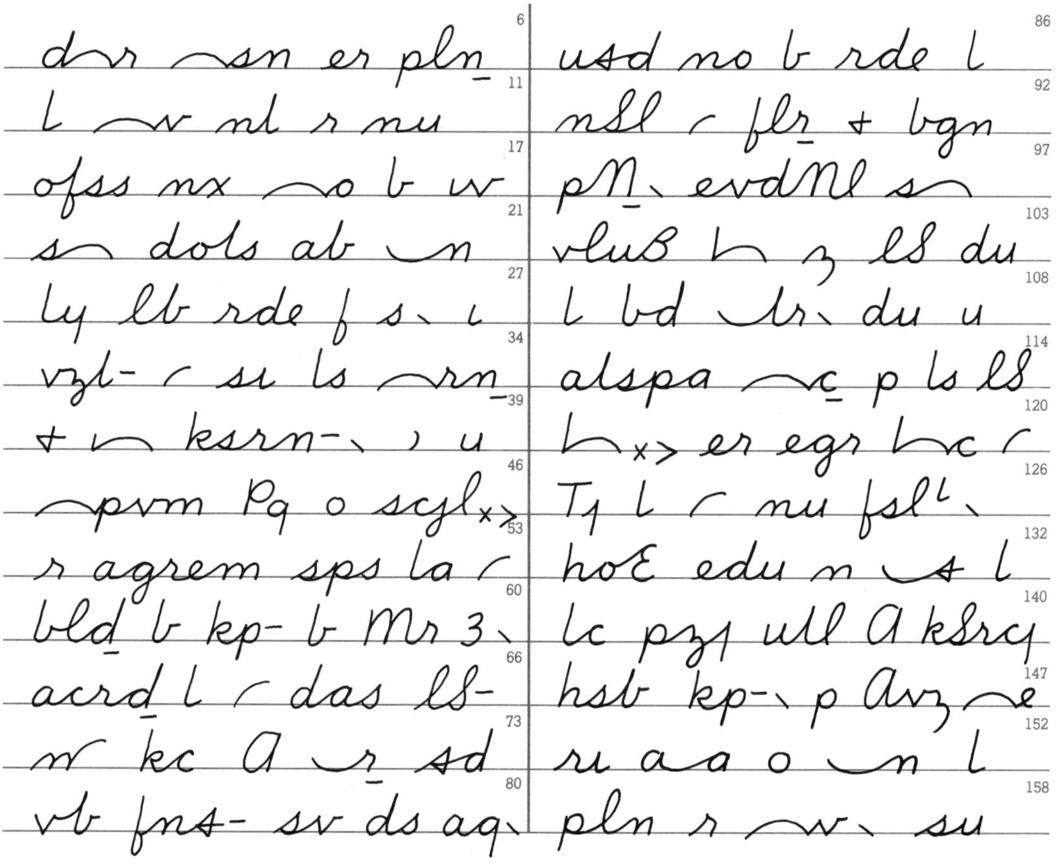

Key

1

Dear Ms. Fields:

Thank you for accepting our invitation. We are extremely pleased that you have agreed to be the[1] guest speaker at our awards banquet.

I hope that you will include some of the material you presented to[2] the personnel managers last month. After I heard your remarks at the national conference, I was determined[3] to bring you before our own group.

We have made the travel arrangements for your visit. The airline ticket is[4] enclosed, and your hotel reservation has been confirmed by our company. I will meet you at the airport and[5] drive you to the hotel. You will have several hours to rest before attending the dinner.

I know that your[6] message will be both helpful and stimulating. Please let me know if I can assist you in any other way.

Yours[7] very truly, (143)

2

Dear Mr. Clark:

I understand that you have conducted much research in energy conservation. I have also[1] heard that you examine residences and businesses to determine how efficiently they operate.[2] Could you come to our building to evaluate our level of efficiency?

Since building our plant nine years ago,[3] we have replaced our heating and cooling system with two separate units. Each was designed to accommodate[4] a radius of 6,000 square feet. Now we are concerned that we may be using an excessive amount[5] of electricity. I believe that a complete analysis is in order.

Please call my office to arrange[6] a day for your visit. I will ask the superintendent of our building to set aside the entire day[7] for you.

Cordially yours, (144)

3

MEMO TO: Debbie Leonard

We are in the process of designing new identification badges for[1] visitors in our building. You will soon receive a box of identification badges to be used in place[2] of the name tags that we have used in the past. Please give extra attention to distributing and collecting the[3] badges. These items are for permanent use, and we do not wish to create an unnecessary expense by[4] having to replace lost badges.

I know that you supervise several people who take over the reception[5] desk when you are away. Would you please see that each of your assistants understands the procedure for issuing[6] badges?

Proper identification is important to the security of our company. I know that[7] we can count on your support, Debbie. (146)

4

MEMO TO: Customer Service Representatives

Many of you already know that Gloria Hastings will be[1] retiring at the end of this month. Please join us on June 30 for a luncheon in honor of her retirement.[2] The luncheon will begin at 11:30 a.m. in the board room.

Needless to say, this friend and associate[3] will be missed by everyone in our department. Those of us who have had the pleasure of working with her know[4] that she has a special skill for solving difficult problems. Fortunately, she has been very generous[5] in passing her knowledge along to the people working with her.

If you wish to attend the luncheon, please complete[6] and return the enclosed form. We hope that you will gather with us for this very special occasion. (138)

5

Dear Mr. Mason:

We are planning to move into our new offices next month, but I have some doubts about when[1] they will be ready for us. I visited the site this morning, and I am concerned. Is your improvement program[2] on schedule?

Our agreement specifies that the building be completed by March 3. According to the dates[3] listed in the contract, all wiring should have been finished several days ago. You should now be ready to install[4] the flooring and begin painting. Evidently, some valuable time was lost due to bad weather. Do you[5] anticipate making up this lost time?

We are eager to make the transition to the new facility.[6] However, we do not wish to take possession until all construction has been completed. Please advise me right away[7] on when to plan our move.

Sincerely yours, (147)

LESSON 10

Word Development

Develop new words from the following brief forms:

with

withdraw 

withstand 

within 

without 

withhold 

work

workshop 

paperwork 

overwork 

network 

framework 

for

forbid 

foreign 

foremost 

forest 

forever 

forgive 

forget 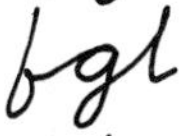

forgotten 

formula 

forge 

Reading and Writing Exercises

——————————————— 1 ———————————————

Preview Words

nearby *nrb*

workday *⌣od*

formal *ffl*

trainees *trnes*

financial *fnnsl*

investigating *nvsga_*

scholarships *sclrss*

representative *rep*

---

d cvn ev ofn lc-
ab ofr_ assN l
⌣pes hu ⌣↙ l ku
lr eycp, lr r vres
⌣as ec q ab ak_
ls, ec pa ⌢ luy
fes f loz ppl ⌣↙
l nrl n · cly nrb,
ls fnnsl hlp ⌢
b apli- l clss hld
nr evn, if ⌢ crs
, scyl- b r coz
pl v jb lrn_ ⌣ hoE,
⌣ db alo- du_ ⌢

⌣od, · ⌣osp n
⌢rd Pss_ or bs ru
db · ex v ls cN
v lrn_, ⌢ nvsga_
⌢ psB l v ofr_ sclrss
f ⌣pes sc_ AvN-
dgres n lr plc aras
v sde, nynrs +
⌢ym lrnes r rep
v ls grp, p lq ab
lz idas, if u lq ⌢
L , ru , idlc l
Ppr · ffl Ppzl
alq ls ln, su

<small>Intro DC · Paren</small>
<small>Intro DC</small>

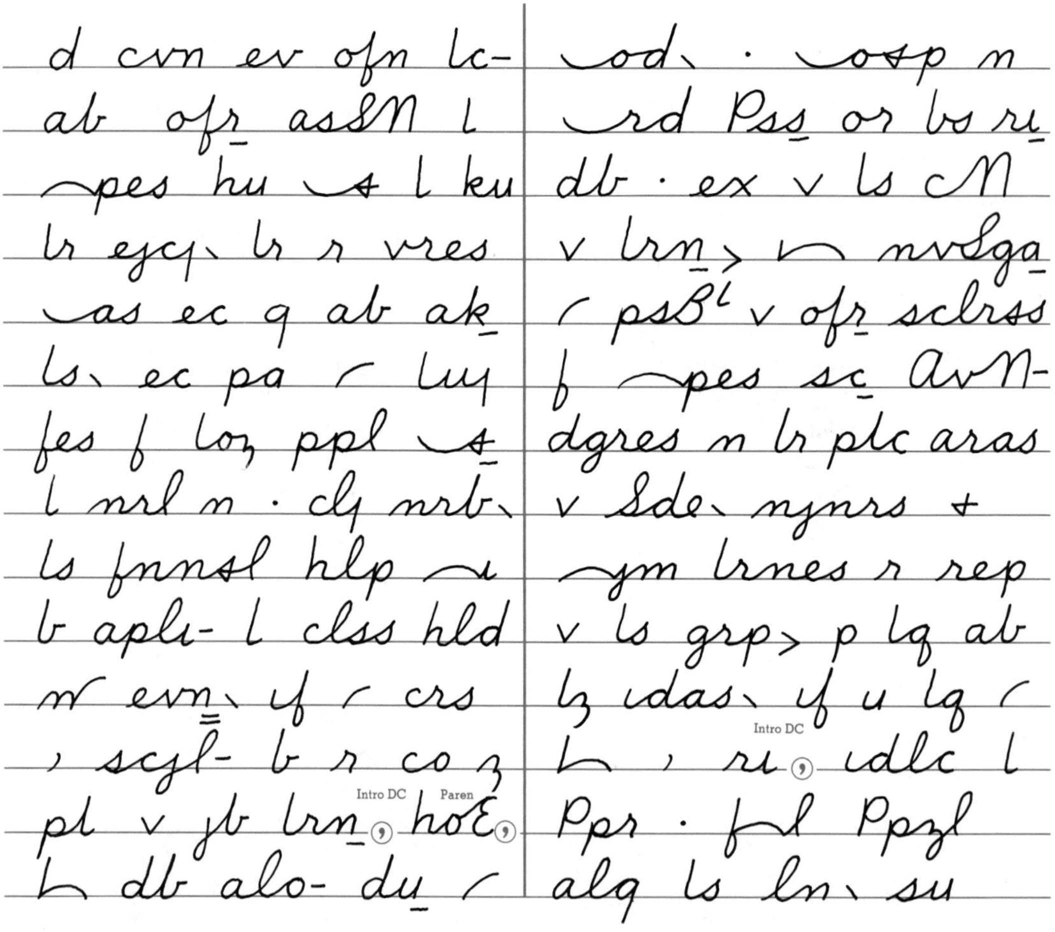

— 2 —

Preview Words

topic	*lpc*	effective	*efcv*
human	*hm*	forthcoming	*flk_*
Coast	*cš*	fundamental	*fNml*
Seattle	*sell*	incorporated	*inc*

[Shorthand passage — two columns]

mo l A dpl hds
ulb gld lno la er
rde l bgn ⌒ lrn_
sjs uv rqš-, aIC-
, . l8 √ Pgs la vb
scgl- so fr, ⌒ lb
flk_, ulfN ⌒ da +
⌐ f eC cls l8-
nx l ⌒ Ul v eC
Nv lpc, ev inc
⌐8 vu sugjs +
v A- . fu vr o,
a⌐q loz l8- r 2
sjs lae šrgl rcm
f El, ⌒ frš , .

⌐osp o ho l ru
efcv Ls, ⌐l iz
vzl r plN ŏ W
cš ₉ iz fCnl enj
l alN . s⌒lr
⌐osp n sell, ₃
. rzll ₉ ⌒u Ls v
⌐pv- grl, ⌒ cls
ksrn hm rljs ,
eqll vluB, bo sjs
Pvd lrn_ la , fNml
l q ⌒ym, p ⌒u
rzrvjs ⌒n ⌒
preds rcm-, ehp
lau njy ⌒ Pgs,

[margin annotations: "Intro DC" and "Paren"]

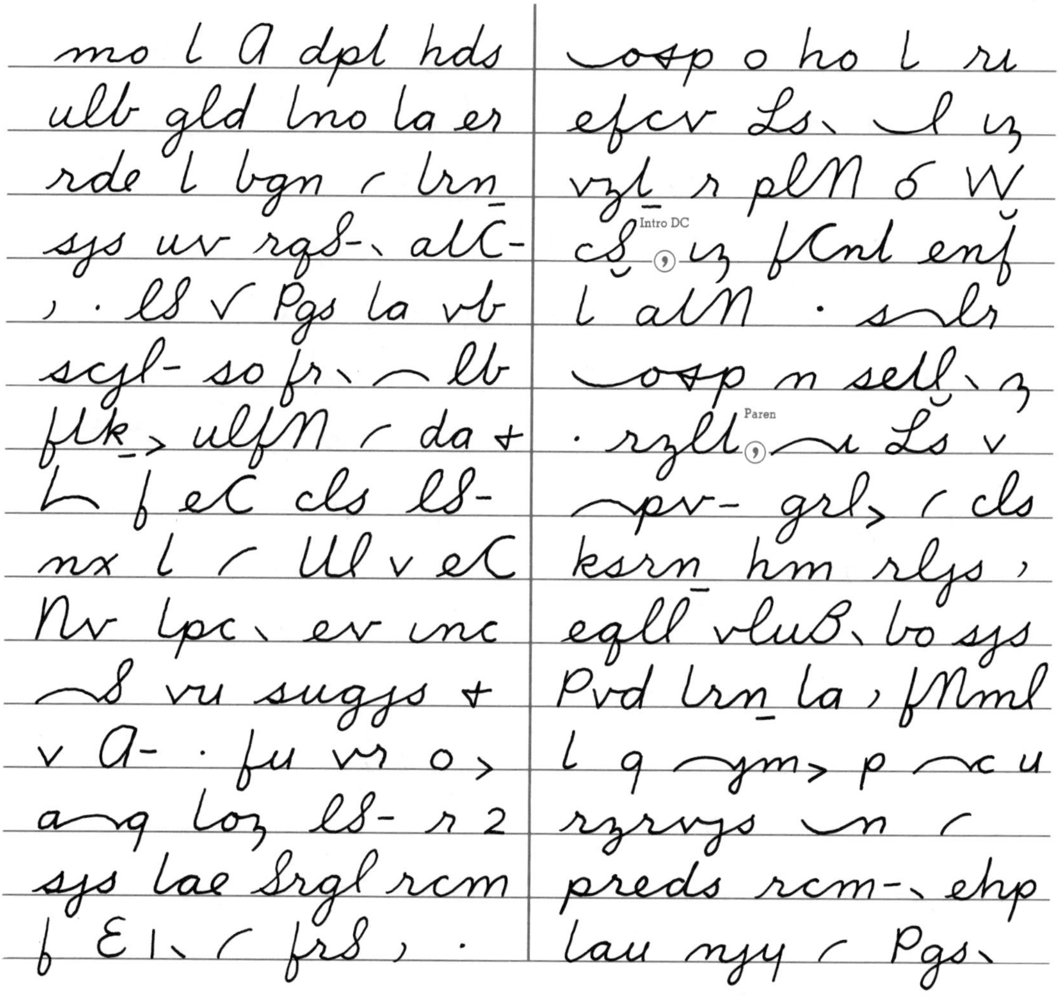

3

Preview Words

vital
routine
ensure
strict

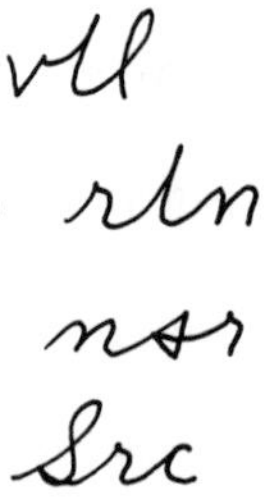

minimal
throughout
paperwork
approximately

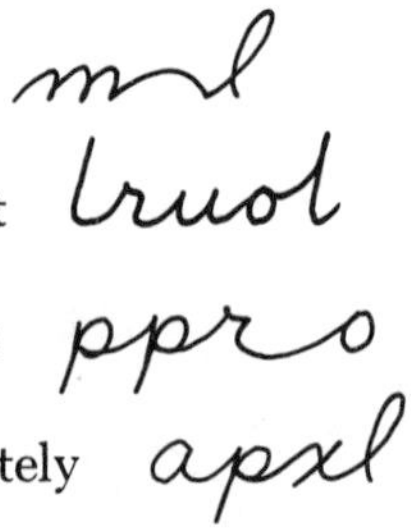

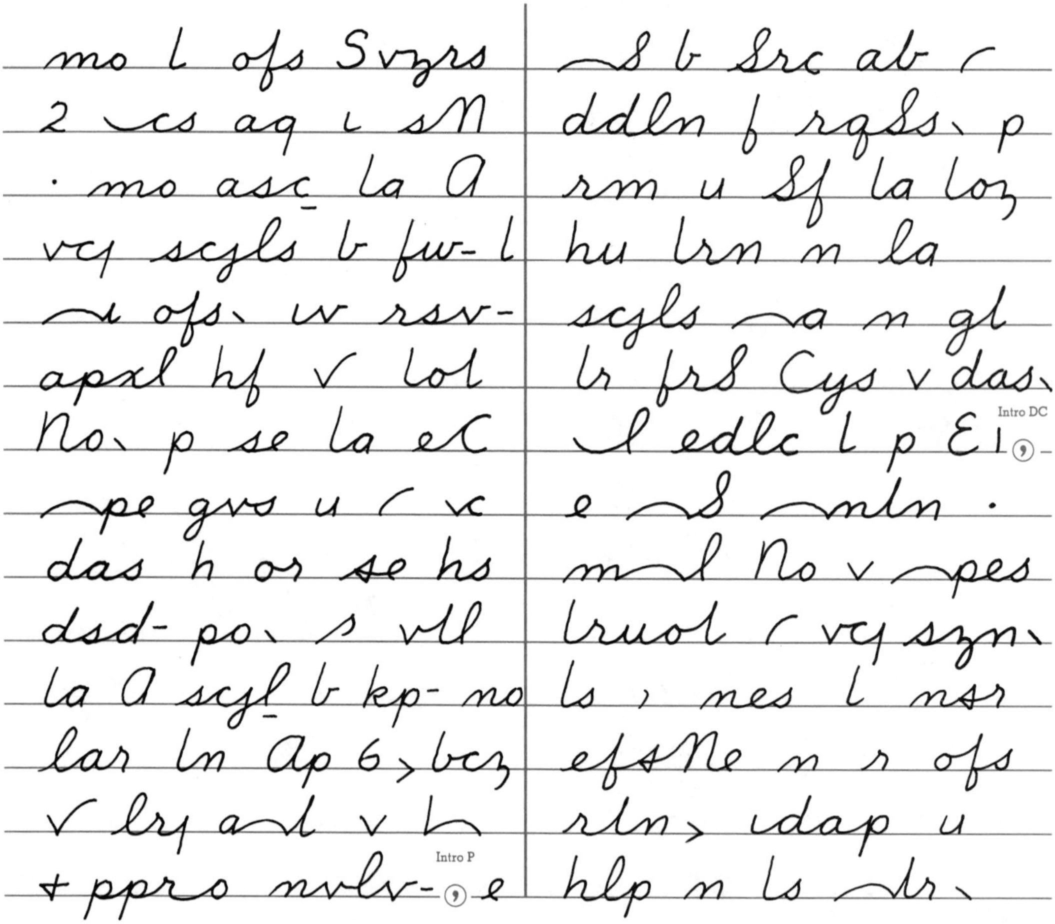

4

Preview Words

Ward	emphasize
aspects	traditional
equally	secretarial
assembling	installing

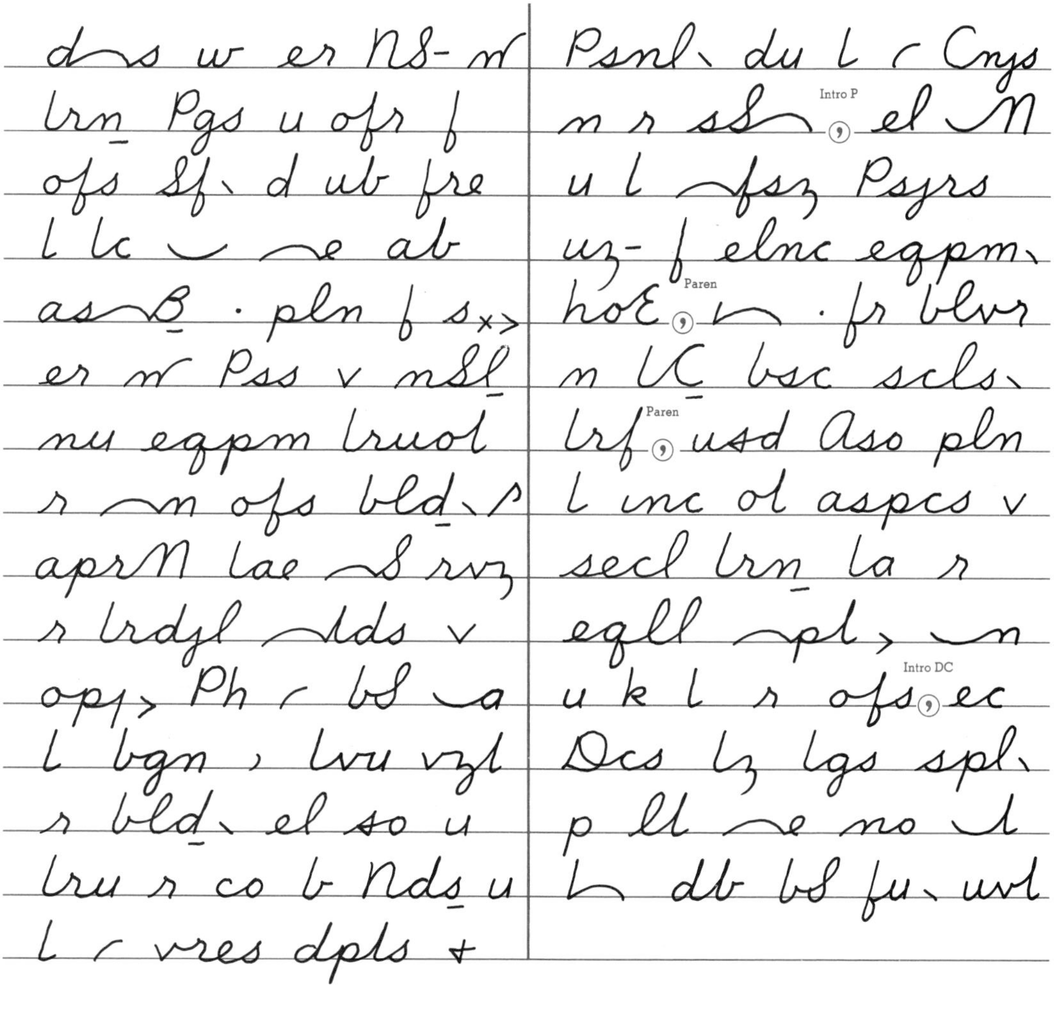

5

Punctuation Study

Add six commas to the following letter to indicate one conjunction, two parenthetical expressions, one introductory dependent clause, and three words in a series.

Preview Words

endure

overlook

activity

confusion

remodeling

construction

concentrate

inconveniences

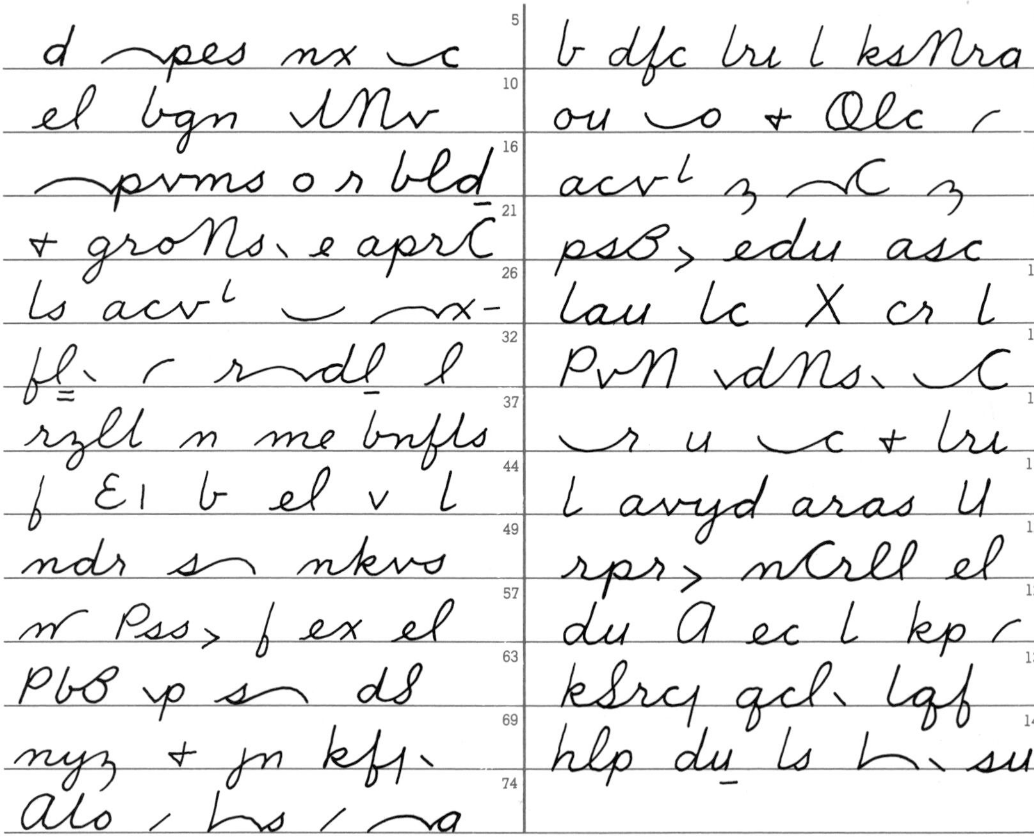

Key

1

Dear Kevin:

We have often talked about offering assistance to employees who wish to continue their[1] education. There are various ways we can go about accomplishing this. We can pay the tuition fees for[2] those people wishing to enroll in a college nearby. This financial help might be applied to classes held in[3] the evenings. If the course is scheduled by our company as part of job training, however, time would be allowed[4] during the workday. A workshop in word processing or business writing would be an example of this kind of[5] training.

I am investigating the possibility of offering scholarships for employees seeking[6] advanced degrees in their particular areas of study. Engineers and management trainees are[7] representative of this group.

Please think about these ideas. If you think the time is right, I would like to prepare[8] a formal proposal along this line.

Sincerely yours, (169)

2

MEMO TO: All Department Heads

You will be glad to know that we are ready to begin the training sessions you[1] have requested. Attached is a list of the programs that have been scheduled so far. More will be forthcoming.

You will[2] find the date and time for each class listed next to the title of each individual topic. We have[3] incorporated most of your suggestions and have added a few of our own.

Among those listed are two sessions[4] that we strongly recommend for everyone. The first is a workshop on how to write effective letters. While I was[5] visiting our plant on the West Coast, I was fortunate enough to attend a similar workshop in Seattle.[6] As a result, my letters have improved greatly.

The class concerning human relations is equally valuable.[7] Both sessions provide training that is fundamental to good management.

Please make your reservations within[8] the periods recommended. We hope that you enjoy the programs. (173)

3

MEMO TO: Office Supervisors

Two weeks ago I sent a memo asking that all vacation schedules be[1] forwarded to my office. I have received approximately half of the total number. Please see that each[2] employee gives you the exact dates he or she has decided upon. It is vital that all scheduling be[3] completed no later than April 6.

Because of the large amount of time and paperwork involved, we must be strict[4] about the deadline for requests. Please remind your staff that those who turn in late schedules may not get their first choice of[5] dates. While we would like to please everyone, we must maintain a minimal number of employees throughout the[6] vacation season. This is necessary to ensure efficiency in our office routine.

I would appreciate[7] your help in this matter. (145)

4

Dear Ms. Ward:

We are interested in the training programs you offer for office staff. Would you be free to talk[1] with me about assembling a plan for us?

We are in the process of installing new equipment throughout our[2] main office building. It is apparent that we must revise our traditional methods of operation.[3]

Perhaps the best way to begin is to have you visit our building. We will show you through our company by[4] introducing you to the various departments and personnel. Due to the changes in our system, we will want[5] you to emphasize procedures used for electronic equipment. However, I am a firm believer in[6] teaching basic skills. Therefore, you should also plan to incorporate other aspects of secretarial training[7] that are equally important.

When you come to our office, we can discuss these things specifically. Please let me[8] know what time would be best for you.

Yours very truly, (169)

5

Dear Employees:

Next week we will begin extensive improvements on our building and grounds. We approach this activity[1] with mixed feelings. The remodeling will result in many benefits for everyone, but we will have to[2] endure some inconveniences in the process.

For example, we will probably experience some dust,[3] noise, and general confusion. Although at times it may be difficult, try to concentrate on your work[4] and overlook the activity as much as possible.

We do ask that you take extra care to prevent accidents.[5] Watch where you walk and try to avoid areas under repair.

Naturally, we will do all we can to complete[6] the construction quickly. Thank you for your help during this time.

Sincerely yours, (134)

unl 3
rtl *

Shorthand Vocabulary Review

Study the following words and the principle they illustrate. You will find these words in the letters and memos in this unit.

1. Write a slightly raised and disjoined l for the word ending *ity* (uh-tee).

quality	ql l	quantities	qN ls
community	kn l	variety	vri l
quantity	qN l	dependability	dpNB l

***Unit Three**
Retailing

2. Write X for the word beginning *extr* and *extra*.

extra X

extreme 

extremely 

extraordinary Xord

3. Write el for the word beginning *electr*.

electric elc

electronic elnc

More About Punctuation

Use a comma to separate two independent adjectives that modify the same noun. The comma is being used in place of the word *and:*

Ellen is an intelligent, dedicated manager.

Do not use a comma if the first adjective modifies both the second adjective and the noun:

Ellen is an intelligent general manager.

If you are in doubt about whether or not to use a comma, consider these two things.

1. Does the sentence still have the same meaning if you replace the comma with the word *and*?

Ellen is an intelligent and dedicated manager.

2. Does the sentence still have the same meaning if you reverse the order of the adjectives?

Ellen is a dedicated and intelligent manager.

If the adjectives meet these tests, they are independent adjectives and should be separated by a comma. Commas used between independent adjectives, where *and* has been omitted, will be identified in your text as **And O.**

LESSON 11

Brief Forms and Derivatives

1. ⌣ *ol Ph Nv pb E*
2. *I f crc spl sucf P₁*

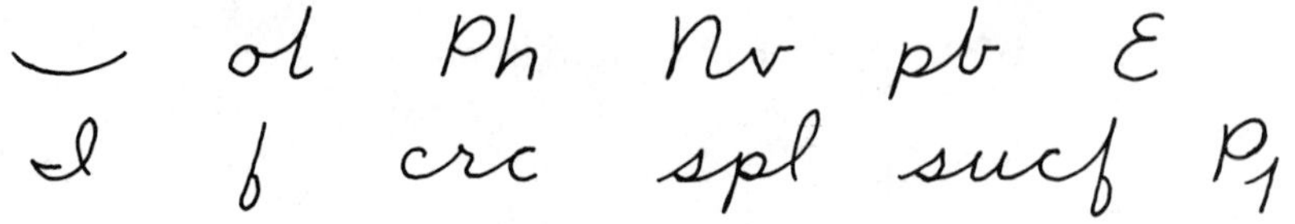

Key

1. were/with, other, perhaps, individual, public, ever/every
2. include, for/full, character/characteristic, specifically, successful, presentation

Phrase Review

1. *id idlc ecd e usd udlc*
2. *lcl lk ⨍ ↗ ou laul*

Key

1. I would, I would like, we could, we were, you should, you would like
2. to call, to come, and the, it is, on you/on your, that you will

Reading and Writing Exercises

————————————— 1 —————————————

Preview Words

hours *hrs*

outfits *olfls*

appeal *apl*

fashions *fjs*

customers *Ks*

entertainment *Nlnm*

profitable *PflB*

establishments *estms*

drs ⌐ w .
ida la ⌐ ~S
egr l Dcs ⌣ u.
i lg ls ida cd
pv Ub v PflB f
bo v s, d ub NS-
n ofr spsl Nlnm
lu Ks du ⌐ lnC
hrs, idlc L P .
Sl so fCr ⌐ laS
fjs f ⌣m, ⌐ arm
⌣os qi ezl if i
Pvd ⌐ ⌐dls +

fjs, ev foN ls Ub
. v sucf Pf n ol
el estms, dN u
lg bo vr bss d
bnfl f ⌐ ida x,
if udlc lk l ⌐
sp ⓥ ecd lc /
vres olfls + dl
⌐ cN + qll v
cll la ⌐ apl lu
Ks, ihp ul sr ⌐
um f lru ls ida,
su

Intro DC

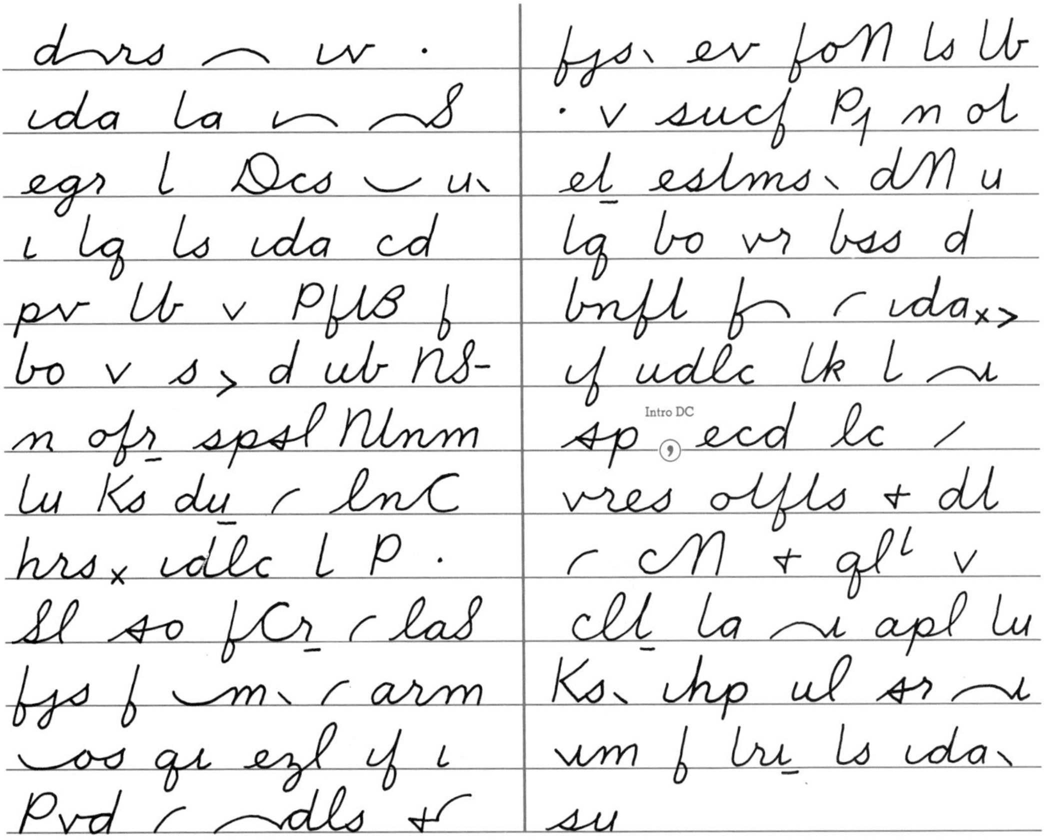

2

Preview Words

image		compliment	kplm
selecting	slc	distinction	Dlgj
clothing	cll	acquainted	aqN-
patronage	plrnj	professional	Pfjl

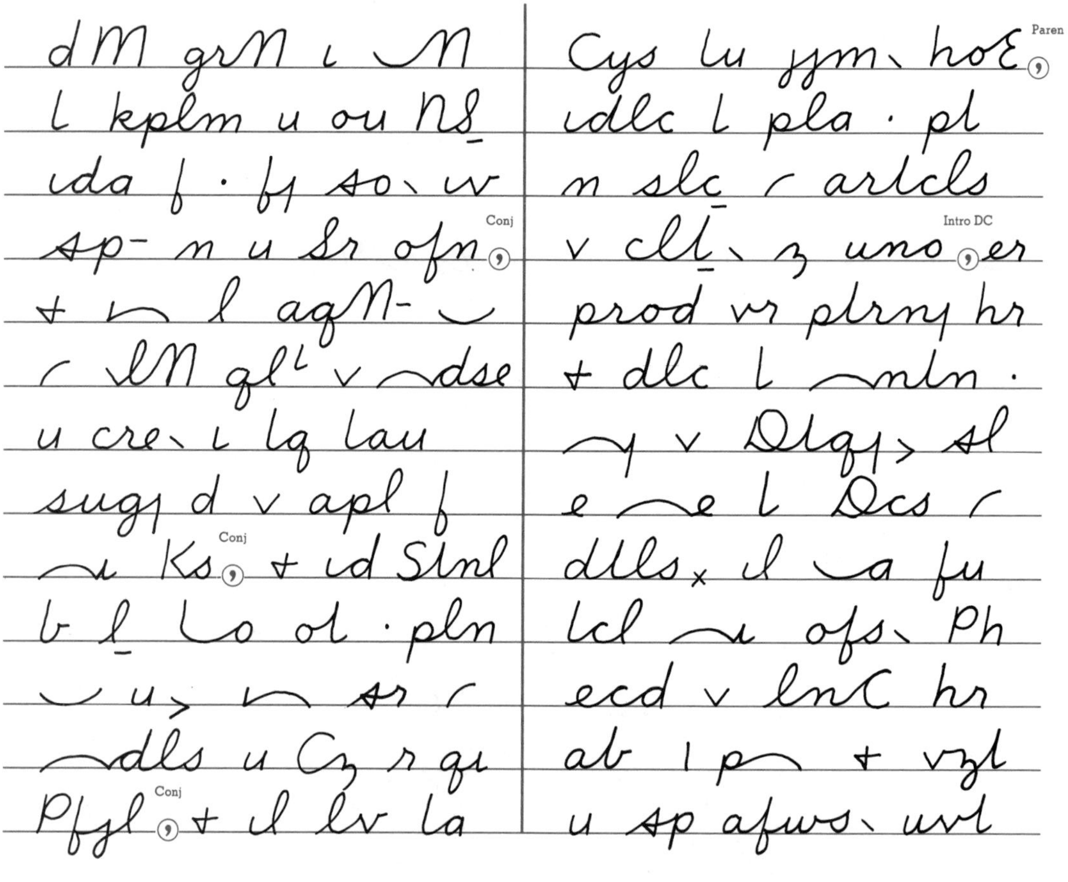

436-5050 Southwest School of Business

Second Chapter Accounting Study Sheets Worksheets

Persuasive Messages Prob. 2

Chapter 3 Accounting

First Prob. Performance Eval. Memo

3

Preview Words

notes	*nts*	stationery	*Syre*
bulletins	*bllns*	attraction	*atrcy*
Janet	*jnt*	handwritten	*hNrtn*
brochures	*brsrs*	typewritten	*tprtn*

mo t jnt — Srs
el hld . sl o
Oc 15 ʒ . spsl
Svs t r G Ks.
d u p ʋsu Psnt
nʋtys t eC K.
ts r sʋ aprCs
avlℬ tu. t8 yr
e sℳ nts o st
Syre— tʒ crds gʋ
ʌ efc ʋ hNrtn
nts ₉ t e Xt
p— ⌣ ʌ rʒtt, n
Pʋes yrs eʋ ⌐t-

ts ta ⌣ tprtn.
eʋ Aso ʋsu- brsrs
t bllns. if uʋ s —
dfrℳ n m ₉ ʋd lk
u ʋdas, ʌ —pt
lau ⌐c r Ks fl
ta ts atrcy , dʒn-
spt f t. ts sl,
t clʒ— t ⌐ jn pt— ₉
t eʋ brq_ n spsl
—dse f sl, ʋdt
gld t Dcs ts ⌐ u
kʋ ₉ jnt.⌐

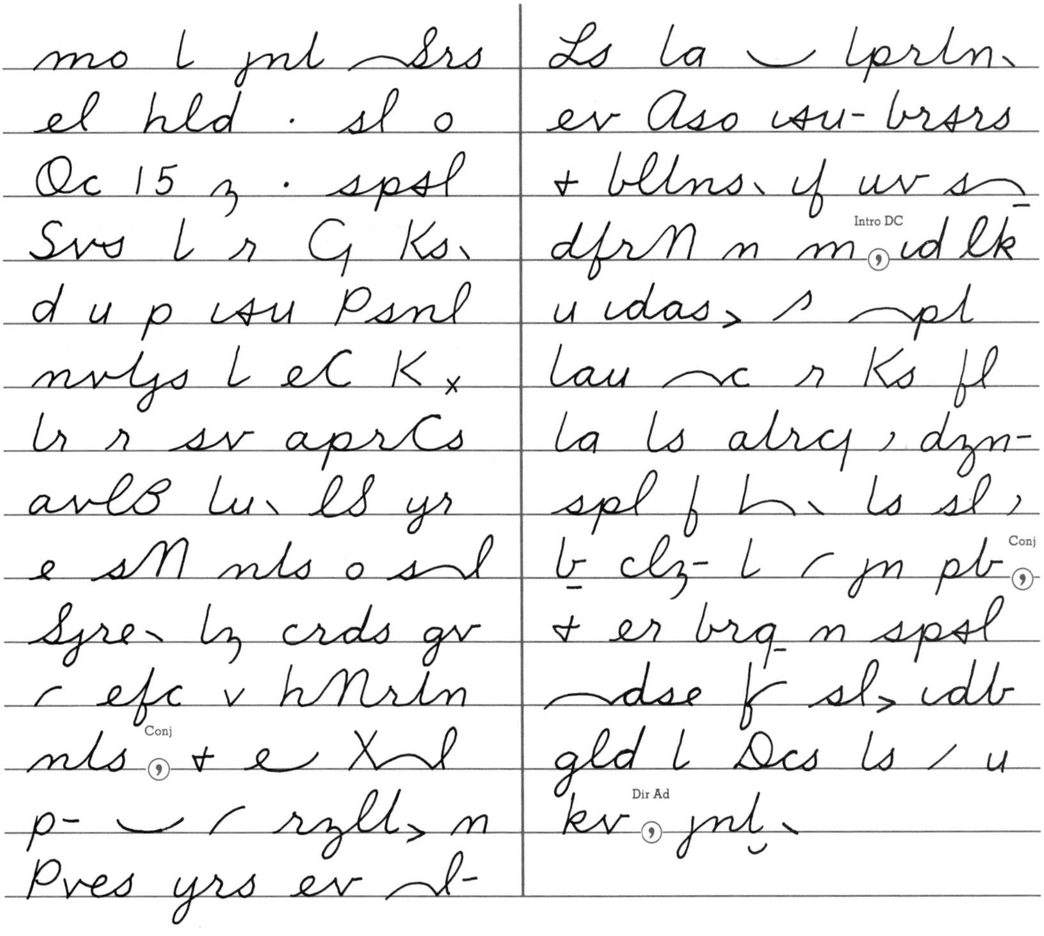

---- 4 ----

Preview Words

single *sgl*   designers *dznrs*
Williams *lyⁱs*   economizing *ecoz_*
instance *nSM*   defining *dfn_*
satisfied *sat-*   unfurnished *ufrns-*

dⁱr lyⁱs me bs exs k l s f hlp n frns_ lr ofss. n E sgl nSM ⁿʳ pd ₍Intro P₎ ev Pds- . Sprz_ + sat- K₎ ⁿr lyⁱs ₍Dir Ad₎ usd se l . lrn-₍And O₎ nlⁱB Psn c du l . ufrns- ofs. lr r ⁿdds v dfn_ sps la l gv . ntrl nu lc lu ⁿa r ⁿ r dznrs

l hlp u Cz . apo y₍Series₎ ly l hlp u ⁿc r bd us v sps uv avlB ₍Series₎ + ly l so u ⁿas v ecoz_, ⁿn r rⁿs r fns-₍Intro DC₎ ul v . efc laul fl prod v + lau clMs l fl kflB ⁿ. M u ll s Avz u× su

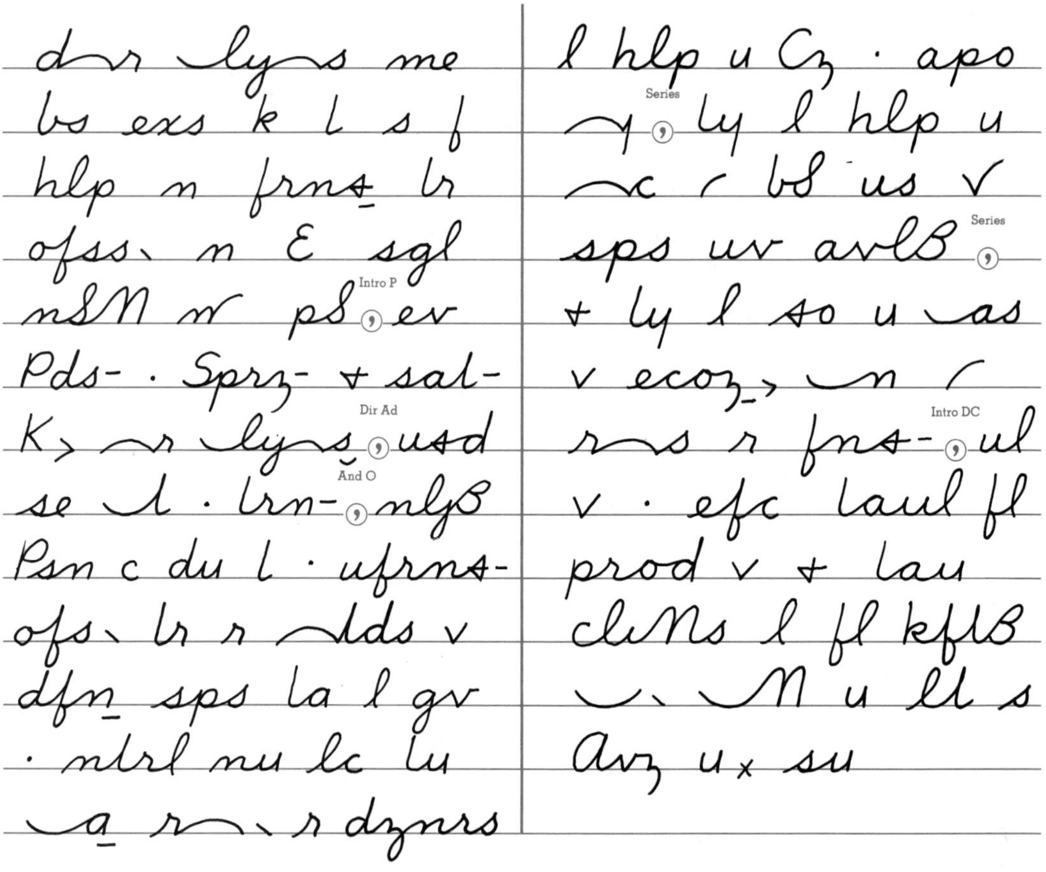

5

Punctuation Study

Add commas to show one conjunction, two parenthetical expressions, one introductory dependent clause, and to show the omission of *and* between adjectives.

Preview Words

dress	drs	amount	a-t
credited	cr-	reliable	rliB
smart	s-rt	account	ak
shoppers	sprs	prospered	Pspr-

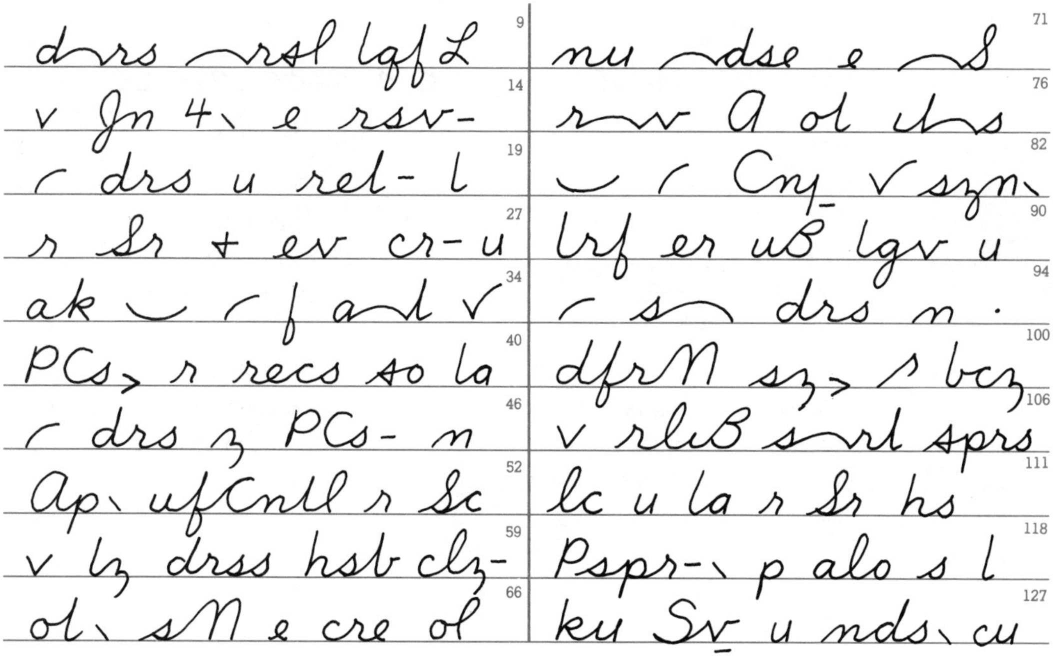

Key

1

Dear Mrs. Moore:

I have an idea that I am most eager to discuss with you. I think this idea could[1] prove to be very profitable for both of us.

Would you be interested in offering special[2] entertainment to your customers during the lunch hours? I would like to present a style show featuring the latest[3] fashions for women. The arrangement works quite easily if I provide the models and the fashions. We have found this[4] to be a very successful presentation in other eating establishments. Don't you think both of our[5] businesses would benefit from the idea?

If you would like to come to my shop, we could look at various[6] outfits and determine the kind and quality of clothing that might appeal to your customers. I hope you will share[7] my excitement for trying this idea.

Sincerely yours, (151)

2

Dear Miss Grant:

I want to compliment you on your interesting idea for a fashion show. I have shopped in[1] your store often, and I am well acquainted with the excellent quality of merchandise you carry. I think[2] that your suggestion would have appeal for my customers, and I would certainly be willing to work out a plan[3] with you.

I am sure the models you choose are quite professional, and I will leave that choice to your judgment. However,[4] I would like to play a part in selecting the articles of clothing. As you know, we are proud of our patronage[5] here and would like to maintain an image of distinction.

Shall we meet to discuss the details? I will wait for[6] you to call my office. Perhaps we could have lunch here about 1 p.m. and visit your shop afterwards.

Yours[7] very truly, (143)

3

MEMO TO: Janet Masters

We will hold a sale on October 15 as a special service to our charge[1] customers. Would you please issue personal invitations to each customer? There are several approaches[2] available to you. Last year we sent notes on small stationery. These cards gave the effect of handwritten notes,[3] and we were extremely pleased with the result.

In previous years we have mailed letters that were typewritten. We have[4] also issued brochures and bulletins. If you have something different in mind, I would welcome your ideas.[5]

It is important that you make our customers feel that this attraction is designed specifically for them. This sale[6] is being closed to the general public, and we are bringing in special merchandise for the sale.

I would be[7] glad to discuss this at your convenience, Janet. (149)

4

Dear Mr. Williams:

Many business executives come to us for help in furnishing their offices. In every[1] single instance in the past, we have produced a surprised and satisfied customer.

Mr. Williams, you should[2] see what a trained, knowledgeable person can do to an unfurnished office. There are methods of defining space[3] that will give an entirely new look to your waiting room. Our designers will help you choose an appropriate image,[4] they will help you make the best use of the space you have available, and they will show you ways of economizing.[5]

When the rooms are finished, you will have an effect that you will feel proud of and that your clients will feel comfortable[6] with. Won't you let us advise you?

Sincerely yours, (131)

5

Dear Mrs. Marshall:

Thank you for your letter of June 4. We received the dress you returned to our store, and we have[1] credited your account with the full amount of the purchase.

Our records show that the dress was purchased in April.[2] Unfortunately, our stock of these dresses has been closed out. Since we carry only new merchandise, we must[3] remove all other items with the changing of the season. Therefore, we are unable to give you the same dress[4] in a different size.

It is because of reliable, smart shoppers like you that our store has prospered. Please allow[5] us to continue serving your needs.

Cordially yours, (109)

LESSON 12

Abbreviations and Derivatives

1. cal ave inv vol cr lit
2. No Hs eslms reps

Key

1. catalog, avenue, invoice, volume, credit, literature
2. number, hundreds, establishments, representatives

Transcription Aids: Typing Numbers

1. When typing sums of money in business letters, omit the decimal point and zeroes.

   The stationery cost $62.

   Our new desk cost nearly $800, but it is very handsome.

2. Type figures and decimal points for uneven sums of money.

   If you order six cases at $24.95 each, the total will be $149.70.

3. When typing even numbers that are extremely large, spell out the numbers—million, billion, or trillion.

   The budget will run a little over our $10 million estimate.

   We may exceed our sales estimates by a quarter of a million dollars.

Your Business Vocabulary	heir *ar* One who inherits property.
	Ownership of all stock will be transferred to his heirs.
	wholesale *hlsl* Sale of goods in large quantities, usually to a retailer.
	We are ordering the merchandise from a wholesale distributor.
	itemize *ulrz* To make a list of, item by item.
	When doing inventory, please itemize the stock on every shelf.

Reading and Writing Exercises

--------------------------------- 1 ---------------------------------

Preview Words

sports	*spls*	colors	*clrs*
formal	*fl*	common	*kn*
examine	*vm*	coordinated	*cordna-*
inventory	*nvnlre*	businesswoman	*bs m*

dK ev q nz f
bs m. er opn_ .
fl dpl js fu> y
ur lc r rs v s ⁹ Intro DC
uv lc- lg + hrd
f apo cll_ f ofs.
me srs c r kn
Mlc v ofr sc la,

elr l fl or n
fl enf. sc slcs
u b fn f . spls
evM or . afnn
le b ly r n / ⁹ Conj
a apo f m
ex> r nu sp l
Cnj a la. dM

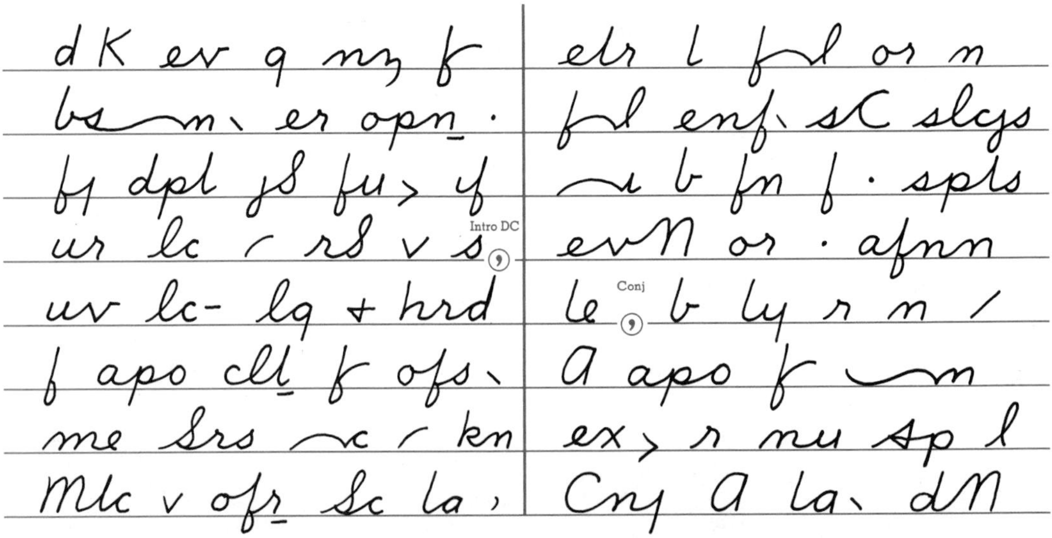

‿a ull ur ps̲ b,
⌒c . spsl lrp l
vm r nvntre, ev

sus, [Series] drss, [Series] cos, [Series] +
sus n dznr Sls
+ cordna- clrs, su

2

Preview Words

social	ssl	Mitchell	mCl
promptly	Pml	wholesale	hlsl
behalf	bhf	character	crc
regularly	rglrl	distributor	Dr

dr clrc n p-
l ru ls L o bhf
v 1 vr mS dpNS
Ks, z . hlsl Dr, [Intro P]
ev dn bs ‿ (
mCl co f me yrs,
ec Slnl lSf la ls
co hs pd s bls
rglrl + Pml, r
recs so la mS
pams ‿ md n
avN v du da n
od l lc avj v

cs Dk, z . bs
yr, [Intro P] mr mCl
dmSras Srq ldrs
+ soN jym, z . Nv, [Intro P]
h , nn f , fn crc,
n adj l r bs rlys, [Intro P] -
iv ‿o- ‿ ls mn
o vres Pjcs w kn
+ v k l ap , NS
n ssl ksrns, n
kfdN lau bq lb p-
l I ls co z 1 vu
lrzr- Ks, uvl

3

Preview Words

heirs	ars	leather	ltr
former	fr	superior	sprer
doors	drs	manufacturer	fr
owner	or	Washington Avenue	WA ave

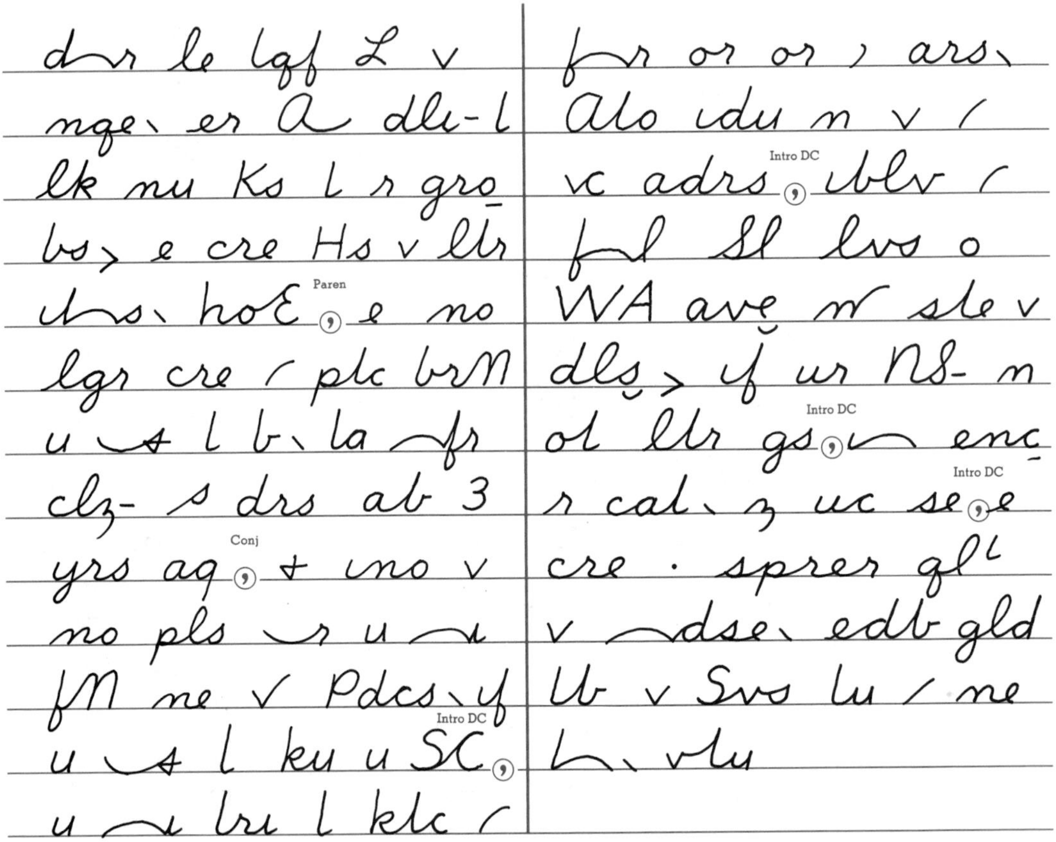

4

Preview Words

itemize	itmz	guarantee	grnte
warranty	—rNe	dealership	dlrs
electric	elc	accordingly	acrdl
relatively	rlvl	commercials	krsls

dr jcsn p sN
s 1H unts vu
No 879 elc hers.
edlc lv r —dse
—l. i USN la
el qlf f . Dk v
10% —n e od /
l8 50 unts. p G
r ak acrdl, + (Conj)
idlc u l itmz r
Dk o inv, —
pls ls od / rqs
v —i Ks. acrd l
r Uvj krsls, u (Intro P)

ofr . —prsv
grnte — u —dse.
—a i as— laul
fw r f dlls v
—rNe — r sm
v —dse. sN —i
dlrs , rlvl nu
+ iv nvr hNl-
u —dse, idap / (Intro DC)
if ud I lil ou
fclre plses, p ll
—e no —n ic pc
dle. ul

5

Punctuation Study

Add commas to show two introductory dependent clauses, one conjunction, and two introductory phrases. Add commas also to show where *and* was omitted and to separate the words in a series.

Preview Words

- simple
- imported
- samples
- beautiful
- beyond
- overhead
- entryway
- affordable

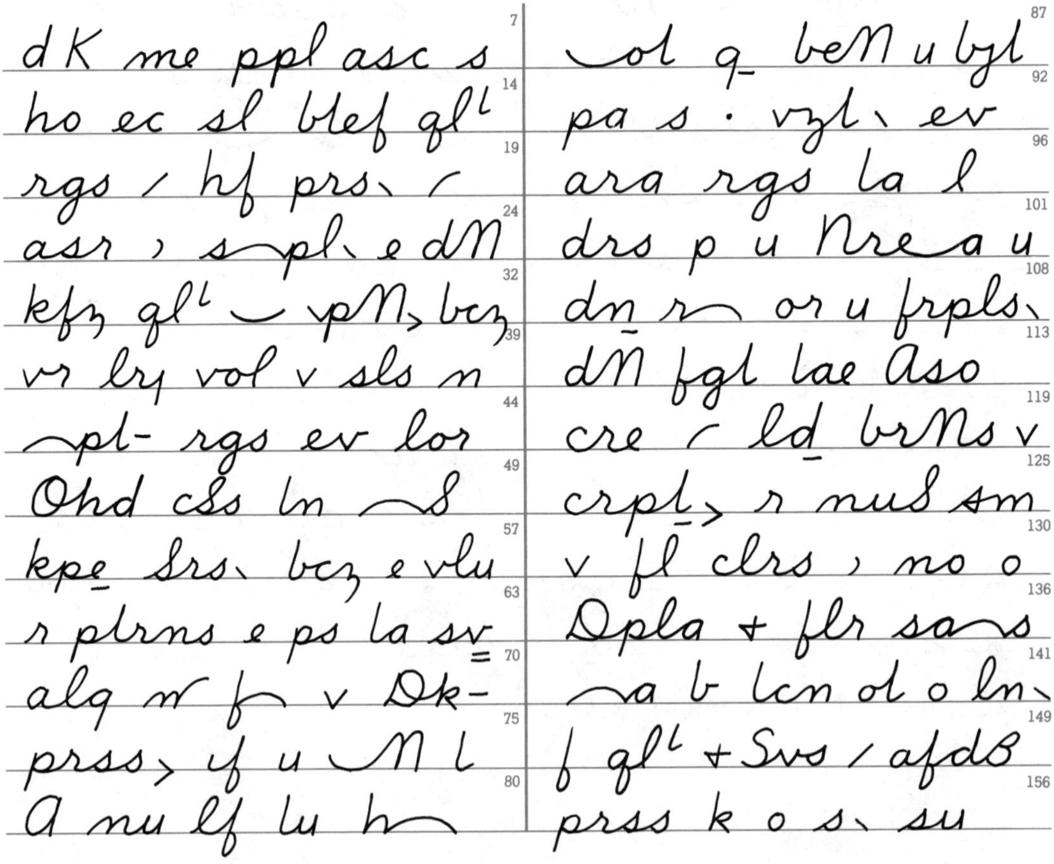

Key

1

Dear Customer:

We have good news for the businesswoman. We are opening a fashion department just for you.[1]

If you are like the rest of us, you have looked long and hard for appropriate clothing for the office. Many stores[2] make the common mistake of offering stock that is either too formal or not formal enough. Such selections[3] might be fine for a sports event or an afternoon tea, but they are not at all appropriate for the woman[4] executive.

Our new shop will change all that. Don't wait until you are passing by. Make a special trip to examine[5] our inventory. We have suits, dresses, coats, and shoes in designer styles and coordinated colors.[6]

Sincerely yours, (122)

2

Dear Mr. Clark:

I am pleased to write this letter on behalf of one of our most dependable customers.[1]

As a wholesale distributor, we have done business with the Mitchell Company for many years. We can certainly[2] testify that this company has paid its bills regularly and promptly. Our records show that most payments were[3] made in advance of the due date in order to take advantage of the cash discount.

As a business manager,[4] Mr. Mitchell demonstrates strong leadership and sound judgment. As an individual, he is known for his fine[5] character. In addition to our business relations, I have worked with this man on various projects in the[6] community and have come to appreciate his interest in social concerns.

I am confident that your[7] bank will be pleased to include this company as one of your treasured customers.

Yours very truly, (158)

3

Dear Mr. Lee:

Thank you for your letter of inquiry. We are always delighted to welcome new customers[1] to our growing business.

We carry hundreds of leather items. However, we no longer carry the particular[2] brand you wish to buy. That manufacturer closed its doors about three years ago, and I know of no place where[3] you might find any of the products. If you wish to continue your search, you might try to contact the former[4] owner or his heirs. Although I do not have the exact address, I believe the family still lives on Washington[5] Avenue in the city of Dallas.

If you are interested in other leather goods, I am enclosing[6] our catalog. As you can see, we carry a superior quality of merchandise. We would be glad[7] to be of service to you at any time.

Very truly yours, (151)

4

Dear Mr. Jackson:

Please send us 100 units of your No. 879 electric heaters. We[1] would like to have the merchandise immediately. I understand that we will qualify for a discount of[2] 10 percent when we order at least 50 units. Please charge our account accordingly, and I would like you to[3] itemize the discount on the invoice.

I am placing this order at the request of my customers. According[4] to the television commercials, you offer an impressive guarantee with your merchandise. May I assume[5] that you will forward the full details of the warranty with the shipment of merchandise? Since my dealership[6] is relatively new and I have never handled your merchandise, I would appreciate it if you would[7] include literature on your factory policies.

Please let me know when I can expect delivery.

Yours[8] truly, (161)

5

Dear Customer:

Many people ask us how we can sell beautiful, quality rugs at half price. The answer is[1] simple. We don't confuse quality with expense.

Because of our large volume of sales in imported rugs, we have[2] lower overhead costs than most competing stores. Because we value our patrons, we pass that savings along in[3] the form of discounted prices.

If you want to add new life to your home without going beyond your budget, pay[4] us a visit. We have area rugs that will dress up your entryway, your dining room, or your fireplace. Don't[5] forget that we also carry the leading brands of carpeting.

Our newest shipment of fall colors is now on[6] display, and floor samples may be taken out on loan. For quality and service at affordable prices, count[7] on us.

Sincerely yours, (144)

LESSON 13

Theory Review

Write money amounts in the following way:

$13.95	13 ^{95}	29 cents	29¢
$400	4H$	$8,425,000	8M425T$
$100,000	1HT$	$2,000,000,000	2B$

Transcription Aids: Similar Words

great *gr* Extremely large; excellent.

The cost of purchasing that equipment is simply too great for our current budget.

Ms. Barnes, manager of the payroll department, is doing a great job in her new position.

grateful *grf* Thankful for benefits received.

We are grateful for the prompt and dependable service you have given us in the past.

Your Business Vocabulary

eliminate *elma* To leave out or remove.

Please proofread the letter carefully to eliminate any possibility of error.

extensive *xtnv* Large in amount or extent; having a wide range.

Professor Randolph has conducted extensive research in the field of genetics.

Reading and Writing Exercises

1

Preview Words

money	me	eliminate	elma
seasonal	sznl	celebrate	slbra
cashier	cAr	anniversary	avrsre
receipt	rse	exclusively	vclsvl

dr flN l slbra
r avrsre vr grN
opn_, ev s_ spsl
n m fu> z . G K,
u Ar no lae ofr gl
dse / lo prss E
d, r rglr Dk
prss elma r nd f
sznl sls, b sp_ n
r Sr, u sv me
E PCs u c>
no er q_ lofr u

s_ evn blr ln r
Ed lo prss, er
nvi_ u l Ar . sp_
vp la, b rzrv-
vclsvl f G Ks,
du r nlr o v
Nv, ulb nlll- l .
adjl Dk v 20%
o E PCs, jS Ao u
crd, & cAr l c
r ajSm ou rse,
su

--- 2 ---

Preview Words

efforts *efls*

grateful *grf*

equally *eqll*

especially *esp*

encouraged *ncry-*

commending *kN̄*

considerate *ksl*

acknowledge *acy*

d ~rs slv&r lgfL
kN̄ r Svo reps、
er grf la uv lcn r
L L acy r Sf、 u L
hsb fw- L (~pes
hu ~ o dle ʃ L
vu vȝl、 ev A ncry-
r reps ll ksl lw
Ks ⟨Conj⟩⊙ b erp- lhr ~n

s ι hsb esp hlpf
+ US N̄、 ʃ eqll rw̄
L lrn la r Ks ap
lȝ X efls lgv q
Svo、 ehp ul ku
L ll s no ab u
ps ~ r eslm、
lqu aq f rī、 uvl

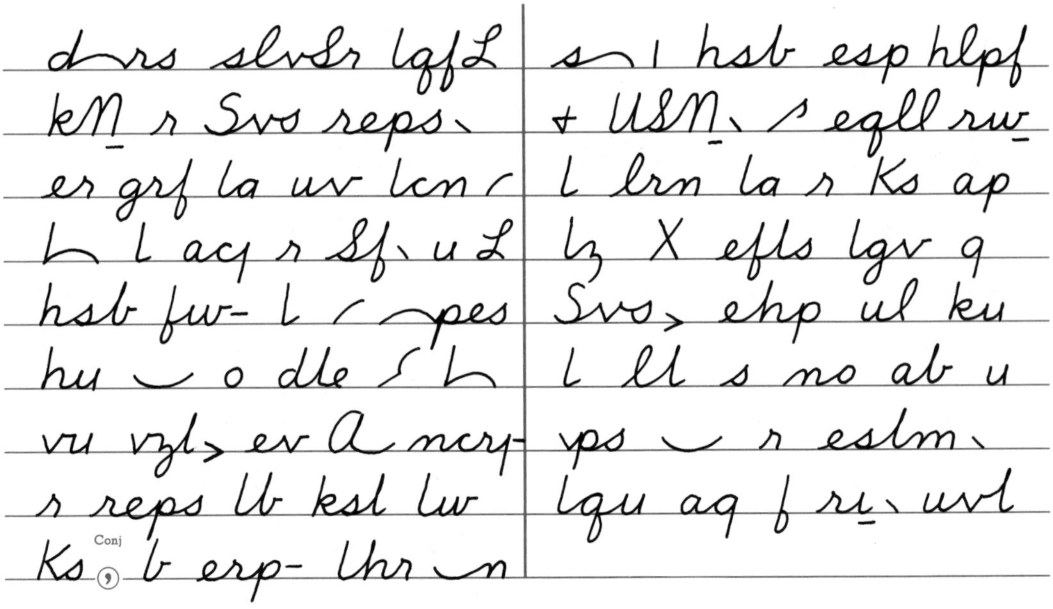

3

Preview Words

once	o𝑁	collection	clcy
truly	trul	entertainment	𝑁lnm
rare	rr	invaluable	nvluß
beauty	ble	extraordinary	Xord

dS o𝑁 n .
gr l (,) . trul
rr opl ks alq,
s r plzr l brq
u r flo ano𝑁m,
f . lt-l ol (,) el c
avlß lu . ol𝑆𝑁
clcy v bcs, lz
vols kln r fnd
slcjs n lil f
a + aro𝑁 r
o, el √ 12
vols ; bo𝑁 n .
hrd cvr v Xord

ble, r sl l bk
. nvluß srs v
nly + 𝑁lnm fu
hl fl, bcz v ls
spsl ofr (,) r nlr
sl cb us f ol
129⁹⁵, p rmbr
la r ofr vprs o
Ja 31 (,) so d𝑁
dla, lz bcs r .
gfl la l ncrs
n vlu z r yrs
q b, cu

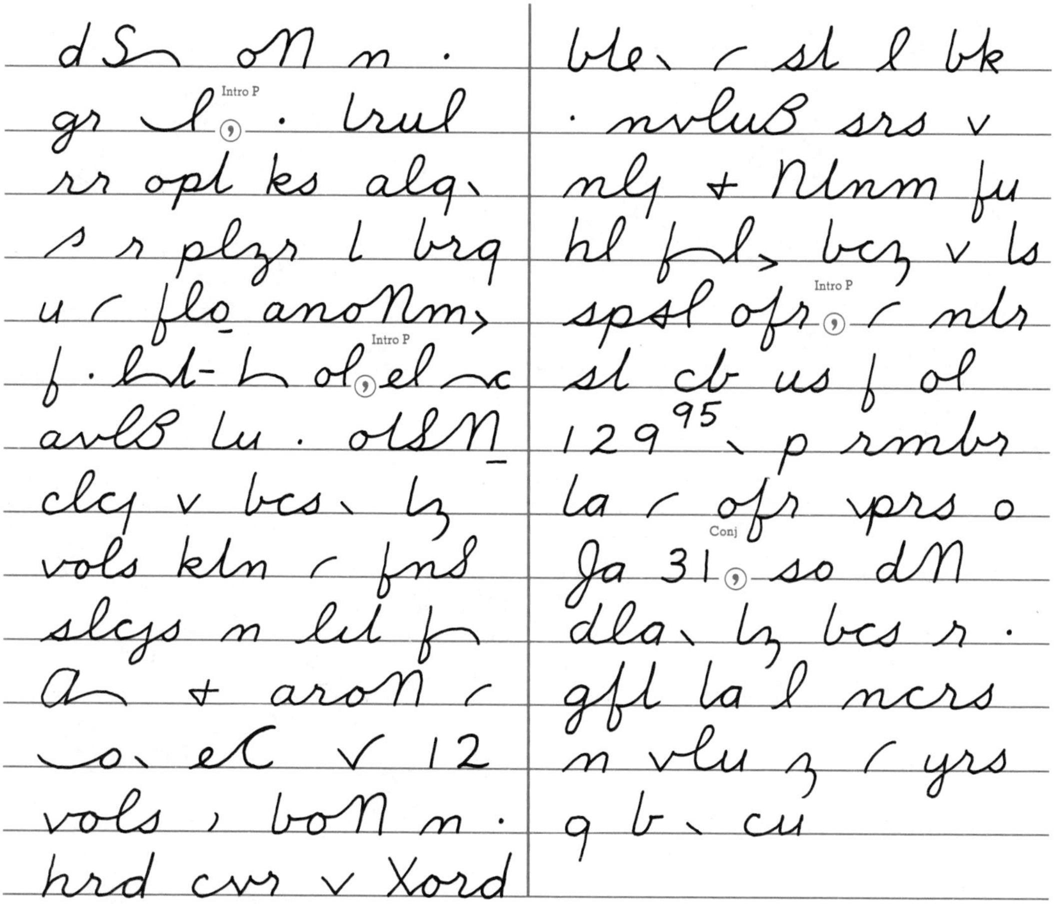

-- **4** --

Preview Words

sinks *sqs*　　　island *eN*

kitchen *cCn*　　　appliances *aplNs*

occupy *ocpe*　　　imagine *ryn*

cabinets *cbnls*　　　photograph *flogrf*

---

d r + rs adrsn
dd uno la uc v
. nu cCn n u
h n 30 ds,
las re u dN v
l PCs . pNr nu
hos lr . blef cCn,
ec nSl nu cbnls ͕ [Series]
nu sqs ͕ [Series] + nu
aplNs r sps
u old frns no
ocpe, ll usf ds
. lll, ryn v A
nu cbnls n .

nu d frns + n
. dfrN Sl, Ph
udlc l Cny r laol
lau no v, b a
eN cbnl ͕ [Intro P] ec gv
u cCn . kpl nu
lc, r cCn sn
r alC- flogrf
cb us f U 2T$,
f uv qs ͕ [Intro DC] k l s
f asrs, el dzn ͕ [Series]
bld ͕ [Series] + nSl u
cbnls rprl
cr, s

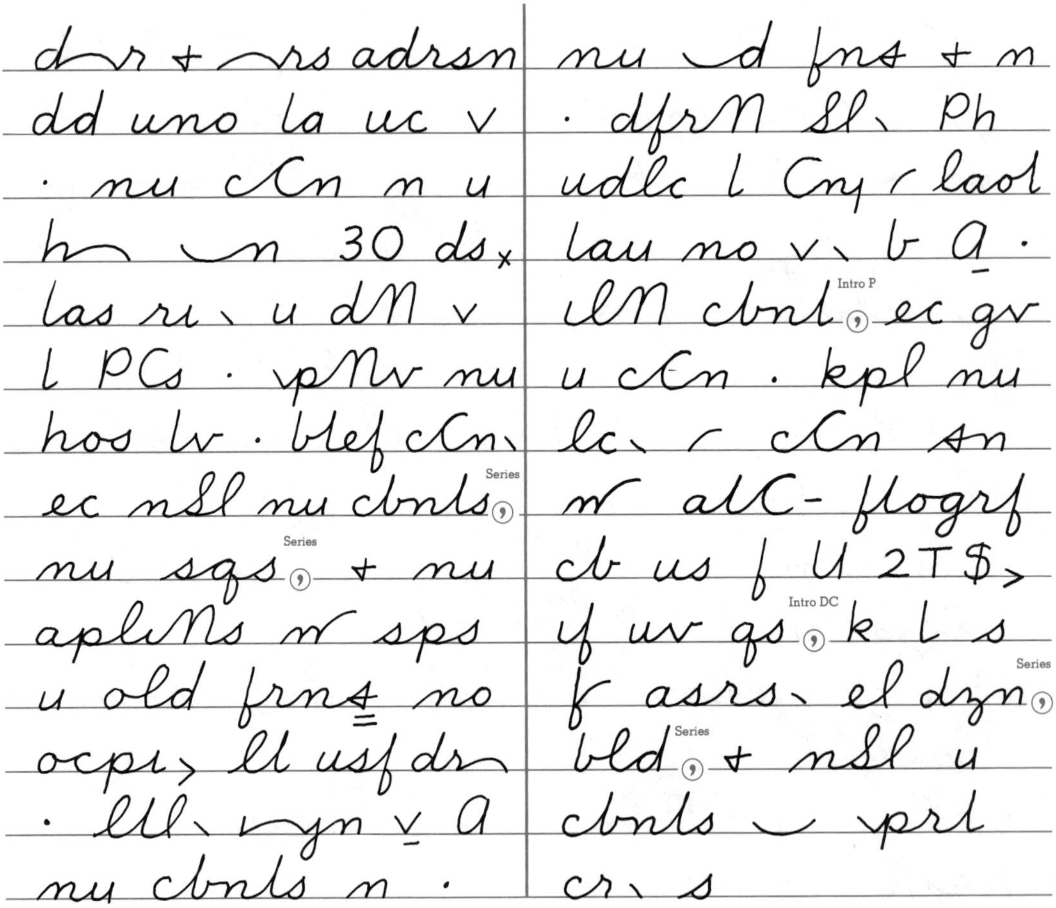

5

Punctuation Study

Add commas to show two conjunctions, one introductory dependent clause, and one parenthetical expression.

Preview Words

spring	sprq	consumer	ksmr
presentation	P1	furnishings	frn4
seating	se	superior	sprer
extensive	xNv	informative	nfmv

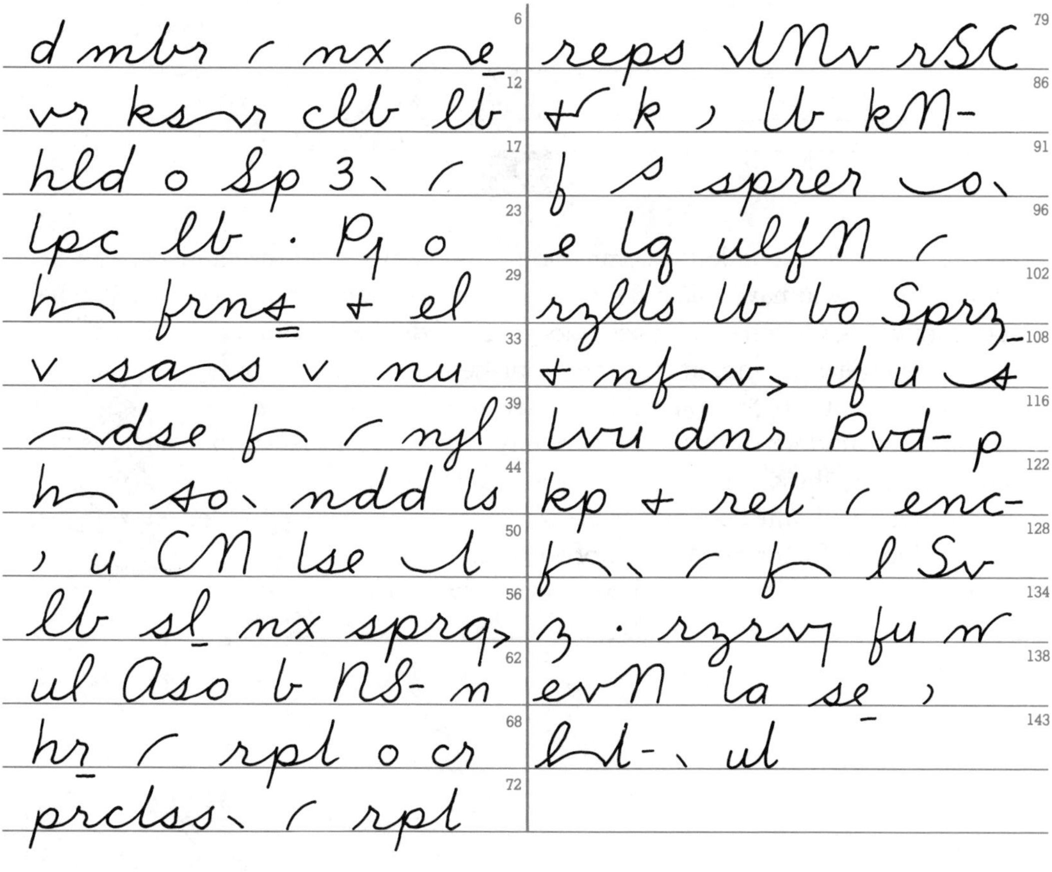

Key

1

Dear Mr. Flint:

To celebrate the anniversary of our grand opening, we have something special in mind[1] for you.

As a charge customer, you already know that we offer quality merchandise at low prices every[2] day. Our regular discount prices eliminate the need for seasonal sales. By shopping in our store, you[3] save money with every purchase you make.

Now we are going to offer you something even better than our[4] everyday low prices. We are inviting you to share a shopping experience that is being reserved[5] exclusively for charge customers. During the entire month of November, you will be entitled to an[6] additional discount of 20 percent on every purchase. Just show your card, and the cashier will make the adjustment[7] on your receipt.

Sincerely yours, (145)

2

Dear Mrs. Sylvester:

Thank you for your letter commending our service representatives. We are grateful that[1] you have taken the time to acknowledge our staff. Your letter has been forwarded to the employees who were on[2] duty at the time of your visit.

We have always encouraged our representatives to be considerate[3] toward customers, but we are pleased to hear when someone has been especially helpful and understanding.[4] It is equally rewarding to learn that our customers appreciate these extra efforts to give good service.[5]

We hope you will continue to let us know about your experiences with our establishment. Thank you again[6] for writing.

Yours very truly, (126)

3

Dear Sir or Madam:

Once in a great while, a truly rare opportunity comes along. It is our pleasure to[1] bring you the following announcement.

For a limited time only, we will make available to you an[2] outstanding collection of books. These volumes contain the finest selections in literature from America[3] and around the world. Each of the 12 volumes is bound in a hard cover of extraordinary beauty. The set[4] will become an invaluable source of knowledge and entertainment for your whole family.

Because of this[5] special offer, the entire set can be yours for only $129.95. Please[6] remember that the offer expires on January 31, so don't delay. These books are a gift that will[7] increase in value as the years go by.

Cordially yours, (149)

4

Dear Mr. and Mrs. Anderson:

Did you know that you can have a new kitchen in your home within 30 days?[1] That's right. You don't have to purchase an expensive new house to have a beautiful kitchen. We can install new[2] cabinets, new sinks, and new appliances in the space your old furnishings now occupy.

Let yourself dream a[3] little. Imagine having all new cabinets in a new wood finish and in a different style. Perhaps you would[4] like to change the layout that you now have. By adding an island cabinet, we can give your kitchen a completely[5] new look. The kitchen shown in the attached photograph can be yours for under $2,000.

If you have[6] questions, come to us for the answers. We will design, build, and install your cabinets with expert care.

Sincerely,[7] (140)

5

Dear Member:

The next meeting of our consumer club will be held on September 3. The topic will be a[1] presentation on home furnishings, and we will have samples of new merchandise from the national home show. Indeed,[2] this is your chance to see what will be selling next spring.

You will also be interested in hearing the report[3] on credit practices. The report represents extensive research, and the committee is to be commended[4] for its superior work. We think you will find the results to be both surprising and informative.

If you[5] wish to have your dinner provided, please complete and return the enclosed form. The form will serve as a reservation[6] for you in the event that seating is limited.

Yours truly, (132)

LESSON 14

Shorthand Vocabulary Review

Write *l* for the word ending *ly* (lee) or *ily* (uh-lee).

early	erl	lovely	lvl
carefully	crfl	rarely	rrl
closely	clsl	definitely	dfnll

Transcription Aids: Spelling

Omit the final *e* when adding *ing* to most words.

din*e*	din*ing*
examin*e*	examin*ing*
creat*e*	creat*ing*
excit*e*	excit*ing*
trac*e*	trac*ing*
confuse	confusing
challenge	challenging
decorate	decorating

Your Business Vocabulary

acknowledge ac To show recognition of.

This letter is to acknowledge your order of March 1.

merchandise dse Goods that may be bought or sold.

That manufacturer produces an excellent quality of merchandise.

Reading and Writing Exercises

1

Preview Words

coat	material
correct	reminding
jacket	situation
leather	acknowledge

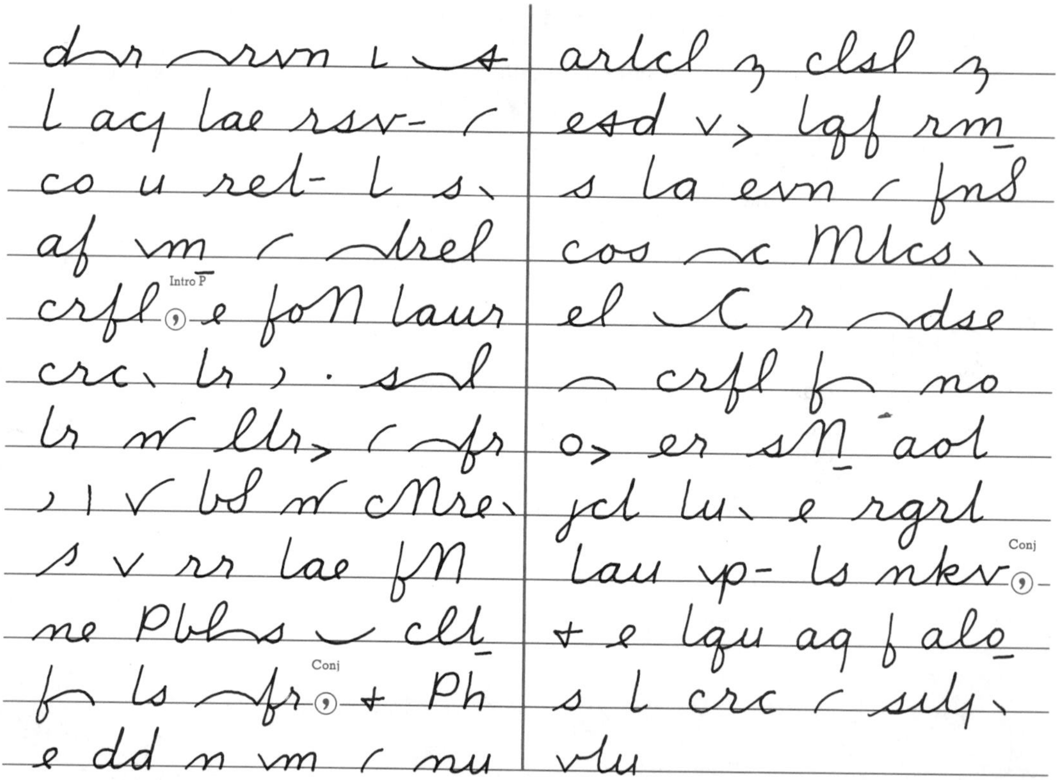

2

Preview Words

bowl	bl	flowers	flors
silver	slvr	basically	bscl
solid	sld	antique	alc
leaves	lvs	decorating	dcra

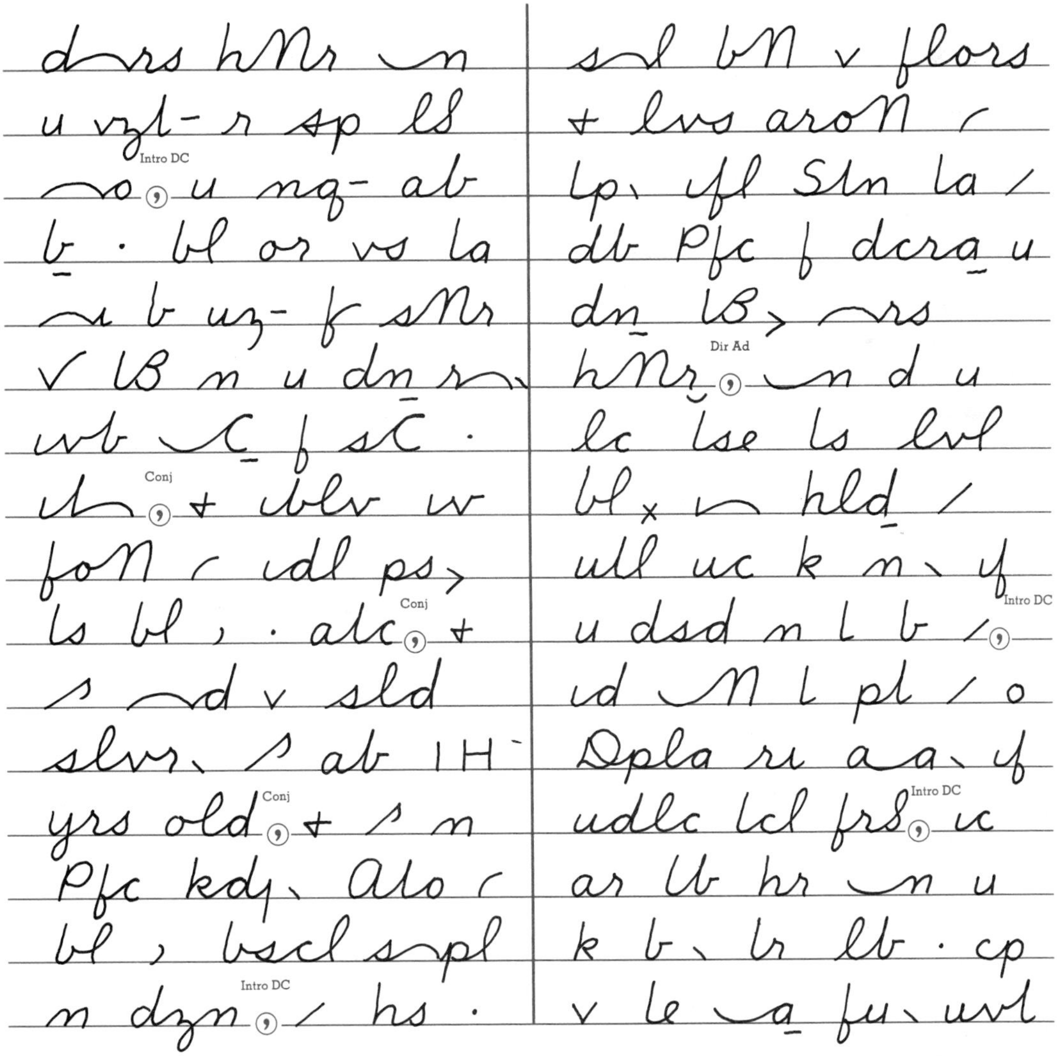

3

Preview Words

Susan *szn*

cooperate *cop*

Sanderson *sNrsn*

challenging *Clny*

effort *efl*

worthwhile *rll*

objective *objcv*

volunteers *vlnlrs*

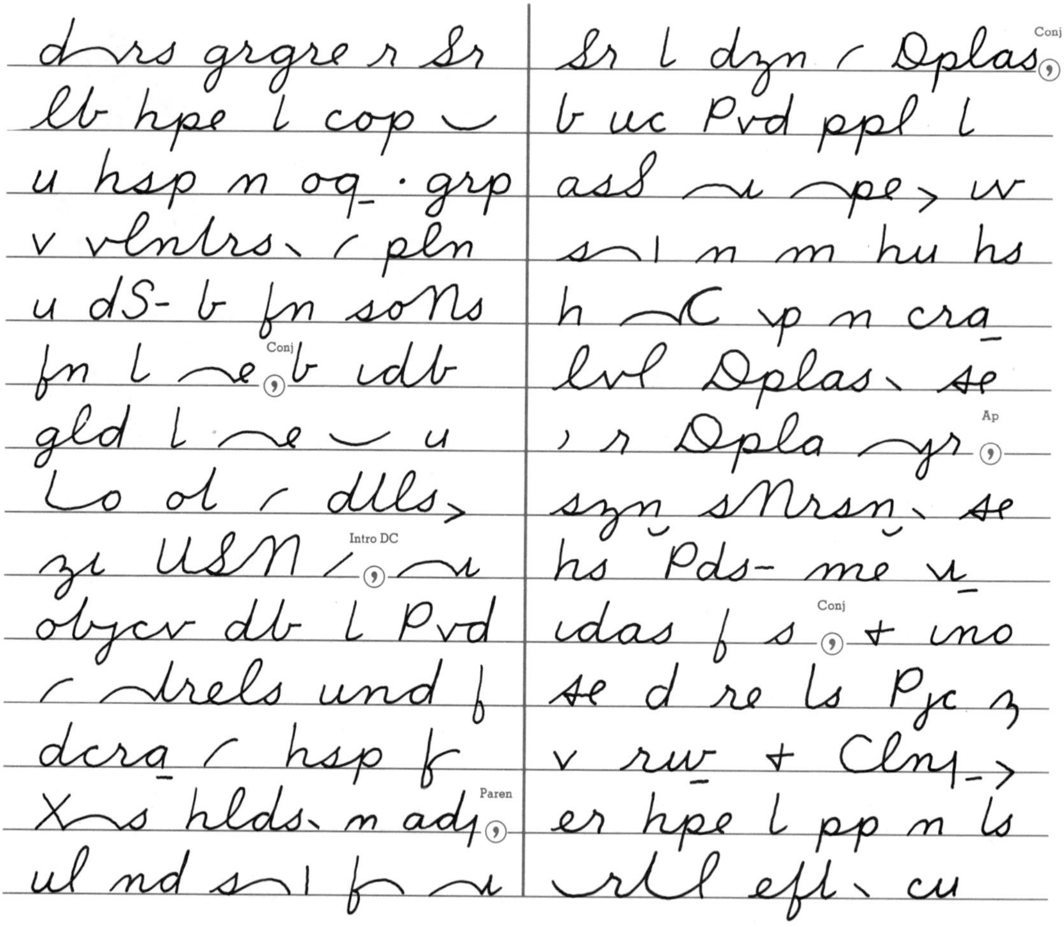

4

Preview Words

owe O

sporting spl̲

brought brl

receipts rses

further frlr

unusual uuz

household hoshld

confusion kf

dr sNfr af Cc̲
r recs crfl, ev (Intro P)
foN la r ad
sn ou 8 rsN
bl̲) crc. r lol
u no o) 76^89.
er enc̲ cpes v
2 sls rses. r
frs PCs z d (Conj)
n r spl̲ gs dpl,
sec z f hoshld

ths, du̲ ls bze
l v yr, s n (Intro P)
uuz f Ks l Olc
. pam. no la ev
dl- r cz v kf, (Intro DC)
eno lau ak lb
brl pda, if uv
frlr gs ab r bl̲
Psyrs, p cl e (Intro DC)
Psnll / 613-2189.
su

5

Punctuation Study

Add commas to show two conjunctions, one direct address, and two introductory dependent clauses.

Preview Words

yard	yd	later	lar
tracing	trs	loading	ld
trees	tres	platform	pltf
touch	tC	evergreen	Egrn

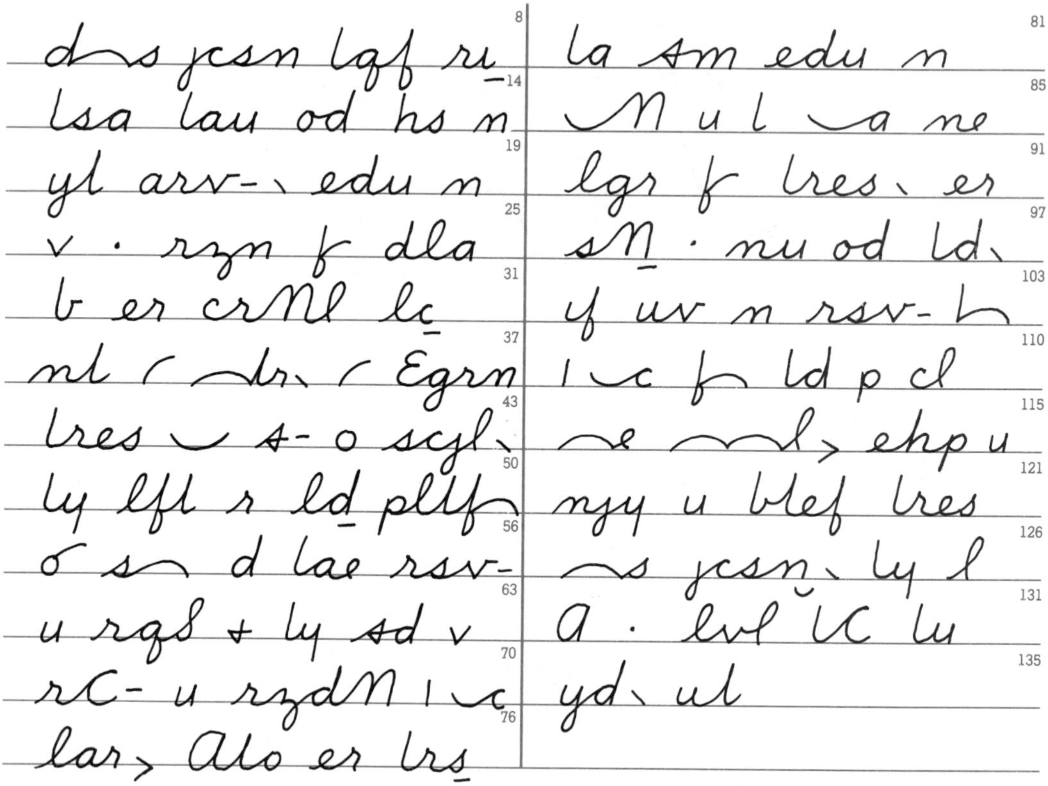

Key

1

Dear Mr. Marvin:

I wish to acknowledge that we received the coat you returned to us. After examining[1] the material carefully, we found that you are correct. There is a small tear in the leather.

The manufacturer[2] is one of the best in the country. It is very rare that we find any problems with clothing from this[3] manufacturer, and perhaps we did not examine the new article as closely as we should have.

Thank you[4] for reminding us that even the finest companies make mistakes. We will watch our merchandise more carefully[5] from now on.

We are sending another jacket to you. We regret that you experienced this inconvenience,[6] and we thank you again for allowing us to correct the situation.

Very truly yours, (137)

2

Dear Mrs. Hunter:

When you visited our shop last month, you inquired about buying a bowl or vase that might be[1] used for the center of the table in your dining room. I have been watching for such an item, and I believe[2] I have found the ideal piece.

This bowl is an antique, and it is made of solid silver. It is about 100[3] years old, and it is in perfect condition. Although the bowl is basically simple in design, it has a[4] small band of flowers and leaves around the top. I feel certain that it would be perfect for decorating your dining[5] table.

Mrs. Hunter, when would you like to see this lovely bowl? I am holding it until you can come in.[6] If you decide not to buy it, I would want to put it on display right away. If you would like to call first, I[7] can arrange to be here when you come by. There will be a cup of tea waiting for you.

Yours very truly, (159)

3

Dear Mrs. Gregory:

Our store will be happy to cooperate with your hospital in organizing a[1] group of volunteers. The plan you described by phone sounds fine to me, but I would be glad to meet with you to work out[2] the details.

As I understand it, my objective would be to provide the materials you need for decorating[3] the hospital for the Christmas holidays. In addition, you will need someone from my store to design the[4] displays, but you can provide people to assist my employee.

I have someone in mind who has had much[5] experience in creating lovely displays. She is our display manager, Susan Sanderson. She has produced[6] many exciting ideas for us, and I know she would regard this project as very rewarding and[7] challenging.

We are happy to participate in this worthwile effort.

Cordially yours, (155)

4

Dear Mr. Sandifer:

After checking our records carefully, we have found that the amount shown on your most[1] recent billing is correct. The total you now owe is $76.89. We are enclosing[2] copies of the two sales receipts. The first purchase was made in our sporting goods department, and the second was for[3] household items.

During this busy time of the year, it is not unusual for customers to overlook[4] a payment. Now that we have determined the cause of confusion, we know that your account will be brought up to date.[5]

If you have further questions about our billing procedures, please call me personally at 613-2189.[6]

Sincerely yours, (124)

5

Dear Ms. Jackson:

Thank you for writing to say that your order has not yet arrived. We do not have a reason for[1] the delay, but we are currently looking into the matter. The evergreen trees were shipped on schedule. They left[2] our loading platform on the same day that we received your request, and they should have reached your residence one week later.[3]

Although we are tracing that shipment, we do not want you to wait any longer for the trees. We are sending[4] a new order today. If you have not received them one week from today, please call me immediately.

We hope[5] you enjoy your beautiful trees, Ms. Jackson. They will add a lovely touch to your yard.

Yours truly, (117)

LESSON 15

Word Development

Develop new words from the following brief forms:

on

only *ol*
onward *ow*
onset *osl*
upon *po*

over

moreover 
overall *Oa*
overdue *Odu*
overhead *Ohd*

firm

affirm *afr*
confirm *kfr*
confirmation *kfrj*
infirmary *nfrre*

part

apartment *aplm*
counterpart *krpl*
depart *dpl*
partner *plnr*

Reading and Writing Exercises

1

Preview Words

before	bf	remember	rmbr
reorder	rod	subtotal	slol
bottom	bh	figure	fgr
catalog	cal	quantity	qNL

dr dvdsn lqf
rsN od f spl gs.
bf ec Pss u od, (Intro DC)
hoE, (Paren) el nd adyl
inf. r cpe v PCs
f sos lau dd n
I cal Nos f ne v
ihs rqS-. p uz r
nu f la ev enc-
l rod r dse.
rmbr l lS r qNL
f eC ih, (Series) r unl
prs, (Series) + cal No.

r bh v pj, (Intro P) so
r lol No v ihs
+ lol cS vu PCss.
a r s fe l ls
slol + so r lol
ad l o-. b sr u
Cc agres r fgr
f lol ad o-.
eap u psN n crc
ls od. el s r dse
zz r kp-f + pam
r rsv-. ul

2

Preview Words

disks   *Dcs*

manual   *nul*

Boulevard   *blvd*

prompt   *Pt*

Lincoln   *lgn*

processor   *Pssr*

electronic   *elnc*

accustomed   *acs—*

[Shorthand text — two columns]

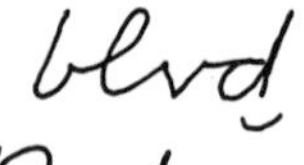

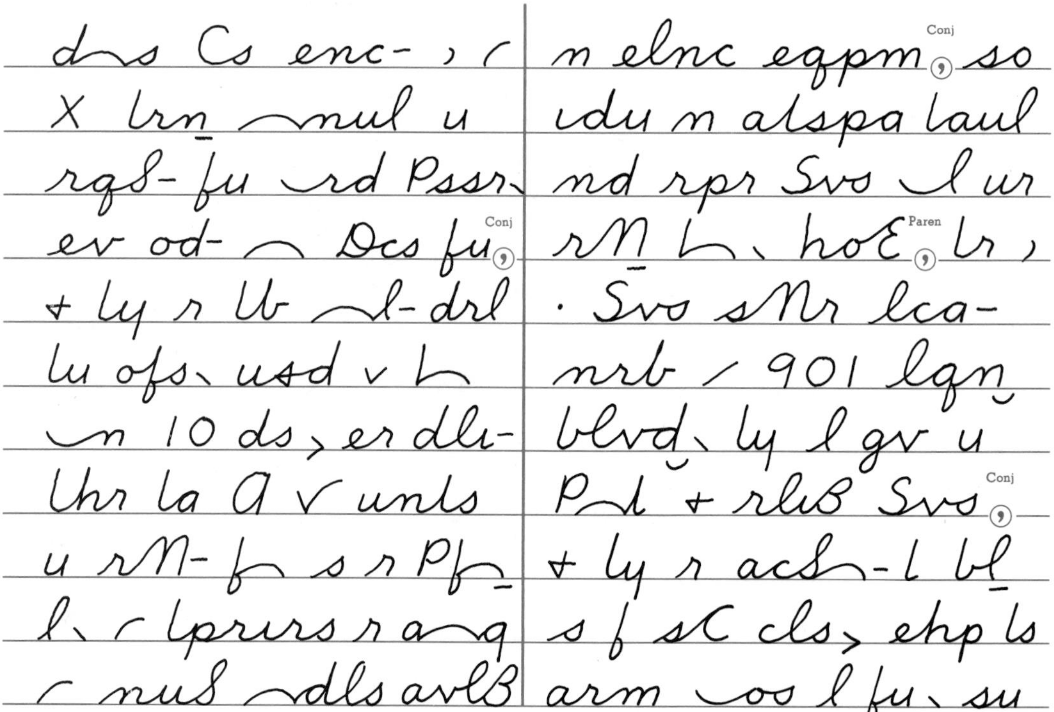

——————————————— **3** ———————————————

Preview Words

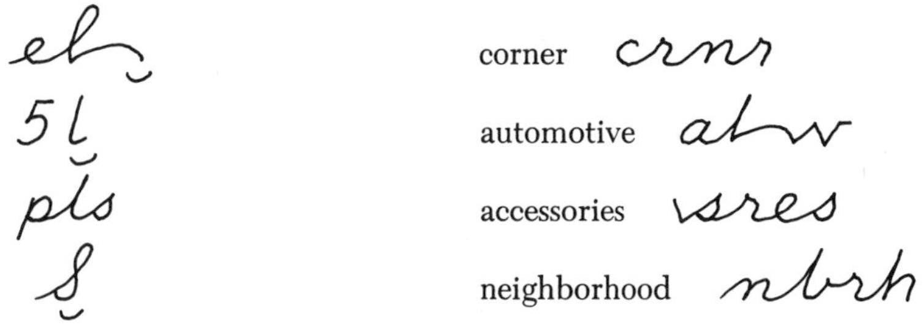

Elm	*el~*
Fifth	*5 l*
parts	*plo*
Street	*S*

corner	*crnr*
automotive	*at~v*
accessories	*vsres*
neighborhood	*nbrh*

dr + ~rs ltrs
erp- l anoM la er
opn . Svs Sj n u
nbrh, uv PbB
drvn b r su frqMl
S lca- S crnr v
5l S + el~ blvd,
edlc u l jyn s f
fre cfe + cc l sltbra
r grM opn, sMer
q- lb nbrs ₉ edlc lb
frMs z l, / Stnl,

. Avj lno r ppl hu
Svs u cr, r Sj l
cre . IMv ln v
at~v plo + vsres,
e P~s fS + rliB
Svs r ecol ras,
M u jyn s o
Mv 8 bln 9a~ +
9 p~ f r grM opn x
u alMM d gv s gr
plzr, vlu

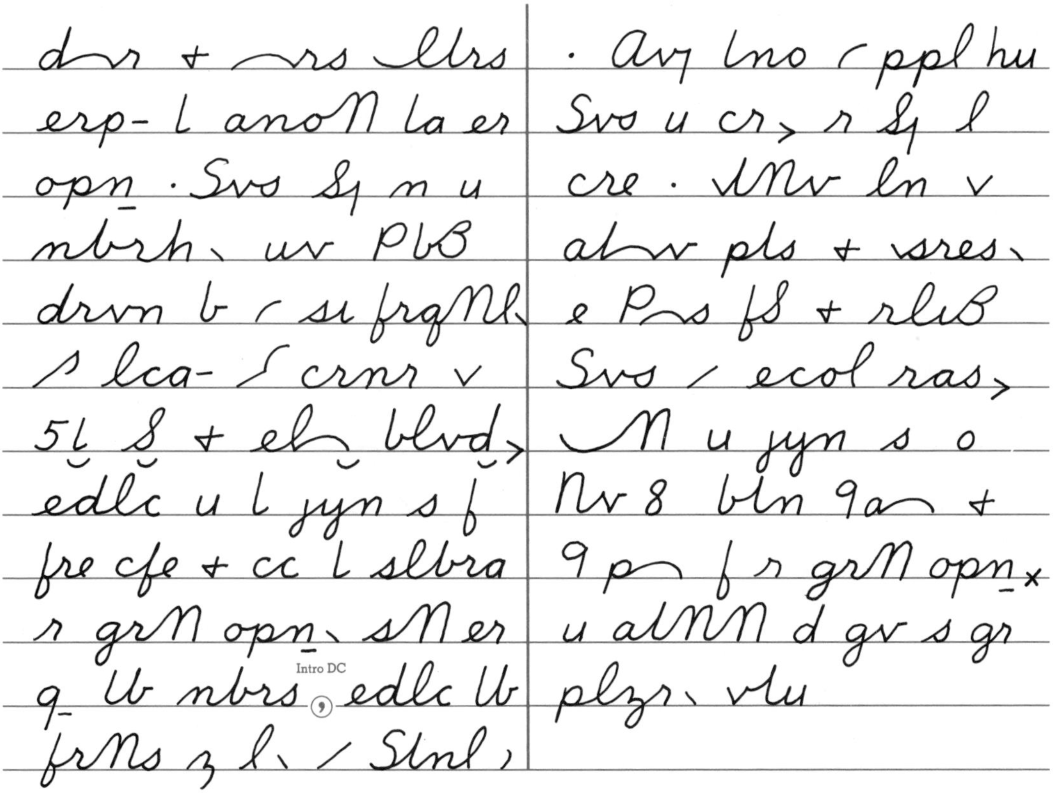

4

Preview Words

water	ltr	edition	edj
section	scj	original	orynl
notice	nls	addition	adj
another	aol	recreation	rcrej

d S— r nu sl cal
, o s —a lu, lc
f / w —l> p nls
la ev vpN- me
aras, (Conj) + ev l- sv
ol lns la r ntrl
nu ls yr, f ex, (Paren) Cc
r scj o c—p gr, e
lq ul apv v lo
prss> aol v adj
l r cal, eqpm
f lr rcrej, —a
ull u se l, no
avlB> ulfN la ls
nul pbls- edj vr
cal hs grn l ls
s orynl sz, y x e
vlu r plrnj vr Ks, (Conj)
+ e —N lofr h r
bs Cyss v —dse>
avryd —c unes
lrps l sp sNrs,
sv me r kv —a
b od / hlsl prss,
uc k o s l olfl u
lu saly, vrı +
dpNB v bk r
spslles, su

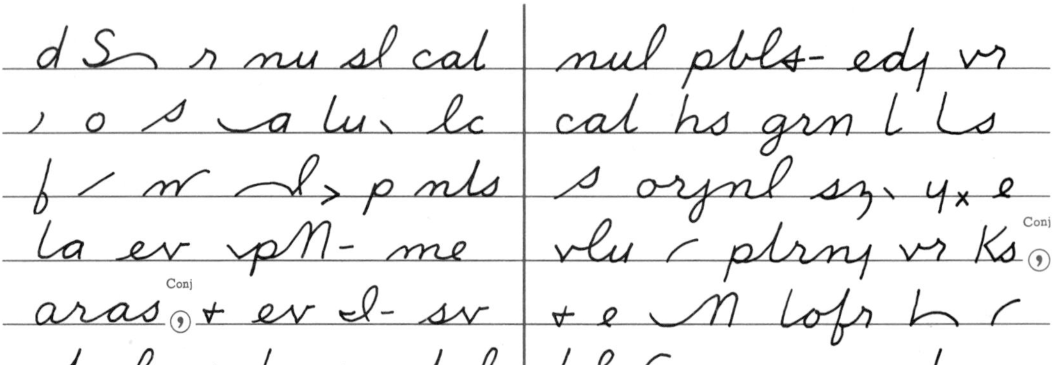

5

Punctuation Study

Add commas to show one appositive, one introductory dependent clause, and two introductory phrases.

Preview Words

fashions *fʃs*

private *prvl*

showroom *ʃor*

presence *prʒN*

American *a*

exclusive *vclsv*

favorite *fvrl*

refreshments *rfrʃms*

d—s evns ⌐ —ym ⁶	—ʃ —prsv dʒnrs ⁷⁴
vr fr rgʃs u prʒN ¹³	n a, brc ⌐ ocɥ ⁸¹
⌐ · prvl ʃo v · u ²⁰	evn ⌐ spʃl ev ⁸⁷
clɥ, ⌐ fCrs · fvrl ²⁸	ar-f Nlnm + rfrʃms, ⁹⁶
a— Pdc dʒnr fʃs, ³⁵	⌐ enc- crd l Sv ʒu ¹⁰³
fʃ —n u lɡ uv sn ⁴²	nvlɥ · p ʃo ⌐ ʒu ¹¹⁰
E · brul r—rcʃ ⁴⁸	N r ʃor, ⌐ gvs ¹¹⁶
ιda ks alɡ, l pv ⁵⁴	s plʒr l hʃ ls ¹²¹
ls py er nvr u l ⁶¹	vclsv ʃo, ehp ¹²⁷
vu orɥnl fʃs f ⌐ ⁶⁷	ulb r gʃ, uvl ¹³⁵

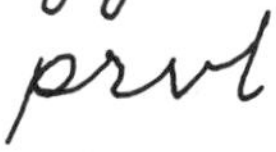

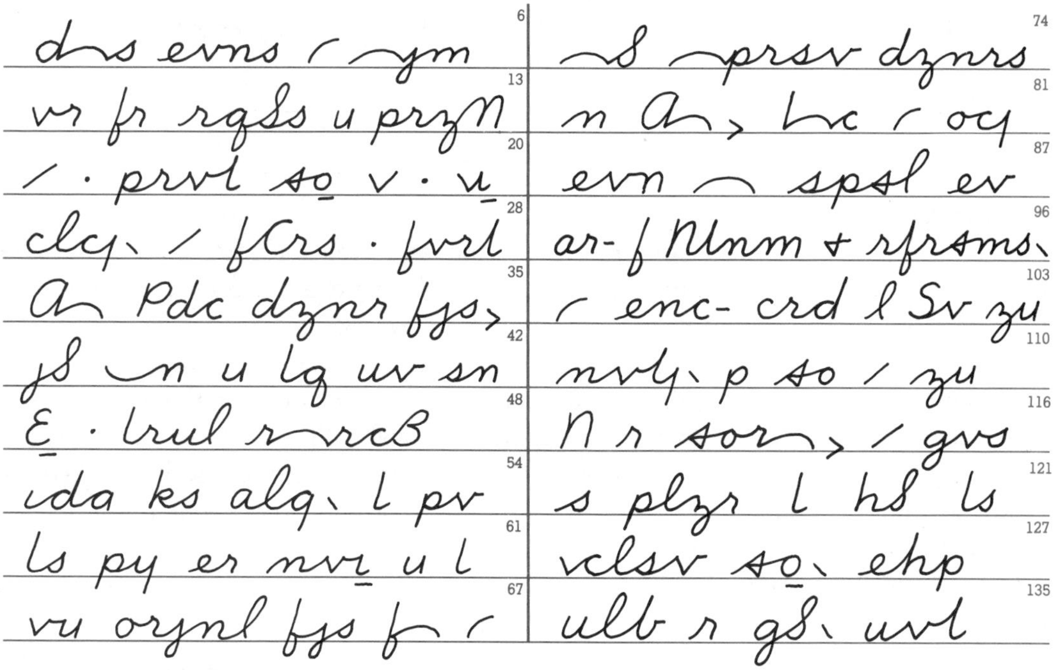

Key

1

Dear Mr. Davidson:

Thank you for your recent order for sporting goods. Before we can process your order,[1] however, we will need additional information. Our copy of the purchase form shows that you did not include[2] catalog numbers for any of the items requested. Please use the new form that we have enclosed to reorder[3] the merchandise.

Remember to list the quantity for each item, the unit price, and the catalog number.[4] At the bottom of the page, show the total number of items and the total cost of your purchases. Add[5] the shipping fee to this subtotal and show the total amount owed. Be sure your check agrees with the figure for[6] the total amount owed.

We appreciate your patience in correcting this order. We will ship the merchandise[7] as soon as the completed form and payment are received.

Yours truly, (152)

2

Dear Ms. Chase:

Enclosed is the extra training manual you requested for your word processor. We have ordered[1] more disks for you, and they are to be mailed directly to your office. You should have them within ten days.

We are[2] delighted to hear that all of the units you rented from us are performing well. The typewriters are among the[3] newest models available in electronic equipment, so I do not anticipate that you will[4] need repair service while you are renting them. However, there is a service center located nearby at[5] 901 Lincoln Boulevard. They will give you prompt and reliable service, and they are accustomed to billing[6] us for such calls.

We hope this arrangement works well for you.

Sincerely yours, (132)

3

Dear Mr. and Mrs. Walters:

We are pleased to announce that we are opening a service station in your[1] neighborhood. You have probably driven by the site frequently. It is located at the corner of Fifth Street and[2] Elm Boulevard.

We would like you to join us for free coffee and cake to celebrate our grand opening. Since we are[3] going to be neighbors, we would like to be friends as well. It certainly is an advantage to know the people[4] who service your car.

Our station will carry an extensive line of automotive parts and accessories. We[5] promise fast and reliable service at economical rates.

Won't you join us on November 8 between[6] 9 a.m. and 9 p.m. for our grand opening? Your attendance would give us great pleasure.

Very truly yours,[7] (140)

4

Dear Sir or Madam:

Our new sale catalog is on its way to you. Look for it in the mail.

Please notice that we[1] have expanded many areas, and we have included several other lines that are entirely new this[2] year. For example, check the section on camping gear. We think you will approve of the low prices.

Another[3] exciting addition to our catalog is equipment for water recreation. Wait until you see what is[4] now available.

You will find that this newly published edition of our catalog has grown to twice its[5] original size. Why? We value the patronage of our customers, and we want to offer them the best choices[6] of merchandise.

Avoid making unnecessary trips to shopping centers. Save money the convenient way by[7] ordering at wholesale prices. You can count on us to outfit you to your satisfaction. Variety and[8] dependability have become our specialties.

Sincerely yours, (172)

5

Dear Ms. Evans:

The management of our firm requests your presence at a private showing of an exciting[1] collection. It features a favorite American product, designer fashions.

Just when you think you have seen[2] everything, a truly remarkable idea comes along. To prove this point, we are inviting you to view[3] original fashions from the most impressive designers in America.

To make the occasion even more[4] special, we have arranged for entertainment and refreshments. The enclosed card will serve as your invitation. Please[5] show it as you enter our showroom.

It gives us pleasure to host this exclusive showing. We hope you will be our[6] guest.

Yours very truly, (124)

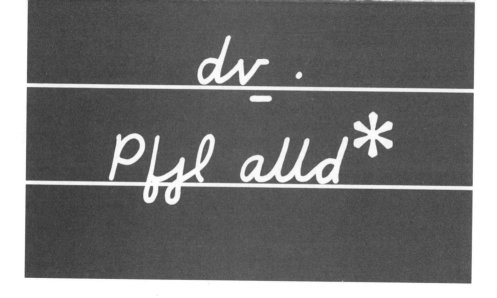

dv . Pfl alld*

Many factors determine how successfully an office worker fits into the total office environment. Technical skills, such as typing, dictation and transcription, word processing, data processing, and computer programming, are essential for performing certain duties. Knowing how to get along well with people is just as important. Because offices are centers for communication, people must be able to work effectively as a team.

In addition to these skills, another quality is important to advancement in office careers. This quality is best described as a *professional image*—an overall image that sets certain office workers apart from others. To project a professional image, you must first develop a professional *attitude*, which determines how you look, work, and interact with other people.

A professional attitude begins with these characteristics:

Enthusiasm. Be willing to accept new responsibilities. Approach each task with energy and seriousness. Be cheerful and courteous to others.

Maturity. Approach your work with dignified behavior. Take your responsibilities seriously and give full attention to your duties.

Competence. Learn your job well. Identify weaker skills and concentrate on improving them on a daily basis.

Confidence. When you are certain that you are giving your best effort to doing a job well, your behavior will reflect the confidence that you have gained from experience.

Cooperation. Office systems depend upon teams of people working together to process communications. Be a cooperative team member.

***Developing a Professional Attitude**

Reliability. Show that you are reliable by being on time, by getting your work done on time, and by consistently producing high quality work.

Positivism. A positive attitude should be evident in everything you say and do. Even when saying "no," learn to say it in a pleasant and positive way.

Unlike technical skills, *professionalism* is not usually taught as a subject in textbooks and classrooms. Yet, it is exhibited in everything you do—how you look, work, and behave. A professional attitude says to everyone around you, "I enjoy my work, I take pride in my work, and I plan to be successful in my career."

unl 4

bq *

Shorthand Vocabulary Review

Study the following words and the principles they illustrate. You will find these words in the letters and memos in this unit.

1. Write a capital  for the sound of *ch, cha* (pronounced *chay*).

check		change	
mutual		future	
branch		structure	
chairman		approaching	
achieve		expenditure	

***Unit Four**
Banking

2. Write f for the word ending *ful*.

grateful	grf	carefully	crfl
helpful	hlpf	successful	sucf
careful	crf	successfully	sucfl

3. Write sf for *self* and svs for *selves*.

yourself	usf	themselves	⌐svs

More About Punctuation

When two or more words are used as one thought to describe a noun, we call them compound adjectives. If these words come immediately before the noun, join them with a hyphen.

Please place an order for a six-foot table.

Where can we find an up-to-date book?

She is a well-known expert.

If these words come after the noun, no hyphen is necessary.

We already have a table that is six feet long.

I believe that this book is up to date.

Her skills are well known.

Do not use a hyphen if the first word ends in "ly."

Can you recommend a highly skilled craftsman?

It was a closely guarded secret.

LESSON 16

Brief Forms and Derivatives

1. *sig   y   ly   dr   n*

2. *apxl   dfce   ac-   yr   ort*

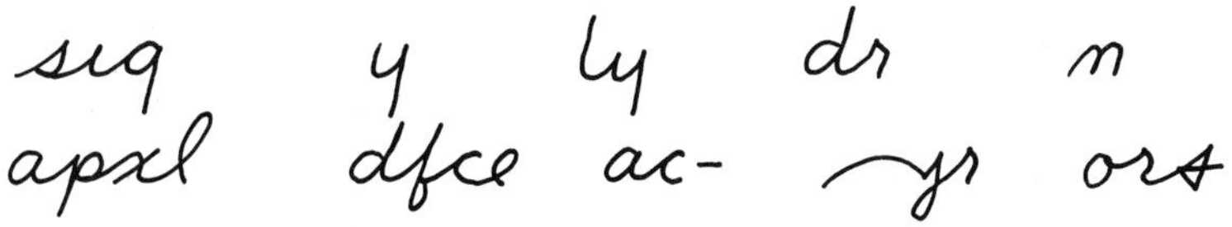

Key

1. signature/significant/significance, why, they, doctor/direct, in/not
2. approximately, difficulty, accepted, manager, ownership

Phrase Review

Easily recognized words are omitted from some phrases:

thank *you* for	*lqf*	as *soon* as	*33*
thank *you* for *your*	*lqf*	time *to* time	*Lh*
thank *you* for *your* letter	*lqfL*	up *to* date	*pda*
never*theless*	*nvrls*	none*theless*	*nnls*

1. *und   ud   lv   lsn   luz   zu*

2. *fu   hsb   n   33   pda*

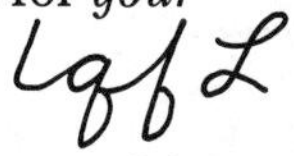

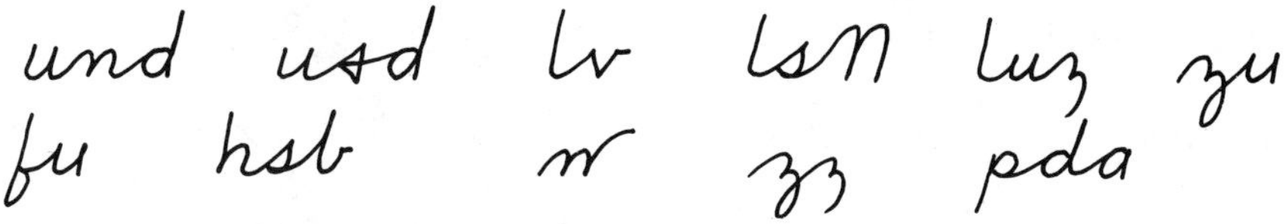

Key

1. you need, you should, to have, to send, to use, as you/as your
2. for you/for your, has been, in the, as soon as, up to date

Reading and Writing Exercises

1

Preview Words

honor	onr	identical	idNcl
reject	rjc	correctly	crcl
destroy	dSry	automatic	al-dc
difficulty	dfce	identification	idNf

dr jcsn er enc . nu idNf crd fu. p dSry u old crd + rpls / ⌣ r nu crd, ze agre- b Ulfn, [Intro DC] r bq l onr r Ccs uv rln uz u f m. n fCr, [Paren] hoE, [Paren] b Sln la r sig u uz ou Ccs , idNcl l la

Sn ou nu idNf crd, e rgrl la 2 vu Ccs ⌣ rel-, [Conj] b r ⌒pes rjc Ccs ⌣C vn b sn-crcl. ls , . al-dc Psyr, [Conj] + s dzn- l Plc u ak, no la uv rsv- u nu crd, [Intro DC] usd v no frlr dfce. uvl

———————— **2** ————————

Preview Words

today   *ld*

goes   *gs*

answer   *asr*

into   *nl*

wonder   *Mr*

transfer   *Tfr*

specified   *sp-*

automatically   *atldcl*

---

dr + rs crlsn s ppl A s lv r me ly nd. dd u E Mr y× r asr , qi s pl f r Ks. ly uz r me ym Svs , b uz r ym Svs ₉ u pa usf bf pa u bls. hr , ho r os. u bgn b dpzt u f pacc r ak.

ln e atldcl Tfr r

Intro P

sp- a l nl u sv ak. ulb a rz- / ho qcl r ak gros , Ph r bS pt v ls pln , s kr. r Ks nsS la ly nvr s l M r me la gs nl sv. e lq s r S sucf pln n bq hSre , uc Srl u ym pln ld. cl 312-4010 f inf. vlu

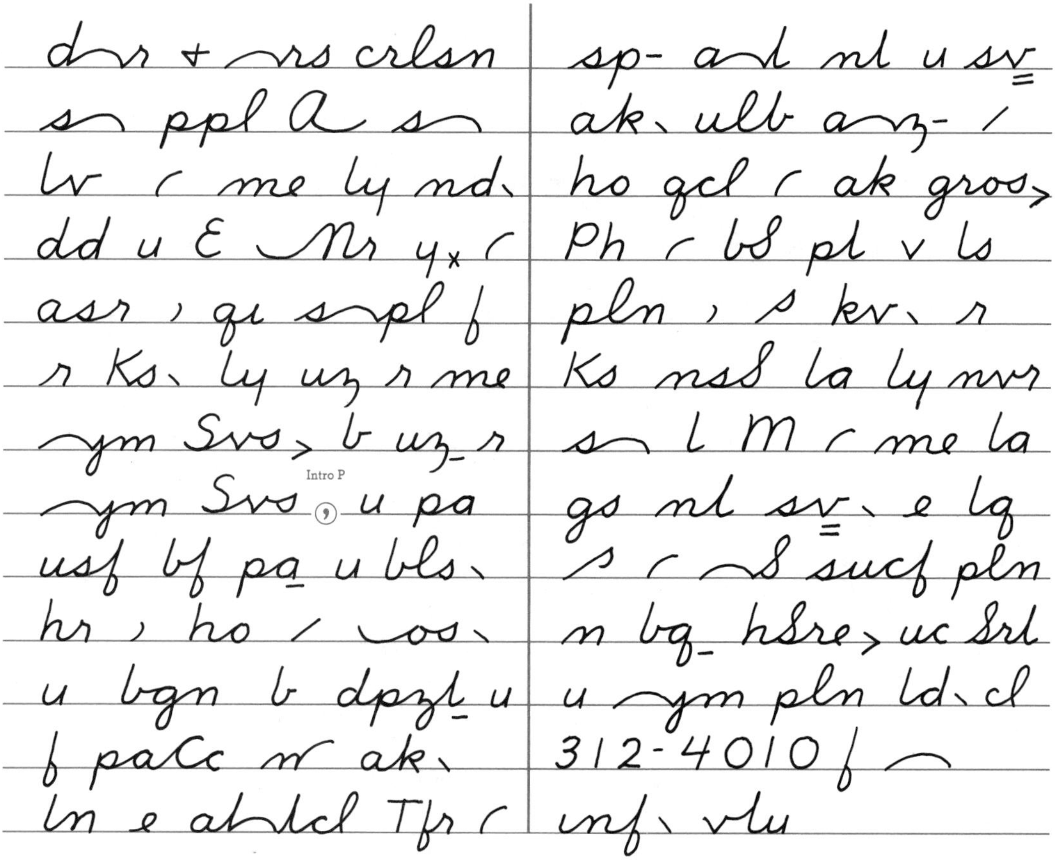

3

Preview Words

peace	ps	greater	grr
stolen	Sln	financial	fnnsl
finances	fnNs	arrangements	arms
vacation	vcj	protection	Plcj

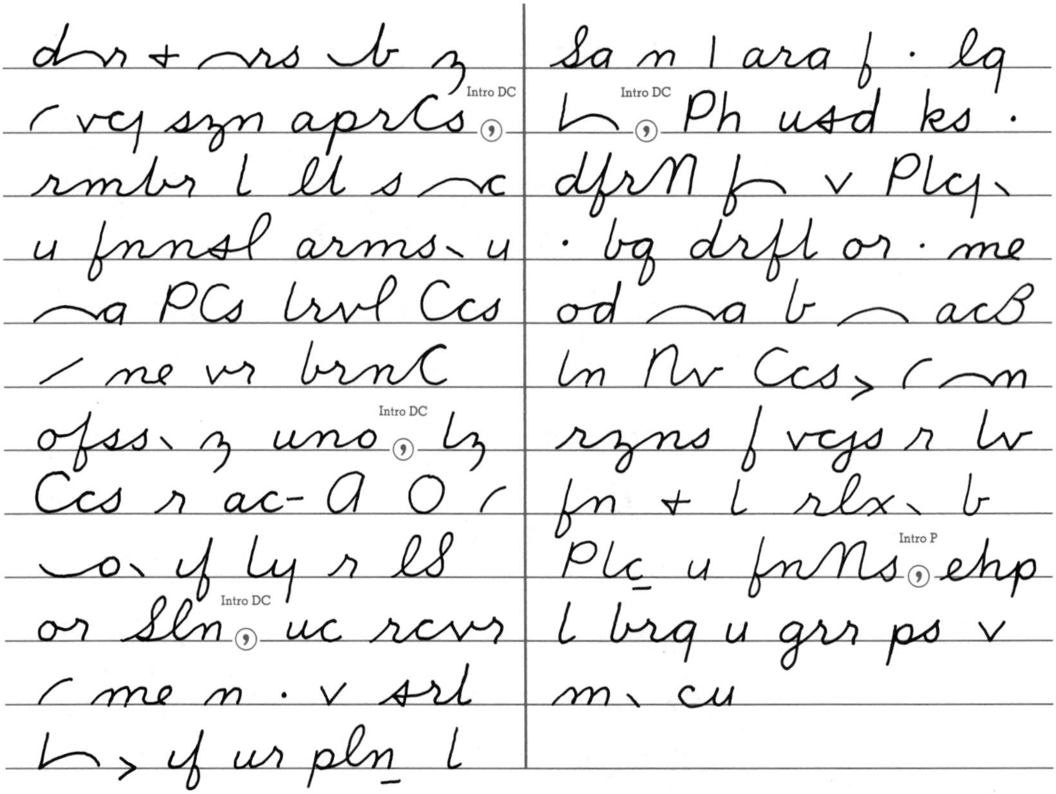

---------------------------- **4** ----------------------------

Preview Words

assign	_asn_	therefore	_lrf_
boxes	_bxs_	possessions	_pzjs_
period	_pred_	safe-deposit	_sf= dpzl_
assured	_asr-_	inexpensive	_nxpNv_

dr hs bcz uv
_lq b . K vr bq_ ⟨Intro DC⟩
e nvr u l lc Avy
v . fre Svs. u ⌢a
uz . sf= dpzl bx /
no cS f . pred v
4 ⌣cs, esl asn
⌢ bxs nr od la
rqSs r rsv-.
lrf ⟨Paren⟩ _yf uv . vcy_
or lrp scyl- ⟨Intro DC⟩ _usd_
gv s u das zz
psO so la ucb

asr- v gl u Cys
v Ls, ehp u
nyy ls Svs. lz
dpzl bxs ofr ⌢
ol sf ⌣a l Plc
⌢pl pprs + pzjs.
u ⌢a evn dsd l
rM l v lz dpzl
bxs o . yrl bss.
⌣n u ks ⌢ snd
_cS_ ⟨Intro DC⟩ _sC Plcy , v_
nxpNv. su

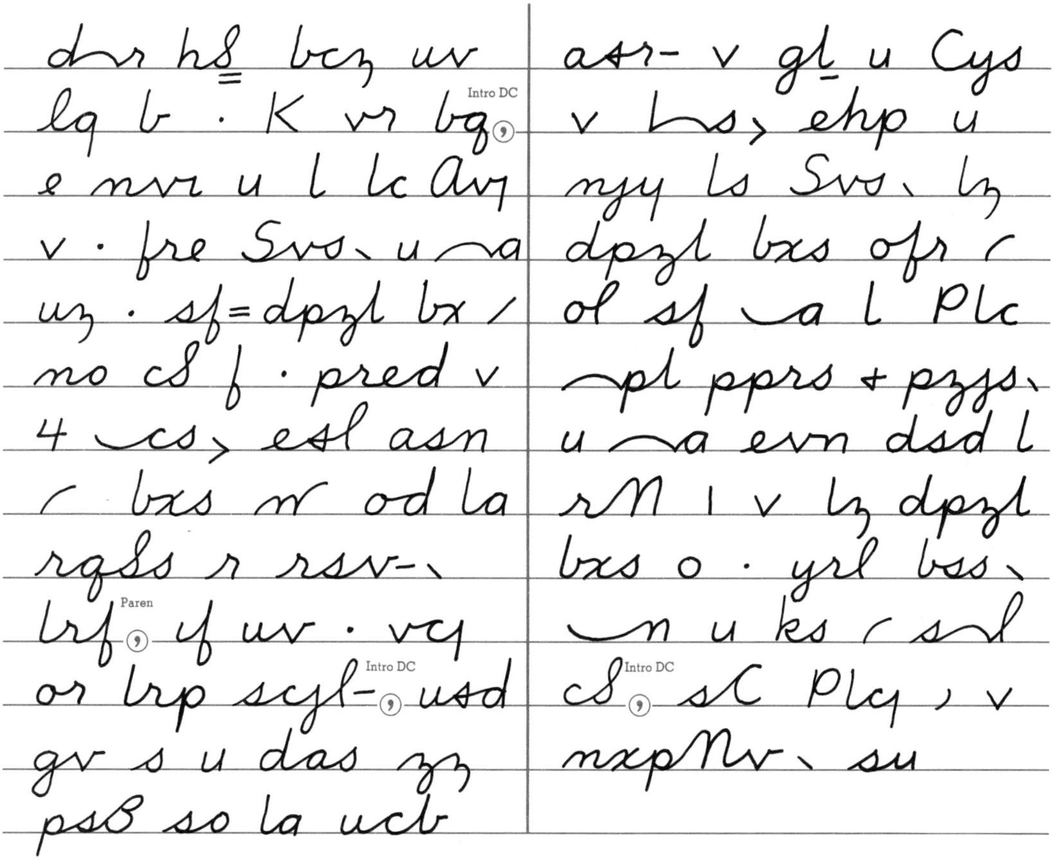

---------- 5 ----------

Punctuation Study

Add commas to set off one series, two introductory dependent clauses, one introductory phrase, and one appositive.

Preview Words

dreams *dr~s*   country *cNre*

burden *brdn*   lending *lN*

yours *us*   reasonable *rznß*

corporation *corp*   ownership *ors*

dS~ erp-l anoN r
opn vr nu brnC
ofs n u nbrh, r
corp hs Sv- Ms
v Ks a O r cMre,
ev ~d r psß f
f~ls lc us l relz
lr dr~s, ev hlp-
l aCv h ors
vcjs cly ejcjs +
ol spsl nds, bcz
r pam plns r so
rznß ly v ej~ r

brdn v rpa lns,
~n und fnnsl
assN usd Cj, lN
co j crfl j ud Cj
. dr, asc u frNs
ab s or brq u qs
l s Psnll, l lrn
~ ab r Svss pa
s . vjl, r ak
yrs r ~S hlpf
ppl n lon lb dli-
l ~e u, ul

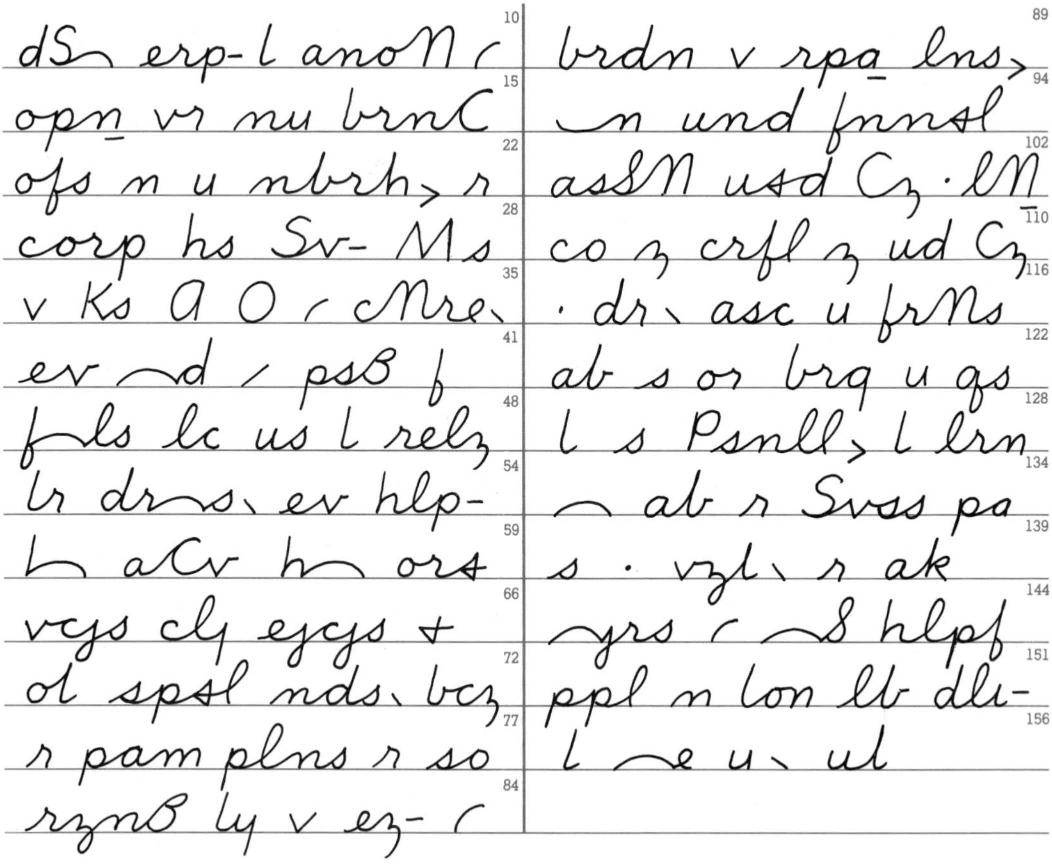

Key

1

Dear Mr. Jackson:

We are enclosing a new identification card for you. Please destroy your old card and[1] replace it with the new card.

As we agreed by telephone, our bank will honor the checks you have written using[2] your full name. In the future, however, be certain that the signature you use on your checks is identical[3] to that shown on your new identification card.

We regret that two of your checks were returned, but our employees[4] reject checks which have not been signed correctly. This is an automatic procedure, and it is designed to[5] protect your account.

Now that you have received your new card, you should have no further difficulty.

Yours very[6] truly, (121)

2

Dear Mr. and Mrs. Carlson:

Some people always seem to have the money they need. Did you ever wonder why?[1] The answer is quite simple for our customers. They use our money management service.

By using our management[2] service, you pay yourself before paying your bills. Here is how it works. You begin by depositing your full[3] paycheck in the account. Then we automatically transfer the specified amount into your savings account.[4] You will be amazed at how quickly the account grows.

Perhaps the best part of this plan is its convenience. Our[5] customers insist that they never seem to miss the money that goes into savings. We think it is the most[6] successful plan in banking history.

You can start your management plan today. Call 312-4010 for[7] more information.

Very truly yours, (146)

3

Dear Mr. and Mrs. Webb:

As the vacation season approaches, remember to let us make your financial[1] arrangements. You may purchase travel checks at any of our branch offices. As you know, these checks are accepted[2] all over the world. If they are lost or stolen, you can recover the money in a very short time.

If you[3] are planning to stay in one area for a long time, perhaps you should consider a different form of[4] protection. A bank draft or a money order may be more acceptable than individual checks.

The main[5] reasons for vacations are to have fun and to relax. By protecting your finances, we hope to bring you greater[6] peace of mind.

Cordially yours, (125)

4

Dear Mr. Hastings:

Because you have long been a customer of our bank, we invite you to take advantage of[1] a free service. You may use a safe-deposit box at no cost for a period of four weeks.

We shall assign[2] the boxes in the order that requests are received. Therefore, if you have a vacation or trip scheduled, you should[3] give us your dates as soon as possible so that you can be assured of getting your choice of times.

We hope you enjoy[4] this service. These deposit boxes offer the only safe way to protect important papers and possessions.[5] You may even decide to rent one of these deposit boxes on a yearly basis. When you consider[6] the small cost, such protection is very inexpensive.

Sincerely yours, (133)

5

Dear Sir or Madam:

We are pleased to announce the opening of our new branch office in your neighborhood.

Our[1] corporation has served millions of customers all over the country. We have made it possible for families[2] like yours to realize their dreams. We have helped them achieve home ownership, vacations, college educations, and[3] other special needs. Because our payment plans are so reasonable, they have eased the burden of repaying loans.[4]

When you need financial assistance, you should choose a lending company as carefully as you would choose a doctor.[5] Ask your friends about us or bring your questions to us personally.

To learn more about our services, pay[6] us a visit. Our account managers, the most helpful people in town, will be delighted to meet you.

Yours[7] truly, (141)

LESSON 17

Abbreviations and Derivatives

1. *a͟d re͟l VP env No fed*
2. *A rep agrl hrs ds*

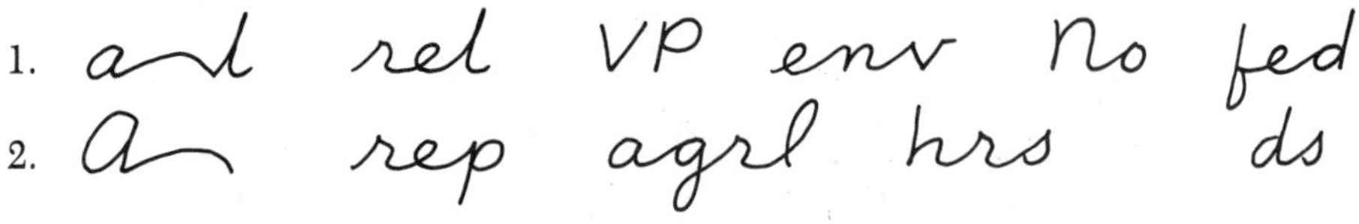

Key

1. amount, return, vice president, envelope, number, federal
2. America/American, represent/representative, agricultural, hours, days

Transcription Aids: Typing Numbers

1. When a number consists of four or more figures, use a comma to set off groups of three digits.

   At least 5,000 people participated in the sports festival.

2. As a general rule, write serial numbers, invoice numbers, and catalog numbers without commas.

   Please refer to Invoice 60843.

Your Business Vocabulary

option *opt*   A choice; in an insurance policy, a clause permitting the policyholder to choose the manner in which payments are to be made or credited to him or her.

Please consider all of the options carefully before deciding upon a particular one.

agenda *ajna*   A list of topics to be discussed or things to be completed at a meeting.

Each board member will receive a copy of the agenda in advance.

Reading and Writing Exercises

——————————————— 1 ———————————————

Preview Words

form $\int$

already a_γ

anything $n\underline{e}$

option $op\gamma$

appointment $apym$

retirement $r\ell rm$

situation $su\gamma$

application $apl\varsigma$

d r lsn hr , (∫ ⌣ ls L , y uv
brsr u rqS- dS r a r dsd- o · plc
rlrm ak , El hs opγ ⑨ jS fl ol (∫
dfrN nds , / db + rel / l s N env
S hlpf lu l ⌣e ev Pvd- , u nu ak
⌣ l vr Sf mbrs l bk acv n apxl
l Dcs u Nv suγ , 10 ds , p ll s no
ec ⌣c · apym / y lr , n⌣e ⌢ ec
u kv , ev l- · aplγ du fu , su

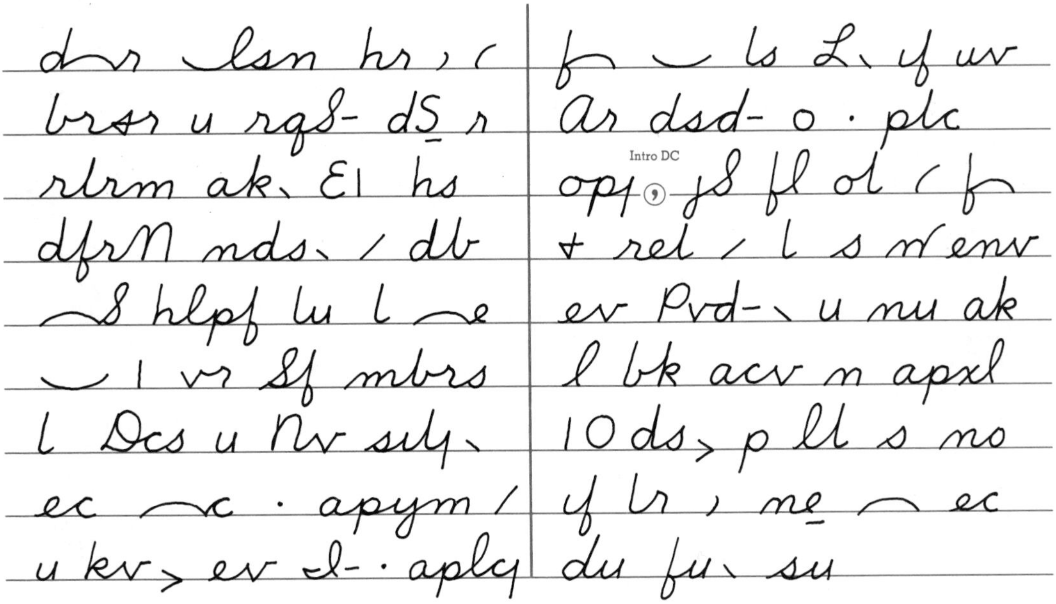

2

Preview Words

dial	dil	access	vs
fire	fr	actually	acCull
per	p	whenever	nE
theft	Tfl	safe-deposit	sf=dpzl

ds rsl r u lc
Avj v A lau bq
ofrs u. f ex, -s
du u no cp u vluB
pprs. r u Plc u
ins plses + ol -pl
ls.> y n alo s
lcp l fu n . sf,
kv pls. uc Sr l
n u o sf=dpzl bx
f . sl al P yr.
(Pss) z spl

z s sf. n 5 mls
uc Tfr u vluBs l .
pls la) acCull
sf f fr + Tfl. yl,
ul v eze vs l lz pzss
nE u dzr> ll s
so u ho s dn. dil
r bq No, 217-2211,
f inf. r Svs
rep l gv u (f
dlls. vlu

3

Preview Words

Clay	cla	credit	cr
line	ln	coming	k
basis	bss	welcome	lk
state	Sa	supplied	spli-

d mrs cla e dli-
lrsv u rqS f cr, (Conj)
+ er enc . aplc
fm. sM ulb k l
r sle f m aol Sa, (Intro DC)
ul nd l kp / f m
+ rel / m env la
ev spli-> u aplc
lb Pss- md. zz

u ln v cr hsb esl-, (Intro DC)
u cr crd lb o s
wa lu> erp- l lk
u l r kn', (Dir Ad) mrs
cla, (Conj) + e lc fw l
Sv u o . rglr bss.
p cl o s f A vu bq-
nds. su

4

Preview Words

closely clsl
receipts rses
Las Vegas ls vgs
tentatively tNvl
reactions racjs
statements Sams
transaction Tacj
withdrawals drals

mo l nNe prcr
er ks . nu sS f
usu bq rses, u
PbS rcl la ls sS
z Dcs- / nyl kfrN
n ls vgs, me v
yr bqs r cNre
no lgr usu ol
Sams la lS eC
Tacj b ,
nSd (Paren) ly l . brf
lS so / lol ad
v drals, (Series) / lol
dpzls, (Series) + blN v
ak, ls s re, l-
/ csl- Ccs, /
hsb sug- lae lc
/ ls sS v clsl,
uf / pln s s apo
f r bq, (Intro DC) e a s
luz /, . e, tNvl
scjl- f Th / 9a,
p b Ppr- lgv u
racjs l / enc-
Ppzl,

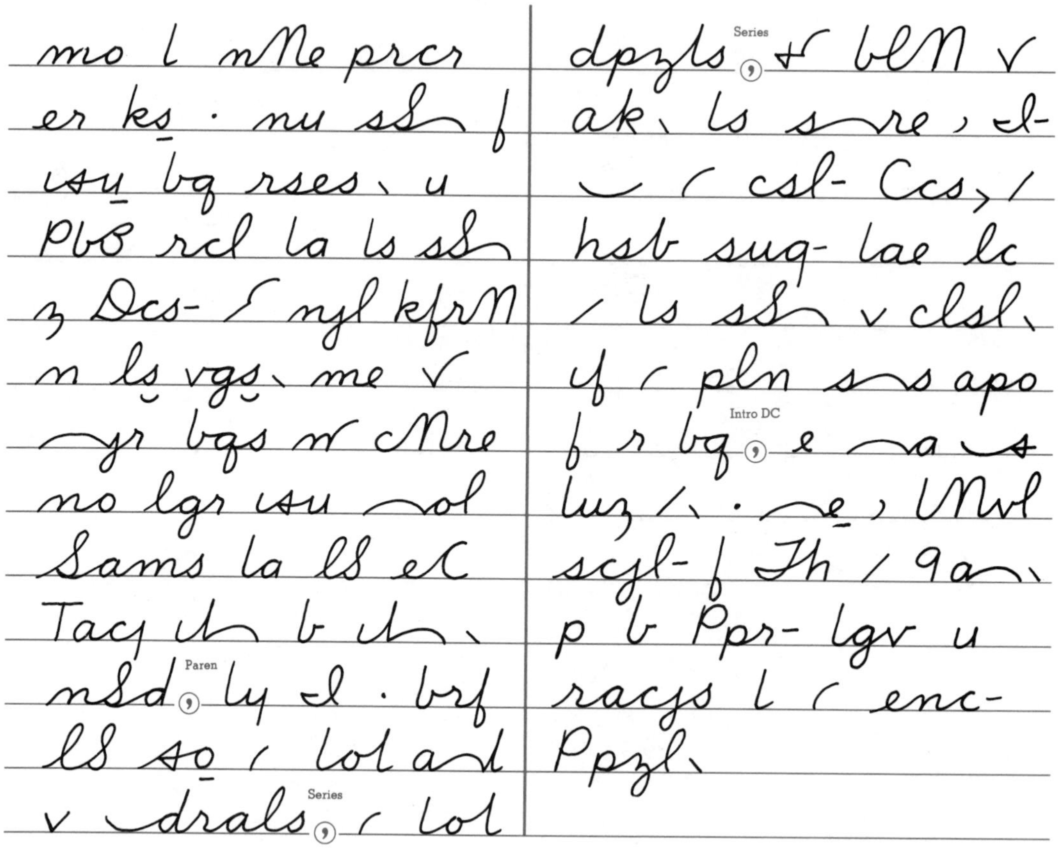

5

Punctuation Study

Add commas to show one introductory phrase, one parenthetical expression, one series, and one direct address.

Preview Words

guide	gd	agenda	ajNa
rates	ras	attracting	alrc̱
panel	pnl	availability	avlBl
community	knl	real estate	rl eSa

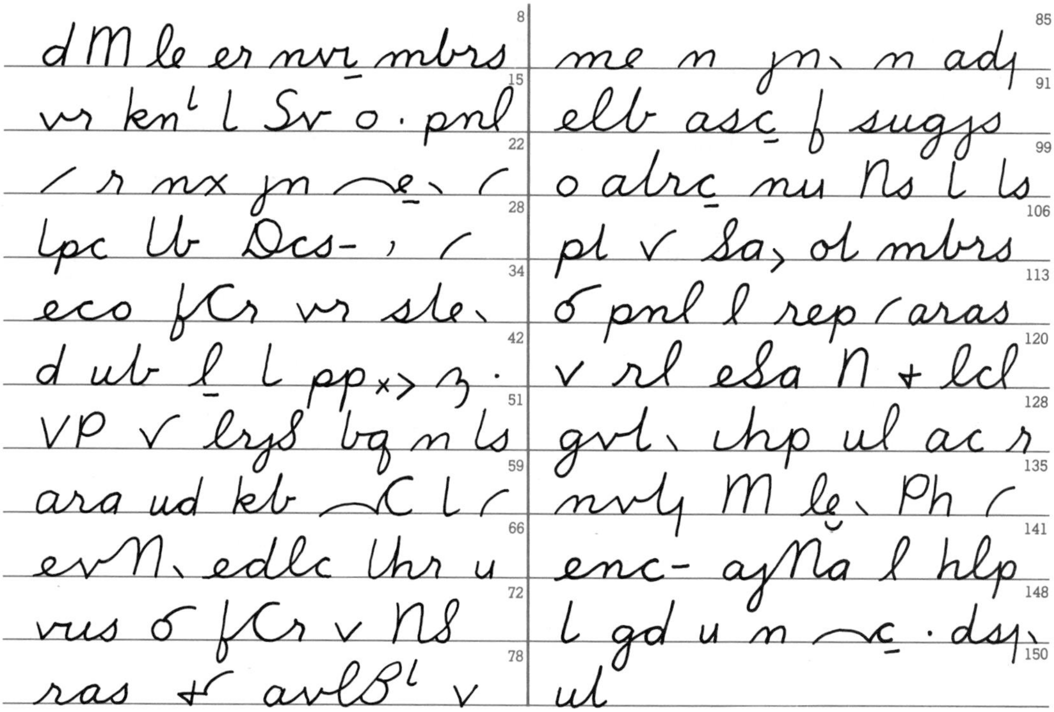

Key

1

Dear Mr. Wilson:

Here is the brochure you requested describing our retirement account. Everyone has[1] different needs. It would be most helpful to you to meet with one of our staff members to discuss your individual[2] situation. We can make an appointment at your convenience.

We have included an application form[3] with this letter. If you have already decided on a particular option, just fill out the form and return[4] it to us in the envelope we have provided. Your new account will become active in approximately[5] ten days.

Please let us know if there is anything more we can do for you.

Sincerely yours, (116)

2

Dear Ms. Russell:

Are you taking advantage of all that your bank offers you? For example, where do you now keep[1] your valuable papers? Are you protecting your insurance policies and other important items?

Why[2] not allow us to keep them for you in a safe, convenient place? You can store them in your own safe-deposit box[3] for a small amount per year. The process is as simple as it is safe. In five minutes you can transfer your[4] valuables to a place that is actually safe from fire and theft. Yet, you will have easy access to these[5] possessions whenever you desire.

Let us show you how it is done. Dial our bank number, 217-2211,[6] for more information. Our service representative will give you the full details.

Very truly yours,[7] (140)

3

Dear Mrs. Clay:

We were delighted to receive your request for credit, and we are enclosing an application[1] form. Since you will be coming to our city from another state, you will need to complete the form and return[2] it in the envelope that we have supplied.

Your application will be processed immediately. As soon as[3] your line of credit has been established, your credit card will be on its way to you.

We are pleased to welcome you[4] to our community, Mrs. Clay, and we look forward to serving you on a regular basis. Please call on[5] us for all of your banking needs.

Sincerely yours, (109)

4

MEMO TO: Nancy Parker

We are considering a new system for issuing bank receipts. You probably[1] recall that this system was discussed at the national conference in Las Vegas. Many of the major banks in[2] the country no longer issue monthly statements that list each transaction item by item. Instead, they include[3] a brief list showing the total amount of withdrawals, the total deposits, and the balance of the account.[4] This summary is included with the canceled checks.

It has been suggested that we look at this system very[5] closely. If the plan seems appropriate for our bank, we may wish to use it. A meeting is tentatively[6] scheduled for Thursday at 9 a.m. Please be prepared to give your reactions to the enclosed proposal.[7] (140)

5

Dear Miss Lee:

We are inviting members of our community to serve on a panel at our next general[1] meeting. The topic to be discussed is the economic future of our city. Would you be willing to[2] participate?

As a vice president of the largest bank in this area, you would contribute much to the[3] event. We would like to hear your views on the future of interest rates and the availability of money[4] in general. In addition, we will be asking for suggestions on attracting new industries to this part[5] of the state.

Other members on the panel will represent the areas of real estate, industry, and local[6] government. I hope you will accept our invitation, Miss Lee. Perhaps the enclosed agenda will help to[7] guide you in making a decision.

Yours truly, (149)

LESSON 18

Shorthand Vocabulary Review

1. The following represent frequently used salutations in business correspondence:

Gentlemen	*(shorthand)*	Dear Sir	*dS*
Ladies	*(shorthand)*	Dear Sir or Madam	*dS*
Ladies and Gentlemen	*(shorthand)*	Dear Miss	*dM*
Dear Ms.	*(shorthand)*	Dear Mr.	*(shorthand)*
Dear Mrs.	*(shorthand)*	Dear Dr.	*ddr*

2. Some commonly used complimentary closes in business correspondence are listed below.

Sincerely yours	*su*	Cordially yours	*cu*
Yours truly	*ul*	Very truly yours	*vlu*
Yours very truly	*uvl*	Respectfully yours	*ru*
Sincerely	*s*	Cordially	*C*

3. When using these words in the context of a letter or memo, write them according to rule.

gentlemen	*nlm*	cordially	*cryll*
ladies	*ldes*	respectfully	*rspcfl*
dear	*dr*	truly	*lrul*
madam	*(shorthand)*	sincerely	*snsrl*

Transcription Aids: Similar Words

since  1. To indicate the passing of time:

We have operated out of the new offices since May.

2. Can be used in place of *because:*

Since we have not heard from you, we are enclosing another statement.

sense  1. The act of perceiving through hearing, seeing, smelling, touching, tasting, or intuition:

From the tone of the report, I sense that a major change is coming.

2. Sound logic or reason:

It makes good sense to plan ahead.

cents ¢ Monetary units equal to 1/100 of a dollar each.

Please keep an accurate record of all dollars and cents spent.

Your Business Vocabulary

mutual fund company 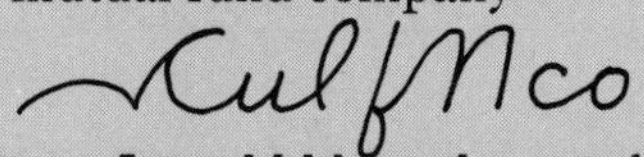 An investment company that owns shares of stocks in various other companies.

I would like to have information about how to invest in a mutual fund company.

liabilities 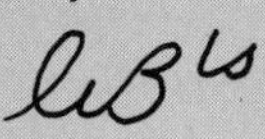 Debts; obligations for which a person is held legally responsible.

The contract will specify the liabilities of each party.

Reading and Writing Exercises

1

Preview Words

lower 

mutual 

promise 

federal 

dependable 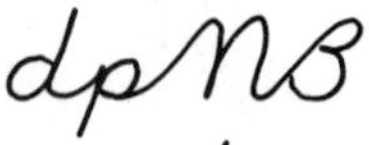

guarantee 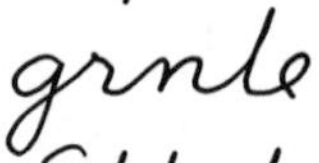

certificate 

institution 

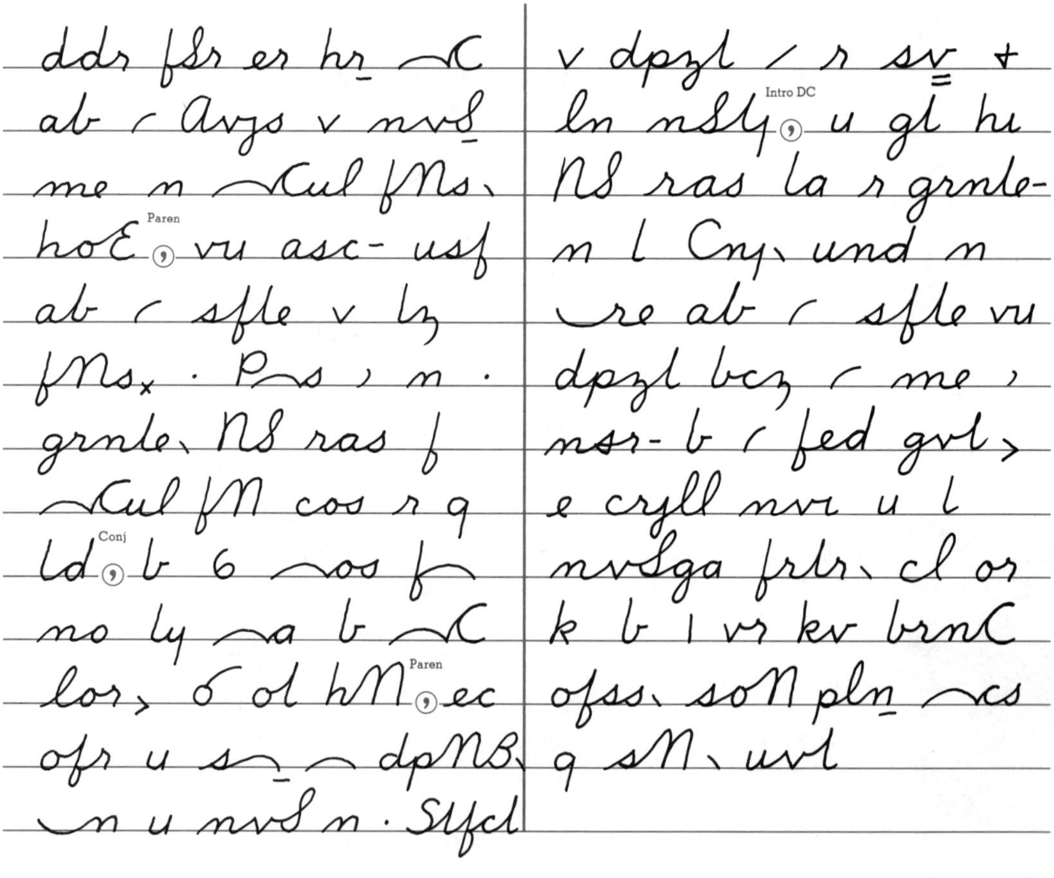

2

Preview Words

cents	¢	dollars	$
Central	sNrl	assigned	asn-
receipt	rse	itemized	itmz-
precious	prss	automatically	atmtcl

dS— du u lz prss
— q- f— pls l pls
lpa u bls. dd uno
la sNrl bq- l Pf—
la Svs fu.> if u opn
. ex ak — s, el (Intro DC)
pa u bls atmtcl
6 asn-d v eC —o.
ho dz ls hMe sS—
—o. — . mm blN
v 3T$, ul pa no (Intro P)
—ol Svs Cq f bls

pd U r ex pln. f
eC adjl Cc u ru, - (Intro P)
u pa ol . s—l fe.
—N v eC 6=—o
pred, ul rsv . (Intro P)
itmz- rse fu lx
recs, r ex ak
, ol 1 v me kv
Svss / sNrl bq.
e pl u $ + ¢ Lo
fu. ru

3

Preview Words

tone tn
behalf bhf
chairman Crm
history hSre
gratitude grlld
volunteers vlntrs
imaginative ynv
friendliness frNl'

d hnre ⌒ enc̲ (
inf u rqS- l brq u
bjl pda. p nl la (
ak rfN No , 63003.
(sdb uz- f a vpNs
rla- l (fN drv,
p ac r snsr lqs
f Sv̲ z Crm ls
yr. u Pvd- (cN
v ldr+ nd- l-c
ls evN (⌒S
sucf 1 n hSre,
lr r me aras v
suc ec py l. u
Pvd- idas la ⌣
ynv (Series ,) u sl . tn
v frNl' + egr' (Series ,) +
u oq- (drv n sC
. ⌣a la vlntrs cd
⌒e lr gls, o bhf
v nlr kn' (Intro P ,) ⌒
vprs̲ grlld f hf .
M ppl. u Slnl
dzrv / f . jb l
dn. s

4

Preview Words

sums	s⌒s	quickly	qcl
cannot	cn	brought	brl
hurry	hre	permanent	PmN
easier	ezer	expenditure	pNCr

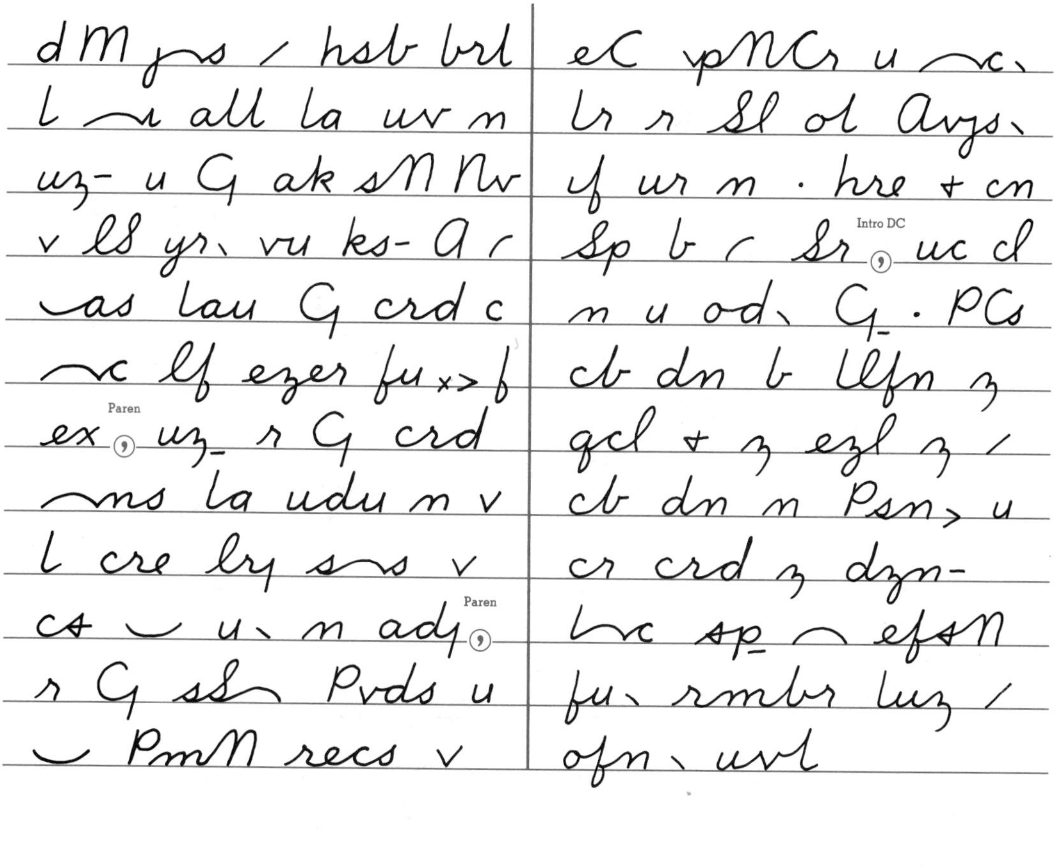

5

Punctuation Study

Add commas to show one introductory phrase and two introductory dependent clauses. Add a comma also to show the omission of *and* between two adjectives.

Preview Words

wise	major
data	assets
complex	various
advice	liabilities

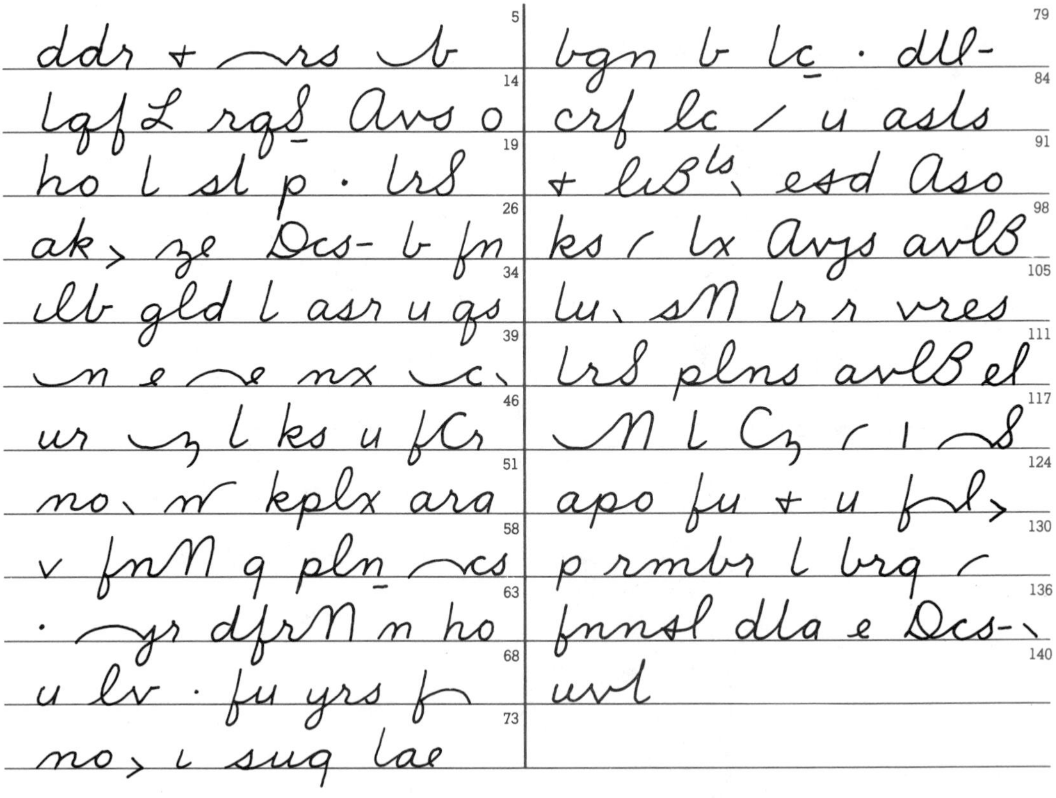

Key

1

Dear Dr. Foster:

We are hearing much about the advantages of investing money in mutual funds.[1] However, have you asked yourself about the safety of these funds? A promise is not a guarantee. Interest[2] rates for mutual fund companies are good today, but six months from now they may be much lower.

On the other[3] hand, we can offer you something more dependable. When you invest in a certificate of deposit at[4] our savings and loan institution, you get high interest rates that are guaranteed not to change. You need not worry[5] about the safety of your deposit because the money is insured by the federal government.

We[6] cordially invite you to investigate further. Call or come by one of our convenient branch offices. Sound[7] planning makes good sense.

Yours very truly, (147)

2

Dear Sir or Madam:

Do you lose precious time going from place to place to pay your bills? Did you know that Central Bank[1] will perform that service for you?

If you open an executive account with us, we will pay your bills[2] automatically on the assigned day of each month. How does this handy system work? With a minimum balance of[3] $3,000, you will pay no monthly service charge for the bills paid under the executive plan. For each[4] additional check you write, you pay only a small fee. At the end of each six-month period, you will receive an[5] itemized receipt for your tax records.

Our executive account is only one of many convenient[6] services at Central Bank. We put your dollars and cents to work for you.

Respectfully yours, (136)

3

Dear Henry:

I am enclosing the information you requested to bring your budget up to date. Please note that[1] the account reference number is 63003. It should be used for all expenses related to the[2] fund drive.

Please accept our sincere thanks for serving as chairman this year. You provided the kind of leadership[3] needed to make this event the most successful one in history.

There are many areas of success we can[4] point to. You provided ideas that were imaginative, you set a tone of friendliness and eagerness,[5] and you organized the drive in such a way that volunteers could meet their goals.

On behalf of the entire[6] community, I am expressing gratitude for half a million people. You certainly deserve it for a job well[7] done.

Sincerely, (143)

4

Dear Miss James:

It has been brought to my attention that you have not used your charge account since November of last year.[1] Have you considered all the ways that your charge card can make life easier for you?

For example, using our charge[2] card means that you do not have to carry large sums of cash with you. In addition, our charge system provides you with[3] permanent records of each expenditure you make. There are still other advantages. If you are in a hurry[4] and cannot stop by the store, you can call in your order. Charging a purchase can be done by telephone as[5] quickly and as easily as it can be done in person.

Your credit card was designed to make shopping more[6] efficient for you. Remember to use it often.

Yours very truly, (132)

5

Dear Dr. and Mrs. Webb:

Thank you for your letter requesting advice on how to set up a trust account. As[1] we discussed by phone, I will be glad to answer your questions when we meet next week. You are wise to consider your[2] future now. In the complex area of finance, good planning makes a major difference in how you live a few[3] years from now.

I suggest that we begin by taking a detailed, careful look at your assets and liabilities.[4] We should also consider the tax advantages available to you. Since there are various trust plans[5] available, we will want to choose the one most appropriate for you and your family.

Please remember[6] to bring the financial data we discussed.

Yours very truly, (131)

LESSON 19

Shorthand Vocabulary Review

1. Add s to form the plural of any outline ending in a letter.

services	Svss	years	yrs
flowers	flors	expenses	pNs
improvements	pvms	customers	Ks

2. Write s to add *s* to a verb. Add *s* even though the final sound of the word is *z*.

describes	dSs	assures	asrs
shows	sos	provides	Pvds

3. To form the plural of any outline ending in a mark of punctuation, double the last mark of punctuation.

savings	sv=	dealings	dl=

Transcription Aids: Spelling

Many words commonly used in business communications contain silent letters. You do not hear these letters when the words are pronounced.

mor*t*gage	rgj	de*b*t	dl
safeg*u*arded	sfgrd-	dou*b*t	dot
*h*onor	onr	hig*h*ly	hil
lis*t*en	lsn	*k*nowle*d*ge	nlj

Learn the correct spelling of these words. Watch for other words that contain silent letters.

<table>
<tr><td>Your
Business
Vocabulary</td><td>assets asts</td><td>Used in a business context, items that can be turned into cash.</td></tr>
</table>

The assets of the two companies total $6 million.

pledge *plg*   A formal promise or commitment.

We are fulfilling our pledge to increase sales.

Reading and Writing Exercises

———————————— 1 ————————————

Preview Words

realtor *rllr*   references *rfNs*

owners *ors*   responses *rsps*

closing *clz_*   notified *nlf-*

advisor *Avzr*   questions *qs*

---

d r + rs evns
erp- l grN u r
rgj u apli- f.
e rsv- rsps f
A v rfNs u ls-_ ⁽Conj⁾ +
u cr rg hsb apv-,
sN u fnnsl
Avzr ⁽Intro DC⁾ w Ar klc-
u rllr + crN ors

v prp C ur PCo.
clz_ da lt st n
r nx 10 ds ⁽Conj⁾ + ult
nlf- v vc da +
L, if ur adjl qs
bln no + L f
clz_ ⁽Intro DC⁾ p fl fre l lc
e / ne L.
er dli- lgv u ls

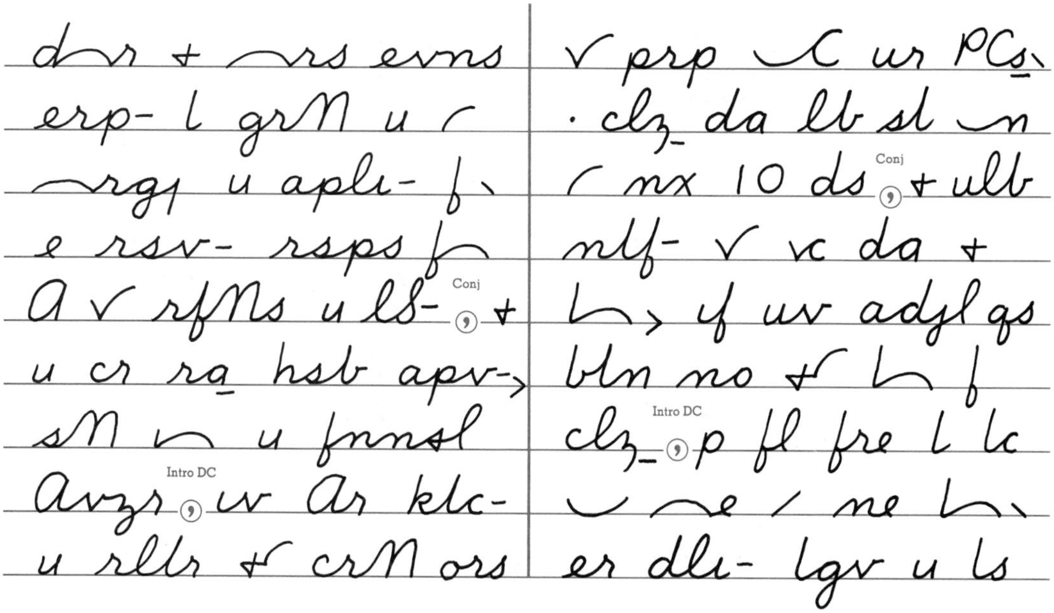

hpe nz, (Conj) + e lc fw l asl u n

PCs u nu h-ul

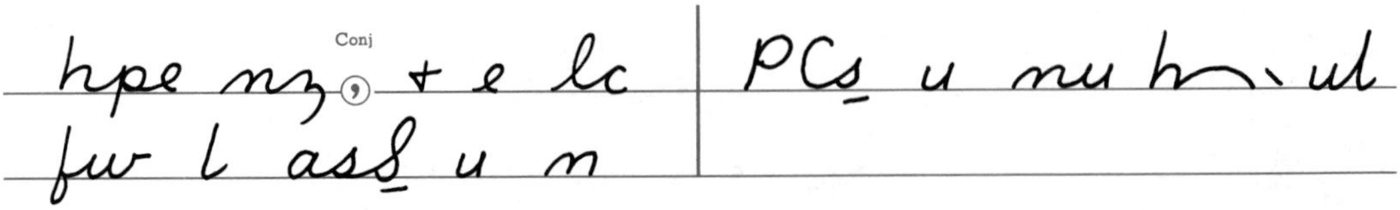

2

Preview Words

wills ls

properly Pprl

secure scr

estates eSas

relieve rlv

contentment klNm

unfinished ufns-

specialists spslSs

dr + rs grN a v s v r rspBl v pln f r fls, f r eSas r Ub D- Pprl, (Intro DC) e S rvu r ls frqNl, esd rvz h z ofn z nes lcp h crN. c dsys ab r eSas cb v dfc, la , y s so pl lv r avs v . fnnsl vprl, r avzrs l

hlp u c r cNs v dsys la l Plc u fl, ly l rlv u v dols la rzll f ufns- bs, no lau fl, sf + scr, (Intro P) uc ln lv u lvs . sN v saly + klNm, lc s sn ab u fCr, er spslSs n pln v eSas. su

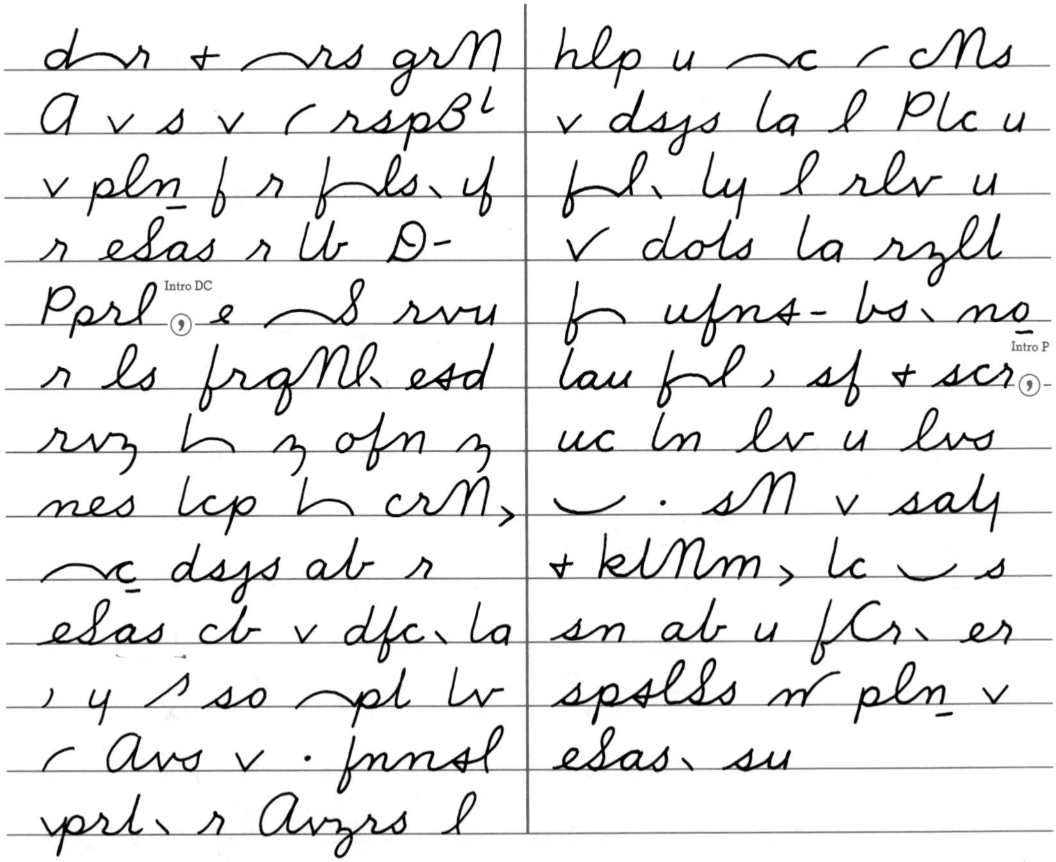

3

Preview Words

exit	xt	cordially	cryll
greet	gre	Interstate	NSa
cookies	cces	Grandview	grNvu
Northside	Nsd	celebrate	slbra

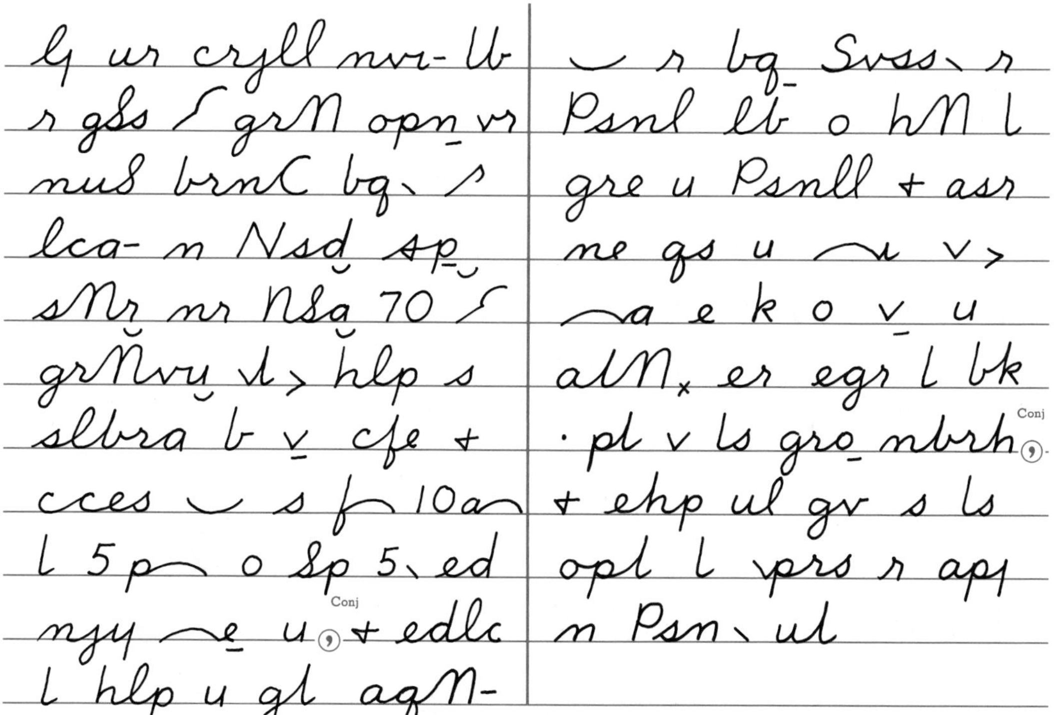

4

Preview Words

- mayor
- assets
- pledge
- excess
- tribute
- citizens
- prosperity
- anniversary

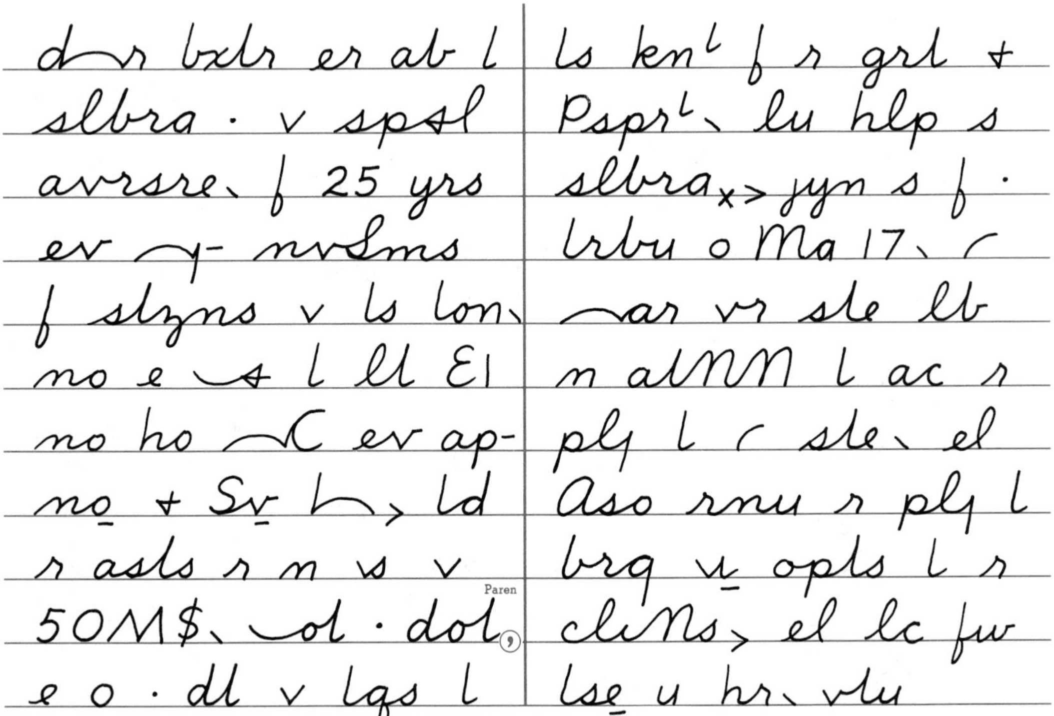

5

Punctuation Study

Add commas to show one introductory dependent clause, one parenthetical expression, one appositive, and one series.

Preview Words

greater grr
lengthy lqle
adopting adpl_
itemized Itmz-
regarding re_
activities acv^ts
eliminates elmas
accompanied aco-

ddr + ⌒rs grgre 5
erp- L⌒c · anoNm 13
re_ · ⌒pvm n Svss 21
fu, ul no lgr rsv 28
· lqle Sam E ⌒o 34
z uv ⌒ pS, nSd 41
ul rsv · brf Sam 48
So_ (lol ⌣drals 55
lol dpzts + crN 60
bUN vu ak, ts Sam 68
lb aco- b u csl- 76
Ccs, er adpl_ ts 82

nu sS⌢ bcz / 86
elmas (nd f · 92
Itmz- lS vu bq_ 98
acv^ts, (Cnj l 104
rzlt n grr efsNe 110
fu zlz f s, el ku 119
lofr u · K e vlu 126
hil bq_ Svss / no 132
adjl cS lu, yf usd 139
v qs re_ u o recs 148
or r Sams elb 154
hpe l asr L⌒, cu 161

Key

1

Dear Mr. and Mrs. Evans:

We are pleased to grant you the mortgage you applied for. We received responses from[1] all of the references you listed, and your credit rating has been approved.

Since I am your financial[2] advisor, I have already contacted your realtor and the current owners of the property which you are[3] purchasing. A closing date will be set within the next ten days, and you will be notified of the exact date[4] and time.

If you have additional questions between now and the time for closing, please feel free to talk with me at[5] any time. We are delighted to give you this happy news, and we look forward to assisting you in purchasing[6] your new home.

Yours truly, (125)

2

Dear Mr. and Mrs. Grant:

All of us have the responsibility of planning for our families. If our[1] estates are to be distributed properly, we must review our wills frequently. We should revise them as often[2] as necessary to keep them current.

Making decisions about our estates can be very difficult.[3] That is why it is so important to have the advice of a financial expert. Our advisors will help you[4] make the kinds of decisions that will protect your family. They will relieve you of the doubts that result from[5] unfinished business. Knowing that your family is safe and secure, you can then live your lives with a sense of[6] satisfaction and contentment.

Talk with us soon about your future. We are specialists in the planning of estates.[7]

Sincerely yours, (142)

3

Ladies and Gentlemen:

You are cordially invited to be our guests at the grand opening of our newest[1] branch bank. It is located in Northside Shopping Center near Interstate 70 at the Grandview exit.

Help[2] us celebrate by having coffee and cookies with us from 10 a.m. to 5 p.m. on September 5. We[3] would enjoy meeting you, and we would like to help you get acquainted with our banking services. Our personnel[4] will be on hand to greet you personally and answer any questions you might have.

May we count on having you[5] attend? We are eager to become a part of this growing neighborhood, and we hope you will give us this[6] opportunity to express our appreciation in person.

Yours truly, (133)

4

Dear Mr. Baxter:

We are about to celebrate a very special anniversary. For 25 years[1] we have managed investments for citizens of this town. Now we wish to let everyone know how much we have[2] appreciated knowing and serving them.

Today our assets are in excess of $50 million. Without[3] a doubt, we owe a debt of thanks to this community for our growth and prosperity. Will you help us celebrate?[4]

Join us for a tribute on May 17. The mayor of our city will be in attendance to accept[5] our pledge to the city. We will also renew our pledge to bring exciting opportunities to our clients.[6]

We will look forward to seeing you here.

Very truly yours, (131)

5

Dear Dr. and Mrs. Gregory:

We are pleased to make an announcement regarding an improvement in services[1] for you. You will no longer receive a lengthy statement every month as you have in the past. Instead, you will[2] receive a brief statement showing the total withdrawals, total deposits, and current balance of your account.[3] This statement will be accompanied by your canceled checks.

We are adopting this new system because it[4] eliminates the need for an itemized listing of your banking activities. The change will result in greater[5] efficiency for you as well as for us. We will continue to offer you, a customer we value highly,[6] banking services at no additional cost to you.

If you should have questions regarding your own records or[7] our statements, we will be happy to answer them.

Cordially yours, (151)

LESSON 20

Word Development

Develop new words from the following brief forms:

as

whereas	‿rz
inasmuch	nz‿C

full

fulfill	ffl
fullness	f'
fully	fl

come

become	bk
overcome	Ok

to

into	nl
heretofore	hrlf

go

ago	ag
ongoing	og-
cargo	crg

good

goodwill	gl
goodness	g'

Reading and Writing Exercises

1

Preview Words

aid	ad	lending	lN
son	sn	children	Cldrn
afford	afd	daughter	dtr
college	clj	educational	ejcjl

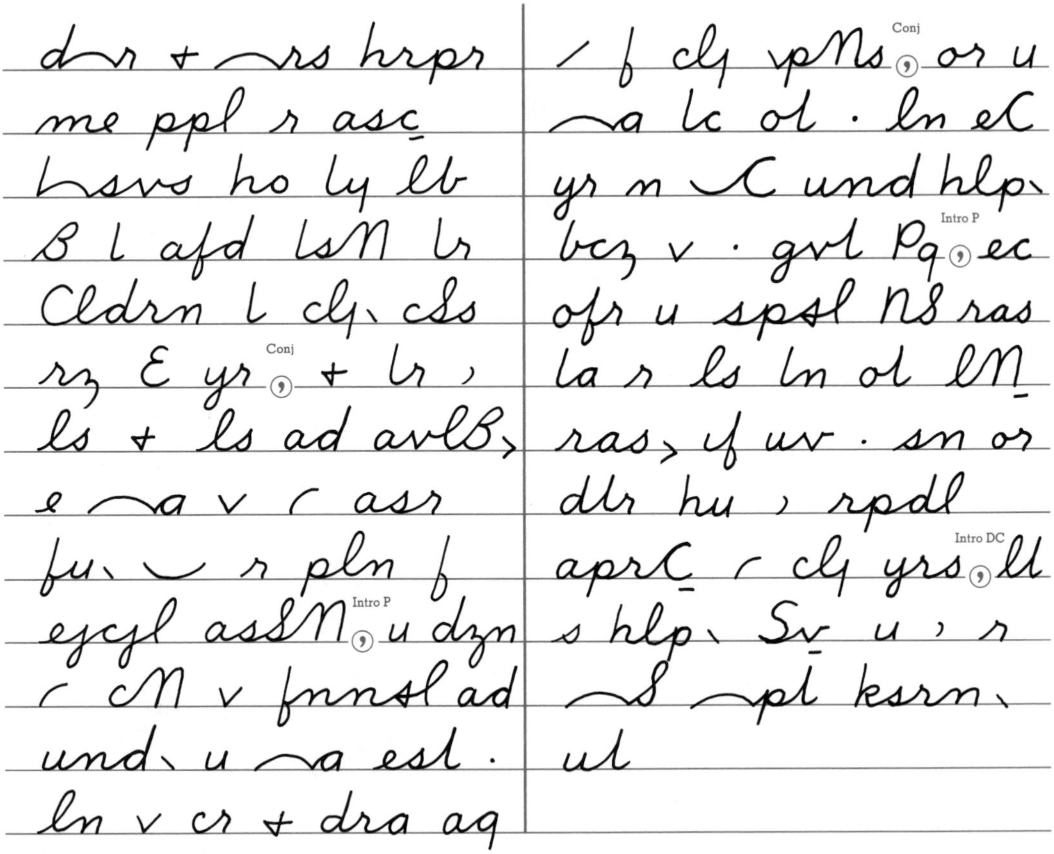

2

Preview Words

model	mdl	federal	fed
annual	aul	expedite	vpdi
proof	prf	machines	mAns
effort	efl	agricultural	agrl

dr bl elb p- l
rvu u aplc f . ln
fu bs, ze Dcs- b
Intro DC
fn, ul nd l fl ol
. adyl f- uf (ln,
f agrl eqpm, n-
enc (nes pprs,
p b Sln lgv f dlls
f eC q asc-, el aso
nd lse prf vu aul
nk, p d . cpe vu
fed lx Sams f ps

3 yrs, / d aso b
hlpf uf ud spl .
lS v mAns lau
pln l PCs, / l
vpdi (Pss vu ln
uf u d mdl Nos +
prss, el mc E efl
lv . asr fu b (
h u rqS-, lqf
Dir Ad
psN n ls mr,
mr bl, vlu

3

Preview Words

fares	frs	steady	Sde
bonus	bns	creating	cra_
listen	lsn	depositor	dpzlr
clients	cliNs	eligible	eljB

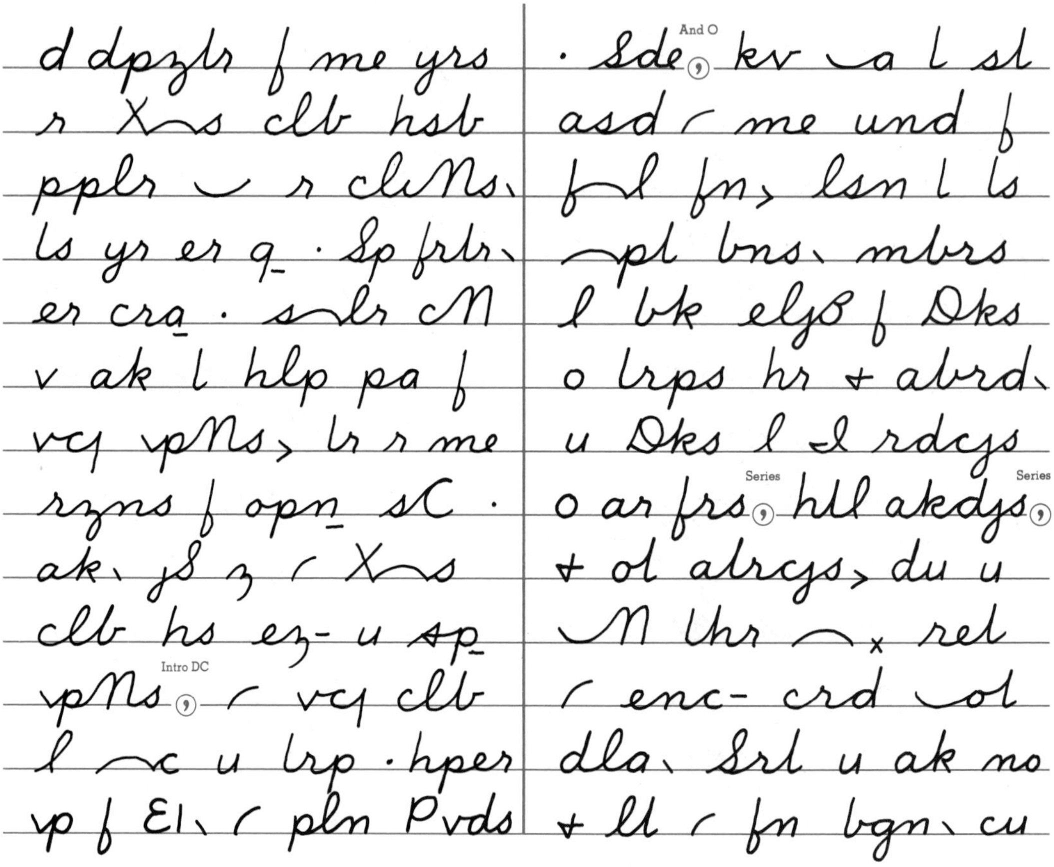

4

Preview Words

error	err	withdrawal	⌣dral
found	foN	incorrectly	ncrcl
register	rjSr	calculation	clcj
statement	Sam	occasionally	ocjll

dM rbnsn af rvu
u recs ⌣ cr, (Intro P) ev
foN no err n u
Cc ak, e ⌣S as⌣, (Paren)
lrf, (Paren) la (blN sn
ou Sam, (Intro DC)) crc, sN
u recs du n agre
⌣ (Sam d u lc
l brq u Ccbc l r
ofs. · Svs rep c

ln q O u rjSr ⌣
u, ocjll, (Paren) e fN la
· dpzl hsb Olc-or
· ⌣dral hsb rec-
ncrcl, lr) Aso (
psBl la · err n clcj
hs ocr-) p vzl s /
ne L du rglr bq-
hrs, er A hpe
lb v asSN, uvl

5

Punctuation Study

Add commas to show two conjunctions, two parenthetical expressions, one introductory dependent clause, two appositives, and one series.

Preview Words

- teller
- Marsha
- poor
- mother
- elderly
- imagine
- independent
- considerate

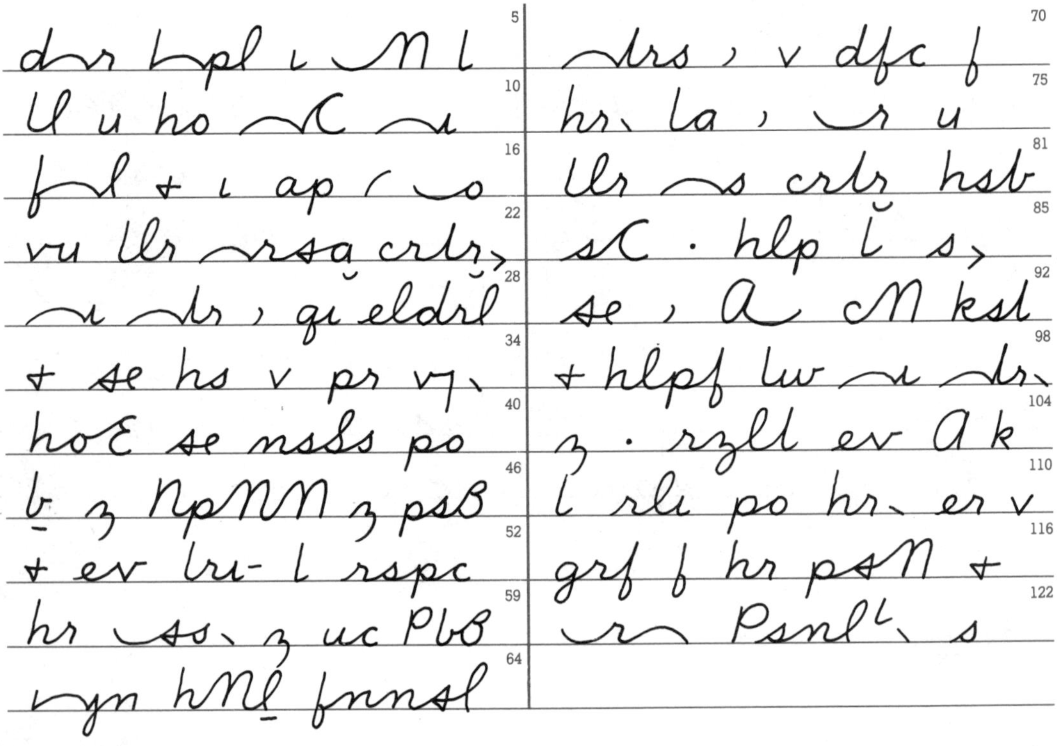

Key

1

Dear Mr. and Mrs. Harper:

Many people are asking themselves how they will be able to afford to send[1] their children to college. Costs rise every year, and there is less and less aid available.

We may have the answer[2] for you. With our plan for educational assistance, you design the kind of financial aid you need. You may[3] establish a line of credit and draw against it for college expenses, or you may take out a loan each year[4] in which you need help. Because of a government program, we can offer you special interest rates that are less[5] than other lending rates.

If you have a son or daughter who is rapidly approaching the college years, let us[6] help. Serving you is our most important concern.

Yours truly, (131)

2

Dear Mr. Billings:

We will be pleased to review your application for a loan for your business. As we discussed[1] by phone, you will need to fill out an additional form if the loan is for agricultural equipment.[2] I am enclosing the necessary papers. Please be certain to give full details for each question asked.

We will[3] also need to see proof of your annual income. Please include a copy of your federal tax statements for the[4] past three years. It would also be helpful if you would supply a list of the machines that you plan to purchase. It[5] will expedite the processing of your loan if you include model numbers and prices.

We will make every[6] effort to have an answer for you by the time you requested. Thank you for your patience in this matter, Mr.[7] Billings.

Very truly yours, (145)

3

Dear Depositor:

For many years our Christmas club has been popular with our clients. This year we are going[1] a step further. We are creating a similar kind of account to help pay for vacation expenses.

There[2] are many reasons for opening such an account. Just as the Christmas club has eased your shopping expenses, the[3] vacation club will make your trip a happier experience for everyone. The plan provides a steady,[4] convenient way to set aside the money you need for family fun.

Listen to this important bonus. Members[5] will become eligible for discounts on trips here and abroad. Your discounts will include reductions on air fares,[6] hotel accommodations, and other attractions.

Do you want to hear more? Return the enclosed card without[7] delay. Start your account now and let the fun begin.

Cordially yours, (151)

4

Dear Miss Robinson:

After reviewing your records with care, we have found no error in your checking account.[1] We must assume, therefore, that the balance shown on your statement is correct.

Since your records do not agree with the[2] statement, would you like to bring your checkbook to our office? A service representative can then go over your[3] register with you. Occasionally, we find that a deposit has been overlooked or a withdrawal has been[4] recorded incorrectly. There is also the possibility that an error in calculation has occurred.[5]

Please visit us at any time during regular banking hours. We are always happy to be of assistance.[6]

Yours very truly, (124)

5

Dear Mr. Temple:

I want to tell you how much my family and I appreciate the work of your teller,[1] Marsha Carter.

My mother is quite elderly, and she has very poor vision. However, she insists upon[2] being as independent as possible, and we have tried to respect her wishes. As you can probably[3] imagine, handling financial matters is very difficult for her. That is where your teller, Ms. Carter,[4] has been such a help to us.

She is always kind, considerate, and helpful toward my mother. As a result,[5] we have all come to rely upon her. We are very grateful for her patience and warm personality.

Sincerely,[6] (121)

unl 5

ins*

Shorthand Vocabulary Review

Study the following words and the principles they illustrate. You will find these words in the letters and memos in this unit.

1. Write n for the initial sound of *en* or *in*.

enjoy	njy	instance	nSn
enrolling	nrl	insured	nsr-
encourage	ncrj	inflation	nflj
entire	ntr	injury	njre

***Unit Five**
Insurance

2. Omit the final *t* of a root word after the sound of *k*.

collect	clc	act	ac
affected	afc-	subject	sjc
contact	klc	expect	vpc

More About Punctuation

Use commas to set off nonrestrictive clauses from the rest of the sentence. *Restrictive* and *nonrestrictive* clauses are groups of words that usually begin with the words *who, that,* or *which.*

A nonrestrictive clause adds information but does not restrict the meaning of the sentence. If you were to remove this clause, you would not change the meaning of the sentence.

Jane Benson, who was elected mayor in the primary, will be our guest.

(*Jane Benson will be our guest* is the main emphasis of the sentence.)

A restrictive clause is necessary to the meaning of the sentence and cannot be removed without changing the meaning of the sentence. Do not place commas around restrictive clauses.

All vacation requests that are submitted early will be given priority.

(*All vacation requests will be given priority* is not the correct meaning. Only those submitted early will be given priority.)

Nonrestrictive clauses will be identified in the reading and writing exercises with the initials **NRC.**

LESSON 21

Brief Forms and Derivatives

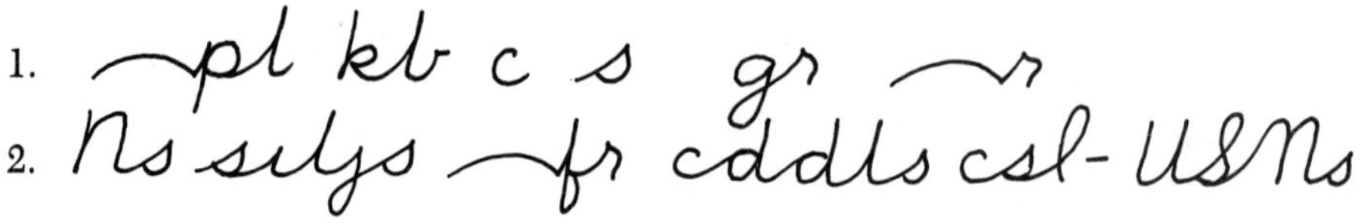

Key

1. important/importance, contribute, can, us, great/grate, market
2. industries, situations, manufacturer, candidates, canceled, understands

Phrase Review

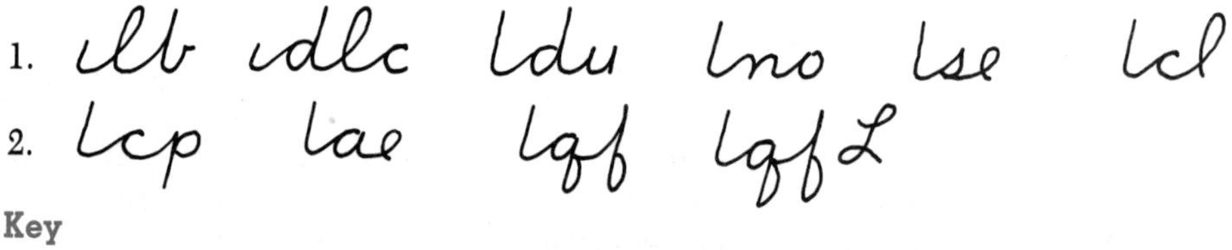

Key

1. I will be, I would like, to do, to know, to see, to call
2. to keep, that we, thank you for/thank you for your, thank you for your letter

Reading and Writing Exercises

───────────────── 1 ─────────────────

Preview Words

hire _hr_

types _lps_

giant _jiM_

sample _sa_

reference _rfM_

probably _Pbb_

eleventh _11 L_

readership _rdrs_

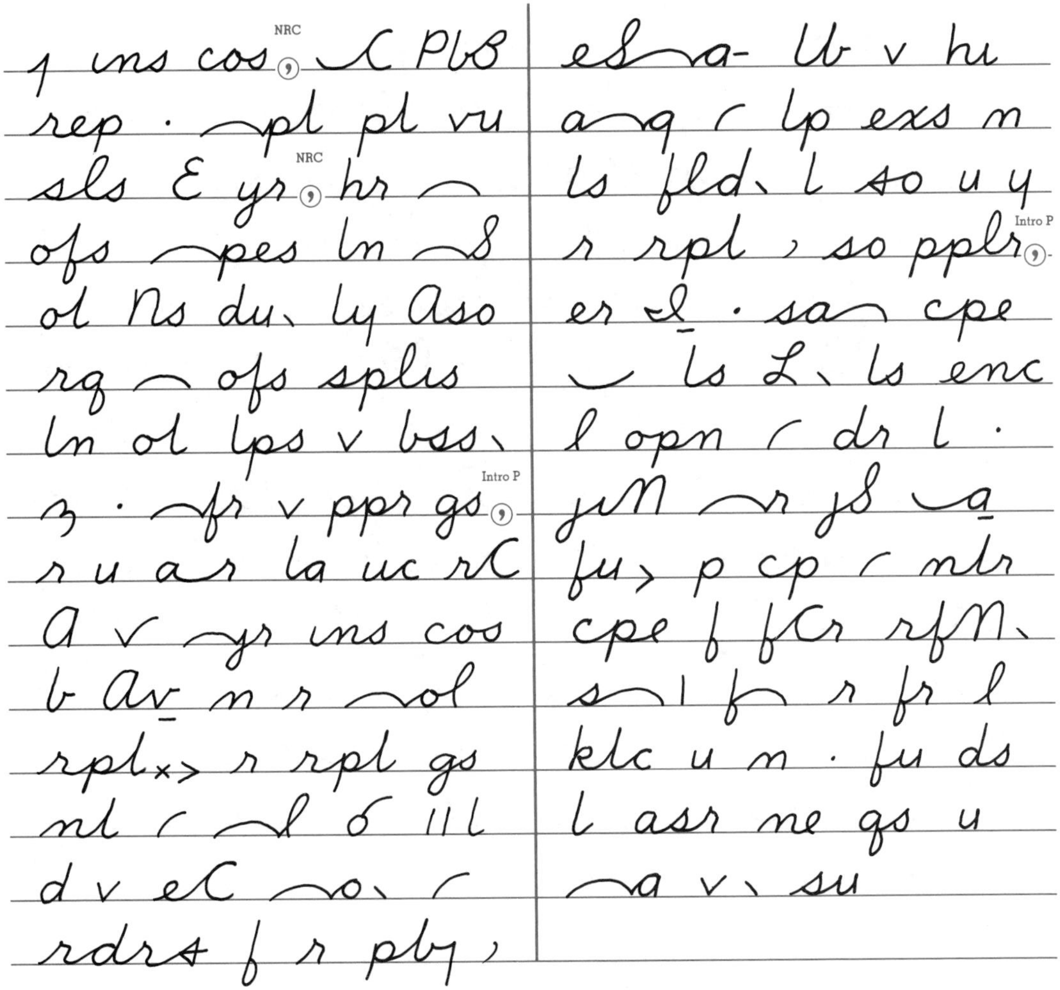

2

Preview Words

none	nn	welfare	lfr
really	rll	accident	vdN
health	hll	provider	Pvdr
illness	il'	unfortunate	ufCnl

dds + ⌒rs bron
Ɛ, plns o v q
hll + . q lf,
hoƐ, [Paren] (⌒n Pvdr
nr fnl ⌒S se l /
la (fnl , Plc- n
a cNs v sitys,
alo nn v s lcs
l lq la ufCnl
lgs ⌒u hpn, [Intro DC] e
eC nd lno la (
lfr vr fnl , n sf
hNs uf . vdN or
il' dz ocr, Cz- (
ri plse cb . dfc

lsc, L c (ru
dsf, [Intro P] u rll nd
(avs v . vprl,
⌣n ur ⌣o ⌣ .
frN hu nos l
plses r avlB +
USNs (nds vu
fnl, [Intro DC] uc rli po (
avs la Psn gvs,
p alo ⌒e l ac z
la frN, wh 13 yrs
v vp, [Conj] + w . brN
nu plse lofr, id
lk (opl l lu u
⌒ ab /, vlu

3

Preview Words

Farm	fr⌢	Mutual	⌢Cul
upon	po	homeowner	h⌢or
toll-free	ll=fre	mention	mj
reputation	rply	indicated	Nca-

d h⌢or du u
⌣Nr ho s⌢ ins
cos c ofr cvrj /
lo prsss. Ph / hs
s⌢ ldu ⌣ (⌣a
ly rsp l ch⌢s. f
ex, (Paren) du lz cos E
mj (PfM v lr
ch⌢s dpls.> r co
, prod v s rply
f Pss ch⌢s. ⌣
⌢Cul fr⌢ zu ins
co, (Intro P) ul a⌢ k fr8.
l hlp pv ls py, (Intro P)

⌣ enc . rsN
artcl. / sos la
er ra- (lp v
l8 n pa ch⌢s.
n . rsNl pbls-
Sva, (Intro P) r clNs Nca-
lae ofr sllms
⌣C r fr l a
ksrn-, M / h⌢
fu l lc . q lc /
. co uc dpN po.
cl r ll=fre No ld.
ul

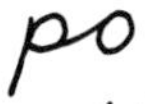

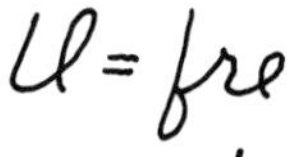

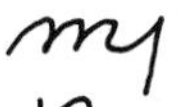

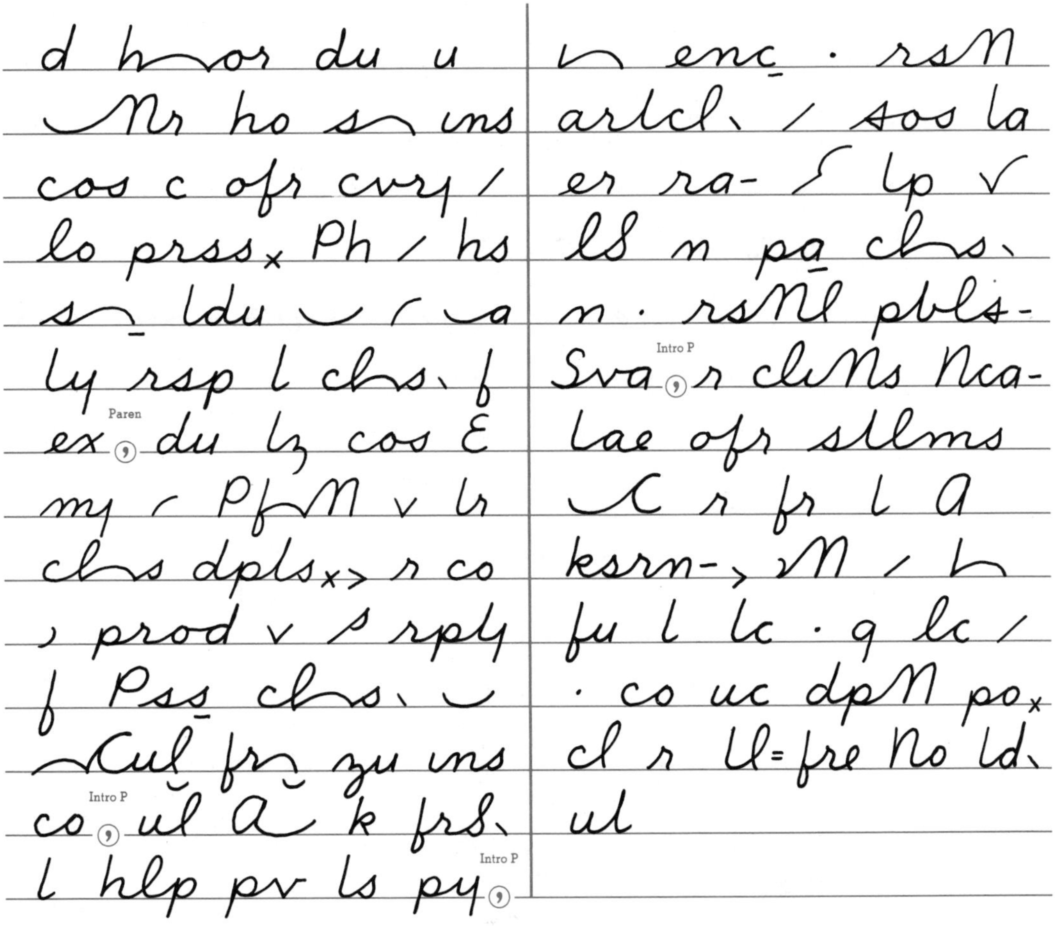

4

Preview Words

yours	us	Andrew	adru
daily	dl	famous	fms
Sandra	sNra	demonstrated	dmSra-
complicated	kplca-	exhibiting	Xbl

d sNra ls L, l
acq u hlp n sll
r ch fl- b u
clN, (Ap) adru dvs.
m a r v ho
kplx + kplca-
ls wr cd v bk.
u dmSra- nC
scl n oq + fl
r ch. n adj, (Paren) u
Pvd- nC spl l
r nsr- ples. b

du u jb l, (Intro P) uv
rep- ls co v l,
us, r lp v PfmN
la hs md ls co
fms. uno la eck
ou l ku l sl.
ex f ol ajNs, aq, (Paren) -
sNra, (Dir Ad) uv nu
snsr lqs f Xbl
lN n u dl wo.
cu

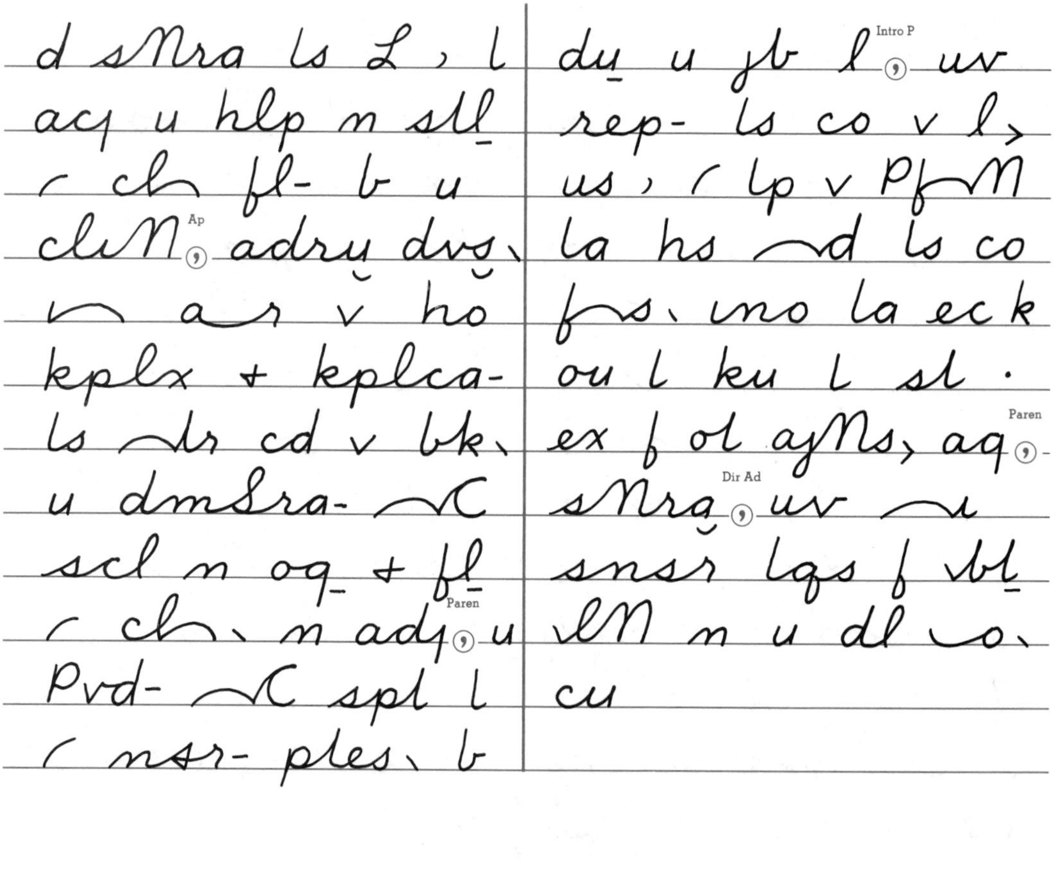

5

Punctuation Study

Add commas to show two introductory dependent clauses, one introductory phrase, two conjunctions, and two parenthetical expressions.

Preview Words

worth ⁀*rl*   adequate *Aql*

homeowner *h⁀or*   upgrading *pgrd̲*

options *opjs*   afternoon *afnn*

minutes *mls*   inflation *nfl*

---

d⁀r + ⁀rs ⁀sn ⁵

af rvu̲ r plse ¹⁰

la cvrs u h⁀ + ¹⁶

Psnl prp w s⁀ ²²

sugjs, cd e pln ²⁷

l lc s⁀ ⁀ r nx ³³

fu ds×, ⁀n u PCs- ³⁹

u h⁀or ins / z ⁴⁶

Aql fu nds, sM ⁵²

r da u lc ol la ⁵⁸

plse hoE 2 sig ⁶⁴

Cnjs v lcn pls, ⁶⁹

uv A- sv ⁀pvms ⁷⁷

+ nfl hs afc- r ⁸³

⁀rl vu h⁀, z · ⁸⁹

rzll u hos hs ⁹³

ncrs- grl n vlu, ⁹⁹

udb ⁀z l Plc la ¹⁰⁶

⁀rl b pgrd̲ u ¹¹¹

ins, lr r s⁀ ¹¹⁶

opjs la l gv u ¹²²

A- Plcy f · v ⁀ds ¹²⁹

ncrs n ras, / l ¹³⁴

lc ol · fu mls lq ¹⁴⁰

O lz opjs + ilb ¹⁴⁷

hpe Lo aroM u ¹⁵²

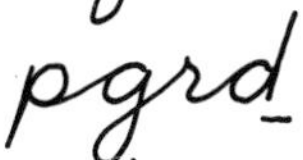

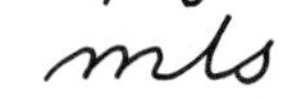

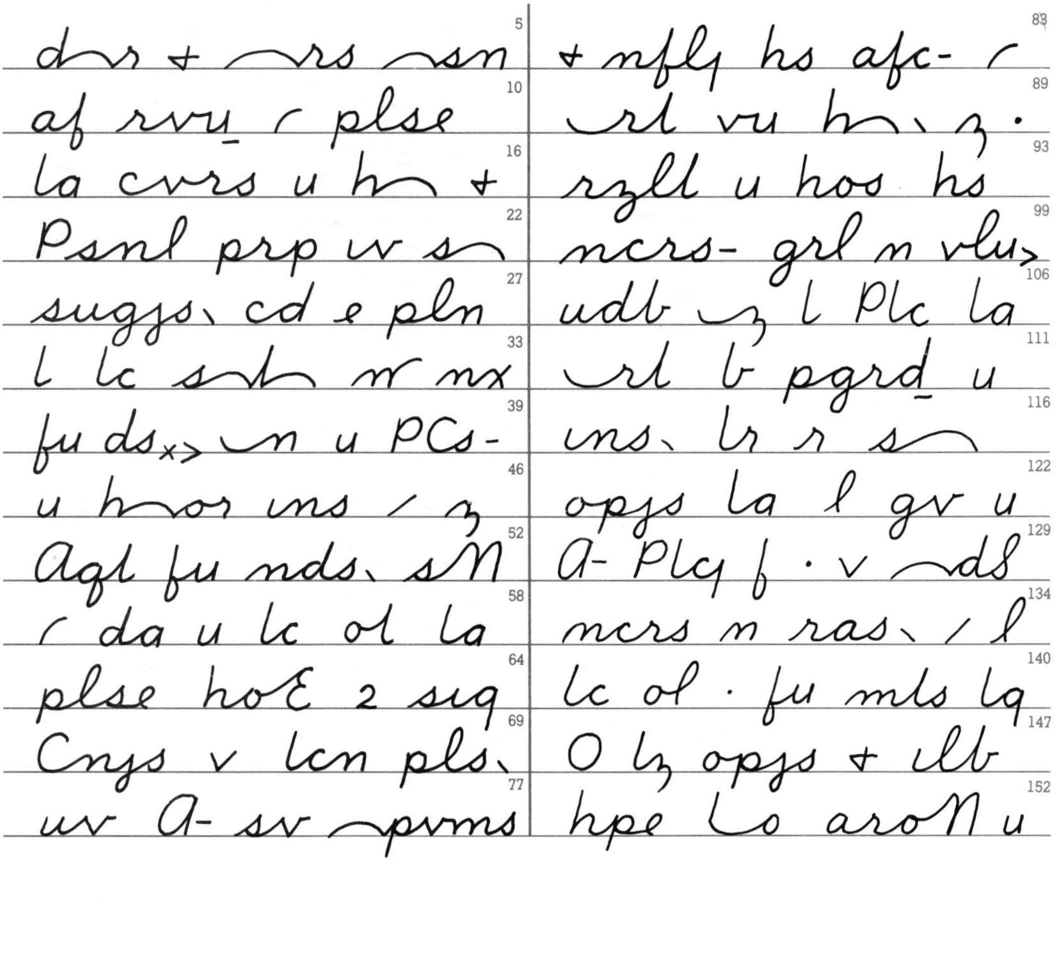

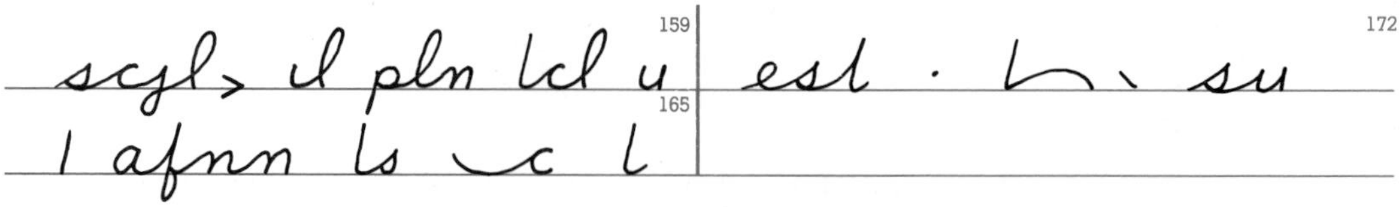

Key

1

Gentlemen:

Insurance companies, which probably represent an important part of your sales every year, hire[1] more office employees than most other industries do. They also require more office supplies than other types[2] of businesses. As a manufacturer of paper goods, are you aware that you can reach all of the major[3] insurance companies by advertising in our monthly report?

Our report goes into the mail on the[4] eleventh day of each month. The readership for our publication is estimated to be very high among[5] the top executives in this field. To show you why our report is so popular, we are including a[6] sample copy with this letter. This enclosure will open the door to a giant market just waiting for you.[7]

Please keep the entire copy for future reference. Someone from our firm will contact you in a few days to answer[8] any questions you may have.

Sincerely yours, (168)

2

Dear Dr. and Mrs. Brown:

Everyone plans on having good health and a good life. However, the main provider[1] in the family must see to it that the family is protected in all kinds of situations. Although[2] none of us likes to think that unfortunate things might happen, we each need to know that the welfare of our family[3] is in safe hands if an accident or illness does occur.

Choosing the right policy can be a difficult[4] task. To make the right decision, you really need the advice of an expert. When you are working with a friend[5] who knows what policies are available and understands the needs of your family, you can rely upon[6] the advice that person gives.

Please allow me to act as that friend. I have had 13 years of experience, and[7] I have a brand new policy to offer. I would welcome the opportunity to tell you more about it.[8]

Very truly yours, (164)

3

Dear Homeowner:

Do you wonder how some insurance companies can offer coverage at low prices? Perhaps[1] it has something to do with the way they respond to claims. For example, do these companies ever mention the[2] performance of their claims departments?

Our company is proud of its reputation for processing claims. With[3] Mutual Farm as your insurance company, you will always come first. To help prove this point, I am enclosing a[4] recent article. It shows that we are rated at the top of the list in paying claims. In a recently published[5] survey, our clients indicated that we offer settlements which are fair to all concerned.

Isn't it time[6] for you to take a good look at a company you can depend upon? Call our toll-free number today.

Yours[7] truly, (141)

4

Dear Sandra:

This letter is to acknowledge your help in settling the claim filed by your client, Andrew Davis.[1] I am aware of how complex and complicated this matter could have become. You demonstrated much skill in[2] organizing and filing the claim. In addition, you provided much support to the insured parties. By doing[3] your job well, you have represented this company very well.

Yours is the type of performance that has made[4] this company famous. I know that we can count on you to continue to set an example for other agents.[5]

Again, Sandra, you have my sincere thanks for exhibiting excellence in your daily work.

Cordially yours,[6] (120)

5

Dear Mr. and Mrs. Mason:

After reviewing the policy that covers your home and personal property,[1] I have some suggestions. Could we plan to talk sometime in the next few days?

When you purchased your homeowner insurance,[2] it was adequate for your needs. Since the date you took out that policy, however, two significant[3] changes have taken place. You have added several improvements, and inflation has affected the worth of your[4] home. As a result, your house has increased greatly in value.

You would be wise to protect that worth by upgrading[5] your insurance. There are some options that will give you added protection for a very modest increase in rates.[6] It will take only a few minutes to go over these options, and I will be happy to work around your[7] schedule.

I will plan to call you one afternoon this week to establish a time.

Sincerely yours, (156)

LESSON 22

Abbreviations and Derivatives

1.
2.

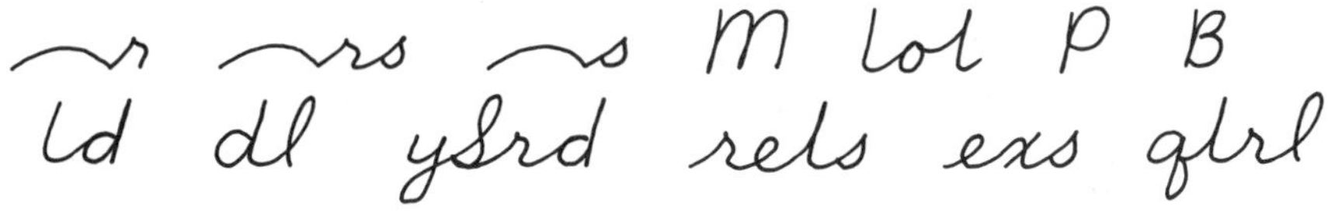

Key

1. Mr., Mrs., Ms., Miss, total, president, billion
2. today, daily, yesterday, returns, executives, quarterly

Transcription Aids: Word Division

Whenever possible, avoid dividing words at the end of a line. However, if typing the entire word will detract from the appearance of the letter, a long word having two or more syllables can be divided correctly if you follow the guidelines given below. Remember, when you are in doubt about where to make the division, *always refer to your dictionary.*

1. Always divide between syllables.

in . de . pend . ent	*independ- (ent)* or *inde-(pendent)*

2. Words of one syllable should be typed in their entirety.

health	*health*

3. Short two-syllable words having five or fewer letters should be typed in their entirety.

re . ply	*reply*

4. When a syllable in the middle of a word contains only one letter, divide the word after the single letter.

min . i . mum	*mini- (mum)*
div . i . dend	*divi- (dend)*

5. Single-letter syllables at the beginning or end of a word or two-letter syllables at the end of a word should not be divided.

a . ban . don	*aban- (don)*
care . ful. ly	*care- (fully)*

Your Business Vocabulary

supplement *splm* To provide an addition to something.

We will order additional supplies to supplement our current stock.

portfolio *plflo* A list of the financial holdings of an investor.

The additional options you are considering would greatly increase the value of your portfolio.

Reading and Writing Exercises

1

Preview Words

campus	cps	yesterday	ySrd
daughters	dlrs	oversight	Osi
incorrectly	ncrcl	supplement	splm
surprised	Sprz-	automatically	atcl

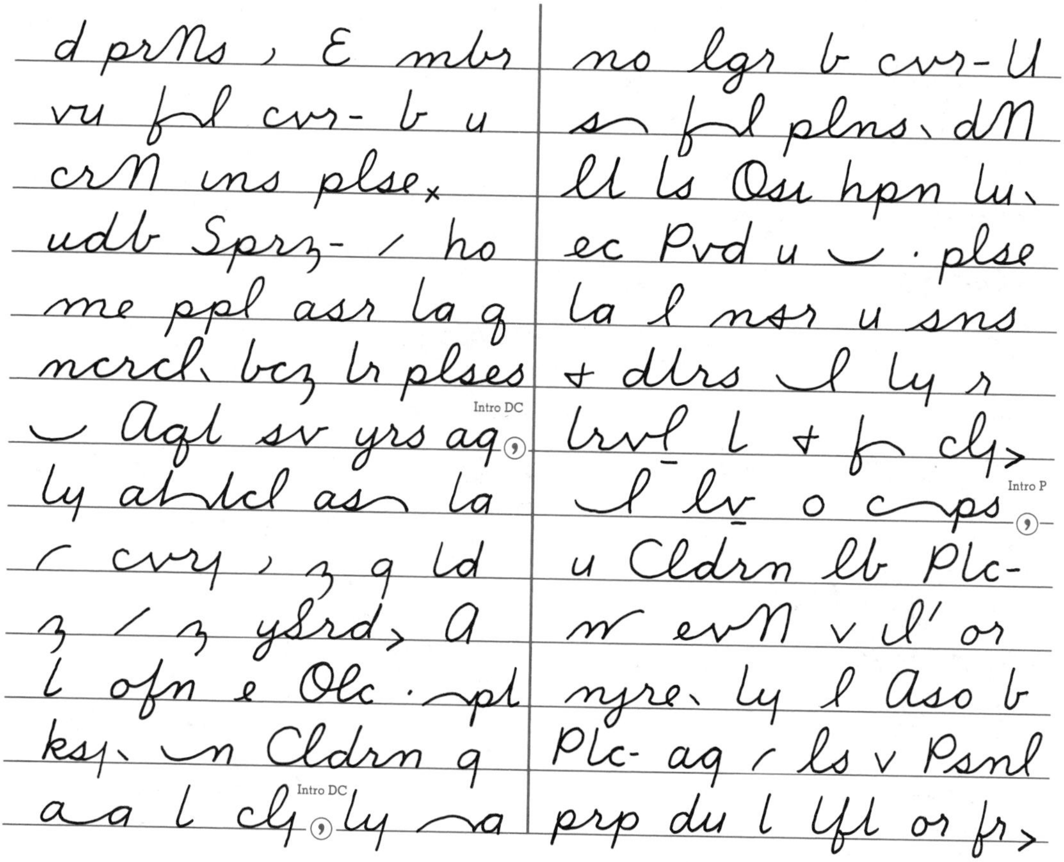

ls , . udl ⌣a l
splm u S cvrj. Intro DC
if udlc lv ⌢ inf ,
sN s c enc-crd
ld. cu

2

Preview Words

gray gra
incur ncr
yellow ylo
weekday ⌣cd
separate sprl
receipts rses
out-patient ol=psN
instructions nSrcjs

drs ⌢rgn lqfL
asc ab c hlt bnfts
u no v. i lq uc
asr A vu qs, uz
c rglr psN cl
f NRC , ⌣C , ylo NRC , f
A Cjs lau ncr z
. ol=psN. du n uz
ls f f dNl cls.
. sprl f NRC , ⌣C ,
gra n clr NRC , sdb
obln- f u bs ofs.
/ l kln . dfrN
sl v nSrcjs f s-d
rqSs, p rmbr la
. sprl f ⌢S b
fl- f eC nsr-ple.
⌢c cpes vu rses
+ cp L n u recs
f lx Ppss, A fl
fre lcl s ne ⌣cd
bln 9a + 5p.
su

3

Preview Words

lapse	*lps*	overdue	*Odu*
force	*fs*	reminder	*rmr*
premiums	*Prems*	security	*scrl*
bracket	*brcl*	together	*lglr*

dM bSr ls, .
rmr lau Prems
r no Odu, acrd
l r brs vu kc ,
u plse l pr f
pam, n rsv- b
Ja 15, r u a r v
l, d cS l rpls
la plse / crM ras
ld, if u Pl u plse
l lps , ul nvr aq
b S l obln ins /

sC . lo cS, E yr
lau a l v u
nl . hir aj brcl,
f E yr lau a ,
ul pa hir Prems,
M bSr, dM alo
u plse it csl-, l
s u pam ld so
lau scrl lb Plc-,
ll s o lglr lcp
u plse n fs, ru

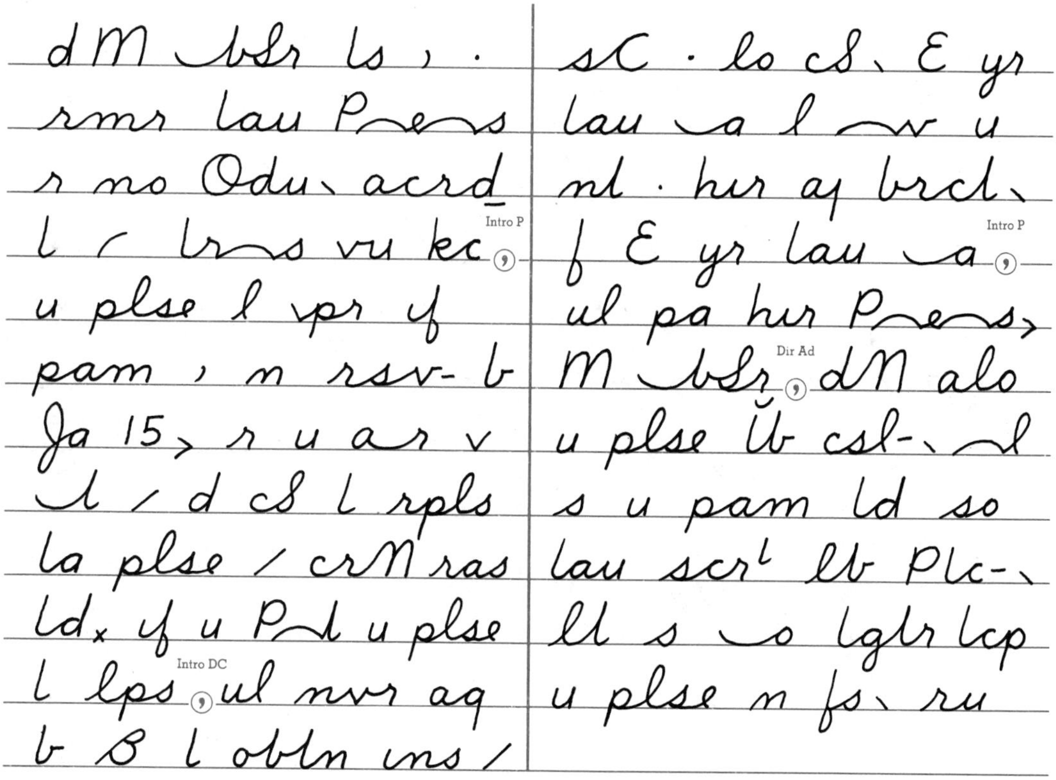

4

Preview Words

Alex	ax	private	prvl
auto	alo	guess	gs
coins	cyns	candidates	cddls
stamps	Sps	congratulations	kgjs

mo l ax lq uv
fns- rd u rpl, + (Conj)
uz v prs- u
rcmys. l agre
u la esd ofr .
grp pln f mbrs
v prvl ogjs, v
crs, / db nes l (Paren)
el ol loz ogjs la
op o . nyl bss + v
. lry enf mbrs
l spl ls cN v
ins pln. cd u
Pvd . lS v loz

ogjs, a q r exs
u lS- alo clbs
+ lrvl clbs. lz r
lN sugjs. id
aso gs la lr r
sv grps la clc
sp ihs. f ex, ppl (Paren)
hu clc Sps or
cyns b cddls
f r plse, uv P- .
u opl f s n .
ara ev lq b NS-
n. kgjs ou fN, (Dir Ad)
ax.

5

Punctuation Study

Add commas to show one series, one nonrestrictive clause, and three introductory dependent clauses.

Preview Words

small	sml	protection	Plcj
whole	hl	flexible	flxB
enough	enf	inability	nBl
qualify	qlf	frustrated	frSra-

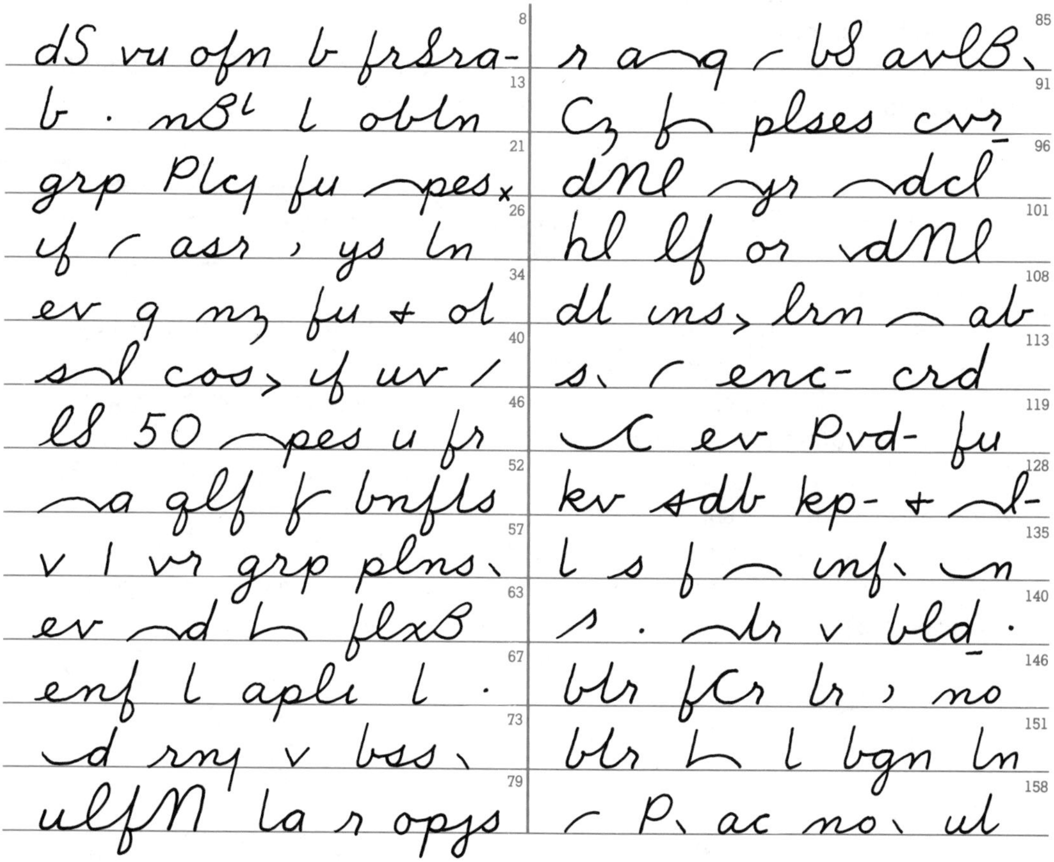

Key

1

Dear Parents:

Is every member of your family covered by your current insurance policy? You would be[1] surprised at how many people answer that question incorrectly. Because their policies were adequate[2] several years ago, they automatically assume that the coverage is as good today as it was[3] yesterday.

All too often we overlook an important consideration. When children go away to college,[4] they may no longer be covered under some family plans. Don't let this oversight happen to you. We can provide[5] you with a policy that will insure your sons and daughters while they are traveling to and from college.

While[6] living on campus, your children will be protected in the event of illness or injury. They will also be[7] protected against the loss of personal property due to theft or fire.

This is an ideal way to supplement[8] your existing coverage. If you would like to have more information, send us the enclosed card today. [9]

Cordially yours, (182)

2

Dear Mrs. Morgan:

Thank you for your letter asking about the health benefits you now have. I think I can answer[1] all of your questions.

Use the regular patient claim form, which is yellow, for all charges that you incur as[2] an out-patient. Do not use this form for dental claims. A separate form, which is gray in color, should be obtained[3] from your business office. It will contain a different set of instructions for submitting requests.

Please remember[4] that a separate form must be filed for each insured party. Make copies of your receipts and keep them in your[5] records for tax purposes.

Always feel free to call us any weekday between 9 a.m. and 5 p.m.[6]

Sincerely yours, (122)

3

Dear Miss Webster:

This is a reminder that your premiums are now overdue. According to the terms of your[1] contract, your policy will expire if payment is not received by January 15.

Are you aware of[2] what it would cost to replace that policy at current rates today? If you permit your policy to lapse, you[3] will never again be able to obtain insurance at such a low cost. Every year that you wait will move you[4] into a higher age bracket. For every year that you wait, you will pay higher premiums.

Miss Webster, don't[5] allow your policy to be canceled. Mail us your payment today so that your security will be protected.[6] Let us work together to keep your policy in force.

Respectfully yours, (134)

4

MEMO TO: Alex Long

I have finished reading your report, and I was very impressed with your recommendations.[1] I agree with you that we should offer a group plan for members of private organizations.

Of course, it[2] would be necessary to include only those organizations that operate on a national basis[3] and have a large enough membership to support this kind of insurance plan. Could you provide a list of those[4] organizations? Among the examples you listed were auto clubs and travel clubs. These are excellent[5] suggestions. I would also guess that there are several groups that collect specific items. For example, people[6] who collect stamps or coins might be candidates for our policy.

You have presented an exciting opportunity[7] for us in an area we have long been interested in. Congratulations on your findings, Alex.[8] (160)

5

Dear Sir:

Have you often been frustrated by an inability to obtain group protection for your employees?[1] If the answer is yes, then we have good news for you and other small companies.

If you have at least 50[2] employees, your firm may qualify for the benefits of one of our group plans. We have made them flexible enough[3] to apply to a wide range of businesses. You will find that our options are among the best available.[4] Choose from policies covering dental, major medical, whole life, or accidental death insurance.

Learn more[5] about us. The enclosed card, which we have provided for your convenience, should be completed and mailed to us for[6] more information. When it is a matter of building a better future, there is no better time to begin[7] than the present. Act now.

Yours truly, (146)

LESSON 23

Theory Review

1. Use an underscore line to indicate the name of a book, magazine, or newspaper.

Sports Illustrated

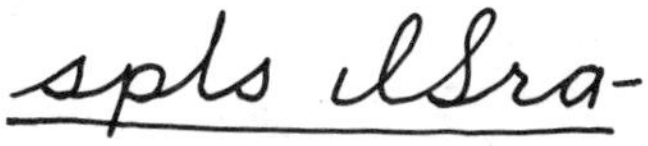

Wall Street Journal

2. Use quotation marks to set off the title of a magazine article, newspaper article, or title of a speech.

I enjoyed reading your article, "Corporate Programs for Stress Management."

Transcription Aids: Similar Words

some  An unspecified amount.

We have some suggestions for you.

sum  The amount obtained from adding figures.

The sum of those figures is $49.85.

Your Business Vocabulary

comprehensive

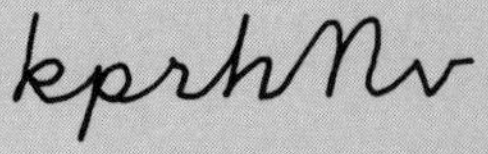

Large in scope; in insurance, coverage for motorized vehicles for a wide range of perils (other than collision), such as fire, wind, theft, hail, vandalism.

We expect to begin a comprehensive advertising campaign in the fall.

Your comprehensive coverage will pay for all damages after you have paid the deductible amount.

liability insurance

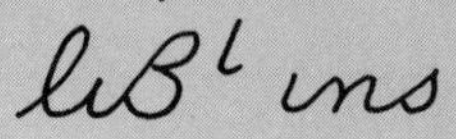

Insurance that covers legal and financial responsibility for the injuries or damaged property of other parties.

The cost of your liability insurance will not be increased this year.

Reading and Writing Exercises

1

Preview Words

expenses	vpNs	paperwork	ppr—o
usually	uzl	laboratory	lbrtre
instance	nSN	substantial	sSnsl
moment	—m	hospitalized	hspz-

dr hNrsn —
enc c fl v 1 vr
—pes, alC- l c
fl , . psN ch
f— , (NRC) —C ehp uc
Pss —l, / uzl
lcs ab 10 ds l
Pss 1 v lz chs,
n ls spsl nSN , (Paren)
hoE , (Paren) ihp la ec
ak c lsc —C
snr, ls —pe lb
hspz- f — ln 2
—cs, h hs Ar pd

. sSnsl ad l ,
dr , (Conj) + h hs Aso
pd sv lbrtre
vpNs, c psN
rsNl PCs- ls c+
plse z . splm l
, ol cvrj, Alo
c ppr—o , n yl
fnl , (Intro DC) ls —pe z cvr-
f— c —m h sn-
c plse, / pas 50$
P d , (Conj) + / db . gr
hlp l h no, vlu

2

Preview Words

adult	adlt	accident	vdN
bonus	bns	liability	liBl
drivers	drvrs	collision	clj
excessive	vsv	comprehensive	kprhNv

drs gra r u pa
l mC f alo ins
alo u ma fN /
hrd l blv, (Intro DC) mS
adlt drvrs du pa
vsv ras. du uno
y ly mc ls ufCnl
Mlc r bcz ly du
n lc r h l sp
aroN f loS psB
ras, Cc r ras +
kpr h u r ras
v ol cos. ul n

fN blr ras f
kprhNv, (Series) clj, (Series) or
liBl ins. la sN
a. lr , . bns f sf
drvrs. if uv n
h . vdN du r lS
5 yrs, (Intro DC) u ma glf
f . adjl Dk, er
hpe l Pvd u w
ls nz, (Dir Ad) ms gra.
. rep l cl sn l
asr qs + ll u m
ab r co. uvl

3

Preview Words

exact	vc	adopting	adpl
input	npl	tomorrow	Lro
publication	pbj	duplicate	dplca
Business Update	bs pda	portfolio	plflo

ded r enc- artcl
apr- rsNl n .
pplr bs pbj, Ap
bs pda\ p rd / +
Ul —e -l u lg ab
r ex pln la , dS-
n Sre> z uno, ev Intro DC
ofn ks- adpl . nu
ins plflo f bs exs\
Alo ed n —s l
dplca ls vc pln, Intro DC
idlc lse s ofr .
s-lr arm\ n od

lofr . plflo la ,
Pprl bln-, e nd Intro P
l vpN nl ol aras
v fnnsl pln\ l
sug lae cra .
Avzre Svs la c
kb ls cN v npl>
— sr ls —c ,
plcl bze fu, b Conj
idlc l Dcs ls
ida b Lro or
r d af\ s

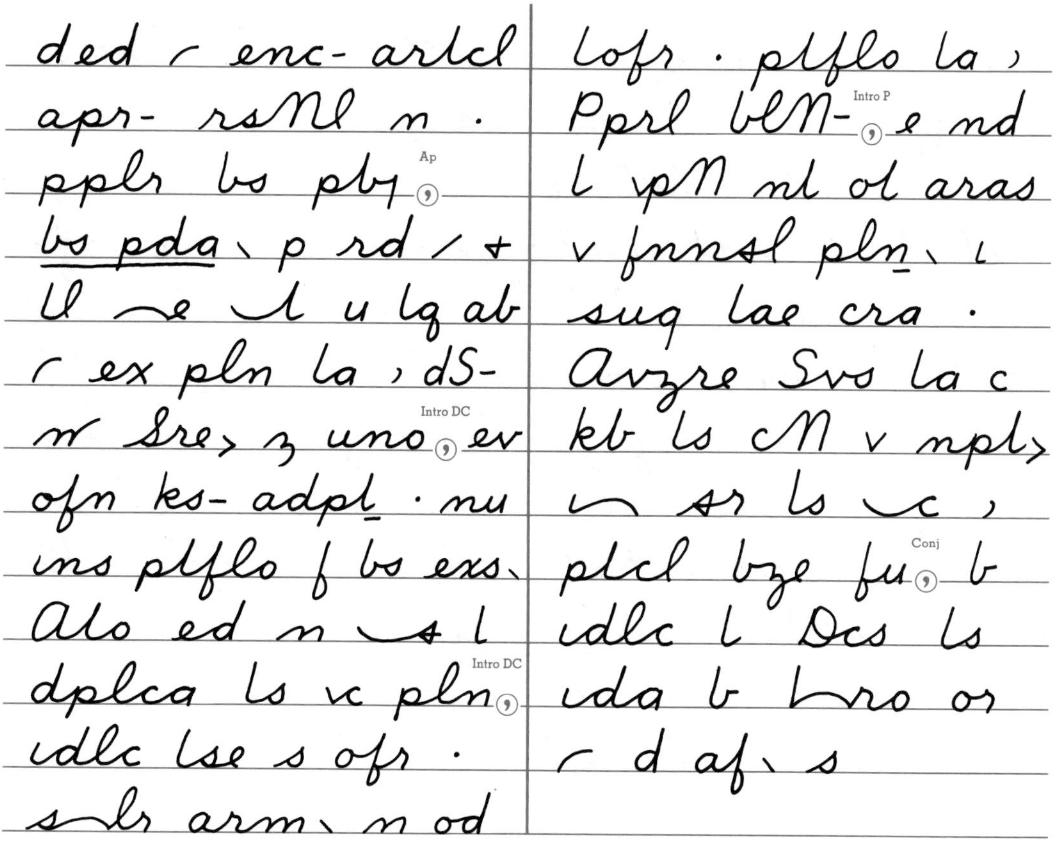

4

Preview Words

sole	sl	support	spl
seek	sc	responding	rsp
attempted	atl-	disability	DBl
serious	sres	self-employed	sfp-

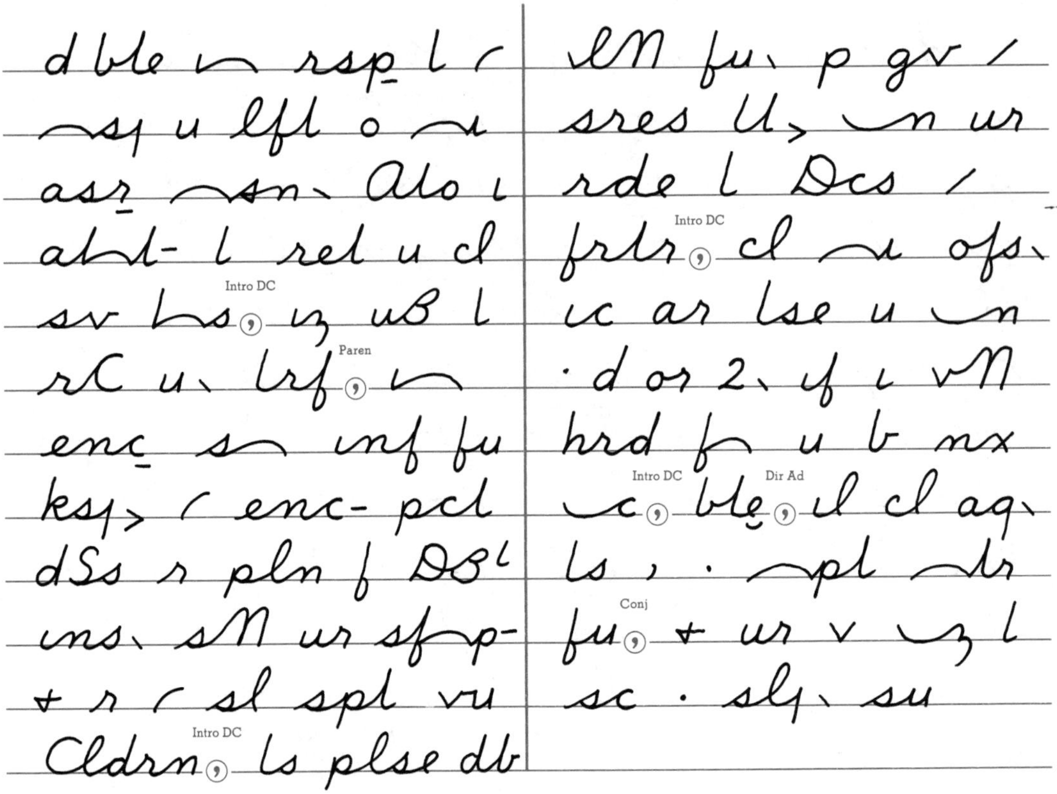

5

Punctuation Study

Add commas to show one introductory phrase, three introductory dependent clauses, and one conjunction.

Preview Words

sum	sm	toward	lw
owed	o-	provider	Pvdr
issued	isu-	physician	fzl
explanation	vplny	acknowledgment	acym

drs N n rel r 7
chs u fl- o Āp 9 13
f mdcl Cys. acrd 19
l r recs chs f 24
loz vpNs v ar b 31
rsv- b r ofs. ly 37
~ fl- b r Pvdr 42
v Svss + . Cc lb 50
isu- l r alN fzl> 57
n r abv pam 62

r nd ul rsv . 67
acym f ls ofs 74
nfn u v sn pd 80
lw ls ch. if lr r 86
Sl upd Cys u fzl 94
l bl u f and Sl 101
o->, if udlc . adyl 109
vplny v bnfls klc 115
ls ofs drl. cu 123

Key

1

Dear Mr. Henderson:

I am enclosing the file of one of our employees. Attached to the file is a patient[1] claim form, which we hope you can process immediately.

It usually takes about ten days to process[2] one of these claims. In this special instance, however, I hope that we can accomplish the task much sooner. This[3] employee will be hospitalized for more than two weeks. He has already paid a substantial amount to his[4] doctor, and he has also paid several laboratory expenses.

The patient recently purchased this cash[5] policy as a supplement to his other coverage. Although the paperwork is not yet final, this[6] employee was covered from the moment he signed the policy. It pays $50 per day, and it would be a[7] great help to him now.

Very truly yours, (146)

2

Dear Ms. Gray:

Are you paying too much for auto insurance? Although you may find it hard to believe, most adult[1] drivers do pay excessive rates. Do you know why they make this unfortunate mistake? It is because they do not[2] take the time to shop around for the lowest possible rates.

Check our rates and compare them with the rates of other[3] companies. You will not find better rates for comprehensive, collision, or liability insurance.[4] That isn't all. There is a bonus for safe drivers. If you have not had an accident during the last five years,[5] you may qualify for an additional discount.

We are happy to provide you with this news, Ms. Gray. A[6] representative will call soon to answer questions and tell you more about our company.

Yours very truly,[7] (140)

3

Dear Ed:

The enclosed article appeared recently in a popular business publication, *Business Update.*[1] Please read it and tell me what you think about the executive plan that is described in the story.

As you know,[2] we have often considered adopting a new insurance portfolio for business executives. Although[3] we would not wish to duplicate this exact plan, I would like to see us offer a similar arrangement. In[4] order to offer a portfolio that is properly balanced, we need to expand into other areas[5] of financial planning. I suggest that we create an advisory service that can contribute this kind[6] of input.

I am sure this week is particularly busy for you, but I would like to discuss this idea[7] by tomorrow or the day after.

Sincerely, (149)

4

Dear Betty:

I am responding to the message you left on my answering machine. Although I attempted to[1] return your call several times, I was unable to reach you. Therefore, I am enclosing some information[2] for your consideration.

The enclosed packet describes our plan for disability insurance. Since you are[3] self-employed and are the sole support of your children, this policy would be excellent for you. Please give it[4] serious thought.

When you are ready to discuss it further, call my office. I can arrange to see you within[5] a day or two. If I haven't heard from you by next week, Betty, I will call again. This is an important matter[6] for you, and you are very wise to seek a solution.

Sincerely yours, (133)

5

Dear Mr. North:

I am returning the claims you filed on April 9 for medical charges. According to our[1] records, claims for those expenses have already been received by our office. They were filed by the provider of[2] the services, and a check will be issued to the attending physician.

When the above payment is made, you[3] will receive an acknowledgment from this office informing you of the sum paid toward this claim. If there are still[4] unpaid charges, your physician will bill you for the amount still owed.

If you would like an additional[5] explanation of benefits, contact this office directly.

Cordially yours, (113)

LESSON 24

Shorthand Vocabulary Review

Write a capital N for the sound of *ent*, *nt*, (pronounced *ent*).

assistant	asSN	accident	vdN
current	crN	different	dfrN
sufficient	sfsN	comment	kN
agent	ajN	evident	evdN

Transcription Aids: Spelling

Learn to distinguish between words that begin with *en* and those that begin with *in*.

encourage	ncrj	invest	nvS
entitled	nttl-	insure	nsr
enrolling	nrl	increase	ncrs
enjoyed	njy-	inquire	nq
enable	nB	involve	nvlv
enact	nac	invitation	nvʃ

Your Business Vocabulary

annuities  Annual payments of income from investments.

As you can see from the report, you can choose your method of payment of annuities.

merger 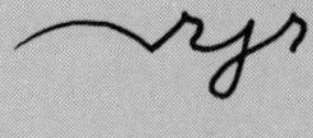 In business, the joining of two or more corporations.

The details of the merger will be announced at a press conference.

Reading and Writing Exercises

---------- 1 ----------

Preview Words

audience   *adeN*

income   *nk*

variety   *vrɪ*

promptly   *P⎯ll*

luncheon   *lnCn*

annuities   *anu ⁱˢ*

competitive   *kplv*

correspondence   *cos*

---

d⎯s dyl ɪdb p-
ll r spcr / ɪ
lnCn o Oc 4, r
lpc v ⎯ɪ adrs
*lt "nvSm pln," *
zu sug- n ɪ cos (Intro DC) (9)
me ppl du n fl
USN r rl v ls
ɪns ayM, r ayM
c hlp ⎯ G,
nvSms la l
ncrs ls nk af
rlrm, ⎯S cos ofr
· vrɪ v anuⁱˢ (Conj) (9)

+ ra v NS ,
kplv ⎯ prvl
fNs, S ⎯ɪ opn
la anuⁱˢ r uzl
· sfr nvSm, ɪl
lc f apxl 15 mls (Conj) (9)
+ ln ɪl alo ⎯l
f qs f r adeN,
sN r ⎯e bgns
P⎯ll / nn, (Intro DC) (9) *ɪl*
ar ll ls ab 20
mls bf ln, lqf
nvly, su

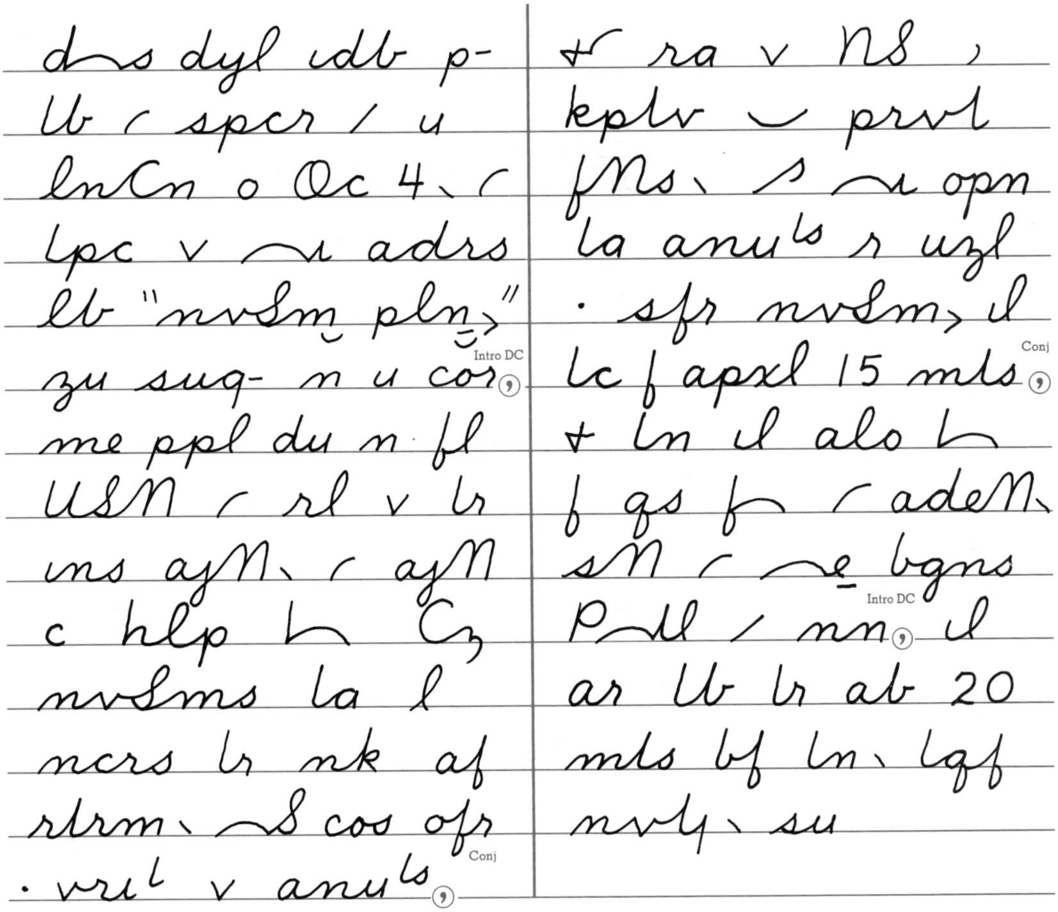

2

Preview Words

upon	po	Hastings	hS
ended	N-	observation	obzrvj
comment	kN	complimenting	kplm
workday	od	encouragement	ncrjm

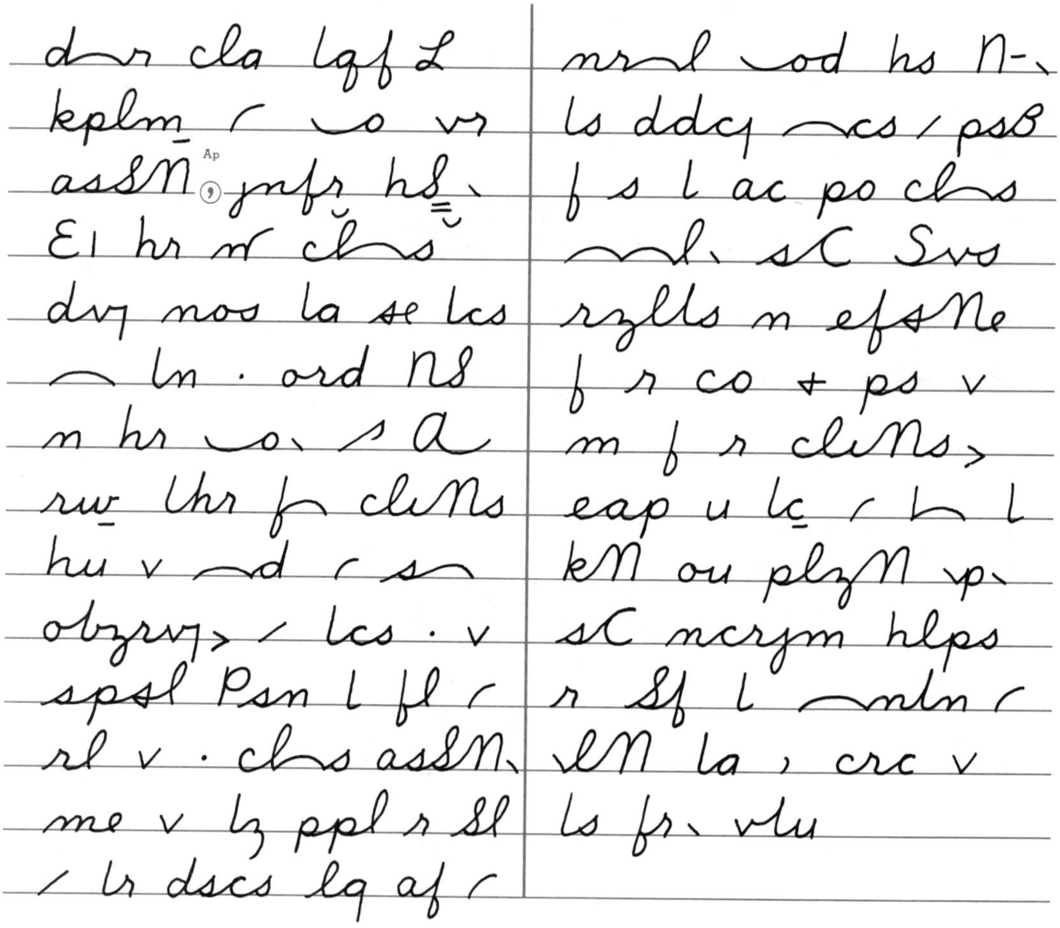

───────── **3** ─────────

Preview Words

merger ～ryʃ   underway ひa

United uni⁻   extensive √Mʋ

evidently evdNl   diversified dʋrsf⁻

announcement anoNm   negotiations ngʃeʃs

---

dɜr hrpɜr ⌣n ız n
ひsa ls ⌣c° ↓ hrd   ᴵⁿᵗʳᵒ ᴰᶜ
s⌣ nz la lb ʋ
Nʃ lu, evdNl°·   ᴾᵃʳᵉⁿ
～ryʃ ‚ ⌐ pln⁻ ∫
2 ⌐yɜ ıns coʃ,
uni⁻ lf ⌣+ ∫n grp⌣
l sn bk ∣ co,
ngʃeʃs ɜr crNl
ひa° ⌣+ ec ʋpc·   ᶜᵒⁿʲ
anoNm ne d no
∫⌣ ⌐ Pɜ ʋ loʒ
coʃ‚ ʒ · ɜrʒll ʋ

ls ～ryʃ° ⌐ nu   ᴵⁿᵗʳᵒ ᴾ
∫r l bk ∣ √ lryʃ
ıns coʃ ɴ ny, ⌐
kbn⁻ asls √ 2
coʃ lol sʋ B$,
alC⁻ ‚ · nzppɜr
artcl √C Ncas
la lɜr hld ɜr bo
dʋrsf⁻ ⌣+ √Mʋ‚
ıllb egɜr lse √l
dʋs ∫⌣ ls nu
ldrɜ ɴ ıns
knl, ul

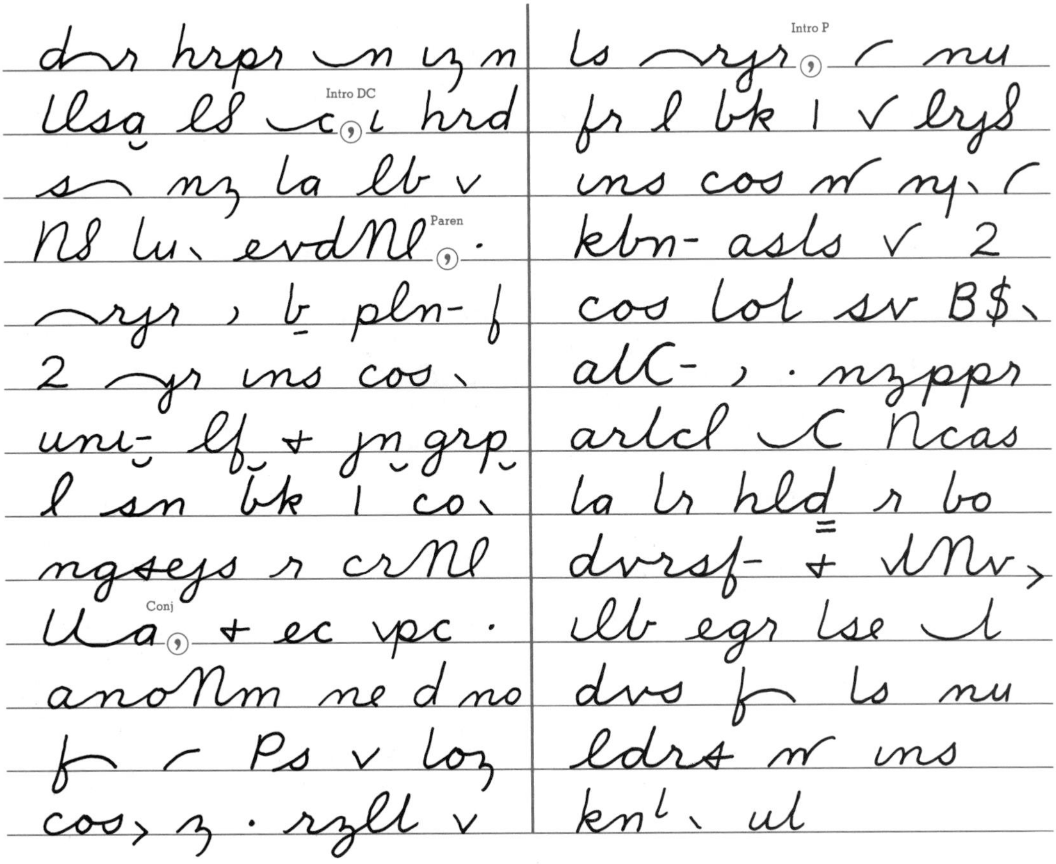

4

Preview Words

main	mn	occasion	ocj
rely	rli	birthday	brld
whom	hm	realize	relz
returns	rels	confidence	kfdN

drs lor hpe
brld! s . plzr
lsN u mu b8
ss o ls spsl
ocj, / aso gvs
me plzr l lqf
ku u plses r
co, uv a fll la
(mn rzn ppl
Cz l ins co O
aol, bcz v ayN
h ly o,
uf uv kfdN w

ayN, (Intro DC) uno uc rli
po (co la h or
se reps, hpe
lsa la uv d
me frNs sN bk
. ayN, (Conj) + l nyy
hNl (ins nds
v loz frNs,
sr u relz lau
a cl o me ne
und hlp, chp
u nyy me hpe
rels, vlu

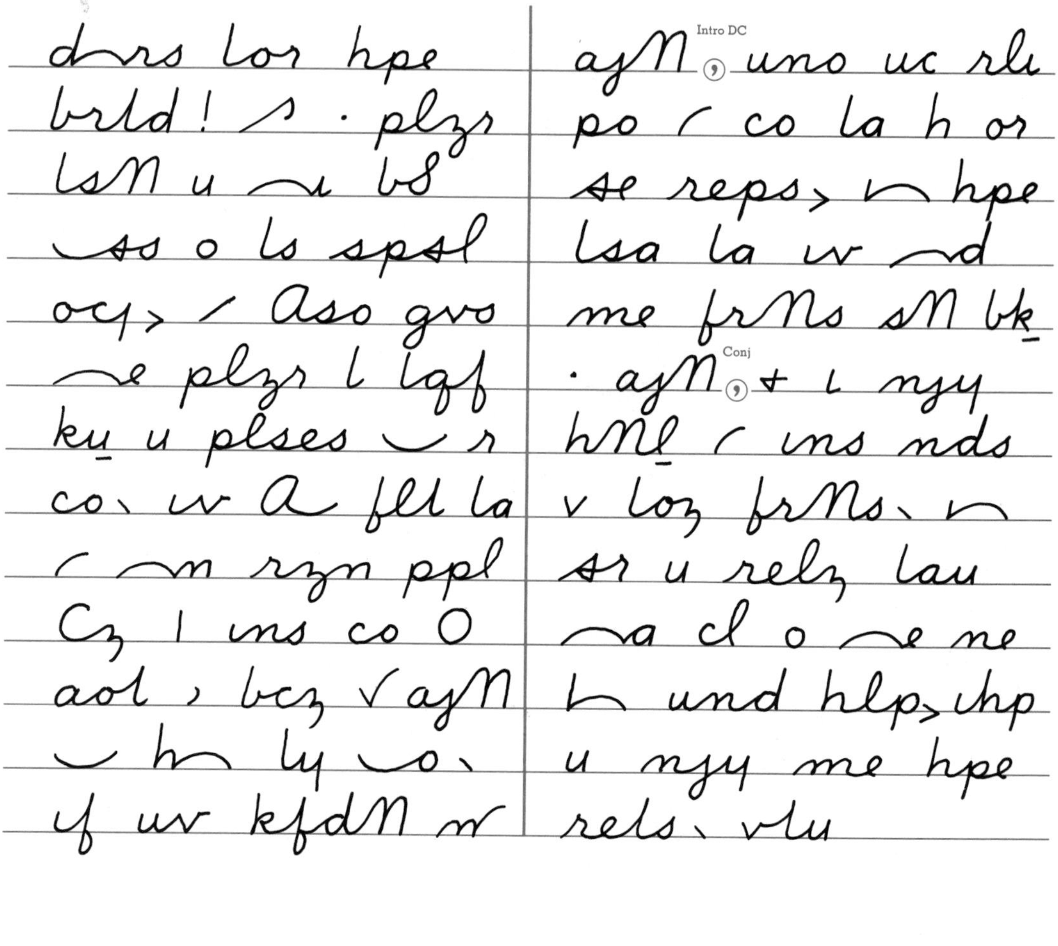

5

Punctuation Study

Add commas to show two conjunctions, one parenthetical expression, and one nonrestrictive clause.

Preview Words

themselves	Lsvs	portfolio	plflo
further	frlr	supporting	spl
enrolling	nrl	thoroughly	lrol
breakfast	brcfs	supplementary	splmre

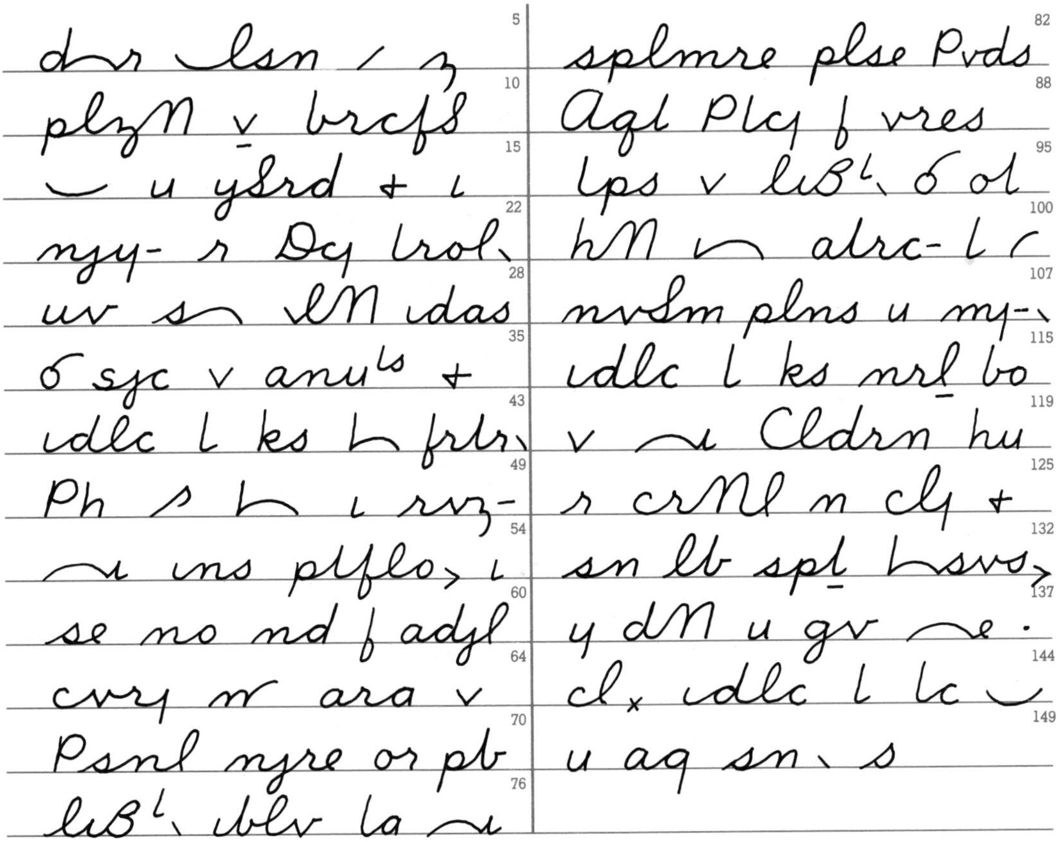

Key

1

Dear Ms. Doyle:

I would be pleased to be the speaker at your luncheon on October 4. The topic of my address[1] will be "Investment Planning."

As you suggested in your correspondence, many people do not fully understand[2] the role of their insurance agent. The agent can help them choose investments that will increase their income after[3] retirement. Most companies offer a variety of annuities, and the rate of interest is[4] competitive with private funds. It is my opinion that annuities are usually a safer[5] investment.

I will talk for approximately 15 minutes, and then I will allow time for questions from the[6] audience. Since the meeting begins promptly at noon, I will arrange to be there about 20 minutes before then.[7] Thank you for your invitation.

Sincerely yours, (149)

2

Dear Mr. Clay:

Thank you for your letter complimenting the work of our assistant, Jennifer Hastings. Everyone[1] here in the claims division knows that she takes more than an ordinary interest in her work. It is always[2] rewarding to hear from clients who have made the same observation.

It takes a very special person to[3] fill the role of a claims assistant. Many of these people are still at their desks long after the normal workday[4] has ended. This dedication makes it possible for us to act upon claims immediately. Such service[5] results in efficiency for our company and peace of mind for our clients.

We appreciate your taking[6] the time to comment on your pleasant experience. Such encouragement helps our staff to maintain the excellence[7] that is characteristic of this firm.

Very truly yours, (151)

3

Dear Mr. Harper:

When I was in Tulsa last week, I heard some news that will be of interest to you. Evidently,[1] a merger is being planned for two major insurance companies. United Life and General Group will[2] soon become one company. Negotiations are currently underway, and we can expect an announcement[3] any day now from the presidents of those companies.

As a result of this merger, the new firm will become[4] one of the largest insurance companies in the nation. The combined assets of the two companies total[5] several billion dollars. Attached is a newspaper article which indicates that their holdings are both[6] diversified and extensive.

I will be eager to see what develops from this new leadership in the[7] insurance community.

Yours truly, (146)

4

Dear Mrs. Tower:

Happy birthday! It is a pleasure to send you my best wishes on this special occasion.[1]

It also gives me pleasure to thank you for continuing your policies with our company. I have always[2] felt that the main reason people choose one insurance company over another is because of the agent[3] with whom they work. If you have confidence in the agent, you know you can rely upon the company that he[4] or she represents.

I am happy to say that I have made many friends since becoming an agent, and I enjoy[5] handling the insurance needs of those friends. I am sure you realize that you may call on me any time[6] you need help.

I hope you enjoy many happy returns.

Very truly yours, (134)

5

Dear Mr. Wilson:

It was pleasant having breakfast with you yesterday, and I enjoyed our discussion thoroughly.[1] You have some excellent ideas on the subject of annuities, and I would like to consider them[2] further. Perhaps it is time I revised my insurance portfolio.

I see no need for additional[3] coverage in the area of personal injury or public liability. I believe that my[4] supplementary policy provides adequate protection for various types of liability. On the[5] other hand, I am attracted to the investment plans you mentioned. I would like to consider enrolling both[6] of my children, who are currently in college and soon will be supporting themselves.

Why don't you give me a call?[7] I would like to talk with you again soon.

Sincerely, (149)

LESSON 25

Word Development

Develop new words using the following brief forms:

operate

- cooperate *cop*
- cooperation *copj*
- operational *opjl*
- inoperative *nopv*

ordinary

- extraordinary *Xord*
- ordinarily *ordl*

other

- another *aol*
- otherwise *olz*

prove

- approve *apv*
- disapproval *Dapvl*
- improved *⌒pv-*
- improvement *⌒pvm*

manage

- manager *⌒jr*
- management *⌒jm*

of

- hereof *hrv*
- thereof *lrv*

Reading and Writing Exercises

1

Preview Words

goods	gs	reimburse	rbrs
sorry	sre	deductible	ddcB
theft	Ufl	depreciation	dprsej
scale	scl	entertainment	Nlnm

dr rsl enc-, . Cc f 950$ l rbrs u f Ufl vu h Nlnm sS. z uno, (Intro DC) (ddcB a-l vu ins , 2H$. la a-l hs Ar b ddc- f (vlu vu Sln gs, n eS-a (lol a-l v ls, (Intro P) e jnl uz . scl v 10% P yr l arv / . fr ra v dprsej. hoE, (Paren) u sls rse

Ncas la (sl z ls ln 2 os old. Lrf, (Paren) er Lre (sl z brN nu dse, (Conj) + ul n b G- . fe f dprsej, er sre lau sfr- ls ls. / reps . Dapym + . nkv fu. er hpe Lc ls sllm fu, (Conj) + e -s u l n fCr. vlu

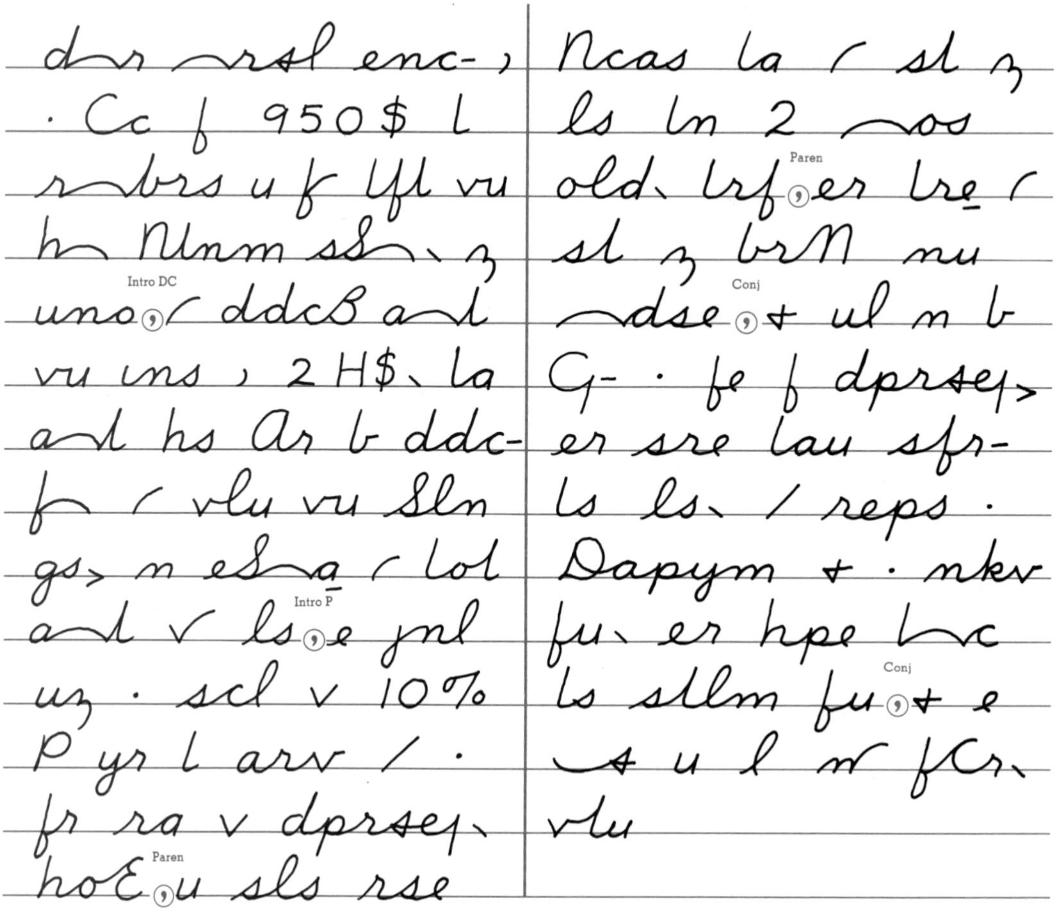

2

Preview Words

annual	aul	defray	dfra
young	yq	tuition	luj
strong	Srq	annuity	anu
accumulate	acla	quarterly	qtrl

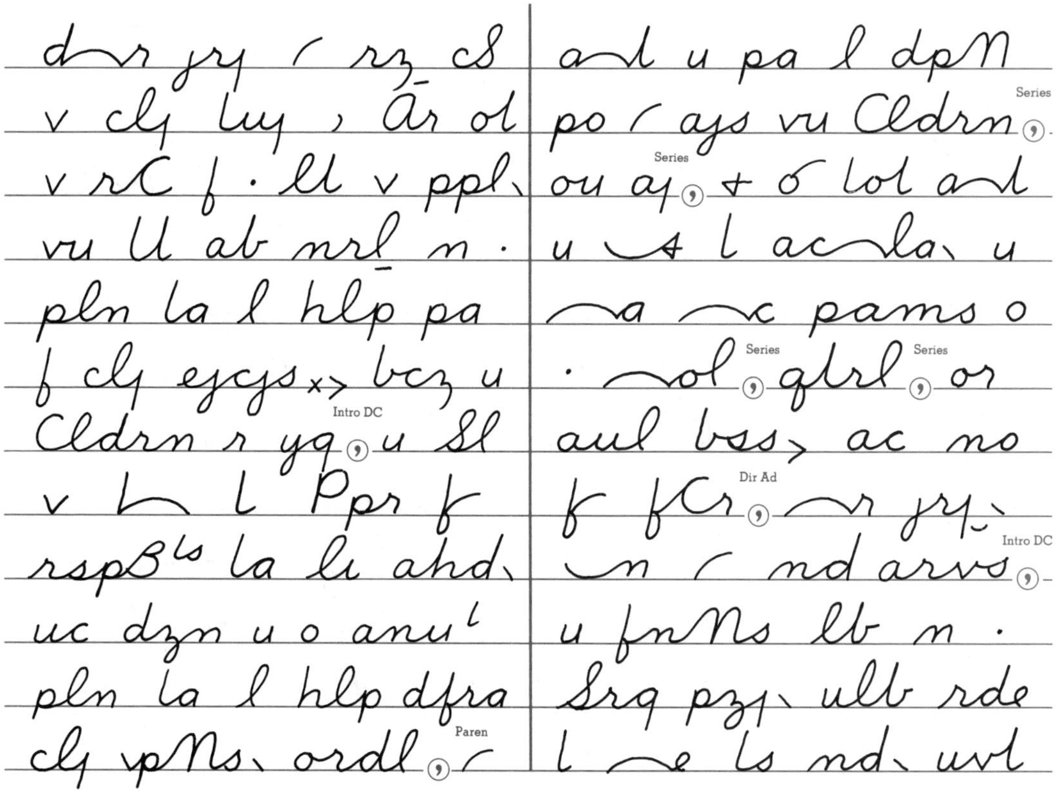
Series
Series
Series
Series
Intro DC
Dir Ad
Intro DC
Paren

3

Preview Words

jaw 

gums 

routine 

examination 

surgery 

resubmit 

submitted 

repayment 

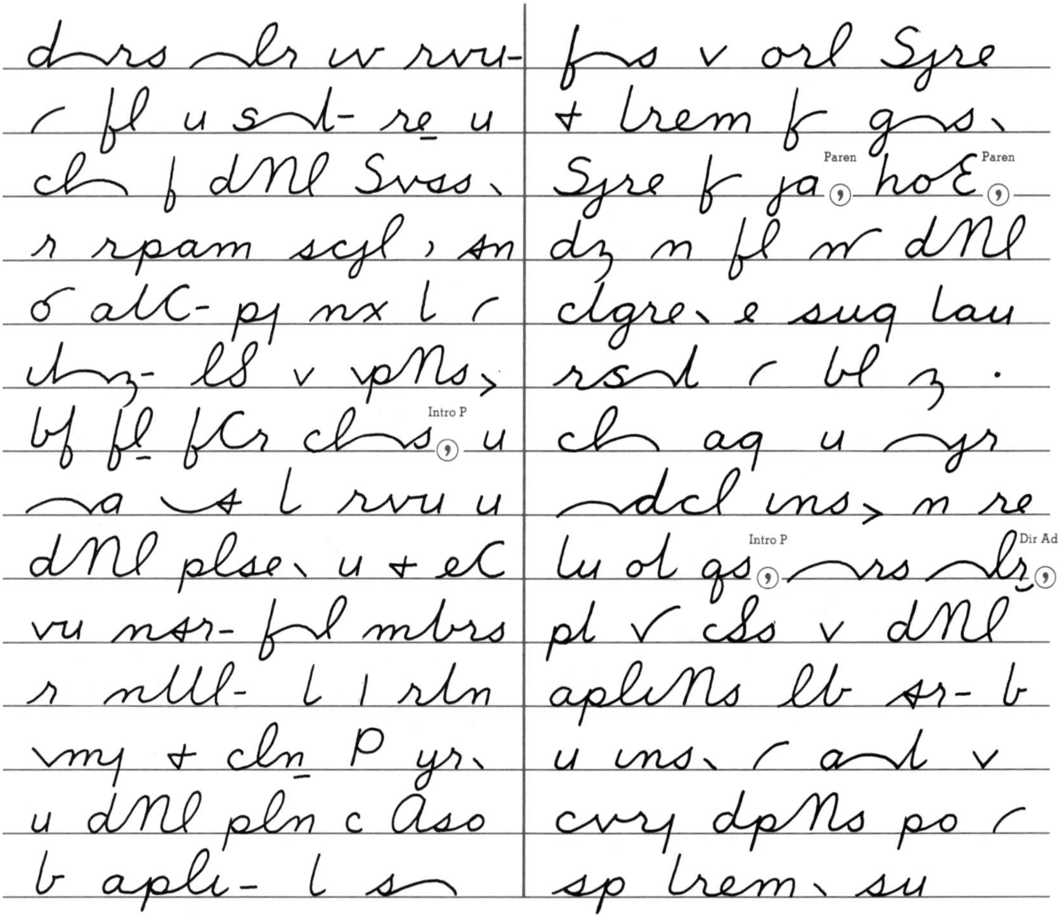

4

Preview Words

forced

lovely

incomes

mortgage

minimal

husband

worries

disability

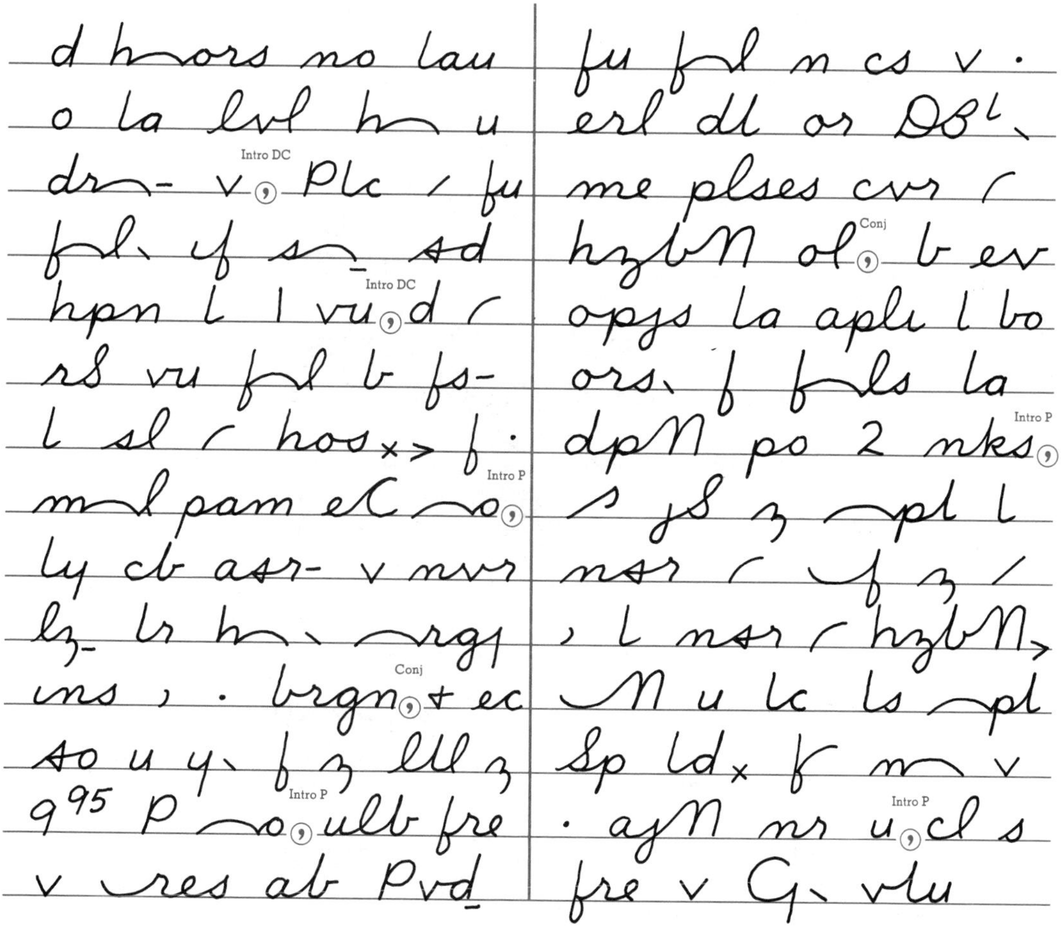

5

Punctuation Study

Add commas to show two parenthetical expressions, three introductory dependent clauses, and one conjunction.

Preview Words

adjust	ajS	springing	sprq-
unless	uls	quotation	qly
salesperson	slsPsn	probably	PbB
automobile	aloB	otherwise	olz

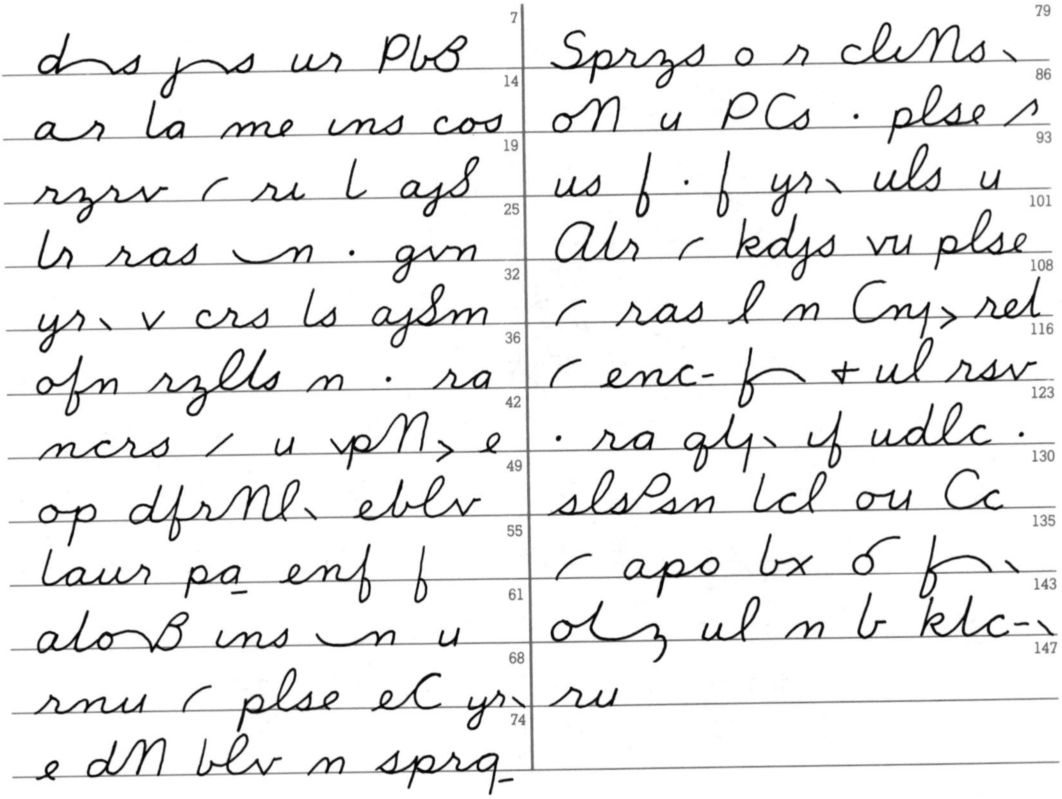

Key

1

Dear Mr. Marshall:

Enclosed is a check for $950 to reimburse you for the theft of your[1] home entertainment system. As you know, the deductible amount of your insurance is $200.[2] That amount has already been deducted from the value of your stolen goods.

In estimating the total[3] amount of the loss, we generally use a scale of 10 percent per year to arrive at a fair rate of[4] depreciation. However, your sales receipt indicates that the set was less than two months old. Therefore, we are[5] treating the set as brand new merchandise, and you will not be charged a fee for depreciation.

We are sorry[6] that you suffered this loss. It represents a disappointment and an inconvenience for you. We are happy to make[7] this settlement for you, and we wish you well in the future.

Very truly yours, (154)

2

Dear Mr. George:

The rising cost of college tuition is already out of reach for a lot of people. Have[1] you thought about enrolling in a plan that will help pay for college educations?

Because your children are young,[2] you still have time to prepare for the responsibilities that lie ahead. You can design your own annuity[3] plan that will help defray college expenses. Ordinarily, the amount you pay will depend upon the[4] ages of your children, on your age, and on the total amount you wish to accumulate. You may make payments[5] on a monthly, quarterly, or annual basis.

Act now for the future, Mr. George. When the need arrives, your[6] finances will be in a strong position. You will be ready to meet this need.

Yours very truly, (138)

3

Dear Mrs. Miller:

I have reviewed the file you submitted regarding your claim for dental services. Our[1] repayment schedule is shown on the attached page next to the itemized list of expenses.

Before filing future[2] claims, you may wish to review your dental policy. You and each of your insured family members are entitled[3] to one routine examination and cleaning per year. Your dental plan can also be applied to some forms[4] of oral surgery and treatment for the gums. Surgery for the jaw, however, does not fall in the dental[5] category. We suggest that you resubmit the bill as a claim against your major medical insurance.[6]

In regard to your other questions, Mrs. Miller, part of the costs of dental appliances will be shared by[7] your insurance. The amount of coverage depends upon the specific treatment.

Sincerely yours, (158)

4

Dear Homeowners:

Now that you own that lovely home you dreamed of, protect it for your family. If something should happen[1] to one of you, would the rest of your family be forced to sell the house?

For a minimal payment each month,[2] they can be assured of never losing their home. Mortgage insurance is a bargain, and we can show you why. For[3] as little as $9.95 per month, you will be free of worries about providing for your[4] family in case of an early death or disability. Many policies cover the husband only, but[5] we have options that apply to both owners. For families that depend upon two incomes, it is just as[6] important to insure the wife as it is to insure the husband.

Won't you take this important step today? For the[7] name of an agent near you, call us free of charge.

Very truly yours, (152)

5

Dear Ms. James:

You are probably aware that many insurance companies reserve the right to adjust their rates[1] within a given year. Of course, this adjustment often results in a rate increase at your expense.

We operate[2] differently. We believe that you are paying enough for automobile insurance when you renew the[3] policy each year. We don't believe in springing surprises on our clients. Once you purchase a policy, it[4] is yours for a full year. Unless you alter the conditions of your policy, the rates will not change.

Return the[5] enclosed form, and you will receive a rate quotation. If you would like a salesperson to call on you, check the[6] appropriate box on the form. Otherwise, you will not be contacted.

Respectfully yours, (136)

unl 6

fnn*

Shorthand Vocabulary Review

Study the following words and the principles they illustrate. Each of these words can be found in the letters and memos in this unit.

1. Write k for the sounds of *com, con, coun* (ow), and *count.*

compare	kpr	convert	kvrl
competition	kpl	consolidating	kslda
computerized	kpurz-	counselors	kslrs
common	kn	contains	klns

***Unit Six**
Finance

confusing kfz-　　encounter nkr

conducting kdc　　account ak

2. Write T for the word beginnings *tran* and *trans*.

transferring Tfr　　transition T1

transactions Tacjs　　transportation Tpl

3. Write sl for the word sounds of *shul* and the word ending *chul* (cial, tial).

financial fnnsl　　essential esnsl

specialists spslss　　potential plnsl

More About Punctuation

Use an apostrophe to show possession. Add *'s* to singular or plural nouns that do not end with an *s* sound.

The employee's check was delivered by mail.
A new children's store is located on Fourth Street.

Nouns ending with an *s* sound that add an extra syllable in the possessive form also require an *'s*.

The class's average was exceptionally high.

Simply add an apostrophe after plural nouns ending with an *s* sound to show possession.

The employees' lounge is being redecorated.

LESSON 26

Brief Forms and Derivatives

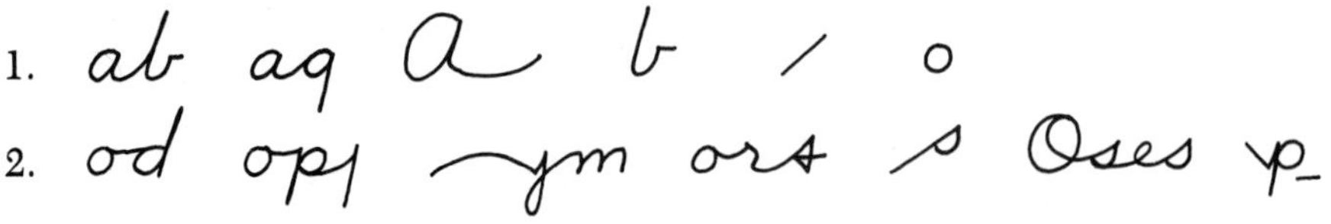

Key

1. about, again/against, always, be/but/been/by/buy, it/at, on/own
2. order, operation, management, ownership, its, overseas, experiencing

Phrase Review

Key

1. I would be, we cannot, we have been, you know, you would like
2. to visit, to you/to your, that you/that your, on the, will be

Reading and Writing Exercises

1

Preview Words

growth	grl	brokers	brcrs
common	kn	counsel	ksl
stocks	Scs	potential	plnsl
reliable	rliB	exchange	√Cnj

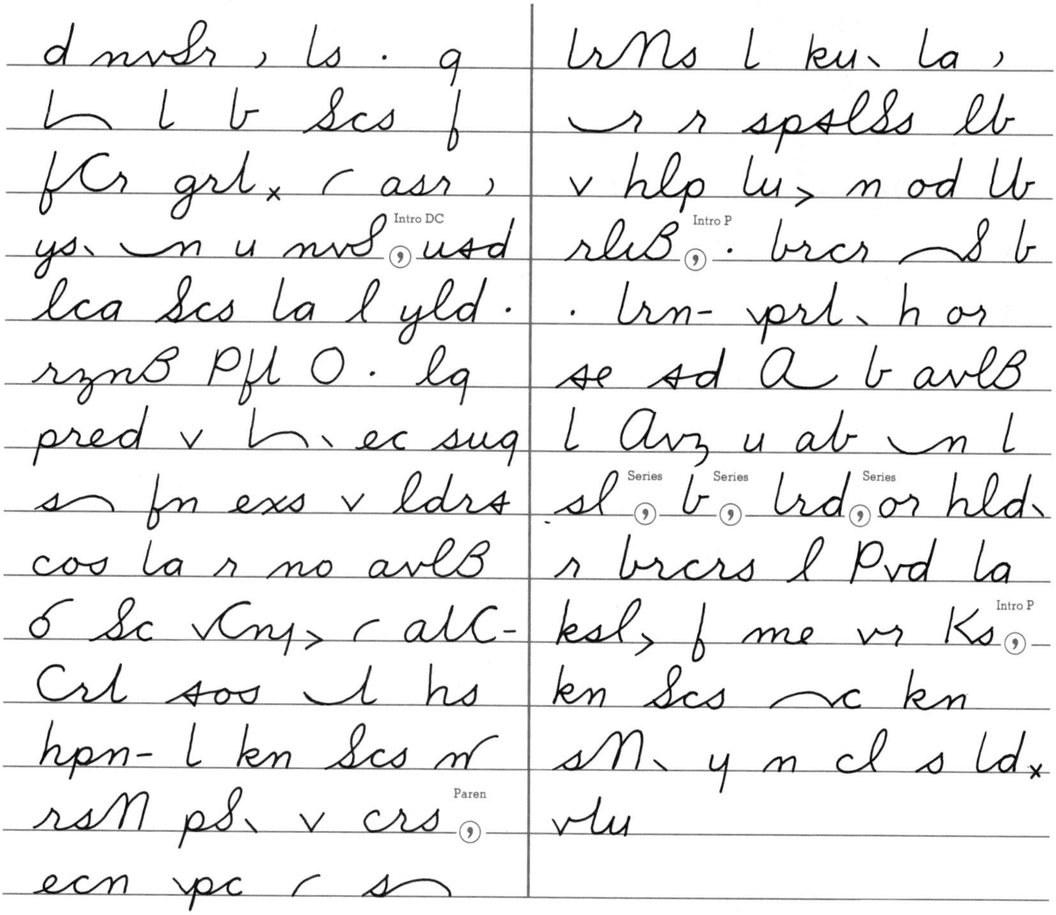

2

Preview Words

natural	nCrl	trusting	lrS
theft	Ufl	disaster	dzSr
dollars	$	security	scrl
practical	prclcl	personalized	Psnlz-

dr grgre lr r
me rzns f lrS s
⌣ u fnnsl scrl,
n adj l r Plcy la
Intro P
er rq- lgv u b la,
ec no nsr u ak f
. adjl 250T$, e
Aso cre Ms v $ v
Plcy aq r ls v
Series Series
scrls b fr, Ufl, or

nCrl dzSr, u gl
a ls Plcy alq ⌣ r
Psnlz- Svs + Pfyl
Avs la evb ofr f
aS 1H yrs, cl +
asc l spc l 1 vr
kslrs, elb gld l hlp
u olln . nvSm pln
la , prclcl fu, cu

3

Preview Words

step	Sp	guidelines	gdlns
series	srz	conducting	kdc̲
confusing	kfz̲	essential	esnsl
security	scrl	uncertainty	uSlnle

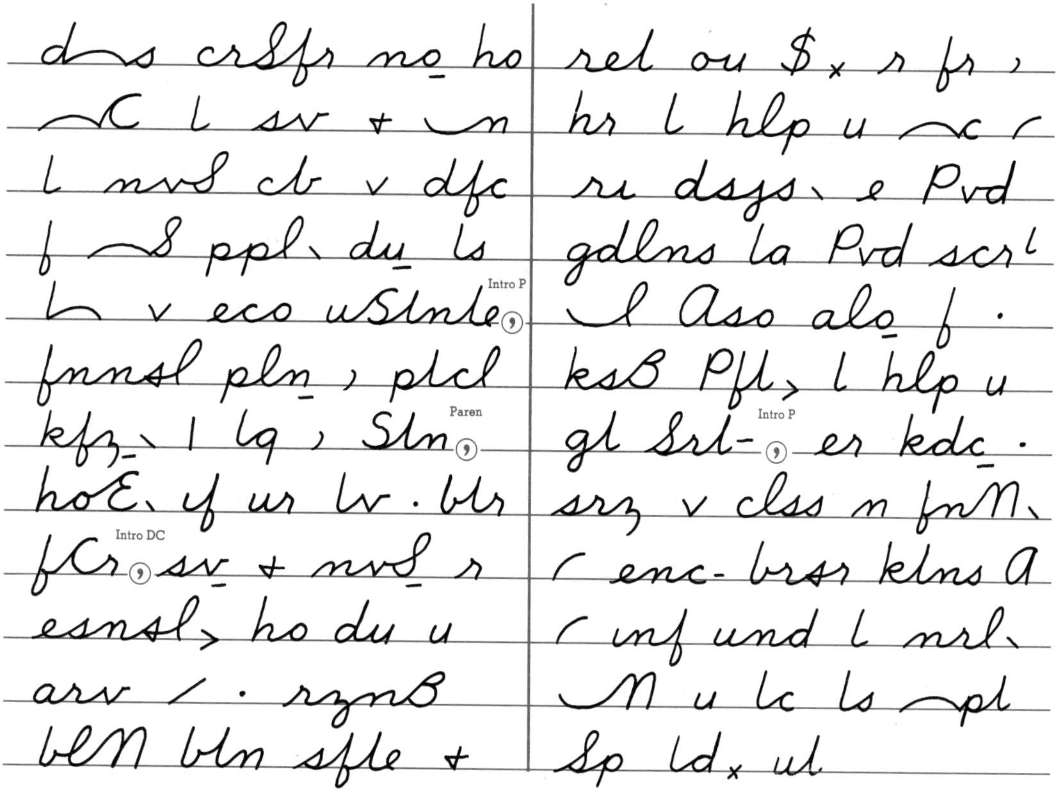

4

Preview Words

status	_Sts_	profitable	_PfLB_
bright	_bru_	fascinating	_fsna_
outlook	_ollc_	computerized	_kpurz-_
vicinity	_vsn^l_	shareholders	_srhldrs_

(shorthand text)

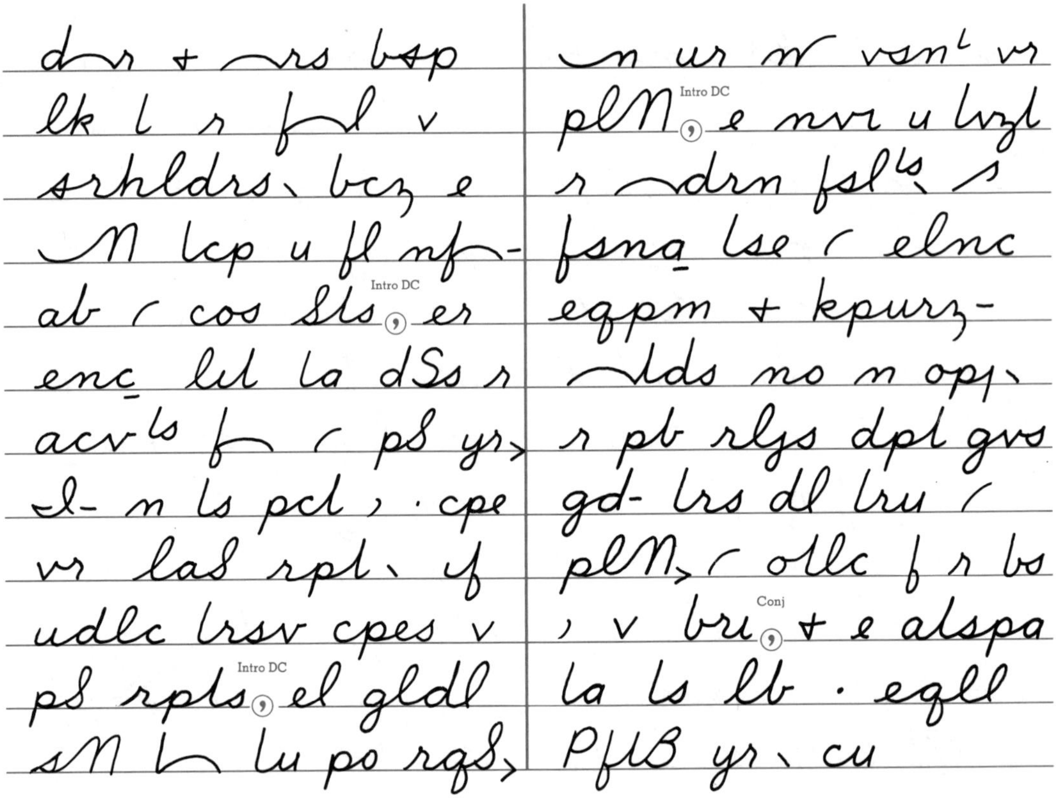

5

Punctuation Study

Add commas to show one introductory dependent clause, two conjunctions, and one omission of *and*.

Preview Words

thud		gambling	
defer		compromise	
solid		supersonic	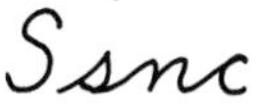
evaluate		predictable	

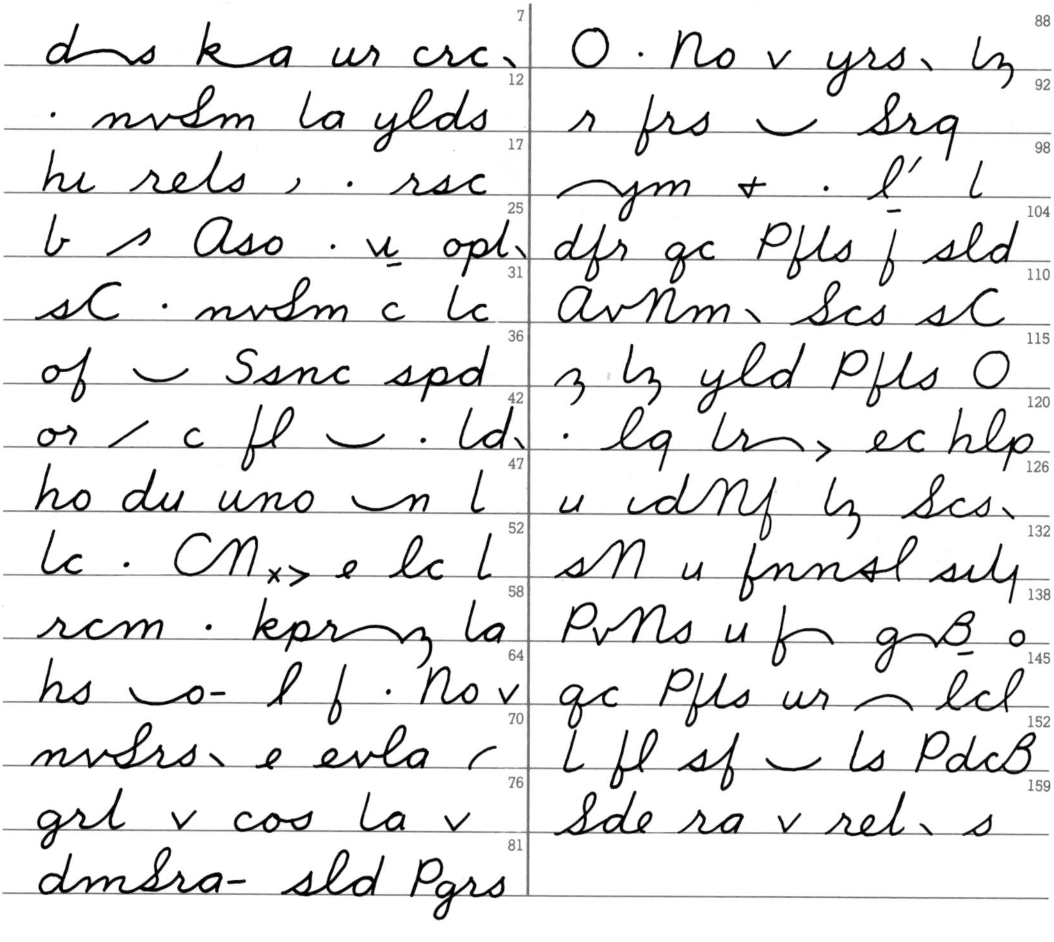

Key

1

Dear Investor:

Is this a good time to buy stocks for future growth? The answer is yes. When you invest, you should locate[1] stocks that will yield a reasonable profit over a long period of time. We can suggest some fine examples[2] of leadership companies that are now available on the stock exchange.

The attached chart shows what has[3] happened to common stocks in the recent past. Of course, we cannot expect the same trends to continue. That is where[4] our specialists will be of help to you.

In order to be reliable, a broker must be a trained expert.[5] He or she should always be available to advise you about when to sell, buy, trade, or hold. Our brokers will[6] provide that counsel.

For many of our customers, common stocks make common sense. Why not call us today?

Very[7] truly yours, (142)

2

Dear Mr. Gregory:

There are many reasons for trusting us with your financial security. In addition[1] to the protection that we are required to give you by law, we can now insure your account for an additional[2] $250,000. We also carry millions of dollars of protection against the loss[3] of securities by fire, theft, or natural disaster.

You get all this protection along with the[4] personalized service and professional advice that we have been offering for almost 100 years. Call and[5] ask to speak to one of our counselors. We will be glad to help you outline an investment plan that is practical[6] for you.

Cordially yours, (125)

3

Dear Ms. Christopher:

Knowing how much to save and when to invest can be very difficult for most people. During[1] this time of economic uncertainty, financial planning is particularly confusing. One thing[2] is certain, however. If you are to have a better future, saving and investing are essential.

How do[3] you arrive at a reasonable balance between safety and return on your dollars? Our firm is here to help[4] you make the right decisions. We provide guidelines that provide security while also allowing for a[5] considerable profit.

To help you get started, we are conducting a series of classes in finance. The[6] enclosed brochure contains all the information you need to enroll. Won't you take this important step today?

Yours[7] truly, (141)

4

Dear Mr. and Mrs. Bishop:

Welcome to our family of shareholders. Because we want to keep you fully[1] informed about the company's status, we are enclosing literature that describes our activities from[2] the past year.

Included in this packet is a copy of our latest report. If you would like to receive copies[3] of past reports, we will gladly send them to you upon request.

When you are in the vicinity of our[4] plant, we invite you to visit our modern facilities. It is fascinating to see the electronic[5] equipment and computerized methods now in operation. Our public relations department gives guided[6] tours daily through the plant.

The outlook for our business is very bright, and we anticipate that this will be an[7] equally profitable year.

Cordially yours, (149)

5

Dear Ms. Conway:

You are correct. An investment that yields high returns is a risk, but it is also an exciting[1] opportunity. Such an investment can take off with supersonic speed, or it can fall with a thud. How[2] do you know when to take a chance?

We like to recommend a compromise that has worked well for a number of[3] investors. We evaluate the growth of companies that have demonstrated solid progress over a number[4] of years. These are firms with strong management and a willingness to defer quick profits for solid advancement. Stocks[5] such as these yield profits over a long term.

We can help you identify these stocks. Since your financial[6] situation prevents you from gambling on quick profits, you are more likely to feel safe with this predictable,[7] steady rate of return.

Sincerely, (146)

LESSON 27

Abbreviations and Derivatives

1. blvd corp $ gvt sec
2. S E S est- hdqtrs aves

Key

1. boulevard, corporation, dollar/dollars, government, second/secretary
2. street, east, south, established, headquarters, avenues

Transcription Aids: The Time of Day

When typing the message of a business letter, use the following guidelines:

1. When typing an even hour followed by the word *o'clock,* you may either spell out the word or use the figure.

   The meeting will begin promptly at 2 o'clock.

2. When showing the exact hour and minutes, use figures and a colon.

   Your appointment is scheduled for 3:15.

3. Use figures with *a.m.* and *p.m.* Never use *a.m.* with *morning* or *p.m.* with *afternoon.* Never use *o'clock* with *a.m.* or *p.m.*

   8 o'clock in the morning or 8 a.m.

   half past three in the afternoon or 3:30 p.m.

4. Noon and midnight may be shown this way:

   12 noon   12 midnight

5. Morning begins after 12 midnight; afternoon begins after 12 noon; evening begins after 6 p.m.

   You may pick up your delivery after 3 o'clock in the afternoon.

   The plane is scheduled to arrive at 12:01 p.m.

6. If a.m., p.m., or o'clock is not used, spell out the hour.

   The meeting begins at seven tonight.

Your Business Vocabulary

capital gains — Profit from the sale of capital assets (holdings such as real estate or stock).

cpll gns

There is an additional tax assessed on all capital gains.

affiliate aflel — An associate having lesser authority; a subsidiary.

The Sunshine Company is now an affiliate of ours.

underwriters Urirs — Agents who assume financial responsibility for a given expense.

The underwriters have agreed to the terms in the contract.

consolidating loans — Combining several loans into one.

kslda lns

There could be a financial advantage in consolidating loans.

Reading and Writing Exercises

——————————————— 1 ———————————————

Preview Words

top _Lp_

automotive _atᴍv_

heritage _hrly_

dependability _dpNBˡ_

reputation _rply_

headquarters _hdqlrs_

innovation _nvᵧ_

craftsmanship _crflsms⁴_

d ᴗr + ᴗᴗrs brnr es
prod l ᴗl u a ᴗq
r nu srhldrs.
eap ᴗ kfdN uv
⌐sn n s b nvᵟ
n r co, enc-ᴗ.
brf hᵟre vr co, es
prod vr hrly (Conj)_ + es_
jᵟ ᴈ prod v kbᵧ
ev ᴗd l ᴗ atᴍv
N, sN Nds r frᵟ
Pdc ᴗ ln 70 yrs
_aq_ (Intro P)_ ev est- , rply_
f nvᵧ + dpNBˡ,

Alo la frᵟ nyn
ᴈ v dfrN f ᴗ
⌐snre no b ᴗf- (Intro DC)
ᴗ rflc- ᴗ rSC
+ fn crflsms⁴ la
d ern s Lp bl n
_, ᴗo ᴗr, e lk u_
ᴈ plnrs nr grl
+ dvm vr corp,
ᴗn ur n ls ara (Intro DC)_-_
_p ᴗ⌐c ᴗ , py_
lvᴈl r hdqlrs,
_ur no , pl v s,_
vlu

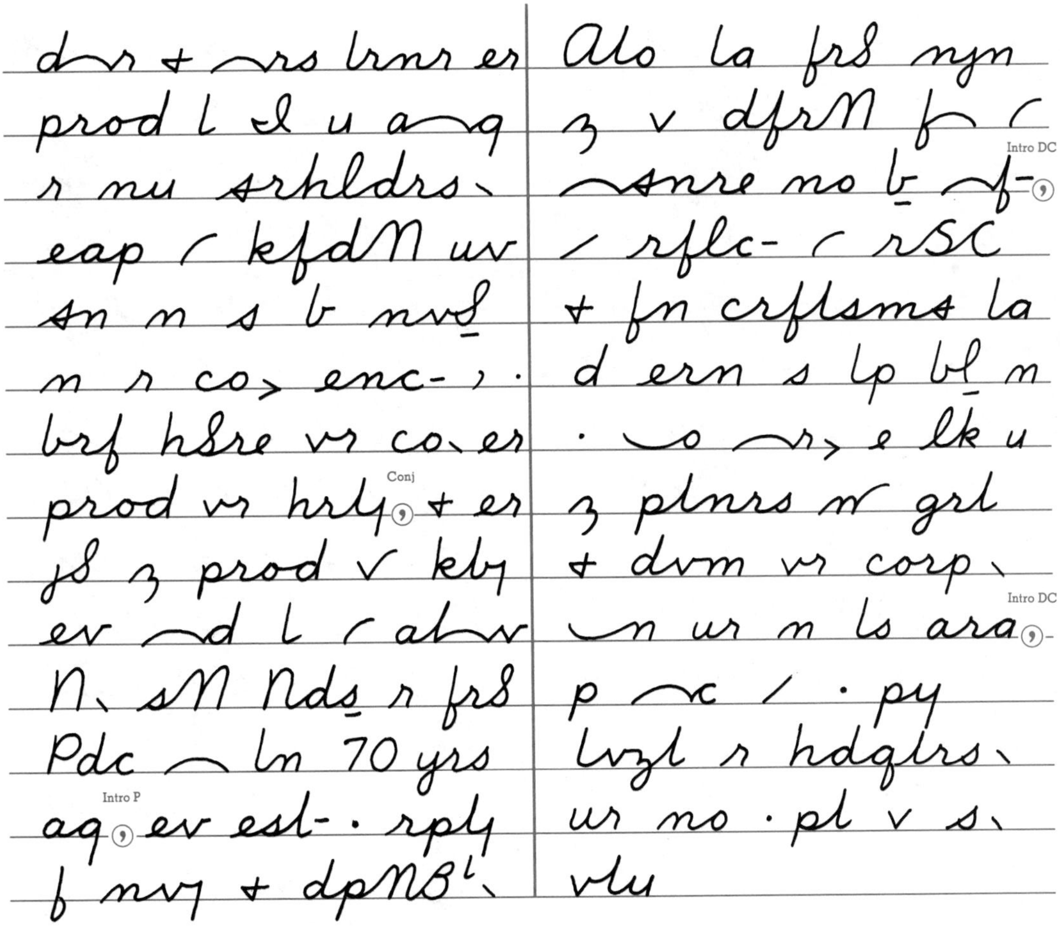

2

Preview Words

Paris prs
foreign fn
summary s-re
overseas Oses
affiliate aflel
primary pr-re
underwriters Urirs
consolidating kslda

d ly- n alC
. mo rln b (
drr vr Nnyl dvj,
/ klns . brf s-re
vr Sd aks + rsN
Tacjs - bqs la r
lca- Oses, z uc
se f- (rpl, r (Intro DC)
bq aflel n prs ,
1 v -S acv Urirs
v fn crNe nr -o,
Ph esd ks kslda
r fn lns + -c

ls bq r pr-re
ajN, p rd (mo
+ gv -e u racjs
l (rcmys olln-
o pj 4, s l-
l-c . dsj re
fCr NSs, (Conj) + idlc
l Dcs sv idas
- u bf e alN (
-e la hsb scyl-
f 10° o Tu, ulb
-S egr lvu rpl,
s

3

Preview Words

fiscal	fscl	stability	SBl
assets	asls	capital gains	cpll gns
abroad	abrd	expansion	vpnj
obvious	obves	Western Europe	Wrnurp

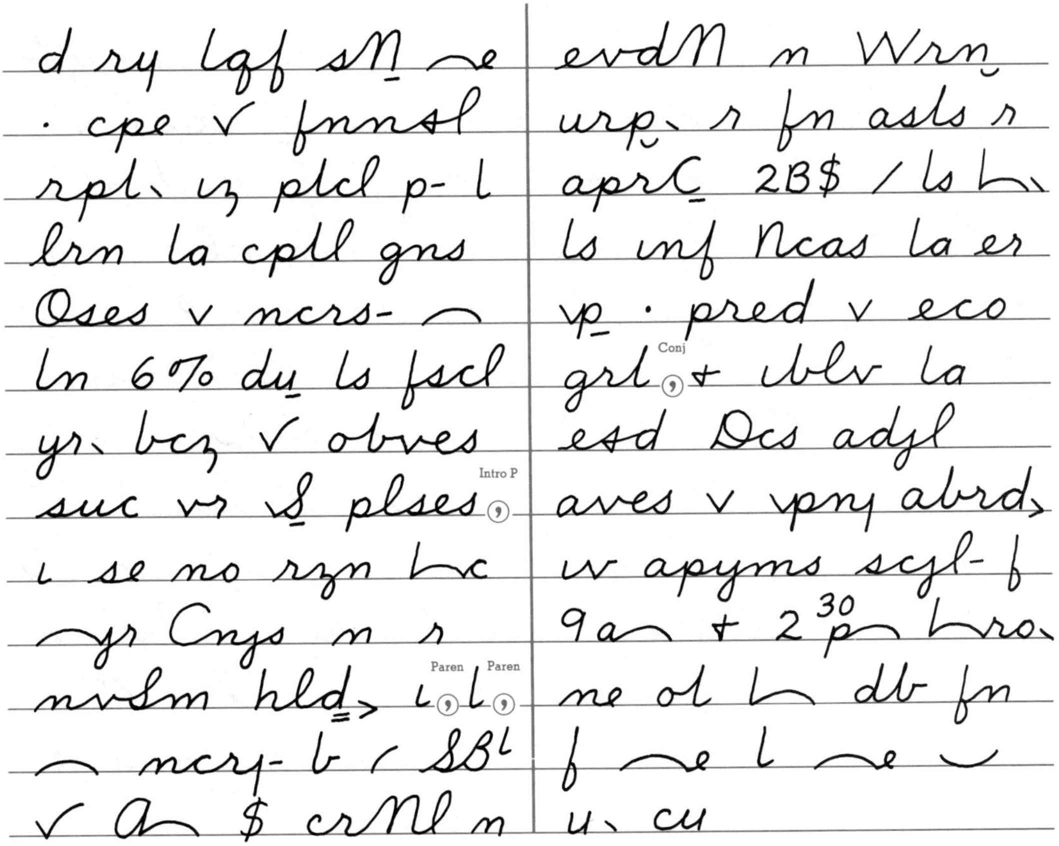

4

Preview Words

bond	bN	reminders	rmrs
sessions	sjs	practices	prclss
lectures	lcCrs	exceptional	vpyl
potential	plnsl	reinvestment	rnvSm

mo l bl ~cls
w asc- la rmrs
b sN l a vr
cliNs re (srz
v lcCrs bgn n
Oc. lz sjs l dl
spl ⌣ Psnl fnN, (Conj)
+ ly l cvr . brd
rny v nvSms.
lpcs l d rscs
+ bnfls, (Series) sv + ln
prclss, (Series) Sc opjs, (Series)
ins plns, (Series) + fCr

bN ylds, zu rqS-, (Intro DC)
n enc cpes v
Ppzl f r dvdN
rnvSm pln. ur
gu ru ab s plnsl.
ls , . lN opl l
so r mbrs la ly
c rnvS dvdNs n
co Sc ⌣ol pa fes
l brcrs, ublv la
me ppl l ⌣N l
lc avj v ls vpyl
opl.

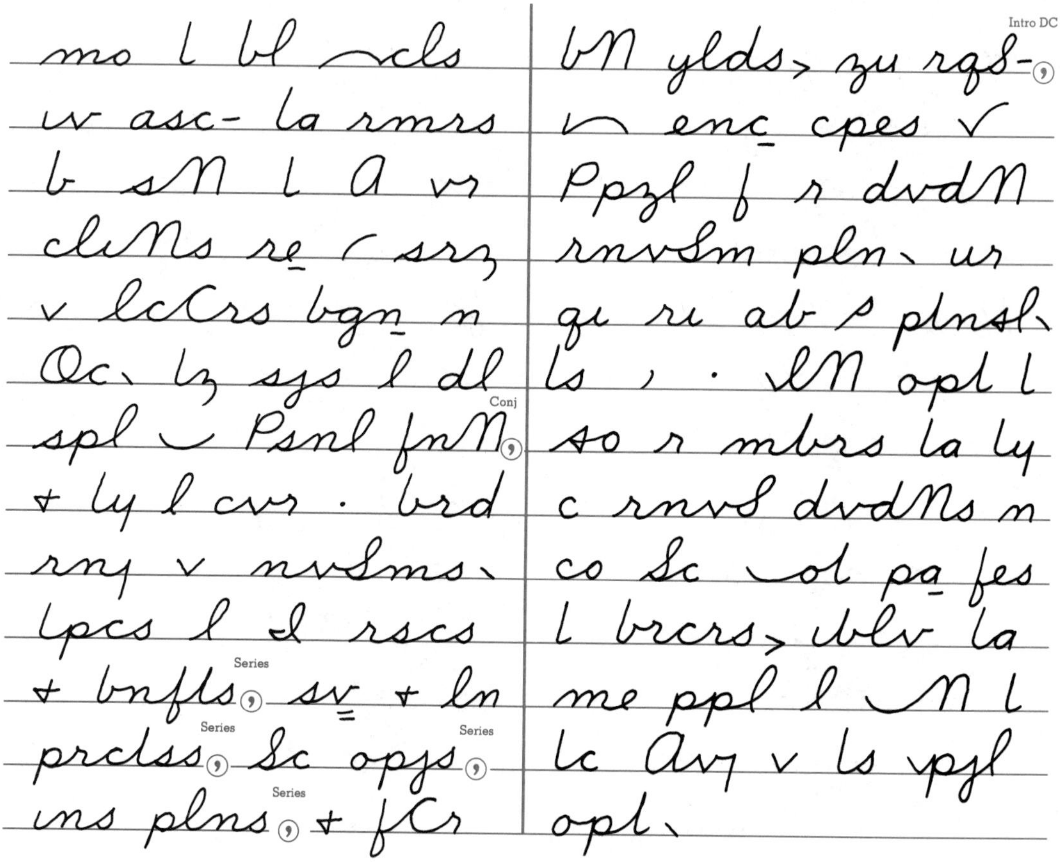

5

Punctuation Study

Add commas to show one parenthetical expression, one introductory phrase, and two introductory dependent clauses.

Preview Words

refer *rf*

enroll *nrl*

toward *lw*

dividends *dvdNs*

guidelines *gdlns*

eligibility *eljßL*

registration *ryßry*

authorization *alrzy*

ddr cx lqfL v
Mr 7, erp- la uv
Nca- · NS n r cos
rnvSm pln, Stnl
ls, · lN L l
apli u dvdNs
lw r PCs v adjl
srs, ldl u eljßL
p rf L r enc-
gdlns, if u Sl
s L pp nr pln

p sN s r m
t ryßry No ls-
ou Sc Slfcl, el
sN u · alrzy f
zz e rsv r inf
ls- abv, oN uv
kp- t rel- r f
l s elb ß l nrl
u nr pln, lqu aq
fu NS n r co, su

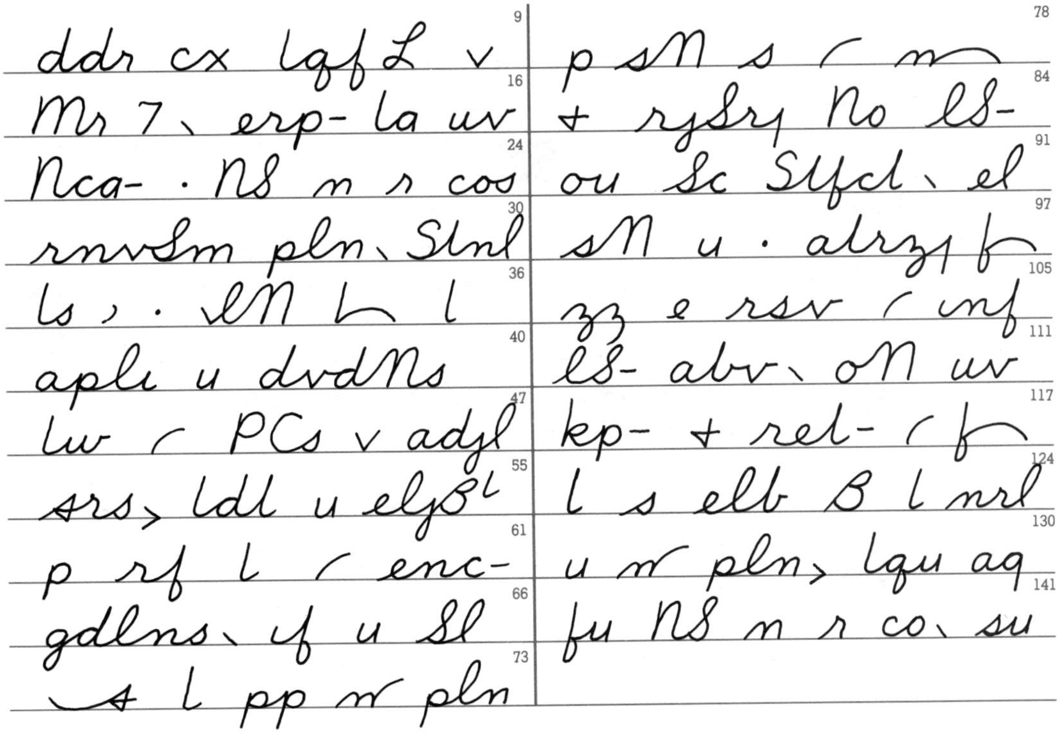

Key

1

Dear Mr. and Mrs. Turner:

We are proud to include you among our new shareholders. We appreciate the[1] confidence you have shown in us by investing in our company.

Enclosed is a brief history of our[2] company. We are proud of our heritage, and we are just as proud of the contribution we have made to the[3] automotive industry. Since introducing our first product more than 70 years ago, we have established[4] a reputation for innovation and dependability. Although that first engine was very different[5] from the machinery now being manufactured, it reflected the research and fine craftsmanship that would[6] earn us top billing in a world market.

We welcome you as partners in the growth and development of our[7] corporation. When you are in this area, please make it a point to visit our headquarters. You are now a part[8] of us.

Very truly yours, (165)

2

Dear William:

I am attaching a memo written by the director of our international division.[1] It contains a brief summary of our existing accounts and recent transactions with banks that are located[2] overseas. As you can see from the report, our banking affiliate in Paris is one of the most active[3] underwriters of foreign currency in the world. Perhaps we should consider consolidating our foreign[4] loans and making this bank our primary agent.

Please read the memo and give me your reactions to the[5] recommendations outlined on page 4. It is time to make a decision regarding future interests, and[6] I would like to discuss several ideas with you before we attend the meeting that has been scheduled for[7] 10 o'clock on Tuesday.

I will be most eager to have your reply.

Sincerely, (153)

3

Dear Roy:

Thank you for sending me a copy of the financial report. I was particularly pleased to learn[1] that capital gains overseas have increased more than 6 percent during this fiscal year. Because of the obvious[2] success of our existing policies, I see no reason to make major changes in our investment holdings.[3]

I, too, am encouraged by the stability of the American dollar currently in evidence[4] in Western Europe. Our foreign assets are approaching $2 billion at this time. This information[5] indicates that we are experiencing a period of economic growth, and I believe that we should[6] discuss additional avenues of expansion abroad.

I have appointments scheduled for 9 a.m. and[7] 2:30 p.m. tomorrow. Any other time would be fine for me to meet with you.

Cordially yours, (157)

4

MEMO TO: Bill Michaels

I have asked that reminders be sent to all of our clients regarding the series of[1] lectures beginning in October. These sessions will deal specifically with personal finance, and they will cover[2] a broad range of investments. Topics will include risks and benefits, savings and loan practices, stock options,[3] insurance plans, and future bond yields.

As you requested, I am enclosing copies of the proposal for our[4] dividend reinvestment plan. You are quite right about its potential. This is an excellent opportunity[5] to show our members that they can reinvest dividends in company stock without paying fees to brokers.[6]

I believe that many people will want to take advantage of this exceptional opportunity. (139)

5

Dear Dr. Cox:

Thank you for your letter of March 7. We are pleased that you have indicated an interest[1] in our company's reinvestment plan. Certainly, this is an excellent time to apply your dividends toward[2] the purchase of additional shares.

To determine your eligibility, please refer to the enclosed[3] guidelines. If you still wish to participate in the plan, please send us the name and registration number listed[4] on your stock certificate. We will send you an authorization form as soon as we receive the information[5] listed above. Once you have completed and returned the form to us, we will be able to enroll you in the[6] plan.

Thank you again for your interest in our company.

Sincerely yours, (134)

LESSON 28

Shorthand Vocabulary Review

Write *a* for the initial and final sound of *aw*.

audit	adl	law	la
authentic	alNc	draw	dra
audience	adeN	saw	sa
awful	af	lawful	laf

Transcription Aids: Similar Words

ensure  To make certain of.

I will make the arrangements myself to ensure that the shipment leaves here on time.

insure  To contract for protection against specified types of losses in return for premiums paid.

I wish to insure every member of my family.

Your Business Vocabulary

tariff trf — A tax imposed by government on imported or exported goods.

A new tariff will be placed on all grain sold abroad.

securities  In reference to stocks and bonds, documents proving ownership, such as stock certificates.

A safe-deposit box will protect your securities from fire or loss.

Reading and Writing Exercises

1

Preview Words

- tariffs
- normal
- imports
- express
- fabrics
- combine
- raw wool
- natural fibers

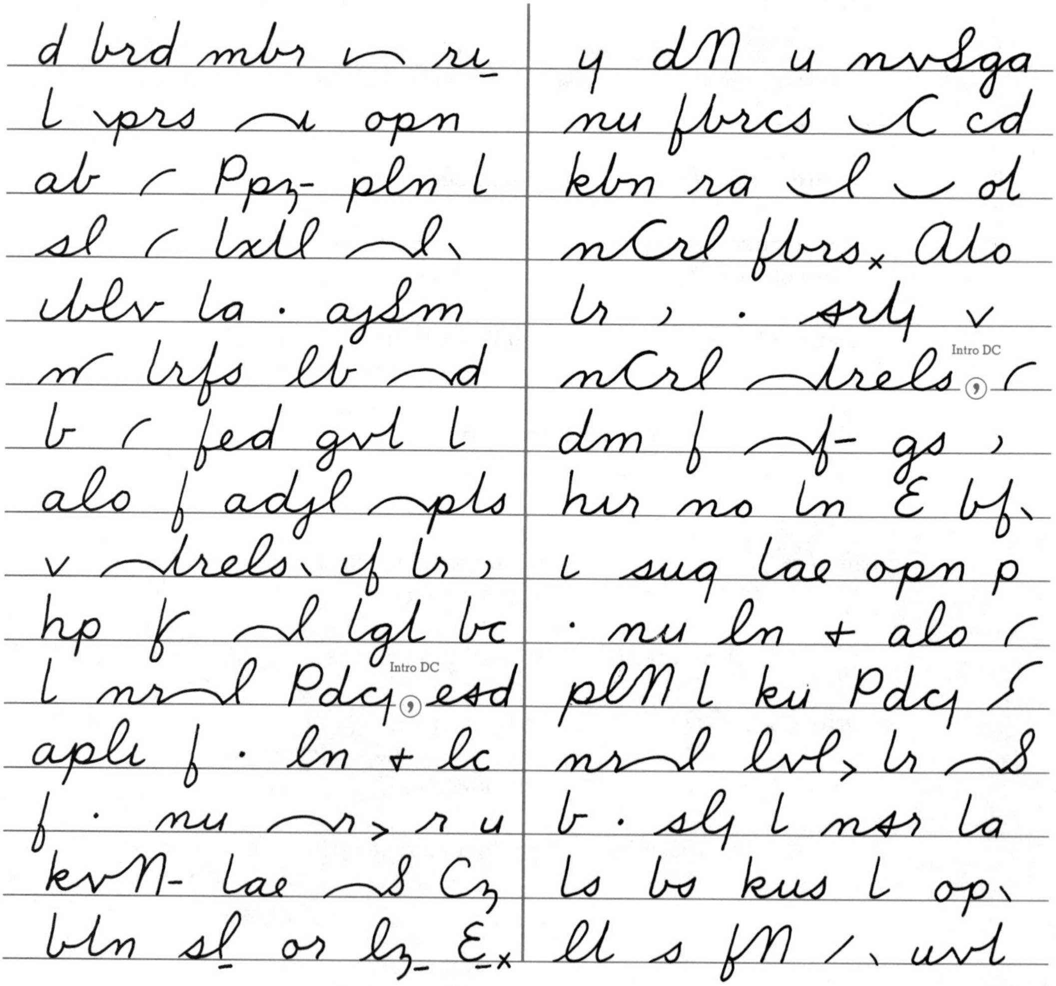

2

Preview Words

Exchange	√Cnj	encounter	nkr
Investors	nvSrs	Washington	WA
Kingston	cgSn	transferring	Tfr
ownership	or4	authenticate	alNca

dr cgSn ls , n
rsp lu nqe ab
Tfr (or4 v Scs
f 1 Nv l aol, (
Pss v Cnj . Ul ,
frl s-pl, usd
frS kp (f la ,
P- 6 rvrs sd v
scr's, b 4r l fl
n A (inf rqS-,
u -S ln asc .
ofsr v . bq l
alNca u siq, lr
, . s-l fe aso-
- (Tfr v eC

4r v Sc > fw (
Slfcls, (NRC) -C vb
ndrs- b (bq
ofsr, (NRC) alq - (
Tfr fe, p l . L
v nSrcj, -l bz
-lrels l -u all
/ nvSrs √Cnj /
300 WA blvd, p
sN ls b rjSr-
-l, nu scr's lb
rel- lu -n 2 -cs, (Intro DC)
if u nkr ne dfces,
p cl -e Psnll,
vlu

3

Preview Words

audits	adls	audience	adeN
timely	l⌒l	refreshing	rfrŧ̲
remarks	r⌒rcs	informative	nf⌒v
aspects	aspcs	stimulating	S⌒la̲

d⌒s hlfld lqf dl̲
sC · nŝ + nf⌒v
spC、 icd ezl se
la (ol nvSrs
nyy- u r⌒rcs z
⌒C zi dd、 z uz, Paren
u idas ⌣ S⌒la̲ +
rfrŧ̲、 / eze lse
y so me ppl nyy
hr̲ u lc, (adeN
lsn-crfl lu Avs、 u
P- s⌒ lN sugjs
o ho l kdc adls、
me v s lv sC

⌒lrs l r ak̲ dpls, Conj
b / l⌒ e ac-Sln
aspcs v la rspBl
f rsvs, i sa me
ppl lc̲ nls du̲ (
evn̲、 ⌒ ŧr la
(sls vu nu bc
l rflc (suc vu
idas、 uv r snss
lqs f · spC la z
l⌒l + usf、 ihp
ulb B l jyn s
aq nx yr、 ul

4

Preview Words

legal lgl
expect vpc
cannot cn
Westport Wpl
reimburse rbrs
expenses vpNs
connected kc-
successfully sucfl

ddr gra er v NS-
n crs ur ofr /
Wpl jr clj acrd l
r Avm n nzppr, Intro P
r sjc v crs lb lgl
gdlns f nvSms
+ scrls, bcz sv
las vb ps-rsNl, Intro DC
ls crs aprs l e
· rl nd n r knl>
ev · lry Sf hu d
bnfl f sC · crs, Conj
+ ru l asc if
ucd akda p l 20

ppl, s r plse l
rbrs pes f A
vpNs kc- clj
crss la r sucfl
kp-, lrf, ed vpc Paren
S pes l lc
Avj v ls opl>
if u fN la ucn
nrl A vr pes
n cls, d u ks Intro DC
opn · sec cls?
idb gld l e
u ne l Dcs
ls v psBl, vlu

5

Punctuation Study

Add commas to show two introductory dependent clauses, one conjunction, and one introductory phrase.

Preview Words

top	Lp	predict	Pdc
status	Sls	restricted	rSrc-
varied	vre-	presently	Pl
neither	nlr	alternatives	alrnvs

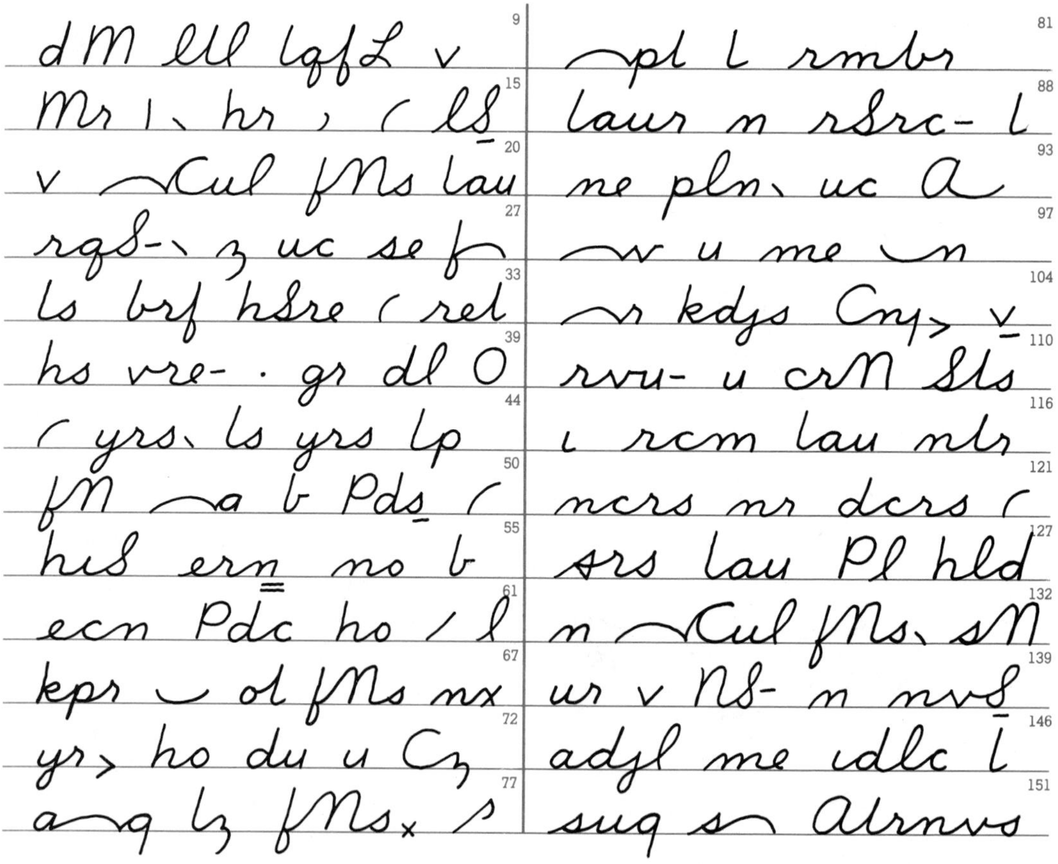

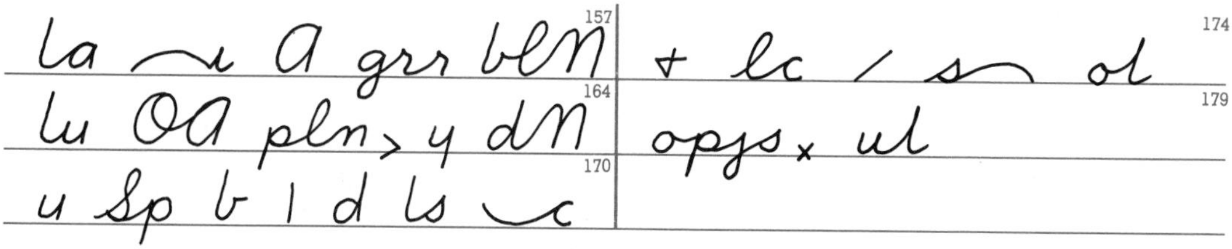

Key

1

Dear Board Member:

I am writing to express my opinion about the proposed plan to sell the textile mill. I[1] believe that an adjustment in the tariffs will be made by the federal government to allow for additional[2] imports of materials. If there is hope for the mill to get back to normal production, we should apply[3] for a loan and look for a new market.

Are you convinced that we must choose between selling or losing everything?[4] Why don't you investigate new fabrics which could combine raw wool with other natural fibers? Although there[5] is a shortage of natural materials, the demand for manufactured goods is higher now than ever[6] before. I suggest that we open up a new line and allow the plant to continue production at the[7] normal level.

There must be a solution to ensure that this business continues to operate. Let us find it.[8]

Yours very truly, (164)

2

Dear Mr. Kingston:

This is in response to your inquiry about transferring the ownership of stocks from one[1] individual to another.

The process of changing a title is fairly simple. You should first complete[2] the form that is presented on the reverse side of the security. Be sure to fill in all the information[3] requested. You must then ask an officer of a bank to authenticate your signature. There is a small[4] fee associated with the transfer of each share of stock.

Forward the certificates, which have been endorsed by[5] the bank officer, along with the transfer fee. Please include a letter of instruction. Mail these materials[6] to my attention at Investors Exchange at 300 Washington Boulevard. Please send this by registered[7] mail. New securities will be returned to you within two weeks.

If you encounter any difficulties, please[8] call me personally.

Very truly yours, (168)

3

Dear Ms. Hatfield:

Thank you for delivering such an interesting and informative speech. I could easily[1] see that the other investors enjoyed your remarks as much as I did. As usual, your ideas were[2] stimulating and refreshing. It is easy to see why so many people enjoy hearing you talk.

The[3] audience listened carefully to your advice. You presented some excellent suggestions on how to conduct[4] audits. Many of us leave such matters to our accounting departments, but it is time we accepted certain[5] aspects of that responsibility for ourselves.

I saw many people taking notes during the evening. I am[6] sure that the sales of your new book will reflect the success of your ideas. You have our sincere thanks for a speech that[7] was timely and useful. I hope you will be able to join us again next year.

Yours truly, (156)

4

Dear Dr. Gray:

We are very interested in the course you are offering at Westport Junior College.[1] According to the advertisement in the newspaper, the subject of the course will be legal guidelines for[2] investments and securities. Because several laws have been passed recently, this course appears to meet a real need[3] in our community.

We have a large staff who would benefit from such a course, and I am writing to ask if you[4] could accommodate up to 20 people. It is our policy to reimburse employees for all expenses[5] connected with college courses that are successfully completed. Therefore, we would expect most employees[6] to take advantage of this opportunity.

If you find that you cannot enroll all of our employees in[7] the class, would you consider opening a second class? I would be glad to meet with you any time to discuss[8] this exciting possibility.

Very truly yours, (170)

5

Dear Miss Little:

Thank you for your letter of March 1. Here is the listing of mutual funds that you requested.[1] As you can see from this brief history, the return has varied a great deal over the years. This year's top fund may[2] be producing the highest earnings now, but we cannot predict how it will compare with other funds next year.[3]

How do you choose among these funds? It is important to remember that you are not restricted to any plan.[4] You can always move your money when market conditions change.

Having reviewed your current status, I recommend[5] that you neither increase nor decrease the shares that you presently hold in mutual funds. Since you are very[6] interested in investing additional money, I would like to suggest some alternatives that might add[7] greater balance to your overall plan.

Why don't you stop by one day this week and look at some other options?

Yours[8] truly, (161)

LESSON 29

Shorthand Vocabulary Review

Write  for the sound of *zh*.

leisure	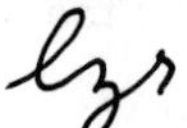	measure	
treasury	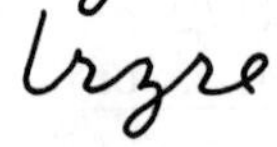	pleasure	
exposure	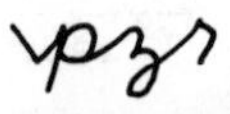	casual	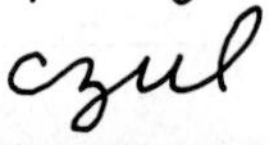

Transcription Aids: Spelling

In general, omit the final *e* of the root word before adding a word ending that begins with a vowel.

approve		approval	
dispose	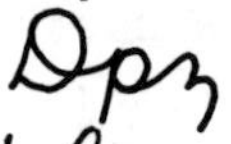	disposal	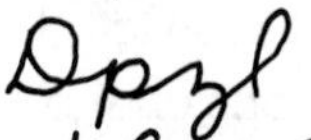
believe		believable	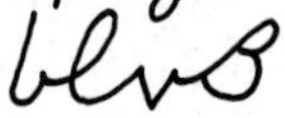
response		responsible	
assure		assurance	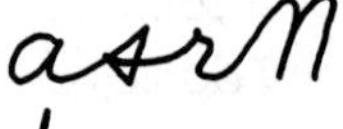
desire		desirous	

Your Business Vocabulary

subject to change — Is likely to change; a condition of possible change exists.

sjc l Cnj

Flight schedules are subject to change.

accessible vsB — Easily approached or obtained.

By moving the master files, we will make them more accessible to everyone.

subsequently ssqNl — Following in time or in sequence of events.

The contract was signed, and the press was subsequently notified.

Reading and Writing Exercises

———————————— 1 ————————————

Preview Words

switch   *s⌣C*

another   *aol*

avenues   *aves*

certificates   *Slfcls*

together   *lglr*

committed   *kl-*

describes   *dSs*

unfortunate   *ufCnl*

dr rbrls lqf L rgs inf ab rlrm plns, (enc- brsr dSs s ⌣ √ me opjs avlB lu, (ufCnl f ppl L bk kl- L 1 nvSm pln, if ur lr fnnsl scrl du u rlrm⊙ und lr sv aves v nk, edb hpe L nvS u fNs n ne

No v Scs⊙ Slfcls⊙ lrzre bls⊙ + √ul fNs, oN ev u apvl⊙ ec s⌣C u fNs f 1 nvSm L aol L obln (bS yld fu, i rcm lae sl don + vplr lz idas lglr, lr r me ⌣as lrc u me ⌣o fu, su

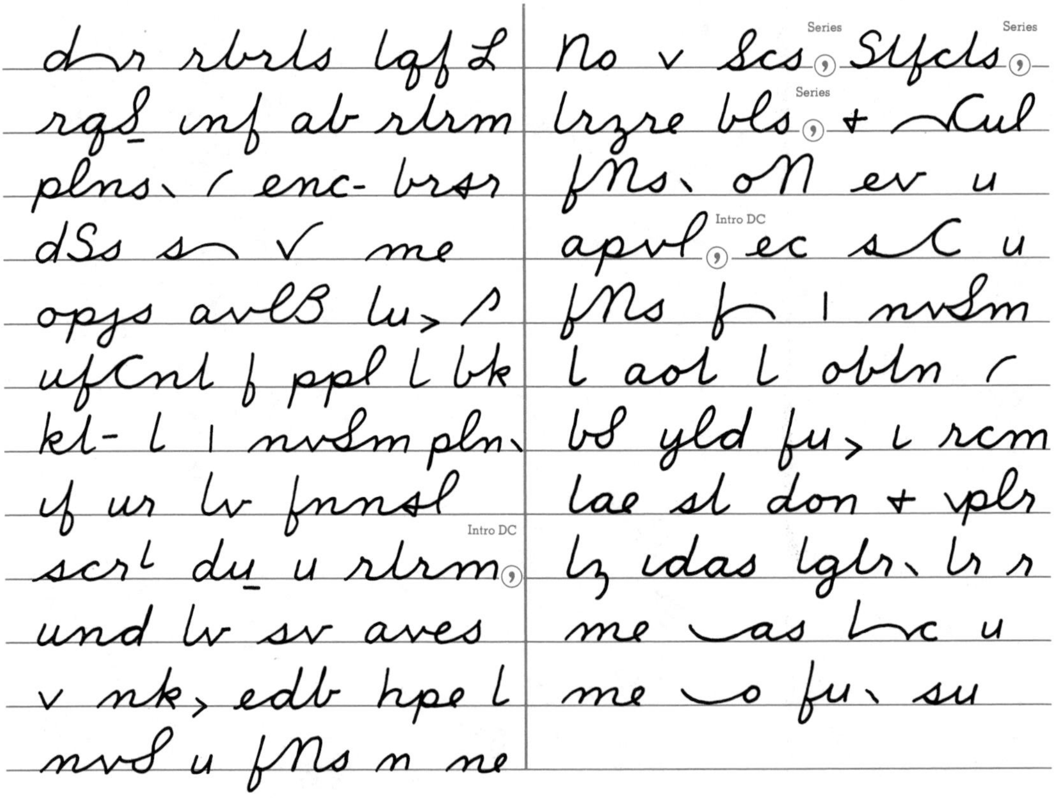

2

Preview Words

host	hS	unstable	uSB
risks	rscs	constantly	kSNl
least	lS	altogether	Algtr
foreign	fn	director	drr

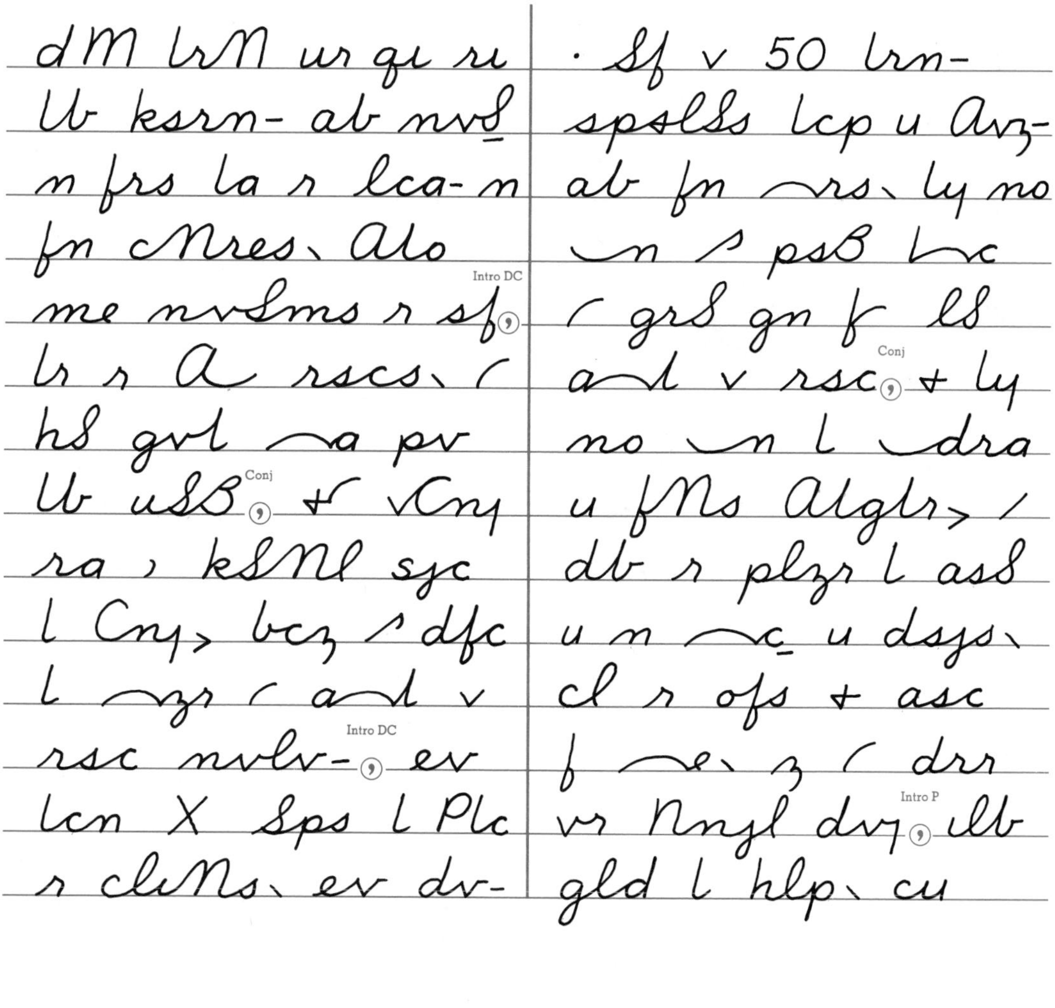

3

Preview Words

urge urj

annual aul

Royal ryl

promptly P-ll

absence absN

nominations nmys

subsequently ssqNl

instructions nSrcys

dr -rsl erp-
l lk u z . nu
Schldr v a-
elncs, (aul
-e v Schldrs
lb hld (ryl
hll n dnvr o
Ma 7, lnC lb
Sv- / 12 30 Conj +.
rvu v yrs acvls
l bgn P-ll / 1o>
lw (N v ls -e Intro P
5 nu drrs lb elc-,
nmys r pc- lb
-d f (flr Conj + .
vo lb lcn ssqNl>

f u pln l alN
(-e Intro DC p -c .
rzrvj acrd l (
rglys sn o alC-
pj, f edu n rsv
vo nSrcys f u Intro DC -
u absN lb ks-z
. vo f adpj v a
Ppzls n agrem -
co -ym> (enc-
rpl plns (sus
lb Dcs- (aul
-e, e urj u l
jyn s n pln f
fCr, vlu

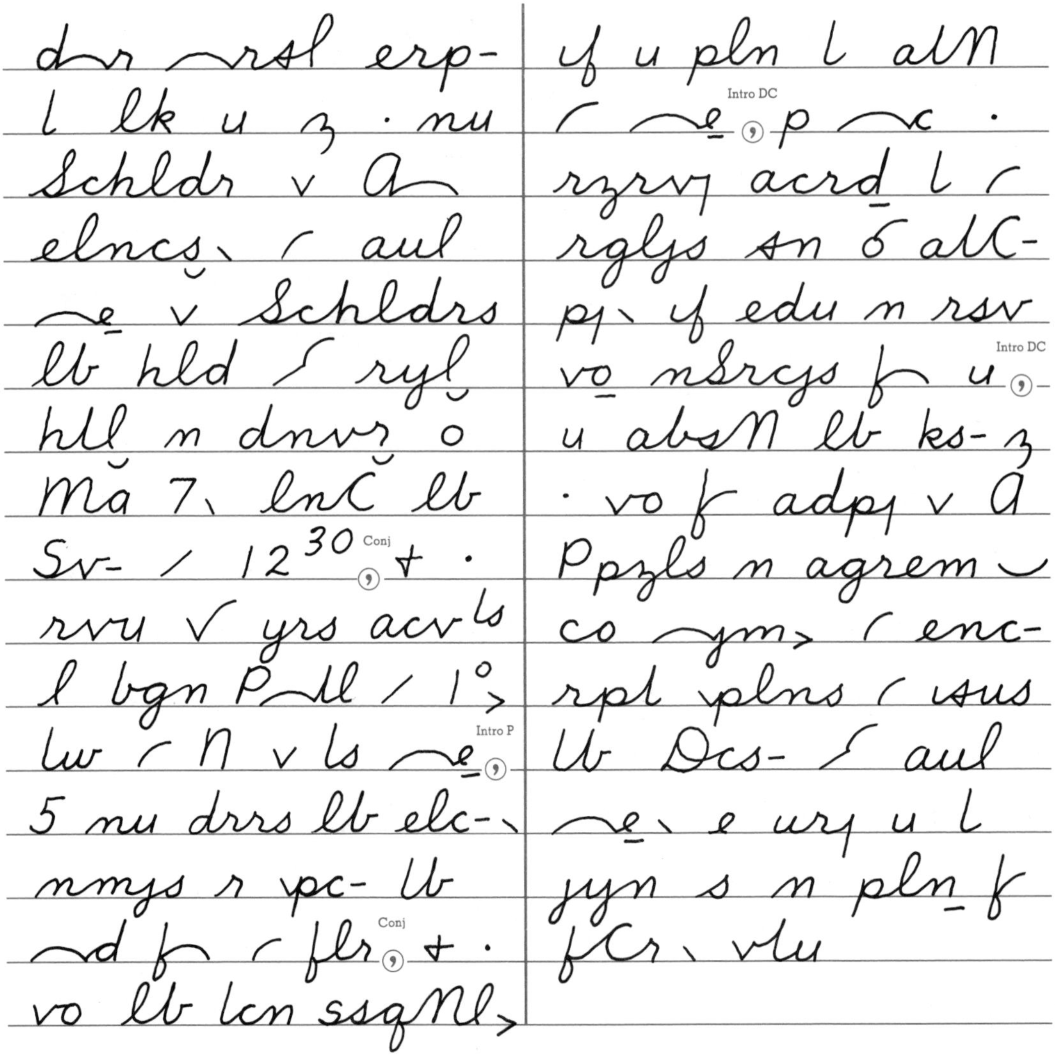

4

Preview Words

respect	*rspc*	accessible	*sB*
researches	*rSCs*	thoroughly	*trol*
attentive	*alnv*	disposition	*Dpzt*
cheerful	*Crf*	greater	*grs*

---

d—r sMrs idlc
l rcm . fnnsl
Avzr fu fr. —s
jnt le hs —o-
— s f — ln 4
yrs. ic asr u la
hr nly , crM₍₉₎ tro₍₉₎—
+ rliB, se hs ern-
r rspc v hr cliMs.
me v — v kM-
la se rSCs opts
v trol bf rcm —
l hr cliMs. ly Aso

rpt la se , alnv
l A v hr aks. evn
o v srt nts₍₉₎ se
, uzl sB l El
se Svs, / hsb
. plzr tv hr —o
f s. el M hr Crf
Dpzt zlz hr Pfjl
nly v —r kdjs,
if u fl la und
grs asrM re hr
glfjs₍₉₎ p tc — —e
Psnll. ut

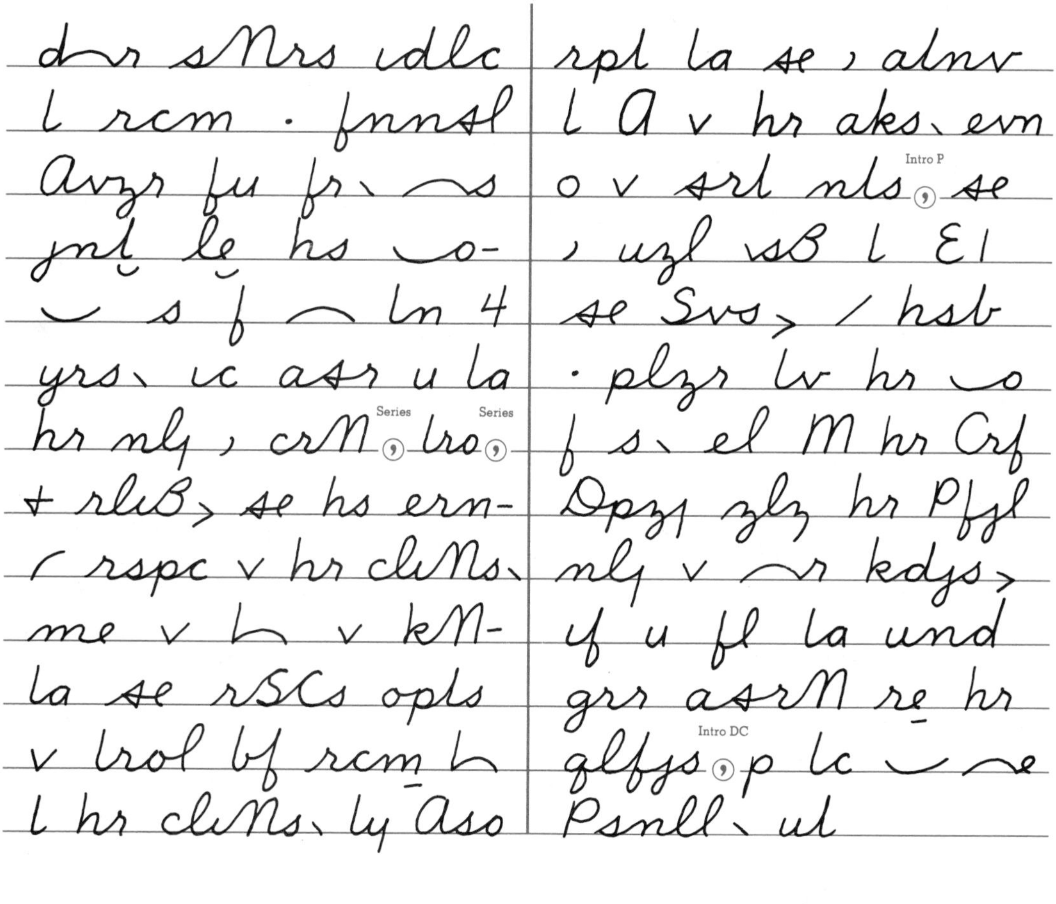

5

Punctuation Study

Add commas to show one appositive, one conjunction, and two introductory phrases.

Preview Words

into	nl	support	spl
energy	nrje	insights	nsis
nearly	nrl	mentioned	mj-
former	fr	foundation	foNj

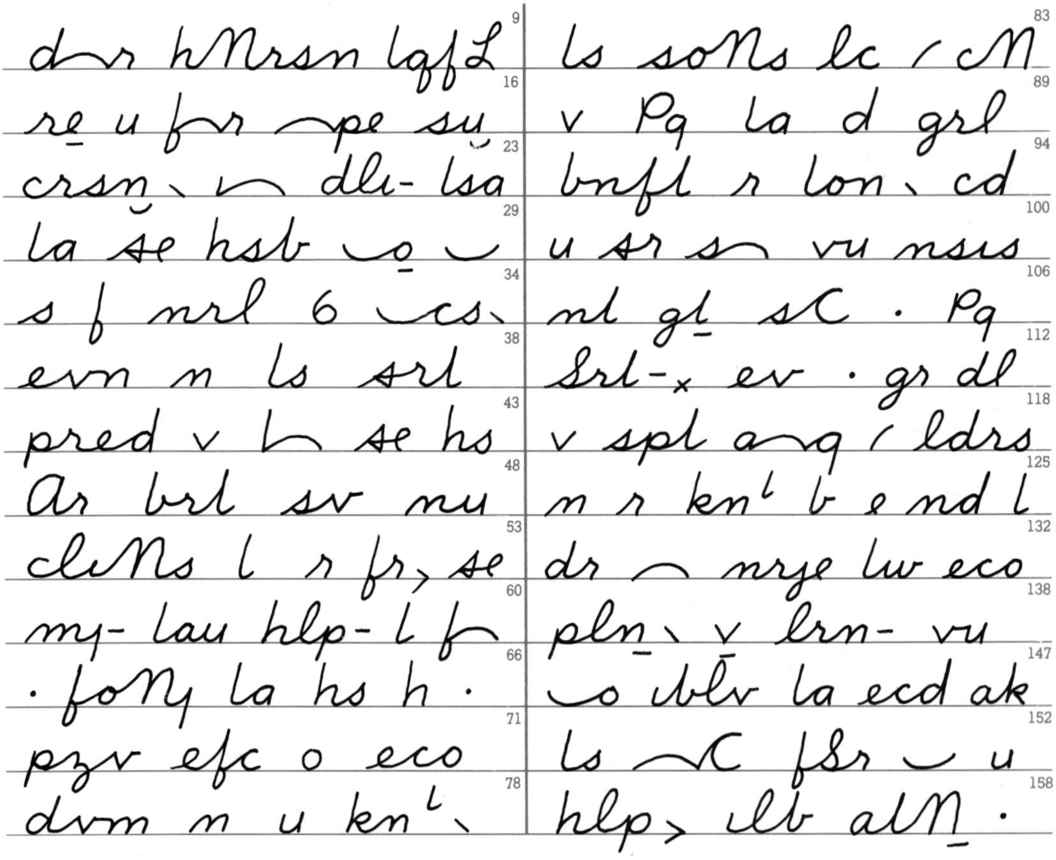

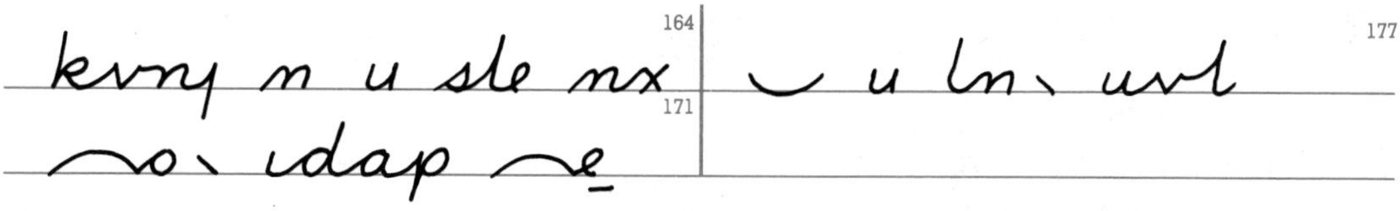

Key

1

Dear Mr. Roberts:

Thank you for your letter requesting information about retirement plans. The enclosed[1] brochure describes some of the many options available to you.

It is unfortunate for people to become[2] committed to one investment plan. If you are to have financial security during your retirement, you[3] need to have several avenues of income.

We would be happy to invest your funds in any number of[4] stocks, certificates, treasury bills, and mutual funds. Once we have your approval, we can switch your funds from one[5] investment to another to obtain the best yield for you.

I recommend that we sit down and explore these[6] ideas together. There are many ways to make your money work for you.

Sincerely yours, (136)

2

Dear Miss Trent:

You are quite right to be concerned about investing in firms that are located in foreign countries.[1] Although many investments are safe, there are always risks. The host government may prove to be unstable, and the[2] exchange rate is constantly subject to change.

Because it is difficult to measure the amount of risk involved,[3] we have taken extra steps to protect our clients. We have developed a staff of 50 trained specialists to keep[4] you advised about foreign markets. They know when it is possible to make the greatest gain for the least amount[5] of risk, and they know when to withdraw your funds altogether.

It would be our pleasure to assist you in making[6] your decisions. Call our office and ask for me. As the director of our international division,[7] I will be glad to help.

Cordially yours, (147)

3

Dear Mr. Marshall:

We are pleased to welcome you as a new stockholder of American Electronics. The[1] annual meeting of stockholders will be held at the Royal Hotel in Denver on May 7. Lunch will be[2] served at 12:30, and a review of the year's activities will begin promptly at 1 o'clock.

Toward the[3] end of this meeting, five new directors will be elected. Nominations are expected to be made from the[4] floor, and a vote will be taken subsequently.

If you plan to attend the meeting, please make a reservation[5] according to the regulations shown on the attached page. If we do not receive voting instructions from you,[6] your absence will be considered as a vote for the adoption of all proposals in agreement with company[7] management.

The enclosed report explains the issues to be discussed at the annual meeting. We urge you[8] to join us in planning for the future.

Very truly yours, (171)

4

Dear Mr. Sanders:

I would like to recommend a financial advisor for your firm. Ms. Janet Lee has worked[1] with us for more than four years. I can assure you that her knowledge is current, thorough, and reliable.

She has[2] earned the respect of her clients. Many of them have commented that she researches opportunities very[3] thoroughly before recommending them to her clients. They also report that she is attentive to all of[4] her accounts. Even on very short notice, she is usually accessible to everyone she serves.

It[5] has been a pleasure to have her work for us. We will miss her cheerful disposition as well as her professional[6] knowledge of market conditions.

If you feel that you need greater assurance regarding her qualifications,[7] please talk with me personally.

Yours truly, (149)

5

Dear Mr. Henderson:

Thank you for your letter regarding your former employee, Sue Carson. I am delighted[1] to say that she has been working with us for nearly six weeks. Even in this short period of time, she has[2] already brought several new clients to our firm.

She mentioned that you helped to form a foundation that has had[3] a positive effect on economic development in your community. This sounds like the kind of[4] program that would greatly benefit our town. Could you share some of your insights into getting such a program started?[5] We have a great deal of support among the leaders in our community, but we need to direct more energy[6] toward economic planning. Having learned of your work, I believe that we could accomplish this much faster[7] with your help.

I will be attending a convention in your city next month. I would appreciate meeting with[8] you then.

Yours very truly, (165)

LESSON 30

Word Development

Develop new words from the following brief forms:

note

notification *nlff*

notified *nlf-*

notation *nly*

notice *nls*

noteworthy *nlrle*

ever

forever *fE*

however *hoE*

whatever *ME*

whenever *nE*

everlasting *ElS*

over

overtime *OL*

overcharge *OG*

overlook *Olc*

turnover *LrnO*

success

successful *sucf*

successfully *sucfl*

successive *sucv*

unsuccessful *usucf*

Reading and Writing Exercises

─────────────────── 1 ───────────────────

Preview Words

servant *SvN*

decades *dcds*

convert *kvrl*

portfolio *plflo*

lifestyle *lfSl*

prosperity *Pspr'*

real estate *rl eSa*

liquid assets *lqd asls*

dr cle kgjs po
u rlrm \ u S fl
v prod v v̲ Sv-
nr fed gvl f nrl
3 dcds > uv aol
rzn l fl hpe \
bcz u d . pl
dsj lq aq l Plc
Intro DC
u fCr (,) uc no njy
(rws \ u + u f
c lc fw l z C
Pspr[L] af rlrm zu
njy- du̲ loz yrs z
. pb SvN > w enc-
. s re vu crN
nvSms \ S vu

ern̲ r f Scs la
v sn . Sde grl
O . lq pred \ e
kN u jjm > no
Intro DC
lau lfSl , Cnj- (,) -
u a + Lc
Cnjs n u plflo \ u
a + l kvrl
s rl eSa nl
lqd asls \ uc rcm
s opjs la l yld
grr Pfls n . srlr
pred v L > p nlf
e n ur rde l
Dcs ls dr \ ul

2

Preview Words

bond	bN	reinvest	rnvS
expected	vpc-	utilities	ull^ls
enjoyable	njyB	letterhead	Lhd
ongoing	oq-	transportation	Tpl

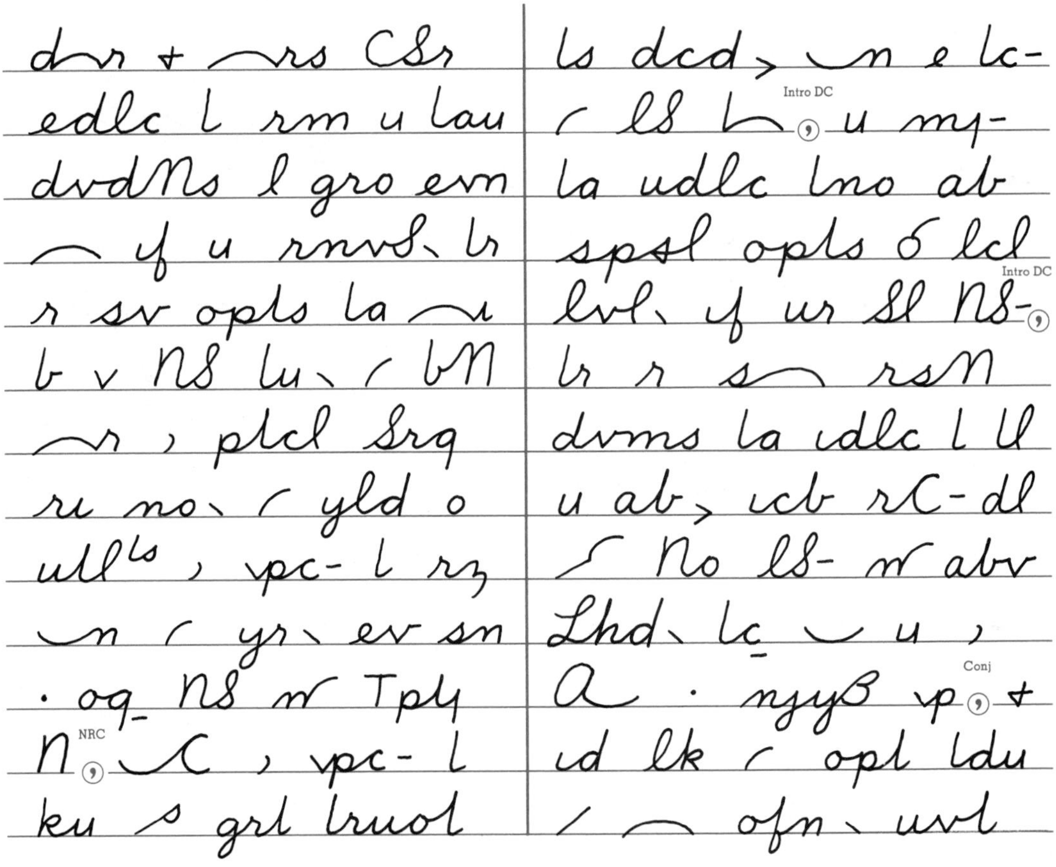

3

Preview Words

capital   *cptl*

access   *vs*

penalty   *pnlle*

exciting   *v̲*

preserve   *Pzrv*

Corporate   *crprl*

evaluations   *evluys*

commission   *kj*

[shorthand text]

d S ev dzn— .
fM la l Pzrv (
cpll la uv o—
hrd L ern, if ur
lc f . sf a l
C u cs gro ks   (Intro DC)
(crprl nk fM
(s h la s
Plc u me ls fM   (Intro P)
alos u lv vs
lu ak, yl (dz   (Paren)
so ol G . kj
fe or . NS pnlle,
ho c e ofr u so

C l G u so
lll, (asr ; s pl.
uv (bnfl v uz u
o nlj v r l Ose
u nvSms, b Pvd
u o evluys + c
u o dsjs ur kvrl   (Intro P)
u nlj nl cs, (
crprl nk fM
ofrs v opls l nel
v . nlj v nvSms,
u Pvd (drj + e   (Conj)
hNl (ppro, lc
nl ls r ld, vlu

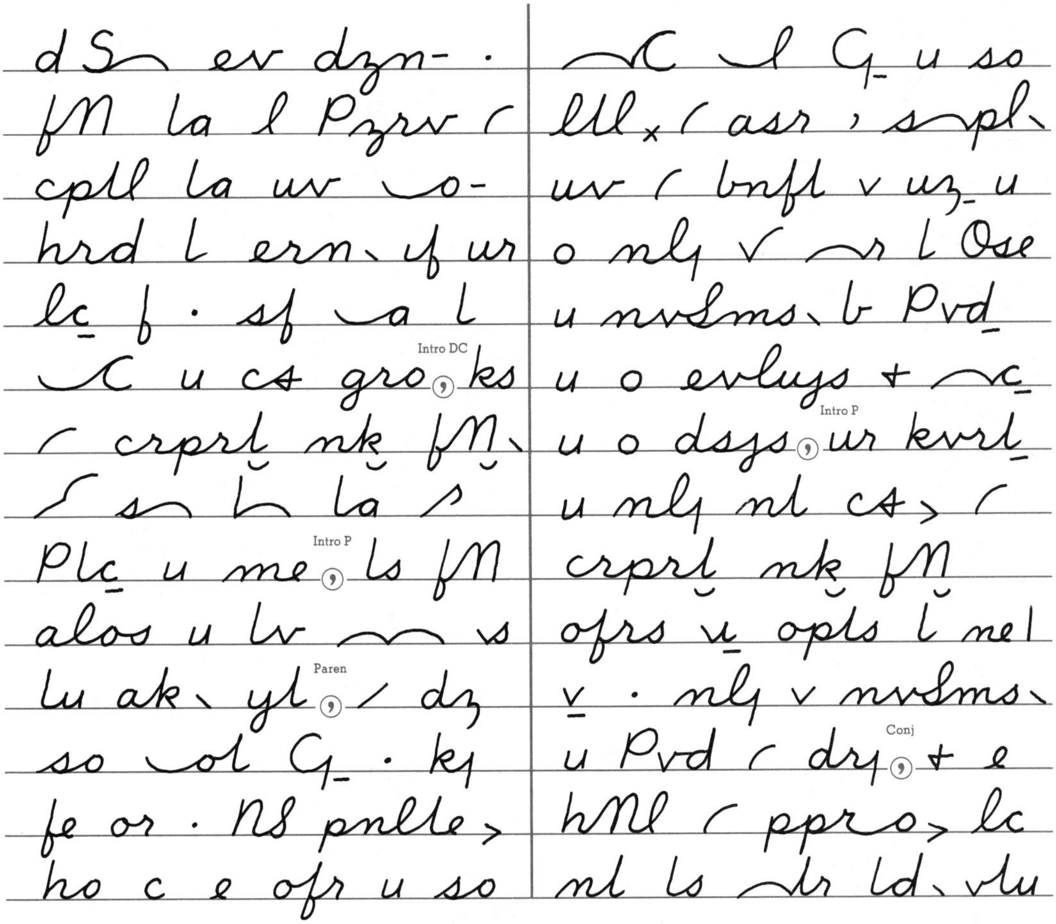

4

Preview Words

depth — *dpt*

America's — *Ans*

subscriber — *sSr*

publication — *pby*

occupants — *ocpNs*

absolutely — *abslul*

competition — *kply*

businessperson — *bsPsn*

---

1 3 ocpNs v . Pfgl ofs, u se me cliNs eC d. vu ks- sS l (ld bs jrnl,× vu l 8, Ans sucf bs pby, fr olsld s kply l8 yr. l hlp u se y, ev l- . sa cpe lo L rd / + ll s l u lg, y udlc lrsv r jrnl ol,
jS ret (enc—

crd. el nrl u 3 . gS sSr, + ul rsv (frS 3 isus abslul fre, lc . fu mls no l kpr r n3 + fl ol pbys uv sn. (dpl + rny v cvry r hlpf l me sres bsPsn. r Pps , l Pvd . rglr Svo o v bs + fnN, b r gS. sS no + rsv 3 isus fre v G. cu

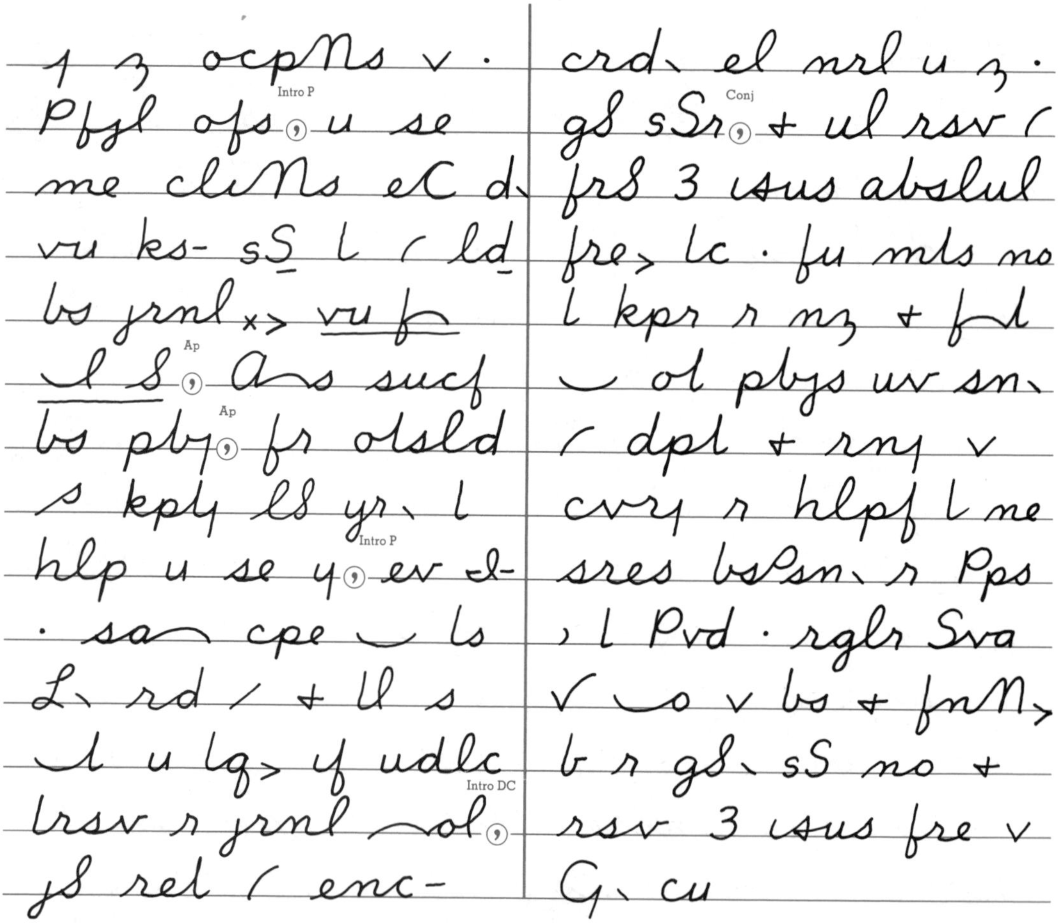

5

Punctuation Study

Add commas to show two introductory phrases, one conjunction, and one introductory dependent clause.

Preview Words

sum, seeking, investigate, accumulated

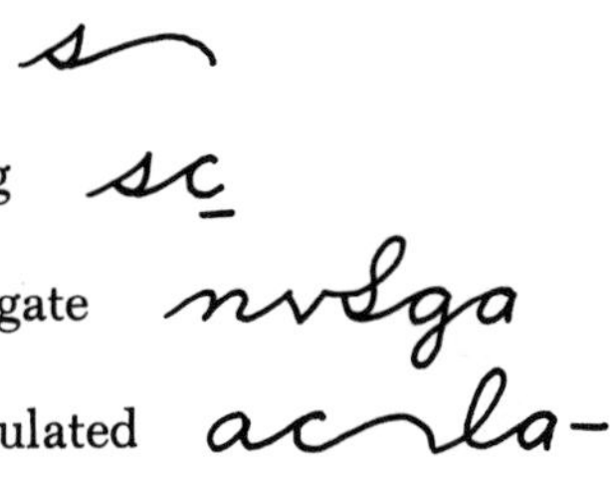

securities, converting, settlement, transition

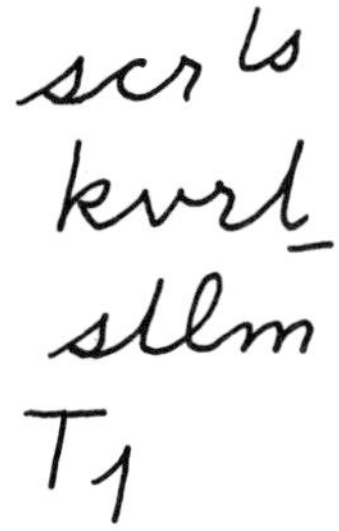

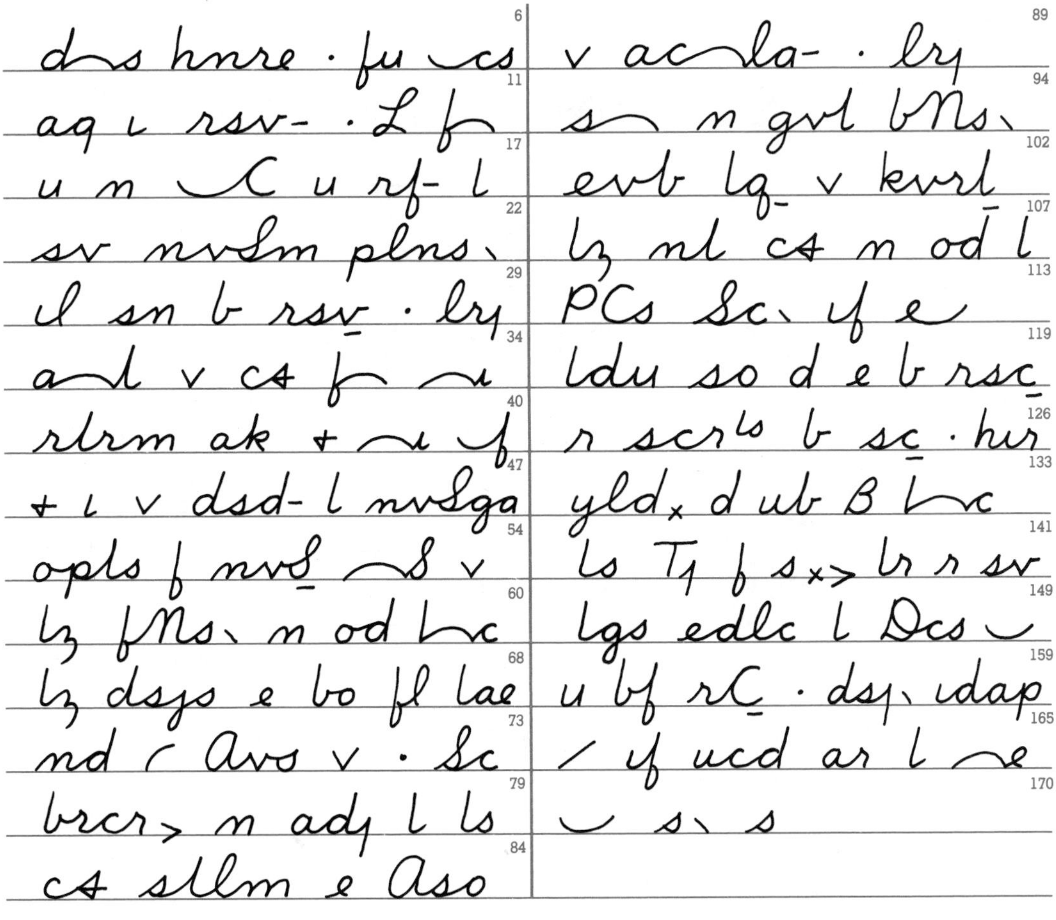

Key

1

Dear Mr. Kelly:

Congratulations upon your retirement. You must feel very proud of having served in the[1] federal government for nearly three decades.

You have another reason to feel happy. Because you made an[2] important decision long ago to protect your future, you can now enjoy the rewards. You and your wife can[3] look forward to as much prosperity after retirement as you enjoyed during those years as a public servant.[4]

I have enclosed a summary of your current investments. Most of your earnings are from stocks that have shown a[5] steady growth over a long period. We commend your judgment.

Now that your lifestyle is changing, you may wish to[6] make changes in your portfolio. You may wish to convert some real estate into liquid assets. I can[7] recommend some options that will yield greater profits in a shorter period of time.

Please notify me when[8] you are ready to discuss this matter.

Yours truly, (169)

2

Dear Mr. and Mrs. Chester:

We would like to remind you that your dividends will grow even more if you[1] reinvest. There are several opportunities that might be of interest to you. The bond market is[2] particularly strong right now. The yield on utilities is expected to rise within the year. We have seen an[3] ongoing interest in the transportation industry, which is expected to continue its growth throughout this[4] decade.

When we talked the last time, you mentioned that you would like to know about special opportunities on the[5] local level. If you are still interested, there are some recent developments that I would like to tell you[6] about.

I can be reached daily at the number listed in the above letterhead. Talking with you is always[7] an enjoyable experience, and I would welcome the opportunity to do it more often.

Yours very[8] truly, (162)

3

Dear Sir or Madam:

We have designed a fund that will preserve the capital that you have worked hard to earn. If[1] you are looking for a safe way to watch your cash grow, consider the Corporate Income Fund. At the same time that[2] it is protecting your money, this fund allows you to have immediate access to your account. Yet, it does so[3] without charging a commission fee or an interest penalty.

How can we offer you so much while charging[4] you so little? The answer is simple. You have the benefit of using your own knowledge of the market to[5] oversee your investments. By providing your own evaluations and making your own decisions, you are[6] converting your knowledge into cash.

The Corporate Income Fund offers exciting opportunities to[7] anyone having a knowledge of investments. You provide the direction, and we handle the paperwork.

Look[8] into this matter today.

Very truly yours, (168)

4

Gentlemen:

As occupants of a professional office, you see many clients each day. Have you considered[1] subscribing to the leading business journal?

View from Wall Street, America's successful business publication,[2] far outsold its competition last year. To help you see why, we have included a sample copy with this letter.[3] Read it and tell us what you think.

If you would like to receive our journal monthly, just return the enclosed card.[4] We will enroll you as a guest subscriber, and you will receive the first three issues absolutely free.

Take a[5] few minutes now to compare our news and format with other publications you have seen. The depth and range of[6] coverage are helpful to any serious businessperson. Our purpose is to provide a regular survey[7] of the world of business and finance.

Be our guest. Subscribe now and receive three issues free of charge.

Cordially yours,[8] (160)

5

Dear Ms. Henry:

A few weeks ago I received a letter from you in which you referred to several investment[1] plans. I will soon be receiving a large amount of cash from my retirement account, and my wife and I have[2] decided to investigate opportunities for investing most of these funds. In order to make these[3] decisions, we both feel that we need the advice of a stock broker.

In addition to this cash settlement, we[4] also have accumulated a large sum in government bonds. We have been thinking of converting these into[5] cash in order to purchase stock. If we were to do so, would we be risking our securities by seeking a[6] higher yield? Would you be able to make this transition for us?

There are several things we would like to discuss[7] with you before reaching a decision. I would appreciate it if you could arrange to meet with us.

Sincerely,[8] (160)

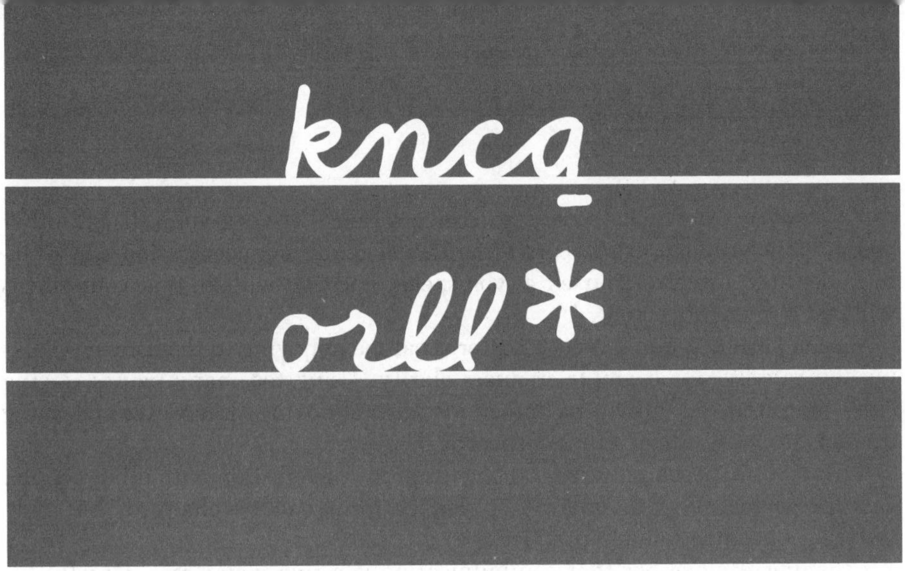

By the time we have learned how to talk, speech seems like the most natural activity in the world. However, if we learned to speak improperly from the beginning, we are faced with two problems. First, our mistakes are easily noticed by other people, and those mistakes detract from a professional image and from our opportunities for success. Second, old habits are difficult to change, especially when we do not notice them ourselves.

Using correct grammar. The most important verbal asset any person possesses is the ability to express thoughts with correct grammar. It is difficult to convince anyone of your competence if you consistently make errors in subject and verb agreement, for example.

Like many other skills, correct English usage can be learned through study and practice. If you are uncertain about your ability to speak correctly, ask a teacher to help you pinpoint the areas in which you have difficulty. Then launch a program to correct bad habits. Concentrate on proper usage and correct yourself as many times as necessary to create new habits.

Voice quality. We are given one voice at birth, which most of us use without questioning. However, have you ever stood next to a person who talked too loudly? Or too softly? Or too harshly? Think of how much more effective that person would be if the quality of his or her voice could be improved. Since we do not hear ourselves as others do, however, it is not easy to detect problems in our own voice quality.

***Communicating Orally**

To analyze your own voice, tape conversations between yourself and other people. If a problem exists, correcting it will require concentration and practice. Learn to listen to yourself as you speak, and you will see that your efforts will result in improvement.

Speech patterns. Some speech patterns can be annoying to the listener. Talking too rapidly, for example, reduces clarity. Using too many pauses, saying "uh" too often, or talking too much is also annoying. Even excessive slang detracts from the effectiveness of speech.

To test your speech patterns, tape yourself in conversation with other people. Like problems of voice quality, speech patterns can be changed, but only through concentration and practice.

Listening. Remember that communication is a two-way street. Careful listening is just as important as good speech habits. Learn to avoid interrupting the speaker. Listen courteously, waiting until the speaker has finished making a point before asking questions. Listen for details. Make certain that you understand all instructions before beginning a task.

unl 7
lrvl*

Shorthand Vocabulary Review

Study the following words and the principles they illustrate. Each of these words is presented in the letters and memos in this unit.

1. For words ending in a long vowel + *t* (*ate, ete, ite, ote, ute/ute*), omit the *t* and write the vowel.

rates	ras	dates	das
fleet	fle	retreat	rtre
might	⌒i	sight-seeing	si = se̲
boats	bos	delighted	dli-

***Unit Seven**
Travel

waiting  greeting 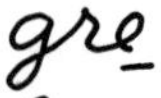

sheet  located 

state  campsites 

2. Write  for the sounds of *ance*, *ence*, *nce*, and *nse*.

agency  expensive 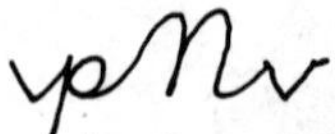

sponsor  conference 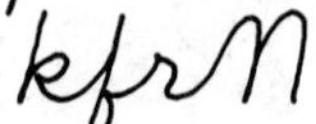

chances  assistance 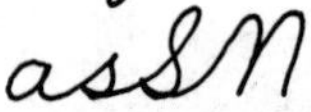

distance  efficiency 

More About Punctuation

In text material, when the name of a state or foreign country follows the name of a city, use a comma to separate the two.

The convention will be held in Dayton, Ohio.

Mr. Nerz is a native of Munich, Germany.

If the city and state combination occurs at the beginning or in the middle of a sentence, place a comma before and after the state name.

The convention will be held in Dayton, Ohio, on February 12.

Seattle, Washington, is a beautiful city.

LESSON 31

Brief Forms and Derivatives

1. *loz prp ⌒ , G rsp*
2. *lrf dle kgjs arpl kfr*

Key

1. those, property, am/more, is/his, charge, respond/response
2. therefore, delivery, congratulations, airport, confirmation

Phrase Review

1. *ic edu elb edap ud*
2. *uvb lgl zlz ze fu lqu*

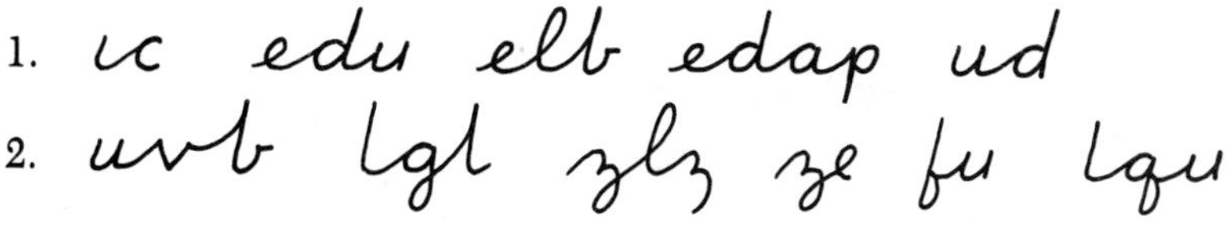

Key

1. I can, we do, we will be, we would appreciate, you would
2. you have been, to get, as well as, as we, for you/for your, thank you

Reading and Writing Exercises

─────────────── 1 ───────────────

Preview Words

tour	*ŀr*	charter	*Crŀr*
rates	*ras*	abroad	*abrd*
fares	*frs*	subject	*sjc*
handy	*hNe*	affordable	*afdß*

[Shorthand passage, two columns]

ddr Nrs hr r r
brŀrs u rgß-, p
nŀ la hll ras +
ar frs r A sjc
l Cny, hoE, r ras   *(Paren)*
lß- n lr ŀrels l
gv u . jn ida v
ŀ l ypc, yf ls ,
u frß ŀrp abrd, u   *(Intro DC)*
⌣ + l ks ŀrvl_
⌣ . ŀr grp, ŀr r
me Crŀr ŀrps avlß.

ly uzl ofr Øk- prss,   *(Conj)*
+ ly Pvd u ⌣ . vp-
ŀr ldr, ⌣ n ur rde
l Øcs sp plss +
das, r ajNe ll   *(Intro DC)*
hpe l Sv u, ec
hlp u pln . ŀrp la
, kv, fn, + afdß,   *(Series) (Series)*
⌣ alC ⌣ bs crd.
p pl / n . hNe pls
so la uc rf l /
⌣ nd-, su

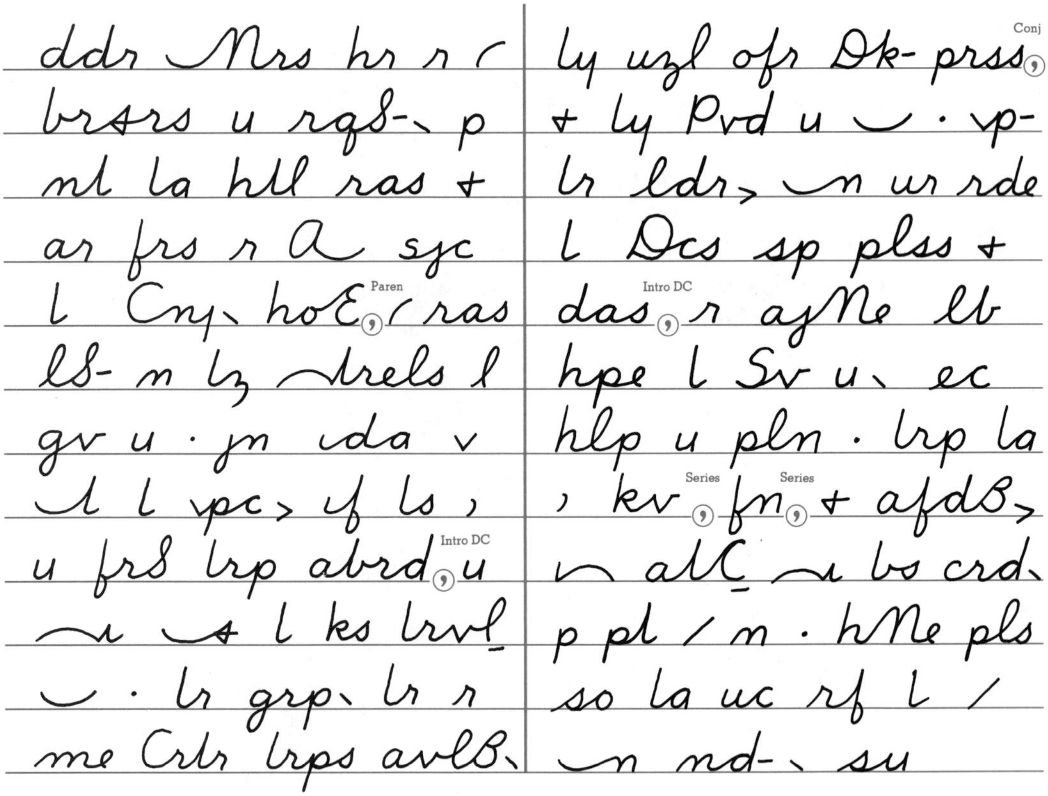

2

Preview Words

meals	~ls	saleswoman	sls~n
honor	onr	Mexico City	~xco slc
airport	arpl	driving tour	drv lr
etc.	elc	miscellaneous	Mlnes

d~s dnldsn kgjs o b n- sls~n v yr, u ~8 fl v prod + u- lrsv ls onr, z (~nr v ls kl8, [Intro P] ul rsv · 1=~c vcj n ~xco slc fu + u hzbN, r lrvl ajNe hsb asc- l~c a v nes arms / no G lu, u fr8=pls aw l pa a vpNs f ar frs, [Series] hll akdjs, [Series] + Tplj l + f~ (arpl, n

adj, [Paren] ul rsv 3H$ n spN me, [Series] 5H$ f ~ls, [Series] + 2H$ f Mlnes vpNs=si=se lrps, [Series] lps, [Series] elc, if udlc l lc · drv lr, [Intro DC] · rNl cr lb ~d avl8 lu / · Dk- ra, u ~a ~c u rzrvjs f ne ~c bln (das v Ma15 + Dc 15, e avz u ldu ls erl n od lgl u Cys v das, vlu

---
3

Preview Words

London *lMn*   informed *nf —*

affect *afc*   occasions *ocjs*

alerting *alrl*   conditions *kdjs*

evaluate *evla*   uncomfortable *ukflB*

---

d r + rs adrsn
lqf ru l Ul s ab u
vps n lMn, s v
pl f s lno ab
r ukflB kdjs u
dS—, ev Sa— n la
hll o vres ocjs +
v foM, Ul lM
m E a, hoE(,)r ^Paren
hll hs Cny— hMs
rsMl, el Slnl

evla r nu ym
bf rcm lz akdjs
l ol cliMs, er sre
lau foM ls hll Ul
usal, ehp la ls
Dapy vp dd n afc
r r8 vu lrp, lqu
aq f alrl s(,) + ^Conj
edap r if ud cp
s nf — ab ol lrvl
vps, uvl

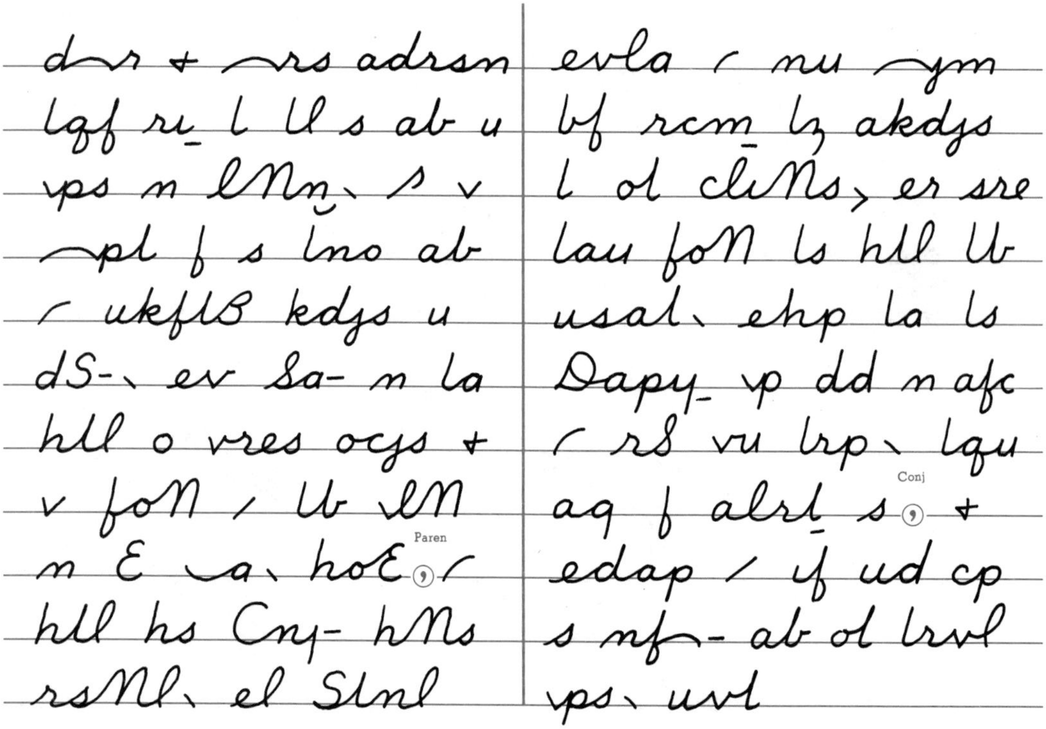

4

Preview Words

fleet	fle	islands	lNs
snacks	sncs	surrounding	SoN
cruise	crz	inspection	nspcj
tickets	tcts	destination	dSnj

d-rs ly-s ys, (Paren)
edu ofr . Dk v
10% f grps v 30
or - ppl. uf udlc
-c rzrvjs f . 3=hr
crz l ne v SoN
lNs, (Intro DC) u -S s-l
u rqS 60 ds n
avN, r rglr prss
v tcts rnj f- 42 50
l 70$. r vc prs
dpNs po r - v
crz zlz r dSnj.
-ls, (Series) sncs, (Series) + drqs

r adjl + r n I-
n ls prs, r fle v
ss, (Ap) r lrjS v s
cN, (Ap) ofrs . -drnj
v scjls. ev me
v s- akdjs la
lrjr oj lnrs ofr.
u lrp lb kflS, (Series)
rlx, (Series) + lrol njyS,
- I adjl lil
fu nspcj. zz uv
dsd- po . da, (Intro DC) lb
hpe l kp r arms.
ul

5

Punctuation Study

Add commas to show one introductory phrase, one introductory dependent clause, and two groups of words in a series.

Preview Words

sponsor 

picnic 

hiking 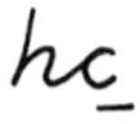

precaution 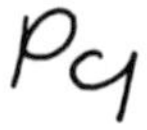

distance 

campsites 

pamphlets 

electricity 

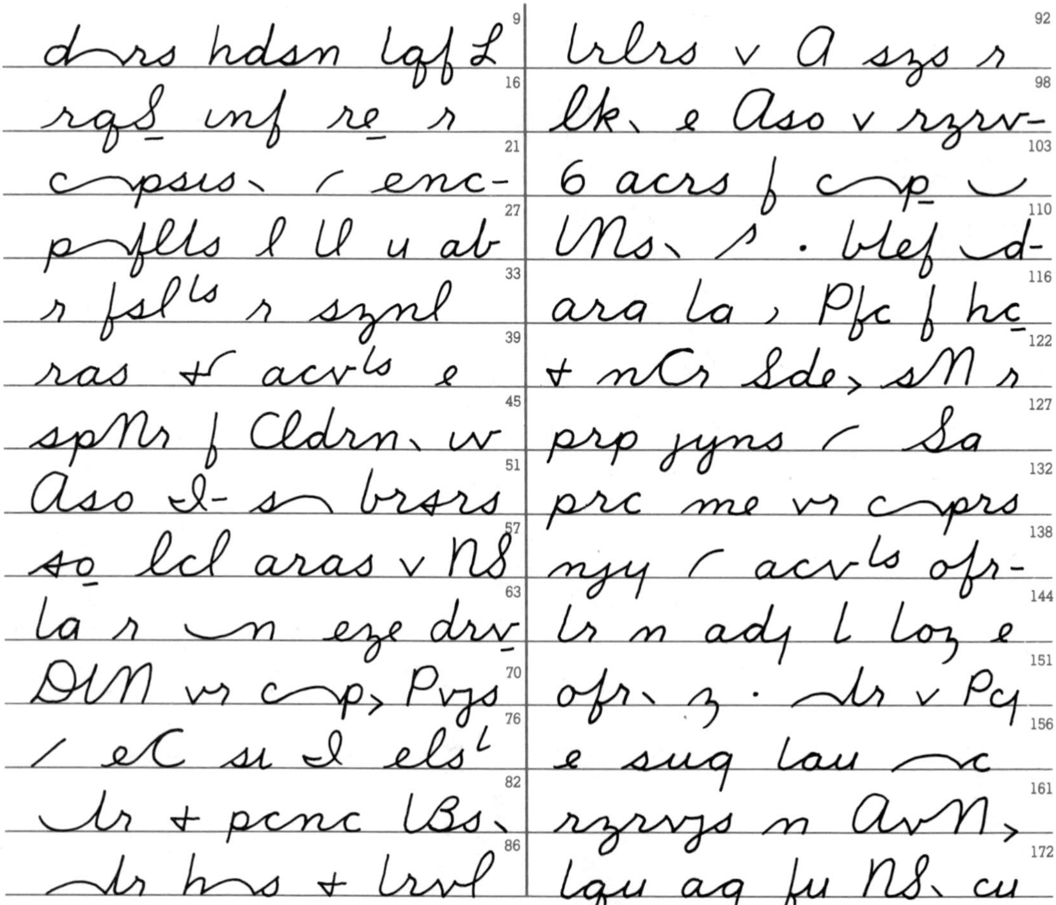

Key

1

Dear Dr. Winters:

Here are the brochures you requested. Please note that hotel rates and air fares are always subject[1] to change. However, the rates listed in these materials will give you a general idea of what to[2] expect.

If this is your first trip abroad, you might wish to consider traveling with a tour group. There are many[3] charter trips available. They usually offer discounted prices, and they provide you with an experienced[4] tour leader.

When you are ready to discuss specific places and dates, our agency will be happy to[5] serve you. We can help you plan a trip that is convenient, fun, and affordable.

I am attaching my business[6] card. Please put it in a handy place so that you can refer to it when needed.

Sincerely yours, (138)

2

Dear Ms. Donaldson:

Congratulations on being named saleswoman of the year. You must feel very proud and[1] excited to receive this honor.

As the winner of this contest, you will receive a one-week vacation in[2] Mexico City for you and your husband. Our travel agency has been asked to make all of the necessary[3] arrangements at no charge to you. Your first-place award will pay all expenses for air fares, hotel accommodations,[4] and transportation to and from the airport.

In addition, you will receive $300 in spending[5] money, $500 for meals, and $200 for miscellaneous expenses—sight-seeing trips,[6] tips, etc. If you would like to take a driving tour, a rental car will be made available to you[7] at a discounted rate.

You may make your reservations for any week between the dates of May 15 and[8] December 15. We advise you to do this early in order to get your choice of dates.

Very truly yours,[9] (180)

3

Dear Mr. and Mrs. Anderson:

Thank you for writing to tell us about your experiences in London.[1] It is very important for us to know about the uncomfortable conditions you described. We have stayed[2] in that hotel on various occasions and have found it to be excellent in every way. However, the[3] hotel has changed hands recently. We will certainly evaluate the new management before recommending[4] these accommodations to other clients.

We are sorry that you found this hotel to be unsatisfactory.[5] We hope that this disappointing experience did not affect the rest of your trip. Thank you again for alerting[6] us, and we would appreciate it if you would keep us informed about other travel experiences.[7]

Yours very truly, (144)

4

Dear Mrs. Williams:

Yes, we do offer a discount of 10 percent for groups of 30 or more people. If you[1] would like to make reservations for a three-hour cruise to any of the surrounding islands, you must submit your[2] request 60 days in advance.

The regular prices of tickets range from $42.50 to[3] $70. The exact price depends upon the time of the cruise as well as the destination. Meals, snacks,[4] and drinks are additional and are not included in this price.

Our fleet of ships, the largest of its kind, offers[5] a wide range of schedules. We have many of the same accommodations that larger ocean liners offer. Your[6] trip will be comfortable, relaxing, and thoroughly enjoyable.

I am including additional[7] literature for your inspection. As soon as you have decided upon a date, I will be happy to complete[8] the arrangements.

Yours truly, (165)

5

Dear Mrs. Hudson:

Thank you for your letter requesting information regarding our campsites. The enclosed pamphlets[1] will tell you about our facilities, our seasonal rates, and the activities we sponsor for children.[2] I have also included some brochures showing local areas of interest that are within easy driving[3] distance of our camp.

Provisions at each site include electricity, water, and picnic tables. Motor[4] homes and travel trailers of all sizes are welcome. We also have reserved six acres for camping with tents.[5] It is a beautiful wooded area that is perfect for hiking and nature study.

Since our property[6] joins the state park, many of our campers enjoy the activities offered there in addition to those we offer.[7] As a matter of precaution, we suggest that you make reservations in advance.

Thank you again for your[8] interest.

Cordially yours, (164)

LESSON 32

Abbreviations and Derivatives

1. etc esp ok E eslms
2. Wrn re ysrd enc- corps

Key

1. et cetera, especially, okay, east, establishments
2. western, regarding, yesterday, enclosed, corporations

Transcription Aids: Capitalization

Do not capitalize the seasons of the year.

We invite you to attend our spring sale.

Do you like winter sports?

Capitalize the names of the time zones or their abbreviations.

Eastern Standard Time (EST) or Eastern Time

Central Standard Time (CST) or Central Time

Mountain Standard Time (MST) or Mountain Time

Pacific Standard Time (PST) or Pacific Time

Daylight-Saving Time (DST)

EDT, CDT, MDT, and PDT may be used to refer to Daylight-Saving Time in each of the time zones.

Your Business Vocabulary	elaborate *elbrl*	Complicated, thorough; created with much care and detail.

He wrote an elaborate report.

tentatively *Invl*   In an uncertain way; not yet definite.

We are tentatively planning to attend, and we will let you know if our plans change.

Reading and Writing Exercises

--- 1 ---

Preview Words

aware	*a r*	confirm	*kfr*
ensure	*nsr*	adjustments	*ajSms*
routes	*rus*	alterations	*alrys*
handle	*hNl*	transportation	*Tply*

d M krd zu nu lrvl ajN₉ i N u lr kfdN r arms i rc fu. lrf₉ n jr Cnjs v Ur d n u lrvl plns₉ hr , r a il hNl L, zz i

bk a r la ajSms r nes₉ il nlf u l. l nsr lau arms r fre v Pbl s₉ il cl r Tply ajN r hll dsc l kfr r rzrvjs, il aso fw inf o prs

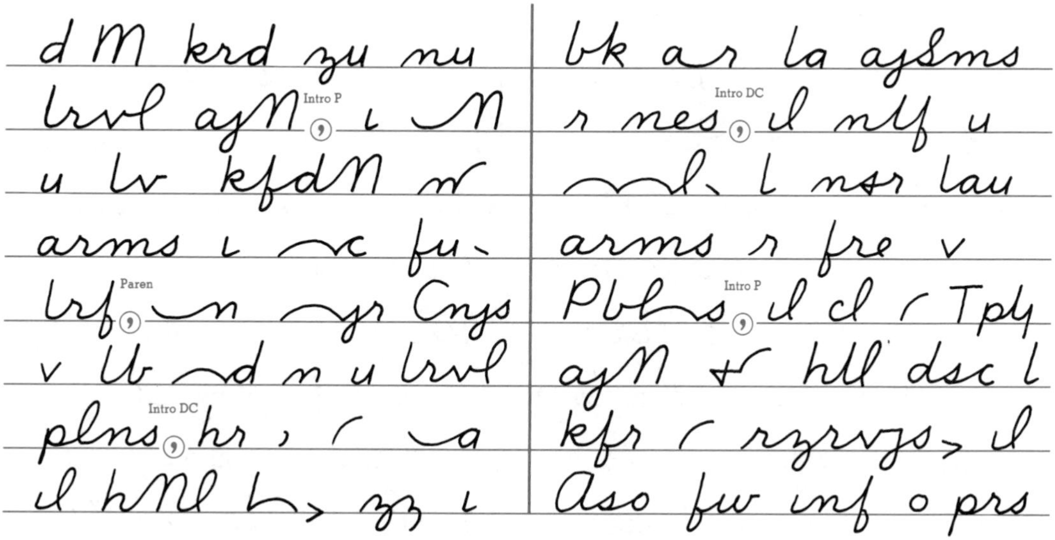

Cnjs + Alrjs n   du ocr f Lth.
Tply rus. Alo e   il du A ic trc u
gr u r ∽S rliB   trp plz∧ fu. c
arms psB, Cnjs

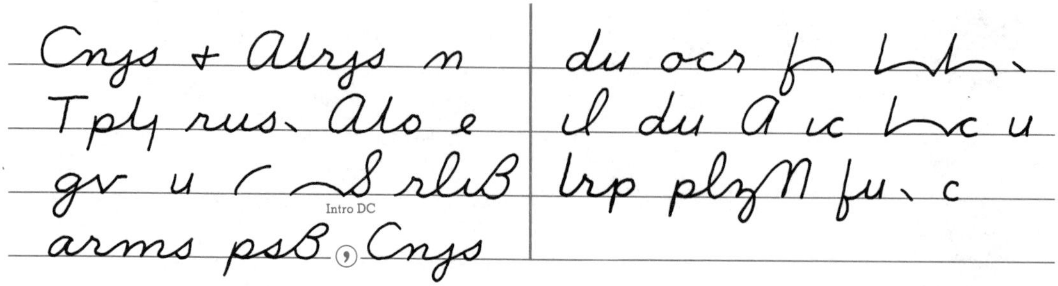

───────────── 2 ─────────────

Preview Words

wife ∤

Japan jpn

Africa afrca

elaborate elbrl

celebrating slbra

Rome, Italy r   ∿ile

Madrid ∽drd

Europe urp

dns ∿dsn il   ur o lz cMres.
rlr f ∽u crM   e Pfr n l Sa n
pzf z Psnl drr   htls la r elbrl
n 6 ∽os. ∿u ∤   + ∿pMr, b edu
+ l r lc fw l   M lr akdjs la
slbra ls ocj b   r sf, kflB, + ezl
lc · vcj s∽r v   sB l Tply, ev
spsl, sM ev nvs   Aso lc- ab vzl
b ol v ls cMre,   Wrn urp, ed esp
er ks lc · lq trp   lc lvzl r ile +
elr l afrca os   ∽drd spn, u
jpn, l inf du   lrvl ajMe hs A

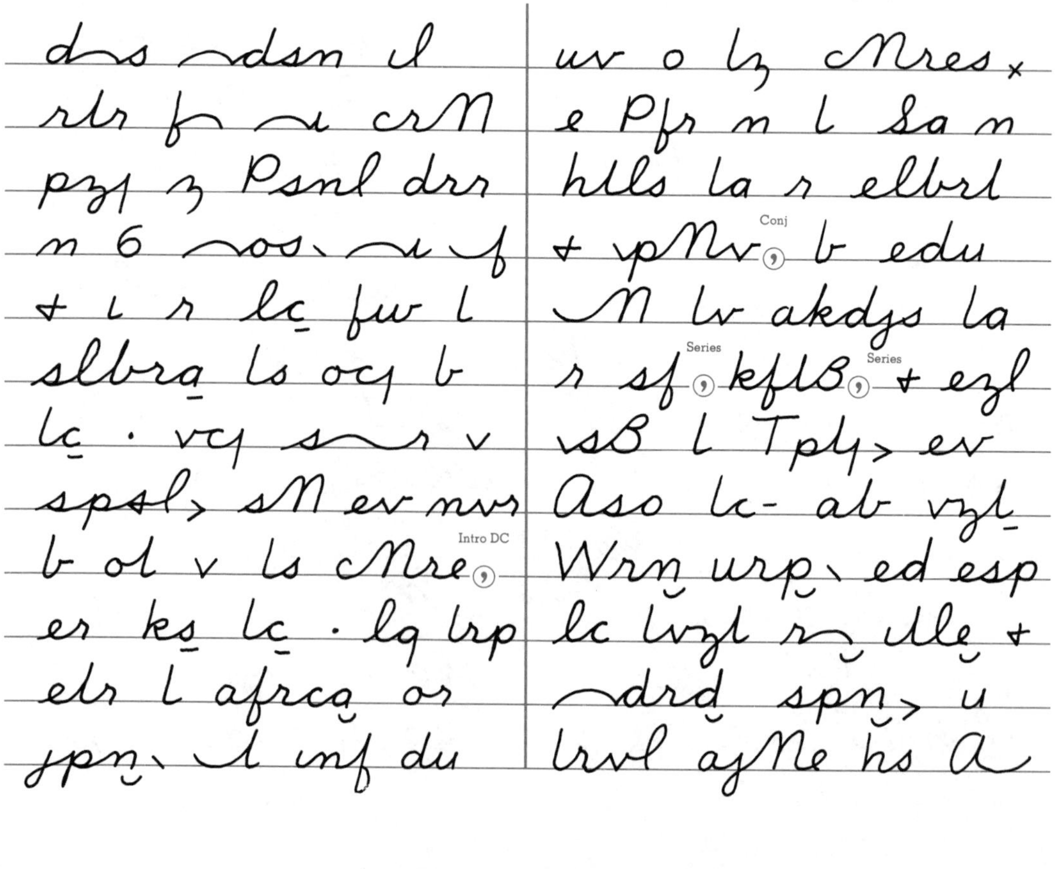

b . gr hlp l ⌒ u
co, ⌒ no lc_
fw Lo ⌣ u
Psnll, s

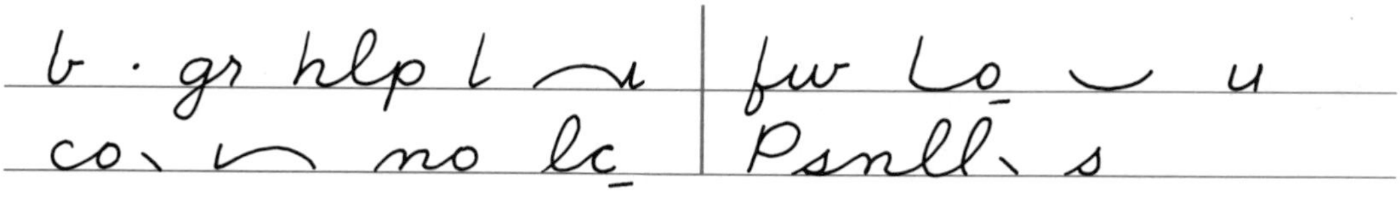

3

Preview Words

theater	lelr
circled	Scl-
elegant	elgN
district	Dlrc
structure	SrcCr
restaurants	rSrNs
Regency Hotel	ryNe hll
businesspersons	bs^sns

dM bcr enc-, .
brsr f ⌒ (ryNe
hll, ev ⌒d u
rzrvj f das u
rgS-, e Stnl hp
lau njy u Sa, zi
vpln- b fn ySrd, Intro DC
ls, I v ⌒S ppls
hlls ang bs^sns,
s kvl lca- n
hrl v bs Dlrc,
yl, Paren s . old + elgN
SrcCr ⌣ . gr dl
v hSre aso- ⌣ /,
s Cr⌒ + kflB,
⌒ aso I . gd
l rSrNs + Nlnm,
ulfN me dlif
Cyss f dn l ur
lr, Conj b v Scl- . fu
la vb rcm- b ol
lrvlrs, i USN
la (dnr lelr
nr u hll, . fvrl
alrcj, Ph ul ⌣N
l pln u evn zz

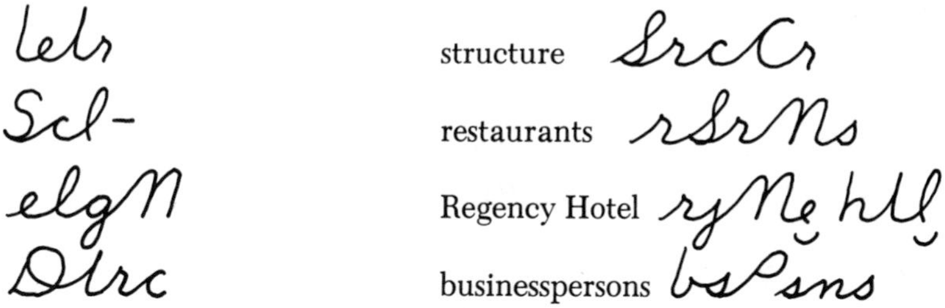

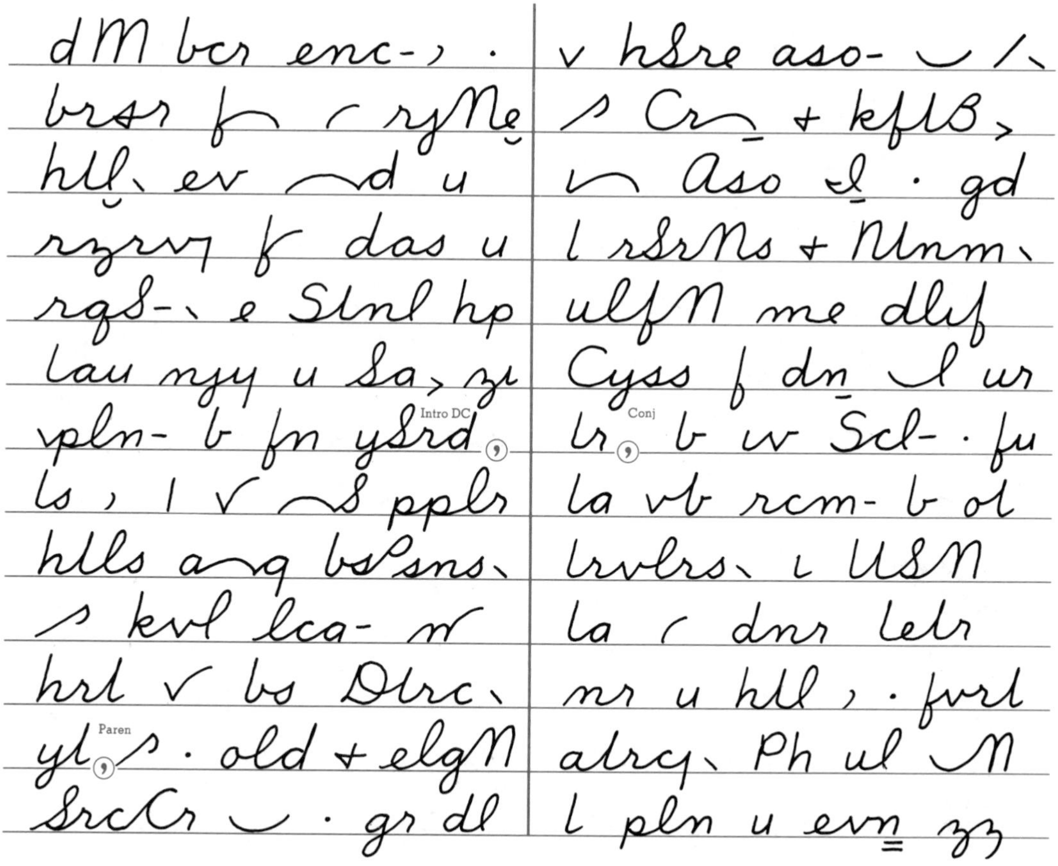

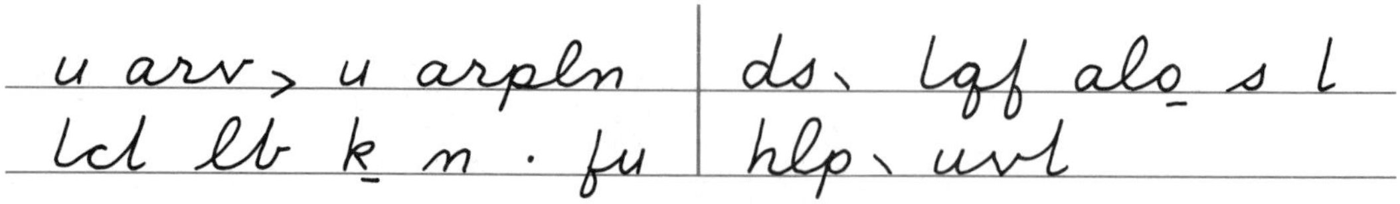

4

Preview Words

- alter 
- resuming 
- realize 
- yourself 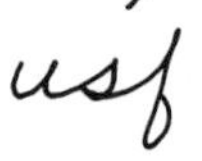
- hometown 
- Tampa, Florida 
- temporary 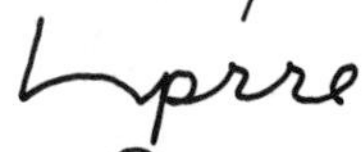
- subscription 

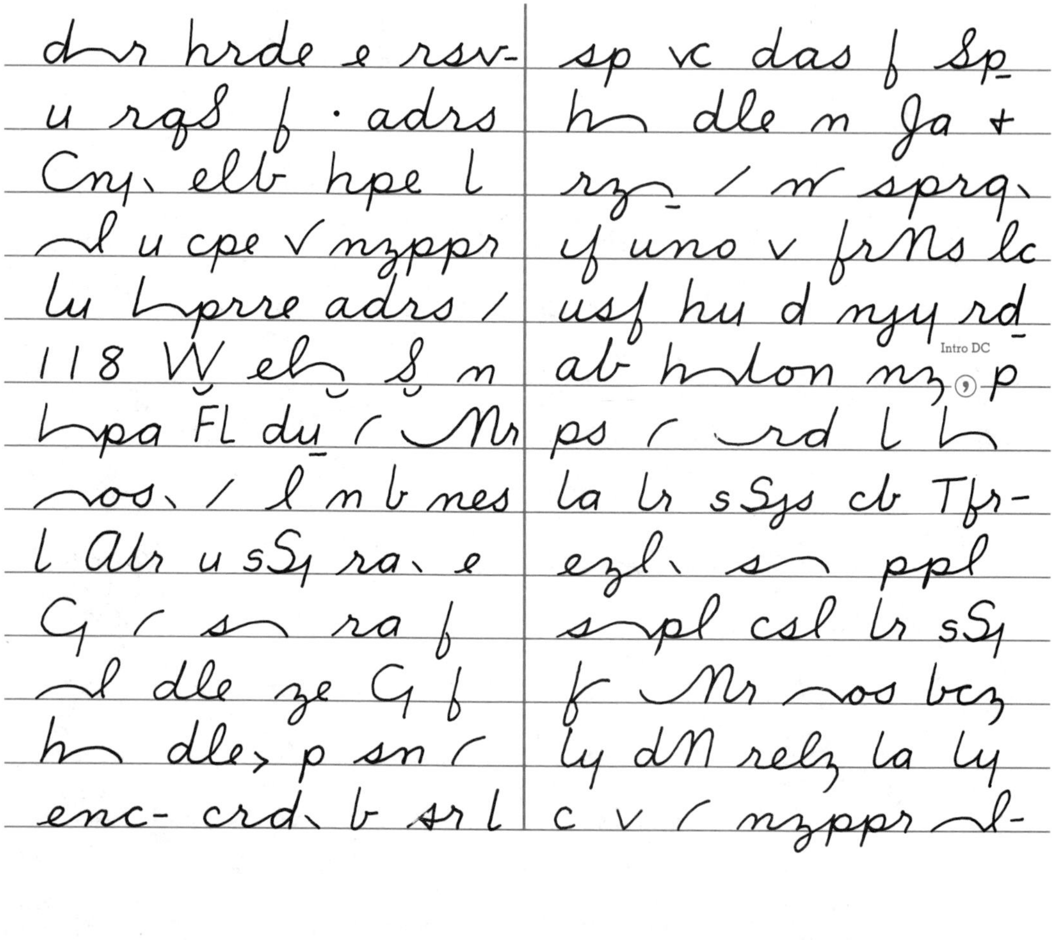

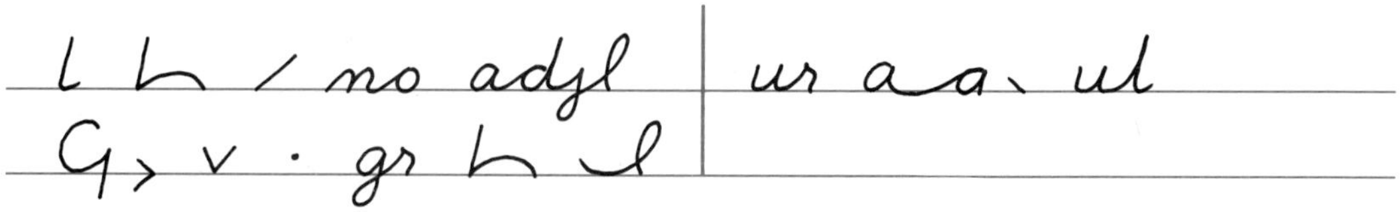

5

Punctuation Study

Add commas to show one introductory dependent clause, one conjunction, one introductory phrase, and one group of words in a series.

Preview Words

lake	lc	projector	Pjcr
boats	bos	facilities	fsl ls
resort	rzrl	recreation	rcre
retreat	rtre	tentatively	tNvl

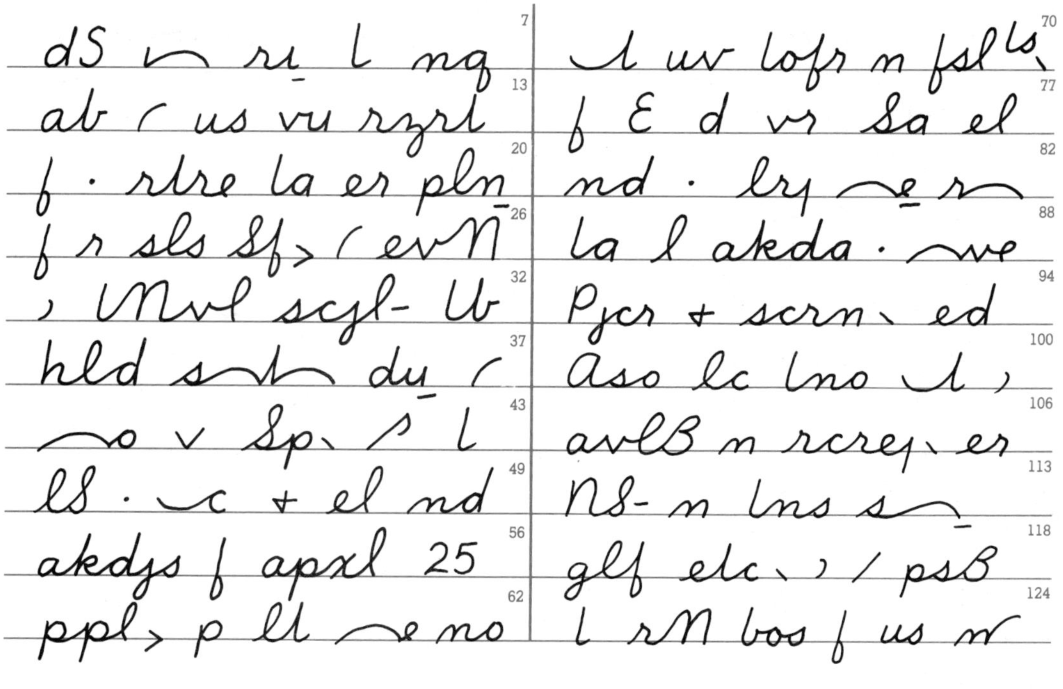

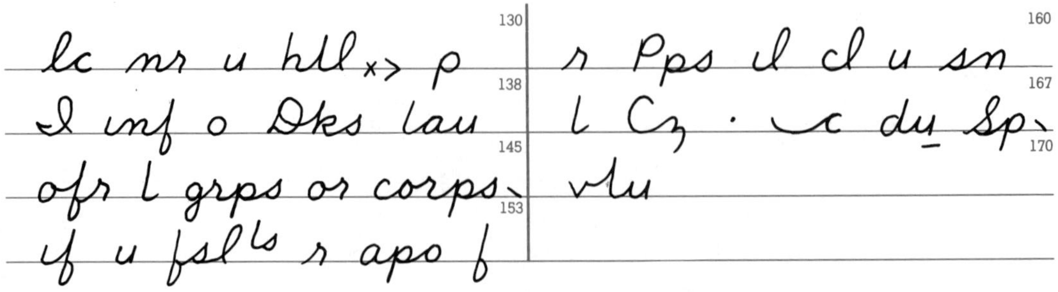

Key

1

Dear Miss Conrad:

As your new travel agent, I want you to have confidence in the arrangements I make for you.[1] Therefore, when major changes have to be made in your travel plans, here is the way I will handle them.

As soon as[2] I become aware that adjustments are necessary, I will notify you immediately. To ensure[3] that your arrangements are free of problems, I will call the transportation agent and the hotel desk to confirm[4] the reservations.

I will also forward information on price changes and alterations in transportation[5] routes. Although we give you the most reliable arrangements possible, changes do occur from time to time.[6] I will do all I can to make your trip pleasant for you.

Cordially, (132)

2

Dear Ms. Madison:

I will retire from my current position as personnel director in six months. My wife[1] and I are looking forward to celebrating this occasion by taking a vacation somewhere very special.[2]

Since we have never been out of this country, we are considering taking a long trip either to Africa[3] or Japan. What information do you have on these countries? We prefer not to stay in hotels that are[4] elaborate and expensive, but we do want to have accommodations that are safe, comfortable, and[5] easily accessible to transportation.

We have also talked about visiting Western Europe. We would[6] especially like to visit Rome, Italy, and Madrid, Spain.

Your travel agency has always been a great help[7] to my company. I am now looking forward to working with you personally.

Sincerely, (156)

3

Dear Miss Baker:

Enclosed is a brochure from the Regency Hotel. We have made your reservation for the dates[1] you requested. We certainly hope that you enjoy your stay.

As I explained by phone yesterday, this is one of the[2] most popular hotels among businesspersons. It is conveniently located in the heart of the business[3] district. Yet, it is an old and elegant structure with a great deal of history associated with it.[4] It is charming and comfortable.

I am also including a guide to restaurants and entertainment.[5] You will find many delightful choices for dining while you are there, but I have circled a few that have been[6] recommended by other travelers. I understand that the dinner theater near your hotel is a[7] favorite attraction. Perhaps you will want to plan your evenings as soon as you arrive.

Your airplane ticket will be[8] coming in a few days. Thank you for allowing us to help.

Yours very truly, (174)

4

Dear Mr. Hardy:

We received your request for an address change. We will be happy to mail your copy of the[1] newspaper to your temporary address at 118 West Elm Street in Tampa, Florida, during the winter[2] months. It will not be necessary to alter your subscription rate. We charge the same rate for mail delivery[3] as we charge for home delivery.

Please sign the enclosed card. Be sure to specify exact dates for stopping[4] home delivery in January and resuming it in the spring. If you know of friends like yourself who would[5] enjoy reading about hometown news, please pass the word to them that their subscriptions can be transferred easily.[6] Some people simply cancel their subscription for the winter months because they don't realize that they can have the[7] newspaper mailed to them at no additional charge.

Have a great time while you are away.

Yours truly, (157)

5

Dear Sir:

I am writing to inquire about the use of your resort for a retreat that we are planning for our[1] sales staff.

The event is tentatively scheduled to be held sometime during the month of September. It is to[2] last a week, and we will need accommodations for approximately 25 people.

Please let me know what[3] you have to offer in facilities. For every day of our stay, we will need a large meeting room that will[4] accommodate a movie projector and screen. We would also like to know what is available in recreation.[5] We are interested in tennis, swimming, golf, etc. Is it possible to rent boats for use in the[6] lake near your hotel?

Please include information on discounts that you offer to groups or corporations. If[7] your facilities are appropriate for our purpose, I will call you soon to choose a week during September.[8]

Very truly yours, (164)

LESSON 33

Shorthand Vocabulary Review

Write N for the sound of *end, nd.*

send	sN	around	aroN
spend	spN	independent	NpNN
fund	fN	understand	USN
friendly	frNl	surroundings	SoN̳

Transcription Aids: Similar Words

all ready a rde Prepared; all in readiness.

The committee members were all ready to begin the meeting.

already ar By this time; previously.

By the time I arrived, the meeting had already begun.

Your Business Vocabulary

convention complex kvny kplx — A cluster of buildings or facilities within a large building designed to accommodate guests for conventions.

The new convention complex will be located in the northern part of our city.

confirmation kfry — The verifying or confirming of information; assurance.

I am requesting confirmation of my hotel reservation for October 15.

Reading and Writing Exercises

1

Preview Words

route	ru	discomfort	Dkfl
tourist	lrS	United States	uni- Sas
lodging	lj-	guided tours	gd- lrs
emphasized	-fsz-	northeastern	NErn

dr lnrd er dli-
l asS u n pln u
f-l vcj. O (yrs
ev lrn- la (bS
vcjs r pln- ahd.
uv Ar lrn- la lc-
CNs o fN akdjs
fr f- h- c ld l
Dkfl + vpN, w
pcl la ev enc-, Intro P
ulfN inf o arln
ras + scjls, Series hlls, Series
+ gd- lrs. zu rqS-, Intro DC
e -fsz- plss w
NErn uni- Sas.

if ud Sl lc l ks
· SWrn ru af so
lz -trels lu f-l, Intro DC
il -l adjl lil lu
-l, n od l nsr
lau gl u Cys v lj-
+ Tplj, Intro P esd bc u
rzrvjs / lS 3
-os n avN. (
lrS szn , vpc- l
bgn erl ls yr, -n
(h- fu vcj arvs, Intro DC
u arms lb A rde
fu. er A egr lb
v asSN. vlu

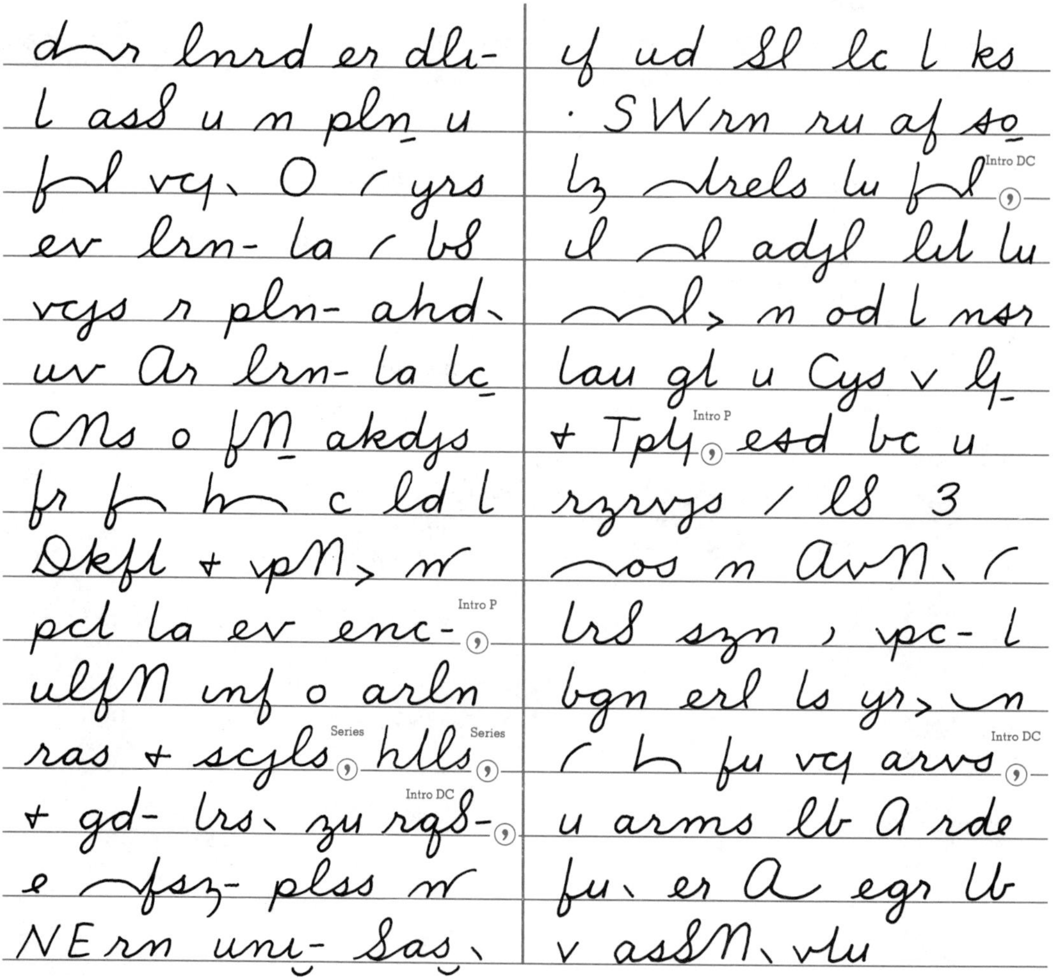

————————————————— 2 —————————————————

Preview Words

Flight *flı̆*

double *dB*

lengthy

lgle

breakfast

brcf8

confirmation *kfrı*

California *CA*

San Francisco

sn frnsscǫ

slide projector

sld Pjcr

d ⌃r crsn p rzrv
· dB r ∫ ⌃e ∫
Nv 5 lru Nv 13،
⌃ ∫ + ι l
arv ⌃r erl afnn
af · lgle lrp ∫
CA، el flı̆ ol v
sn frnsscǫ o flı̆
Nǫ 217، / l arv
n nu hvn / 1⁰⁵
Ern Sd ⌃، p ⌃c
Sln la ⌃ hll ⌃
، rde ∫ s b 2 p ⌃،
l Aso nd · kfrN
⌃ ∫ ⌃rn̲ v Nv 7،
⌃ r ⌃ sdb lrı

enf l se ab 15
ppl kflB، el nd
· lrı lB + · sld
Pjcr + scrn، llb
od brcf8 lb Sv-/
8 ³⁰ la ⌃rn̲ ⌃، p
sN kfrı v lȝ
arms rı a a، ι
USN la lȝ lb·
lrı kvrı n lon
la ⌃c ⌃₉ + ι ⌃
lb Sln la Agl
akdjs lb avlB
∫ s، lgu v ⌃C
∫ Ose̲ lȝ ⌃lr، c

3

Preview Words

smell	sml	horseback	hrsbc
cooking	cc	trail boss	lrl bs
mountains	moNns	fun-filled	fn = fl-
wranglers	rglrs	Happy Valley	hpe vle

dmrs msn lqf
NS n hpe vle
rnC, ehp (enc-
bcll asrs u qs,
z uc se, E d /
r rnC , . lq +
fn = fl- ocq, uc jyn
. lrl rd nl (
moNns lse (sn
k p, + uc cc frs
bf O . opn fr wn
(sn gs don, ev
hrd / sd b ppl
don hr la ly c

sml la q Wrn cc
f mls aroN, loz
hu dN lc hrsbc
rd c njy s m, lns,
. hll clb, + mC
m, lll rglrs U
(aj v 5 r U (
cr v . glf- lrl
bs, mrs msn, -
er gld laur lq-
ab b w s du
u vcj, e lc fw
lu vzl, uvl

4

Preview Words

inns 

slightly 

rustic 

lodges 

resorts 

private 

informative 

campsights 

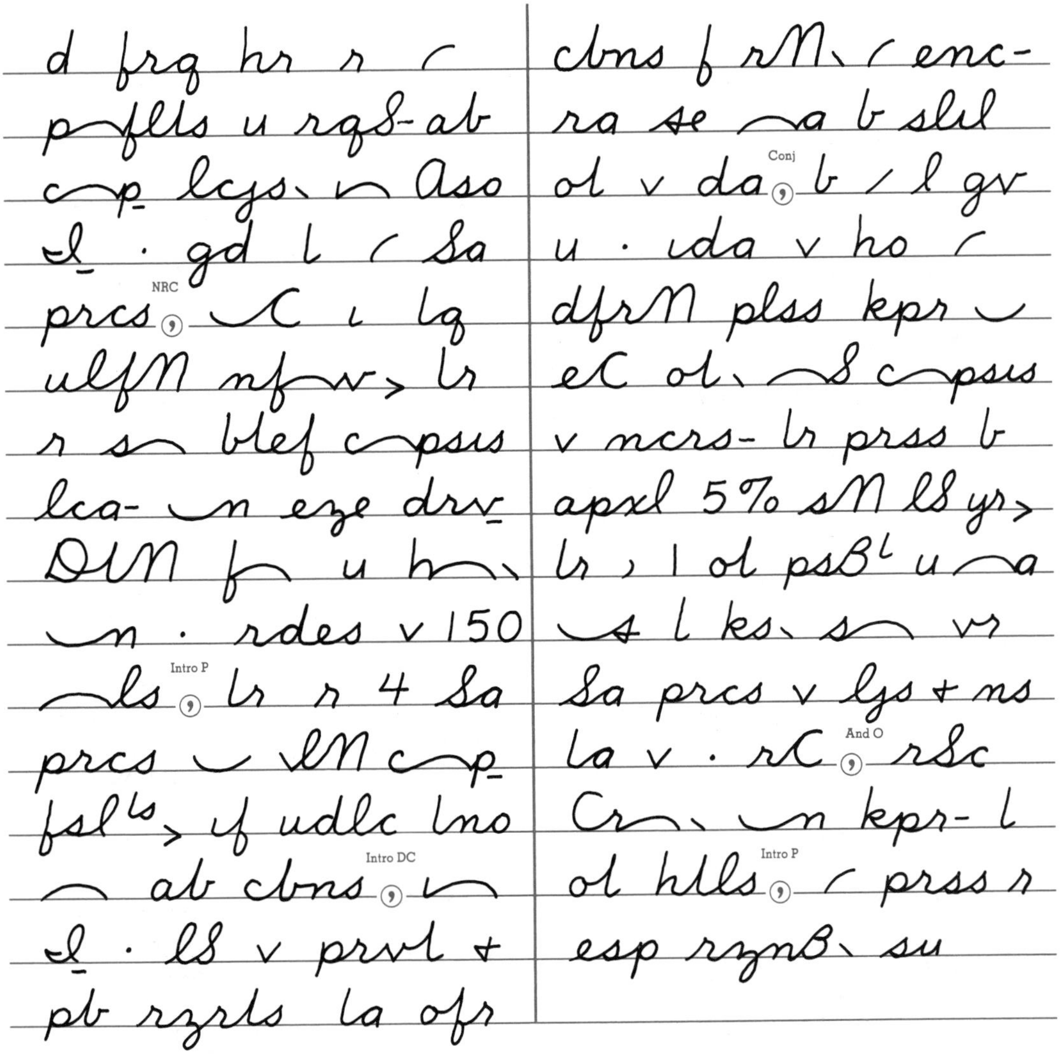

5

Punctuation Study

Add commas to set off one group of words in a series, one introductory dependent clause, and one parenthetical expression, and the name of a city.

Preview Words

- campus
- complex
- theaters
- favorably
- convention
- alternative
- merchandising
- Austin, Texas

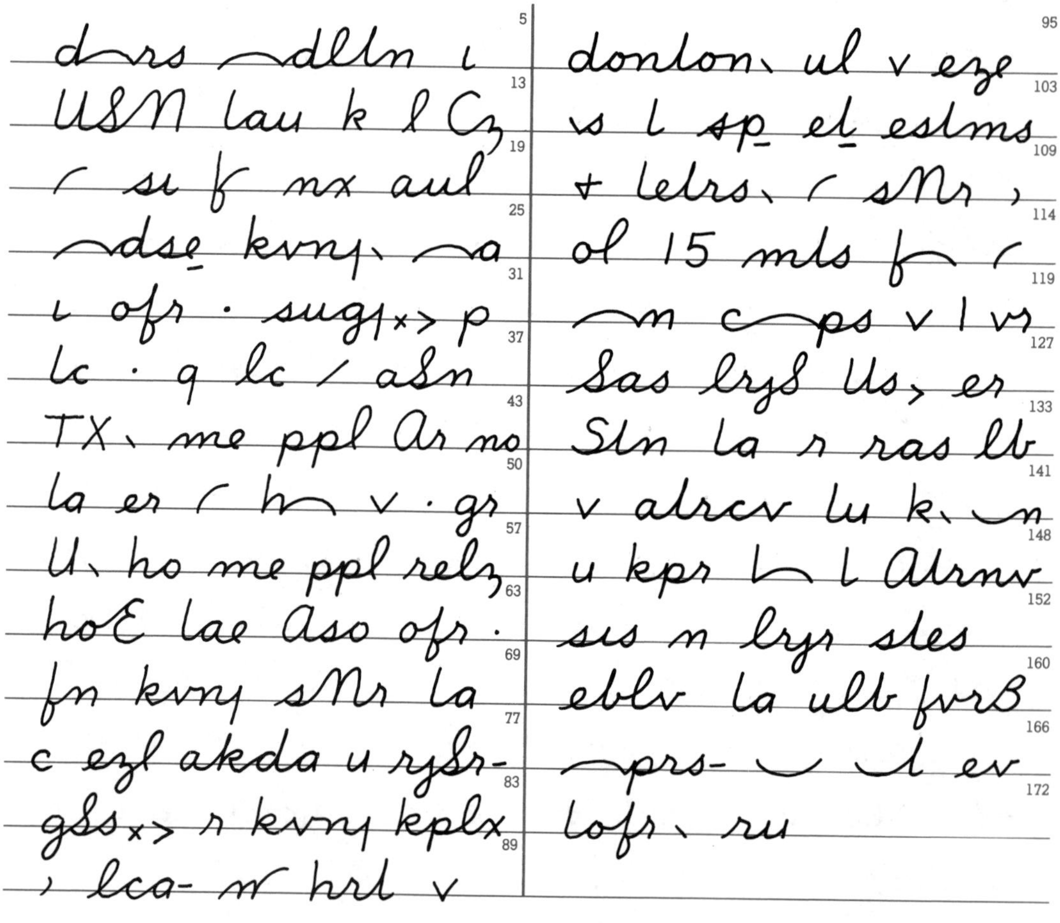

Key

1

Dear Mr. Leonard:

We are delighted to assist you in planning your family vacation. Over the years[1] we have learned that the best vacations are planned ahead. You have already learned that taking chances on finding[2] accommodations far from home can lead to discomfort and expense.

In the packet that we have enclosed, you will find[3] information on airline rates and schedules, hotels, and guided tours. As you requested, we emphasized places[4] in the northeastern United States. If you would still like to consider a southwestern route after showing these[5] materials to your family, I will mail additional literature to you immediately.

In[6] order to ensure that you get your choice of lodging and transportation, we should book your reservations at least[7] three months in advance. The tourist season is expected to begin early this year.

When the time for your vacation[8] arrives, your arrangements will be all ready for you. We are always eager to be of assistance.

Very[9] truly yours, (182)

2

Dear Mr. Carson:

Please reserve a double room for me for November 5 through November 13. My wife and[1] I will arrive in the early afternoon after a lengthy trip from California. We will fly out of[2] San Francisco on Flight No. 217. It will arrive in New Haven at 1:05 p.m. Eastern[3] Standard Time. Please make certain that the hotel room is ready for us by 2 p.m.

I will also need a[4] conference room for the morning of November 7. The room should be large enough to seat about 15 people[5] comfortably. We will need a large table and a slide projector and screen. I will be ordering breakfast to be[6] served at 8:30 that morning.

Please send confirmation of these arrangements right away. I understand that there[7] will be a large convention in town that week, and I wish to be certain that adequate accommodations will[8] be available for us.

Thank you very much for overseeing this matter.

Cordially, (176)

3

Dear Mrs. Mason:

Thank you for your interest in Happy Valley Ranch. We hope the enclosed booklet answers your[1] questions.

As you can see, every day at our ranch is a long and fun-filled occasion. You can join a trail ride[2] into the mountains to see the sun come up, and you can cook fresh beef over an open fire when the sun goes down.[3] We have heard it said by people down here that they can smell that good western cooking for miles around.

Those who don't like[4] horseback riding can enjoy swimming, tennis, a health club, and much more. Little wranglers under the age of five are[5] under the care of a qualified trail boss.

Mrs. Mason, we are glad that you are thinking about being with us[6] during your vacation. We look forward to your visit.

Yours very truly, (134)

4

Dear Frank:

Here are the pamphlets you requested about camping locations. I am also including a guide to[1] the state parks, which I think you will find informative.

There are some beautiful campsites located within easy[2] driving distance from your home. Within a radius of 150 miles, there are four state parks with excellent[3] camping facilities.

If you would like to know more about cabins, I am including a list of private[4] and public resorts that offer cabins for rent. The enclosed rate sheet may be slightly out of date, but it will give[5] you an idea of how the different places compare with each other. Most campsites have increased their prices[6] by approximately 5 percent since last year.

There is one other possibility you may wish to consider.[7] Some of our state parks have lodges and inns that have a rich, rustic charm. When compared to other hotels, the prices[8] are especially reasonable.

Sincerely yours, (170)

5

Dear Mrs. Middleton:

I understand that your committee will choose the site for the next annual merchandising[1] convention. May I offer a suggestion?

Please take a good look at Austin, Texas. Many people already[2] know that we are the home of a great university. How many people realize, however, that we[3] also offer a fine convention center that can easily accommodate your registered guests?

Our convention[4] complex is located in the heart of downtown. You will have easy access to shopping, eating establishments,[5] and theaters. The center is only 15 minutes from the main campus of one of our state's largest[6] universities.

We are certain that our rates will be very attractive to your committee. When you compare them[7] to alternative sites in larger cities, we believe that you will be favorably impressed with what we have[8] to offer.

Respectfully yours, (166)

LESSON 34

Shorthand Vocabulary Review

1. Write city names according to principle.

Galveston	glvSn	New Haven	nu hvn
Houston	hSn	Saint Louis	sN lus
Cambridge	kbrj	Oxford	vfd
Acapulco	acplco	Fairbanks	frbqs

2. Write the names of countries and geographical regions according to principle.

Scotland	scllN	Middle East	mdl E
England	eglN	Western Europe	W rn urp
Greece	grs	West Coast	W cS
Soviet Union	svel unyn	Philippine Islands	flpn lNs

3. Use state initials to indicate the names of states.

Georgia	GA	New York	NY
Indiana	IN	Michigan	MI
Nebraska	NE	Pennsylvania	PA
Wyoming	WY	Vermont	VT

Transcription Aids: Spelling

The following words contain silent letters. Learn to spell them correctly.

a*d*joins	ajyns	begin*n*ing	bgn
a*d*just	ajS	Pitt*s*burg*h*	plsbrq
condem*n*	kd	fas*c*inate	fsna
clim*b*ed	cl-	*is*land	iN
recom*m*end	rcm	com*m*ent	kN

Your Business Vocabulary

itinerary Inrre — A plan used for travel arrangements; a schedule of events, times, and places that are part of the trip.

Have you prepared the itinerary for my trip to Boston?

expand your horizon xpN u hrzn — Increase your knowledge and experience.

Reading and travel are activities that help to expand your horizon.

Reading and Writing Exercises

1

Preview Words

realize	confirm
ocean	originally
motion	courteous
seaside	accommodations

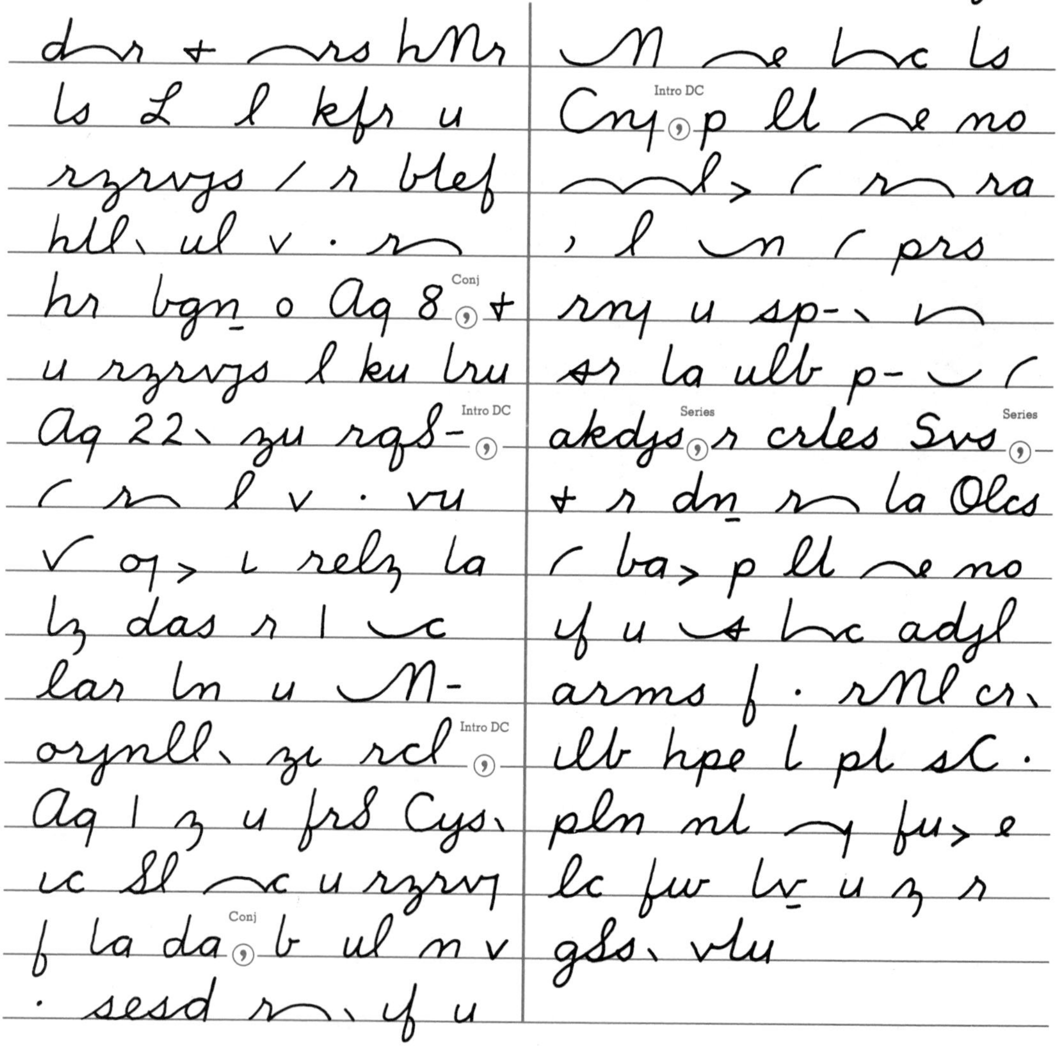

2

Preview Words

sponsor	spNr	weekend	cN
initial	insl	confined	kfn-
minimal	ml	administrative	Amv
Los Angeles	ls ajls	Air Travel	ar trvl

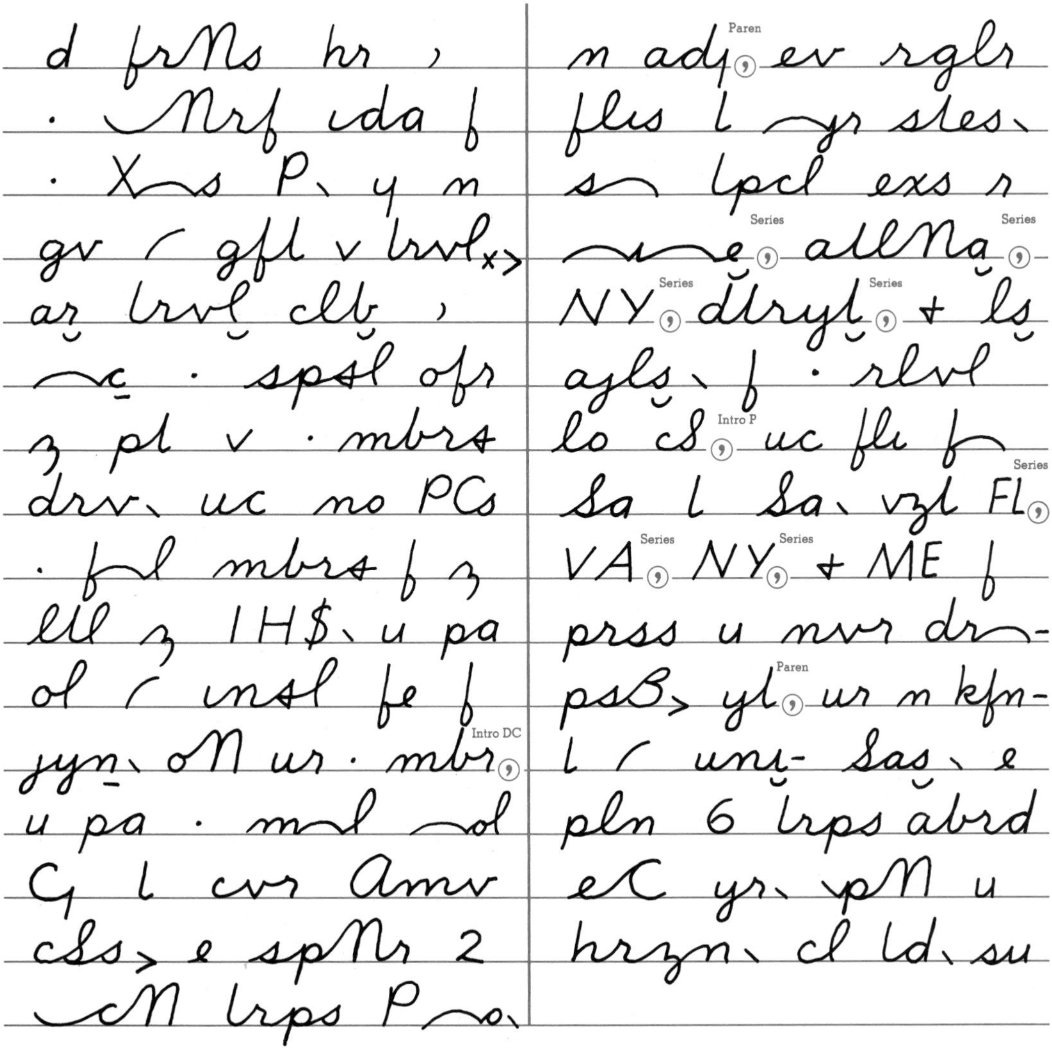

--- **3** ---

Preview Words

Eagle	*egl*	minimize	*m̃ʒ*
coupon	*cpn*	cooperate	*cop*
booking	*bc̲*	discomfort	*Dkfl*
accurate	*acrl*	destination	*dSny*

d ∿rs flps enc-
, . Slfcl la
nllls u l . Dk
ou nx lrp ∿
egl arlns⹁ e
aplʒ f nkv
cʒ- u b r rsN
MUSN⹁ Alo e
lri llⱱ v acrl
n bc̲ flus Ꝺ Mlcs
du hpn f ⱢⱢ⹁
∿n . sily lc us
dvs Ꝺ edu A ec
l m̃ʒ u Dkfl
+ gl u lu dSny ʒ
qcl ʒ psB⹁ n u

Dir Ad
cs Ꝺ ∿rs flps Ꝺ evn
lo ecd n gl u o
brd u rglrl scyl-
flu ∿ s Ꝺ e dd
∿c r arms l
se u o . pln ∿
aol arln⹁ r r
uʒ plse l cop ∿
r nbrs ∿n /
∿ns gv̲ blr Svs
l r Ks⹁ ∿n u bc
u nx flu Ꝺ p nlf r
rʒrvʒ dsc la ulb
apli̲ r crlse cpn⹁
e lqf psN n ls
∿lr⹁ uvl

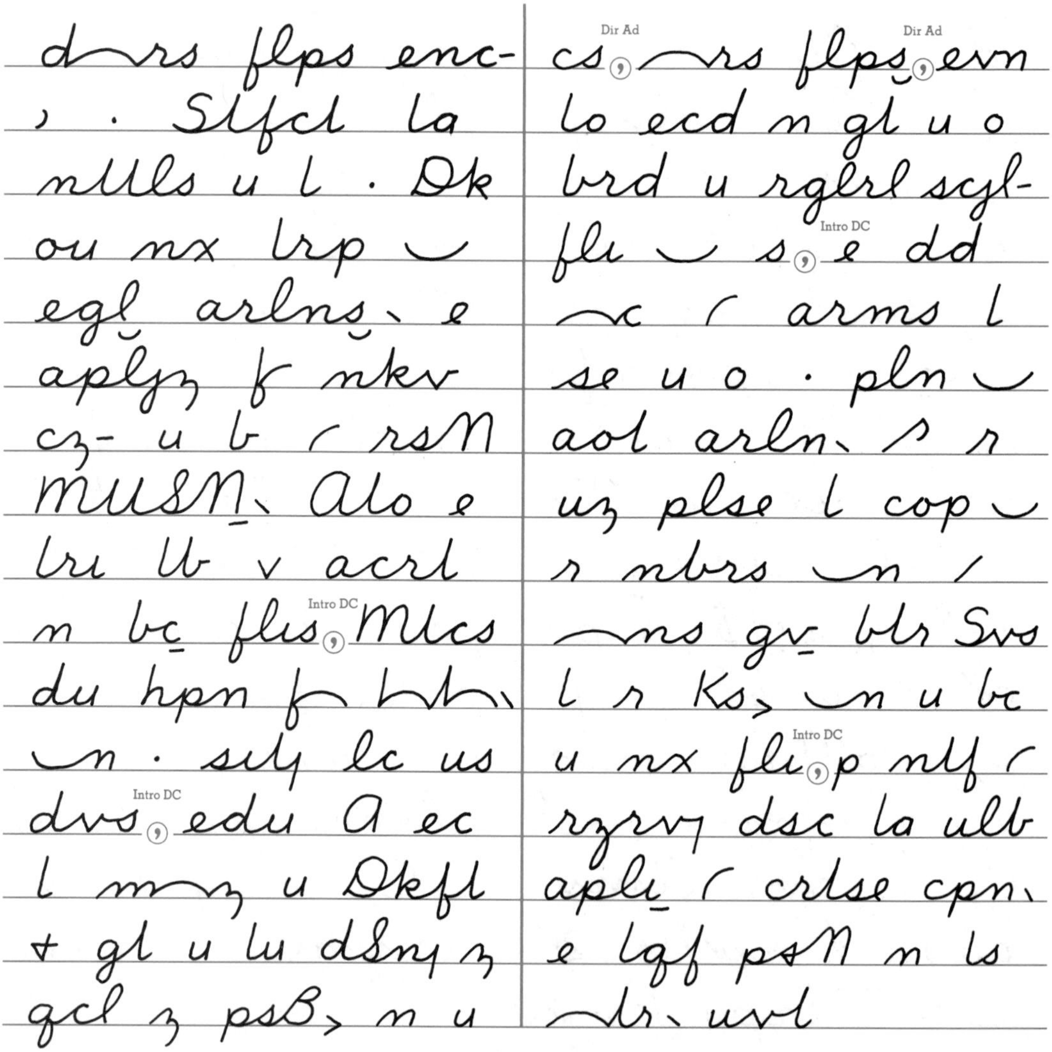

4

Preview Words

visa vza
birth brl
itinerary Unrre
passport pspl
distant DIN
festive fsv
photographs flogrfs
particularly plcl

d M ra ev Ppr-
(enc- Unrre fu
lrp l jpn. if u
apv v lz arms, [Intro DC]
el ~c u rzrvjs
/ oN> er enc
inf l asr u qs
ab Ppr f lrp.
z vpln- w gvl
hNbc, [Intro P] ul nd . vza
n ad lu pspl. if
uv n Ar dn so, [Intro DC] p
lc u brl Slfcl + 2

blc = + = ~ i flogrfs
l (ps ofs. ls lb
. ~dS fe, [Conj] + u pspl
lb ~l- lu ~n . fu
~cs> i USN la
ulb vzl ls DIN
cNre ~n / plcl
fsv. if uv ne ~
qs, [Intro DC] dN hzla l
asc. p ll ~e no
~l if (arms
lc ok lu. ul

5

Punctuation Study

Add commas to show one nonrestrictive clause, two groups of words in a series, and three introductory dependent clauses.

Preview Words

drama 

aiding 

abroad 

portion 

academic 

politics 

tuition 

lifetime 

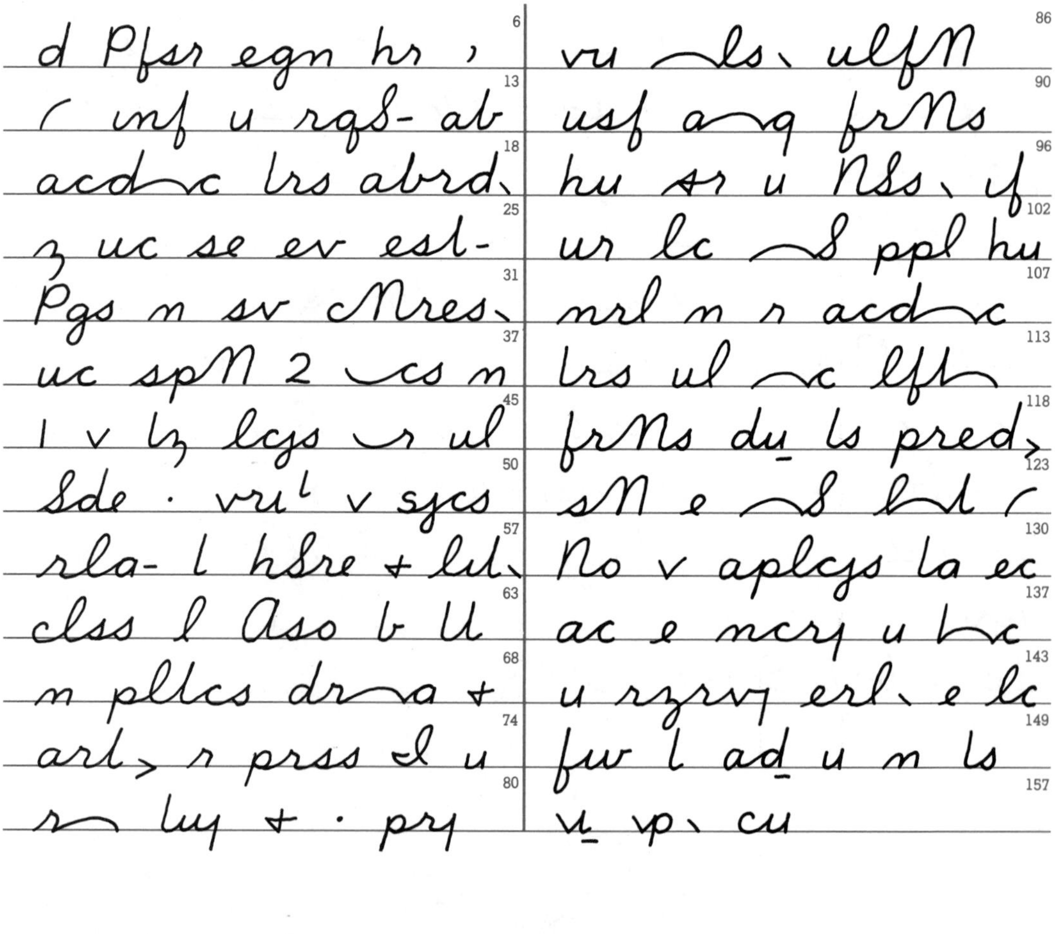

Key

1

Dear Mr. and Mrs. Hunter:

This letter will confirm your reservations at our beautiful hotel. You will[1] have a room here beginning on August 8, and your reservations will continue through August 22. As[2] you requested, the room will have a view of the ocean.

I realize that these dates are one week later than you[3] wanted originally. As I recall, August 1 was your first choice. I can still make your reservation for[4] that date, but you will not have a seaside room. If you want me to make this change, please let me know immediately.[5]

The room rate is well within the price range you specified. I am sure that you will be pleased with the accommodations,[6] our courteous service, and our dining room that overlooks the bay.

Please let me know if you wish to make[7] additional arrangements for a rental car. I will be happy to put such a plan into motion for you.[8]

We look forward to having you as our guests.

Very truly yours, (171)

2

Dear Friends:

Here is a wonderful idea for a Christmas present. Why not give the gift of travel?

Air Travel[1] Club is making a special offer as part of a membership drive. You can now purchase a family membership[2] for as little as $100. You pay only the initial fee for joining. Once you are a member,[3] you pay a minimal monthly charge to cover administrative costs.

We sponsor two weekend trips per month.[4] In addition, we have regular flights to major cities. Some typical examples are Miami, Atlanta,[5] New York, Detroit, and Los Angeles. For a relatively low cost, you can fly from state to state. Visit[6] Florida, Virginia, New York, and Maine for prices you never dreamed possible.

Yet, you are not confined to the[7] United States. We plan six trips abroad each year. Expand your horizon. Call today.

Sincerely yours, (157)

3

Dear Mrs. Phillips:

Enclosed is a certificate that entitles you to a discount on your next trip with[1] Eagle Airlines. We apologize for the inconvenience caused you by the recent misunderstanding. Although we[2] try to be very accurate in booking flights, mistakes do happen from time to time. When a situation like[3] yours develops, we do all we can to minimize your discomfort and get you to your destination as quickly[4] as possible.

In your case, Mrs. Phillips, even though we could not get you on board your regularly scheduled[5] flight with us, we did make the arrangements to seat you on a plane with another airline. It is our usual[6] policy to cooperate with our neighbors when it means giving better service to our customers.

When[7] you book your next flight, please notify the reservation desk that you will be applying the courtesy coupon.[8] We thank you for your patience in this matter.

Yours very truly, (171)

4

Dear Miss Ray:

We have prepared the enclosed itinerary for your trip to Japan. If you approve of these[1] arrangements, we will make your reservations at once.

We are enclosing information to answer your questions[2] about preparing for the trip. As explained in the government handbook, you will need a visa in addition[3] to your passport. If you have not already done so, please take your birth certificate and two black-and-white photographs[4] to the post office. There will be a modest fee, and your passport will be mailed to you within a few weeks.

I[5] understand that you will be visiting this distant country when it is particularly festive. If you have[6] any more questions, don't hesitate to ask. Please let me know immediately if the arrangements look okay[7] to you.

Yours truly, (143)

5

Dear Professor Egan:

Here is the information you requested about academic tours abroad. As you[1] can see, we have established programs in several countries. You can spend two weeks in one of these locations, where[2] you will study a variety of subjects related to history and literature. Classes will also[3] be taught in politics, drama, and art.

Our prices include your room, tuition, and a portion of your meals.[4] You will find yourself among friends who share your interests. If you are like most people who enroll in our academic[5] tours, you will make lifetime friends during this period.

Since we must limit the number of applications that[6] we can accept, we encourage you to make your reservation early. We look forward to aiding you in[7] this exciting experience.

Cordially yours, (149)

LESSON 35

Word Development

Develop new words using the following brief forms:

part

- apart apl
- party ple
- imparted ⌒pl-
- compartment kplm
- particle plcl
- partnership plnr+

port

- carport crpl
- export ✓pl
- reporters rplrs
- airport arpl
- passport pspl
- portfolio plflo

more

- moreover ⌒O
- evermore E⌒
- furthermore frlr⌒

with

- herewith hr⌒
- withholding ⌒hld̲
- withstand ⌒SN

Reading and Writing Exercises

1

Preview Words

whom hm
loss ls
remedy rmde
inconvenienced nkv-
instruct nSrc
intention ntnj
briefcase brfcs
identification idNfj

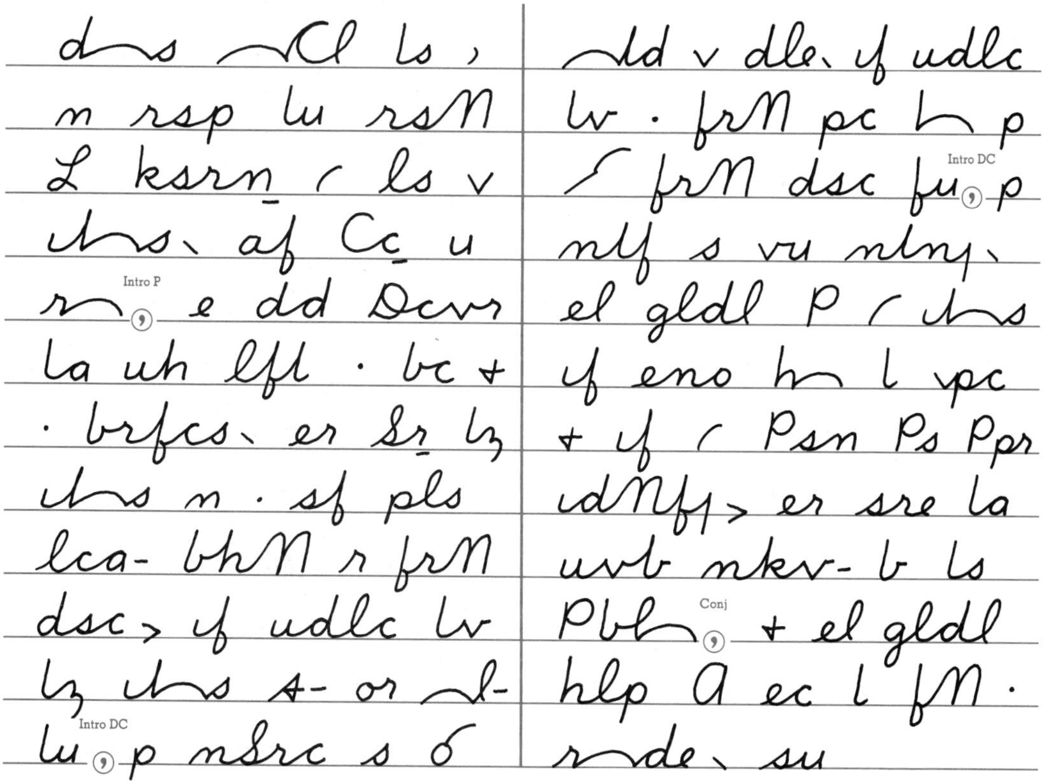

2

Preview Words

kitchen	cCn	minimum	mm
await	a-a	100 yards	1H yds
laundry	lNre	sofa bed	sfa bd
islands	lNs	vacationed	vcj-

dr + rs crlsn
e N- u lno ab
. spsl fl pln
er ofr ls sr.
sN uv vcj- s
w pS, usd no la (Intro DC)
er Nds . nu efsNe
ra f fls v 4 or
ppl> l glf f
ls ra, u S Sa . (Intro P)
mm v 14 ds. du
ls l ul v (us
v . frns- aplm
kp cCn, dn (Series)
lB + Crs, lv r (Series)

sfa bd, + (Series)
bdr 2 dB
bds. lNre fsl ls
r lca- n c
DUN v eC aplm>
f ur NS- n gl (
S ecol ra psB, (Intro DC)
ec pls u n . ns, (And O)
kflB aplm lca-
ab 1H yds f (or>
c u plns no +
nyy (lNs du (
os v Jn, Jl, + Ag. (Series) (Series)
(sn + fn a-a u
/ brgn prss. cu

3

Preview Words

Miami	⌇e	Emerald	⌇rld
fly-sail	flı = sl	highlight	hılı
cruise	crz	registered	rȷšr–
departs	dpls	international	Nnȷl

d⌇r cršfr ⌇rld
arlnš lb p– l lk
u abrd r hld flı
No 336⌇ / dpls
f r Nnȷl arpl o
Dc 20 f ⌇e⌇ e
nls lau dd n lc
Avȷ √ sd lrp la
ev ar–⌇ ȝ pl vu
flı pln _{Intro P} ⌇ ur eȷß l
lc · l = d lrp l r
lMs / hf r rglr

fr⌇ ls ⌇ r flı = sl
pcȷ la ho gn– s
so ⌇C nȷl all⌇ /
hsb v sucf w
pš ^{Conj} ⌇ + me Ks ll s
la r crz ⌇ r hılı
v lr lrp⌇ uf u ⌇
llr rȷšr– f crz _{Intro DC} p
rel r enc–rzrvȷ⌇
r lcls lb hld fu
/ r flı rzrvȷ dsc⌇
lȷf flı ⌇rld⌇ su

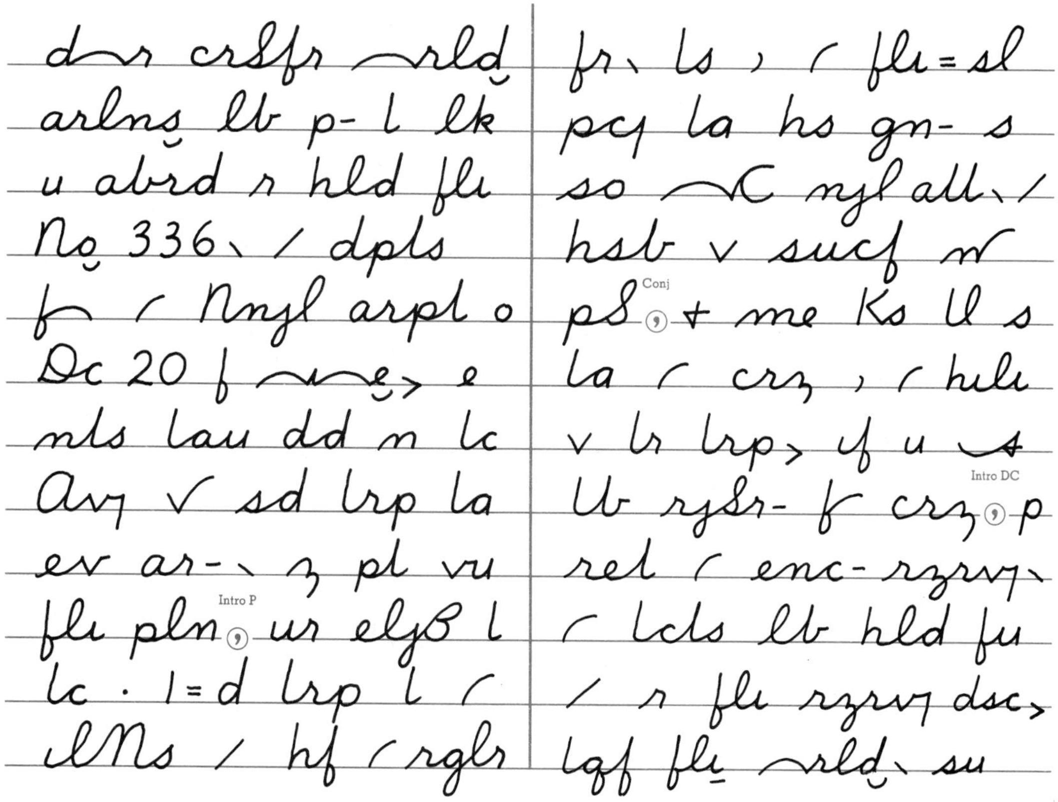

4

Preview Words

Athens	alns	duration	drj
varying	vre	round-trip	roN=trp
departure	dplr	exceptionally	vpjll
returnable	retB	colleagues	clgs

d cls mbrs er hpe
l anoN la Crtr
flis r b ar- f
smr, z . sr / nu
hvn clj, (Intro P) u qlf f
spsl roN=trp frs
+ Dk ras / me
htls, flis vb scjl-
l arv n m, (Series) lNn, (Series)
+ alns. lz Crtr
flis r v vre drj
+ cs, Crtr flis ofr
ejcjl opls l SdNs

/ vpjll lo prss. if
u pls u rzrvj bf
Mr 7, (Intro DC) ulb nlll- l
. adjl Dk v 50$.
Lc u rzrvj, (Intro P) l .
dpzl v 2H$. dpzls
r retB p l 30 ds
prir l dplr, lr r
ol . lml- No v ses
avlB o a flis. pln
no lq abrd - frNs
+ clgs. e dN - N l
lv h - ol u. vlu

5

Punctuation Study

Add commas to show two groups of words in a series, one conjunction, one introductory phrase, and one instance where *and* has been omitted.

Preview Words

woods	famous
angle	mountains
customs	textbooks
climbed	mining car

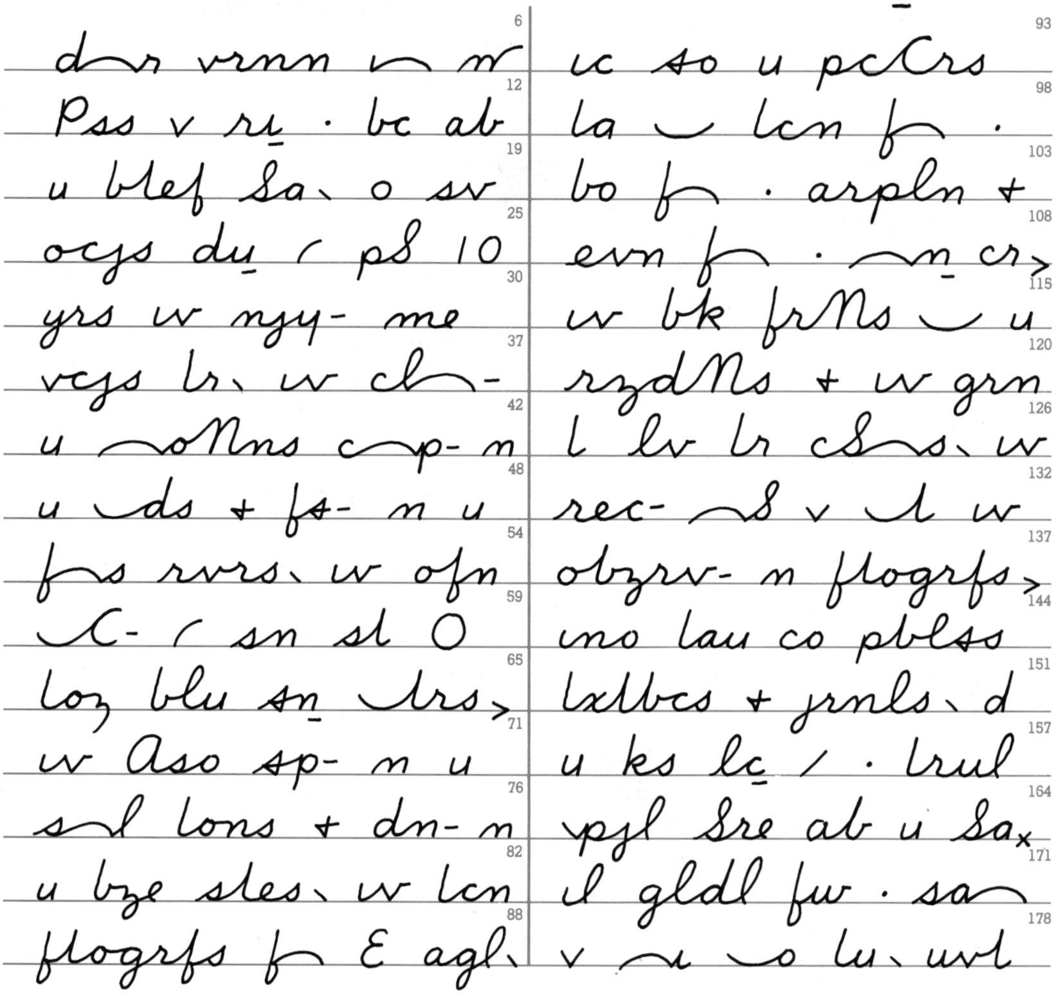

Key

1

Dear Ms. Mitchell:

This is in response to your recent letter concerning the loss of items. After checking your[1] room, we did discover that you had left a book and a briefcase. We are storing these items in a safe place[2] located behind our front desk.

If you would like to have these items shipped or mailed to you, please instruct us on the[3] method of delivery. If you would like to have a friend pick them up at the front desk for you, please notify us[4] of your intention. We will gladly present the items if we know whom to expect and if the person presents[5] proper identification.

We are sorry that you have been inconvenienced by this problem, and we will[6] gladly help all we can to find a remedy.

Sincerely yours, (131)

2

Dear Mr. and Mrs. Carlson:

We wanted you to know about a special family plan we are offering[1] this summer. Since you have vacationed with us in the past, you should know that we are introducing a new efficiency[2] rate for families of four or more people.

To qualify for this rate, you must stay a minimum of[3] 14 days. During this time you will have the use of a furnished apartment complete with kitchen, dining table[4] and chairs, living room with sofa bed, and bedroom with two double beds. Laundry facilities are located[5] within walking distance of each apartment.

If you are interested in getting the most economical[6] rate possible, we can place you in a nice, comfortable apartment located about 100 yards from[7] the ocean.

Make your plans now and enjoy the islands during the months of June, July, and August. The sun and fun[8] await you at bargain prices.

Cordially yours, (168)

3

Dear Mr. Christopher:

Emerald Airlines will be pleased to welcome you aboard our holiday flight No.[1] 336. It departs from the international airport on December 20 for Miami.

We notice[2] that you did not take advantage of the side trip that we have arranged. As part of your flight plan, you are eligible[3] to take a one-day trip to the islands at half the regular fare. This is the fly-sail package that has gained[4] us so much national attention. It has been very successful in the past, and many customers tell us[5] that the cruise is the highlight of their trip.

If you wish to be registered for the cruise, please return the enclosed[6] reservation. The tickets will be held for you at our flight reservation desk.

Thank you for flying Emerald.[7]

Sincerely yours, (143)

4

Dear Class Member:

We are happy to announce that charter flights are being arranged for the summer. As a senior[1] at New Haven College, you qualify for special round-trip fares and discount rates at many hotels. Flights have been[2] scheduled to arrive in Rome, London, and Athens. These charter flights are of varying duration and cost.

Charter[3] flights offer educational opportunities to students at exceptionally low prices. If you place[4] your reservation before March 7, you will be entitled to an additional discount of $50.[5] To make your reservation, include a deposit of $200. Deposits are returnable[6] up to 30 days prior to departure.

There are only a limited number of seats available on[7] all flights. Plan now to go abroad with friends and colleagues. We don't want to leave home without you.

Very truly yours,[8] (160)

5

Dear Mr. Vernon:

I am in the process of writing a book about your beautiful state. On several[1] occasions during the past ten years, I have enjoyed many vacations there. I have climbed your mountains, camped in your woods,[2] and fished in your famous rivers. I have often watched the sun set over those blue, shining waters.

I have also[3] shopped in your small towns and dined in your busy cities. I have taken photographs from every angle. I can show[4] you pictures that were taken from a boat, from an airplane, and even from a mining car.

I have become friends with[5] your residents, and I have grown to love their customs. I have recorded most of what I have observed in photographs.[6]

I know that your company publishes textbooks and journals. Would you consider looking at a truly[7] exceptional story about your state? I will gladly forward a sample of my work to you.

Yours very truly,[8] (160)

unl 8

av*

Shorthand Vocabulary Review

Study the following words and the principles they illustrate. Look for these words in the letters and memos in this unit.

1. Write [sh symbol] for the sound of *ish* or *sh*.

sharp	wish
should	shown
sure	issue
ensuring	publisher
brochure	furnishings

***Unit Eight**
Advertising

2. Write  for the word beginning *sub*.

submit		substitute	
subscribe		subsequently	

More About Punctuation

1. Place a period after an abbreviation that is part of a company name. *Inc.* (Incorporated) and *Ltd.* (Limited) are the most common examples.

Hawksworth, Inc.

Harrison Imports, Ltd.

Use a comma to separate the first part of the name from the abbreviation unless the company omits the comma and includes the *Inc.* or *Ltd.* as part of its official name.

The delivery was arranged by Murray and Sons, Ltd.

Send this letter to Manufacturer's Trust Inc.

When a name using *Inc.* or *Ltd.* occurs at the beginning or in the middle of a sentence, use a comma to separate the abbreviation from the rest of the sentence.

Barnes and Barnes, Inc., will handle the case for us.

Commas used to set off abbreviations will be designated by the letters **Ab** in the reading and writing exercises in this text.

2. Place a period after an initial if it is used as an abbreviation for a proper name.

The report was made by J. B. Harper.

You can get that information from the U. S. Department of Agriculture.

In some instances, a person is given an initial as a middle name. This initial is not an abbreviation and should not be followed by a period.

The bill was signed by President Harry S Truman.

LESSON 36

Brief Forms and Derivatives

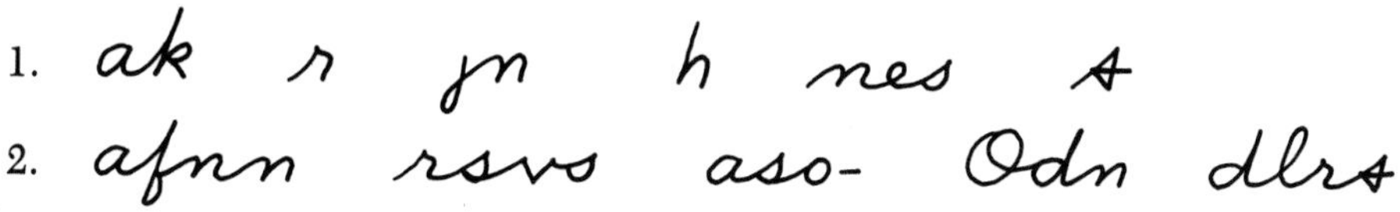

Key

1. accomplish, are/our, general, he/had/him, necessary, ship
2. afternoon, ourselves, associated, overdone, dealership

Phrase Review

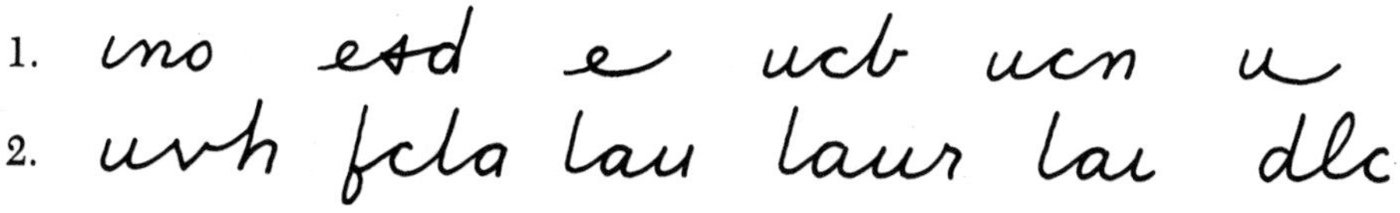

Key

1. I know, we should, we were, you can be, you cannot, you were
2. you have had, fact that, that you/that your, that you are, that I, would like

Reading and Writing Exercises

_____ 1 _____

Preview Words

space _sps_   section _scy_

notice _nls_   nominal _nml_

exposure _pzr_ magazine _gzn_

regardless _rels_   decorating _dcra_

---

d M ⌐rln lgf
nge ab PCo av̱
sps n r ⌐gzn.
r rdrs n v ns̱-
m h dcra̱ Conj + u
Pdcs l v lM pzr
n r ⌐gzn rels
v ⌐r e pls u a.
hoE Paren ⌐ rcm lae
Cz . spsl scy
dvo- l arls +
crfls. sM u Pdcs
r fbrcs Intro DC . ly r Sln
l alrc all ls, ⌐
enc̱ . ra crd fu
inf. z uc se Intro DC ls,

· adjl G rq- f
pls̱ u a m · sp
scy. uf u fl la r
rdrs , ⌐C bls
f la scy . r plsm
fe , nml n kprsn
l r ncrs m sls
la l rzll, p nls
la r ⌐S pNv a
, r l la rns lh
ol. r ⌐S ecol
pln avlB , r aul
kc pln. e ncry u
lgv r crf ksy, p
ll s no l uv
dsd-, vlu

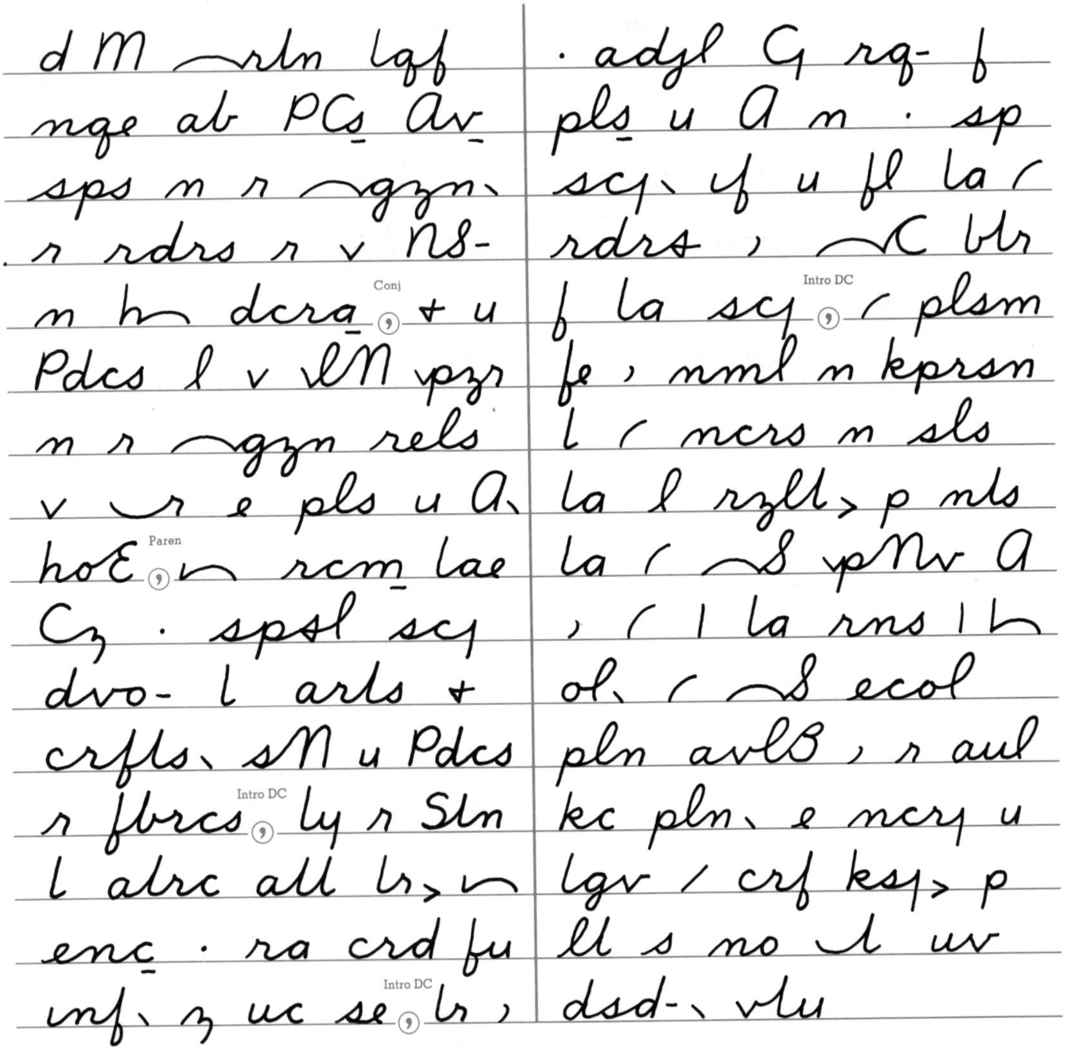

2

Preview Words

aired	ar-	listening	lsn̲
familiar	flr	commercials	krsls
noonday	nnd	talk show	lc so
advertiser	avr	prime time	pr- l-

dr edwds i ⌣M
l lk u z . nu
avr, aso (Paren ,) wb
asc- l hlp pln u
av̲ scjl zz psBs
ur no rn̲ 15 krsls
. ⌣c (Conj ,) + a v lz r
ar- du̲ pr- l-
w erl ⌒rn̲ or
w la afnn, idlc
fu l lq ab scjl̲
s- adjl anoMms
du̲ r ⌒dl v d,
⌒ sr laur flr
⌣ r ⌒rn̲ lc so (Paren ,)

f ex, ls pplr Pq (NRC ,) —
⌣C , hS- b 1 1
nlsn̲ (NRC ,) ks 6 ar /
10° Mn lru Fr, s
nt- f s suc n sl̲
hoshld Pdcs (Conj ,) + i
lq ud gl lM rzlts
f u krsls, r nnd
rpl , aol so ⌣C
hs . lry lsn̲ adeM,
i USM laur k̲ nt
r Sj nx ⌣c, ilc
fw lgl̲ lglr ⌣ u
l-c r plns, ul

3

Preview Words

assume, sessions, underway, invitation, solution, campaign, acceptable, extended

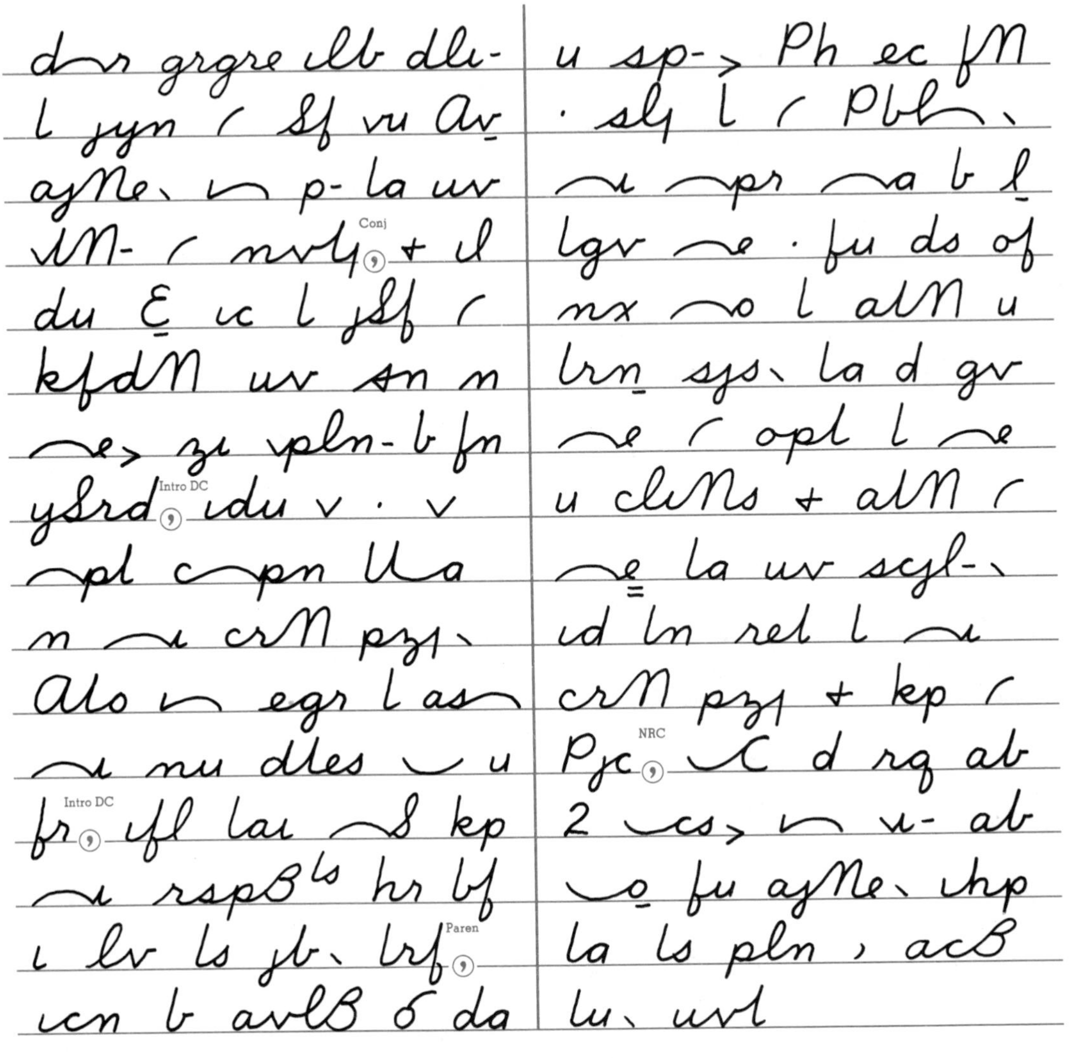

4

Preview Words

color	clr	projector	Pjcr
latest	laS	video tape	vdo lp
artwork	arlo	audio-visual	ado=vzul
justice	jSs	sophisticated	sfSca-

And O

1 du u no o (laS, -S efcv eqpm f so ado=vzul -drels x r u sls Pjs b-d- b u eqpm x> ucn du jSs l blef slds uf u Pjcr brcs don w -dl v . dmSry . . vdo lp , n q- lb efcv uf (ql^L v clr , pr or uf (pcCrs r n srp. uf u - lse . dmSry vr Pdcs, ud se -l . dfrN fn ql^L d

Intro DC

-c. eqpm -f- b bron, inc, , (-S sfSca- 6 -r> l pv ls py, edlc l ar . spsl vu fu. e nvr u l brq (bS -o lau arl dpl hs Pds-. uf u dN agre la r eqpm aprs l -pv (ql^L vu arlo, el lN u (us vr eqpm f 1 -o fre v G> lc . -pl Sp lw suc. cl s ld. cu

Ab Ab Intro P Intro DC

---------- 5 ----------

Punctuation Study

Add commas to show one conjunction, one parenthetical expression, one introductory dependent clause, and one instance of *and* omitted.

Preview Words

gowns	*gons*	substitute	*sStu*
classic	*clsc*	hair styles	*hr Sls*
creative	*crav*	conservative	*ksrvv*
wondering	*Nr*	traditional	*trdjl*

[Shorthand text passage follows, numbered by line: 5, 12, 19, 23, 30, 34, 40, 46, 53, 60, 66, 73, 82, 89 in the left column and 96, 104, 111, 118, 124, 131, 136, 144, 151, 158, 164, 169, 173 in the right column.]

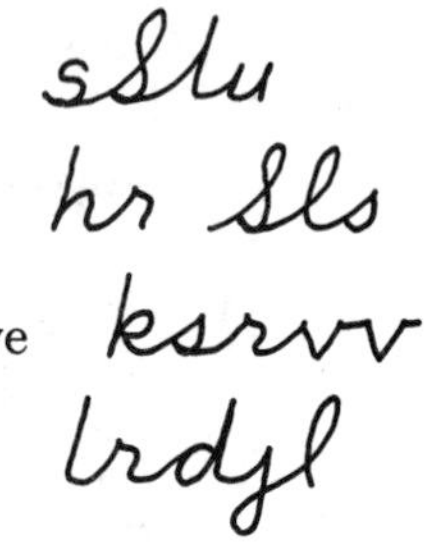

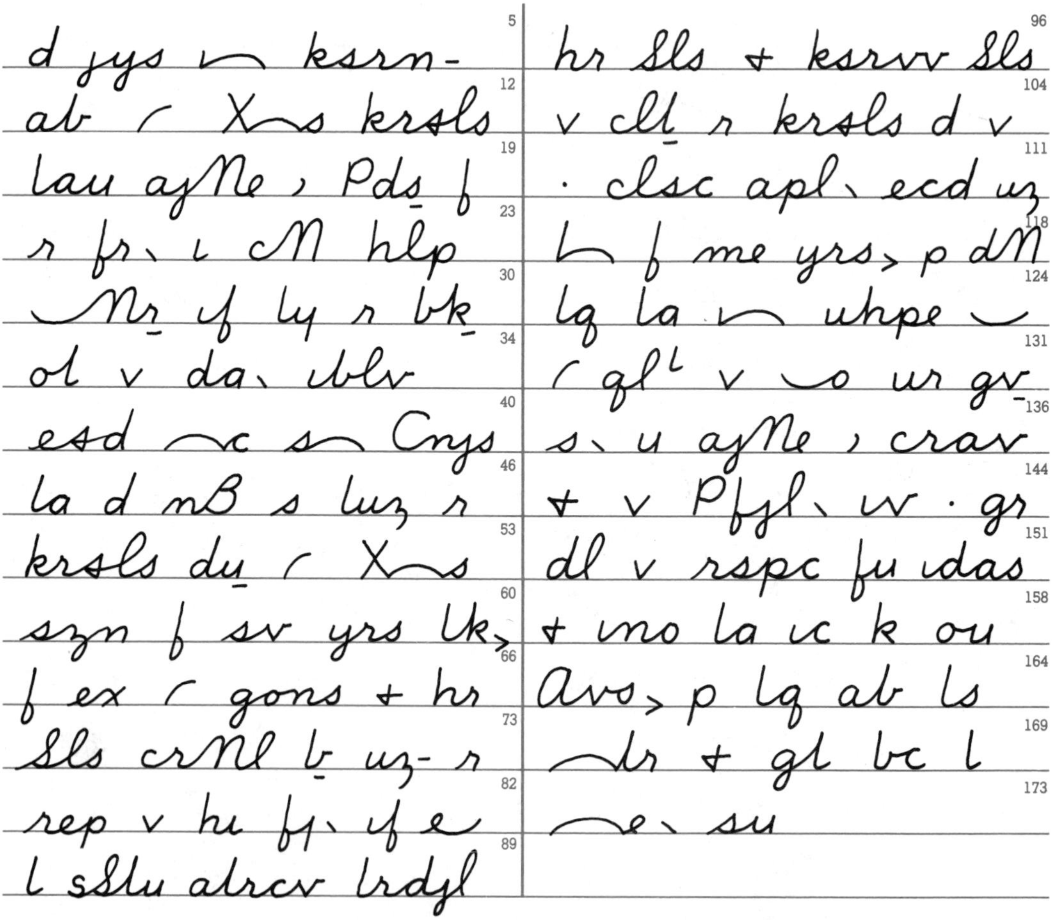

Key

1

Dear Miss Martin:

Thank you for your inquiry about purchasing advertising space in our magazine. Our readers[1] are very interested in home decorating, and your products will have excellent exposure in our[2] magazine regardless of where we place your ad. However, I am recommending that we choose a special section[3] devoted to arts and crafts. Since your products are fabrics, they are certain to attract attention there.

I am[4] enclosing a rate card for your information. As you can see, there is an additional charge required for placing[5] your ad in a specific section. If you feel that the readership is much better for that section, the placement[6] fee is nominal in comparison to the increase in sales that will result.

Please notice that the most expensive[7] ad is the one that runs one time only. The most economical plan available is our annual[8] contract plan. We encourage you to give it careful consideration.

Please let us know what you have decided.[9]

Very truly yours, (184)

2

Dear Mr. Edwards:

I want to welcome you as a new advertiser. Also, I have been asked to help plan your[1] advertising schedule as soon as possible.

You are now running 15 commercials a week, and all of these[2] are aired during prime time in the early morning or in the late afternoon. I would like for you to think about[3] scheduling some additional announcements during the middle of the day. I am sure that you are familiar[4] with our morning talk show, for example. This popular program, which is hosted by J. J. Nelson, comes on the[5] air at 10 o'clock Monday through Friday. It is noted for its success in selling household products, and I think[6] you would get excellent results from your commercials.

Our noonday report is another show which has a large[7] listening audience. I understand that you are coming into our station next week. I look forward to getting[8] together with you to make our plans.

Yours truly, (169)

3

Dear Mr. Gregory:

I will be delighted to join the staff of your advertising agency. I am pleased[1] that you have extended the invitation, and I will do everything I can to justify the confidence[2] you have shown in me.

As I explained by phone yesterday, I do have a very important campaign underway[3] in my current position. Although I am eager to assume my new duties with your firm, I feel that I must[4] complete my responsibilities here before I leave this job. Therefore, I cannot be available on the[5] date you specified.

Perhaps we can find a solution to the problem. My employer may be willing to give[6] me a few days off next month to attend your training sessions. That would give me the opportunity to meet your[7] clients and attend the meetings that you have scheduled. I would then return to my current position and complete[8] the project, which would require about two weeks.

I am excited about working for your agency. I hope that[9] this plan is acceptable to you.

Yours very truly, (190)

4

Gentlemen:

Do you now own the latest, most effective equipment for showing audio-visual materials?[1] Are your sales presentations limited by your equipment?

You cannot do justice to beautiful slides if[2] your projector breaks down in the middle of a demonstration. A video tape is not going to be[3] effective if the quality of the color is poor or if the pictures are not sharp. If you were to see a[4] demonstration of our products, you would see what a difference fine quality would make. Equipment manufactured[5] by Brown, Inc., is the most sophisticated on the market.

To prove this point, we would like to[6] arrange a special viewing for you. We invite you to bring the best work that your art department has produced. If[7] you don't agree that our equipment appears to improve the quality of your artwork, we will lend you the use[8] of our equipment for one month free of charge.

Take an important step toward success. Call us today.

Cordially[9] yours, (181)

5

Dear Joyce:

I am concerned about the Christmas commercials that your agency is producing for our firm. I can't[1] help wondering if they are becoming out of date. I believe we should make some changes that would enable us[2] to use our commercials during the Christmas season for several years to come.

For example, the gowns and hair[3] styles currently being used are representative of high fashion. If we were to substitute attractive,[4] traditional hair styles and conservative styles of clothing, our commercials would have a classic appeal. We could use[5] them for many years.

Please don't think that I am unhappy with the quality of work you are giving us. Your[6] agency is creative and very professional. I have a great deal of respect for your ideas, and[7] I know that I can count on your advice.

Please think about this matter and get back to me.

Sincerely yours, (158)

LESSON 37

Abbreviations and Derivatives

1. M in invs nnd qtrl qs
2. Ts avrs av ecol est-

Key

1. million, inch, invoices, noonday, quarterly, questionnaire
2. thousands, advertisers, advertising, economical, established

Transcription Aids: Capitalization

As a general rule, do not capitalize divisions of a company, such as shipping department or manufacturing division, within a sentence.

Please send a copy of your report to the marketing division.

In general, do not capitalize titles of committees, boards, or employment positions.

The board of directors will meet in the conference room.

Please send your inquiries to the personnel director.

When these terms are used in an inside address, an envelope address, or a signature reference, they should be capitalized.

Mrs. Judith Murray, Marketing Director
Sycamore Valley Press
101 North Street
New York, NY 10015

When referring to a specific president of the United States (or other specific persons who hold high offices in government), always use a capital.

The President will address the nation at 6 o'clock.

Please ask the Senator to return the President's call.

Remember that some rules regarding capitalization may vary among companies. Follow the style used by your employer.

Your Business Vocabulary

ethical

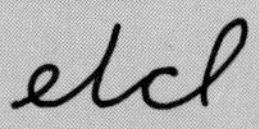

Judged to be "right" according to the accepted standards of conduct.

Our advertising must be based on ethical principles.

quoted price

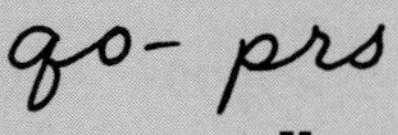

The amount of money stated as a price of goods or services.

You may purchase that equipment at the quoted price.

market penetration

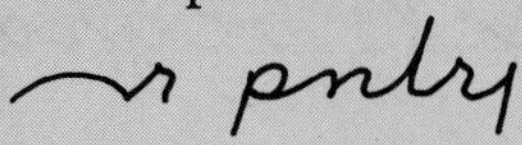

The extent of entry into an area of sales or marketing for the purpose of selling goods or services.

When we introduce the new line of electronic products next spring, can we expect to have good market penetration right away?

Reading and Writing Exercises

1

Preview Words

won 

mayor 

single 

honor 

ethical 

ceremony 

historical 

background 

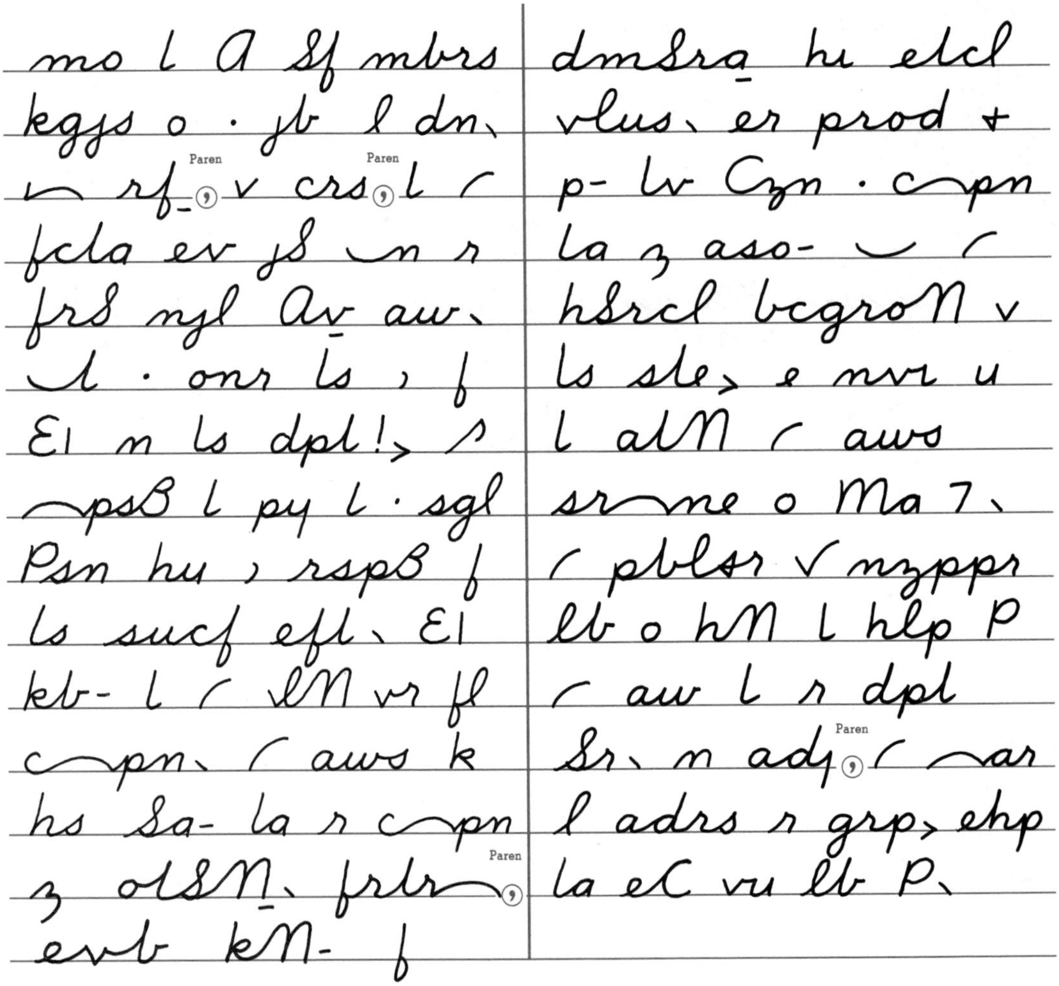

2

Preview Words

spot spl
goals gls
Patricia plrsa
television tlvj
newscast nzcs
audience adeN
supposed spz-
rescheduled rscjl-

d plrsa … ru ls
L l kfr la ev
rscjl- (krsl
anoNm la z spz-
lb sn o Sp 3. bcz
v . spsl adrs b
(P, (Intro P) e uB l ar
u 30=sec spl z
scjl- / 7p 13 > el
… c p la … b
rn u anoNm du
(evn nzcs o Sp 9.

ls , . lN Pq, (Conj) + /
hs . v hi vu adeN.
ifl Sln la ulb p-
… (tlvj vpzr
ul rsv> ihp ls
arm lb sal. / z
. plzr lc … u
ySrd, (Conj) + ilc fw lse
u aq sn. z a, (Paren)
… avlB l … e …
u ne … l rvu
u Av gls. s

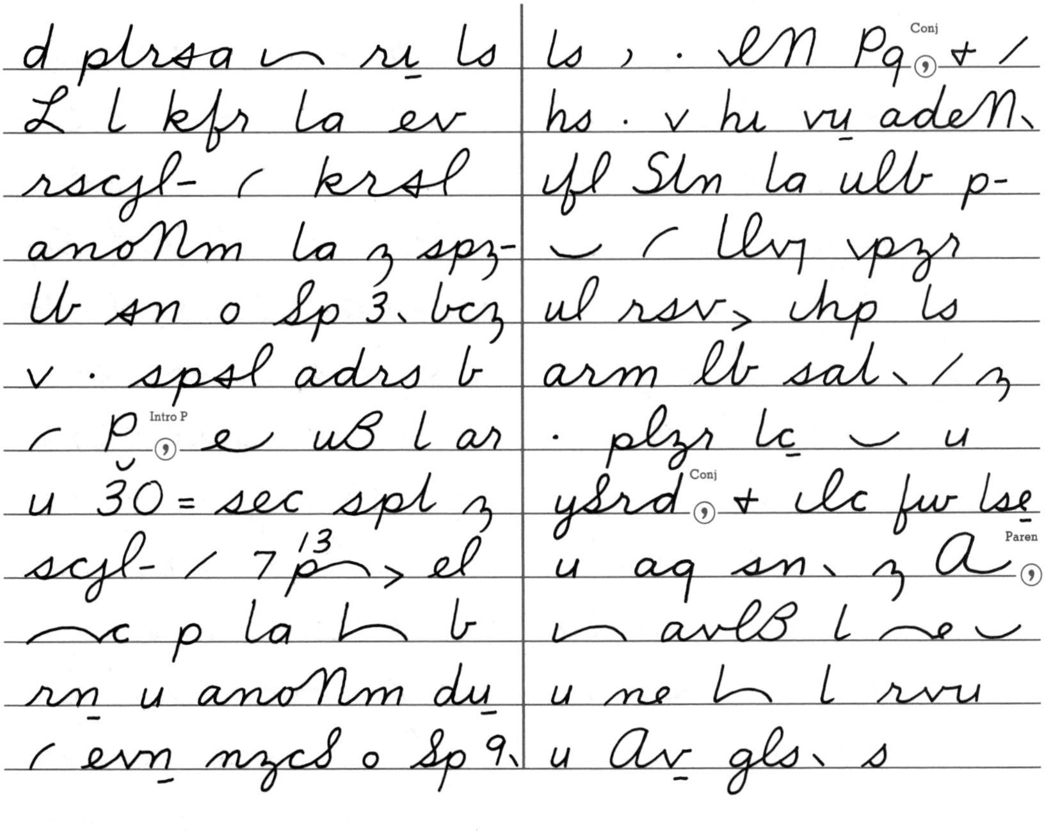

3

Preview Words

trial   *lril*

solid   *sld*

stories   *Sres*

nominal   *nml*

accurate   *acrl*

elsewhere   *els ⌐*

researchers   *rSCrs*

complicated   *kplca-*

dS r u l nf—
at l , hpn w
bs ⌐ o× if u rd
Av rvu eC ⌐ c ⑼   [Intro DC]
uct kfdN lau
nly , acrl + pda,
l ⌐ , · vluß asl f
Pfjl, la , y e ⌐ p
· Sf v rurs + rSCrs
l fN ⌐ mz fu, ly
srl lru ⌐ ⌐ cs
hpn + P ⌐ ⌐ S
siq inf n · f l
la , kv fu l rd,
uc ezl lca ⌐ artcls

la r ⌐ S ⌐ pl lu,
⌐ s ⌐ l ⌐ hoE ⑼   [Paren] [Paren]
uc se l , hpn
els r ⌐ ol rd lq ⑼   [And O]
kplca- Sres, l so
u l e ⌐ m ⑼ es   [Intro P]
⌐ c ls lril ofr,
if u sS f 4 ⌐ oo ⑼—   [Intro DC]
el sN ⌐ frS 4
sus lu fre v G,
kp ⌐ enc— crd ld,
f ol · nml nvSm ⑼—   [Intro P]
ul rsv · M$ ⌐ rl
v sld inf, vlu

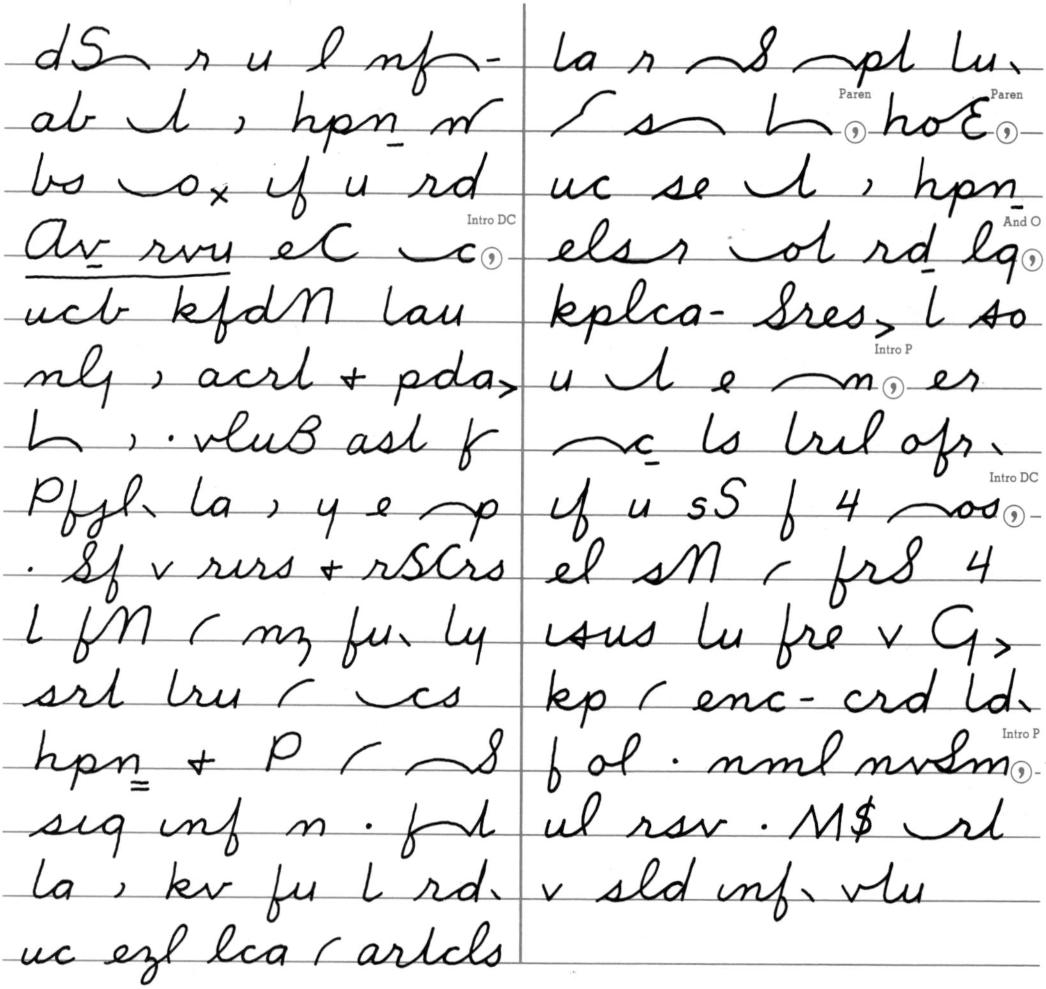

———————————— **4** ————————————

Preview Words

York	*yrc*	promised	*P⌢s-*
image	*⌐ɣ*	extremely	*X⌐l*
stressed	*Srs-*	stability	*SBˡ*
preserve	*Pzrv*	direction	*dry*

[Shorthand outlines — dictation exercise]

mo l p⌢la Svns
iv ß k f⌢ . ⌐e
⌣ u nuß cliⁿ ᴬᵖ⁽⁹⁾
yrc No⌣ ₃ ch vpc-⁽⁹⁾ ᴵⁿᵗʳᵒ ᴰᶜ
ly ⌣ Xⁿl p- ⌣ r
Pɣ u ⌐d lS ⌣c⌣
ly r v- ab r plns
u olln- f lr ak⁽⁹⁾ ᶜᵒⁿʲ +
ly dlc fu l ku n
la s⌢ dry, r Av
⌐ɣr Srs- la ly ⌣+
l Pzrv r ⌐ɣ la ly
v est-⌣ lr Avms

+d rflc SBˡ + qlˡ
v Svo⌣ sⁿ uvh ⌣
gr dl v p ⌣ ls
ⁿ v ak⁽⁹⁾ ᴵⁿᵗʳᵒ ᴰᶜ idu n
alspa laul v ne
Pblⁿs, yf u Sl ⁿ
l rvu r byl f ls
ak⁽⁹⁾ ᴵⁿᵗʳᵒ ᴰᶜ ilb hpe l lc /
u sugyo⌣ ʃ no p
lu l +o la ec dl
r ⁿ v c⌢pn la
ev P⌢s-⌣ clo ⌐e
yf icb v asSⁿ⌣

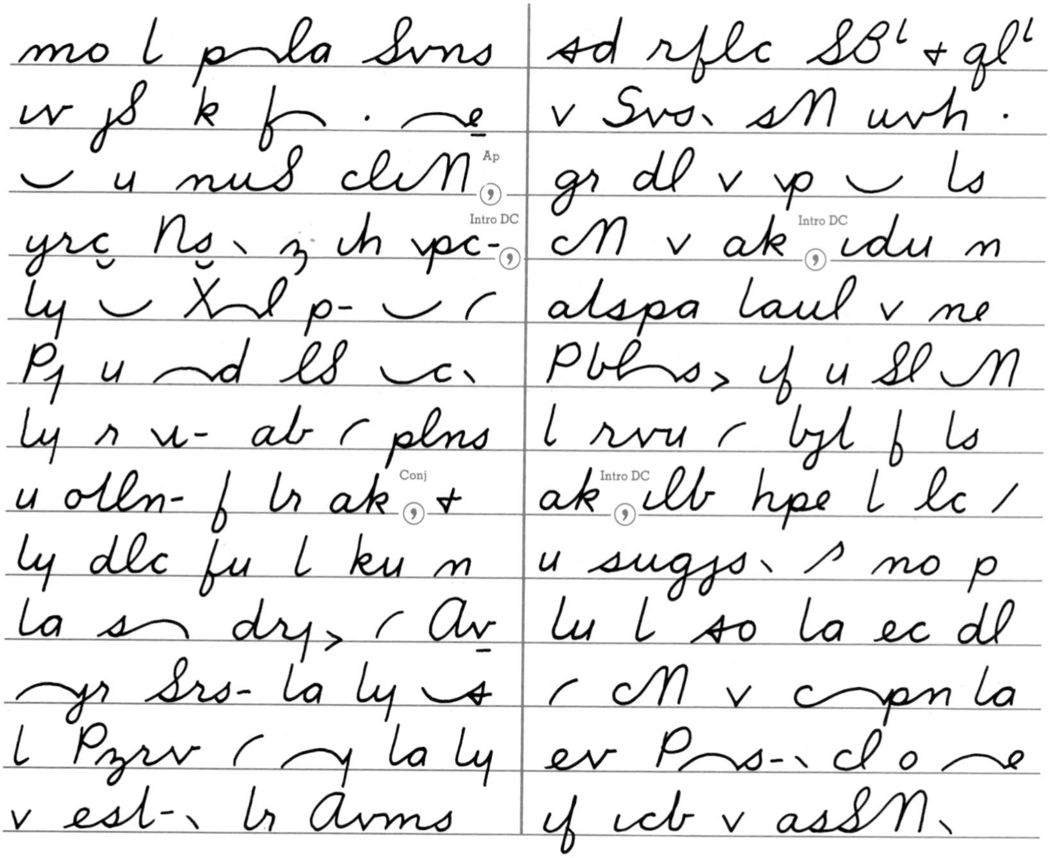

5

Punctuation Study

Add commas to show one direct address, one conjunction, and two introductory dependent clauses.

Preview Words

exceed	vd	sponsored	spNr-
actual	acCul	penetration	pnlry
glance	glN	accordingly	acrdl
estimated	eS-a-	subsequently	ssqNl

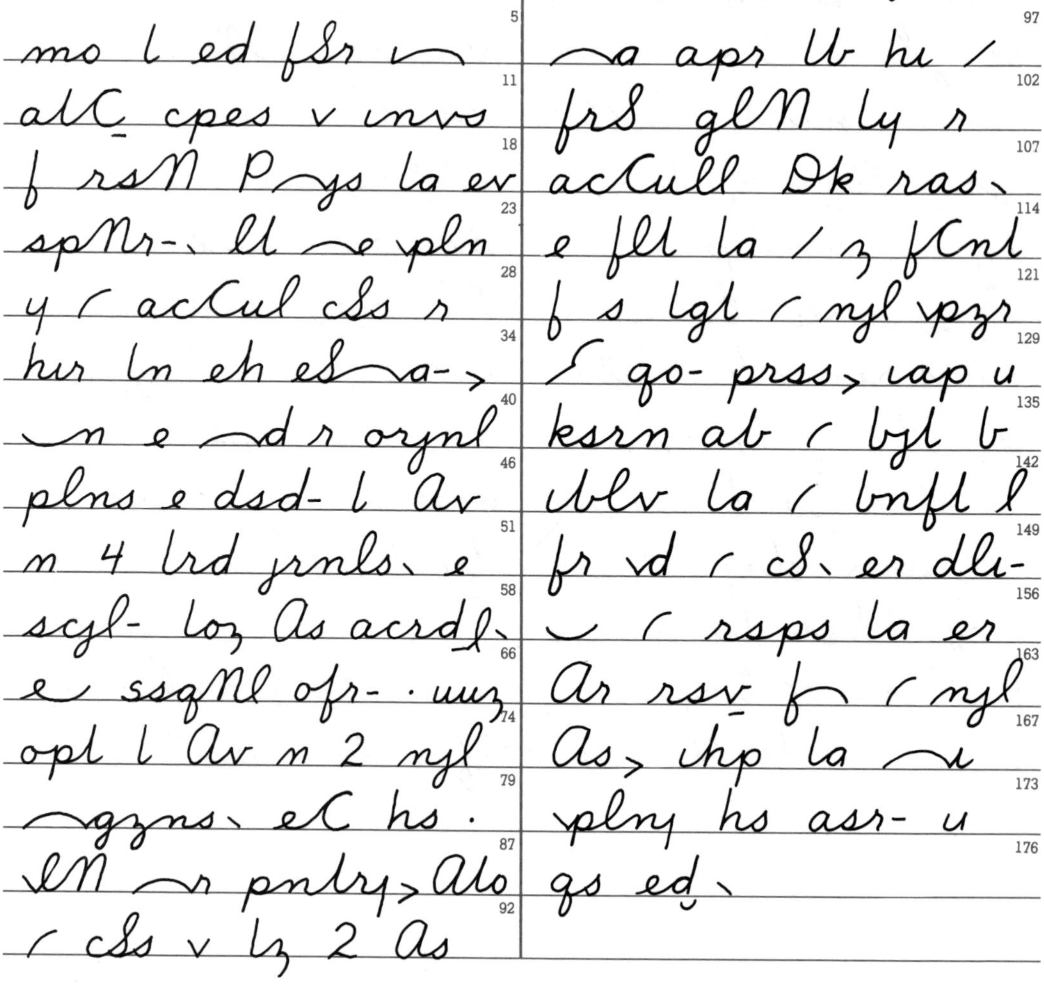

Key

1

MEMO TO: All Staff Members

Congratulations on a job well done. I am referring, of course, to the fact that[1] we have just won our first national advertising award. What an honor this is for everyone in this[2] department!

It is impossible to point to a single person who is responsible for this successful[3] effort. Everyone contributed to the excellence of our fall campaign. The awards committee has stated[4] that our campaign was outstanding. Furthermore, we have been commended for demonstrating high ethical values.[5] We are proud and pleased to have chosen a campaign that was associated with the historical background of[6] this city.

We invite you to attend the awards ceremony on May 7. The publisher of the[7] newspaper will be on hand to help present the award to our department store. In addition, the mayor will[8] address our group.

We hope that each of you will be present. (169)

2

Dear Patricia:

I am writing this letter to confirm that we have rescheduled the commercial announcement that[1] was supposed to be shown on September 3. Because of a special address by the President, we were unable[2] to air your 30-second spot as scheduled at 7:13 p.m.

We will make up that time by running[3] your announcement during the evening newscast on September 9. This is an excellent program, and it has a[4] very high viewing audience. I feel certain that you will be pleased with the television exposure you will[5] receive.

I hope this arrangement will be satisfactory. It was a pleasure talking with you yesterday, and[6] I look forward to seeing you again soon. As always, I am available to meet with you any time to[7] review your advertising goals.

Sincerely, (148)

3

Dear Sir or Madam:

Are you well informed about what is happening in the business world? If you read *Advertising*[1] *Review* each week, you can be confident that your knowledge is accurate and up to date.

Time is a valuable[2] asset for the professional. That is why we employ a staff of writers and researchers to find the news[3] for you. They sort through the week's happenings and present the most significant information in a format[4] that is convenient for you to read. You can easily locate the articles that are most important to you.[5] At the same time, however, you can see what is happening elsewhere without reading long, complicated stories.[6]

To show you what we mean, we are making this trial offer. If you subscribe for four months, we will send the first four[7] issues to you free of charge.

Complete the enclosed card today. For only a nominal investment, you will[8] receive a million dollars worth of solid information.

Very truly yours, (174)

4

MEMO TO: Pamela Stevens

I have just come from a meeting with your newest client, York Industries. As I had[1] expected, they were extremely pleased with the presentation you made last week. They are excited about the[2] plans you outlined for their account, and they would like for you to continue in that same direction.

The advertising[3] manager stressed that they wish to preserve the image that they have established. Their advertisements should reflect[4] stability and quality of service. Since you have had a great deal of experience with this kind of account,[5] I do not anticipate that you will have any problems.

If you still want to review the budget for this[6] account, I will be happy to look at your suggestions. It is now up to you to show that we can deliver[7] the kind of campaign that we have promised. Call on me if I can be of assistance. (155)

5

MEMO TO: Ed Foster

I am attaching copies of invoices for recent promotions that we have sponsored.[1] Let me explain why the actual costs are higher than we had estimated.

When we made our original[2] plans, we decided to advertise in four trade journals. We scheduled those ads accordingly. We were subsequently[3] offered an unusual opportunity to advertise in two national magazines. Each has an[4] excellent market penetration.

Although the costs of these two ads may appear to be high at first glance, they are[5] actually discount rates. We felt that it was fortunate for us to get the national exposure at the[6] quoted prices.

I appreciate your concern about the budget, but I believe that the benefit will far[7] exceed the cost. We are delighted with the responses that we are already receiving from the national[8] ads.

I hope that my explanation has answered your questions, Ed. (171)

LESSON 38

Shorthand Vocabulary Review

1. Write N for the word beginnings *enter, inter, intra,* and *intro.*

enter	N	entertain	Ntn
introduce	Nds	enterprise	Nprz
interview	Nvu	international	Nnjl
interesting	NS̲	introduction	Ndj

2. Write q for the medial or final sound of any vowel + *ng* when the sound is part of the root word and is not a suffix (*ang, eng, ing, ong, ung*).

young	yq	single	sgl
younger	yqr	along	alq
strong	Srq	bring	brq
long	lq	among	a-q

Transcription Aids: Similar Words

sometime  An unspecified point in time.

Bill will visit us sometime soon.

some time  An unspecified amount of time.

I think we should spend some time reorganizing the files.

<table>
<tr><td>Your
Business
Vocabulary</td><td>media

~da</td><td>Plural for *medium*. In mass
communications, *media* refers to
newspapers, magazines, radio and television
stations, etc.</td></tr>
</table>

Please notify all media of our change in plans.

free enterprise

fre Nprz

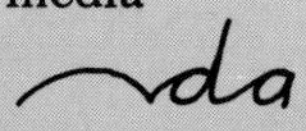

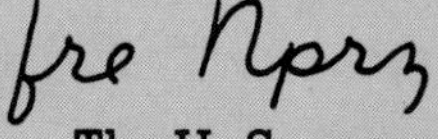

Freedom of individuals to operate businesses
with minimal government regulations.

The U. S. economy is based upon the principle of free enterprise.

Reading and Writing Exercises

―――――――――― 1 ――――――――――

Preview Words

cannot *cn*

system *ss*

buyers *bro*

careers *crrs*

consumer *ks~r*

materials *~drels*

deadline *ddln*

enterprise *Nprz*

d~r bsr lgf
brsr ab r rl v
Av n r eco~n .
ss v fre Nprz _{Intro P} ⑨
Av_ hlps l eyca r
ks~r, me brs dpM
po Avms l U L

E ly M lno ab
r Pdco ly +l
*PCs, r scl, spMr_*
. Ndcy l crrs nx
~o, + Av_ , a~q _{Conj} ⑨
r aras U P_, cd
u sM s 2H cpes

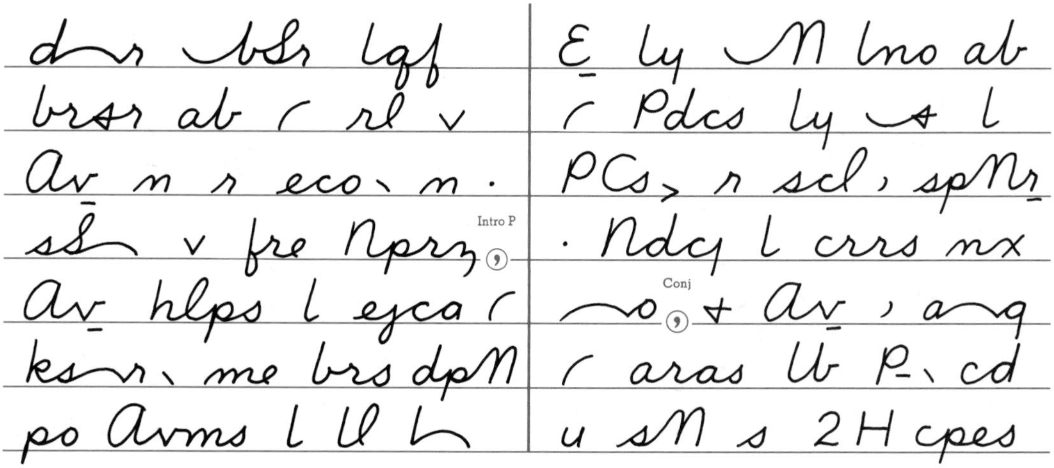

vu brↄr x, уf uc ‿, p
sN ⌒ brↄrↄ l ‿e
∫ adrs gvn abv.
p d · bↄl f ‿d
fes zlz f ‿lrels.

chp uc ‿e ↄ ddln
v Nv 12, уf ucn ‿,
d u p ll ‿e no x,
e Slnl lb B ‿c
q us vu ‿lrels, cu

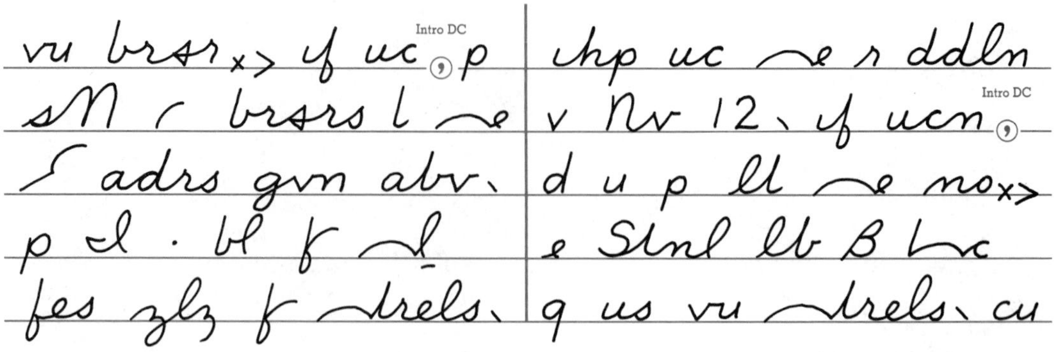

─────────── 2 ───────────

Preview Words

trial	*lril*	political	*plldl*
coffee	*cfe*	surprise	*Sprz*
country	*cNre*	authorities	*alↄ ᵗ⁶*
up-to-date	*pda*	*Wall Street Post*	*l ∫ p∫*

d rdↄ lↄ , · Sprz
n Sↄ fu‿, s‿ nu
l arv ⁄ u dↄ nx
‿c , + edlc u l ac
⁄ z · gfl f‿ s, ⁄
⌒ l ∫ p∫ , ⌒ plↄy
uz‿ lↄ fnnↄl vprls
acrↄ ⌒ ny, y , ⌒
p∫ so pplↄ x frↄ v
a , ⌒ rln lↄ sv

ld alↄ ᵗ⁶, sec , ⁄
klns pda inf, 3d ,
∫ rlↄB, lↄ ↄ me
‿ rzns , lↄ eↄ
nvↄ u l f‿ u o
opn, spN ↄ‿ ‿
rd ls N∫ plↄy, ⁄ l
brq u clsↄ l ⌒
plldl + fnnↄl
dvms la ↄp ↄ eco,

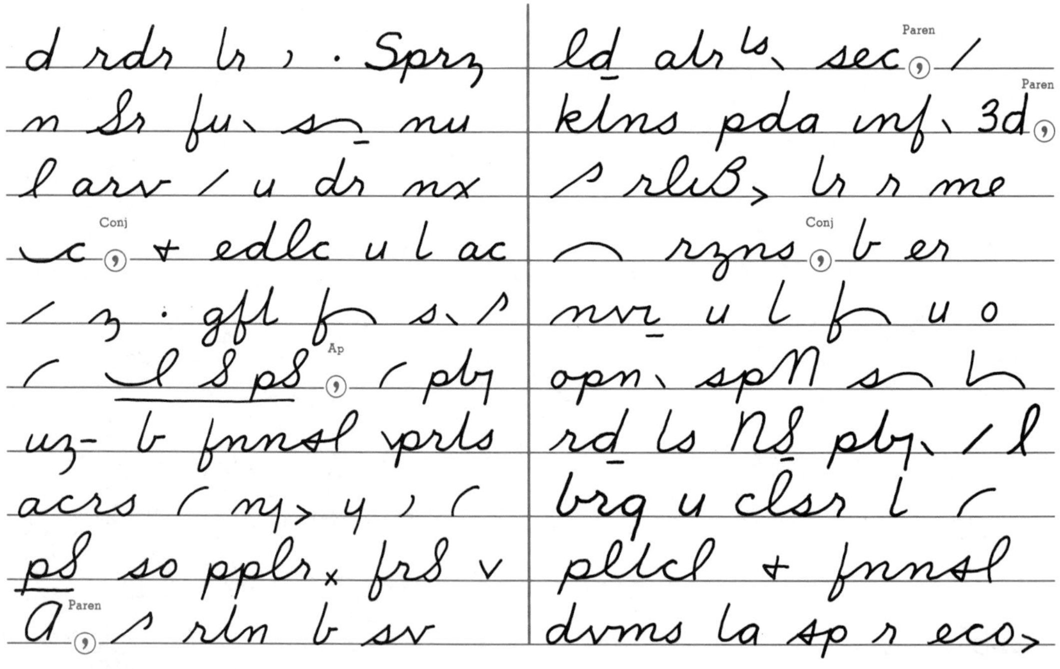

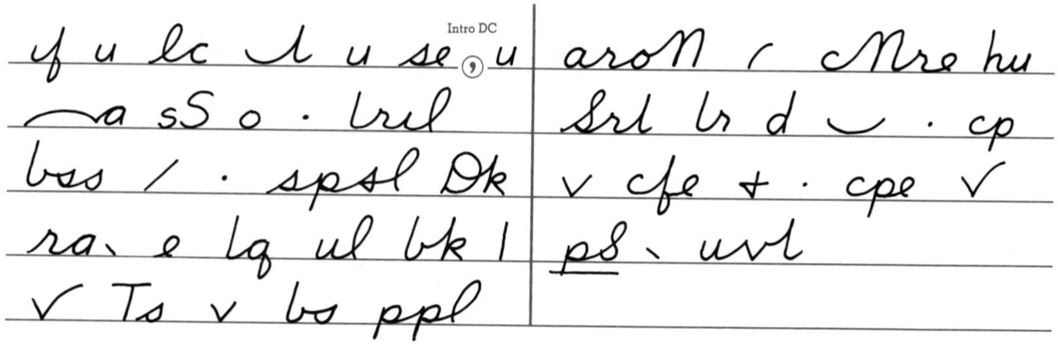

3

Preview Words

top	magazine
topics	businesswomen
edition	reservation
another	professional

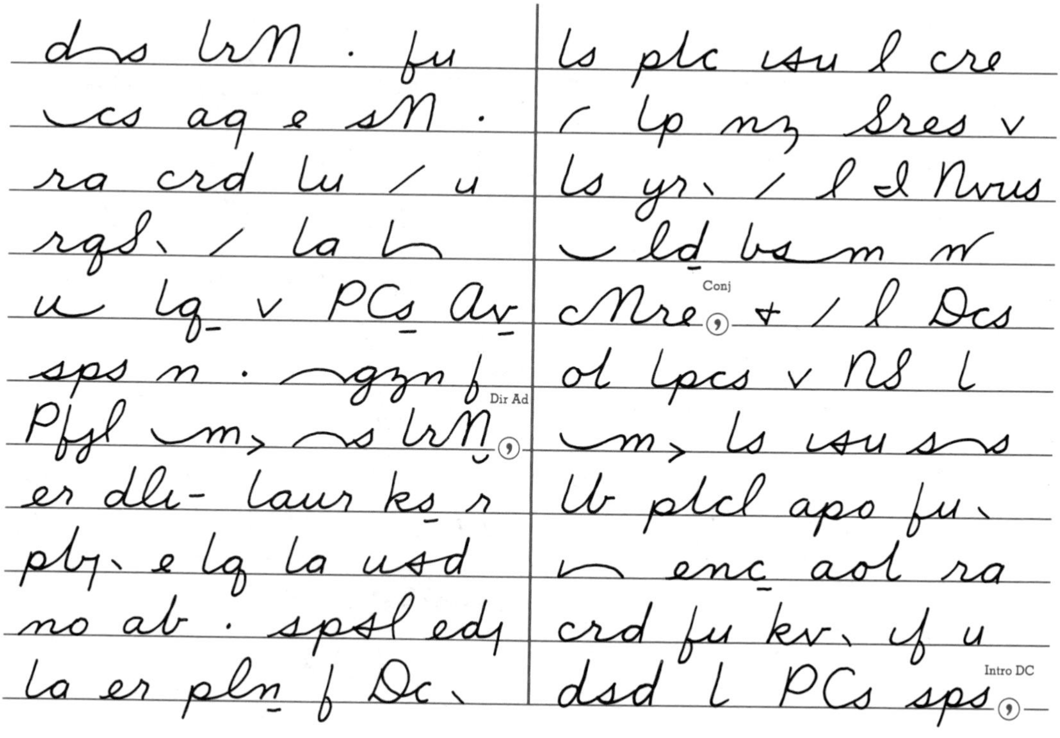

[shorthand outlines]

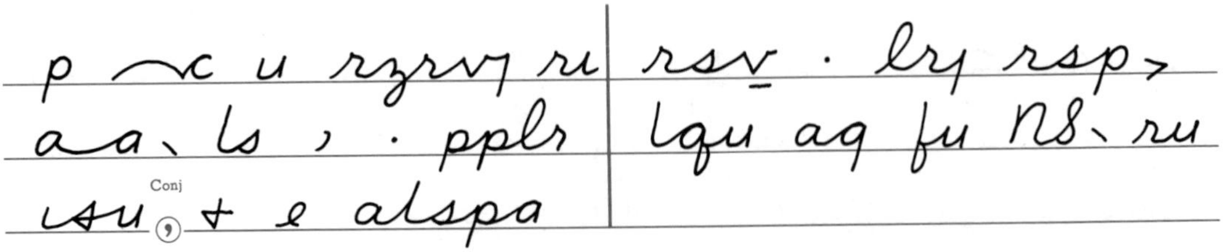

— **4** —

Preview Words

scene	*sn*	reinforce	*rnfs*
media	*da*	sketches	*sccs*
script	*S*	goodwill	*gl*
rough	*rf*	international	*Nnjl*

[shorthand outlines]

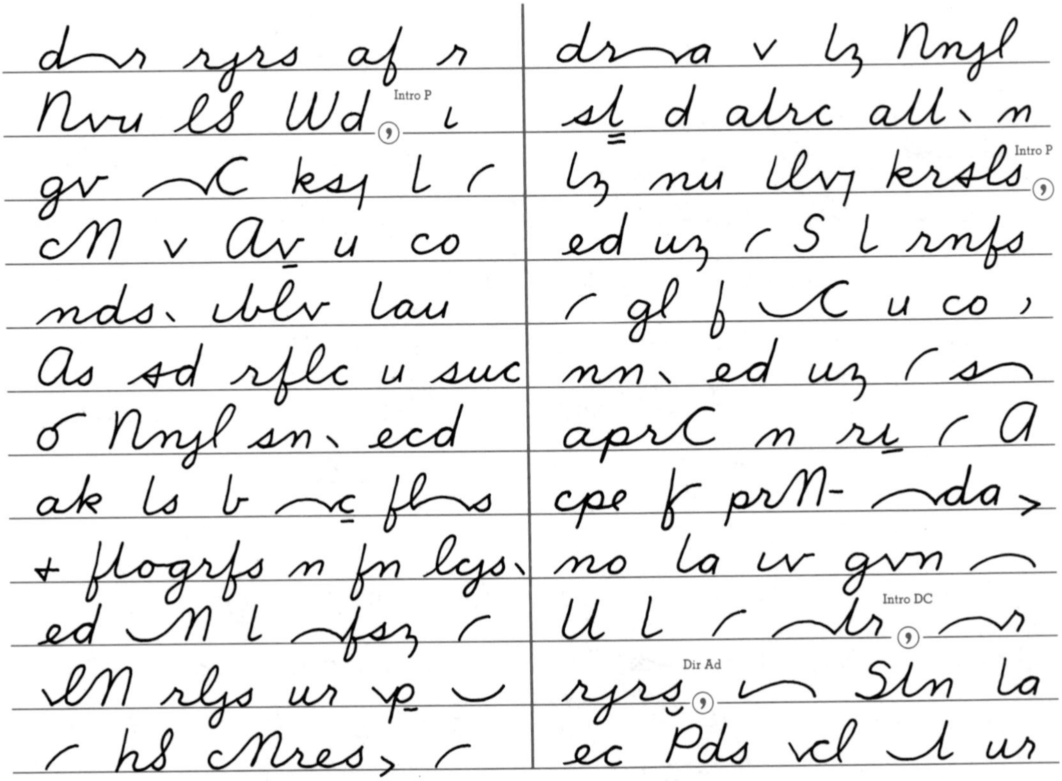

lc f d ub avlß | rf scℓs, ✓lu
_s ✓l ℓ lc ✓ s_

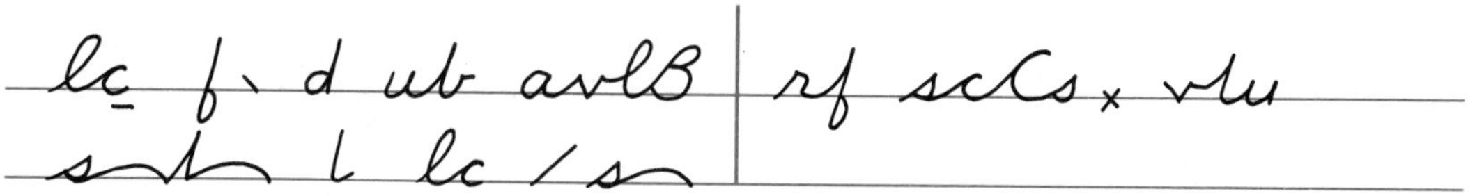

———————— **5** ————————

Punctuation Study

Add commas to show one conjunction, one nonrestrictive clause, one introductory phrase, and one omission of *and*. Also add commas to separate one group of words in a series.

Preview Words

ability _ß ℓ_

skilled _scℓ—_

artists _arℓ§s_

veterans _✓lrns_

fascinating _fsna_

work pace _⌣o ps_

communicate _knca_

photographers _flgrfrs_

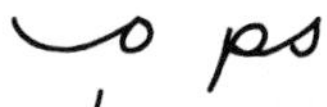

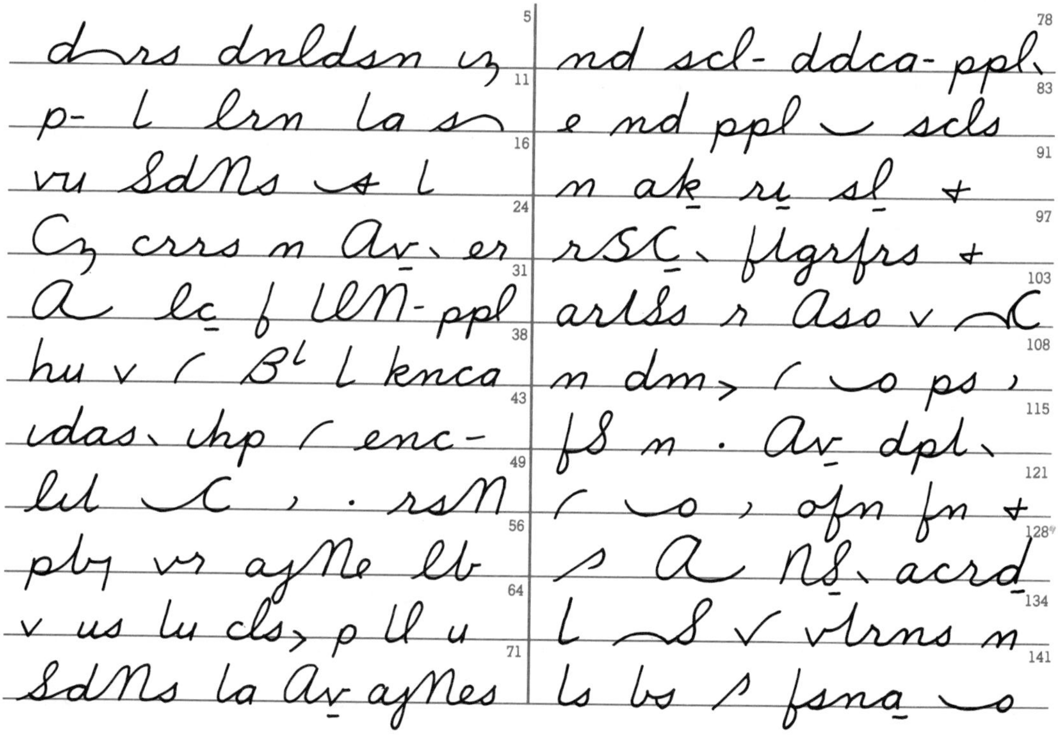

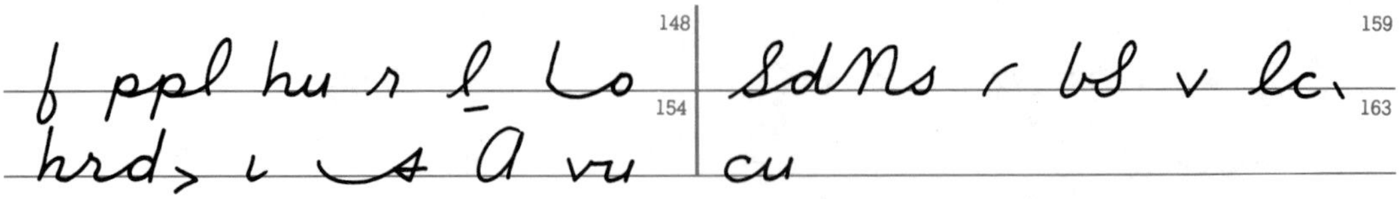

Key

1

Dear Mr. Webster:

Thank you for your brochure about the role of advertising in our economy. In a[1] system of free enterprise, advertising helps to educate the consumer. Many buyers depend upon[2] advertisements to tell them everything they want to know about the products they wish to purchase.

Our school is[3] sponsoring an introduction to careers next month, and advertising is among the areas to be[4] presented. Could you send us 200 copies of your brochure?

If you can, please send the brochures to me at the[5] address given above. Please include a bill for the mailing fees as well as for the materials. I hope you can[6] meet our deadline of November 12. If you cannot, would you please let me know?

We certainly will be able to make[7] good use of your materials.

Cordially yours, (149)

2

Dear Reader:

There is a surprise in store for you. Something new will arrive at your door next week, and we would like you[1] to accept it as a gift from us. It is the *Wall Street Post,* the publication used by financial experts across[2] the nation.

Why is the *Post* so popular? First of all, it is written by several leading authorities.[3] Second, it contains up-to-date information. Third, it is reliable.

There are many more reasons, but[4] we are inviting you to form your own opinion. Spend some time reading this interesting publication. It[5] will bring you closer to the political and financial developments that shape our economy.

If you[6] like what you see, you may subscribe on a trial basis at a special discount rate. We think you will become one[7] of the thousands of business people around the country who start their day with a cup of coffee and a copy[8] of the *Post.*

Yours very truly, (166)

3

Dear Ms. Trent:

A few weeks ago we sent a rate card to you at your request. At that time you were thinking of[1] purchasing advertising space in a magazine for professional women.

Ms. Trent, we are delighted that[2] you are considering our publication. We think that you should know about a special edition that we are[3] planning for December. This particular issue will carry the top news stories of this year. It will include[4] interviews with leading businesswomen in the country, and it will discuss other topics of interest to[5] women.

This issue seems to be particularly appropriate for you. I am enclosing another rate card[6] for your convenience. If you decide to purchase space, please make your reservation right away. This is a popular[7] issue, and we anticipate receiving a large response.

Thank you again for your interest.

Respectfully[8] yours, (161)

4

Dear Mr. Rogers:

After our interview last Wednesday, I gave much consideration to the kind of advertising[1] your company needs. I believe that your ads should reflect your success on the international scene. We could[2] accomplish this by making films and photographs in foreign locations. We would want to emphasize the excellent[3] relations you are experiencing with the host countries.

The drama of these international settings[4] would attract attention. In these new television commercials, we would use the script to reinforce the goodwill[5] for which your company is known. We would use the same approach in writing the ad copy for the printed media.[6]

Now that I have given more thought to the matter, Mr. Rogers, I am certain that we can produce exactly[7] what you are looking for. Would you be available sometime to look at some rough sketches?

Very truly yours,[8] (160)

5

Dear Mrs. Donaldson:

I was pleased to learn that some of your students wish to choose careers in advertising.[1] We are always looking for talented people who have the ability to communicate ideas. I hope[2] the enclosed literature, which is a recent publication of our agency, will be of use to your class.[3]

Please tell your students that advertising agencies need skilled, dedicated people. We need people with skills in[4] accounting, writing, selling, and researching. Photographers and artists are also very much in demand.[5]

The work pace is fast in an advertising department. The work is often fun, and it is always interesting.[6] According to most of the veterans in this business, it is fascinating work for people who are willing[7] to work hard.

I wish all of your students the best of luck.

Cordially yours, (153)

LESSON 39

Shorthand Vocabulary Review

Write *a* for the word beginning *an*.

answer	*asr*	analyze	*alz*
anniversary	*avrsre*	annual	*aul*
another	*aol*	anticipate	*alspa*
Anderson	*adrsn*		

Transcription Aids: Spelling

Usually, when adding a word ending that begins with a consonant to a word that ends in an *e*, retain the *e*.

mov*e*, mov*e*ment	hop*e*, hop*e*less
arrang*e*, arrang*e*ment	car*e*, car*e*less
advertis*e*, advertis*e*ment	car*e*, car*e*ful
effectiv*e*, effectiv*e*ness	forc*e*, forc*e*ful

Your Business Vocabulary

full-color ad

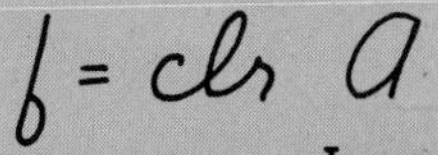

Printed advertisement containing four or more colors.

I am ordering a full-color ad for our fall campaign.

contemporary

Current in style; modern.

We are moving away from a traditional image and toward a contemporary image.

free-lance

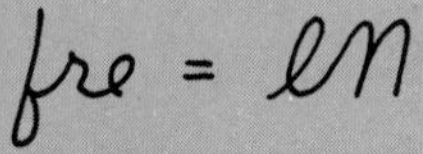

The practice of selling professional services (usually writing or art) to a company without entering into a long-term commitment.

We will ask a free-lance photographer to provide illustrations for the book.

Reading and Writing Exercises

1

Preview Words

manner	mnr	population	ppl
region	ryn	regardless	rels
positive	pzv	questionnaire	qr
cleaners	clnrs	random sample	rN sa

d rCrd ev kp- /
rSC o hoshld
clnrs la evb kdç
fu fr, n enç .
cpe v qr + . cpe
v Sva rzlts, z
uc se f / dla, / (Intro DC)
yrl v ppl Sva-
rsp- lu Pdc n .
pzv mnr, ln
60% sd la ly d
pa / asç prs, l
aS 20% sd la
ly lc- / Pdc +

foN / Ub efcv, (Intro DC)
ly U / suq-rtl
prs z l hi, of 15%
sd la ly d n b /
h rels v prs,
ls Sva z bs- o .
rN sa v ppl
n ls ryn, + / sdb (Conj)
ks- . rliB sa,
n uvh . CN l
Sde lz rzlts crfl, (Intro DC)
p gv e . d, l
ar l Dcs u
/ lql, s

2

Preview Words

sports	spls	type style	tp Sl
itself	sf	full-color	f = clr
original	orjnl	columns	clms
follow-up	flo = p	artwork	arwk

drs jcsn lqf od, zu rqS- (Intro DC) ev rzrv- sps f · f=clr a, / lb 4 clms d b 30 ins dp, (Conj) + / lb pzj- n spls pjs, if udlc l rn · flo=p avm, (Intro DC) esd rzrv sps f la a no, me avrs Cz luz r sn arwk + tp Sl uz- n orjnl a, n od l cl cSs, (Intro P) hoE, (Paren) / psB l rn r sec a n 1 or 2 clrs,

dpN po r arwk sf, (Intro P) / ma b psB l rn r sec a n blc + w l ol, r lrj, (And O) f=clr a, r mS pNv opj avlB, (Conj) + / ofn v efcv, smlms, (Paren) hoE, (Paren) uc aCv r sn efcv' m · flo=p a v · rds- sz, id sug la r sec a b 3 clms d b 20 ins dp, p ll me no l uv dsd- ldu, ul

---
3

Preview Words

designs *dzns*

counties *kes*

colored *clr –*

ink *ıq*

surrounding *SoŊ*

decisions *dsjs*

objective *objcv*

miscellaneous *Mlnes*

d–r dvs es NS– m v u aŊe dzn · sls brsr f s. Alo ev p– Sde grt (Intro DC) r objcv , l ncrs sls b 30% ls yr, z pl v ls pln (Intro P) edlc lsN brsrs l E hoshld n ls sle + n 5 SoŊ kes, es l l Dcs vres dzns + pro rnjs, bf –c

ne dsjs (Intro P) edlc lno u Sd fes f dzn (Series) f Pvd orjnl arls (Series) + f Pds (brsr. / d hlp s lno (cSs v uz clr– ıq (Series) v prŊ (Series) + v ne adjl Mlnes pŊs, wb prs– (o vu aŊe f qs l. ılc fw lhr f u n re l ls lr. vlu

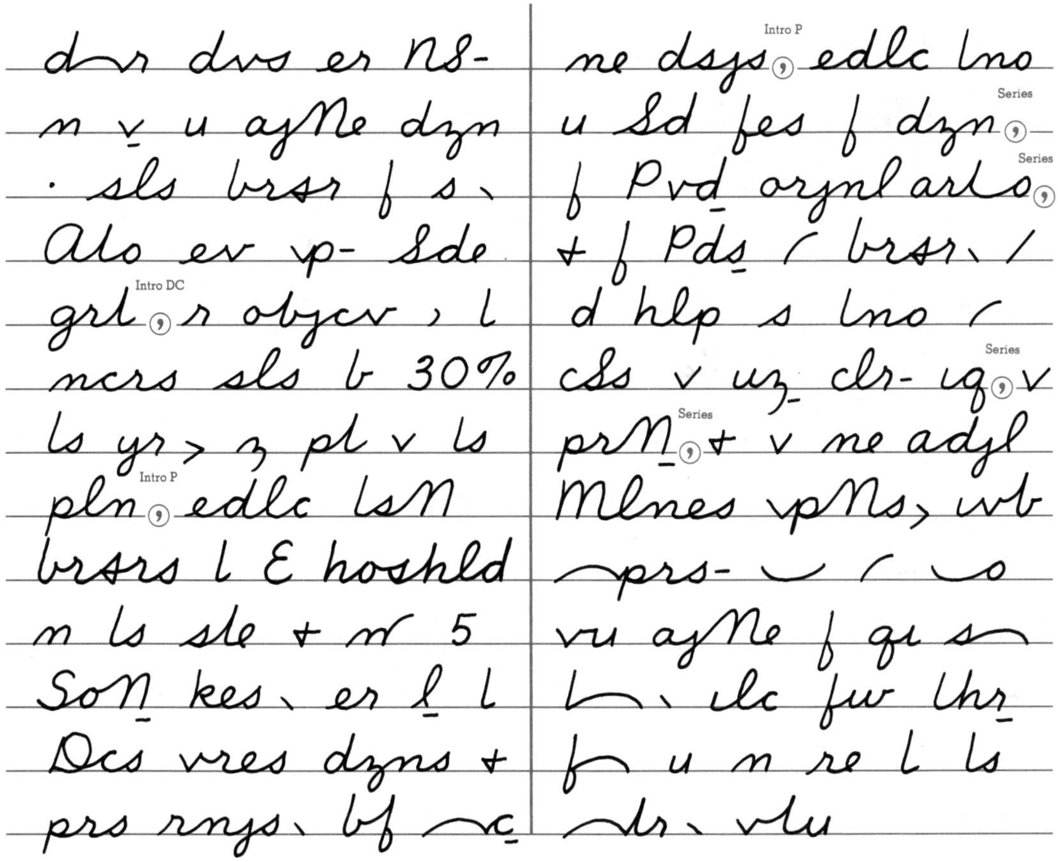

4

Preview Words

bold	bld	crowded	crod-
image	ı	compliment	kplm
owners	ors	dealership	dlrs
sketches	scCs	contemporary	kl prre

mo l bl hrsn idlc
l kplm u o As ur
dy f alo B dlrs.
i lc r jn aprC
uv uz-, n lc f
scCs, (Intro P) hoE, (Paren) ih s
sugjs l ps o lu.
sN r ors v sp-
la ly r lc f .
kl prre ı, (Intro DC) i lq
esd Cz nu clrs. r
drc bron + grn
uv uz- r alrcv, (Conj)
b ly du n kb l .
kl prre ı. i lq

ly sdb Cny- l bri, (And O)
bld clrs, — Aso
ksrn- ab r Cys
+ sz v lp uz- f
cpe. r lp) . hve
Sl la rqs . ll v
sps. / crNl lcs
crod- o pj. esd
elr rds r a l v
cpe so la ls lp
hs lb uz-, (Conj) or esd
slc . dfrN Sl la
db — apo, idlc
lse r scCs aq af
uv adrs- lz Pbls.

5

Punctuation Study

Add commas to show one direct address, one introductory dependent clause, one parenthetical expression, and two conjunctions. Add commas to separate one group of words in a series.

Preview Words

aware

phase

prospect

generously

free-lance

technical

writers

electronics

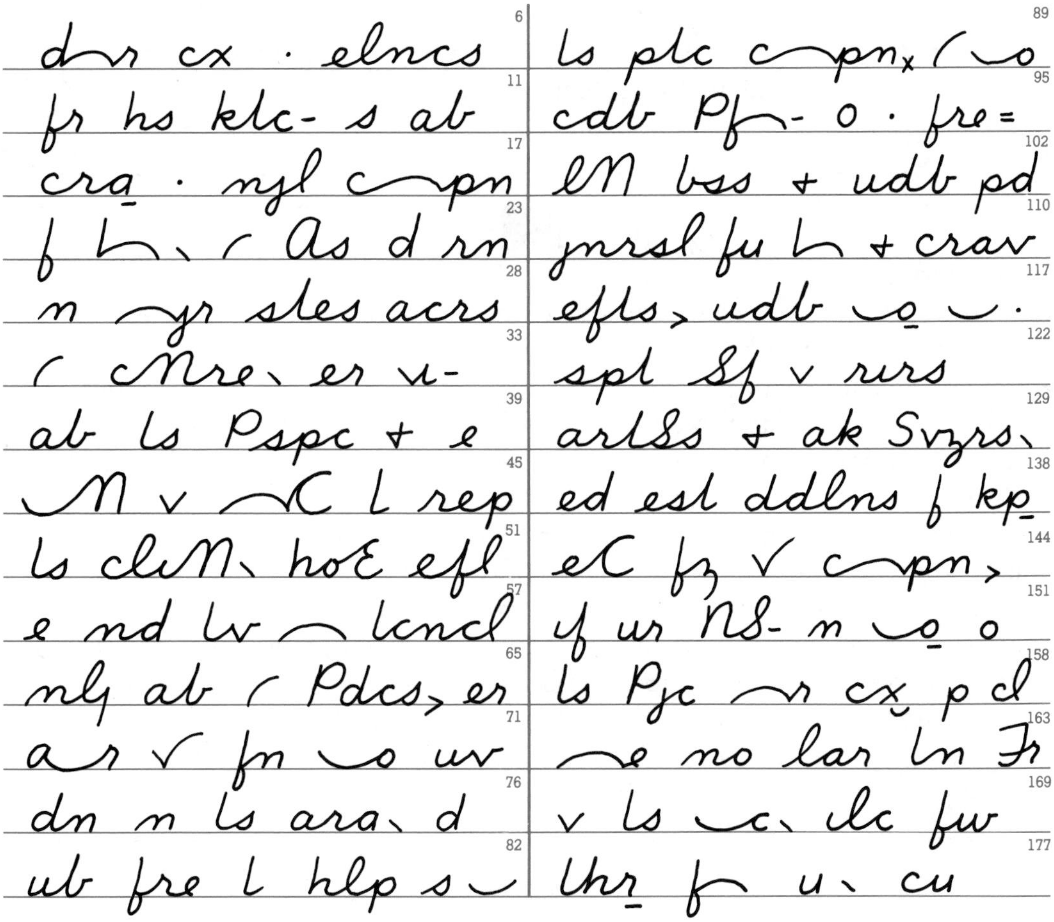

Key

1

Dear Richard:

We have completed the research on household cleaners that we have been conducting for your firm. I am[1] enclosing a copy of the questionnaire and a copy of the survey results.

As you can see from the data,[2] the majority of the people surveyed responded to your product in a positive manner. More than[3] 60 percent said that they would pay the asking price. While almost 20 percent said that they liked the product and[4] found it to be effective, they thought the suggested retail price was too high. Only 15 percent said that they[5] would not buy the item regardless of price.

This survey was based on a random sample of the population[6] in this region, and it should be considered a reliable sample.

When you have had a chance to study these[7] results carefully, please give me a call. I will arrange to discuss them with you at length.

Sincerely, (158)

2

Dear Mrs. Jackson:

Thank you for your order. As you requested, we have reserved space for a full-color ad. It[1] will be four columns wide by 30 inches deep, and it will be positioned in the sports pages.

If you would like[2] to run a follow-up advertisement, we should reserve space for that ad now. Many advertisers choose to use[3] the same artwork and type style used in the original ad. In order to cut costs, however, it is possible[4] to run the second ad in one or two colors. Depending upon the artwork itself, it may be possible[5] to run the second ad in black and white only.

The large, full-color ad is the most expensive option[6] available, and it is often very effective. Sometimes, however, you can achieve the same effectiveness[7] with a follow-up ad of a reduced size. I would suggest that the second ad be three columns wide by[8] 20 inches deep.

Please let me know what you have decided to do.

Yours truly, (173)

3

Dear Mr. Davis:

We are interested in having your agency design a sales brochure for us. Although[1] we have experienced steady growth, our objective is to increase sales by 30 percent this year.

As part of[2] this plan, we would like to send brochures to every household in this city and in the five surrounding counties.[3] We are willing to discuss various designs and price ranges. Before making any decisions, we would like[4] to know your standard fees for design, for providing original artwork, and for producing the brochure. It would[5] help us to know the costs of using colored ink, of printing, and of any additional miscellaneous[6] expenses.

I have been impressed with the work of your agency for quite some time. I look forward to hearing from[7] you in regard to this matter.

Very truly yours, (149)

4

MEMO TO: Bill Harrison

I would like to compliment you on the ads you are doing for the automobile[1] dealership. I like the general approach you have used.

In looking at the sketches, however, I had some[2] suggestions to pass on to you. Since the owners have specified that they are looking for a contemporary[3] image, I think we should choose new colors. The dark brown and green you have used are attractive, but they do not contribute[4] to a contemporary image. I think they should be changed to bright, bold colors.

I am also concerned about[5] the choice and size of type used for the copy. The type is a heavy style that requires a lot of space. It currently[6] looks crowded on the page. We should either reduce the amount of copy so that less type has to be used, or[7] we should select a different style that would be more appropriate.

I would like to see the sketches again[8] after you have addressed these problems. (166)

5

Dear Mr. Cox:

An electronics firm has contacted us about creating a national campaign for them.[1] The ads would run in major cities across the country. We are excited about this prospect, and we want very[2] much to represent this client. However, we feel we need to have more technical knowledge about the products.[3]

We are aware of the fine work you have done in this area. Would you be free to help us with this particular[4] campaign? The work could be performed on a free-lance basis, and you would be paid generously for your time and[5] creative efforts.

You would be working with a support staff of writers, artists, and account supervisors.[6] We would establish deadlines for completing each phase of the campaign.

If you are interested in working on[7] this project, Mr. Cox, please call me no later than Friday of this week. I look forward to hearing from you.[8]

Cordially yours, (162)

LESSON 40

Word Development

Develop new words from the following brief forms:

market

- marketing
- marketable
- marketplace
- supermarket

letter

- letterhead
- newsletter

up

- updated
- upon
- upcoming
- upward
- upper

suggest

- suggestion
- suggesting
- suggestive
- suggestible

not

- cannot
- notwithstanding

work

- workbook
- workday
- workload
- workmen
- workweek

Reading and Writing Exercises

---------- 1 ----------

Preview Words

loses *lzs*

danger *dnjr*

luncheon *lnCn*

reputation *rply*

gaining *gn*

pharmacies *fr—ses*

retail outlets *rll ollls*

sporting goods *spl go*

[shorthand notes]

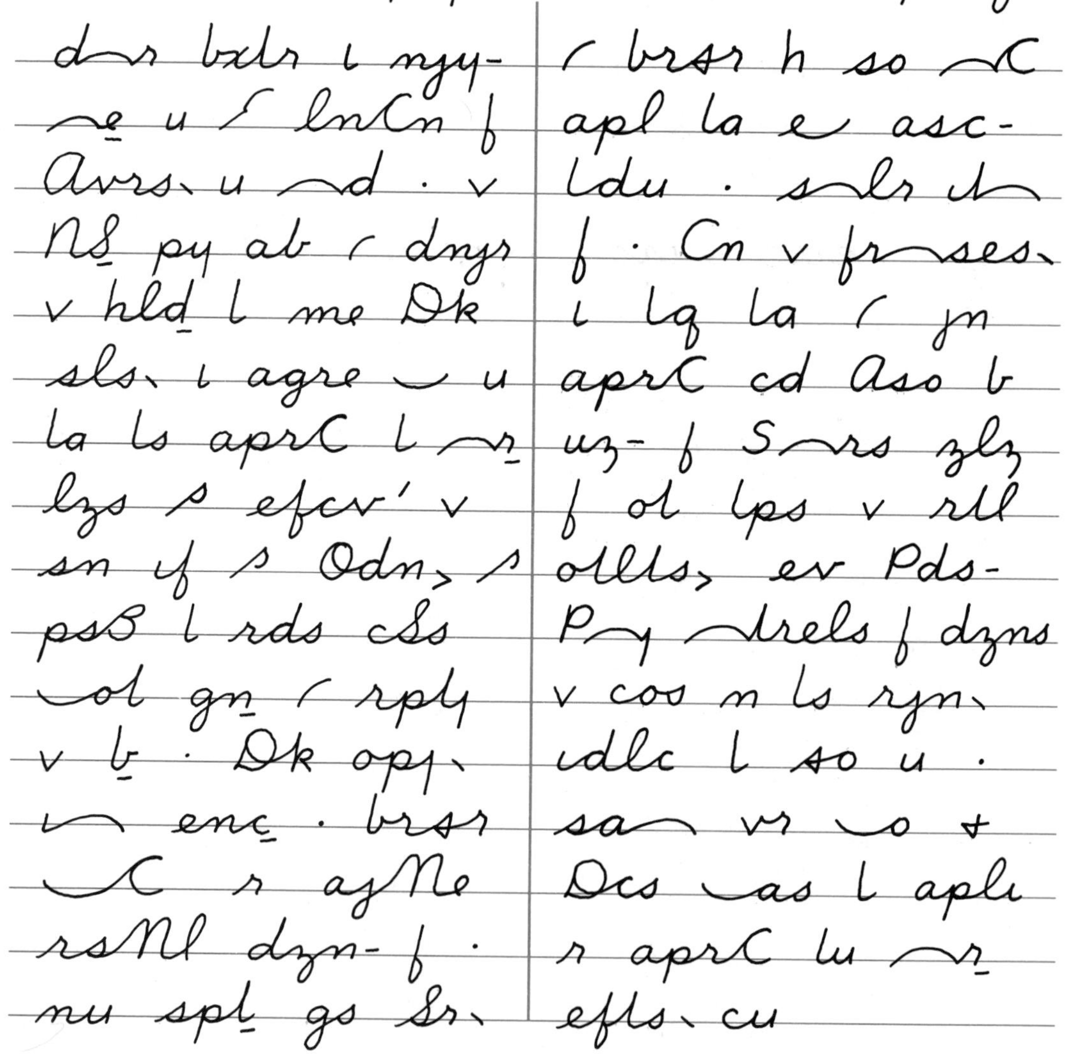

2

Preview Words

radius *rdes*

analysis *anlss*

command *kN*

evaluation *evluy*

ensuring *nsr*

glassware *glsr*

Stanford *Snfd*

home furnishings *h frns*

---

d M rgn lqf
nqe ab r rSC
n h frns. ur
z l kdc · lro
r anlss. Av
dsjs r ofn d
f hbl rlr ln
f crf evluy. e
o s lN
rSC frs Conj + ec
Slnl ar lvu qs
asr-, sN u pln
l sl u ln v glsr
n · rdes v 2H
ls Intro DC rcm

fr v Snfd Ab inc.
ly v kp- slr
asnms Conj + lr fN
vb v rluB. ly l
obln (inf und
lc dsjs ab Dj
+ prs, b klc s Intro P
ur lcn (frS Sp
lw nsr lau Pdc
l kN · q sr v
r. y dN u klc
u ofs ls c so
la ec c plns
f cpn ahd. ul

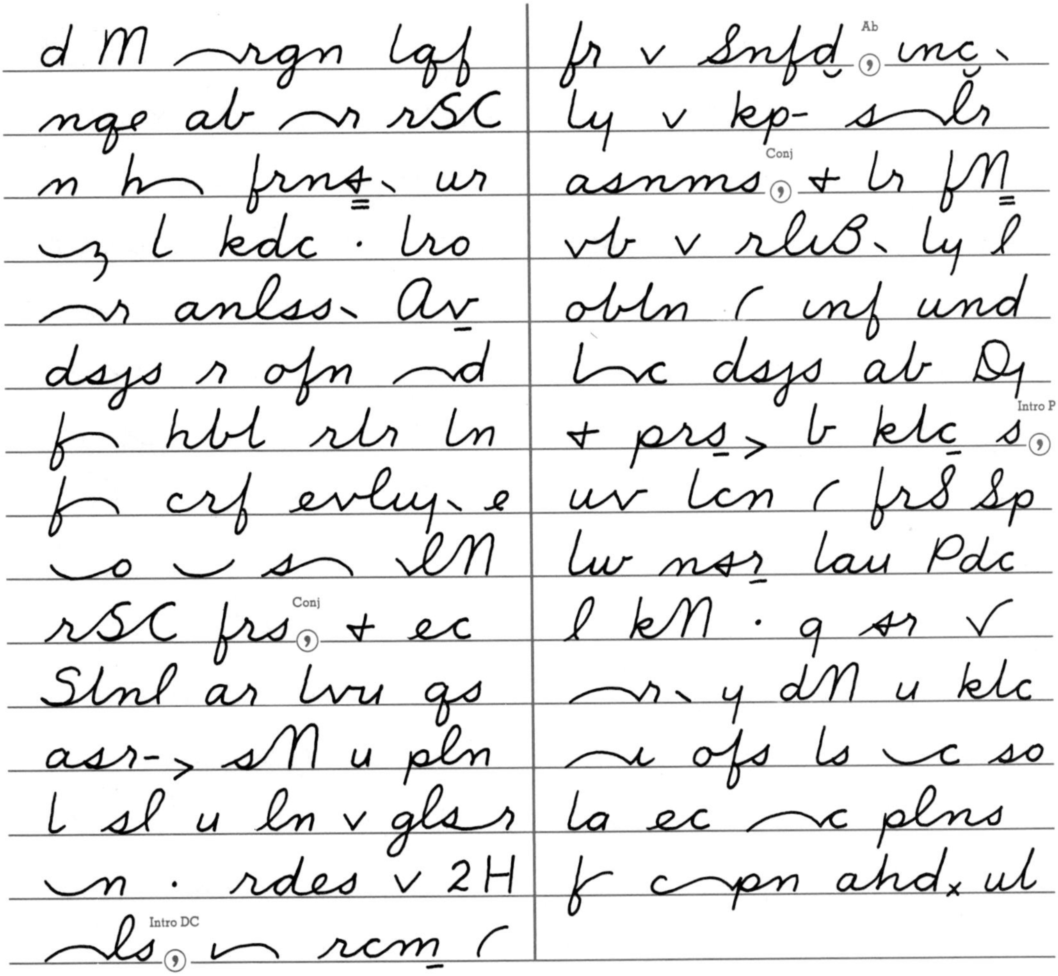

3

Preview Words

space	sps	economical	ecol
daily	dl	day-to-day	d=l=d
options	opjs	classified	clsf-
quarterly	qtrl	circulation	Scl

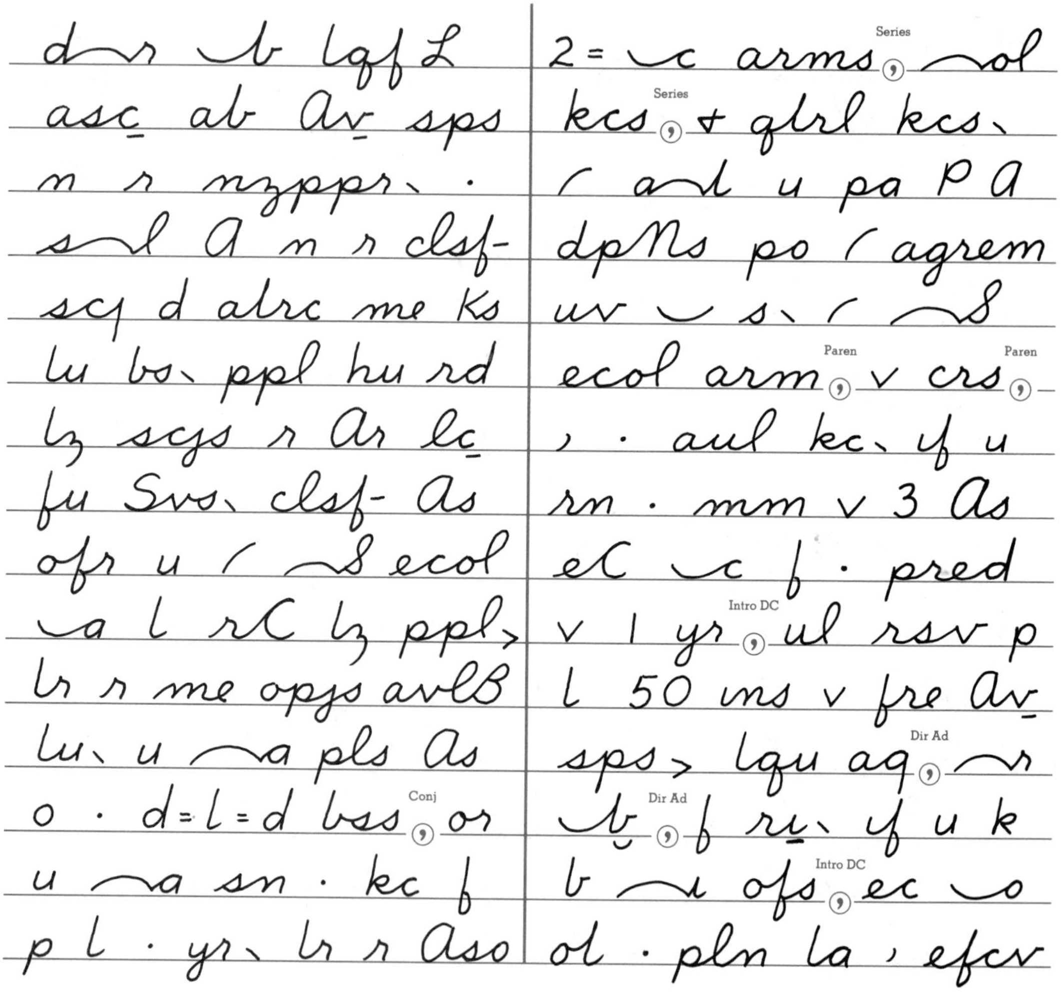

+ ecol fu. r dl
Sclj, no O /HT.

uno ec hlp u. uvl

4

Preview Words

media	~da	meantime	~nt
prefer	Pfr	priority	prirl
conduct	kdc	contacted	klc-
emphasis	~fss	Midwestern	~d Wrn

d~s hord edb
dli- l Dcs u av
plns. ec ~e ◡
u du lnC o Mn, Date
Ja 5, Date zu sug-.
◡n e ~e ◡ u, Intro DC
el nd lv sp inf
ab u Pdcs + ~fss
u Pfr, ev klc-. ~r
rSC fr, Ap ~d Wrn
rSC, Conj + ex ~yr
hs agre- lgv u
Pjc prirl. i lq

s psB l lS u nu
Pdcs, Series kdc . Sva, Series
+ v (rzlts ~n
6 ~os, n ~nt, Paren
el bgn lq ol plns
f Nds u Pdc l (
pb. b (L (lS
rzlts r n, Intro P el v
~d (nes arms
◡ (~da, / lb
. plzr Lo ◡ u
aq. su

5

Punctuation Study

Add commas to show one parenthetical expression, two introductory dependent clauses, and two introductory phrases.

Preview Words

- beyond
- Senator's
- candidate
- workload
- capacity
- ourselves
- committed
- supportive

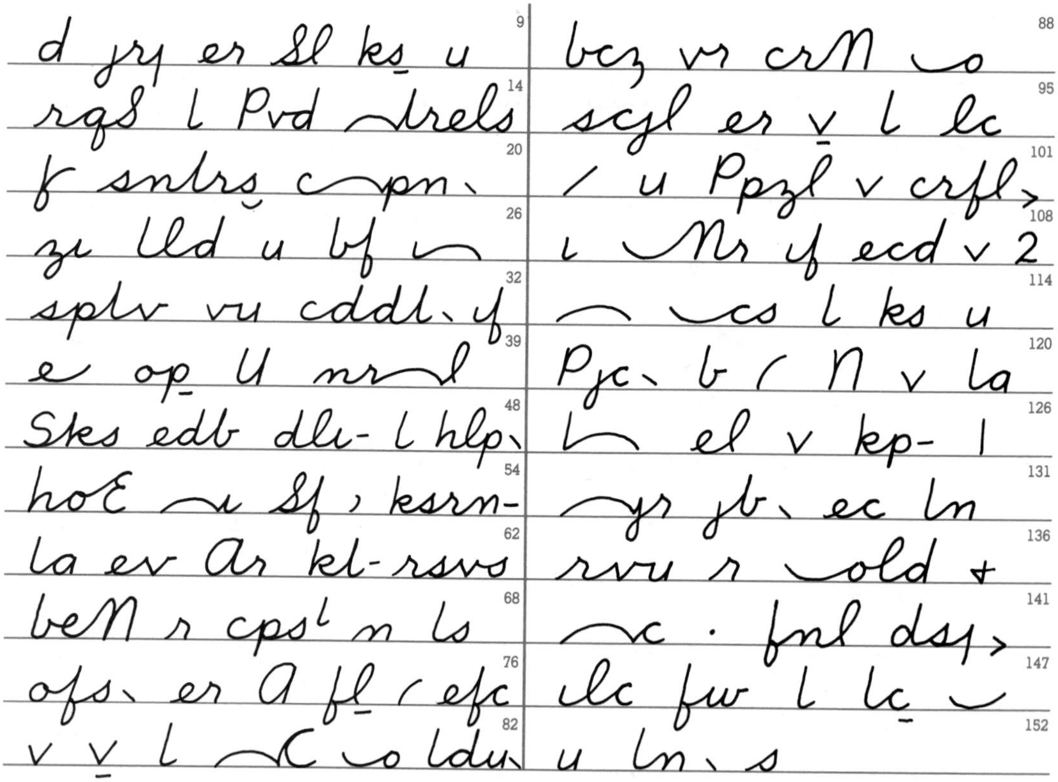

Key

1

Dear Mr. Baxter:

I enjoyed meeting you at the luncheon for advertisers. You made a very interesting[1] point about the danger of holding too many discount sales. I agree with you that this approach to marketing[2] loses its effectiveness very soon if it is overdone.

It is possible to reduce costs without[3] gaining the reputation of being a discount operation. I am enclosing a brochure which our[4] agency recently designed for a new sporting goods store. The brochure had so much appeal that we were asked to do[5] a similar item for a chain of pharmacies. I think that the general approach could also be used for[6] supermarkets as well as for other types of retail outlets.

We have produced promotion materials for[7] dozens of companies in this region. I would like to show you a sample of our work and discuss ways to[8] apply our approach to your marketing efforts.

Cordially yours, (171)

2

Dear Miss Morgan:

Thank you for your inquiry about market research in home furnishings. You are wise to conduct[1] a thorough market analysis. Advertising decisions are often made from habit rather than from[2] careful evaluation. We work with some excellent research firms, and we can certainly arrange to have your[3] questions answered.

Since you plan to sell your line of glassware within a radius of 200 miles, I am[4] recommending the firm of Stanford, Inc. They have completed similar assignments, and their findings[5] have been very reliable. They will obtain the information you need to make decisions about distribution[6] and pricing.

By contacting us, you have taken the first step toward ensuring that your product will command[7] a good share of the market. Why don't you contact my office this week so that we can make plans for the campaign[8] ahead?

Yours truly, (164)

3

Dear Mr. Webb:

Thank you for your letter asking about advertising space in our newspaper. A small ad in[1] our classified section would attract many customers to your business. People who read these sections are already[2] looking for your service. Classified ads offer you the most economical way to reach these people.

There[3] are many options available to you. You may place ads on a day-to-day basis, or you may sign a contract[4] for up to a year. There are also two-week arrangements, monthly contracts, and quarterly contracts. The amount[5] you pay per ad depends upon the agreement you have with us. The most economical arrangement, of course,[6] is an annual contract. If you run a minimum of three ads each week for a period of one year, you[7] will receive up to 50 inches of free advertising space.

Thank you again, Mr. Webb, for writing. If you[8] come by my office, we can work out a plan that is effective and economical for you. Our daily[9] circulation is now over 100,000. I know we can help you.

Yours very truly, (196)

4

Dear Ms. Howard:

We would be delighted to discuss your advertising plans. We can meet with you during lunch on[1] Monday, January 5, as you suggested. When we meet with you, we will need to have specific information[2] about your products and the emphasis you prefer.

We have contacted a marketing research firm, Midwestern[3] Research, and the executive manager has agreed to give your project priority. I think it is[4] possible to test your new products, conduct a survey, and have the results within six months.

In the meantime,[5] we will begin laying out plans for introducing your product to the public. By the time the test results are in,[6] we will have made the necessary arrangements with the media.

It will be a pleasure to work with you[7] again.

Sincerely yours, (144)

5

Dear George:

We are still considering your request to provide materials for the Senator's campaign. As I[1] told you before, I am supportive of your candidate. If we were operating under normal circumstances,[2] we would be delighted to help. However, my staff is concerned that we have already committed ourselves[3] beyond our capacity in this office. We are all feeling the effect of having too much work to do.[4] Because of our current work schedule, we are having to look at your proposal very carefully.

I wonder if[5] we could have two more weeks to consider your project. By the end of that time, we will have completed one major[6] job. We can then review our workload and make a final decision.

I look forward to talking with you then.[7]

Sincerely, (142)

unl 9
rl eSa*

Shorthand Vocabulary Review

Study these words and the principles they illustrate. Look for these words as you read the letters and memos in this unit.

1. Write m for the word endings *mand*, *mend*, *mind*, and *ment*.

demand	dm	basement	bsm
recommend	rcm	retirement	rlrm
remind	rm	achievement	aCvm
apartment	aplm	arrangements	arms
appointment	apym	requirement	rqm

***Unit Nine**
Real Estate

2. Omit *p* in the sound of *mpt*.

empty 

attempt 

prompt 

exemptions 

More About Punctuation

1. A semicolon can be used to connect two short statements when the two thoughts are very closely related in meaning.

Thank you for your letter; it explained the problem quite well.

(Thank you for your letter. It explained the problem quite well.)

Use a semicolon to connect two **independent** clauses (two complete thoughts that can stand alone) when the conjunctions *and*, *or*, or *but* have been omitted.

The delivery is scheduled for Tuesday; we will have someone here to sign for it.

(The delivery is scheduled for Tuesday, and we will have someone here to sign for it.)

2. Use a semicolon to separate two independent clauses when the two clauses are joined by a parenthetical expression, such as those listed below. These transitional expressions are sometimes called conjunctive adverbs and are usually followed by a comma, especially if they contain more than one syllable.

therefore 

however 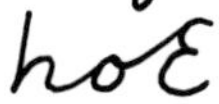

consequently 

thus 

meanwhile 

nevertheless 

furthermore 

indeed 

hence 

still 

We had planned to meet Mr. Turner at school; however, his plane did not arrive until 1:30.

Other common parenthetical expressions include the following phrases. Note that a semicolon comes before the parenthetical expression in this construction and that a comma follows the parenthetical expression.

in addition 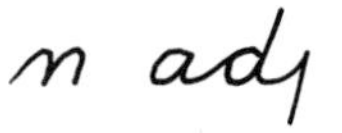

as a result 

in fact 

in other words 

on the contrary 

by the way 

for example 

at any rate 

at the same time 

on the other hand 

Your promotion has been approved; in addition, you will receive a bonus for your superior performance this year.

3. Use the semicolon also to separate items in a complicated series.

Send a copy of the report to Sam Johnson, marketing; Ann Hudson, promotion; and Jim Williams, personnel.

The notation **Semi** will be highlighted in the reading and writing exercises.

LESSON 41

Brief Forms and Derivatives

1. *Ar bln kc dl , q nx*
2. *Sks dvms ⁓l dfces aq*

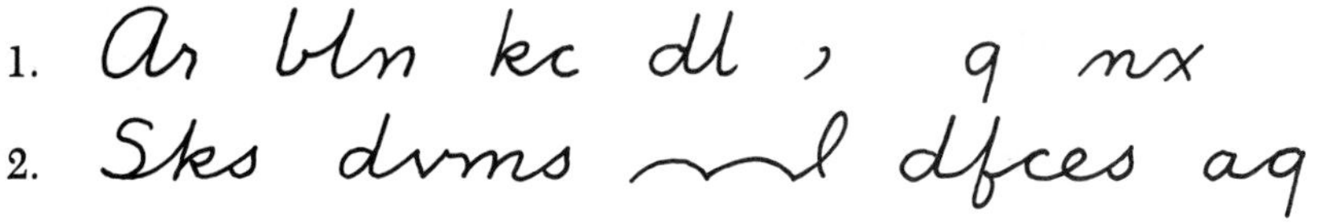

Key

1. already, between, contract, determine, is/his, go/good, next
2. circumstances, developments, immediately, difficulties, ago

Phrase Review

1. *idu ilc ed ulfN lvu*
2. *Uhr lrsv cdb vb laul dlc*

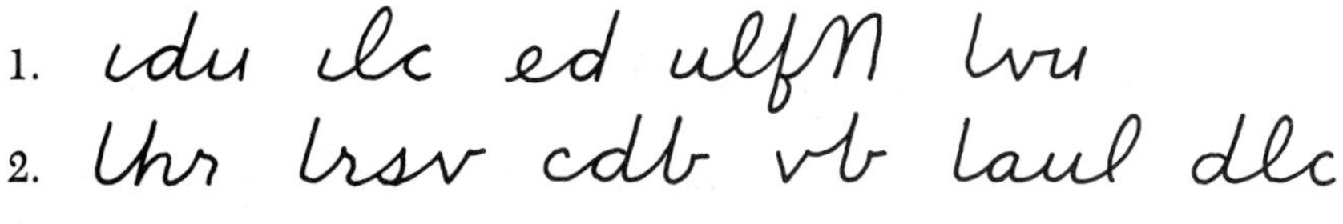

Key

1. I do, I look, we would, you will find, to have you/to have your
2. to hear, to receive, could be, have been, that you will, would like

Reading and Writing Exercises

1

Preview Words

empty, unique, tenants, supplier, previous, relocate, opportune, industrial

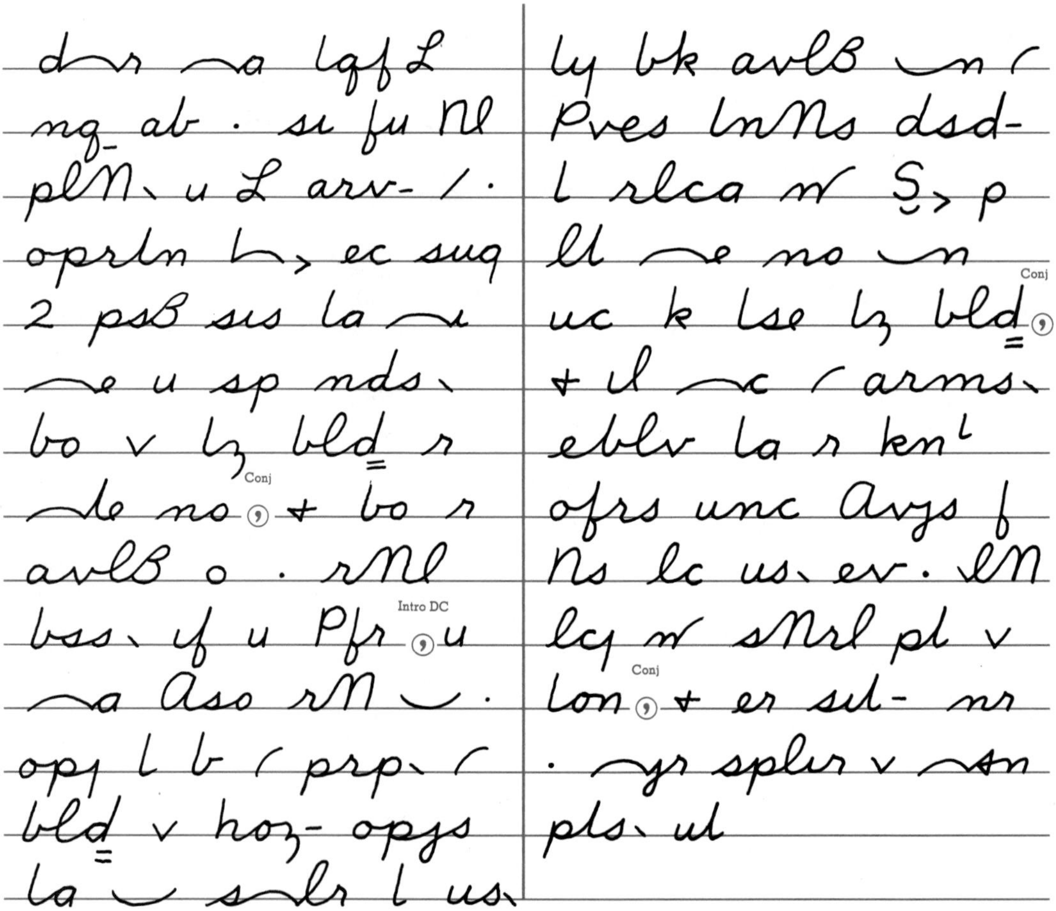

----------------- **2** -----------------

Preview Words

sports	*spts*	occupancy	*ocpNe*
luxury	*lxre*	connected	*kc-*
complex	*kplx*	recreation	*rcrey*
walkway	*⌣a*	Twin Towers	*Ln lors*

d s hrsn ⌒
dli- laus N8- m
se . aplm lca- m
s fnd kplx [Ap] *Ln*
lors, ⌣blv lae ofs
A ✓ fCrs lau sp-
m u L, aplms lb
rde f ocpNe ab r
L us pln L ⌢
l lo sle, s unls
ofs me lxre fCrs
m ady l L . blef

vu ✓ sle, e Aso
ofs sp fsl [Series] *rcrey* [Series] *-*
+ fd Svss, . mu
spts sNs , b bll
mx ds [NRC] *C lb kc-*
l s bld b . prvl
⌣a, ⌒dl aplms
s mo opn fu
nspcy, cl ⌢e r
mx L us w sle [Conj]
+ cl as l so u .
aplm, su

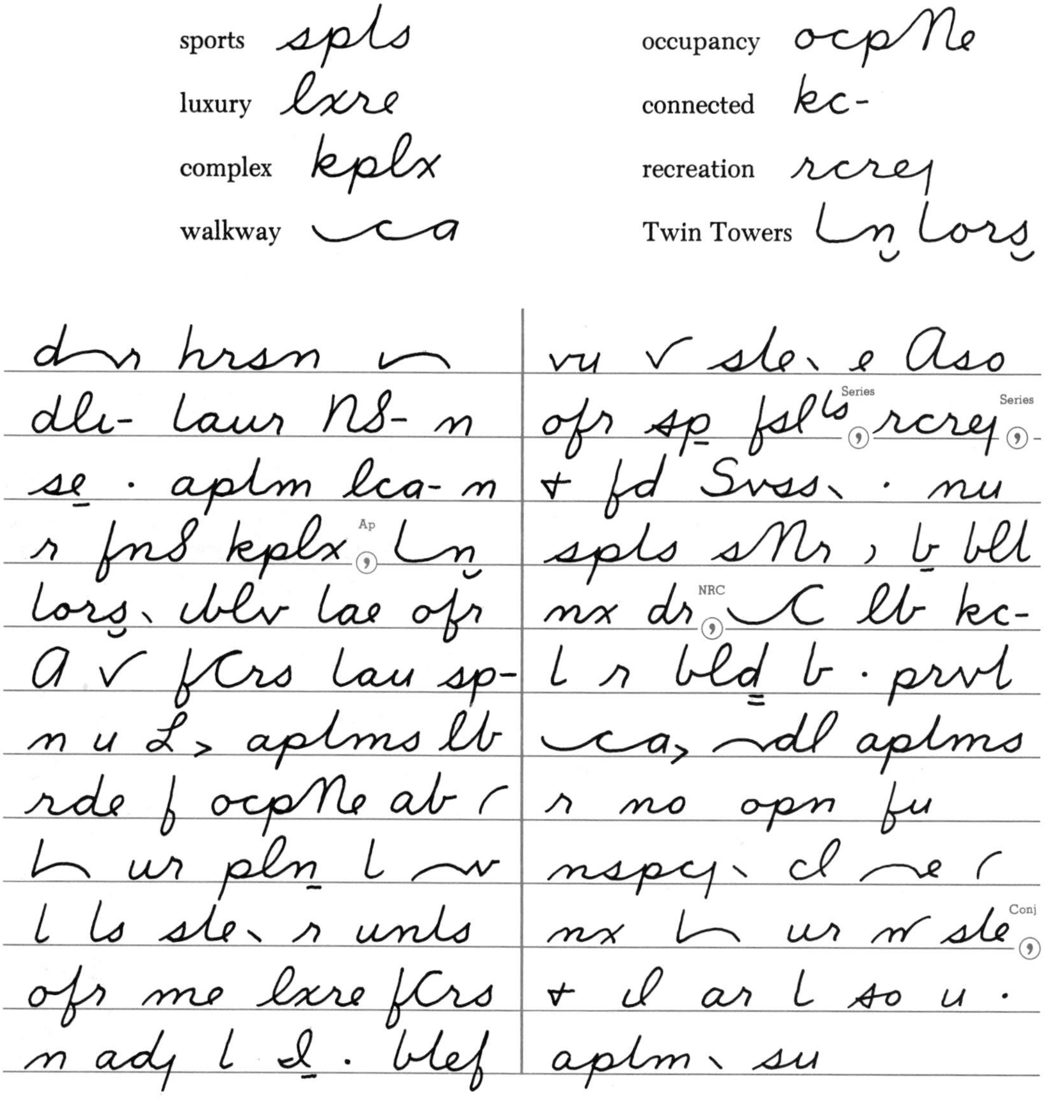

────────── **3** ──────────

Preview Words

acre
acr

Ford *fd*

active *acv*

district *Dtrc*

multiple-listing
llpl=lS

basement *bsm*

Jefferson *jfrsn*

subdivision *sdvj*

---

d rs fd w sv
hoss l so u n
u vzl nx c.
hoo lau N- l
nspc o adrsn S
, no lgr . psO l ⌣ (Semi) ;
(z sld lS c,
hoO (Paren) ; y u ptcl
lc la nbrh (Intro DC) ; w
g nz fu. lr r
sv hoss crNl
O r n la ara.
n enc s pjs
f r llpl=lS
Svs. (hos o

jfrsn ln db .
lN (Paren) ; b f ex. /
ho apxl 25H sq
fl v lv sps C
Is . fns- bsm,
(bc yd , apxl
l = hf acr v lN,
ls sdvj , lca- n
. Cys scl Dtrc.
/ ho . acv grp
v rzdNs (Conj) ; + i lg
ud njy lv lr.
lc fw lse u nx
c. su

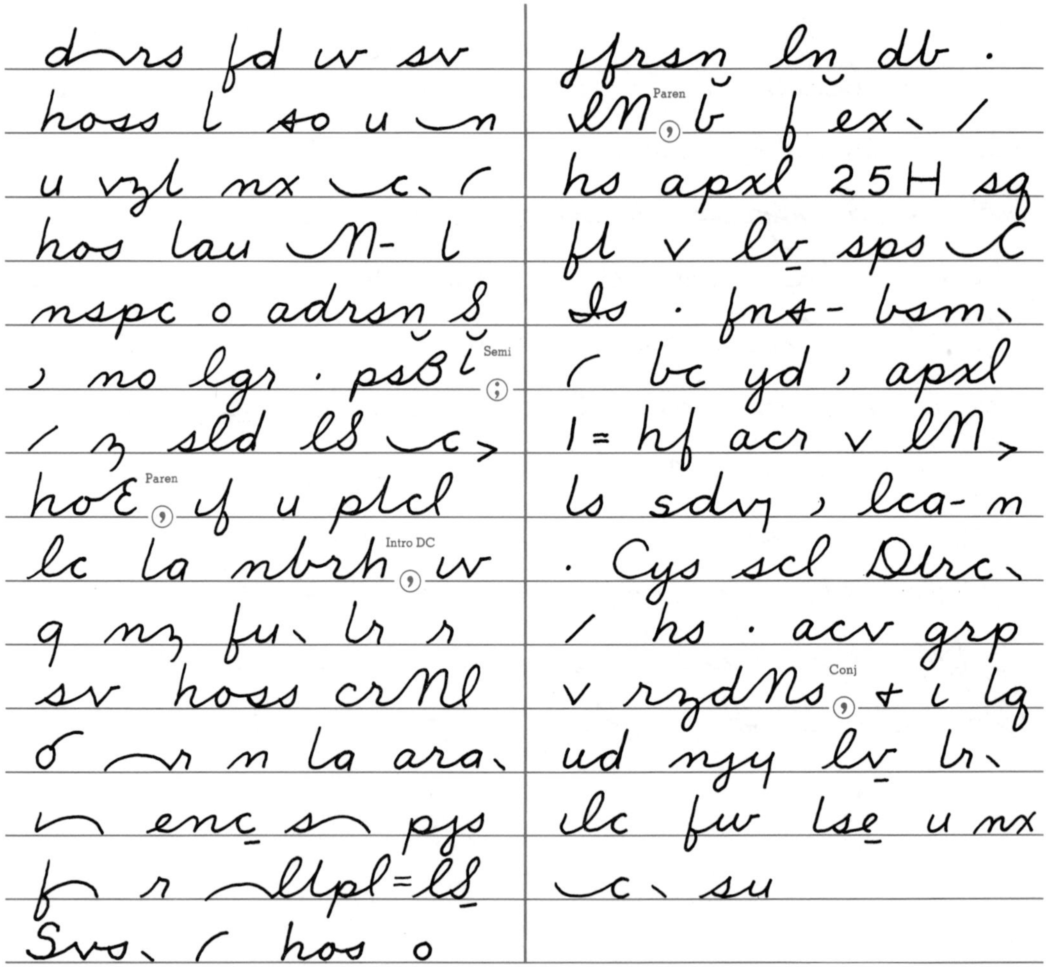

———————————— **4** ————————————

Preview Words

submit — _s—l_

reopen — _ropn_

lowered — _lor-_

definitely — _dfnll_

reasonable — _rznß_

subdivision — _sdvʼ_

negotiations — _ngseʼ̣s_

Hidden Valley — _hdn̦ vle̦_

d—r + —rs grgre
ι suq lae s—l .
ofr f prp n hdn̦
vle̦ , u s—- l lc
la sdvʼ . gr dl °(Conj)
+ ιdlc u lrsv u
frß Cys v sιs,
_sM e lß lc-_ °(Intro DC) _r_
sily ho Cnʼ-, r
sl prs hsb lor- °(Conj)
+ ι lq la ulb ß
l b r prp f . v

rznß a—l, r
crM ors klc-—e
yßrd lse f u Sl
Nß- n PCs̲ r lM,
ly r dfnll n Nß-
n bld̲ . hoo ð sι °(Conj)
+ ly dlc l ropn
ngseʼ̣s — u, ιdlc
lvu Avo bf ι lc
aq — r ors, p
_ll —e no l u_
— + ldu, c

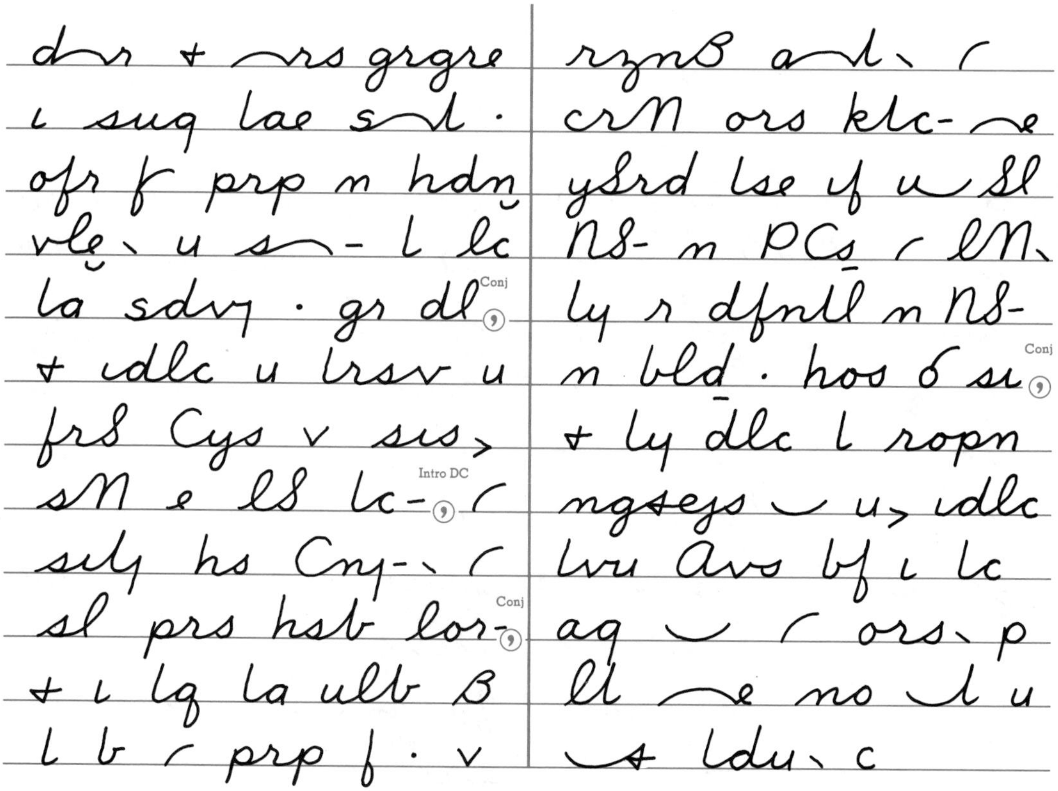

5

Punctuation Study

Add commas to show one parenthetical expression, one direct address, and two conjunctions.

Preview Words

goals	endeavors
dollars	remarkable
Margaret	progresses
yourself	furthermore

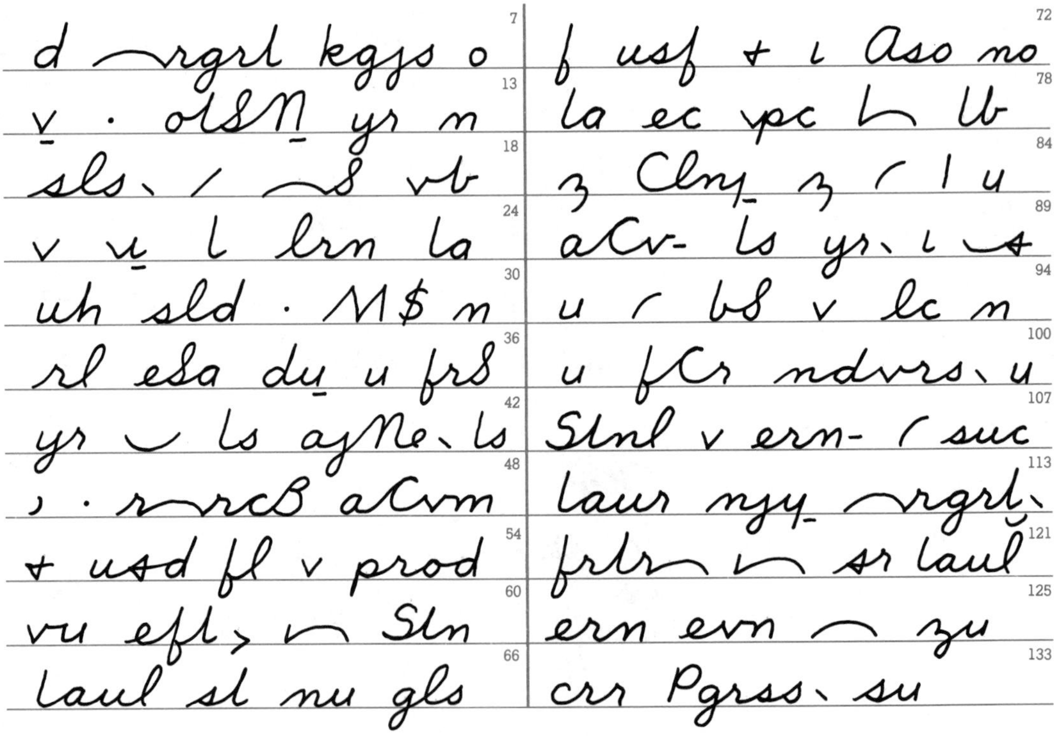

Key

1

Dear Mr. May:

Thank you for your letter inquiring about a site for your industrial plant. Your letter arrived[1] at an opportune time.

We can suggest two possible sites that might meet your specific needs. Both of these buildings[2] are empty now, and both are available on a rental basis. If you prefer, you may also rent with[3] an option to buy the property. The buildings have housed operations that were similar to yours. They became[4] available when the previous tenants decided to relocate in the South.

Please let me know when you can[5] come to see these buildings, and I will make the arrangements. We believe that our community offers unique[6] advantages for industries like yours. We have an excellent location in the central part of town, and we are[7] situated near a major supplier of machine parts.

Yours truly, (153)

2

Dear Mr. Harrison:

I am delighted that you are interested in seeing an apartment located[1] in our finest complex, Twin Towers. I believe that we offer all of the features that you specified in your[2] letter.

Apartments will be ready for occupancy about the time you are planning to move to this city.[3] Our units offer many luxury features in addition to including a beautiful view of the city.[4] We also offer shopping facilities, recreation, and food services. A new sports center is being[5] built next door, which will be connected to our buildings by a private walkway.

Model apartments are now open[6] for your inspection. Call me the next time you are in the city, and I will arrange to show you an apartment.[7]

Sincerely yours, (144)

3

Dear Mrs. Ford:

I have several houses to show you when you visit next week. The house that you wanted to[1] inspect on Anderson Street is no longer a possibility; it was sold last week.

However, if you[2] particularly like that neighborhood, I have good news for you. There are several houses currently on the[3] market in that area. I am enclosing some pages from our multiple-listing service. The house on[4] Jefferson Lane would be an excellent buy, for example. It has approximately 2500 square feet[5] of living space which includes a finished basement. The back yard is approximately one-half acre of land.

This[6] subdivision is located in a choice school district. It has an active group of residents, and I think you would[7] enjoy living there. I look forward to seeing you next week.

Sincerely yours, (153)

4

Dear Mr. and Mrs. Gregory:

I suggest that we submit an offer for the property in Hidden Valley.[1] You seemed to like that subdivision a great deal, and I would like you to receive your first choice of sites.

Since we[2] last talked, the situation has changed. The sale price has been lowered, and I think that you will be able to buy the[3] property for a very reasonable amount. The current owners contacted me yesterday to see if[4] you were still interested in purchasing the land. They are definitely not interested in building a[5] house on the site, and they would like to reopen negotiations with you.

I would like to have your advice[6] before I talk again with the owners. Please let me know what you wish to do.

Cordially, (135)

5

Dear Margaret:

Congratulations on having an outstanding year in sales. It must have been very exciting[1] to learn that you had sold a million dollars in real estate during your first year with this agency. This is a[2] remarkable achievement, and you should feel very proud of your effort.

I am certain that you will set new goals[3] for yourself, and I also know that we can expect them to be as challenging as the one you achieved this year.[4] I wish you the best of luck in your future endeavors. You certainly have earned the success that you are enjoying,[5] Margaret. Furthermore, I am sure that you will earn even more as your career progresses.

Sincerely yours,[6] (120)

LESSON 42

Abbreviations and Derivatives

1. S yd ok sq ft corp N
2. inc ex VP re aco

Key

1. superintendent, yard, okay, square, feet, corporation, north
2. incorporate/incorporated, example/executive, vice president, regarding, accompany

Transcription Aids: Typing Addresses

1. When typing addresses in a sentence, use figures for house numbers and spell out such words as *Street, Avenue, Road, Drive, Lane,* and *Boulevard.*

Please mail the order to my home address, 3115 Harrison Boulevard.

2. Spell out numbers from one through ten when they are street names.

Our new address will be 410 Fifth Street.

3. Use figures for numbers greater than ten when they are used as street names. If no word separates these street numbers from the building numbers, use *th, st,* or *d* for clarity.

The package was delivered to 101 54th Street.

4. If a word such as *North, South, East,* or *West* separates the two groups of numbers, the *th, st,* or *d* is not necessary for the second number.

Send the book to 518 South 21 Street.

Your Business Vocabulary

fixed rate of interest

fx-ra ⌄ n8

A rate of interest that is not subject to change during the duration of a contract.

A mortgage will be granted to you at a fixed rate of interest.

subdivision *sdvy*

In real estate, a tract of land that has been divided into smaller lots for individual houses.

We will be happy to show you a model home in our new subdivision.

Reading and Writing Exercises

––––––––––––––––––– 1 –––––––––––––––––––

Preview Words

access *ʋ*

stated *Sa-*

utility *ullᴸ*

estimates *eʃ ʌs*

carefully *crfl*

favorable *fvr8*

suitable *su8*

parking lot *prc̲ ll*

dʋr dʋnpl w ⌐-
⌐ ara nr ⌐ arpl
crfl ⁽Conj⁾₉ + vblv la
w lca- ⌐ cN ⌄
ofs bld̲ u ⌐ ʌ l
lʋ. Alo s sz , su8 ⁽Intro DC⁾₉
⌐ bld̲ c of lʋ PCs-

⌣ . kc sl. ʌ du
u lq ⌄ ls ida ₓᵧ ⌐
lʋʌs r fvr8 ⁽Conj⁾₉ + ud
⌄ . fx- ra ⌄ n8.
⌐ bld̲ ⌐es Ɛ rqm
Sa- n u L. ⌐ prc̲
ll , lry ⁽Conj⁾₉ + lʋ r

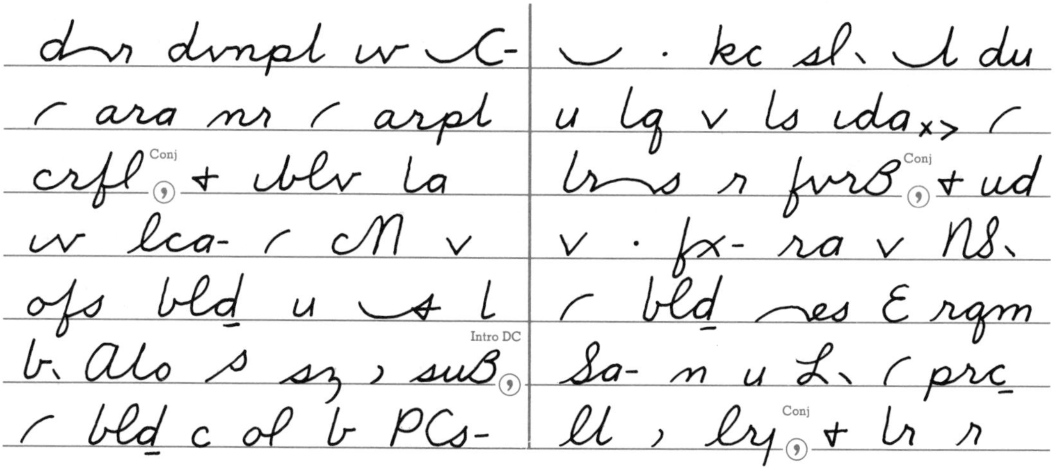

sv vs rds lca-
nrb. s lca- n .
ara la hs n yl
b inc nl r ste
blds, d u lc lsN
. rep lse ls bld.

ic pl lglr s—
eS ls v ull cSs
if ur NS- n b r
prp. lb —a lhr
f— u. vlu

2

Preview Words

owns	os	undecided	udsd-
pursue	Psu	alternative	Alrnv
Grant	grN	warehouse	—rhos
factory	fclre	instructions	nSrcjs

drs bSr w spcn
— js grN, hu os (NRC)
r —rhos / 23 E
71 S. h , no ks r
ofr u —d l ls ,
bld. hoE, r ex VP (Paren)
v fclre nx dr hs
—d . ofr l b r
bld. [P L—, —r (Intro P)

grN , udsd- ab l
ldu, d ub NS- n ls
— . opj l b. —n
u ks la r dm f
prp , ncrs n ls
ara, . opj agrem (Intro DC)
—a b r bS slj
f E1. if u —t l
Psu ls pln, p ll (Intro DC)

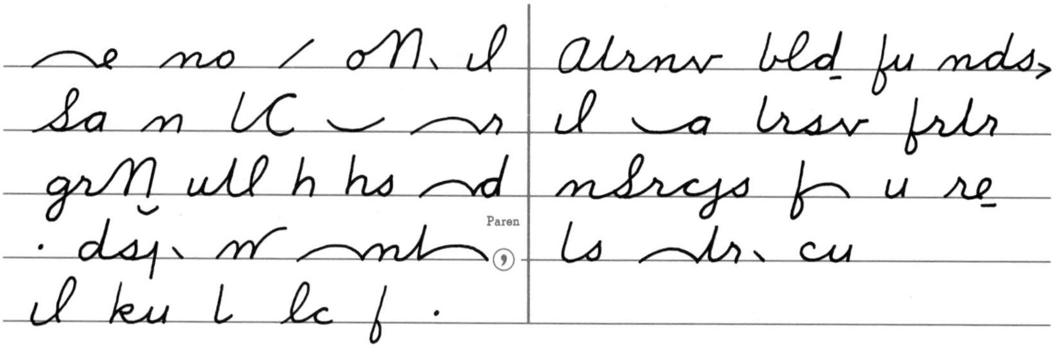

3

Preview Words

buyer

twice

slowly

minor

weather

Orlando, Florida

permission

maintenance

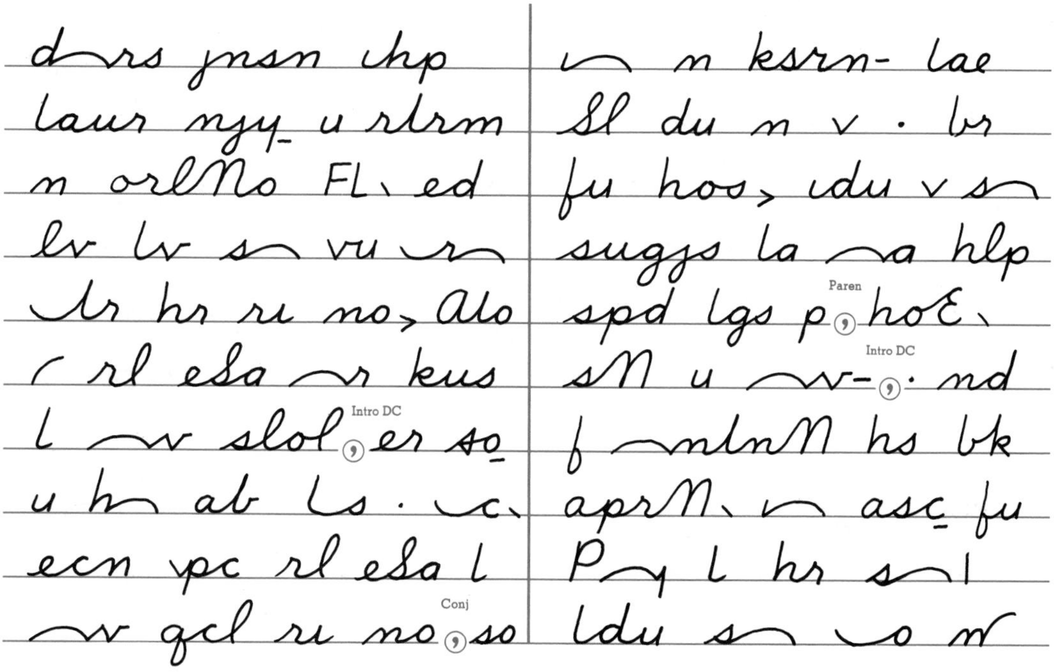

hos; (Semi) (yd rqs
s— ⌣o z l, · fu
—ns rprs l du
⌣Nrs f · hos la
, vcN> lz rprs
cdb ak- f · —d8
G, p ll —e no
if s ok lq ahd
⌣ (⌣o, uvl

4

Preview Words

swimming	s—	bedrooms	bdr—s
liberty	lbrle	basement	bsm
private	prvl	beautiful	blef
another	aol	furthermore	frlr—

d—s + —rs dyl
af e lc- ySrd, (Intro DC) l
lrn- v aol hos
la hs jS bk avlB,
bcz / soNs lc (
cN v pls laur
lc f, (Intro DC) ⌣ hpf
laul fN (l—
lse / ls ⌣cN, (
hos l n b avlB
f so ull Sl —rn, (Conj)
so — lc (lbrle
v —c · apym f
9a—> uno ls —ns
laul v l Sa n lon
· adyl ni, (Conj) b ublv
laul ⌣N lse ls
hos, / hs 6 bdr—s, (Series)
· fns- bsm, (Series) + ·
s— pl, s sil-

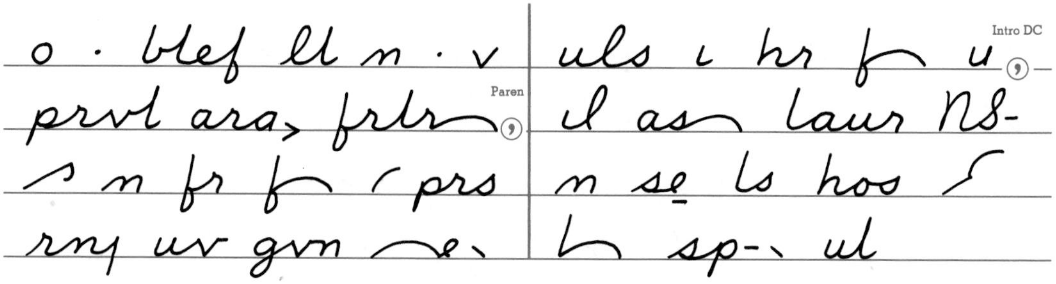

5

Punctuation Study

Add commas to show four introductory dependent clauses and one group of words in a series.

Preview Words

lease		either	
sites		negotiate	
space		expansion	
shorter		consultation	

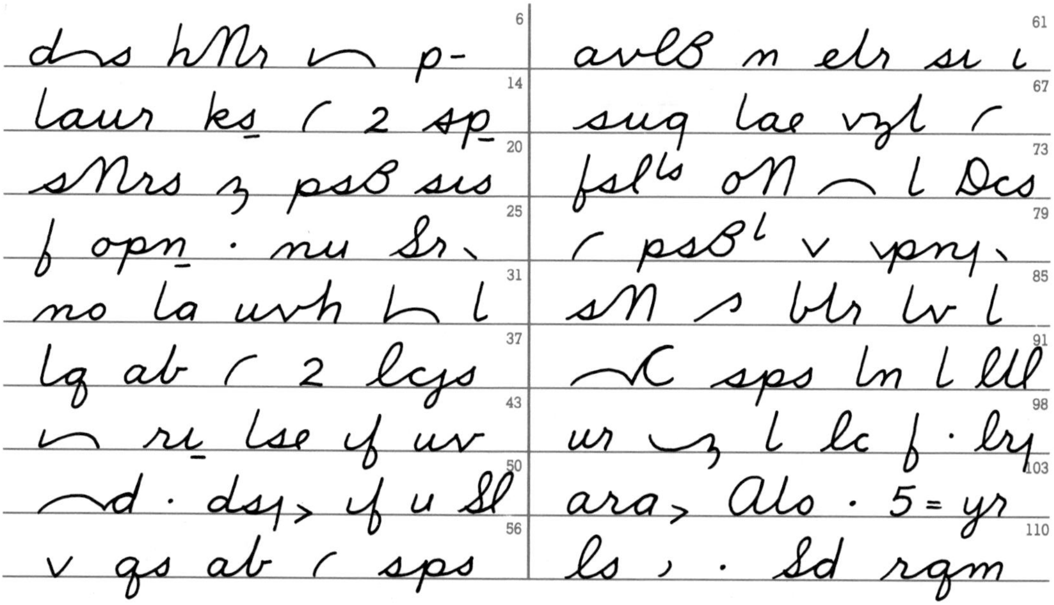

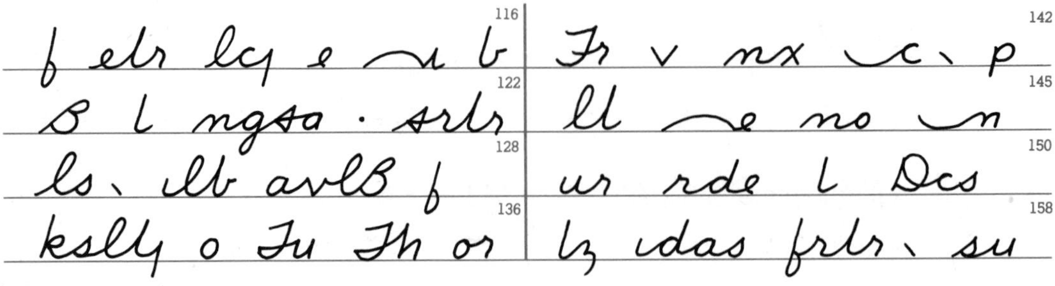

Key

1

Dear Mr. Davenport:

I have watched the area near the airport carefully, and I believe that I have[1] located the kind of office building you wish to buy. Although its size is suitable, the building can only be[2] purchased with a contract sale. What do you think of this idea?

The terms are favorable, and you would have a[3] fixed rate of interest. The building meets every requirement stated in your letter. The parking lot is large, and[4] there are several access roads located nearby. It is located in an area that has not yet been[5] incorporated into the city limits.

Would you like to send a representative to see this building?[6] I can put together some estimates of utility costs if you are interested in buying the[7] property. I will be waiting to hear from you.

Very truly yours, (151)

2

Dear Mrs. Webster:

I have spoken with James Grant, who owns the warehouse at 23 East 71 Street.[1] He is now considering the offer you made to lease his building. However, the executive vice president[2] of the factory next door has made an offer to buy the building. At the present time, Mr. Grant is[3] undecided about what to do.

Would you be interested in leasing with an option to buy? When you consider[4] that the demand for property is increasing in this area, an option agreement may be the best[5] solution for everyone. If you wish to pursue this plan, please let me know at once. I will stay in touch with Mr.[6] Grant until he has made a decision. In the meantime, I will continue to look for an alternative[7] building for your needs.

I will wait to receive further instructions from you regarding this matter.

Cordially yours,[8] (160)

3

Dear Mrs. Johnson:

I hope that you are enjoying your retirement in Orlando, Florida. We would love to[1] have some of your warm weather here right now.

Although the real estate market continues to move slowly, we are showing[2] your home about twice a week. We cannot expect real estate to move quickly right now, so I am not concerned[3] that we still do not have a buyer for your house.

I do have some suggestions that may help speed things up, however.[4] Since you moved, a need for maintenance has become apparent. I am asking for your permission to hire someone[5] to do some work in the house; the yard requires some work as well. A few minor repairs will do wonders for a house[6] that is vacant.

These repairs could be accomplished for a modest charge. Please let me know if it is okay to go[7] ahead with the work.

Yours very truly, (147)

4

Dear Mr. and Mrs. Doyle:

After we talked yesterday, I learned of another house that has just become available.[1] Because it sounds like the kind of place that you are looking for, I am hopeful that you will find the time to see[2] it this weekend. The house will not be available for showing until Saturday morning, so I am taking[3] the liberty of making an appointment for 9 a.m.

I know this means that you will have to stay in town[4] an additional night, but I believe that you will want to see this house. It has six bedrooms, a finished basement,[5] and a swimming pool. It is situated on a beautiful lot in a very private area.

Furthermore,[6] it is not far from the price range you have given me. Unless I hear from you, I will assume that you are[7] interested in seeing this house at the time specified.

Yours truly, (152)

5

Dear Ms. Hunter:

I am pleased that you are considering the two shopping centers as possible sites for opening[1] a new store. Now that you have had time to think about the two locations, I am writing to see if you have[2] made a decision.

If you still have questions about the space available in either site, I suggest that we[3] visit the facilities once more to discuss the possibility of expansion. Since it is better to[4] have too much space than too little, you are wise to look for a large area.

Although a five-year lease is a[5] standard requirement for either location, we might be able to negotiate a shorter lease. I will be[6] available for consultation on Tuesday, Thursday, or Friday of next week. Please let me know when you are ready[7] to discuss these ideas further.

Sincerely yours, (149)

LESSON 43

Shorthand Vocabulary Review

Practice writing the names of the following cities. When you hear difficult or unusual names, it may be helpful to spell out the name in full.

Omaha	omha	Memphis	mfs
Phoenix	fnx	Lincoln	lgn
Des Moines	d myn	Atlanta	atlNa
Pittsburgh	ptsbrg	Salt Lake City	slt lc ste
Los Angeles	ls ajls	Philadelphia	fldlfa
New Orleans	nu orlns	Indianapolis	Nenpls
Chicago	scg	Nashville	nsvl
Trenton	trNn	Springfield	sprgfld

Transcription Aids: Similar Words

do du — To perform an action.

I know you will do everything you can to help.

due du — (1) Payable immediately (2) expected (3) because of.

(1) The payment is due on January 2.

(2) The train is due at 11 o'clock.

(3) Due to bad weather, the flight was delayed.

dew du — Moisture condensed from the air.

The grass was moist with the morning dew.

Your Business Vocabulary	closing *clz*	In real estate, a meeting in which the sale is finalized and the deed to property changes hands.

The closing will be held at Central State Bank on May 1.

	escrow *escro*	A written agreement or financial amount placed in the hands of a third party, such as a bank, and held ineffective until certain conditions are met.

The deed will be held in escrow until the heir reaches his 18th birthday.

	earnest money *ernS me*	Money paid in advance as partial payment to bind a contract or bargain.

He paid $500 in earnest money to the current owners.

Reading and Writing Exercises

─────────────── 1 ───────────────

Preview Words

deed *dd*

rather *rlr*

closing *clz*

lending *eN*

valuable *vluB*

optional *opjl*

officially *ofsll*

institution *nSly*

d r + ~rs scl   enc- , · cpe v

u ~S b p- lau   kc la ulb asc-l

ofr hsb ac-, ur   sn ʃ L v clz,

ab l bk r ors v   if uv ne qs ab

· nu aplm bld,   r lr~s p cl ~e

Intro DC

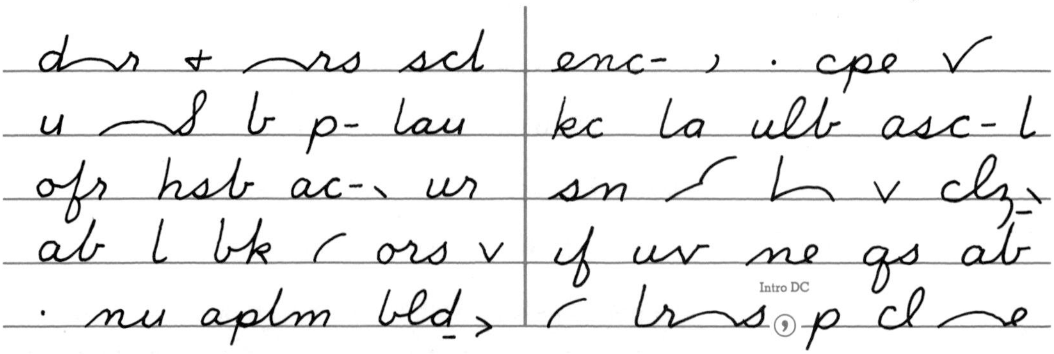

(— l so la ic (rec Pss , opyl ⟨Conj⟩ ⟨9⟩
asr ⌐ bf e ⟍e bi rcm la ev
ofʃll, ⟍n u b / dn, b du so ⟨Intro P⟩ ⟨9⟩-
prp o · kc bss el Plc u nvSm
rlr ln PCs · r prp, idu hp
⟍rgi f · lM laur p- ⟍ ls PCs.
nSly ⟨Intro DC⟩ ⟨9⟩ (dd l (s vluB prp ⟨9⟩ +
prp , n rec- / l Slnl pv lb
ull (kc , pd of · ⟍lM nvSm fu.
hoE ⟨Paren⟩ ⟨9⟩ ec pa · fe + su
v (kc rec- ,

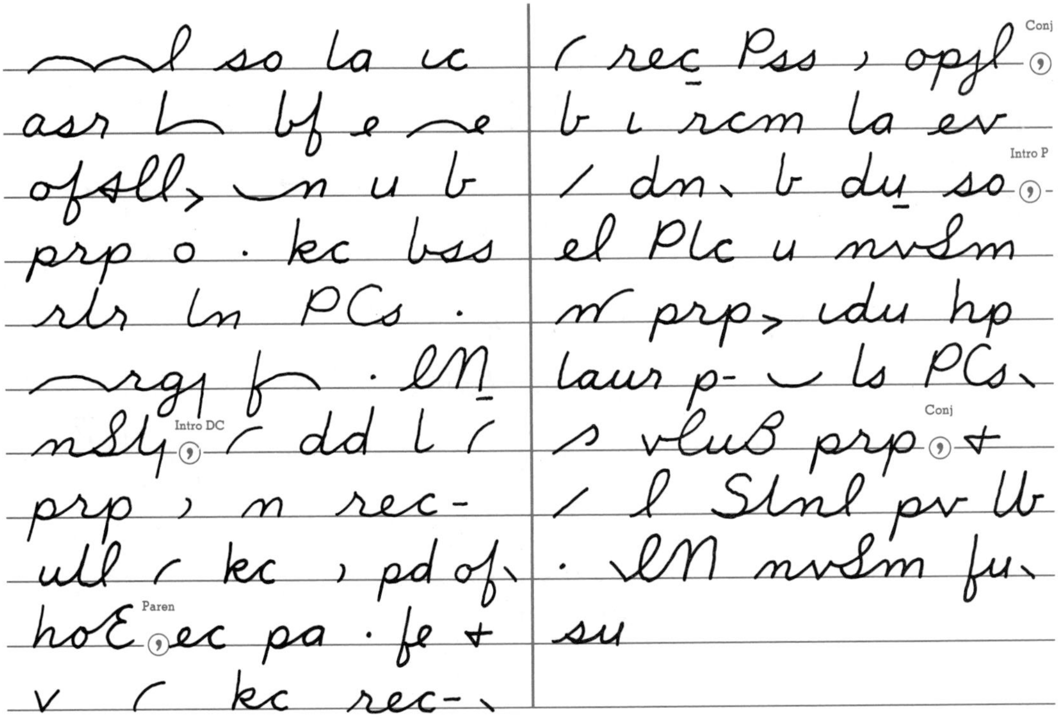

2

Preview Words

alert alrl   postpone pSpn

Detroit dlryl   computer kpur

radically rdcll   potential plnsl

meantime ⟍nl⟍   initiate insa

d ⟍r brcr (Slnl Cny- rdcll ⟨9⟩ ⟨Conj⟩ + /
USM u dzr l db blr fu l Sa
pSpn (sl vu r ur ull uvh
h ⟍, u Sks v ⌐ ⌐c u dsy,

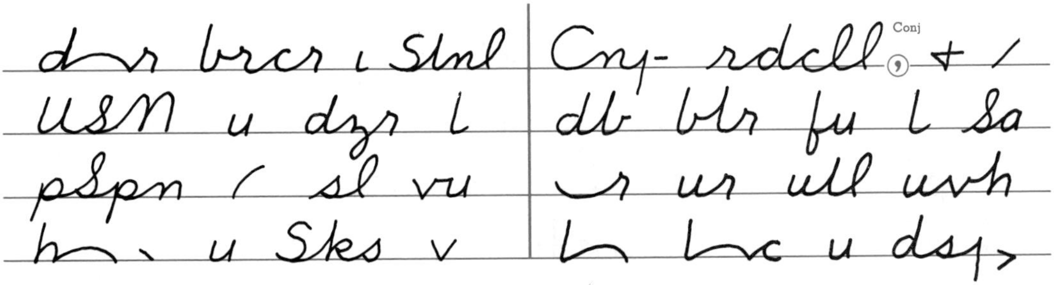

Paren

Intro DC

Paren

Intro DC

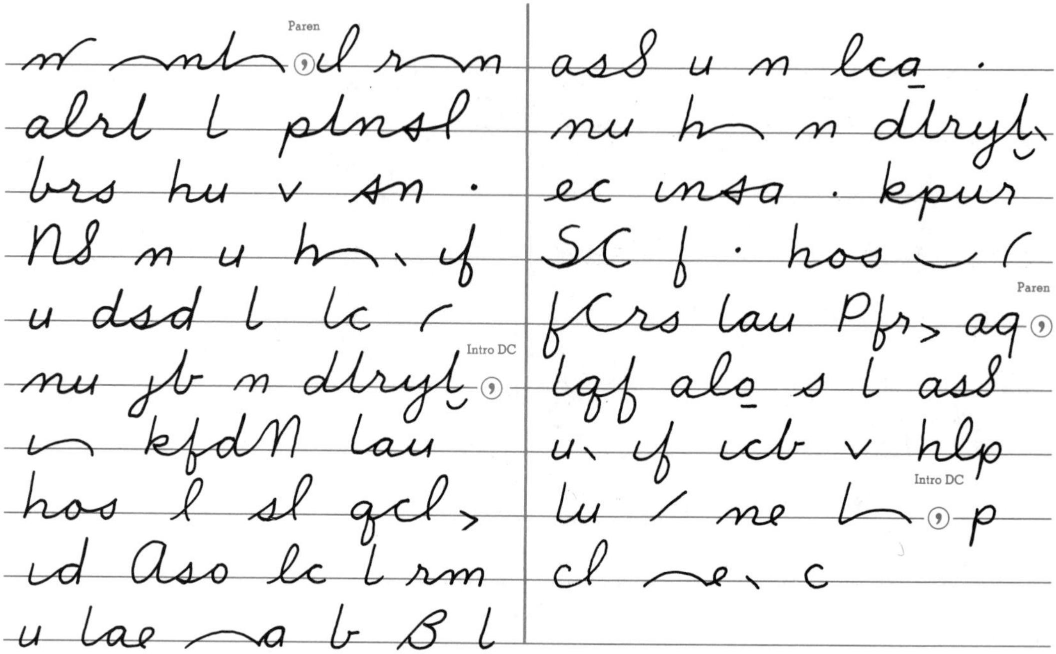

3

Preview Words

title	*Ul*	procedures	*Psjro*
escrow	*escro*	Stevenson	*Svnsn*
transfer	*Tfr*	withdrawn	*drn*
earnest	*ernS*	possession	*pzj*

Intro P

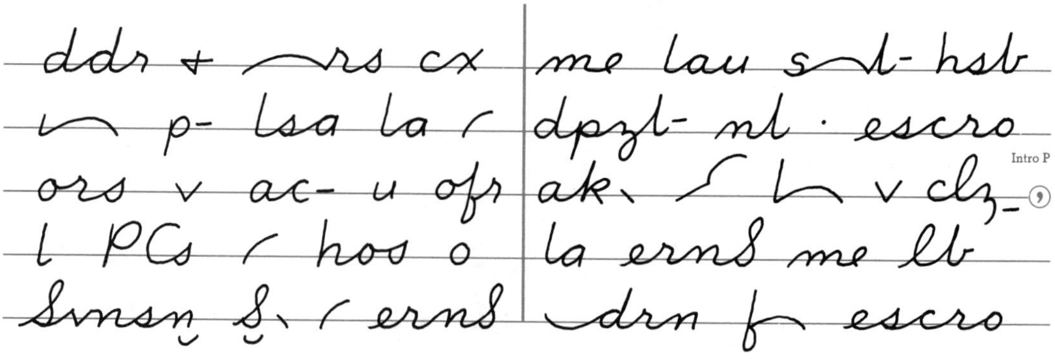

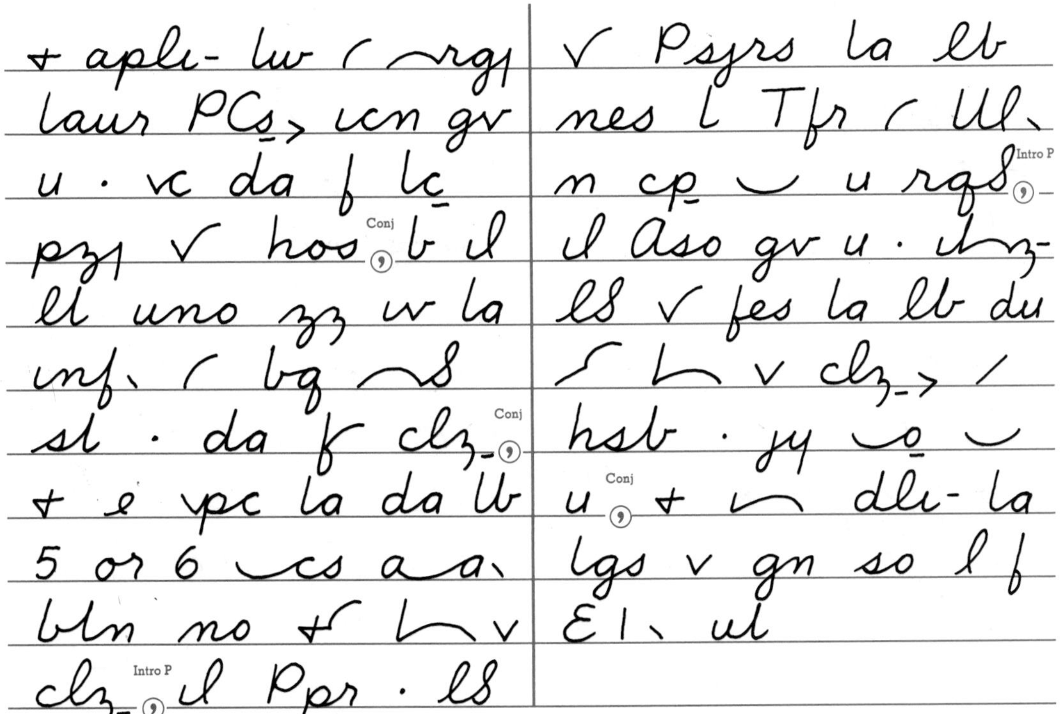

———— 4 ————

Preview Words

aspects	*aspcs*	licensed	*lsN-*
realtor	*rllr*	appraisal	*aprzl*
amateur	*a—lr*	ownership	*ors*
attempt	*atl*	prospective	*Pspcv*

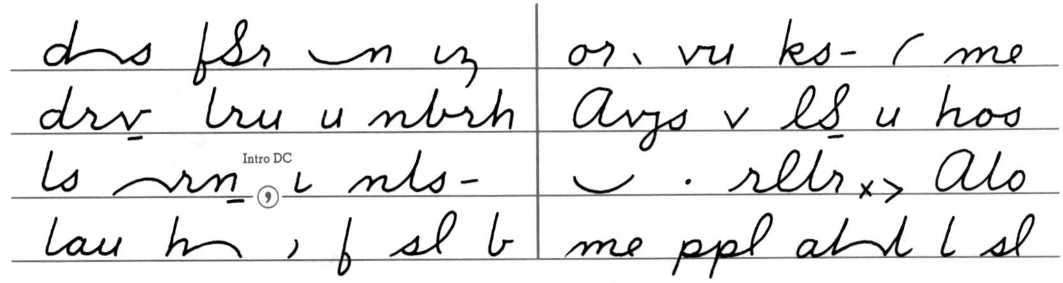

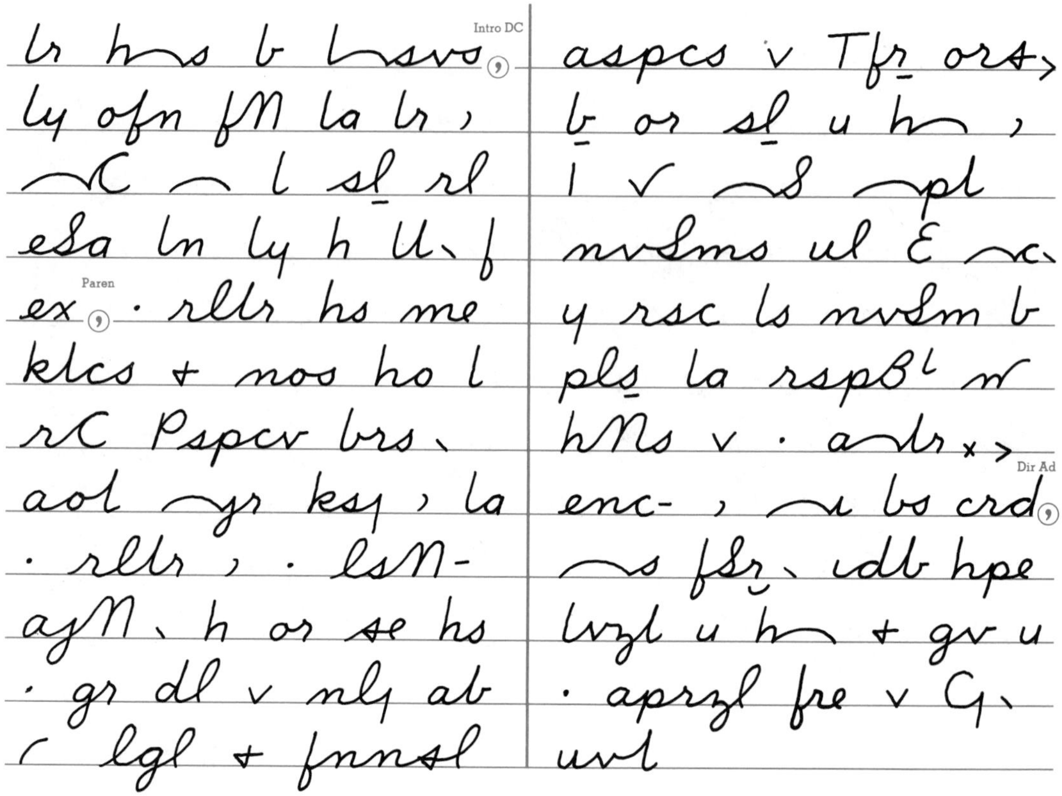

5

Punctuation Study

Add commas to show one nonrestrictive clause, one group of words in a series, two introductory phrases, and two introductory dependent clauses.

Preview Words

title	Ul	accompany	aco
points	pys	originating	orjna
routine	rtn	institution	nStu
appraisal	aprzl	verification	vrfi

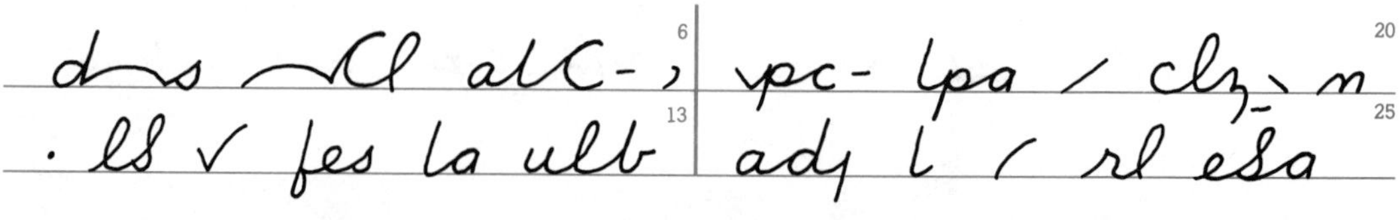

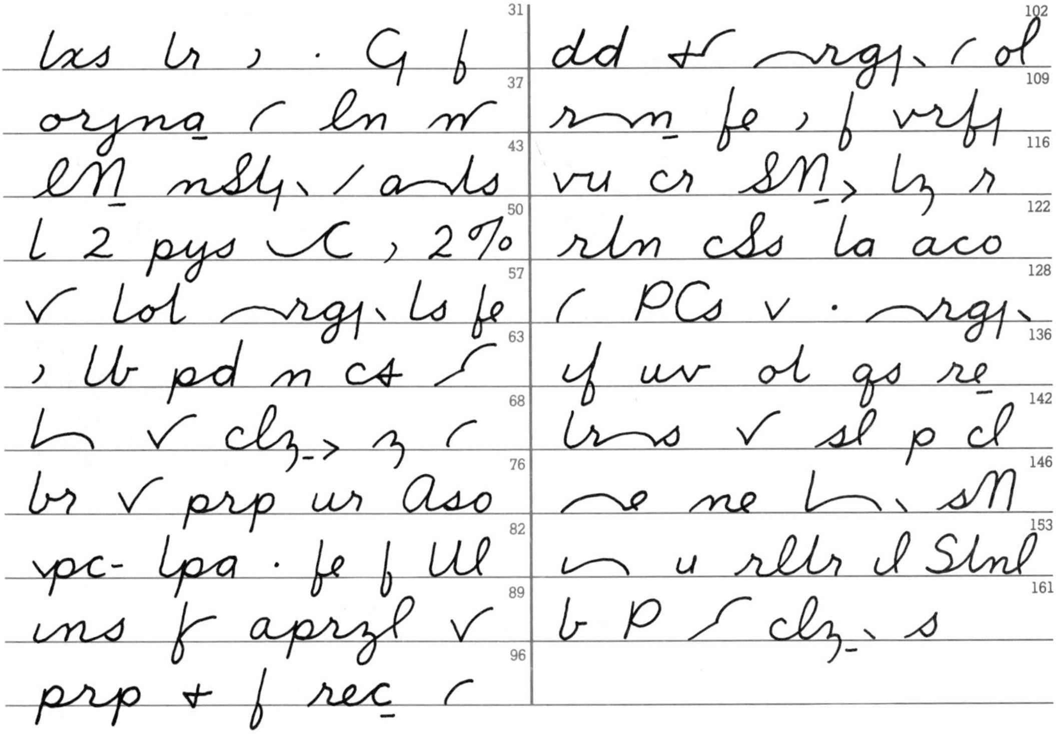

Key

1

Dear Mr. and Mrs. Scott:

You must be pleased that your offer has been accepted. You are about to become the[1] owners of a new apartment building.

Enclosed is a copy of the contract that you will be asked to sign at[2] the time of closing. If you have any questions about the terms, please call me immediately so that I can[3] answer them before we meet officially.

When you buy property on a contract basis rather than purchase[4] a mortgage from a lending institution, the deed to the property is not recorded until the contract[5] is paid off. However, we can pay a fee and have the contract recorded. The recording process is optional,[6] but I recommend that we have it done. By doing so, we will protect your investment in the property.[7]

I do hope that you are pleased with this purchase. It is valuable property, and it will certainly prove to[8] be an excellent investment for you.

Sincerely yours, (170)

2

Dear Mr. Barker:

I certainly understand your desire to postpone the sale of your home. Your circumstances[1] have changed radically, and it would be better for you to stay where you are until you have had time to make your[2] decision.

In the meantime, I will remain alert to potential buyers who have shown an interest in your[3] home. If you decide to take the new job in Detroit, I am confident that your house will sell quickly.

I would[4] also like to remind you that we may be able to assist you in locating a new home in Detroit.[5] We can initiate a computer search for a house with the features that you prefer.

Again, thank you for[6] allowing us to assist you. If I can be of help to you at any time, please call me.

Cordially, (138)

3

Dear Dr. and Mrs. Cox:

I am pleased to say that the owners have accepted your offer to purchase the house[1] on Stevenson Street. The earnest money that you submitted has been deposited into an escrow account.[2] At the time of closing, that earnest money will be withdrawn from escrow and applied toward the mortgage that you are[3] purchasing.

I cannot give you an exact date for taking possession of the house, but I will let you know[4] as soon as I have that information. The bank must set a date for the closing, and we expect that date to be[5] five or six weeks away. Between now and the time of closing, I will prepare a list of the procedures that will be[6] necessary to transfer the title. In keeping with your request, I will also give you an itemized list[7] of the fees that will be due at the time of closing.

It has been a joy working with you, and I am delighted[8] that things have gone so well for everyone.

Yours truly, (170)

4

Dear Ms. Foster:

When I was driving through your neighborhood this morning, I noticed that your home is for sale by owner.[1] Have you considered the many advantages of listing your house with a realtor?

Although many people[2] attempt to sell their homes by themselves, they often find that there is much more to selling real estate than they had thought.[3] For example, a realtor has many contacts and knows how to reach prospective buyers. Another major[4] consideration is that a realtor is a licensed agent. He or she has a great deal of knowledge[5] about the legal and financial aspects of transferring ownership.

Buying or selling your home is one of[6] the most important investments you will ever make. Why risk this investment by placing that responsibility[7] in the hands of an amateur?

Enclosed is my business card, Ms. Foster. I would be happy to visit your[8] home and give you an appraisal free of charge.

Yours very truly, (171)

5

Dear Ms. Mitchell:

Attached is a list of the fees that you will be expected to pay at closing. In addition[1] to the real estate taxes, there is a charge for originating the loan in the lending institution. It[2] amounts to two points, which is 2 percent of the total mortgage. This fee is to be paid in cash at the time of[3] the closing.

As the buyer of the property, you are also expected to pay a fee for title insurance,[4] for the appraisal of the property, and for recording the deed and the mortgage. The only remaining[5] fee is for verification of your credit standing.

These are routine costs that accompany the purchase of[6] a mortgage. If you have other questions regarding terms of the sale, please call me any time. Since I am your[7] realtor, I will certainly be present at the closing.

Sincerely, (152)

LESSON 44

Shorthand Vocabulary Review

Write $\mathcal{S}$ for the word beginnings *cer, cir, ser, sur* (sir).

certain	*Sčn*	surveyed	*Svā-*
service	*Svs*	search	*SC*
certificate	*Sčfcl*	surprise	*Sprz*
circular	*Sclr*	surcharge	*SC*
surplus	*Spls*	surgery	*Syre*

Transcription Aids: Spelling

Learn to spell the following words which end in *al* or *le*. When you are in doubt about the spelling of these words, use your dictionary.

al

practical	*prclcl*
survival	*Svvl*
vital	*vtl*
personal	*Psnl*
chemical	*cvcl*
legal	*lgl*

le

title	*ttl*
vehicle	*vhcl*
settle	*stl*
article	*artcl*
assemble	*asB*
cable	*cB*

Your Business Vocabulary

easement 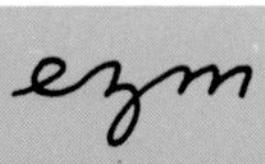 In real estate, the legal right of a party to have limited use of another person's property.

The water company requests that nothing be planted within the boundaries of its easement.

abstract  In real estate, a legal document containing the complete written history of a deeded parcel of land.

I have requested that a copy of the abstract be sent to you.

Reading and Writing Exercises

1

Preview Words

county	ke	commercial	krsl
partner	ptnr	newcomer	nukr
resolve	rzlv	residential	rzdnsl
surrounding	SoN	school system	scl sS

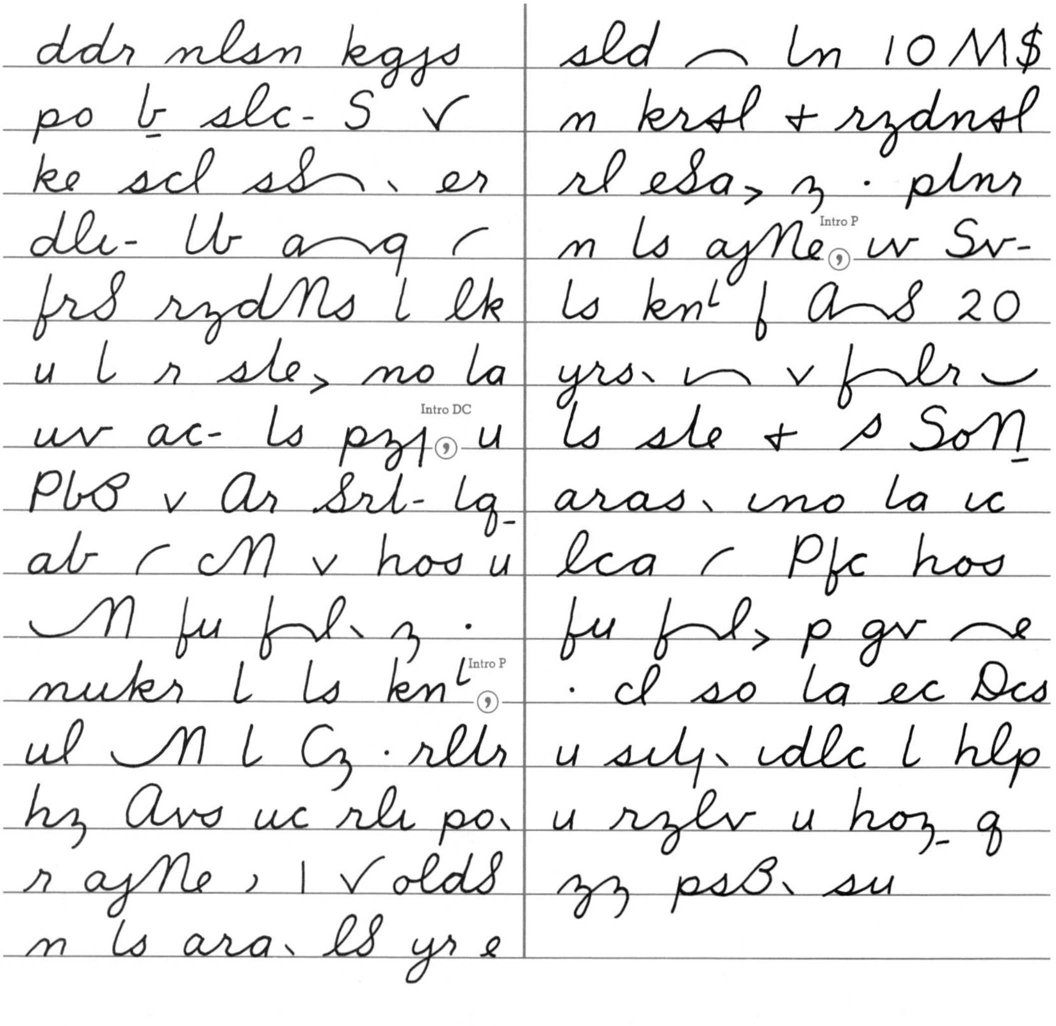

―――――――――― **2** ――――――――――

Preview Words

bet   *bl*

keys   *ces*

arises   *arzs*

residing   *rzd*

effect   *efc*

exemption   *⌣⌐y*

acquainted   *aqM-*

River Road   *rvr rd*

---

d ⌐r ⌐rfe ⌐ enc‾
(X sl v ces
lu nu h⌐⌐ no‾
u ß^l lgl lgs dn
gcl ₍,₎ ιdb l l bl
laur kpl stl- b no,
rvr rd , · blef
ara ₍,₎ Conj + ⌐ ⌐sr ul
nyy rzd lr, l hlp
u gl aqM- ⌣ u
nbrs ₍,₎ Intro P ιv sM crds
l lr h⌐s anoM u
arvl, n re lu q ab

(prp lxs ₍,₎ Intro P u ⌐a fl
f ι ⌐⌐y af Ja l ι u
lxs f ls yr v Ar b
pd n f ₍,₎ Conj + ⌐⌐y dz
n q nl efc ull
6 ⌐os af (Ul l
(prp hsb Tfr-l
(nu or, / hsb
⌐ι plzr l rep u
n ⌐c lz arms,
⌐n (nd arzs ₍,₎ Intro DC
⌐ a rde l hlp,
ul

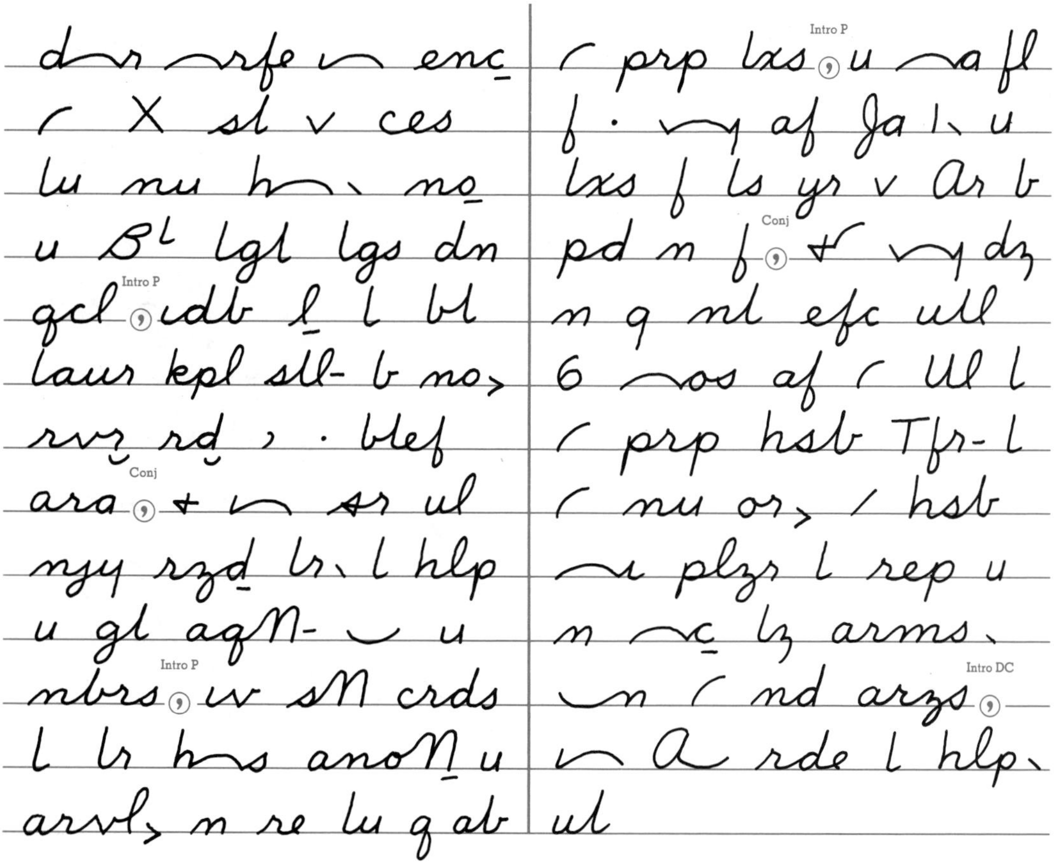

3

Preview Words

lengthy	*lqle*	abstract	*abSrc*
verified	*vrf-*	acquiring	*aq-*
breakdown	*brcdon*	homeowner	*h⌢or*
principal	*prNpl*	installments	*nSlms*

d M lnrd ⌐ brd
v ⌐yrs apv- u ln
ls afnn, ⌐ prp
hsb aprz-₍,₎ ✝ u cs   *Conj*
rq hsb vrf-, ul
rsv · 20 = yr ⌐rgj
la , paß n ⌐ol
nSlms, yf u dsd
l ⌐ u h⌢or ins
✝ prp lxs ◡ u
hoo pams₍,₎ ec   *Intro DC*
⌐c loz arms,
ino la uh s⌐ qs
ab aq- · abSrc f

prp, bcz · abSrc
c bk qi lqle ✝
vpNv-₍,₎ ι rcm lau   *Intro DC*
PCo Ul ins nSd,
⌐ Ul ins l grnle
lau fnnsl nvSm
, Plc-, ⌐ ⌐ v
clz-₍,₎ ul rsv · scjl   *Intro P*
v pams, la scjl
l so · brcdon √
nS ✝ prNpl O ⌐
20 = yr pred, ilb lc
fw l lc ◡ u aq.
cu

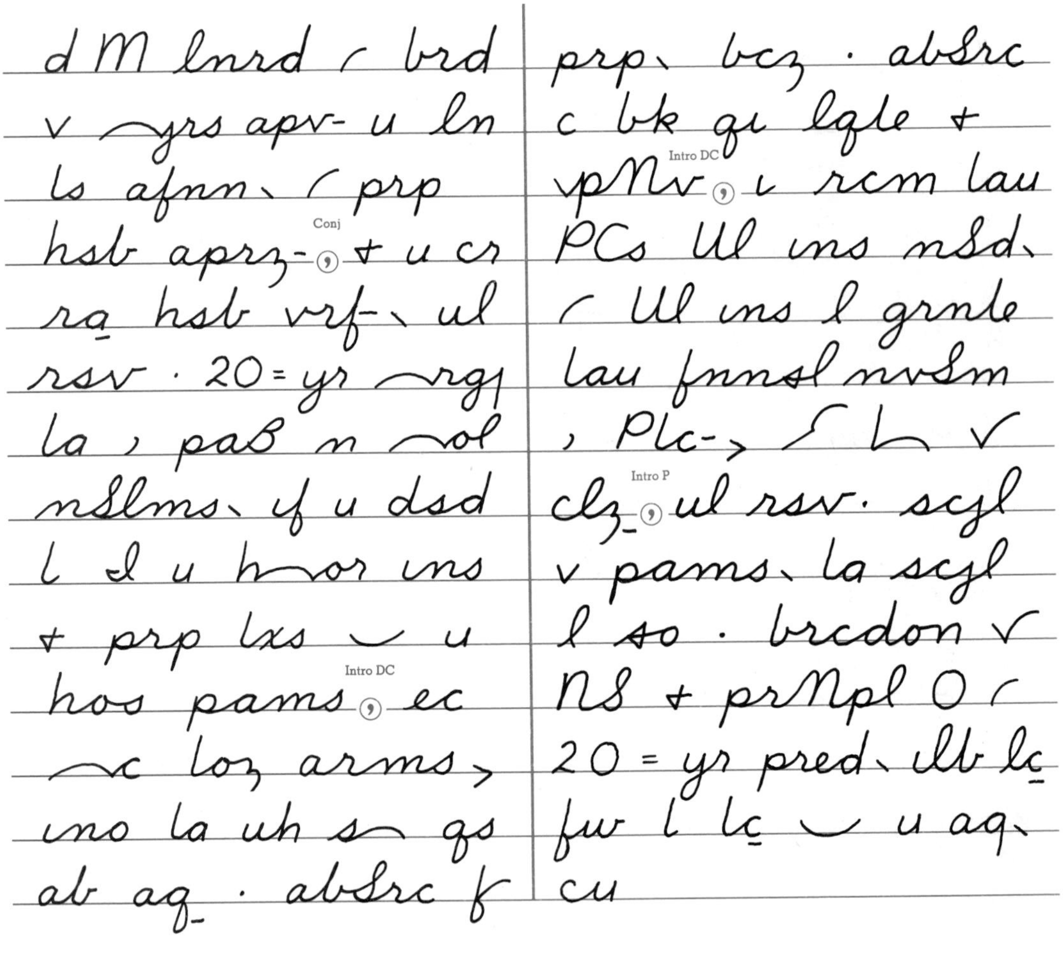

---- **4** ----

Preview Words

creek	*crc*	practical	*prclcl*
adjoins	*ajyns*	boundaries	*boNres*
smaller	*s—lr*	subdivided	*sdvd-*
zoned	*zn-*	County Road	*ke rd*

[Shorthand practice passage — two columns of shorthand outlines]

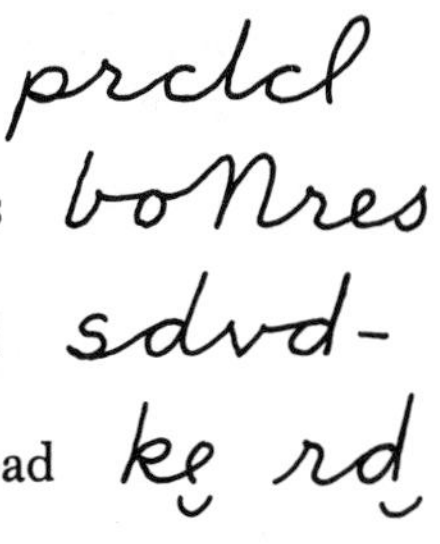

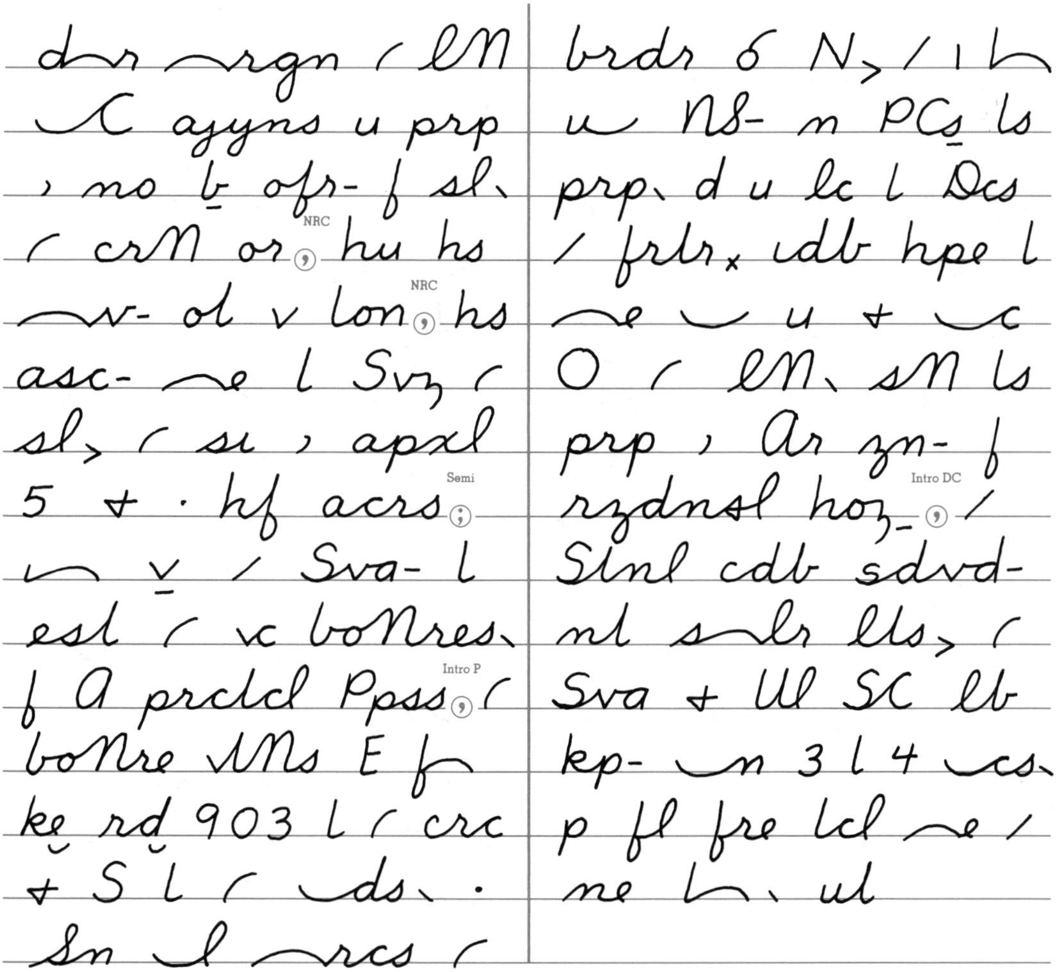

5

Punctuation Study

Add commas to show two introductory phrases, two introductory dependent clauses, and two parenthetical expressions.

Preview Words

lot	ll	electric	elc
exists	Ss	bordering	brdr
title	Ul	easement	ezm
likely	lcl	county clerk	ke clrc

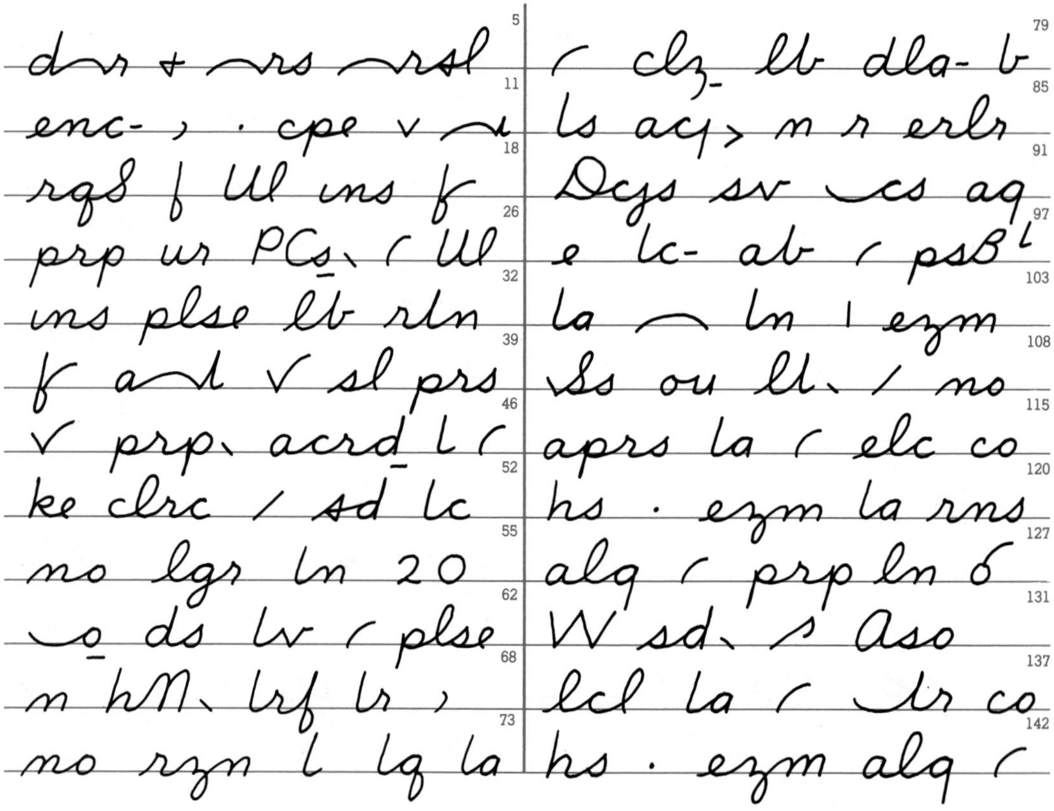

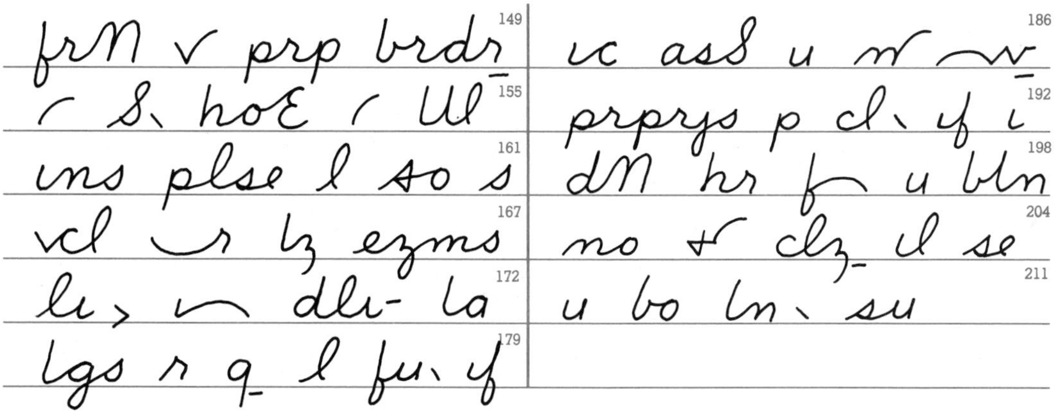

Key

1

Dear Dr. Nelson:

Congratulations upon being selected superintendent of the county school[1] system. We are delighted to be among the first residents to welcome you to our city.

Now that you have[2] accepted this position, you probably have already started thinking about the kind of house you want for your[3] family. As a newcomer to this community, you will want to choose a realtor whose advice you can[4] rely upon. Our agency is one of the oldest in this area. Last year we sold more than $10 million[5] in commercial and residential real estate.

As a partner in this agency, I have served this community[6] for almost 20 years. I am very familiar with this city and its surrounding areas. I know[7] that I can locate the perfect house for your family.

Please give me a call so that we can discuss your[8] situation. I would like to help you resolve your housing question as soon as possible.

Sincerely yours,[9] (180)

2

Dear Mr. Murphy:

I am enclosing the extra set of keys to your new home. Knowing your ability to[1] get things done quickly, I would be willing to bet that you are completely settled by now.

River Road is a[2] beautiful area, and I am sure you will enjoy residing there. To help you get acquainted with your neighbors,[3] I have sent cards to their homes announcing your arrival.

In regard to your question about the property taxes,[4] you may file for an exemption after January 1. Your taxes for this year have already been paid[5] in full, and the exemption does not go into effect until six months after the title to the property[6] has been transferred to the new owner.

It has been my pleasure to represent you in making these arrangements. When[7] the need arises, I am always ready to help.

Yours truly, (151)

3

Dear Miss Leonard:

The board of managers approved your loan this afternoon. The property has been appraised, and your[1] credit rating has been verified. You will receive a 20-year mortgage that is payable in monthly[2] installments. If you decide to include your homeowner insurance and property taxes with your house payments,[3] we can make those arrangements.

I know that you had some questions about acquiring an abstract for the property.[4] Because an abstract can become quite lengthy and expensive, I recommend that you purchase title insurance[5] instead. The title insurance will guarantee that your financial investment is protected.

At the time of the[6] closing, you will receive a schedule of payments. That schedule will show a breakdown of the interest and principal[7] over the 20-year period. I will be looking forward to talking with you again.

Cordially yours,[8] (160)

4

Dear Mr. Morgan:

The land which adjoins your property is now being offered for sale. The current owner, who[1] has moved out of town, has asked me to supervise the sale.

The site is approximately five and a half acres;[2] I am having it surveyed to establish the exact boundaries. For all practical purposes, the boundary[3] extends east from County Road 903 to the creek and south to the woods. A stone wall marks the border on the north.[4]

At one time you were interested in purchasing this property. Would you like to discuss it further? I would[5] be happy to meet with you and walk over the land. Since this property is already zoned for residential[6] housing, it certainly could be subdivided into smaller lots.

The survey and title search will be[7] completed within three to four weeks. Please feel free to call me at any time.

Yours truly, (155)

5

Dear Mr. and Mrs. Marshall:

Enclosed is a copy of my request for title insurance for the property[1] you are purchasing. The title insurance policy will be written for the amount of the sale price of the[2] property. According to the county clerk, it should take no longer than 20 working days to have the policy[3] in hand. Therefore, there is no reason to think that the closing will be delayed by this action.

In our earlier[4] discussions several weeks ago, we talked about the possibility that more than one easement exists[5] on your lot. It now appears that the electric company has an easement that runs along the property[6] line on the west side. It is also likely that the water company has an easement along the front of the[7] property bordering the street. However, the title insurance policy will show us exactly where these[8] easements lie.

I am delighted that things are going well for you. If I can assist you in the moving[9] preparations, please call. If I don't hear from you between now and the closing, I will see you both then.

Sincerely yours,[10] (200)

LESSON 45

Word Development

Develop new words using the following brief forms:

contract

contracting *kc̣*

contracts *kcs*

contracted *kc-*

contractor *kcr*

contractual *kcul*

accept

accepted *ac-*

accepting *ac̣*

acceptance *acɱ*

acceptable *acß*

acceptability *acß^l*

for

format *frl*

formation *frm*

formerly *frrl*

fortunate *fcnl*

formulated *frla-*

effort *efl*

conform *kf*

forecast *fcs*

comfortable *kflß*

enforcement *nfsm*

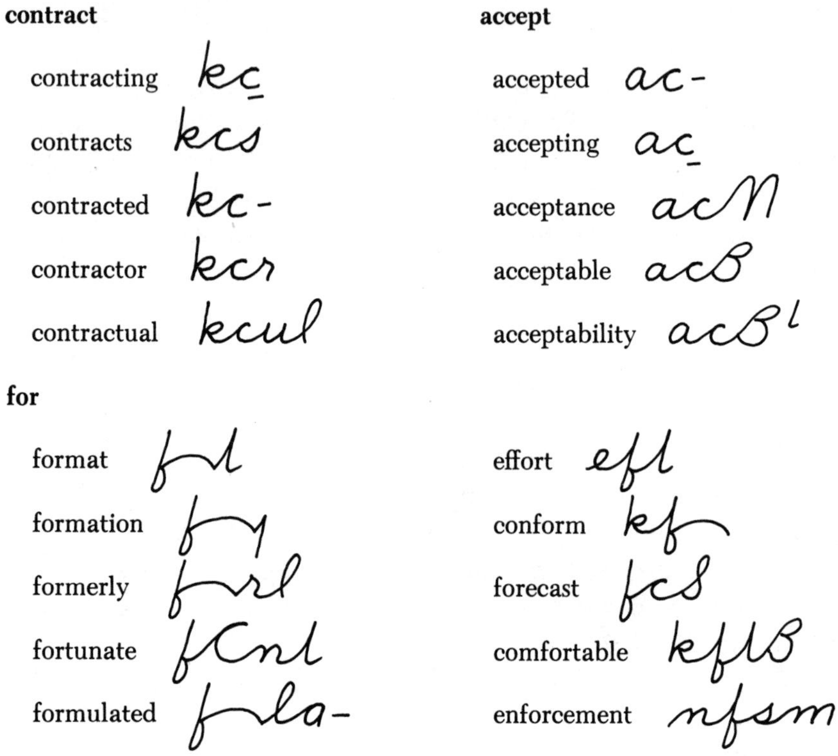

Reading and Writing Exercises

1

Preview Words

appeal	apl	donations	dnys
rezone	rzn	treasurer	trzrr
priority	prir l	commission	kj
rejected	ryc-	transactions	Tacys

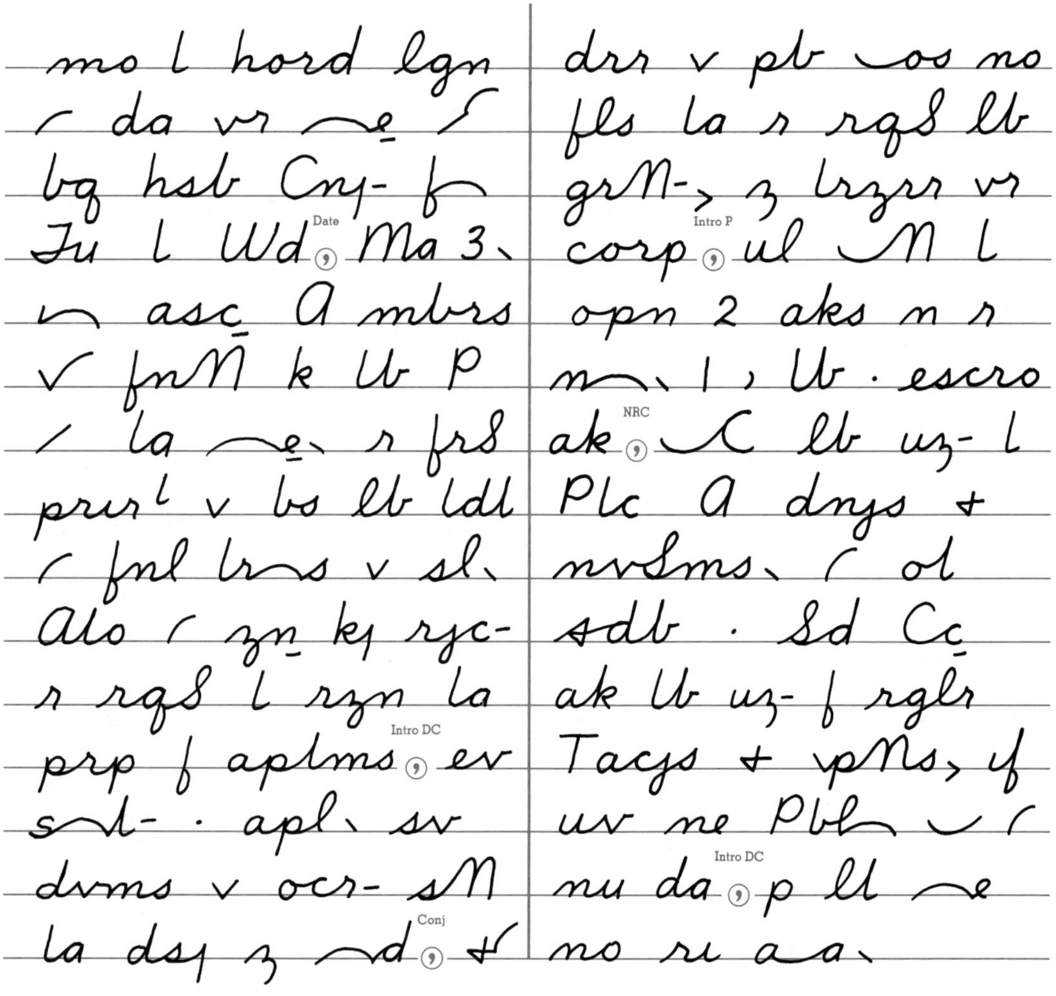

2

Preview Words

expires	vprs	renovate	rnva
indoor	ndr	extension	vtnj
athletic	alllc	initiated	insa-
formerly	frl	expiration	vprj

d jrld hr , (Pgrs
rpl u rqS- (bld
la frl z o- b (
alllc clb. Ul l (
prp , Sl n hNs
v bq. srll af (
fsl z clz- (Intro DC ,) . grp
v lcl nvSrs d
. ofr l PCs /. la
ofr z rfz- b (bq.
3 os aq . sec
grp v nvSrs
aprC- (bq. ls
grp obln- . 90=d
opj l PCs (NRC ,) C
vprs Fb 9 > (trs
v opj agrem clrl

Sa la / l n b
psB lgl . vtnj
af (vprj da. (
nvSrs v insa- .
efl l rz adyl fNs
l rnva (bld.
plns r b d l
opn . fl fl' sNr
la l l ndr s (Series ,)
jq (Series ,) lns (Series ,) + ol Pgs >
if udlc adyl inf (Intro DC ,)
ic pl u n lC
(P v ls grp. (
mbrs drv l bgn
l (Conj ,) so id Avz
u l ac qcl. s

3

Preview Words

earnest

escrow

progress

summary

withdrawn

down payment

conversation

Central Savings

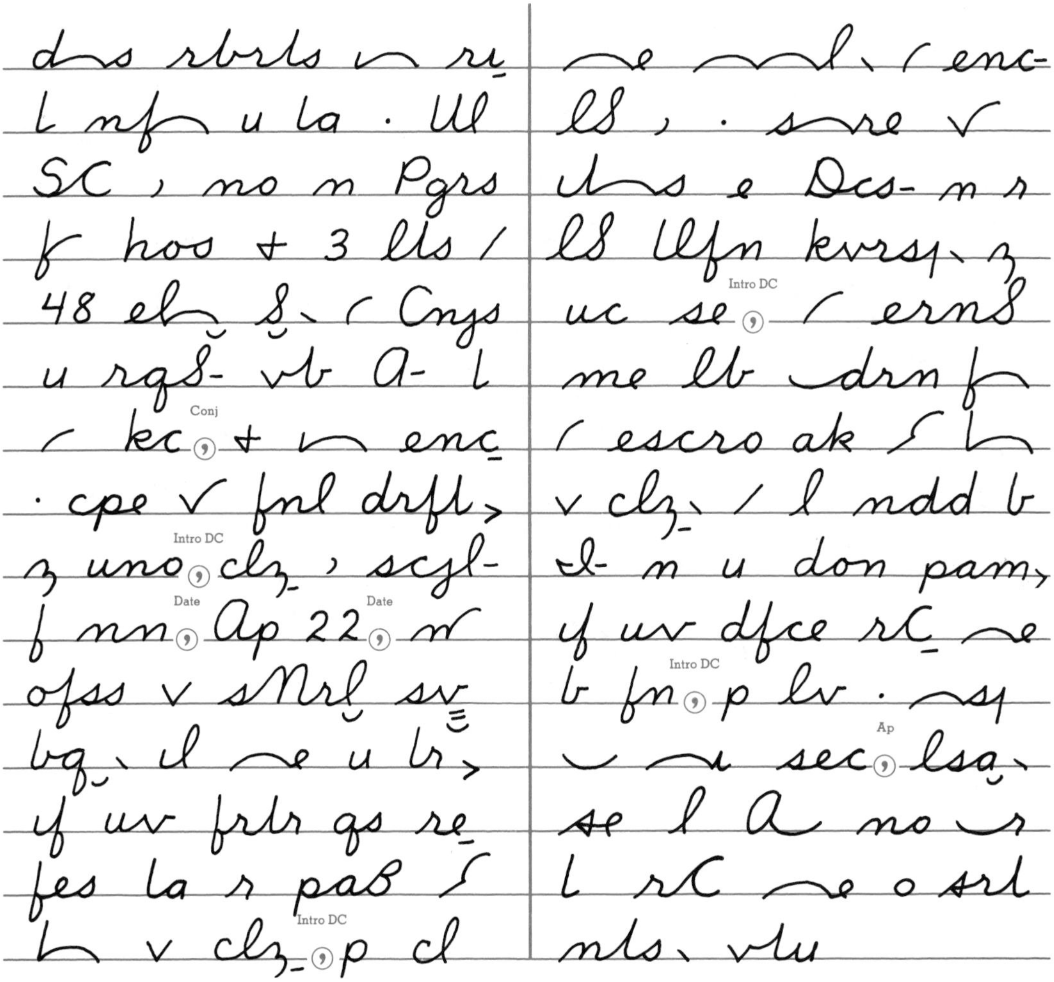

4

Preview Words

exact	possession
quiet	relinquish
whenever	neighborhood
alternative	conveniently

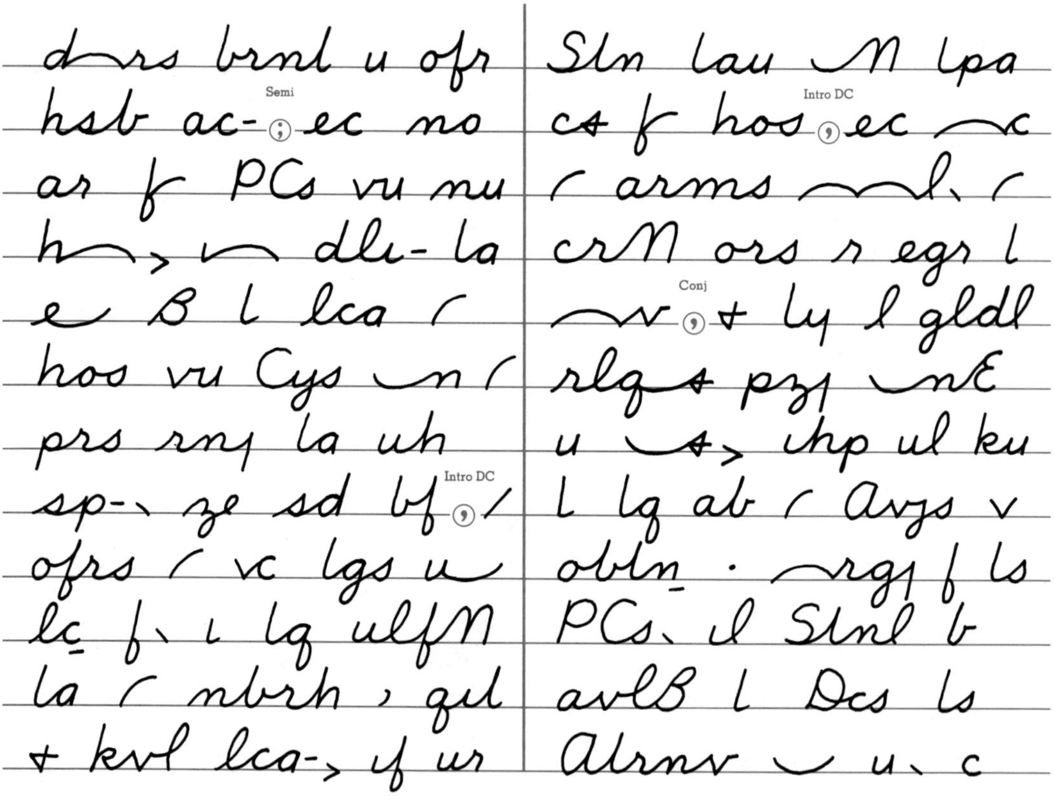

5

Punctuation Study

Add commas to show one conjunction, one introductory phrase, one appositive, one introductory dependent clause, and one parenthetical expression.

Preview Words

owners	ors	another	aol
resale	rsl	terminate	trma
couple	cpl	subsequent	ssqN
assumed	as-	conventional	kvnjl

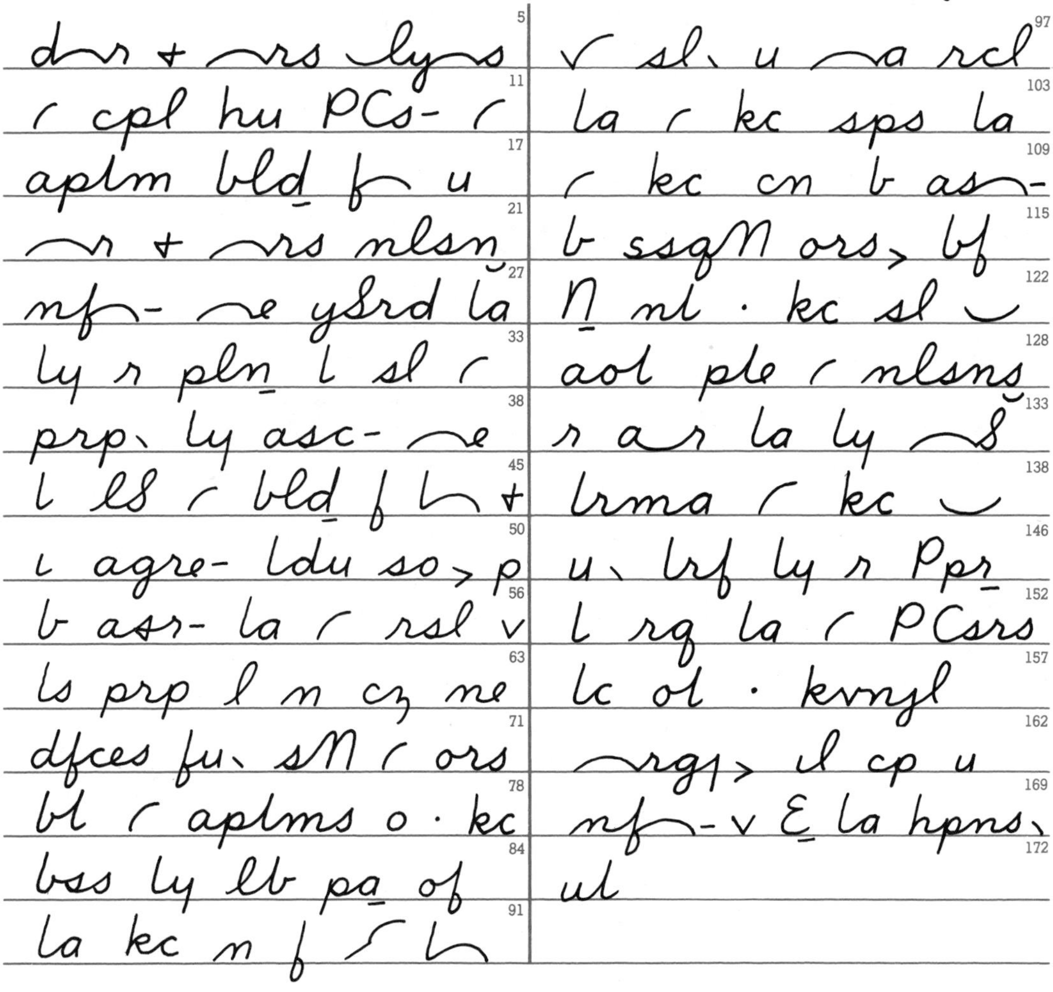

Key

1

MEMO TO: Howard Logan

The date of our meeting at the bank has been changed from Tuesday to Wednesday, May 3. I[1] am asking all members of the finance committee to be present at that meeting. Our first priority of[2] business will be to determine the final terms of sale. Although the zoning commission rejected our request[3] to rezone that property for apartments, we have submitted an appeal. Several developments have occurred[4] since that decision was made, and the director of public works now feels that our request will be granted.

As[5] treasurer of our corporation, you will want to open two accounts in our name. One is to be an escrow[6] account, which will be used to protect all donations and investments. The other should be a standard checking account[7] to be used for regular transactions and expenses.

If you have any problem with the new date, please let[8] me know right away. (164)

2

Dear Gerald:

Here is the progress report you requested on the building that formerly was owned by the athletic[1] club. Title to the property is still in the hands of the bank. Shortly after the facility was closed,[2] a group of local investors made an offer to purchase it. That offer was refused by the bank. Three months ago[3] a second group of investors approached the bank. This group obtained a 90-day option to purchase, which expires[4] February 9.

The terms of the option agreement clearly state that it will not be possible to get[5] an extension after the expiration date. The investors have initiated an effort to raise[6] additional funds to renovate the building. Plans are being made to open a family fitness center that[7] will include indoor swimming, jogging, tennis, and other programs.

If you would like additional information,[8] I can put you in touch with the president of this group. The membership drive will begin immediately, so[9] I would advise you to act quickly.

Sincerely, (189)

3

Dear Ms. Roberts:

I am writing to inform you that a title search is now in progress for the house and three lots[1] at 48 Elm Street. The changes you requested have been added to the contract, and I am enclosing a[2] copy of the final draft.

As you know, closing is scheduled for noon, April 22, in the offices of[3] Central Savings Bank. I will meet you there.

If you have further questions regarding fees that are payable at the[4] time of closing, please call me immediately. The enclosed list is a summary of the items we discussed[5] in our last telephone conversation. As you can see, the earnest money will be withdrawn from the escrow account[6] at the time of closing. It will indeed be included in your down payment.

If you have difficulty reaching[7] me by phone, please leave a message with my secretary, Lisa. She will always know where to reach me on short[8] notice.

Very truly yours, (165)

4

Dear Mrs. Barnett:

Your offer has been accepted; we can now arrange for the purchase of your new home.

I am[1] delighted that we were able to locate the house of your choice within the price range that you had specified.[2] As we said before, it offers the exact things you were looking for. I think you will find that the neighborhood is[3] quiet and conveniently located.

If you are certain that you want to pay cash for the house, we can make the[4] arrangements immediately. The current owners are eager to move, and they will gladly relinquish possession[5] whenever you wish.

I hope you will continue to think about the advantages of obtaining a mortgage[6] for this purchase. I will certainly be available to discuss this alternative with you.

Cordially,[7] (140)

5

Dear Mr. and Mrs. Williams:

The couple who purchased the apartment building from you, Mr. and Mrs. Nelson,[1] informed me yesterday that they are planning to sell the property. They asked me to list the building for them,[2] and I agreed to do so.

Please be assured that the resale of this property will not cause any difficulties[3] for you. Since the owners bought the apartments on a contract basis, they will be paying off that contract in[4] full at the time of the sale. You may recall that the contract specifies that the contract cannot be assumed by[5] subsequent owners.

Before entering into a contract sale with another party, the Nelsons are aware[6] that they must terminate the contract with you. Therefore, they are preparing to require that the purchasers take out[7] a conventional mortgage.

I will keep you informed of everything that happens.

Yours truly, (156)

gre̱ clrs b llfn*

In today's electronic world, more and more communication takes place by telephone. Since we do not have the advantage of seeing the person and using nonverbal clues to send and receive messages, we must rely strictly upon our voices to do that job for us. Because the persons we are speaking with will form impressions of us on the basis of our telephone manners, it becomes increasingly important to use our oral communication skills as effectively as possible.

Be courteous. Assume a personal tone and make the caller feel that he or she is the most important person in the world.

Speak clearly and listen carefully. Speak distinctly so that your message will be received without difficulty by the listener. Listen carefully for the correct pronunciation of the caller's name and for the name of the party she or he wishes to speak to.

Identify yourself immediately. When answering a call coming from outside your organization, begin with a pleasant greeting, followed by your organization's name and then your name:

"Good afternoon, Westcott Enterprises, Chris Bergman speaking."

If you are answering a call from inside your building or if your organization has a switchboard operator who has answered the outside call before directing it to you, simply answer by identifying the department or your supervisor's name before giving your name:

"Purchasing department, Julie Randolph speaking."
"Mr. Marshall's office, John Moore speaking."

***Greeting Callers by Telephone**

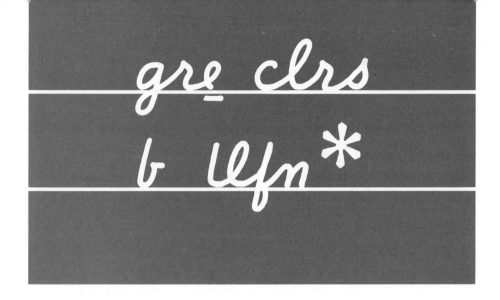

Get complete information. If you are answering the phone for someone else in your department, be certain to get the correct name of the caller and the caller's organization. Phrase the question politely:

> "May I ask who's calling, please?" Or "Who shall I say is calling, please?"

Offer assistance. Be as helpful as you can. If you cannot connect the caller with the appropriate party, give the caller an explanation and options.

> "I'm sorry, Mr. Ryan is on another line. Would you like to hold a few moments, or shall I take a message and have him return your call?"
> "I'm sorry, Ms. Summerville will not be in the office today. Could someone else help you?"

If the caller prefers to wait on the line, go back on the line after one minute and ask if the person wishes to continue waiting. It is irritating to be placed on "hold" and forgotten.

Conclude by verifying information. Be certain that a complete exchange of information has taken place. If you are taking a message, read the information back to ensure its completeness and accuracy. End with a pleasant and direct tone.

> "Thank you, Mr. Morgan. I will ask Mrs. Chandler to return your call at 302-4000, extension 201, concerning the budget proposal. Good-bye."

unl 10

(shorthand symbols) *

Shorthand Vocabulary Review

Study the following words and the principles they illustrate. Look for these words in the letters and memos presented in this unit.

1. Write *(symbol)* for the word ending *ify*. Write *(symbol)* for the word ending *ification*.

justify	*(shorthand)*	qualified	*(shorthand)*
clarifies	*(shorthand)*	justified	*(shorthand)*
gratifying	*(shorthand)*	qualifications	*(shorthand)*
certified	*(shorthand)*	modifications	*(shorthand)*

*Unit Ten
Manufacturing

2. Write *u* for the word beginning *un*.

unusual	*uuz*	uncommon	*ukn*
unpaid	*upd*	unexpected	*uxpc-*
unlikely	*ulcl*	unnecessary	*unes*
unless	*uls*	unfortunately	*ufCnll*

More About Punctuation

Use a colon to introduce lists, tabulations, explanations, or quotations. Some words that commonly precede colons are given below:

the following	listed below
as follows	such as

> Please order the following: file folders, disks, ballpoint pens, and typewriting paper.

> The committee members are as follows: Alexander Haley, Sylvia Carmichael, Andrew Simpson, and Deborah Easterby.

LESSON 46

Brief Forms and Derivatives

1. *D kl ho h nl uz*
2. *uuz Dr Drs nl⁻ nlf⁻*

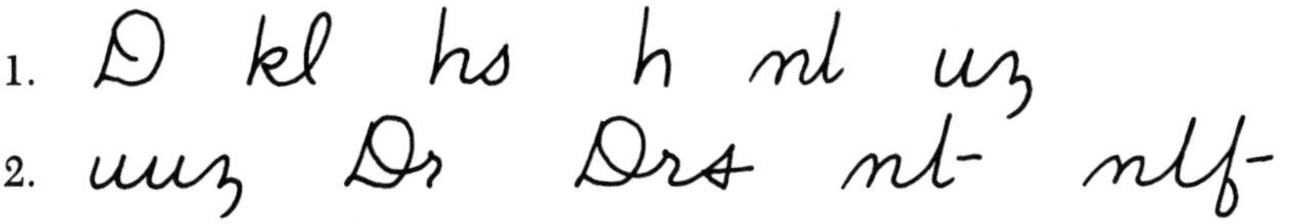

Key

1. distribute, control, has, he/had/him, note, usual
2. unusual, distributor, distributorship, noted, notified

Phrase Review

1. *ihd iz efl erp⁻ ecd*
2. *edb ucn uvh lvzl Lo*
3. *zi cb vn vu ou*

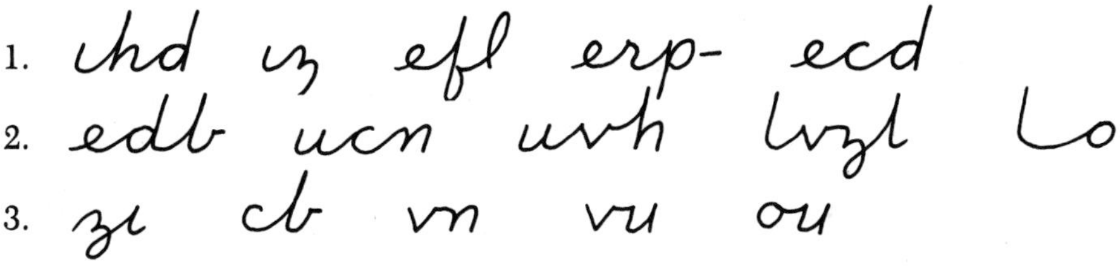

Key

1. I had, I was, we feel, we are pleased, we could
2. we would be, you cannot, you have had, to visit, to work
3. as I, can be, have not, of you/of your, on you/on your

Reading and Writing Exercises

1

Preview Words

avoid	heavier
rapid	regularly
mechanical	prosperity
emergencies	replacement

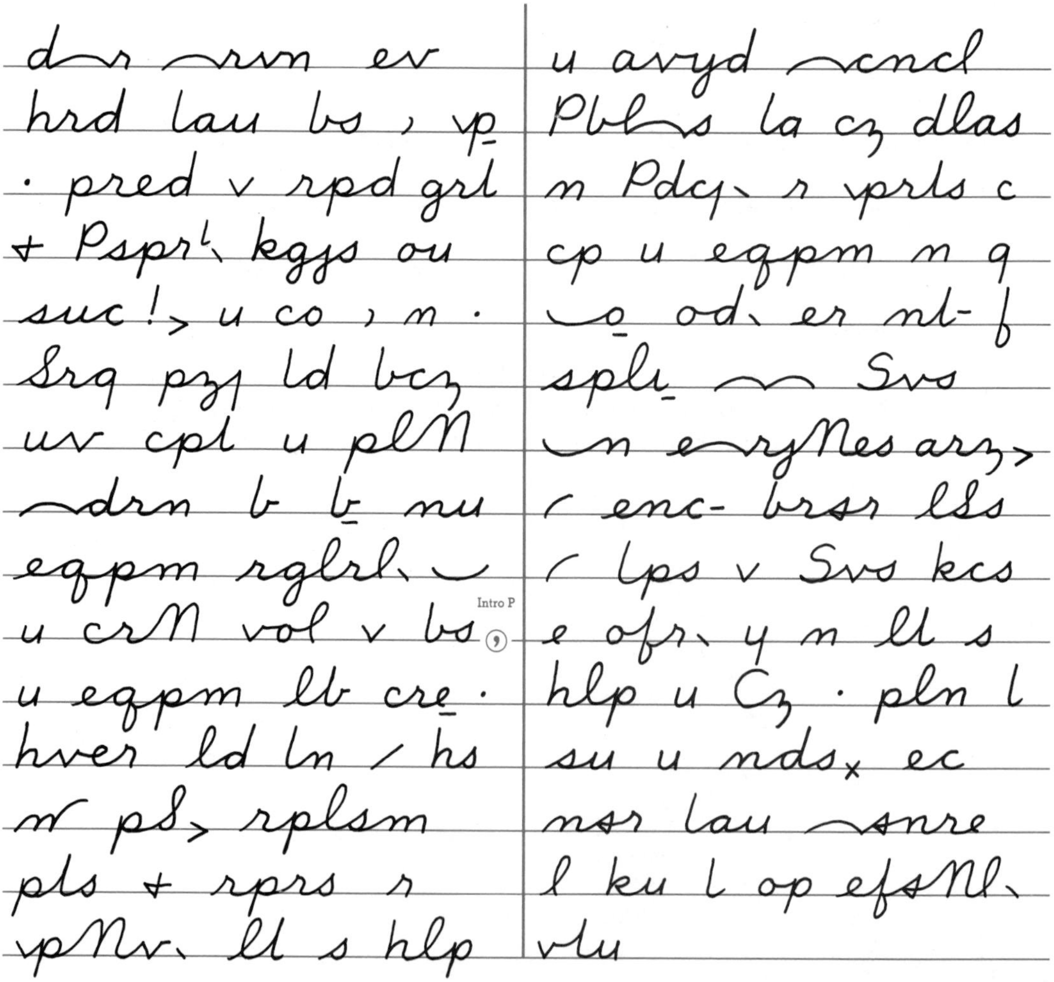

————————————— **2** —————————————

Preview Words

Ltd. $\mathcal{L}\,\mathcal{l}\underset{\sim}{\bar{}}$

roof $\mathcal{rf}$

operation opj

computer $kpur$

thorough $\mathcal{bro}$

flexibility $flx\mathcal{B}^{l}$

orientation $ore\mathcal{Ny}$

technology $\mathcal{lcnlje}$

---

d n hrve hr ,
(dla u rqd-. ,
uc se ⑼ / klns .
kp ld √ nu eqpm
u ⌐4 l ndl n
fr v jcsn + jcsn ⑼
l l-ͧ idlc l suq
lau brq u ⌐pes
l n plN lse (
eqpm n opj. ev
. v ⌐prsv Dpla
v kpur lcnlje U
l rf, edb hpe l

dmSra (flxB^l vr
unls. ι lq ecd
Aso kvN u ⌐pes
la n Pqs n eze
luz. ec hlp l
pln (lps v ⌐o
Sjs la n apo f lr
nds, e nvr u +
u ⌐pes lvzl s /.
l la , ⌐S kv fu
grp. el pln l Pvd
. lro oreN l n
eqpm. uvl

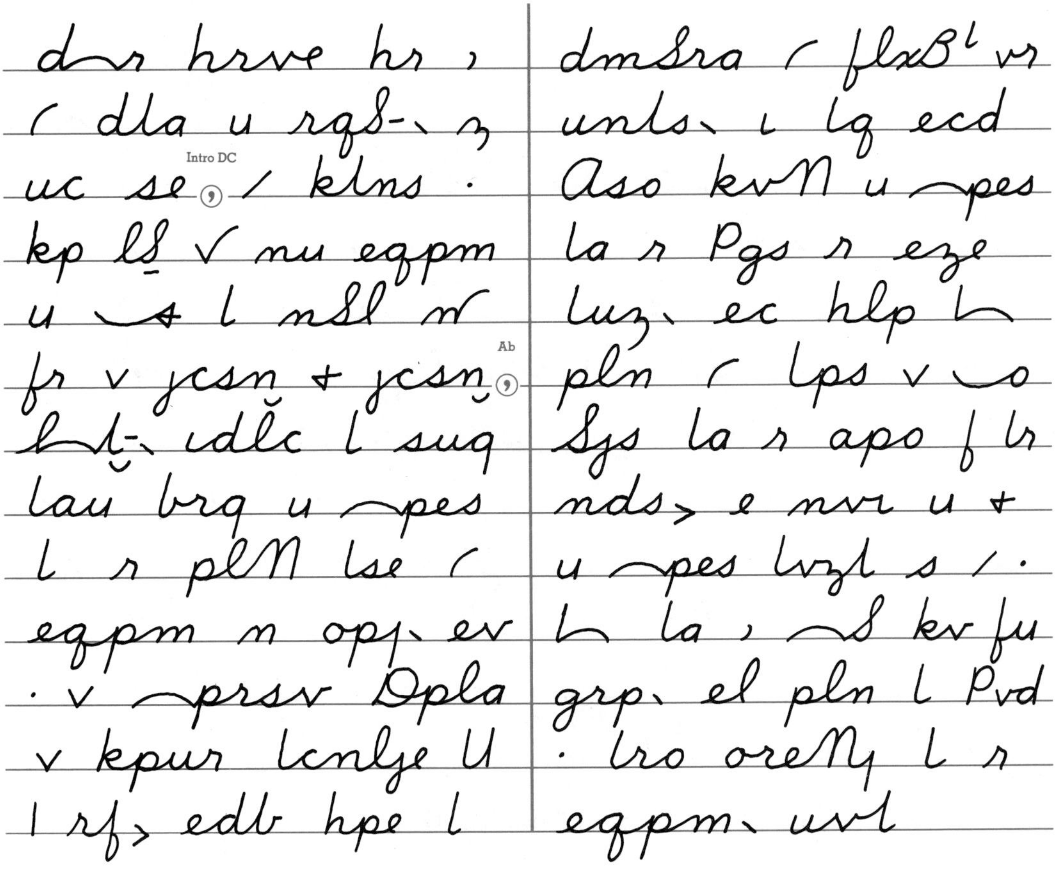

--- **3** ---

Preview Words

teams	ᴸ—ᵒ	doorways	*dr as*
rules	*rls*	walkways	*c as*
careless	*crls*	regulations	*rgljs*
enforce	*nfs*	obstructions	*obSrcjs*

(shorthand text — two columns)

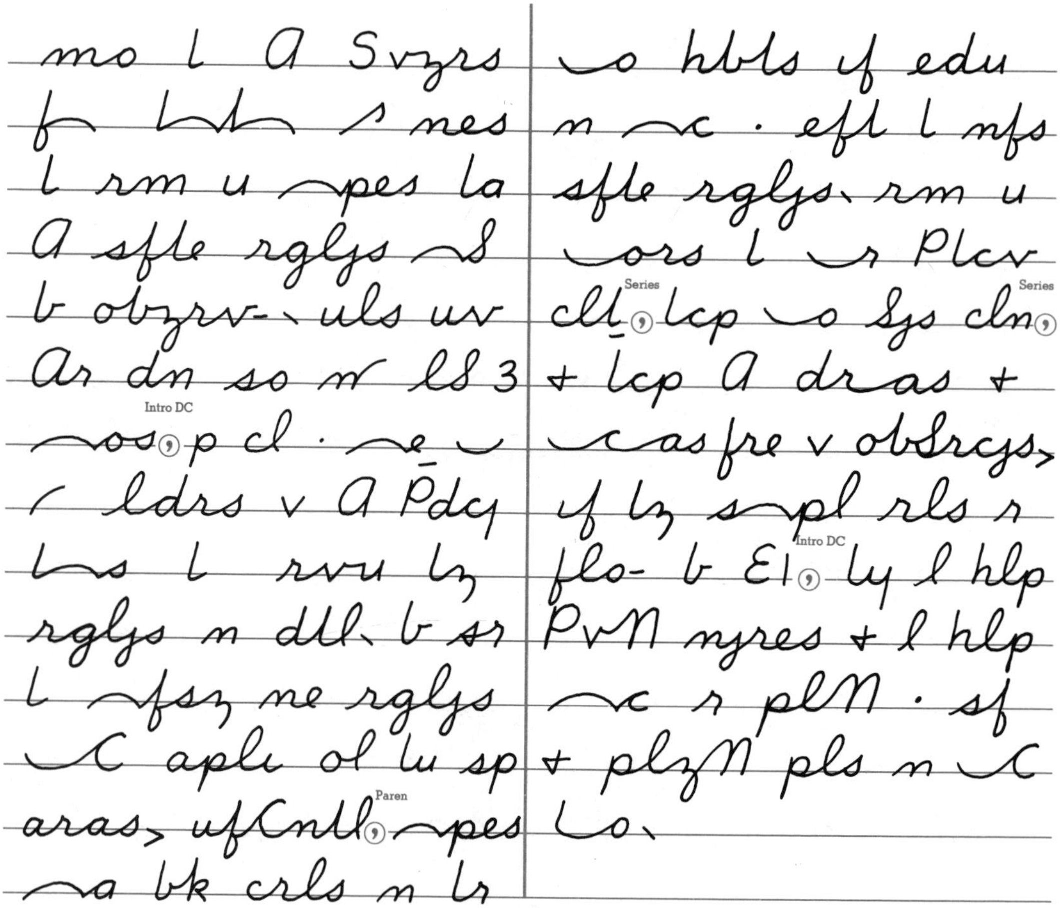

4

Preview Words

basis bss

elected elc-

clarify clrf

document dcm

stock item Sc ith

obligations oblgjs

distributors Drs

responsibilities rspBls

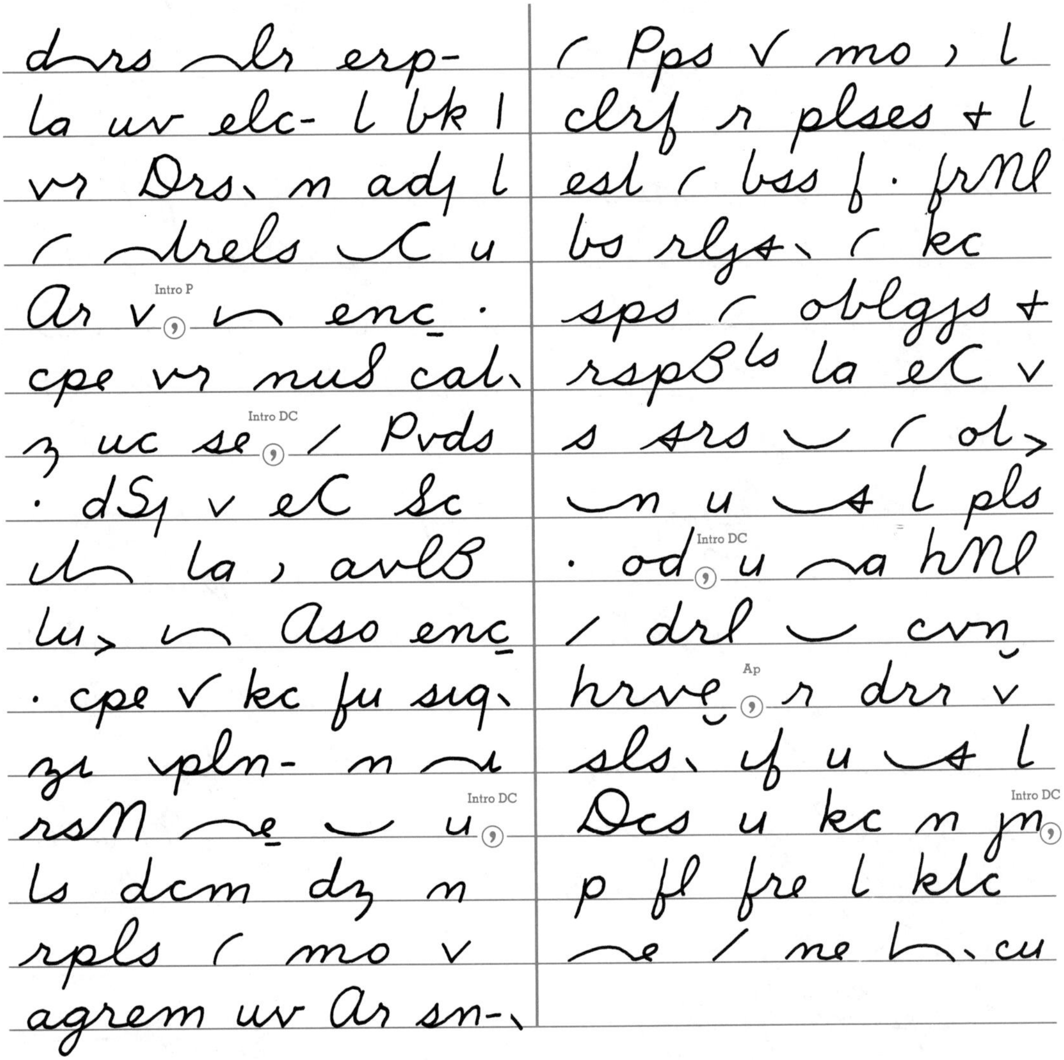

5

Punctuation Study

Add commas to show one introductory phrase, one introductory dependent clause, one appositive, and one series.

Preview Words

rare 

says 

contributor 

participants 

pledges 

donation 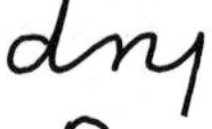

distinction 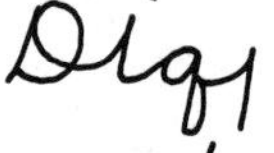

worthwhile 

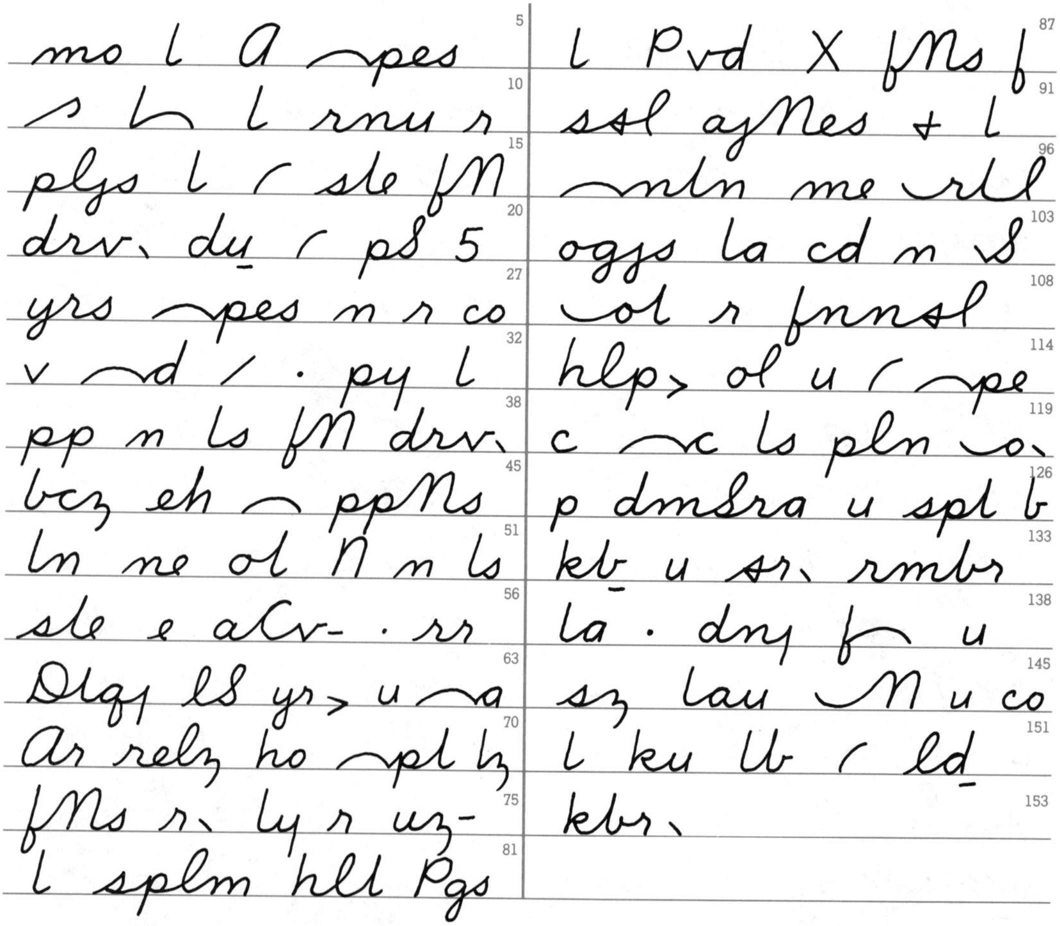

Key

1

Dear Mr. Marvin:

We have heard that your business is experiencing a period of rapid growth and[1] prosperity. Congratulations on your success!

Your company is in a strong position today because[2] you have kept your plant modern by buying new equipment regularly. With your current volume of business, your[3] equipment will be carrying a heavier load than it has in the past.

Replacement parts and repairs are[4] expensive. Let us help you avoid mechanical problems that cause delays in production. Our experts can keep your[5] equipment in good working order. We are noted for supplying immediate service when emergencies[6] arise.

The enclosed brochure lists the types of service contracts we offer. Why not let us help you choose a plan to suit[7] your needs? We can ensure that your machinery will continue to operate efficiently.

Very truly[8] yours, (161)

2

Dear Mr. Harvey:

Here is the data you requested. As you can see, it contains a complete listing of the[1] new equipment you wish to install in the firm of Jackson and Jackson, Ltd. I would like to suggest that[2] you bring your employees to our plant to see the equipment in operation. We have a very impressive[3] display of computer technology under one roof.

We would be happy to demonstrate the flexibility[4] of our units. I think we could also convince your employees that our programs are easy to use. We can[5] help them plan the types of work stations that are appropriate for their needs.

We invite you and your employees to[6] visit us at a time that is most convenient for your group. We will plan to provide a thorough orientation[7] to our equipment.

Yours very truly, (148)

3

MEMO TO: All Supervisors

From time to time it is necessary to remind your employees that all safety[1] regulations must be observed. Unless you have already done so in the last three months, please call a meeting[2] with the leaders of all production teams to review these regulations in detail. Be sure to emphasize any[3] regulations which apply only to your specific areas.

Unfortunately, employees may become[4] careless in their work habits if we do not make an effort to enforce safety regulations. Remind your[5] workers to wear protective clothing, to keep work stations clean, and to keep all doorways and walkways free of obstructions.[6]

If these simple rules are followed by everyone, they will help prevent injuries and will help make our plant a[7] safe and pleasant place in which to work. (146)

4

Dear Mrs. Miller:

We are pleased that you have elected to become one of our distributors. In addition[1] to the materials which you already have, I am enclosing a copy of our newest catalog.[2] As you can see, it provides a description of each stock item that is available to you.

I am also[3] enclosing a copy of the contract for your signature. As I explained in my recent meeting with you, this[4] document does not replace the memo of agreement you have already signed. The purpose of the memo is to[5] clarify our policies and to establish the basis for a friendly business relationship. The contract[6] specifies the obligations and responsibilities that each of us shares with the other.

When you wish to[7] place an order, you may handle it directly with Kevin Harvey, our director of sales. If you wish to[8] discuss your contract in general, please feel free to contact me at any time.

Cordially yours, (176)

5

MEMO TO: All Employees

It is time to renew our pledges to the city fund drive. During the past five years,[1] employees in our company have made it a point to participate in this fund drive. Because we had more[2] participants than any other industry in this city, we achieved a rare distinction last year.

You may[3] already realize how important these funds are. They are used to supplement health programs, to provide extra[4] funds for social agencies, and to maintain many worthwhile organizations that could not exist without our[5] financial help.

Only you, the employee, can make this plan work. Please demonstrate your support by contributing your[6] share. Remember that a donation from you says that you want your company to continue to be the leading[7] contributor. (143)

LESSON 47

Abbreviations and Derivatives

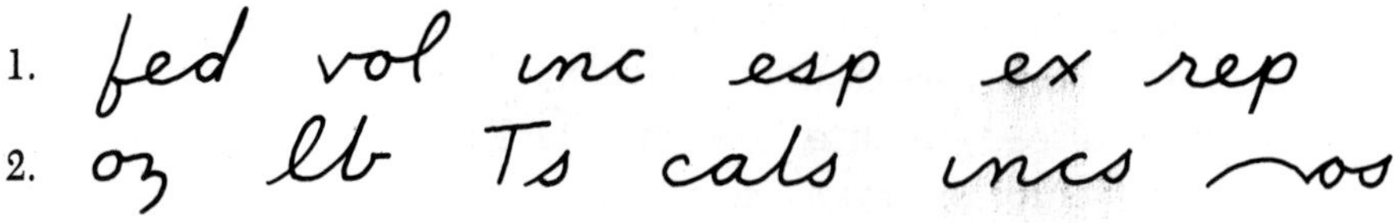

Key

1. federal, volume, incorporate/incorporated, especially, example/executive, represent/representative
2. ounce, pound, thousands, catalogs, incorporates, months

Transcription Aids: Proofreading

Careful proofreading is as important to successful transcription as any other part of the transcription process. Before producing the final copy of your letter, look at its general appearance. Ask yourself these questions:

1. Is the letter arranged attractively on the pages so that the margins are well balanced?
2. Is the printed material free of smudges and noticeable corrections?
3. Have I spaced correctly after punctuation marks and between parts of the letter?

If the answer to each of these questions is yes, your next step should be to read each word carefully to determine the following:

1. Is each word spelled correctly?
2. Are all numbers accurate?
3. Are all names, addresses, and special terms correct?
4. Have I punctuated and capitalized correctly?
5. Does this letter reflect well on my skills and on the image of my company?

Your Business Vocabulary

uniformity *unf* ᴸ   Sameness; the condition of being consistent.

That series of books will have uniformity of design.

ultimate *ult* ↲   The conclusive step in a process; the furthest possible extent.

Our ultimate objective is to increase sales by 20 percent.

Reading and Writing Exercises

— 1 —

Preview Words

step *Sp*

colorful *clrf*

counters *krs*

windows *Nos*

subscribed *s S-*

imaginative *ynv*

preferences *prfrNs*

disassemble *Das B*

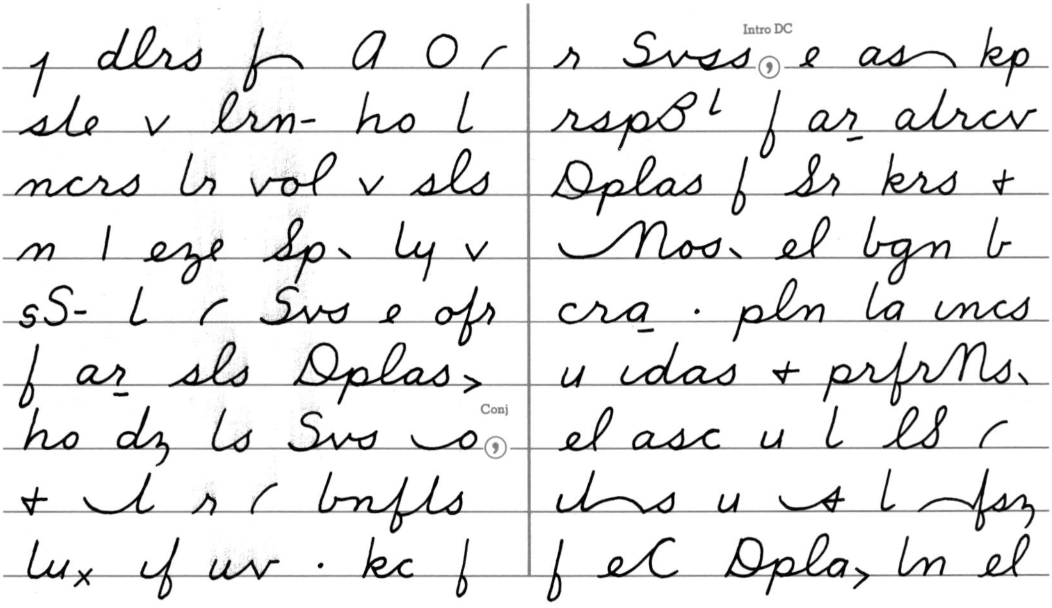

[Shorthand outlines]

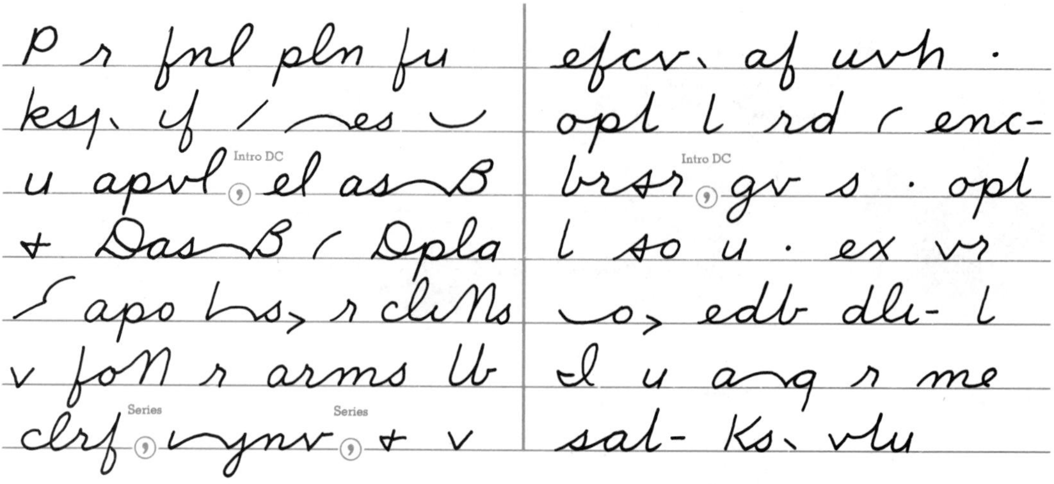

— **2** —

Preview Words

cart	_crl_
correct	_crc_
aiding	_ad_
powered	_por-_

hallways	_hl as_
mail room	_l r_
electronic	_elnc_
unnecessarily	_unesl_

[Shorthand outlines]

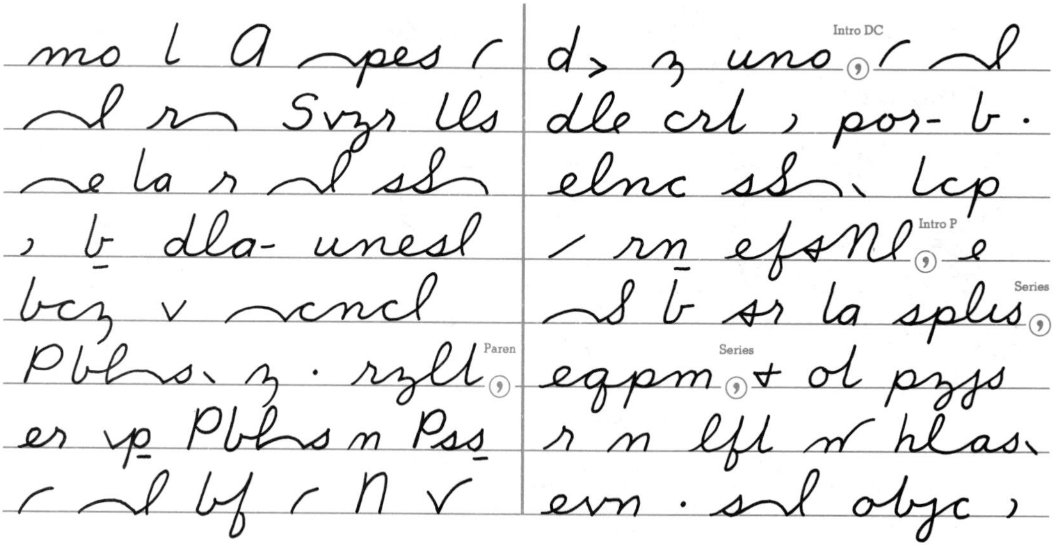

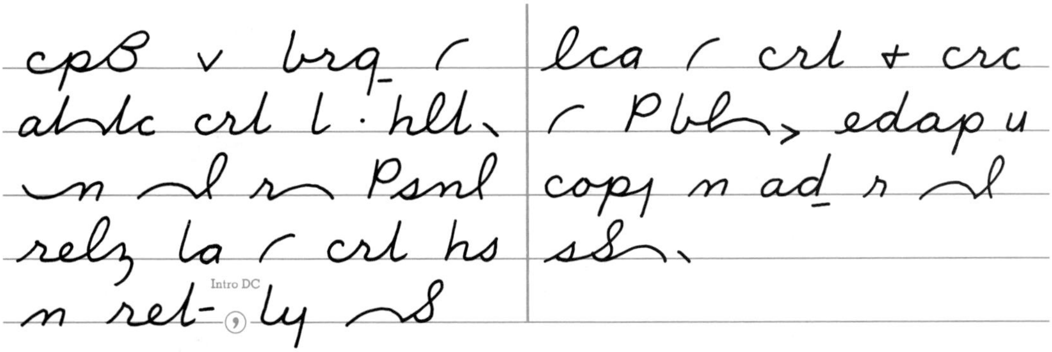

3

Preview Words

recruit	*rcru*	via	*va*
variety	*vri*	Parcel	*prsl*
support	*spl*	partnership	*plnrs*
welcome	*lk*	dealerships	*dlrss*

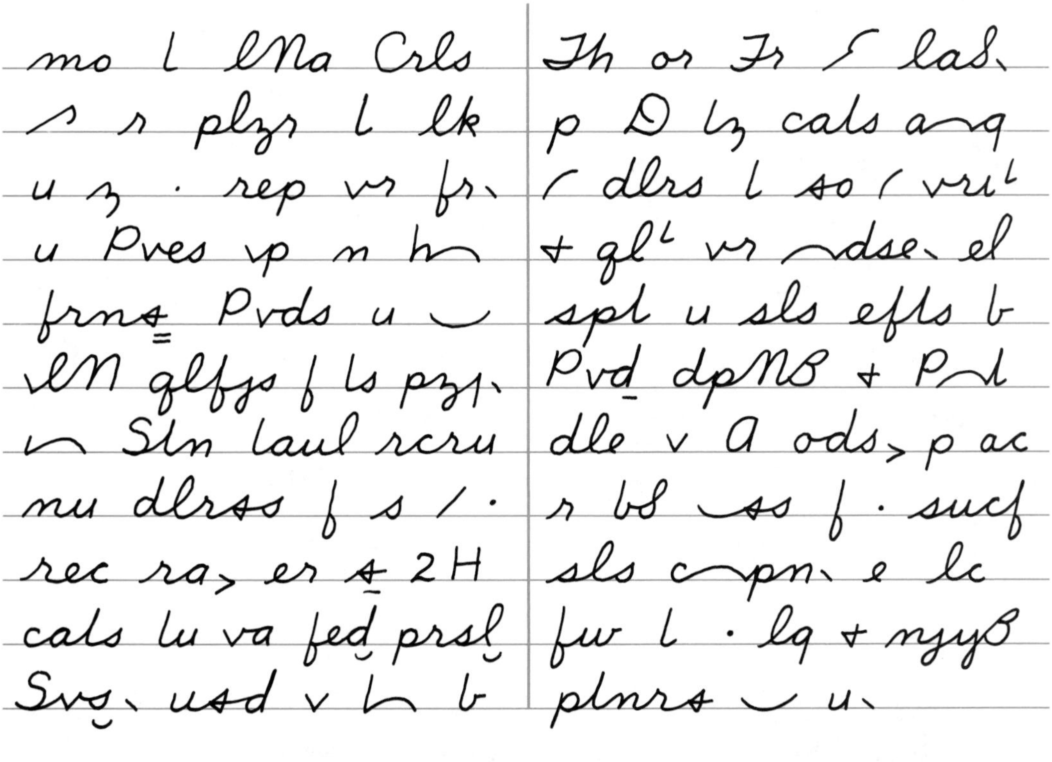

4

Preview Words

unlikely	ulcl	precision	Psj
regional	rjnl	supplement	splm
assembly	asB	engineering	njnr
ultimate	ultt	operation	opj

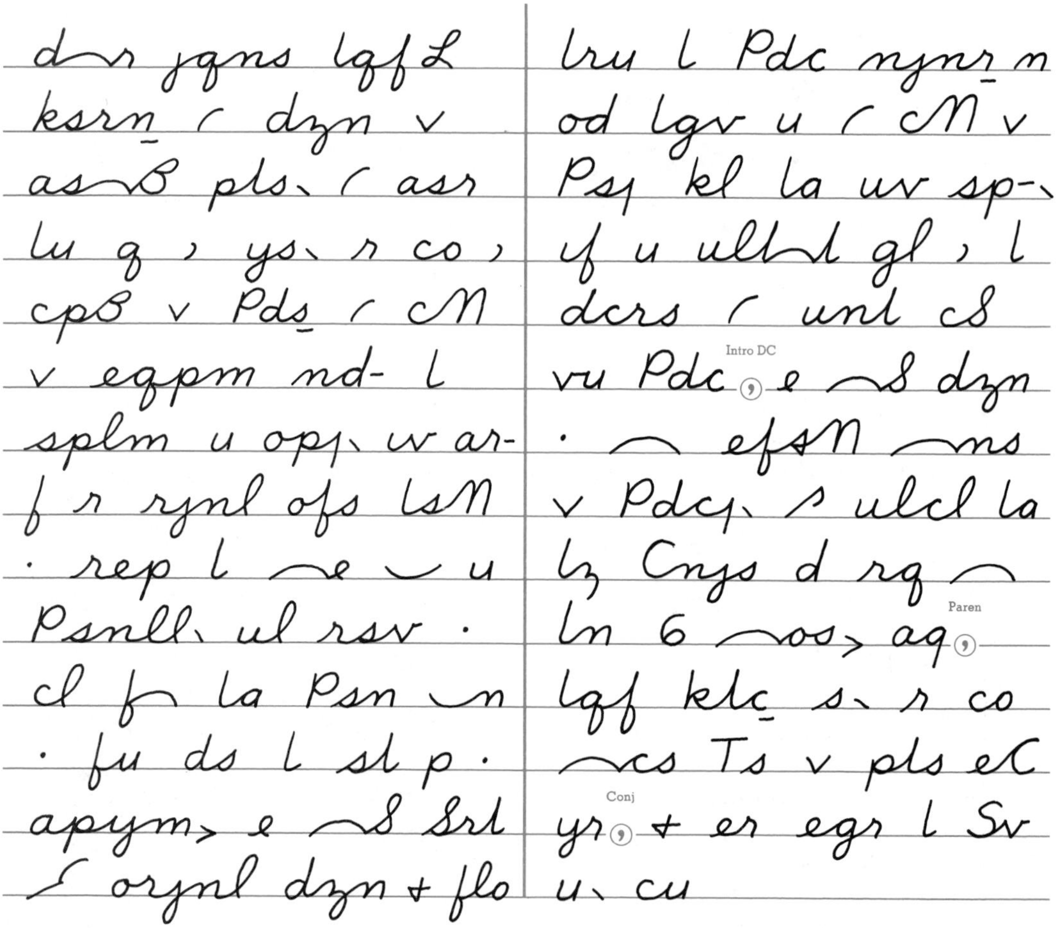

5

Punctuation Study

Add commas to show one appositive, one direct address, one introductory dependent clause, and two groups of words in a series.

Preview Words

gas	gs	nuclear	ncler
fuel	ful	Bestway	bSa
powder	podr	generators	jnrars
whose	hz	uniformity	unf⌒'

d⌒r hdsn ls , . 6
kl sS⌒ la c sv 11
me n ful efsNe 16
+ ern me fu b 22
ncrs̲ Pdcs, er lc̲ 29
ab (nyl ldr n 35
sls + Svs bSa kl 42
sS⌒ > ⌒ls u Pdcs 48
r ⌒d f⌒ gs lqd 54
or podr ⌒trel ls 59
sS⌒ Pvds lcnlye 64
la l ⌒pv (OA 70
opj vu plN, ec 77
rds u cSs ⌒pv 82

Pdc unf⌒' + ncrs 89
u Pfls> ⌒a e 93
dmSra ho r ⌒pv- 99
sS⌒ cb apli- lu 105
⌒f- plN× ev . Sf 113
v vprls hu l kdc 118
. Sde / no G lu, 124
ev Pvd- lz Svss 131
l me lps v Ns 136
hz Pdcs vre f⌒ 141
plScs l ncler 145
por jnrars> ul cl 151
u ofs l⌒c . apym 159
⌒r hdsn, ul 164

Key

1

Gentlemen:

Dealers from all over the city have learned how to increase their volume of sales in one easy step.[1] They have subscribed to the service we offer for arranging sales displays.

How does this service work, and what are the[2] benefits to you? If you have a contract for our services, we assume complete responsibility for[3] arranging attractive displays for store counters and windows. We will begin by creating a plan that incorporates[4] your ideas and preferences. We will ask you to list the items you wish to emphasize for each[5] display.

Then we will present our final plan for your consideration. If it meets with your approval, we will[6] assemble and disassemble the display at the appropriate times.

Our clients have found our arrangements[7] to be colorful, imaginative, and very effective. After you have had an opportunity to read[8] the enclosed brochure, give us an opportunity to show you an example of our work.

We would be delighted[9] to include you among our many satisfied customers.

Very truly yours, (195)

2

MEMO TO: All Employees

The mail room supervisor tells me that our mail system is being delayed[1] unnecessarily because of mechanical problems. As a result, we are experiencing problems in[2] processing the mail before the end of the day.

As you know, the mail delivery cart is powered by an[3] electronic system. To keep it running efficiently, we must be sure that supplies, equipment, and other[4] possessions are not left in the hallways. Even a small object is capable of bringing the automatic cart[5] to a halt. When mail room personnel realize that the cart has not returned, they must locate the cart and correct the[6] problem.

We would appreciate your cooperation in aiding our mail system. (135)

3

MEMO TO: Linda Charles

It is our pleasure to welcome you as a representative of our firm. Your previous[1] experience in home furnishings provides you with excellent qualifications for this position. I am[2] certain that you will recruit new dealerships for us at a record rate.

We are shipping 200 catalogs[3] to you via Federal Parcel Service. You should have them by Thursday or Friday at the latest. Please distribute[4] these catalogs among the dealers to show the variety and quality of our merchandise. We will[5] support your sales efforts by providing dependable and prompt delivery of all orders.

Please accept[6] our best wishes for a successful sales campaign. We look forward to a long and enjoyable partnership with[7] you. (141)

4

Dear Mr. Jenkins:

Thank you for your letter concerning the design of assembly parts. The answer to your question[1] is yes. Our company is capable of producing the kind of equipment needed to supplement your[2] operation. I have arranged for our regional office to send a representative to meet with you[3] personally. You will receive a call from that person within a few days to set up an appointment.

We must start[4] at the original design and follow through to product engineering in order to give you the kind of[5] precision control that you have specified. If your ultimate goal is to decrease the unit cost of your product,[6] we must design a more efficient means of production. It is unlikely that these changes would require more[7] than six months.

Again, thank you for contacting us. Our company makes thousands of parts each year, and we are eager[8] to serve you.

Cordially yours, (165)

5

Dear Mr. Hudson:

There is a control system that can save money in fuel efficiency and earn money[1] for you by increasing production. We are talking about the national leader in sales and service, Bestway[2] Control System.

Whether your products are made from gas, liquid, or powder material, this system provides[3] technology that will improve the overall operation of your plant. We can reduce your costs, improve product[4] uniformity, and increase your profits.

May we demonstrate how our improved system can be applied to your[5] manufacturing plant? We have a staff of experts who will conduct a study at no charge to you. We have[6] provided these services to many types of industries whose products vary from plastics to nuclear power[7] generators.

I will call your office to make an appointment, Mr. Hudson.

Yours truly, (156)

LESSON 48

Shorthand Vocabulary Review

1. Write q for the sound of *kw* and for the word ending *quire*.

quite	qi	require	rq
requested	rqs-	inquiries	nqes
quantity	qNt	acquiring	aq-

2. Write v for the medial and final sound of *tive*.

active	acv	positive	pzv
objective	objcv	effective	efcv
competitive	kptv	attractive	atrcv
incentive	nsnv	collectively	clcvl

Transcription Aids: Similar Words

complimentary
kplmre

Expressing praise; the presentation of a free gift.

Please accept this complimentary copy of our magazine.

complementary
kplmre

Supplying a part that is needed to make up a whole; producing an effect in which all parts are well coordinated.

Is the new perfume complementary to the rest of our line of cosmetics?

Your Business Vocabulary	replenish *rplns* To refill; make complete again.
	Has anyone ordered new stock to replenish that sold during the sale?
	initiate *insa* To begin or originate.
	We will initiate a training program for new employees.

Reading and Writing Exercises

―――――――――――――――― 1 ――――――――――――――――

Preview Words

lotion *ly*	disturbed *Dlrb-*
shelf *slf*	compensate *kpNa*
replenish *rplns*	complimentary *kplmre*
patronage *plrny*	top-selling *lp = sl*

drs lrpl b no
usd v rsv- r
nu sm v ~dse.
~ ru l vpro r
apr fu psN + USN.
~n l hrd la r
orynl sm kln-
sv dy- drs ⑼ *ur*   Intro DC

v Dlrb-. l nu la
und- ly drs l
rplns u slf Sc
+ la ch grnle- .
erl dle lu, edlc
Lc . spsl ofr l
hlp kpNa f ne
nkv lau ~a v
vp-. fu nx PCs
vr Pdcs ⑼ *el I .*   Intro P

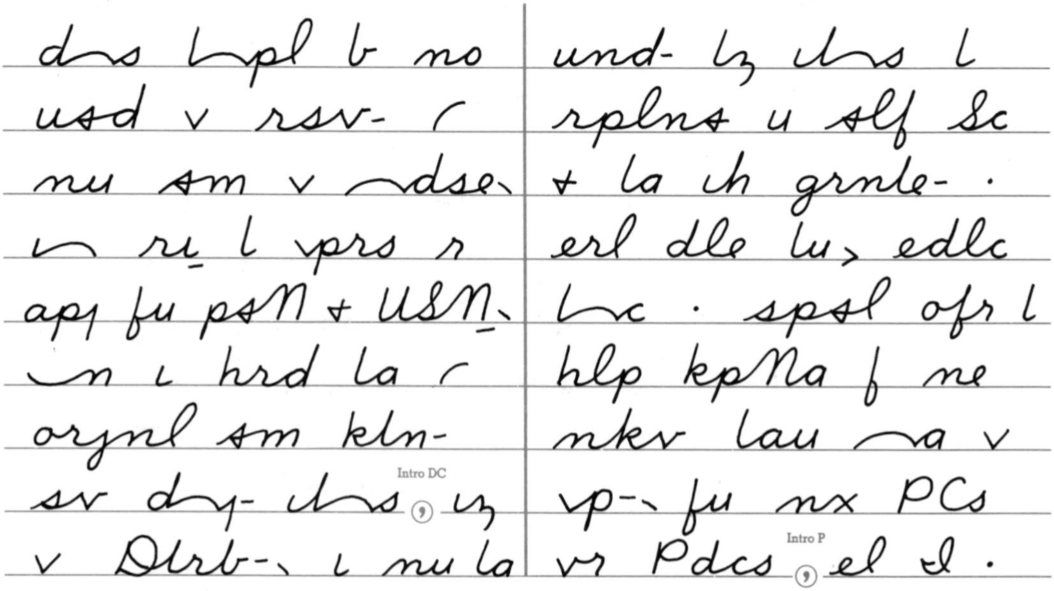

kplmre cs vr lp=
sl Pdc, Ap r hN +
bde lj. u ~a v
ls Pdc n elr v
2 szs. uno lau

nr—ll Sc r 32=oz
bll + r 4=oz jr. el
kpli — CE rqS
u ~c> lqu aq fu
ku- plrnj. su

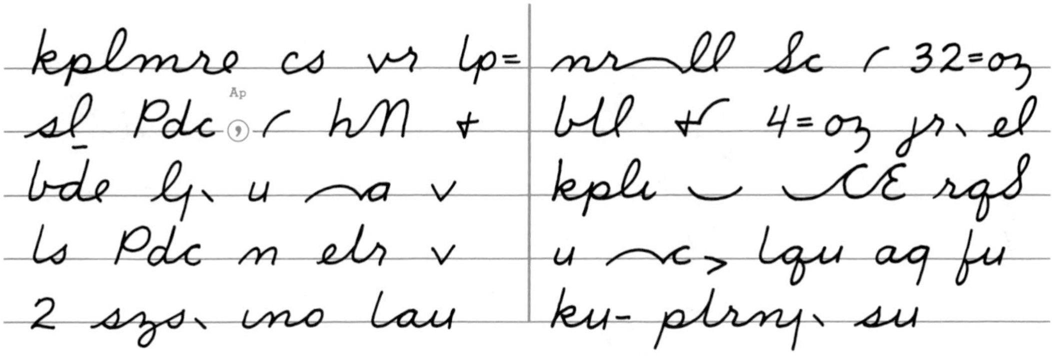

2

Preview Words

sorry	sre	initiate	insa
forced	fs-	remainder	r~Mr
partial	prsl	certified	Sf-
receipt	rse	collection	clcj

dr jsn lsL, l
rm u lau pams
f invs 342 + 701
r no Odu. r lol
a-l o- l s, 5682 49 >
w orjnl agrem
sn- b r ~jr vu
Sr, Intro P u ~ c prsl
pams 6 frS d v

Mr, Series Ap, Series + Ma l
brq u ak pda. e
rsv- l pam o Mr 7
f IT5H$. sN la
da, Paren hoE, Paren uv n
rsp- l r Ls or
cls> r r~Mr vu
ak ~S b pd n f.
if edu n rsv ls

(shorthand outlines)

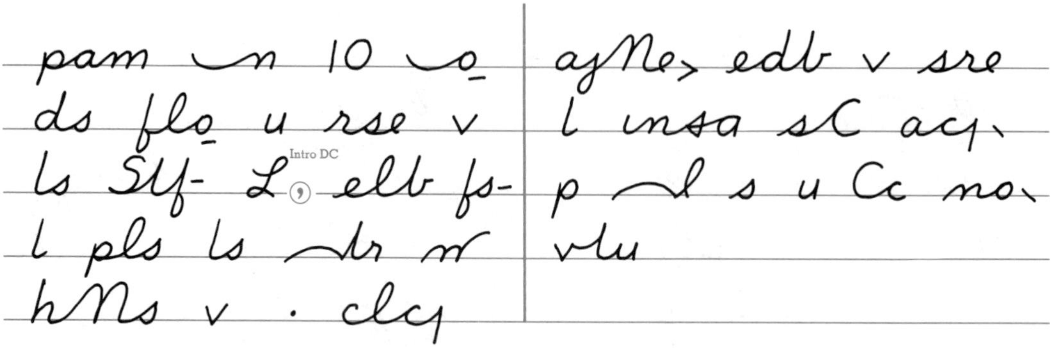

3

Preview Words

line	*ln*	uncommon	*ukn*
lawn	*ln*	competitive	*kplv*
garden	*grdn*	promotions	*P—ys*
grass seed	*grs sd*	gratifying	*grlf_*

(shorthand outlines)

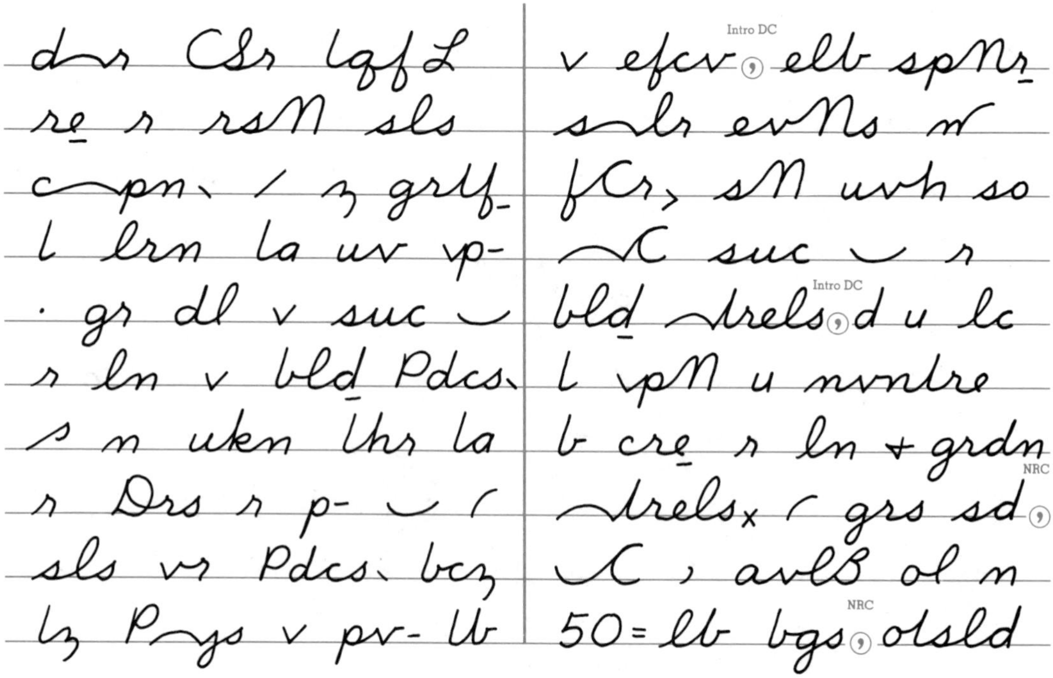

me kplv Pdcs
lS yrs, ~ I . pcl
v ~lrels dS_ (
ln + grdn Pdcs.

ev foN r grdn
Pdcs lb v kplmre
~ r bld_ ~lrels.
uvl

4

Preview Words

data	dla	warranty	~rNe
force	fs	factory	fclre
relating	rla_	convention	kvnj
conducted	kdc-	teleconference	lLkfrN

d~r lrns ev rvu-
. rpl f~ (reps
hu alN- (fclre
dmSrj u kdc- /
njl kvnjs, z . rzll
v se_ (dla u P- ,
ev dsd- l a (
ln v Pdcs u Nds-
/ kvnj. efl la r
sls fs c brq n
ods la l jSf (

adj v ls eqpm l
r ln, edu v sv
qs rla_ l (kdjs
uv lS- f ~rNe
Plcj. d ub avlB
l Dcs lz dlls ~
r sls + ~r_ Sf.
if ucn vzl r ofss
Psnll, Ph ucd ar
f . lLkfrN cl. sC
. cl d alo a ples

Intro P

Intro DC

l knca frel, p
ll ~e no ho isd

Psd. vlu

5

Punctuation Study

Add commas to show two introductory dependent clauses, two parenthetical expressions, and one appositive.

Preview Words

loan ln
draw dra
forth fl
tomorrow lro
directly drl
Sterling Srlq
extensions Vnjs
debt service dl Svs

dM Srlq lqfL 9
vpln u fnnsl Sks, 17
Alo edu n uzl 23
grN Vnjs o aks 29
efl la ls , . spsl 35
cs. lrf er grN . 43
adjl 90 ds v cr 48
ou ln. sN edu 54
n pln l ncrs r 59
ra v NS f ls adjl 66
dl Svs / l n b 72
nes l dra p . 77

nu kc. hoE . 82
fl agrem , b 87
Ppr- l sl fl r 92
lns v Vnj. ul 99
v l sn ls agrem 105
bf / c q nl efc, 111
l USN la r grl 117
vu co l dpN drl 124
po aq r nu fsl 130
laur n Pss v b. 138
r ol rqS ev , 144
lau Pvd s ~ . 149

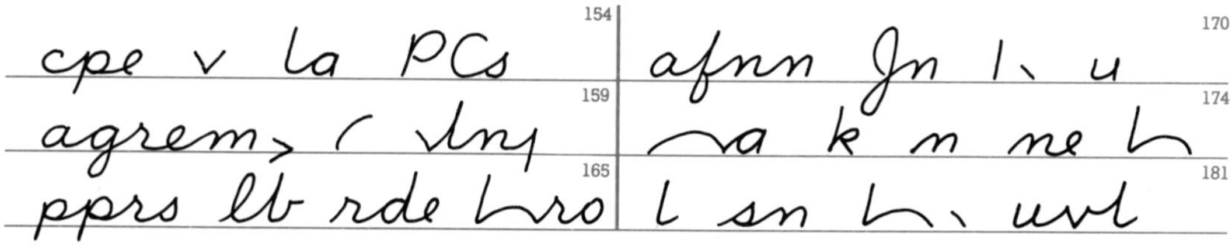

Key

1

Dear Ms. Temple:

By now you should have received the new shipment of merchandise. I am writing to express our[1] appreciation for your patience and understanding. When I heard that the original shipment contained[2] several damaged items, I was very disturbed. I knew that you needed these items to replenish your shelf stock[3] and that I had guaranteed an early delivery to you.

We would like to make a special offer to help[4] compensate for any inconvenience that you may have experienced. For your next purchase of our products, we will[5] include a complimentary case of our top-selling product, the hand and body lotion. You may have this[6] product in either of two sizes. I know that you normally stock the 32-ounce bottle and the 4-ounce jar.[7] We will comply with whichever request you make.

Thank you again for your continued patronage.

Sincerely yours,[8] (160)

2

Dear Mr. Jason:

This letter is to remind you that your payments for Invoices 342 and 701 are[1] now overdue. The total amount owed to us is $5,682.49.[2]

In the original agreement signed by the manager of your store, you were to make partial payments[3] on the first day of March, April, and May to bring your account up to date. We received one payment on March 7 for[4] $1,500. Since that date, however, you have not responded to our letters or calls.[5]

The remainder of your account must be paid in full. If we do not receive this payment within ten working days[6] following your receipt of this certified letter, we will be forced to place this matter in the hands of a[7] collection agency.

We would be very sorry to initiate such action. Please mail us your check now.

Very[8] truly yours, (162)

3

Dear Mr. Chester:

Thank you for your letter regarding our recent sales campaign. It was gratifying to learn[1] that you have experienced a great deal of success with our line of building products. It is not uncommon to[2] hear that our distributors are pleased with the sales of our products. Because these promotions have proved to be very[3] effective, we will be sponsoring similar events in the future.

Since you have had so much success with our[4] building materials, would you like to expand your inventory by carrying our lawn and garden[5] materials? The grass seed, which is available only in 50-pound bags, outsold many competitive products[6] last year.

I am including a packet of materials describing the lawn and garden products. We have[7] found our garden products to be very complementary with our building materials.

Yours very truly,[8] (160)

4

Dear Mr. Turner:

We have reviewed a report from the representatives who attended the factory[1] demonstration you conducted at the national convention.

As a result of seeing the data you[2] presented, we have decided to add the line of products you introduced at the convention. We feel that our sales[3] force can bring in orders that will justify the addition of this equipment to our line.

We do have several[4] questions relating to the conditions you have listed for warranty protection. Would you be available[5] to discuss these details with our sales and marketing staff? If you cannot visit our offices personally,[6] perhaps I could arrange for a teleconference call. Such a call would allow all parties to communicate[7] freely.

Please let me know how I should proceed.

Very truly yours, (151)

5

Dear Miss Sterling:

Thank you for your letter explaining your financial circumstances.

Although we do not usually[1] grant extensions on accounts, we feel that this is a special case. Therefore, we are granting an additional[2] 90 days of credit on your loan. Since we do not plan to increase the rate of interest for this additional[3] debt service, it will not be necessary to draw up a new contract. However, a formal agreement[4] is being prepared to set forth the terms of the extension. You will have to sign this agreement before it[5] can go into effect.

I understand that the growth of your company will depend directly upon acquiring[6] the new facility that you are in the process of buying. The only request we have is that you provide[7] us with a copy of that purchase agreement.

The extension papers will be ready tomorrow afternoon,[8] June 1. You may come in any time to sign them.

Yours very truly, (173)

LESSON 49

Shorthand Vocabulary Review

1. Write a capital D for the word beginning *dis*.

Write a capital M for the word beginning *mis*.

discussion	Dcj	misleading	Mld
displays	Dplas	mistake	Mlc
disposal	Dpzl	misinformed	Mnf-
disturbance	DlrbN	misunderstood	MUSd

2. Word beginnings, word endings, and sound blends that can also be individual words may be used to express those words.

end	N	men	m
all	a	ad, add	a
extra	X	per	p
miss	M	mind	m

Transcription Aids: Spelling

Learn to distinguish between words that end in *cial* and words that end in *tial*. When in doubt, consult your dictionary.

cial		tial	
special	spsl	potential	plnsl
crucial	crsl	substantial	sSnsl
judicial	jdsl	partial	prsl

official *ofsl* sequential *sqnsl*

financial *fnnsl* influential *nflunsl*

Your Business Vocabulary	remittance *∽lM* Money or credit sent as a payment on a bill.
	Please mail us your remittance of $15.33.
	collectively *clcvl* Assembled or accumulated into a whole; a number of individuals acting as a group.
	The money for this donation was raised collectively by our employees.

Reading and Writing Exercises

--- 1 ---

Preview Words

sturdy *Srde* competitive *kplv*

predict *Pdc* constructed *kSrc-*

indoor *ndr* moneymakers *me crs*

reorder *rod* folding chairs *fld_ Crs*

---

d K r enc- bcll brNs n la ly

l Nds u l r nu r kSrc- f r

ln v fld_ Crs. p fnS drels. ly

nl la ly r n r dzn- f bo ndr

ord Crs. ly dfr + oldr us, u Ks l

f me kplv lc ⌐ f me rzns.

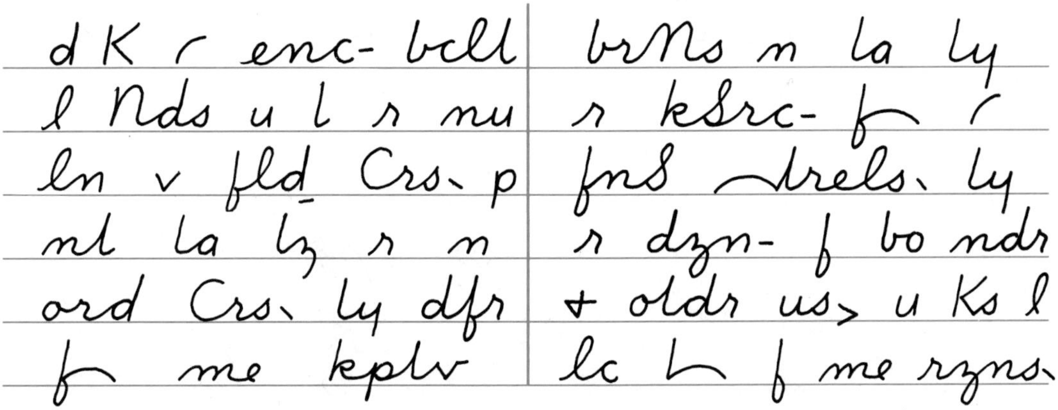

lz Crs r apo f
bs us, b ly l lc (Conj)
aS z q n .
rzdnsl sl. ly
dN rq X Plcy; (Semi)
ly r z Srde z
ly r alrcv, er
ac lul ods f .
mm v 12 Crs
pam du n 90
ds. er kfdN laul
sr r vm oN uv

sn r Pdc. rel (
Crs n 30 ds f
ly du n pv Lb
mecrs. l lSra
i kfdN n ls
Pdc, i Pdc la (Intro P)
ulb rde l rod
n 30 ds, u a
pls u od ne l
bln 8 a + 4 30 p.
el lc fw lu cl.
su

2

Preview Words

small sl

options opjs

directly drl

previously Pvesl

improvements pvms

health care hll cr

modifications dfjs

oral surgery orl Syre

mo l a pes
lqs l (efls vr
rSC k, ec no (Intro P)
anoN nu opjs

n u ins bnfls.
lz opjs rep pl
dfjs n u lol
hll cr pln, bgn

o Jl 1, (Intro P) dNl cvrj
lb A- f . s~l
~ol fe. r a~l
v fe l dpN po
r No v mbrs
n u f~l, n adj, (Paren)
u plse l cvr sp
lps v orl Syre
la vn Pvesl b
I-. p rd r alC-

bcll crfl ldl
~l vpNs lb cvr-.
if uv sp qs, (Intro DC) p
brq l drl l r
Psnl ofs, aq, (Paren) e
~t l lq r rSC
k f hlp s aCv
lz ~pvms n r
ins Pq.

3

Preview Words

period	pred	meantime	~nl
notation	nly	letterhead	Lhd
unpaid	upd	remittance	r~lN
latter	llr	installment	nSlm

dr hrsn lqf Cc
f 895^{17} n pam
vr inv 8093. u
r~lN arv- 15 ds
af r N v Dk
pred. lrf, (Paren) u pam

sd vb 913^{44}. u
~a fu . Cc f
adjl 18^{27} or l
la a~l ~ u nx
~ol pam. if u
Cz r llr ~ld

v pam, (Intro DC) p Pvd .
nlj la r adjl
a-l , lb cr- lu
upd blN f Ap>
w mt, (Paren) er cr
u ak f . lol v
895^17. u nx nSlm

sdb rsv- b Ma 6
n od l glf u f
Dk f la ~o> if
u rq frlr asSN, (Intro DC)
p cl s r No lS-
abv n r Lhd.
vlu

4

Preview Words

ago	aq	incentive	nsnv
surpassed	Sps-	year-end	yr=N
expectations	vpcjs	collectively	clcvl
substantial	sSnsl	profit sharing	Pfl sr

mo l A pes 6
cs aq e anoN-
. nu nsnv pln
bs- 6 kspl v Pfl
sr. er dli- l rpl
la r suc v ls
pln hs Sps- A
vpcjs. bcz v kbn-

efls v E l, (Intro P) Pdcj
hs ncrs- b 18%.
kgjs o . jb l dn>
n adj l ncrs-
Pdcj, (Intro P) . fss o pv-
Psyrs hs rds- r
ra v errs b .
sSnsl ryn. if

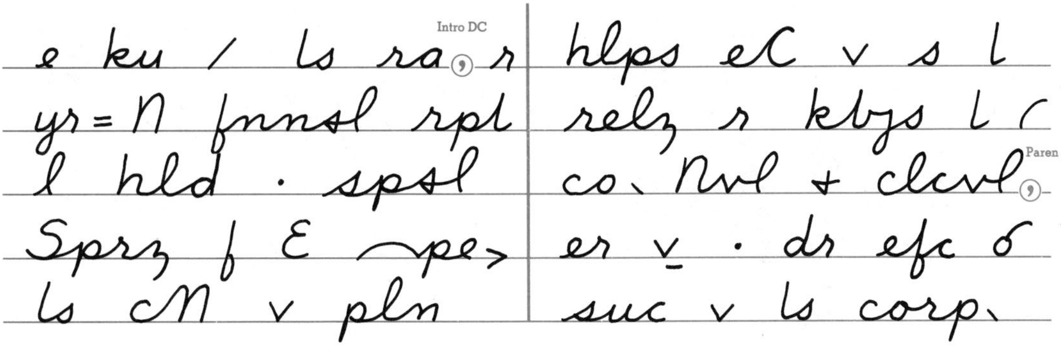

5

Punctuation Study

Add commas to show two introductory dependent clauses, one direct address, and two conjunctions.

Preview Words

depart
image
young
audience

direction
traditional
emphasize
workmanship

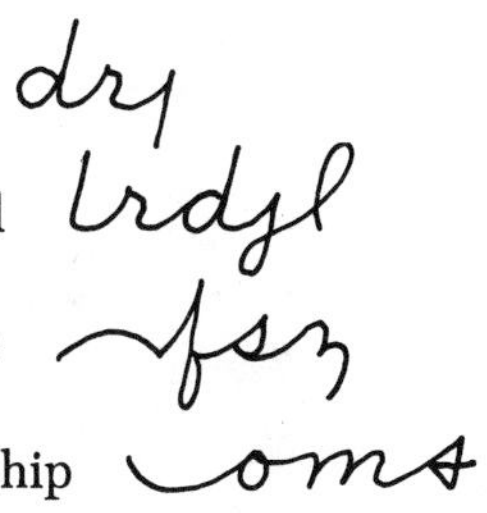

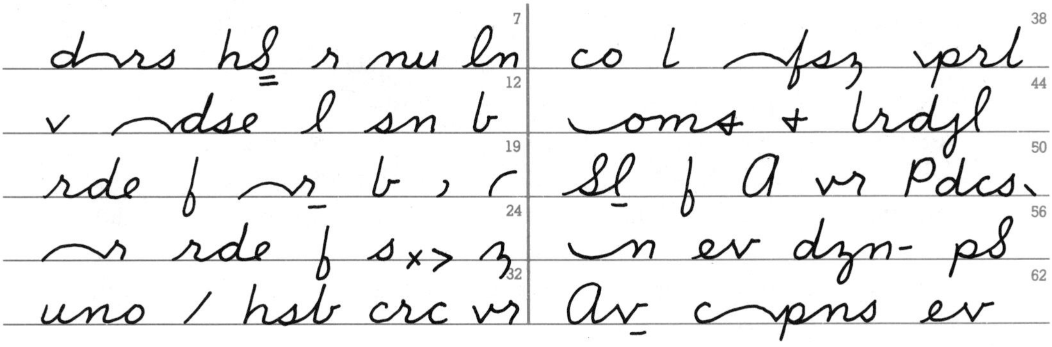

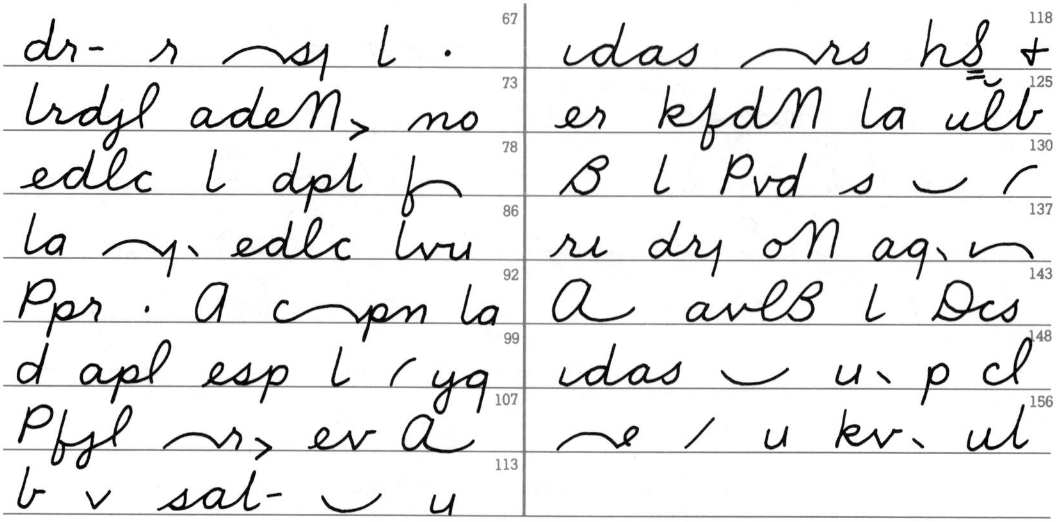

Key

1

Dear Customer:

The enclosed booklet will introduce you to our new line of folding chairs. Please note that these are not[1] ordinary chairs. They differ from many competitive brands in that they are constructed from the finest[2] materials. They are designed for both indoor and outdoor use.

Your customers will like them for many reasons.[3] These chairs are appropriate for business use, but they will look almost as good in a residential setting. They[4] don't require extra protection; they are as sturdy as they are attractive.

We are accepting trial orders for[5] a minimum of 12 chairs with payment due within 90 days. We are confident that you will share our excitement[6] once you have seen our product. Return the chairs within 30 days if they do not prove to be moneymakers.[7] To illustrate my confidence in this product, I predict that you will be ready to reorder within[8] 30 days.

You may place your order any time between 8 a.m. and 4:30 p.m. We will look forward to[9] your call.

Sincerely yours, (184)

2

MEMO TO: All Employees

Thanks to the efforts of our research committee, we can now announce new options in[1] your insurance benefits. These options represent important modifications in your total health care plan.[2]

Beginning on July 1, dental coverage will be added for a small monthly fee. The amount of the fee[3] will depend upon the number of members in your family.

In addition, your policy will cover[4] specific types of oral surgery that have not previously been included. Please read the attached booklet[5] carefully to determine what expenses will be covered. If you have specific questions, please bring them directly[6] to the personnel office.

Again, we wish to thank the research committee for helping us achieve these improvements[7] in our insurance program. (146)

3

Dear Mr. Harrison:

Thank you for your check for $895.17 in payment of[1] our Invoice 8093. Your remittance arrived 15 days after the end of the discount period.[2] Therefore, your payment should have been $913.44. You may forward a check for the[3] additional $18.27 or include that amount with your next monthly payment. If you[4] choose the latter method of payment, please provide a notation that the additional amount is to be[5] credited to your unpaid balance for April.

In the meantime, we are crediting your account for a total of[6] $895.17. Your next installment should be received by May 6 in order to[7] qualify you for the discount for that month.

If you require further assistance, please call us at the number listed[8] above in our letterhead.

Very truly yours, (168)

4

MEMO TO: All Employees

Six weeks ago we announced a new incentive plan based on the concept of profit[1] sharing. We are delighted to report that the success of this plan has surpassed all expectations. Because of[2] the combined efforts of everyone, production has increased by 18 percent. Congratulations on a job[3] well done.

In addition to increased production, an emphasis on improved procedures has reduced the rate of[4] errors by a substantial margin. If we continue at this rate, our year-end financial report will hold a[5] special surprise for every employee.

This kind of plan helps each of us to realize our contributions to[6] the company. Individually and collectively, we are having a direct effect on the success[7] of this corporation. (144)

5

Dear Mrs. Hastings:

Our new line of merchandise will soon be ready for marketing, but is the market ready[1] for us?

As you know, it has been characteristic of our company to emphasize expert workmanship and[2] traditional styling for all of our products. When we have designed past advertising campaigns, we have directed[3] our message to a traditional audience.

Now we would like to depart from that image. We would like to[4] have you prepare an ad campaign that would appeal especially to the young professional market.

We have always[5] been very satisfied with your ideas, Mrs. Hastings, and we are confident that you will be able[6] to provide us with the right direction once again. I am always available to discuss ideas with[7] you. Please call me at your convenience.

Yours truly, (149)

LESSON 50

Word Development

Develop new words from the following brief forms:

every

everybody Ebde

everyday Ed

everyone E 1

everything E_

everywhere Ēr

control

controls kls

controllable klB

uncontrollable uklB

controllability klBˡ

controller klr

ship

leadership ldrꞩ

membership mbrꞩ

fellowship floꞩ

township lonꞩ

scholarship sclrꞩ

friendship frNꞩ

hardship hrdꞩ

salesmanship slsmꞩ

sponsorship spNrꞩ

shipyard ꞩyd

Reading and Writing Exercises

—————————————— 1 ——————————————

Preview Words

flowing　*flo_*

assembly　*as B*

automated　*al a-*

procedures　*Psyrs*

scheduling　*scyl_*

adjustments　*ajSms*

maintenance　*nlnM*

administered　*AmSr-*

mo l A yrs . od hsb plo- f nu as B ~Ans Conj + e ypc dle n 3 cs. sM ly ~Ans l ncrs Pdcy b 13 l 15% Intro DC A yrs l nd Lc ajSms n scyl. sC Cnys lb nes lcp plo flo_ l (as B ~Ans, l sug lau e u pes n s l grps l ypln y Psyrs S b

Cny-, p asr El la ly al a- ~Ans l n cy (lo v ne ybs. y . Ar v fc Intro P el nd L hr adyl ppl n sv aras, er ar spsl lrn sys C lb kdc- srll af (eqpm , nSl-. ly sys lb AmSr- b reps v fr. n yn Paren (opy + nlnM v lo nu ~Anre l n dfr grl f la

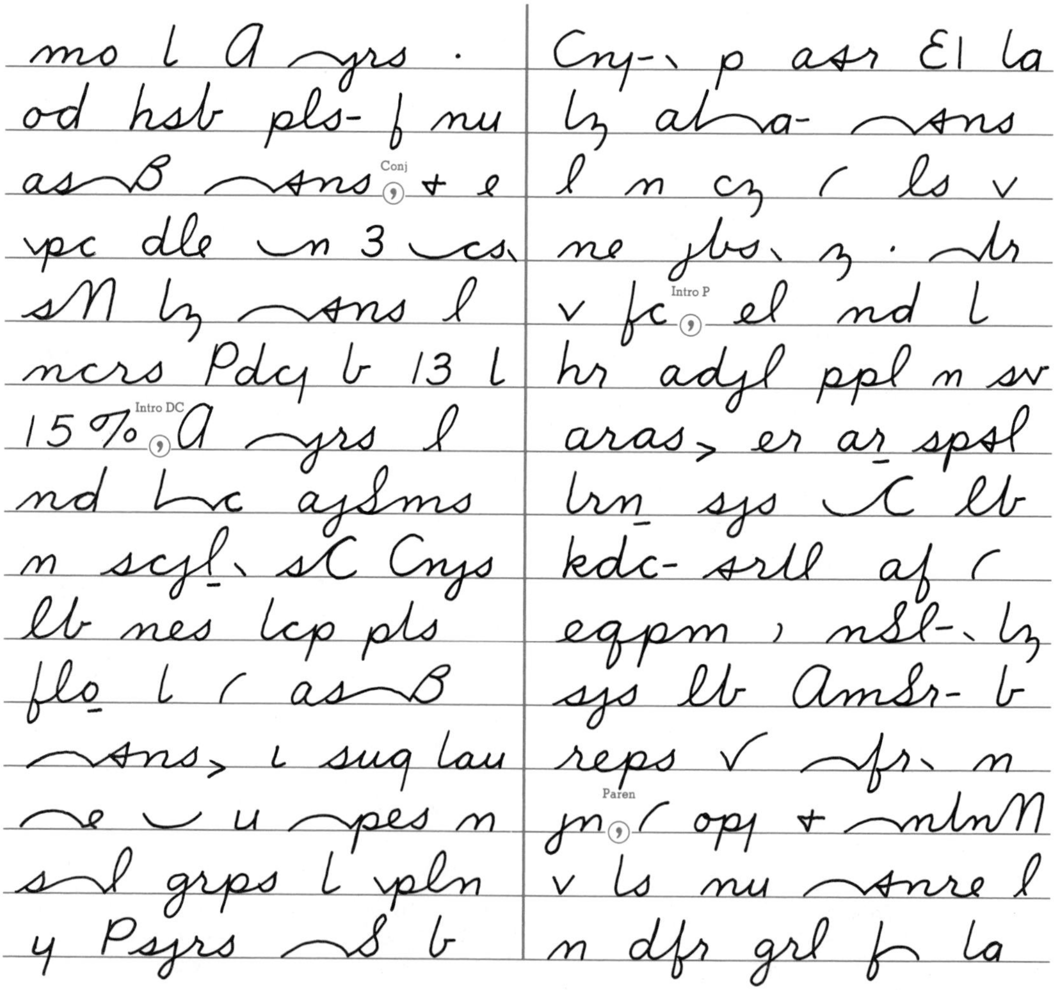

v pS> f u 4 lv
asSN n vpln lz
lrs lu pes, .
Intro DC

mbr vr nynr Sf
lb hpe l hlp.

2

Preview Words

coats	cos	transit	Tl
c.o.d.	cod	freight	fra
loading	ld	trucking	lrc
unusual	uuz	minimum	mm

ds dyl lgf od v
Ag 7. (30 cos u
rqS- lb 4- lu
ol dla. Alo ecn
gv u . vc da f dle,
Intro DC
el du A ec lv (
dse lu n L
fu fl sl> / l lc
s apxl 10 ds l Pss
u od + Ppr (ds
f 4. oN . 4m
lvs r ld ara, /
Intro DC
lcs ab 5 ds n

Tl. f A lgs q
acrd l scyl, usd
Intro DC
v (cos n 2
cs> el sN (od
cod. Alo du n
no vcl ho C (
fra Gs lb, ic U
Intro DC
u la (lrc co e
uz Gs . mm v
50$ f A dse U
1H lbs> f lr r ne
uuz dlas, lb Sln
Intro DC
l ll uno. vlu

3

Preview Words

phone *fn*

routine *rtn*

contacting *ktc*

analysis *anlss*

qualifications *qlfjs*

retail outlet *rll olll*

Empire Roofing *pr rf*

distributorship *Drs*

---

dr h lltn lqf ktc pr rf inc eap u NS n bk . Dr f r fr, r Sd Psr , lsN . rep lvzl u rll olll. du ls vzl r rep l vpln r plses + clc (inf e nd lc . rtn anlss, ul v (opl l asc

qs / la h, el ktc u Psnll apxl 3 cs flo (vzl. f u pls v bs hs (qlfjs nes l bk . Drs el asc u l sn . kc agrem la l bk efcv l, ulb ktc- b fn l st p . apym f vzl, cu

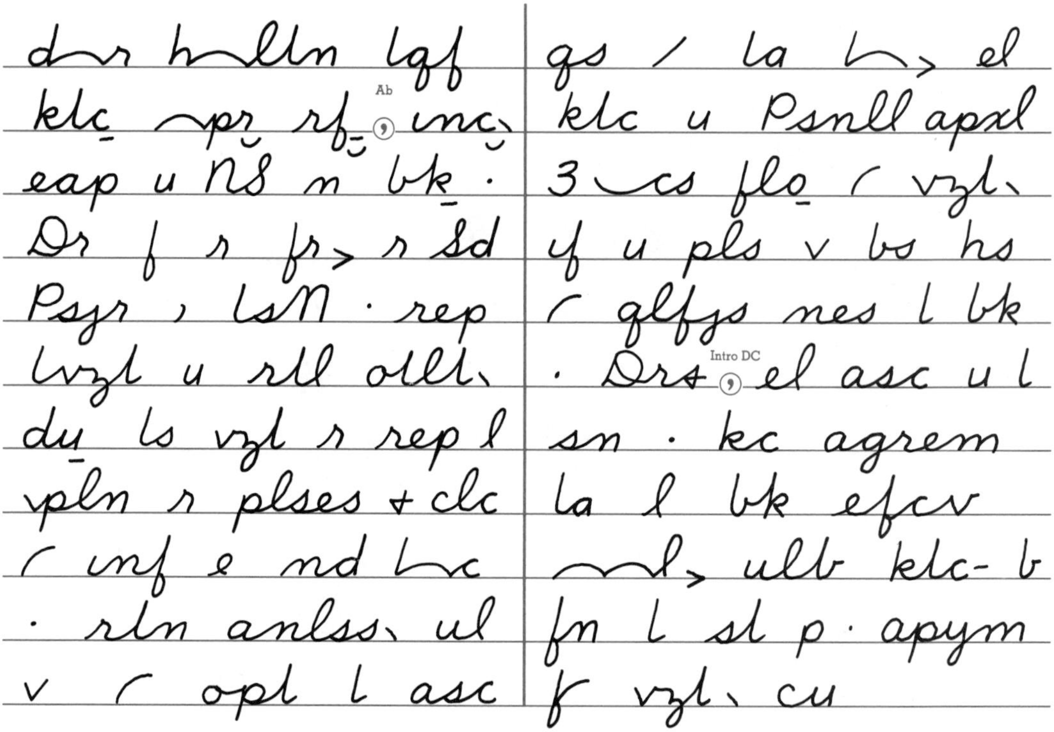

4

Preview Words

sheet	se	higher	hir
goods	gs	incurred	ncr-
leather	llr	projected	Pjc-
shortage	srly	raw materials	ra -trels

y ls L, l nf
u v rsN prs
Cnys f a llr
Pdcs. bcz v rz-
cSs v ra -trels, Intro P
ev ncr- hir -f-
cSs. z . rzll, Paren e
-S no ncrs r
fclre prss b 15%,
er enc . cS se
la lSs r prs Cnys
f eC il- v Sc.

p b Sln luz r
fgrs o ls se n
pls a fCr ods,
er ky lse . hi dm
f llr gs. bcz v .
Pjc- srly n ra
-trels, Intro P la dm lb
evn grr, e ncry
u l pls u ods z
erl z psB. el du
r bS l fl - lu
saly. ul

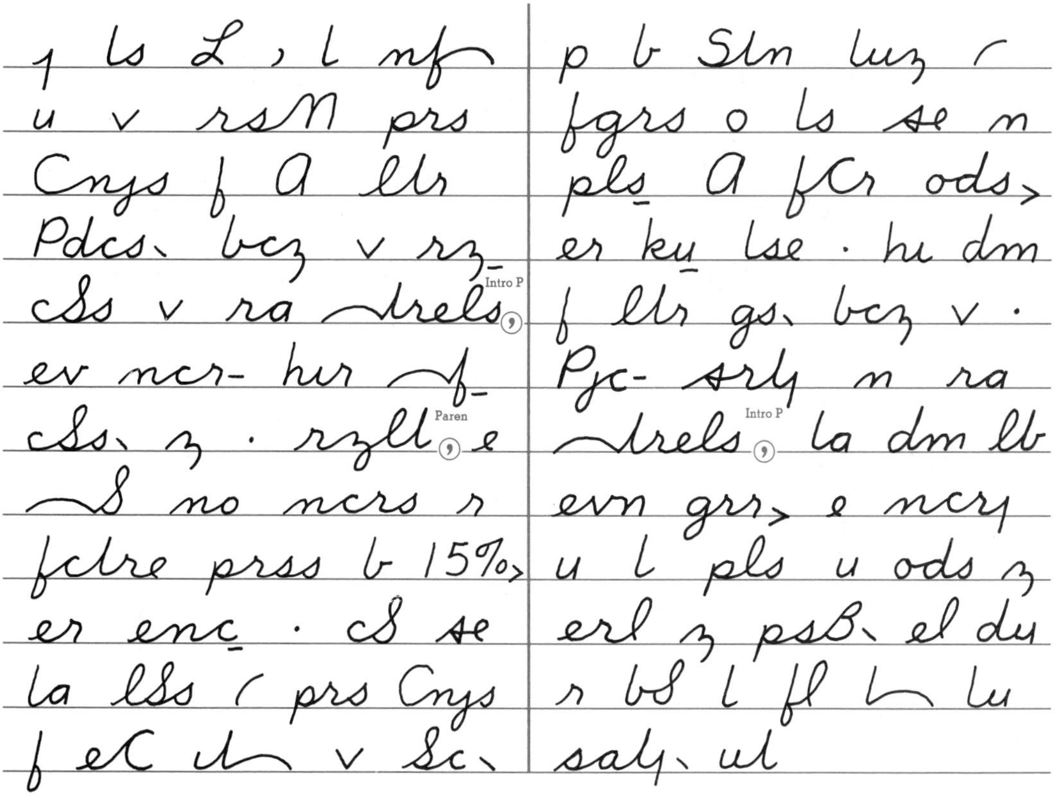

5

Punctuation Study

Add commas to show one parenthetical expression, one introductory dependent clause, two conjunctions, and one series.

Preview Words

fallen

process

spite

unusual

repeated

explanation

understanding

bookkeeping

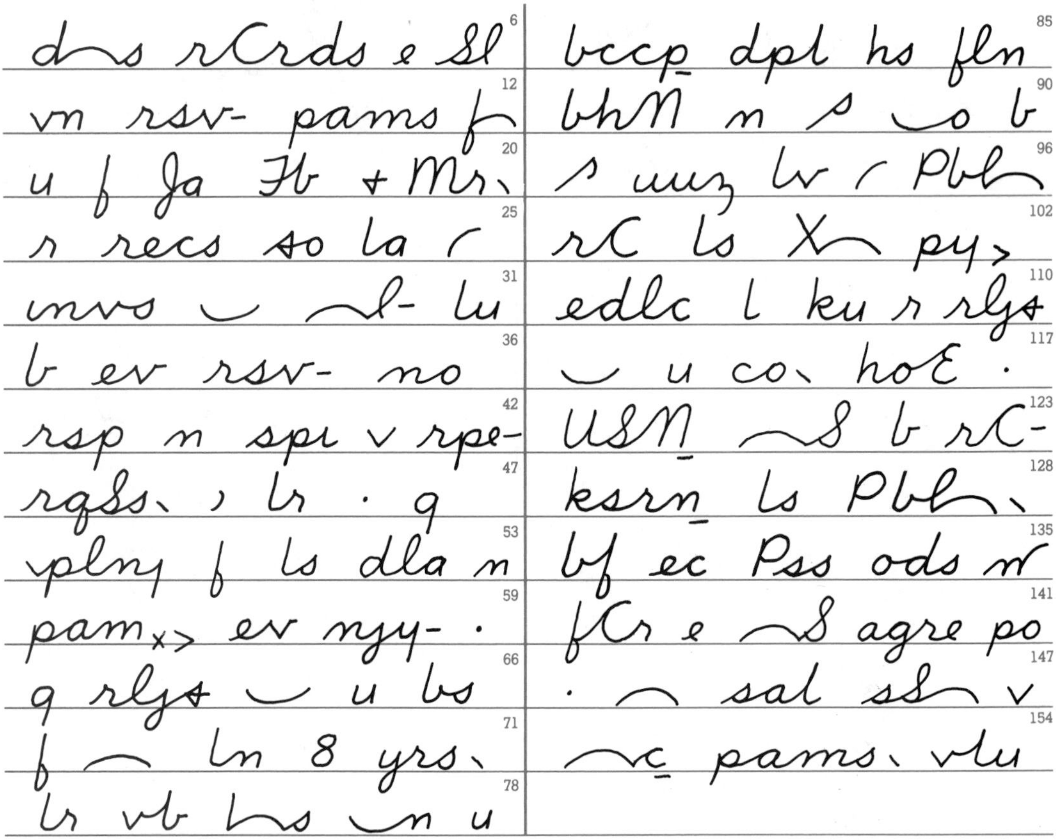

Key

1

MEMO TO: All Managers

An order has been placed for new assembly machines, and we expect delivery[1] within three weeks. Since these machines will increase production by 13 to 15 percent, all managers will need[2] to make adjustments in scheduling. Such changes will be necessary to keep parts flowing to the assembly[3] machines.

I suggest that you meet with your employees in small groups to explain why procedures must be changed. Please[4] assure everyone that these automated machines will not cause the loss of any jobs. As a matter of fact,[5] we will need to hire additional people in several areas.

We are arranging special training sessions[6] which will be conducted shortly after the equipment is installed. These sessions will be administered by[7] representatives of the manufacturer. In general, the operation and maintenance of this new[8] machinery will not differ greatly from that of the past.

If you wish to have assistance in explaining these[9] matters to your employees, a member of our engineering staff will be happy to help. (196)

2

Dear Ms. Doyle:

Thank you for your order of August 7. The 30 coats you requested will be shipped to you without[1] delay. Although we cannot give you an exact date for delivery, we will do all we can to have the[2] merchandise to you in time for your fall sale.

It will take us approximately ten days to process your order[3] and prepare the items for shipping. Once a shipment leaves our loading area, it takes about five days in transit.[4] If all things go according to schedule, you should have the coats within two weeks.

We will send the order c.o.d.[5] Although I do not know exactly how much the freight charges will be, I can tell you that the trucking company[6] we use charges a minimum of $50 for all merchandise under 100 pounds.

If there are[7] any unusual delays, I will be certain to let you know.

Very truly yours, (156)

3

Dear Mr. Hamilton:

Thank you for contacting Empire Roofing, Inc. We appreciate your[1] interest in becoming a distributor for our firm.

Our standard procedure is to send a representative[2] to visit your retail outlet. During this visit our representative will explain our policies and[3] collect the information we need to make a routine analysis. You will have the opportunity to[4] ask questions at that time.

We will contact you personally approximately three weeks following the visit.[5] If your place of business has the qualifications necessary to become a distributorship, we will[6] ask you to sign a contract agreement that will become effective immediately.

You will be contacted[7] by phone to set up an appointment for the visit.

Cordially yours, (152)

4

Gentlemen:

This letter is to inform you of recent price changes for all leather products. Because of rising[1] costs of raw materials, we have incurred higher manufacturing costs. As a result, we must now increase[2] our factory prices by 15 percent.

We are enclosing a cost sheet that lists the price changes for each item[3] of stock. Please be certain to use the figures on this sheet in placing all future orders.

We are continuing[4] to see a high demand for leather goods. Because of a projected shortage in raw materials, that demand[5] will be even greater.

We encourage you to place your orders as early as possible. We will do our[6] best to fill them to your satisfaction.

Yours truly, (129)

5

Dear Ms. Richards:

We still have not received payments from you for January, February, and March. Our records[1] show that the invoices were mailed to you, but we have received no response in spite of repeated requests. Is there[2] a good explanation for this delay in payment?

We have enjoyed a good relationship with your business for[3] more than eight years. There have been times when your bookkeeping department has fallen behind in its work, but it is[4] unusual to have the problem reach this extreme point.

We would like to continue our relationship with your[5] company. However, an understanding must be reached concerning this problem. Before we can process orders[6] in the future, we must agree upon a more satisfactory system of making payments.

Very truly yours,[7] (140)

unt 11

inf Pss *

Shorthand Vocabulary Review

Study the following words and the principles they illustrate. Look for these words in the letters and memos that follow.

Write *m* for the sounds of *mem, mum, men, mon,* and *mun.*

memo	*mo*	terminal	*trml*
members	*mbrs*	minimum	*mm*
eliminate	*elma*	monitor	*mlr*
minutes	*mls*	Germany	*jrme*
memory	*mre*	money	*me*
seminar	*smr*	mention	*my*

More About Punctuation

Set off academic degrees and other abbreviated titles with commas.

Alice Stewart, Ph.D., is a leading authority in English literature.

Please send all contributions to James Stein, Jr.

Academic degrees and other abbreviated titles will be highlighted **Ab** in the reading and writing exercises.

LESSON 51

Brief Forms and Derivatives

1. * acy cor p L san*
2. *Amy pv- pv opls po pgrd*

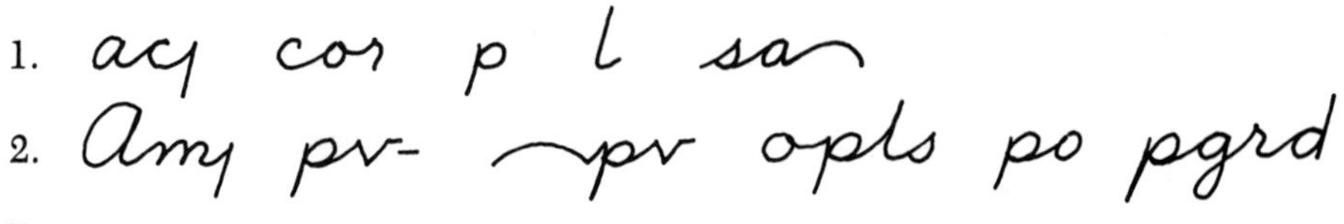

Key

1. acknowledge, correspond/correspondence, please/up, to/too, sample
2. administration, proved, improve, opportunities, upon, upgrade

Phrase Review

1. *yl ino isd idap eh*
2. *evh eap ern ucd uno*
3. *u lk ldl lvu ou sdb*

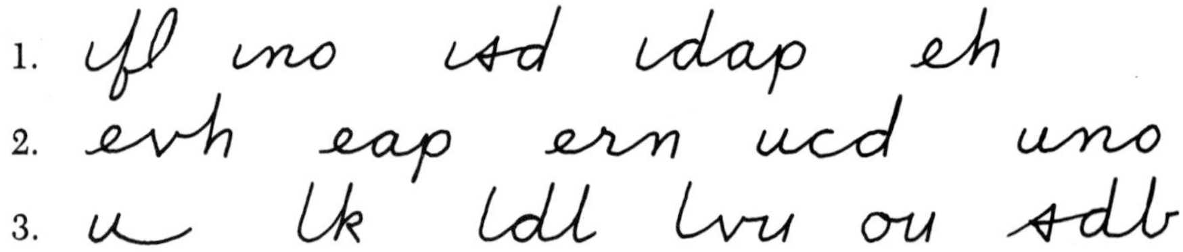

Key

1. I feel, I know, I should, I would appreciate, we had
2. we have had, we appreciate, we are not, you could, you know
3. you were, to come, to determine, to have you/to have your, on you/on your, should be

Reading and Writing Exercises

1

Preview Words

yours	Vincent
within	confirm
greater	operation
accuracy	short notice

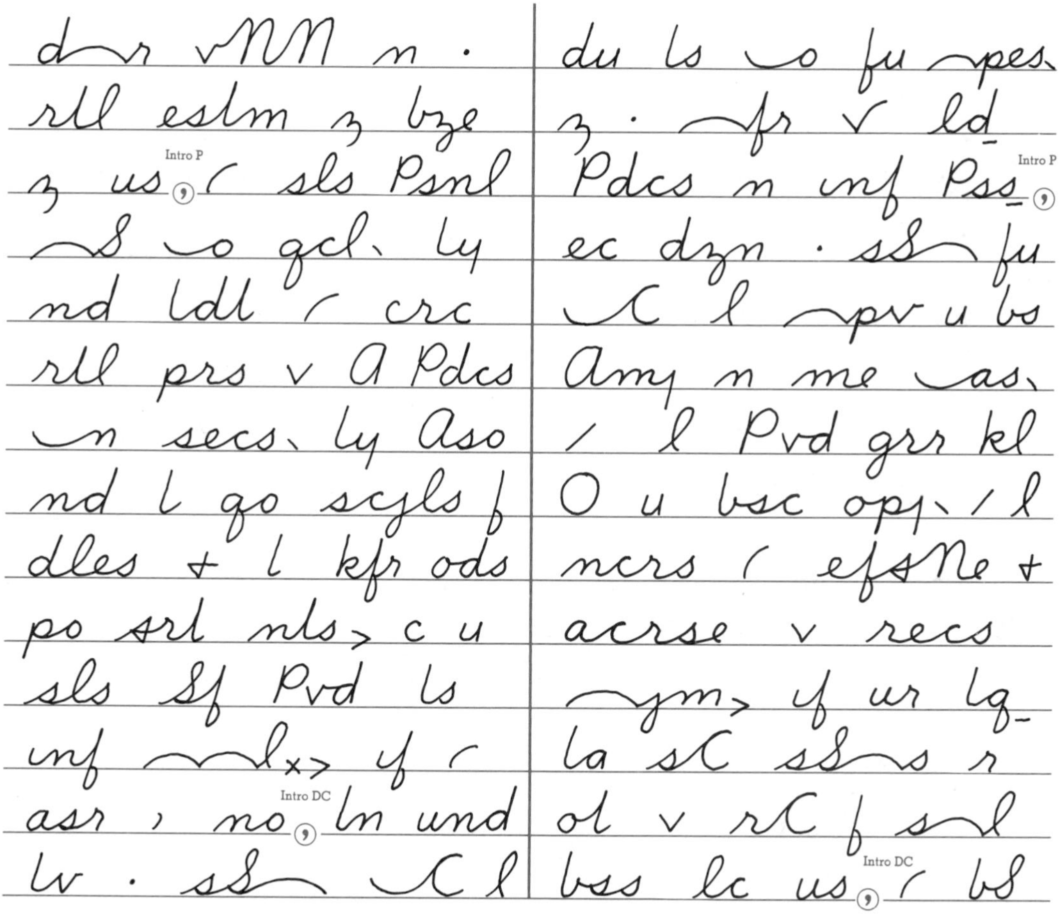

nz , yl Uk. r	c . apym nol
sS s uzl pa f	lc eqpm la ev
Lsvs n 5 yrs,	avlB. su

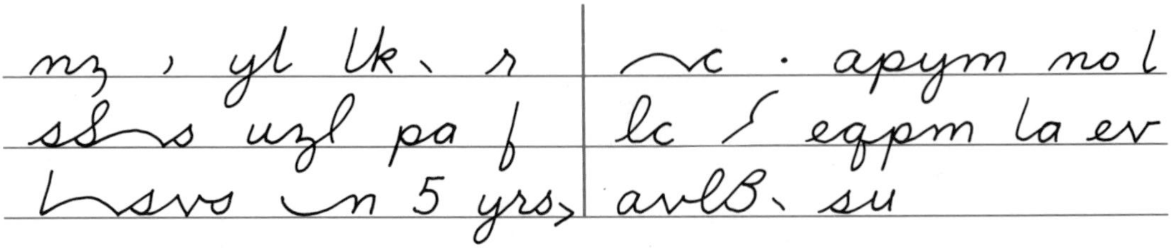

2

Preview Words

master	Sr	temporary	Lprre
clearly	clrl	implementing	plm
printout	prNol	previously	Pvesl
confusion	kf	transmitted	Tl-

mo l rCrd lgn	n Tl- nl c sNrl
ySrd i rsv- .	mre bq. plm nu
mo f u Sa la	sS s c cz Pbls, (Conj)
uv n b gvn cr	b sC Pbls r
f sls kcs u dl-	Lprre. Aso, (Paren) c
n Ja. uv rqS- .	N rzll , jnl rl
prNol vu sls	c kf cra- b Cn
rpls l Cc L ag	r Psyrs, s clrl
r Sr recs. usd	. Av Ub B l Pss
v . asr fu b Lro,	u ods n hf c L
evb df r inf	Pvesl rq-. if uv
sS, (Conj) + s psB	ne frlr Pbls, (Intro DC)
la s vu sls	cl e ri a a.

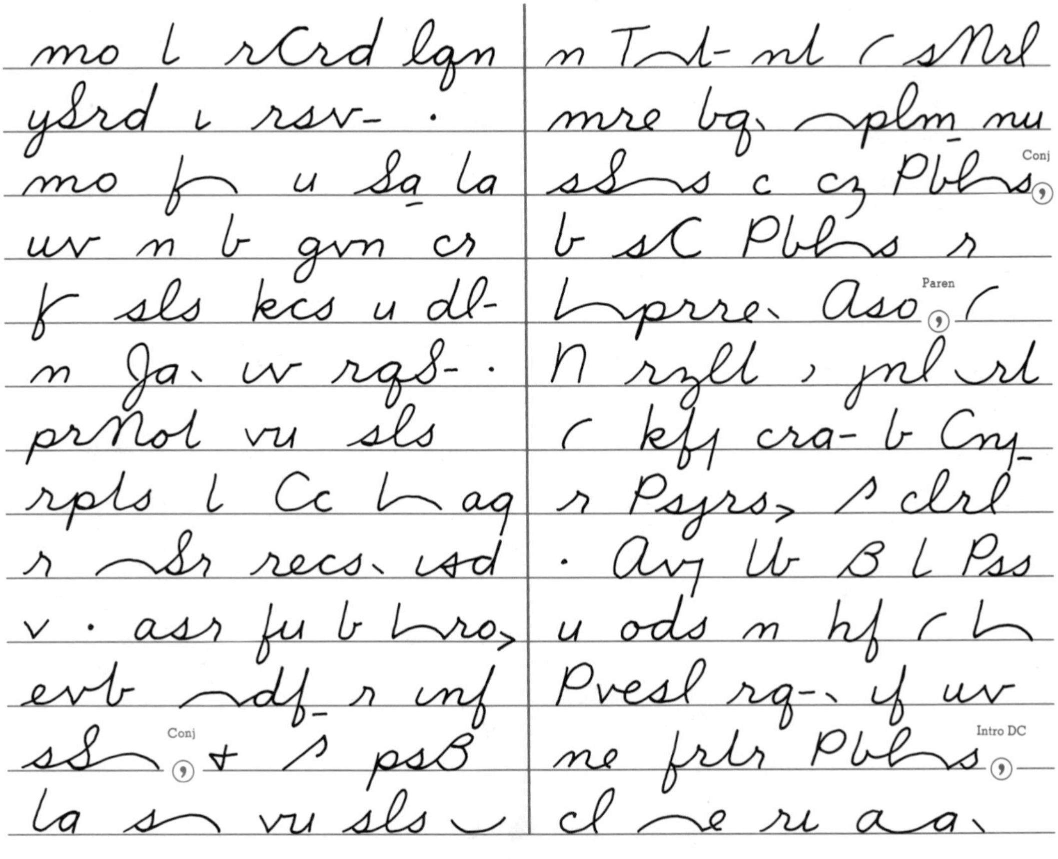

3

Preview Words

existed *S-* computers *kpurs*

software *sflr* wondering *Mr*

orientation *oreNy* competing *kpe*

demonstrations *dmSrys* knowledgeable *nlgŎ*

---

d ex vu b lc S
nu sflr Pgs
crNl ϭ ᴧr +
Mr Ṟ d ofr
ᴦ bŎ Avys fu
Psnl + Pfyl us x,>
r fclre reps ᴧc
Psnl vyls l bs
lcys f bs ᴧyrs
lc u, ly brg ᴦ
eqpm nes l Pvd
dmSrys vr kpurs
+ sflr Pdcs, ᴧa

e pl l vr reps n
LC ᴗ u x n ls
bye ay v kpe Pdcs
+ Svss ⑨ S ᴧpl lv Intro P
• lro oreNy la ,
gvn b • vprl ᴧr
fld, la , y e ᴧp
ol nlgŎ ppl Lᴧc
ly dmSrys f s,•
ayŊ lb klc u sm,
• vyl fᴧ ls Psn
l ofr opls lau
ddN no S-, uvl

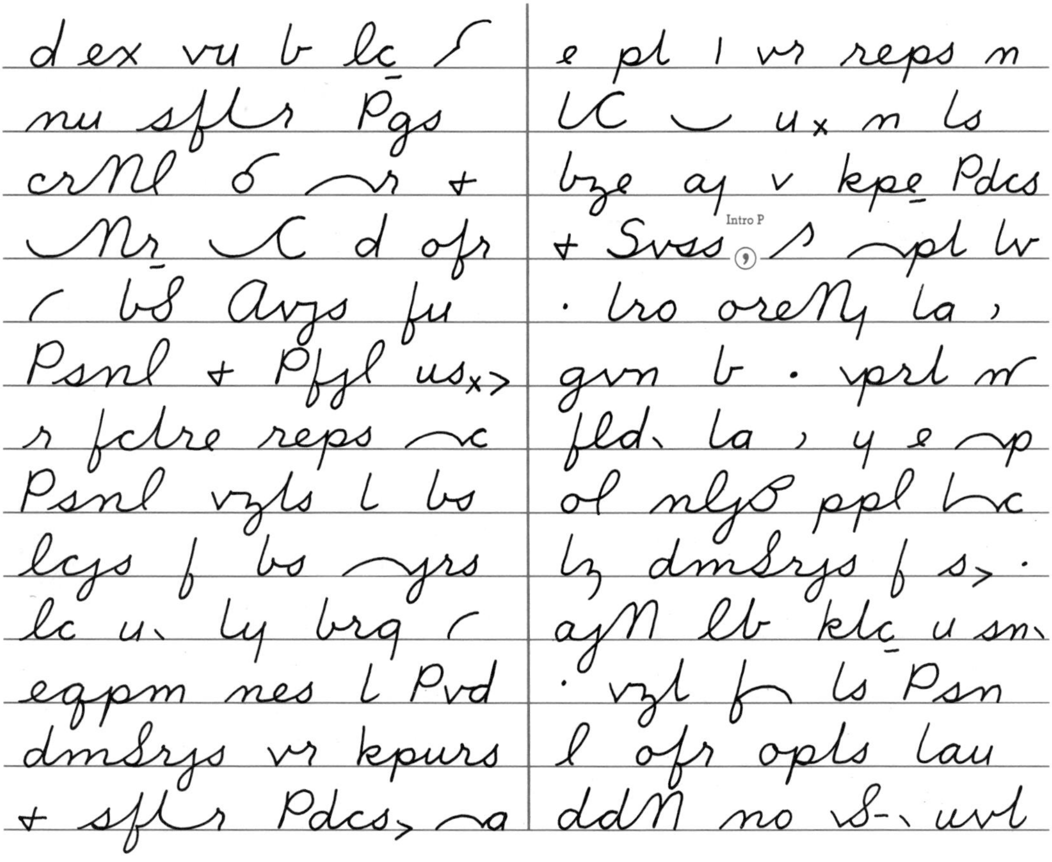

4

Preview Words

analysis	anlss	solutions	slys
upgrade	pgrd	throughout	truol
serious	sres	modifications	-dfys
conduct	kdc	documentation	dcmj

mo l elzbt prSn
lqf lM sugjs u
-d / lnC ySrd.
i agre la s- Cnjs
r nd- n flo v
inf truol r ofss.
d ub l l Sv o .
k l lc nl -dfys
vr sS x> idlc (k
l kdc . kp Sde v
nds v eC ofs. id
hp lau rpl d I

. anlss v efsNe, (Series)
acrse, (Series) + kl. id Aso
lc lv rcmjs f
slys l (Pbls la
r idNf- n rpl,
if s (rcmj v
k lae nd l pgrd
r eqpm, (Intro DC) la sugj
lb gvn sres ksj.
hoE, (Paren) id vpc lse
dcmj f ls rqS.

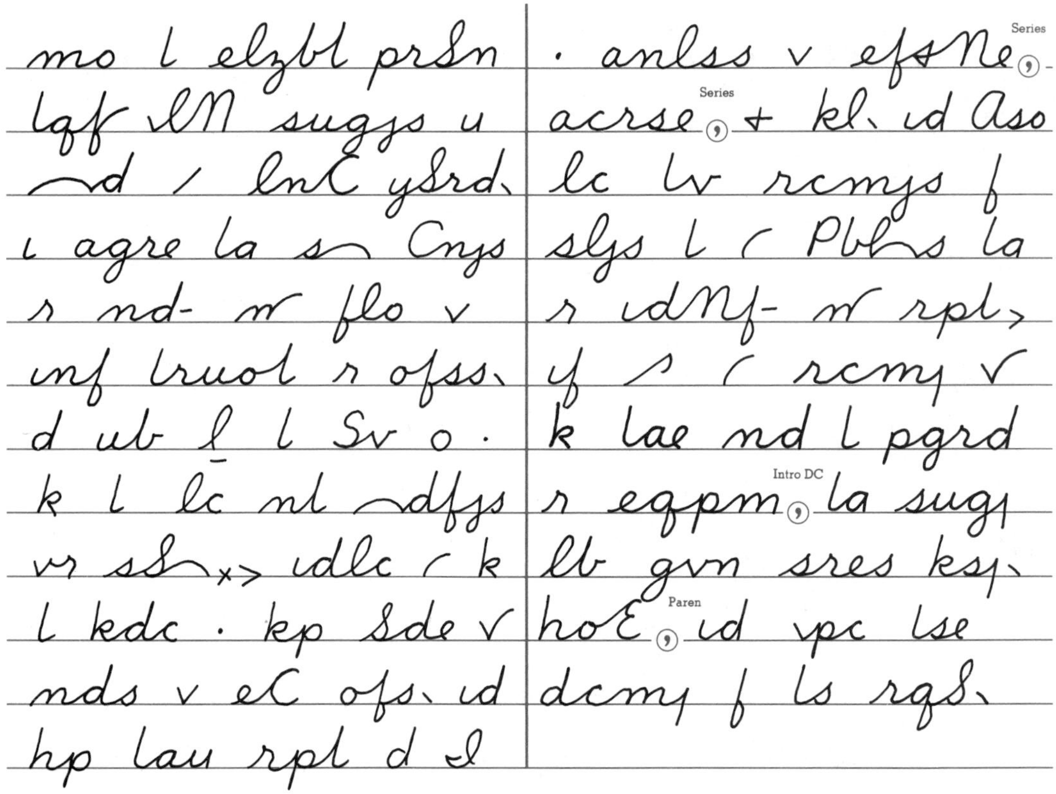

5

Punctuation Study

Add commas to show one conjunction, one introductory phrase, and three introductory dependent clauses.

Preview Words

- carry
- layout
- modular
- showroom
- terminal
- component
- attractive
- reasonably

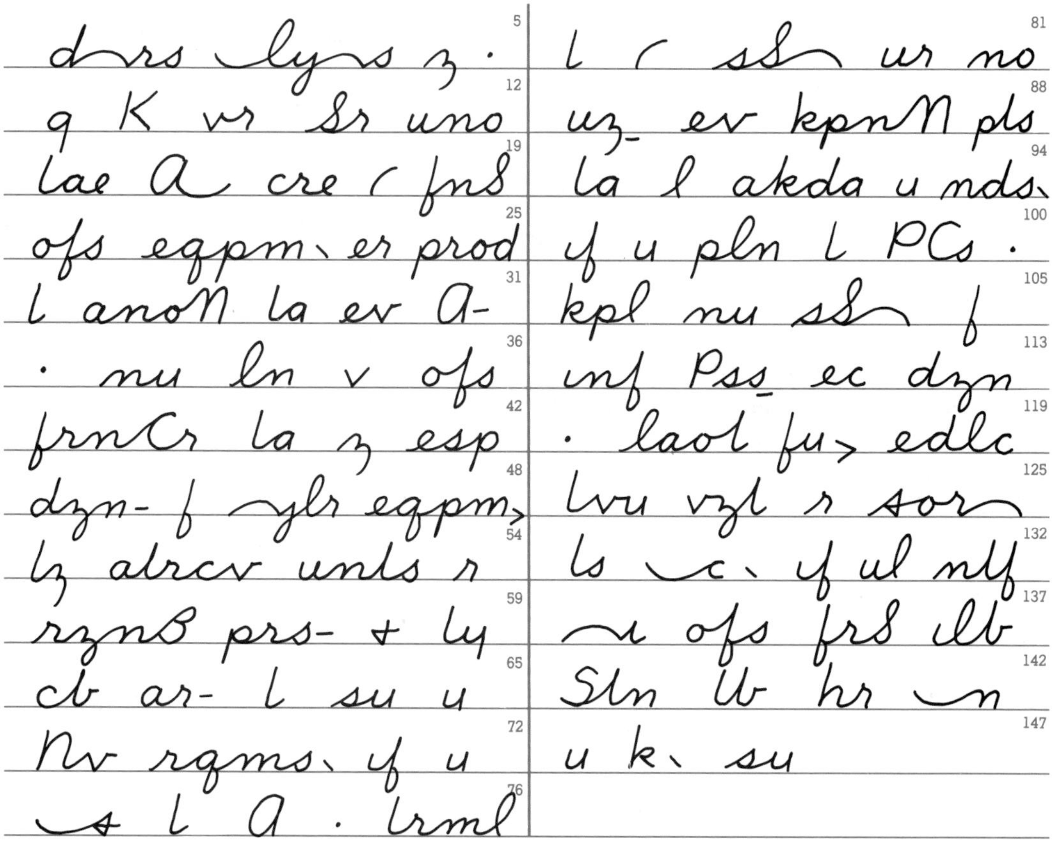

Key

1

Dear Mr. Vincent:

In a retail establishment as busy as yours, the sales personnel must work quickly. They[1] need to determine the correct retail price of all products within seconds. They also need to quote schedules[2] for deliveries and to confirm orders upon short notice.

Can your sales staff provide this information[3] immediately?

If the answer is no, then you need to have a system which will do this work for your employees.[4] As a manufacturer of the leading products in information processing, we can design a system[5] for you which will improve your business administration in many ways. It will provide greater control over your[6] basic operation. It will increase the efficiency and accuracy of records management.

If you[7] are thinking that such systems are out of reach for small businesses like yours, the best news is yet to come. Our systems[8] usually pay for themselves within five years.

Make an appointment now to look at the equipment that we have[9] available.

Sincerely yours, (186)

2

MEMO TO: Richard Lincoln

Yesterday I received a memo from you stating that you have not been given credit[1] for the sales contracts you delivered in January. I have requested a printout of your sales reports[2] to check them against our master records. I should have an answer for you by tomorrow.

We have been modifying[3] our information system, and it is possible that some of your sales were not transmitted into the central[4] memory bank. Implementing new systems can cause problems, but such problems are temporary. Also, the[5] end result is generally worth the confusion created by changing our procedures.

It is clearly an[6] advantage to be able to process your orders in half the time previously required. If you have any[7] further problems, call me right away. (146)

3

Dear Executive:

Have you been looking at the new software programs currently on the market and wondering[1] which would offer the best advantages for your personal and professional use?

Our factory representatives[2] make personal visits to business locations for business managers like you. They bring the equipment[3] necessary to provide demonstrations of our computers and software products.

May we put one of our[4] representatives in touch with you? In this busy age of competing products and services, it is important[5] to have a thorough orientation that is given by an expert in the field. That is why we employ only[6] knowledgeable people to make these demonstrations for us.

An agent will be contacting you soon. A visit[7] from this person will offer opportunities that you didn't know existed.

Yours very truly, (159)

4

MEMO TO: Elizabeth Preston

Thank you for the excellent suggestions you made at lunch yesterday. I agree[1] that some changes are needed in the flow of information throughout our offices. Would you be willing to[2] serve on a committee to look into modifications of our system?

I would like the committee to conduct[3] a complete study of the needs of each office. I would hope that your report would include an analysis[4] of efficiency, accuracy, and control. I would also like to have recommendations for solutions[5] to the problems that are identified in the report.

If it is the recommendation of the committee[6] that we need to upgrade our equipment, that suggestion will be given serious consideration. However,[7] I would expect to see documentation for this request. (151)

5

Dear Mrs. Williams:

As a good customer of our store, you know that we always carry the finest office[1] equipment. We are proud to announce that we have added a new line of office furniture that was especially[2] designed for modular equipment.

These attractive units are reasonably priced, and they can be arranged to[3] suit your individual requirements. If you wish to add a terminal to the system you are now using,[4] we have component parts that will accommodate your needs. If you plan to purchase a completely new system for[5] information processing, we can design a layout for you.

We would like to have you visit our showroom this week.[6] If you will notify my office first, I will be certain to be here when you come.

Sincerely yours, (138)

LESSON 52

Abbreviations and Derivatives

1. *dpl ex rel % amt blvd*
2. *estm ecol Wrn rel̠ recs*

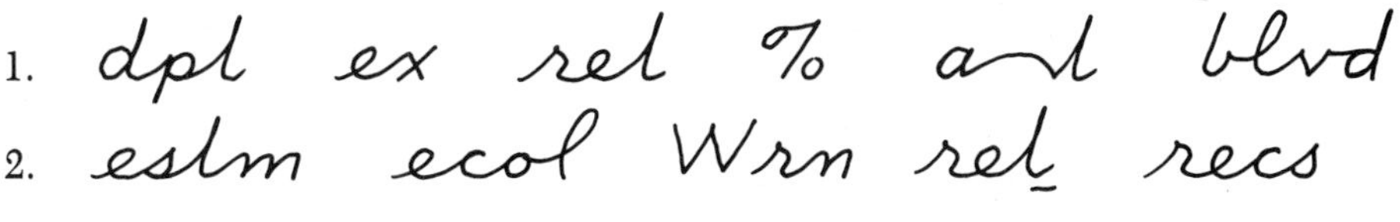

Key

1. department, example/executive, return, percent, amount, boulevard
2. establishment, economical, western, returning, records

Transcription Aids: Omitted Outlines

When taking dictation at a rapid speed, it is not uncommon to omit an outline because of the speed or difficulty of the dictation. An omitted outline need not be a serious problem. When the omission occurs in a common expression, you will be able to identify the missing word by reading the context of the sentence. For example:

Did you identify the missing word? The sentence should be transcribed as follows:

I will put the check in the mail today.

In some instances, you will find that more than one word can be used in place of the missing outline without changing the meaning of the sentence. For example:

The missing outline could be *response* or *regard*.

I am writing in response to your letter of April 2.

As your transcription skills grow, you will learn to supply these missing outlines as you transcribe the letter. In situations in which the missing outline represents a common expression, choose a word that fits the meaning of the sentence.

In the lessons that follow, Letter 4 will contain two omitted outlines. When you transcribe these sentences, supply the word that you think is most appropriate. An acceptable choice for the missing word will be italicized in your key, and appropriate alternate choices will be shown at the bottom of each letter.

Your Business Vocabulary

hardware  In computer systems, the physical parts and equipment, such as the printer, the cathode ray tube (CRT), or the keyboard.

Please provide a price list for all hardware that is available.

printout 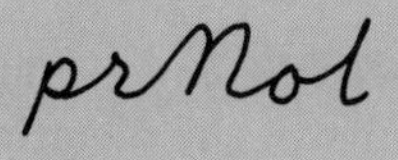 The printed product (output) of a computer. A printout is sometimes referred to as "hard copy."

When may I have a printout of everything that is contained on that disk?

software  Computer programs, routines, and symbolic languages that are essential to the operation of computers.

Our company produces excellent software programs.

Reading and Writing Exercises

——————————— 1 ———————————

Preview Words

poor *pr*

unclear *uclr*

message *~sy*

awkward *acw*

dictating *dcla_*

originates *orynas*

unnecessarily *unesl*

introductory *Ndclre*

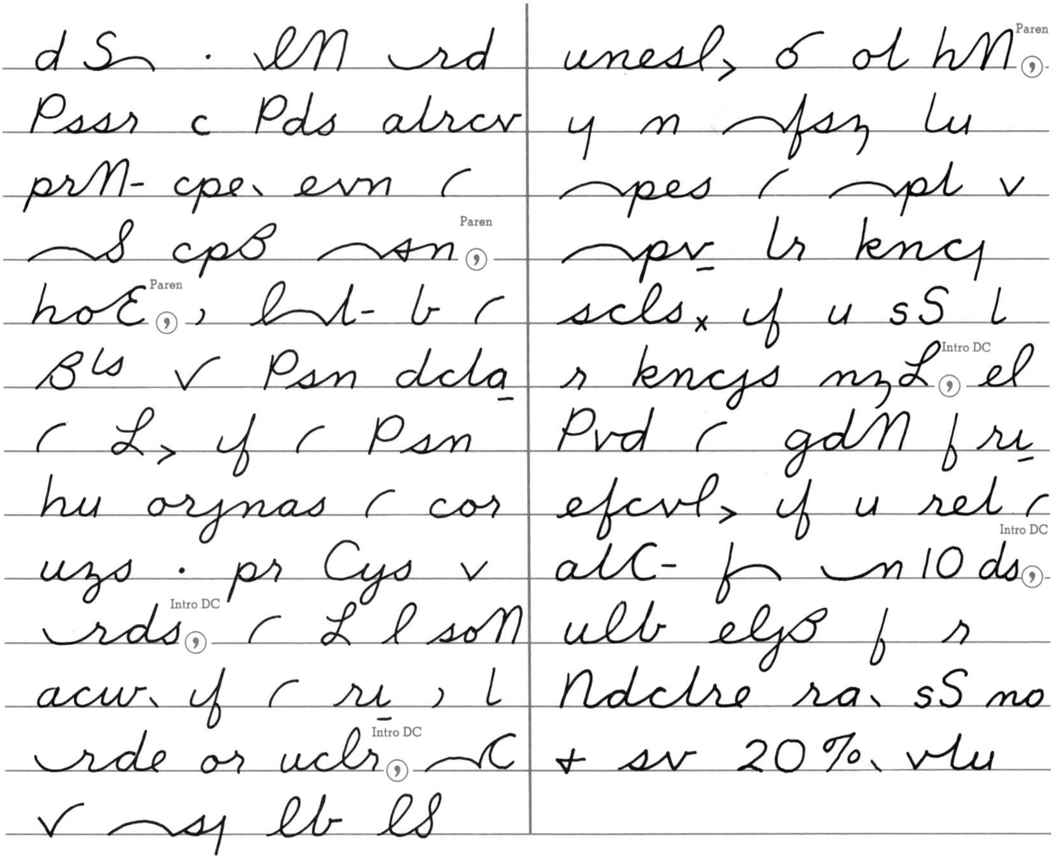

2

Preview Words

disks	Dcs	cartons	crlns
cloth	cll	omitted	ol-
habit	hbl	incomplete	nkp
ribbons	rbns	daisy wheel	dze ⌣l

dS ⌣ ru l acy
la (Am e rsv-
f u ls ⌣rn
arv- o scyl. hoE, Paren
/ z nkp. eh
asc- f flo ⌣s:
1. 4 crlns v cll
rbns f ⌣dl 7H
prNr, 2. 1 No 9H
dze ⌣l, 3. 9 bxs v
Dcs, alo (inv
ls- (⌣s anabv, Intro DC

e Dcvr- lar la 2
bxs v Dcs h b ol-.
lrf, Paren ⌣ rqs lau fw
(⌣n Dcs l r
ofs, udap / u ucd
A (M ⌣s ⌣ol
dla. alo ern ⌣
hbl v pls rA ods, Intro DC
eh alspa- v lz n
Sc b no. p ll s
no ⌣n l vpc dle.
su

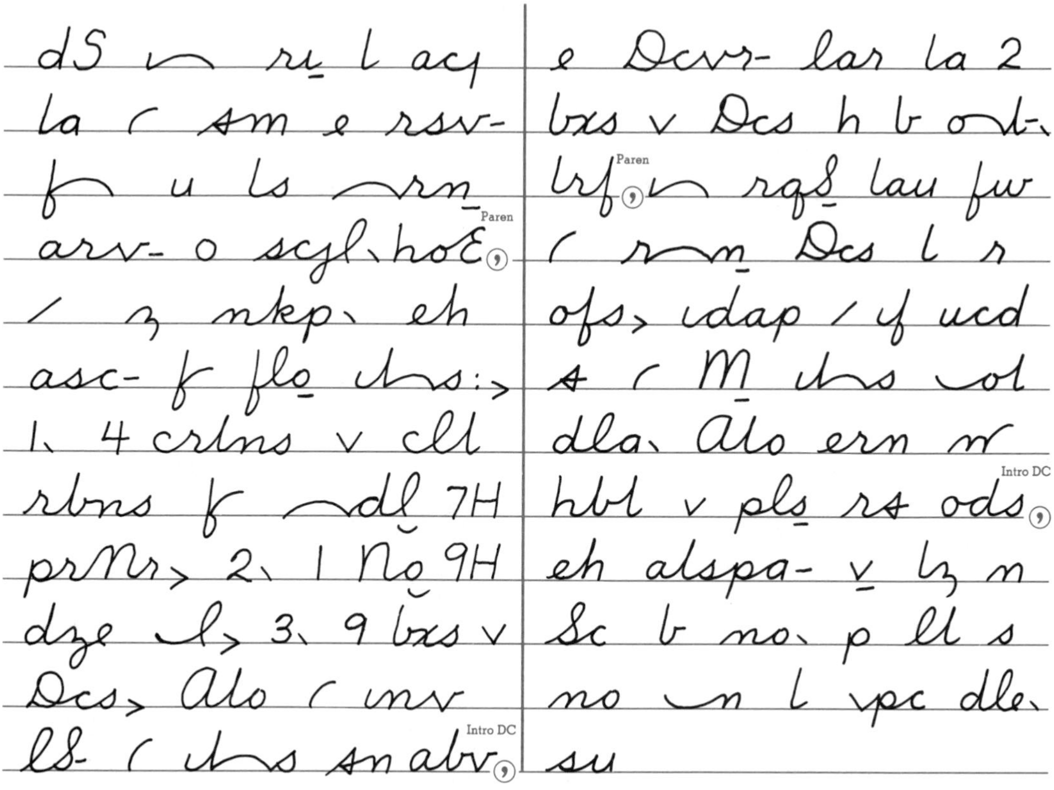

3

Preview Words

miss _M_

serious _sres_

isolate _isla_

data base _dla bs_

inventory _nvnlre_

unexpected _uxpc-_

dangerously _dnyrsl_

20-pound _20=lb_

---

mo l szn crls
_lu p Cc hc sr_
la r kpur Pq e
uz f nvnlre kl,
o Pprl x, ysrd l
lrn- la er nrl ol
v 20= lb ppr. ls
l c e Dcvr- la ol
splis v dnyrsl
ls. yf r dla bs v
crM, ls uxpc-
srlys d n v ocr-,

Intro DC

z uno, ecn afd
l rn srl v ofs
splis, sC . srly
rzlls n dlas +
cd cz s l M dle
ddlns, ne la PvMs
s f ofs dpMB
Svs , . sres Pbl
f s, mo la lc rlu
ou, n u isla r
Pbl, p ll e no
_ru a a,_

Intro DC

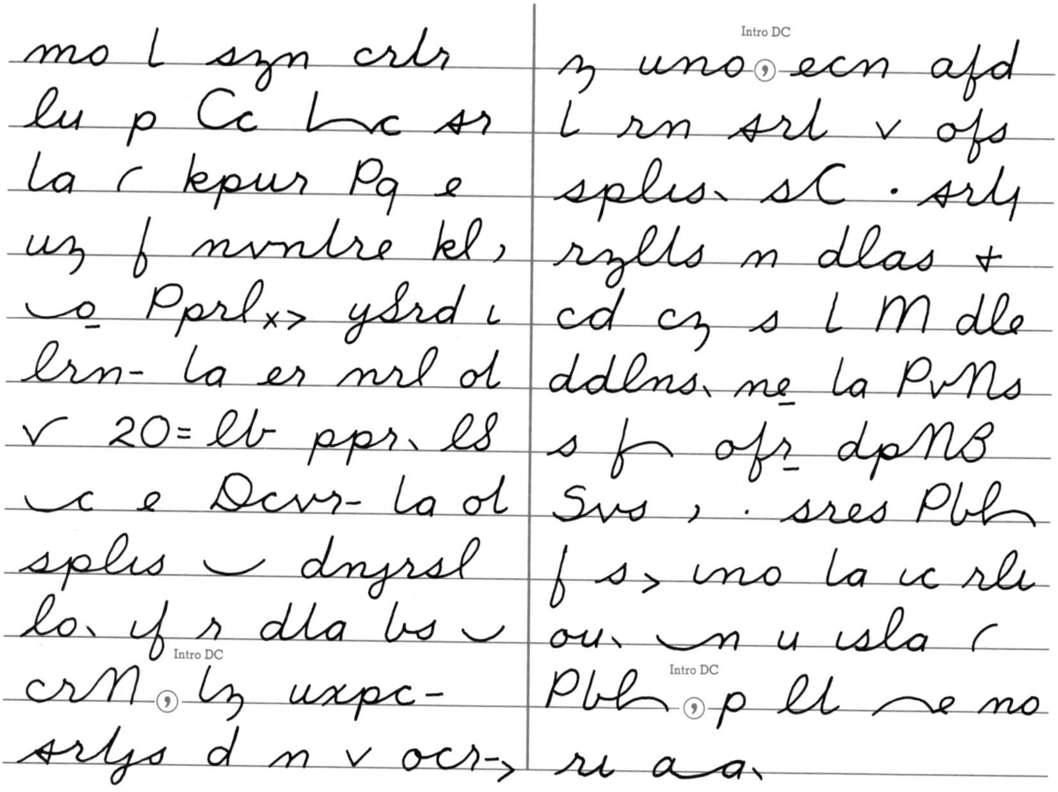

4

Supply two words that are missing in the following letter.

Preview Words

various	vres	surpassed	Sps-
hardware	hrdr	capabilities	cpBls
regional	rjnl	tremendously	trmdsl
analysis	anlss	up-to-date	pda

dr rbrts sM
nSl (nu kpur
hrdr 2 yrs aq, (Intro P)
r nds v grn
trmdsl. n fc, r (Paren)
nds v fr Sps- (
cpBls v hrdr>
bf A nu trmls
+ prMrs t r crM
eqpm, (Intro P) edlc tv .
pda anlss vr nds.
n adj t (dla Ar
b Pss-, (Intro P) edlc t A

nvntre kl + vres
sls Pgs. Aso, (Paren) r
rjnl sls ppl sdb
B tv dr ls t (
sNrl kpur> d ub
l t ____ ts anlss
f s× e nvi u tk
t r ofs + Dcs
lz Pbls - s.
idap / if ucd lt
-e no ____ (nx
fu ds. su

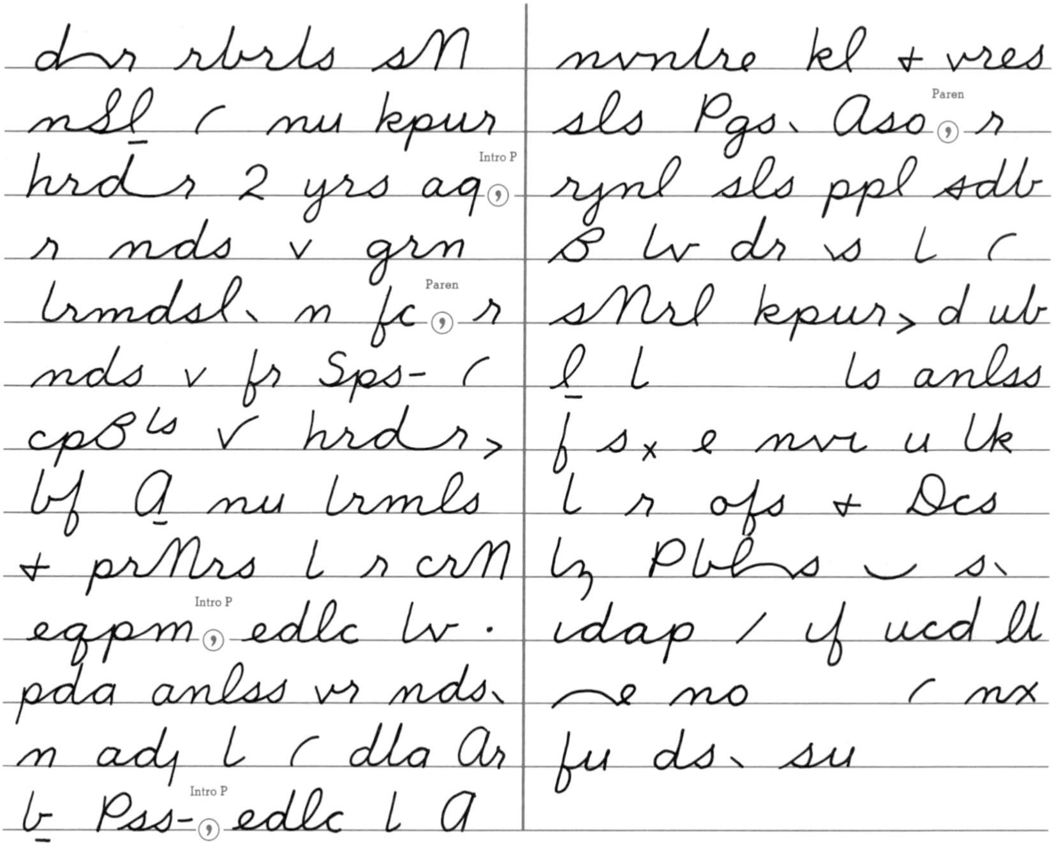

5

Punctuation Study

Add commas to show two introductory dependent clauses, one introductory phrase, one parenthetical expression, and one direct address.

Preview Words

initial
figures
thought
distributors
functions
finalized
technical
follow-up

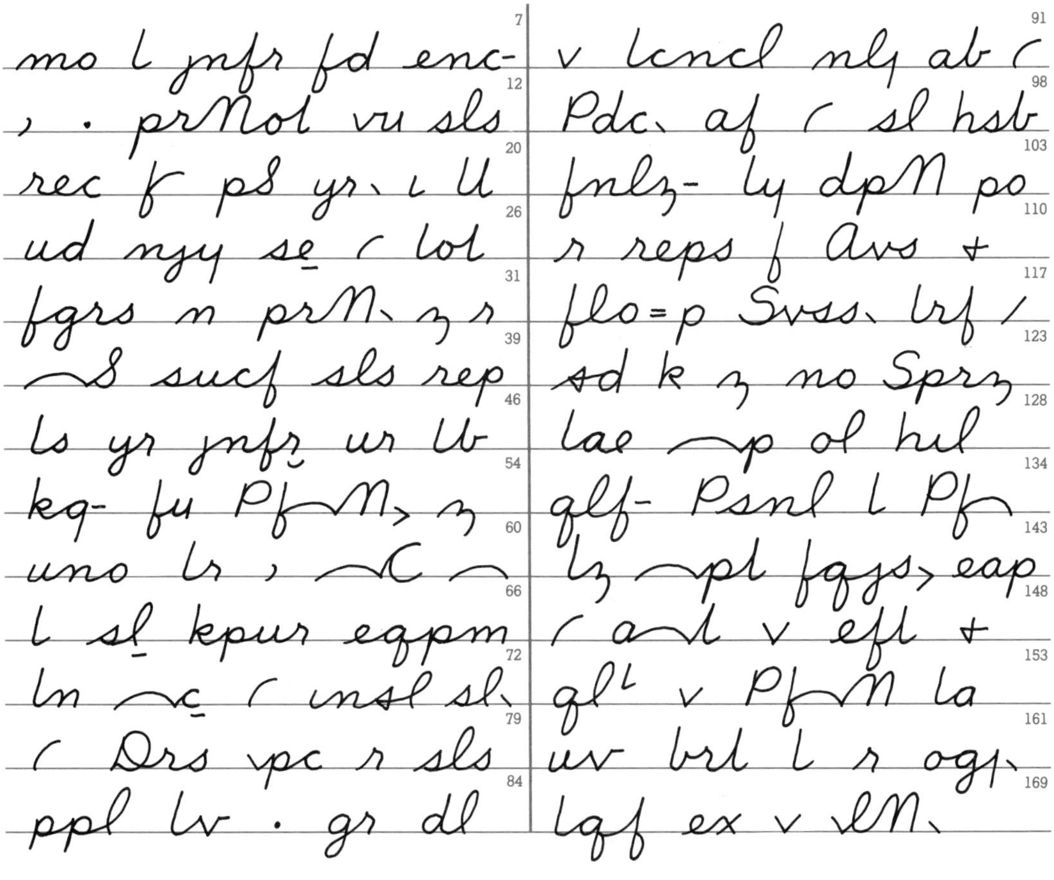

Key

1

Dear Sir or Madam:

An excellent word processor can produce attractive printed copy. Even the most[1] capable machine, however, is limited by the abilities of the person dictating the letter.[2]

If the person who originates the correspondence uses a poor choice of words, the letter will sound awkward.[3] If the writing is too wordy or unclear, much of the message will be lost unnecessarily.

On the other[4] hand, why not emphasize to your employees the importance of improving their communication skills? If you[5] subscribe to our communications newsletter, we will provide the guidance for writing effectively.

If you[6] return the attached form within ten days, you will be eligible for our introductory rate. Subscribe now[7] and save 20 percent.

Very truly yours, (148)

2

Dear Sir:

I am writing to acknowledge that the shipment we received from you this morning arrived on schedule.[1] However, it was incomplete. We had asked for the following items:

1. Four cartons of cloth ribbons for the[2] Model 700 printer.
2. One No. 900 daisy wheel.
3. Nine boxes of disks.

Although the invoice[3] listed the items shown above, we discovered later that two boxes of disks had been omitted. Therefore,[4] I am requesting that you forward the remaining disks to our office.

I would appreciate it if you could[5] ship the missing items without delay. Although we are not in the habit of placing rush orders, we had[6] anticipated having these in stock by now. Please let us know when to expect delivery.

Sincerely yours,[7] (140)

3

MEMO TO: Susan Carter

Will you please check to make sure that the computer program we use for inventory[1] control is working properly?

Yesterday I learned that we are nearly out of the 20-pound paper. Last week[2] we discovered that other supplies were dangerously low. If our data base were current, these unexpected[3] shortages would not have occurred.

As you know, we cannot afford to run short of office supplies. Such a shortage[4] results in delays and could cause us to miss delivery deadlines. Anything that prevents us from offering[5] dependable service is a serious problem for us.

I know that I can rely on you. When you isolate[6] the problem, please let me know right away. (128)

4

Dear Mr. Roberts:

Since installing the new computer hardware two years ago, our needs have grown tremendously.[1] In fact, our needs have far surpassed the capabilities of the hardware.

Before adding new terminals and printers[2] to our current equipment, we would like to have an up-to-date analysis of our needs. In addition[3] to the data already being processed, we would like to add inventory control and various sales programs.[4] Also, our regional sales people should be able to have direct access to the central computer.

Would[5] you be willing to *provide* this analysis for us? We invite you to come to our office and discuss these[6] problems with us. I would appreciate it if you could let me know *within* the next few days.

Sincerely yours,[7] (140)

provide: conduct, do, perform

within: during, in

5

MEMO TO: Jennifer Ford

Enclosed is a printout of your sales record for the past year. I thought you would enjoy[1] seeing the total figures in print. As our most successful sales representative this year, Jennifer, you are[2] to be congratulated for your performance.

As you know, there is much more to selling computer equipment[3] than making the initial sale. The distributors expect our sales people to have a great deal of technical[4] knowledge about the product. After the sale has been finalized, they depend upon our representatives for[5] advice and follow-up services. Therefore, it should come as no surprise that we employ only highly qualified[6] personnel to perform these important functions.

We appreciate the amount of effort and quality[7] of performance that you have brought to our organization. Thank you for your example of excellence. (159)

LESSON 53

Shorthand Vocabulary Review

1. Write  for the medial or final sound of any vowel + *nk* (*ank, enk, ink, onk, unk*).

thank 

bank 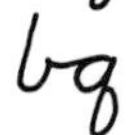

length 

junk 

linked 

thinking 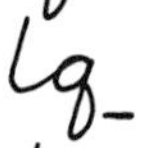

function 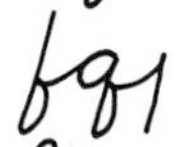

Lincoln 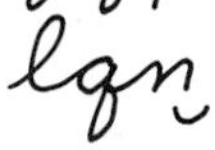

2. Write a printed, disjoined capital  for the word beginning *super*.

Also write a printed, disjoined capital  for the word endings *scribe* and *script* and for the sound of *scrip*.

super 

supermarket 

supervise 

superstar 

described 

subscribe 

subscription 

manuscript 

Transcription Aids: Similar Words

ware 

A word used to describe goods or articles of the same general type. For example, glassware, software, hardware, housewares.

We are ordering new software for the data processing department.

wear 

A word used to describe clothing or the act of clothing oneself.

You will find leather belts in the men's wear department.

Your Business Vocabulary	main frame *m fr*	The part of a computer system that contains the central processing unit and control elements.
	All data will be processed automatically through the main frame.	
	projected earnings *Pjc- ern*	Estimated income for the future; the amount of income that is estimated in advance of a target date or action.
	What are the projected earnings for this corporation for next year?	

Reading and Writing Exercises

1

Preview Words

goes	*gs*	discount	*Dk*
various	*vres*	exceeded	*vd-*
options	*opjs*	minimum	*mm*
reflect	*rflc*	selecting	*slc*

d~rs sldn lgf ngе
ksrn nu sflr fu
ofs inf ss~. ec
Pvd u ~ vres Pgs
l ~e r nds dS-
m u L ~ enc.
cal C dSs r opjs

la r avlB, r kc ~
u sps laul rsv .
Dk o E od pls-
af u ods v rC-
. mm v 2T$ P
yr. bcz u vd- la
a l ~ r plsm

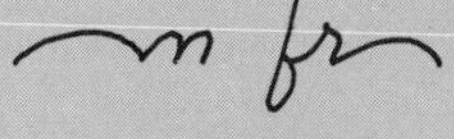

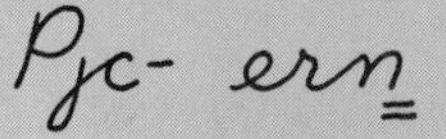

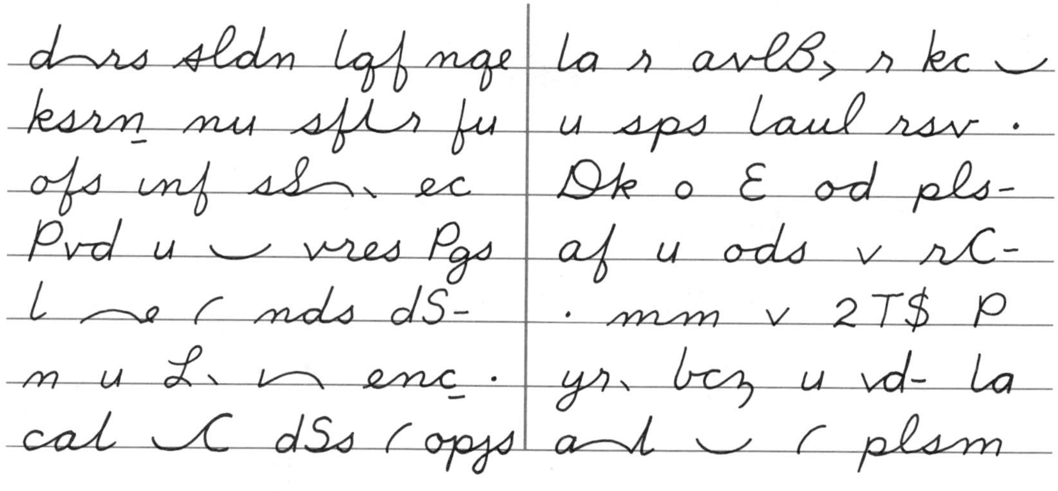

vu lS od, (Intro DC) ls Dk
gs nl efc ~nl,
lrf, (Paren) a fCr invs
f ls yr l rflc.
Dk v 20%, eap
u ku- spl f r Pdcs,
p ll ~e no if
und frlr inf n
slc sfl-r Pgs, su

2

Preview Words

endure ndr

wear ~r

major ~yr

sturdiest SrdeS

entered N-

maintenance ~nlnN

postage-paid pS = pd

productivity Pdcv L

1 ~n u PCs- (
kpur eqpm n u
ofs, (Intro DC) u PbS sn- .
Svs kc, ~n u N-
nl la agrem, (Intro DC) u
hp- lau Svs Pbl-s
db slv-, vu foN
lau no rsv (qc
+ rliS Svs nd-
lcp u eqpm op
efsNl? vu foN la
(Svs agrem u
sn- ~ (~fr vu
eqpm, z ecol +
sal z / sdb?, if
ucn asr ys l bo
v lz gs, (Intro DC) ev . sly la
l grl ncrs Pdcv L
n u ofs, s r bs
lcp inf sS-s op

/ lr lp lvl v
efsNe, e Svs
hrdr + ~c
rprs ~n nes, e
cre . f ln v pls
+ vsres f~ 9 ~yr
~frs> Alo ~S
eqpm , bll l

ndr . gr dl v
~r, (Intro DC) evn r SrdeS
unl rqs rglr
~nlnN lcp / n
q kdj> l lrn ~
ab r Svss, (Intro P) p rel
r pS=pd crd la
ev enc-, ul

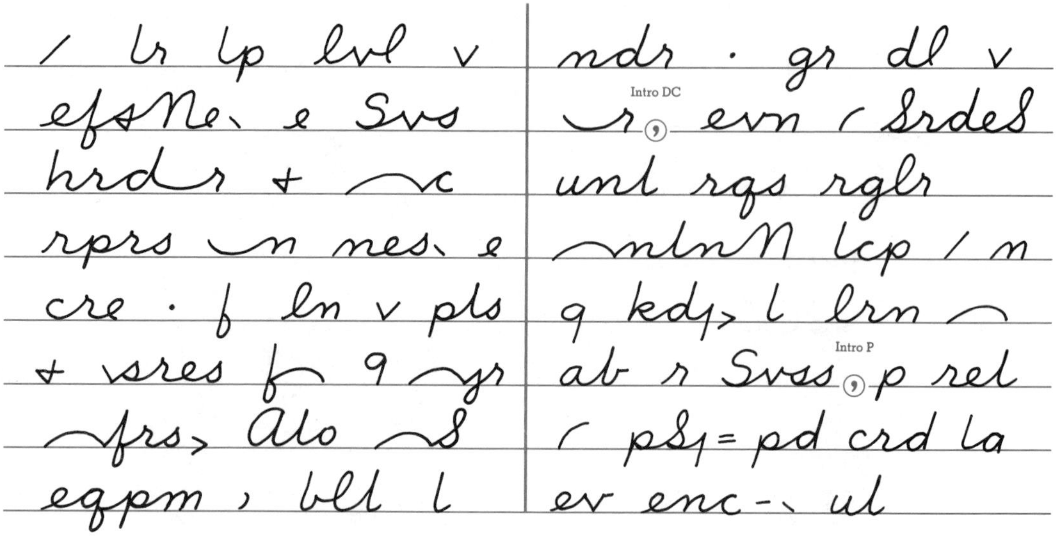

3

Preview Words

usage	usj	inclined	ncln-
network	nlo	flat rate	fll ra
relatively	rlvl	time-share	h = Ar
inexpensive	nxpNv	main frame	~n fr

mo l rlf lsn v-
jS rd u rpl, (Intro P) i
agre ~ u rcmys
f Ar kpur h ~
ol cos, uf e sS l
. h = Ar sSh, (Intro DC)

ecd v r us v .
v vpNv ~n fr
f . cS la , rlvl
nxpNv> z . mbr
v ls nlo, (Intro P) ho d
e b G- f r usj x

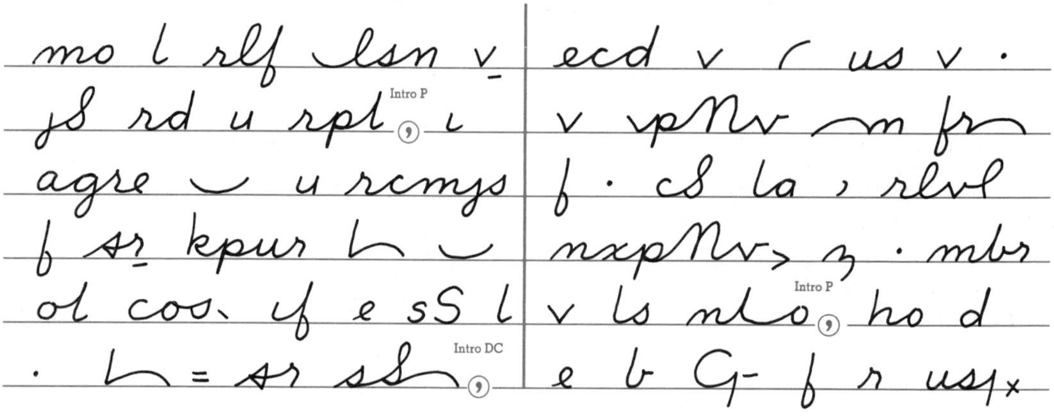

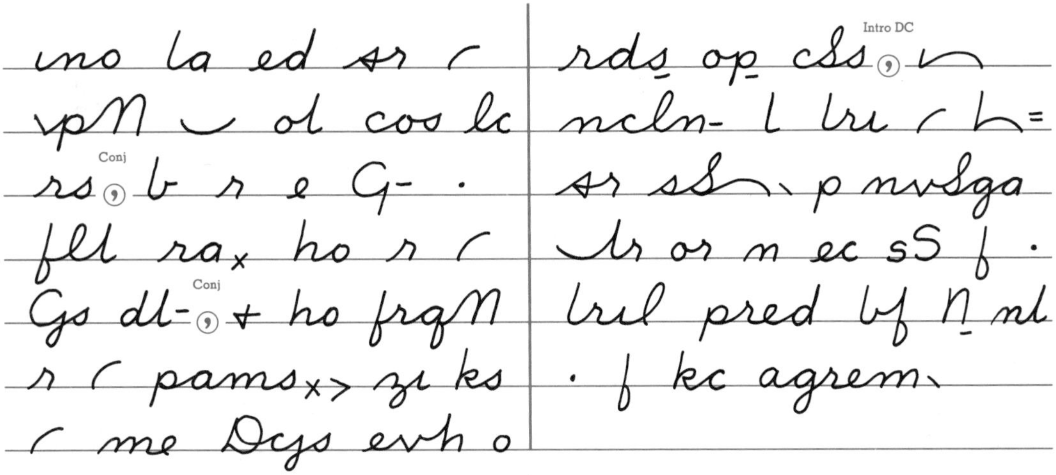

4

Supply two words that are missing in the following letter.

Preview Words

assigning	asn_	projected	Pjc-
compares	kprs	preparation	prpy
previous	Pves	substantial	sSnsl
earnings	ern=	color graphs	clr grfs

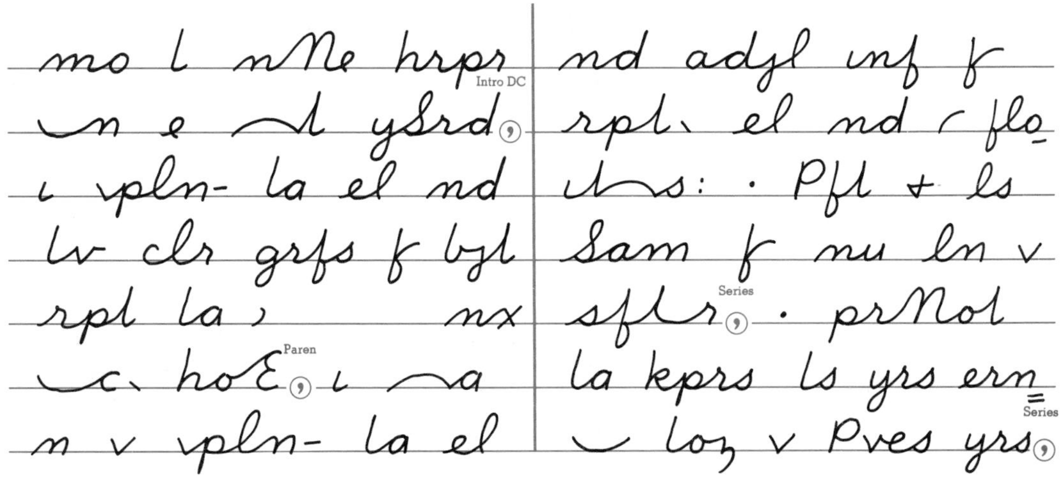

+ Pjc- ern = f nx | asn = 2 ~pes f
5 yrs, (rpl sdb | r ~rd Pss= dpl
prN- + boN, ino la | Lo ~ u, ul Aso
ls reps · sSnsl | v f us v · kfrN
al v ~o + prpry ⒐ *(Conj)* | r ull u ~o ,
b r nes lae P | , f uv gs ⒐- *(Intro DC)*
ls inf, L hlp u | p brq h L ~e
~ ls Pjc ⒐ ~ *(Intro P)* | (ne h,

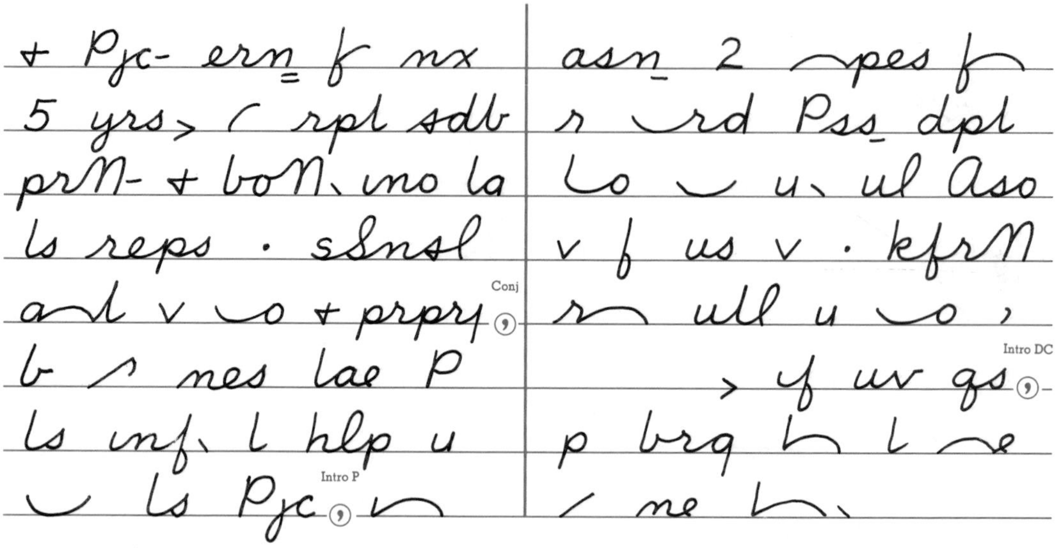

———————————— 5 ————————————

Punctuation Study

Add commas to show one conjunction, two parenthetical expressions, one
introductory dependent clause, and one introductory phrase.

Preview Words

wrong	rq	reactions	racys
hesitant	hzlN	experiment	prm
worthwhile	rll	furthermore	frlr
performance	PfN	comprehensive	kprhNv

mo L ~rgrl ry ⁴ | ls isu w dsd- ³⁴
evh me Pbl~s ¹⁰ | la ls sflr cn ³⁹
~ (ak sflr ¹⁶ | du (~o e rq, ⁴⁴
e PCs- n Fb, af ²² | r n kprhNv ⁴⁹
gv ~C ksy L ²⁸ | enf L ~e r nds, ⁵⁴

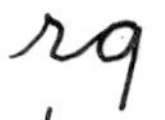

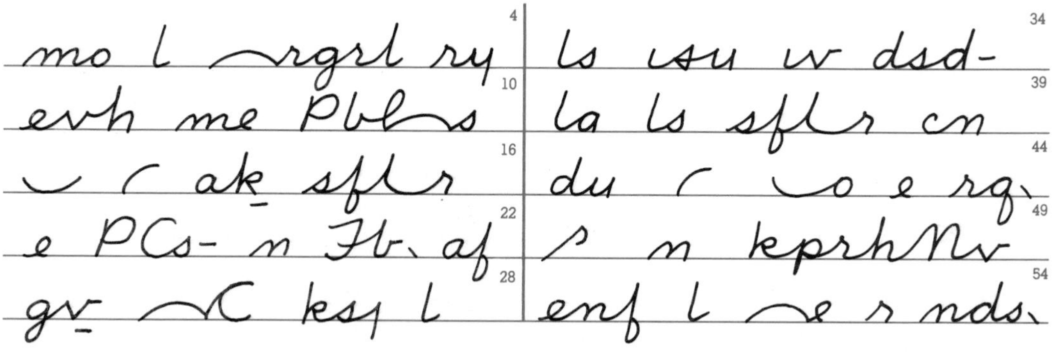

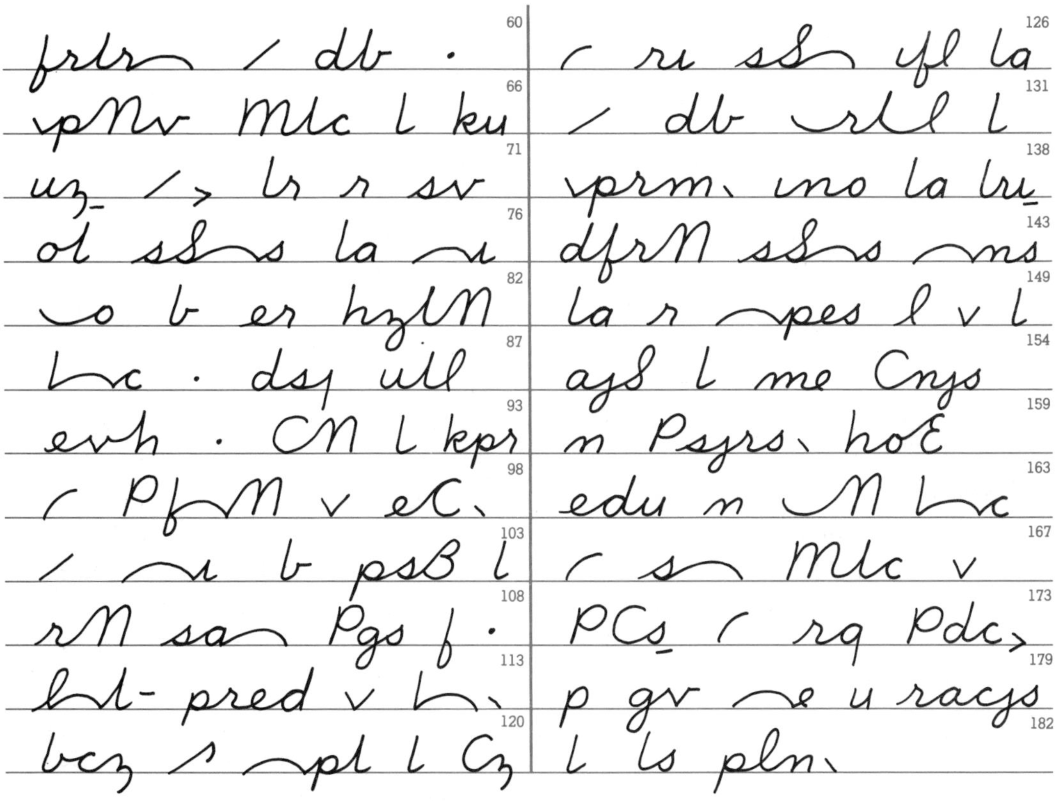

Key

1

Dear Mrs. Sheldon:

Thank you for your inquiry concerning new software for your office information system.[1] We can provide you with various programs to meet the needs described in your letter. I am enclosing a[2] catalog which describes the options that are available.

Our contract with you specifies that you will receive a[3] discount on every order placed after your orders have reached a minimum of $2,000 per year. Because[4] you exceeded that amount with the placement of your last order, this discount goes into effect immediately.[5] Therefore, all future invoices for this year will reflect a discount of 20 percent.

We appreciate[6] your continued support for our products. Please let me know if you need further information in selecting[7] software programs.

Sincerely yours, (146)

2

Gentlemen:

When you purchased the computer equipment in your office, you probably signed a service contract.[1] When you entered into that agreement, you hoped that your service problems would be solved. Have you found that you now receive[2] the quick and reliable service needed to keep your equipment operating efficiently? Have you[3] found that the service agreement you signed with the manufacturer of your equipment is as economical[4] and satisfactory as it should be?

If you cannot answer yes to both of these questions, we have a solution[5] that will greatly increase productivity in your office. It is our business to keep information systems[6] operating at their top level of efficiency. We service hardware and make repairs when necessary.[7] We carry a full line of parts and accessories from nine major manufacturers.

Although most equipment[8] is built to endure a great deal of wear, even the sturdiest unit requires regular maintenance[9] to keep it in good condition.

To learn more about our services, please return the postage-paid card that we have[10] enclosed.

Yours truly, (204)

3

MEMO TO: Ralph Wilson

Having just read your report, I agree with your recommendations for sharing computer[1] time with other companies. If we subscribe to a time-share system, we could have the use of a very expensive[2] main frame for a cost that is relatively inexpensive.

As a member of this network, how would we be[3] charged for our usage? I know that we would share the expense with other companies like ours, but are we charged a[4] flat rate? How are the charges determined, and how frequent are the payments?

As I consider the many discussions[5] we have had on reducing operating costs, I am inclined to try the time-share system. Please investigate[6] whether or not we can subscribe for a trial period before entering into a full contract agreement.[7] (141)

4

MEMO TO: Nancy Harper

When we met yesterday, I explained that we will need to have color graphs for the budget[1] report that is *due* next week. However, I may not have explained that we will need additional information[2] for the report. We will need the following items: a profit and loss statement for the new line of software,[3] a printout that compares this year's earnings with those of previous years, and projected earnings for the next five years.[4]

The report should be printed and bound. I know that this represents a substantial amount of work and preparation,[5] but it is necessary that we present this information. To help you with this project, I am assigning[6] two employees from our word processing department to work with you. You will also have full use of a conference[7] room until your work is *completed.* If you have questions, please bring them to me at any time. (158)

due: needed, expected

completed: finished, done

5

MEMO TO: Margaret Roy

We have had many problems with the accounting software we purchased in February.[1] After giving much consideration to this issue, I have decided that this software cannot do the[2] work we require. It is not comprehensive enough to meet our needs. Furthermore, it would be an expensive mistake[3] to continue using it.

There are several other systems that might work, but we are hesitant to make[4] a decision until we have had a chance to compare the performance of each. It might be possible to rent[5] sample programs for a limited period of time. Because it is important to choose the right system,[6] I feel that it would be worthwhile to experiment. I know that trying different systems means that our employees[7] will have to adjust to many changes in procedures. However, we do not want to make the same mistake of[8] purchasing the wrong product.

Please give me your reactions to this plan. (172)

LESSON 54

Shorthand Vocabulary Review

1. Retain the initial and root-word vowel when adding prefixes and suffixes. When a prefix contains a long vowel followed by a root-word vowel, omit the prefix vowel.

truly	trul	reorder	rod
payable	paB	uneasy	ueze
unusable	uuzB	disappoint	Dapy
cooperation	copj	reorganize	rog

2. Write h for the word ending *hood.* Write g for the word ending *gram.*

neighborhood	nbrh	cablegram	cBg
childhood	Cldh	telegram	tlg
likelihood	lclh	program	Pg

3. Write w for the word ending *ward.*

award	aw	toward	tw
reward	rw	forward	fw
onward	ow	awkward	acw

Transcription Aids: Spelling

Learn to distinguish between words ending in *ent* and *ant*.

ent		**ant**	
prevent	PvN	tenant	tnN
recent	rsN	warrant	◡rN
confident	kfdN	constant	kSN
apparent	aprN	rampant	r—pN
current	crN	pursuant	PsuN
consistent	ksSN	errant	erN

Your Business Vocabulary

functioning fqN- Performing an assigned duty or action; operating.

The photocopier is now functioning correctly.

hard copy hrd cpe Information that has been printed on paper.

Electronic mail eliminates much of the need for hard copy.

Reading and Writing Exercises

1

Preview Words

unused	uuz-	reliability	rliB^l
entirely	ntrl	functioning	fqj-
actually	acCull	substantial	sSnsl
damaged	dj-	compensated	kpNa-

dr Cbrs ev
vp- sres Pblms
— r l8 od v Dcs
lae rsv- f u, ev
uz- 47 v 1H Dcs
lae od-, ufCnll, 3 Paren
v loz uz- v pv-
lb dj-, ly apr-
lb fqj- w bgn, b Conj
ev acCull l8 ntr
fls o loz Dcs> er
rel r dj- Dcs
alq — r 53 uuz-

Dcs, ehp la uc
rcvr r inf kln-
o dj- Dcs, edlc
lvu rpls r Dcs er
rel — ntrl nu
dse, lu l8 r nu
Dcs l esl lr rliB^l x>
r Pblms cz- b lz
dj- Dcs v rzll-
n . sSnsl vpN +
nkv f r co, edlc
lb kpNa- f ls vpN,
l du u suq x vlu

2

Preview Words

bids	bds	renovation	rnvj
defined	dfn-	remodeling	r⌒dl
media	⌒da	electronic	elnc
forgotten	fgln	structural	SrcCrl

mo l brNa ⌒Cl
lgf lM r⌒rcs (
Sf ⌒e ls ⌒rn.
u⌒ qi ri l brq
p (sugj lae rvu
r plns f r⌒dl (
sMrl recs ofs. Alo
e dru p lz plns
nrl . yr aq, e s⌒ (Intro DC)
lv fgln l flo p
o ls ⌒lr, idlc
lvu Sde loz plns
crfl. if u blv la
ly r apo + aql
f r crM + fCr
nds, il v (bs (Intro DC)
ofs sM h⌒ ol f

bds ⌒l. sM
dra p loz plns, - (Intro P)
ev Cnj- r Psyrs
f Sr recs. ev k
l rli ⌒ po Dcs
f Srj, + e no rli (Conj)
ls po hrd cpe. du
(rnvj plns alo
enf sps f Srj v
elnc ⌒da, + , la (Conj)
sps aqll dfn-x>
⌒n e ⌒c lz
SrcCrl Cnjs, (Intro DC)
esd b Sln la (
Cnjs l akda r
nds f sv yrs lk.

3

Preview Words

series

error

Germany

warranty

overseas

consequences

transmitting

mechanical

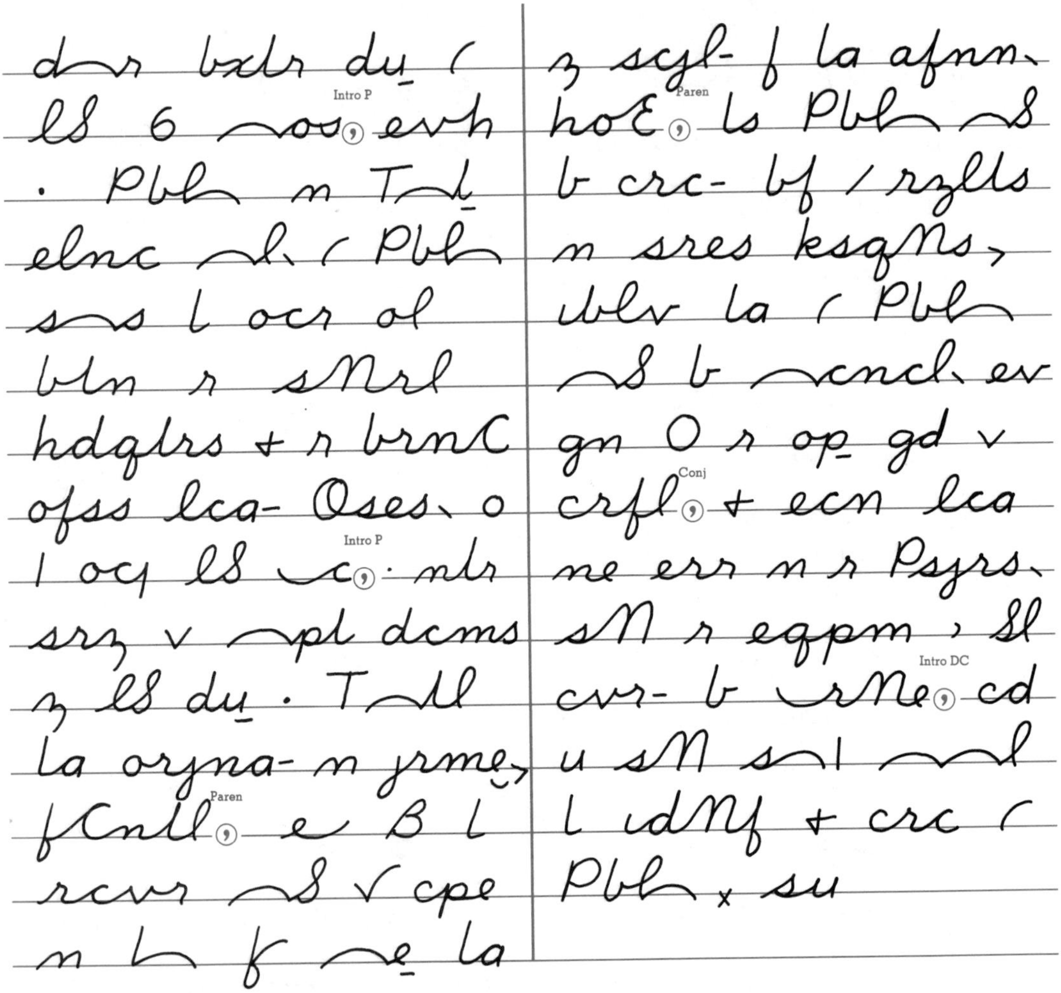

4

Supply two words that are missing in the following letter.

Preview Words

terminal *Lrml*	exercises *vszs*
creating *cra_*	previously *Pvesl*
welcome *lk*	independently *NpNNl*
confidently *kfdNl*	training manual *Lrn_ mul*

---

mo L rd Pss_
oprs lk L ls Lrn_
sy, ur hr L rsv
. Ndy L r nu
sflr f r rd
Pss_ dpl, r alC-
Lrn_ mul l so
u ho luz u Lrml
f cra_ ₍Series₎ edl_ ₍Series₎ prN_ ₍Series₎
+ Sr_ dcms, af kp_
ls mul, ₍Intro P₎ ulb B
luz u o fy L
Pds dcms la lc v
Pfyl, yl ₍Paren₎ lz dcms

l rq ls Ln hf
r L uv Pvesl
L Pds fns-
cpe, ulb B ls
gcl ₍Series₎ NpNNl ₍Series₎ +
kfdNl, ls eqpm
, dzn- L c u
o z eze +
fre v z
psB, p fl fre L
asc qs ze o
Lru r vszs kln-
n ls mul,

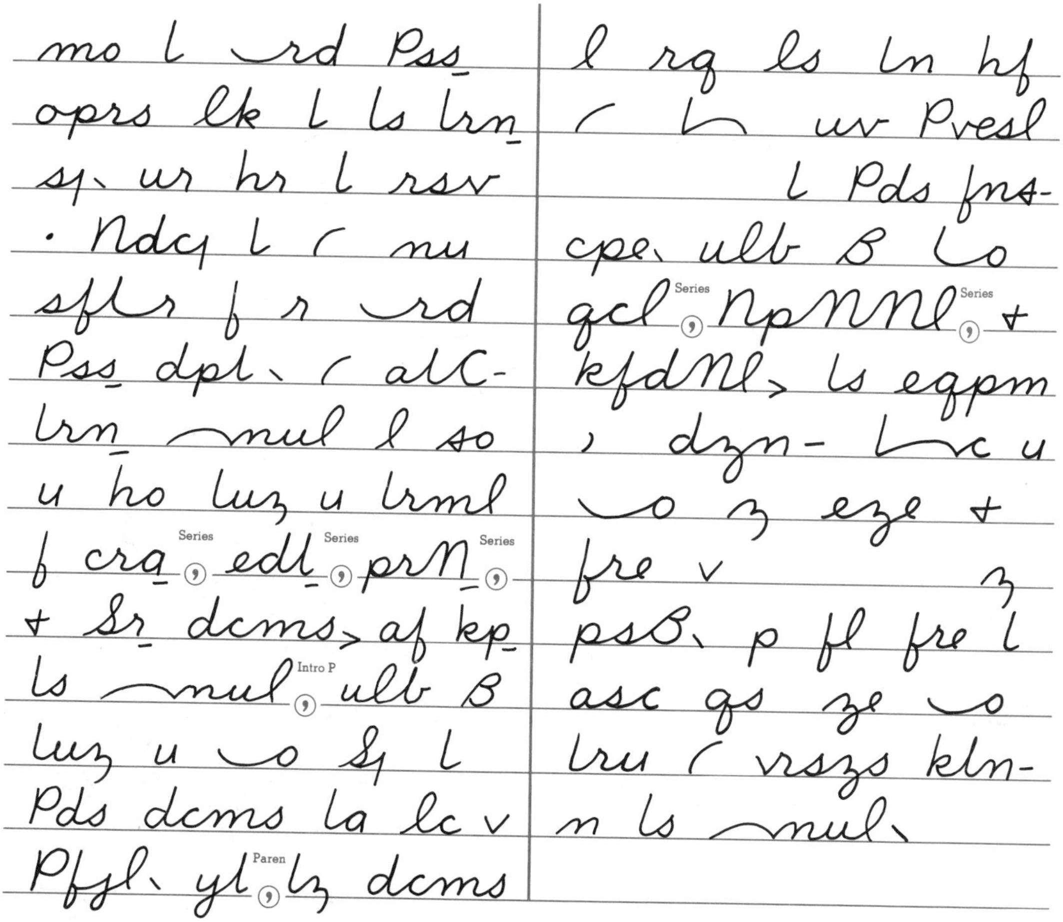

5

Punctuation Study

Add commas to show one parenthetical expression and three introductory dependent clauses.

Preview Words

index Nx

worry ⌣re

analysts alSs

improper ⌒Ppr

greatly grl

damaged dy-

aggravation agrvj

occasionally ocyll

ds evns enc- r 6
3 nu Dcs kln_ 11
cpe ⌣C e Tfr- 16
f (dy- Dcs, 21
⌣n u rvu (25
dcm Nx f eC 30
Dc ul se la e⌣ 37
B l rcvr ⌒S 41
√ M_ cpe la z 47
lS ⌣n u old 50
Dcs ⌣ dy-> r 55
alSs blv la (61
dy rzlt- f⌒ 65

⌒Ppr cr √ Dcs, 70
ze vpln- dy_ (76
lrn_ sys Dcs rq 83
crf hNl_ + spsl 88
arms f Sry, if u 95
Sr l⌒ Pprl ul 101
grl rds (rsc 106
√ dy> ocyll hoE 113
. Dc , dy- f 117
no aprN rzn, 121
la , y ^ avzB 127
l⌒c ⌒ ln l cpe 133
√ E Dc u uz, 137

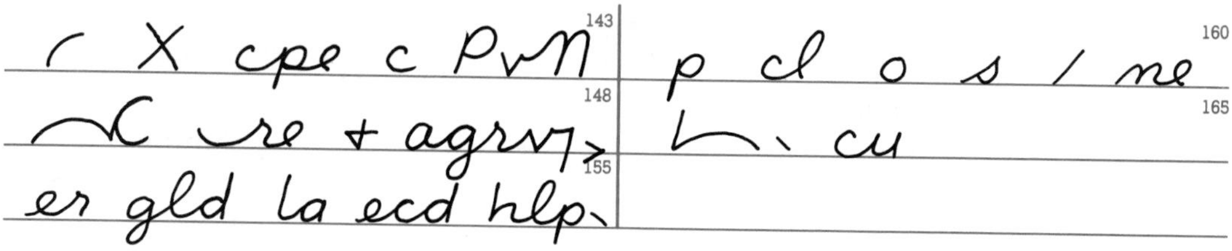

Key

1

Dear Mr. Chambers:

We have experienced serious problems with the last order of disks that we received from[1] you. We have used 47 of the 100 disks that we ordered. Unfortunately, three of those used have[2] proved to be damaged. They appeared to be functioning in the beginning, but we have actually lost entire[3] files on those disks.

We are returning the damaged disks along with the 53 unused disks. We hope that you can[4] recover the information contained on the damaged disks. We would like to have you replace the disks we are[5] returning with entirely new merchandise. Will you test the new disks to establish their reliability?[6]

The problems caused by these damaged disks have resulted in a substantial expense and inconvenience for our[7] company. We would like to be compensated for this expense. What do you suggest?

Very truly yours, (157)

2

MEMO TO: Brenda Mitchell

Thank you for your excellent remarks at the staff meeting this morning. You were quite right[1] to bring up the suggestion that we review our plans for remodeling the central records office. Although we[2] drew up these plans nearly a year ago, we seem to have forgotten to follow up on this matter.

I would like[3] to have you study those plans carefully. If you believe that they are appropriate and adequate for our current[4] and future needs, I will have the business office send them out for bids immediately. Since drawing up those[5] plans, we have changed our procedures for storing records. We have come to rely more upon disks for storage, and we[6] now rely less upon hard copy. Do the renovation plans allow enough space for storage of electronic[7] media, and is that space adequately defined?

When we make these structural changes, we should be certain[8] that the changes will accommodate our needs for several years to come. (173)

3

Dear Mr. Baxter:

During the last six months, we have had a problem in transmitting electronic mail. The problem[1] seems to occur only between our central headquarters and our branch offices located overseas. On[2] one occasion last week, an entire series of important documents was lost during a transmittal that[3] originated in Germany.

Fortunately, we were able to recover most of the copy in time[4] for the meeting that was scheduled for that afternoon. However, this problem must be corrected before it results[5] in serious consequences.

I believe that the problem must be mechanical. We have gone over our[6] operating guide very carefully, and we cannot locate any error in our procedures. Since our[7] equipment is still covered by warranty, could you send someone immediately to identify and correct[8] the problem?

Sincerely yours, (164)

4

MEMO TO: Word Processing Operators

Welcome to this training session. You are here to receive an introduction[1] to the new software for our word processing department. The attached training manual will show you how[2] to use your terminal for creating, editing, printing, and storing documents.

After completing this[3] manual, you will be able to use your work station to produce documents that look very professional. Yet,[4] these documents will require less than half the time you have previously *needed* to produce finished copy. You[5] will be able to work quickly, independently, and confidently.

This equipment is designed to make your[6] work as easy and free of *errors* as possible. Please feel free to ask questions as we work through the exercises[7] contained in this manual. (146)

needed: taken, required

errors: mistakes, problems

5

Dear Ms. Evans:

Enclosed are three new disks containing copy which we transferred from the damaged disks. When you review[1] the document index for each disk, you will see that we were able to recover most of the missing copy[2] that was lost when your old disks were damaged.

Our analysts believe that the damage resulted from improper care[3] of the disks. As we explained during the training sessions, disks require careful handling and special arrangements[4] for storage. If you store them properly, you will greatly reduce the risk of damage.

Occasionally, however,[5] a disk is damaged for no apparent reason. That is why it is advisable to make more than one copy[6] of every disk you use. The extra copy can prevent much worry and aggravation.

We are glad that we[7] could help. Please call on us at any time.

Cordially yours, (150)

LESSON 55

Word Development

Develop new words from the following brief forms:

present

presents	*Ps*
presenting	*P̠*
presently	*Pl*
presentations	*Pjs*
presentable	*PB*

general

generals	*jns*
generally	*jnl*
generalist	*jnS*
generalize	*jnz*
generality	*jnl*

under

underscore	*Uscr*
underwriter	*Urir*
undertaking	*Uc̱*
understandable	*USNB*
misunderstand	*mUSN*

underneath	*Unl*
underlying	*Uli̱*
underline	*Uln*
Underwood	*Ud̠*
undergraduate	*Ugrjul*

Reading and Writing Exercises

1

Preview Words

team		operation	opj
aspect	aspc	functions	fqjs
workshop	osp	registration	rjSrj
seminar	smr	enrollments	nrlms

d ex erp- l nvr
u l . smr f rll
bss, (Pps v ls
smr lb l so
ors + yrs ho
ly c uz lr kpur
eqpm l aCv grr
efsNe n lr OA
opj> (enc- brsr
dSs (vres fqjs
la lb Dcs-, z uc
se, (Intro DC) lr r me as
n C u eqpm

cb uz- l vrsz
kl O E aspc
vu opj> Alo uc
alN ls osp
f . v rznB fe, (Intro DC)
nrlms r bl-,
sN u rjSrj ld,
n od l rzrv .
pls fu + ol mbrs
vu ym l, (Intro P) . dpzl
S b l- f eC
Psn, elb lc fw
lv u jyn s, su

–––––––––––––––––––––––– **2** ––––––––––––––––––––––––

Preview Words

noon *nn*   priority *prurˡ*

payroll *parl*   activities *acv ᴸ*

inventory *nvnlre*   imperative *prv*

analysis *anlss*   particularly *plcl*

---

*mo L bl crvr du
L ncrss w cS v
ppr + prM Svss⊙
e ⌐a nd Lⁿc
Cnjs n r op‾
byl, ls dsy lb
⌐d ⌠ byl ⌐e‾
o Fr, p rn · anlss
v parl⊙ nvnlre⊙
Av‾⊙ + ol Ohd cSs,
Ppr 6 cpes vu rpl
+ D L L A dpl*

*hds b nn o Th,
af ev A h · opl
L Sde ⌐ rpl + l
Ppr s rcmys⊙ el
esl · pln f rds‾
cSs, p gv ls Pjc
prurˡ O A ol acv ᴸ.
ino la ls, · plcl
bze L ru no⊙ b
s prv la ev
ls inf sn,*

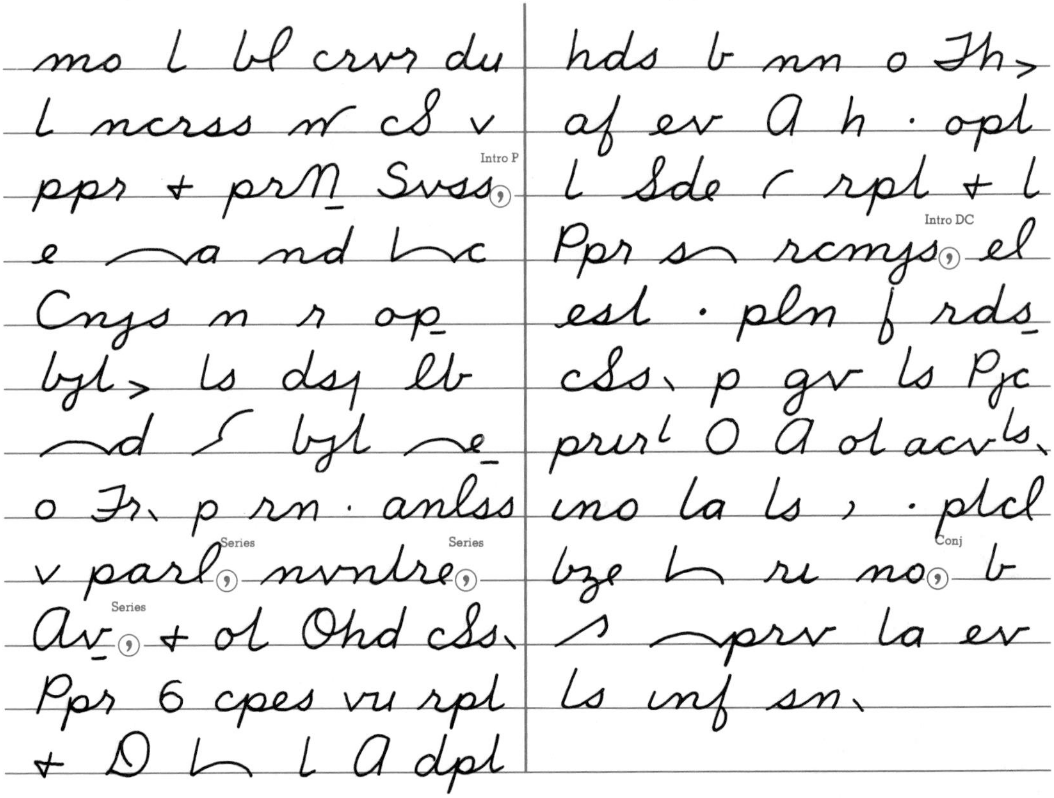

3

Preview Words

trace

worth

color

functions

graphic

original

wherever

highlight

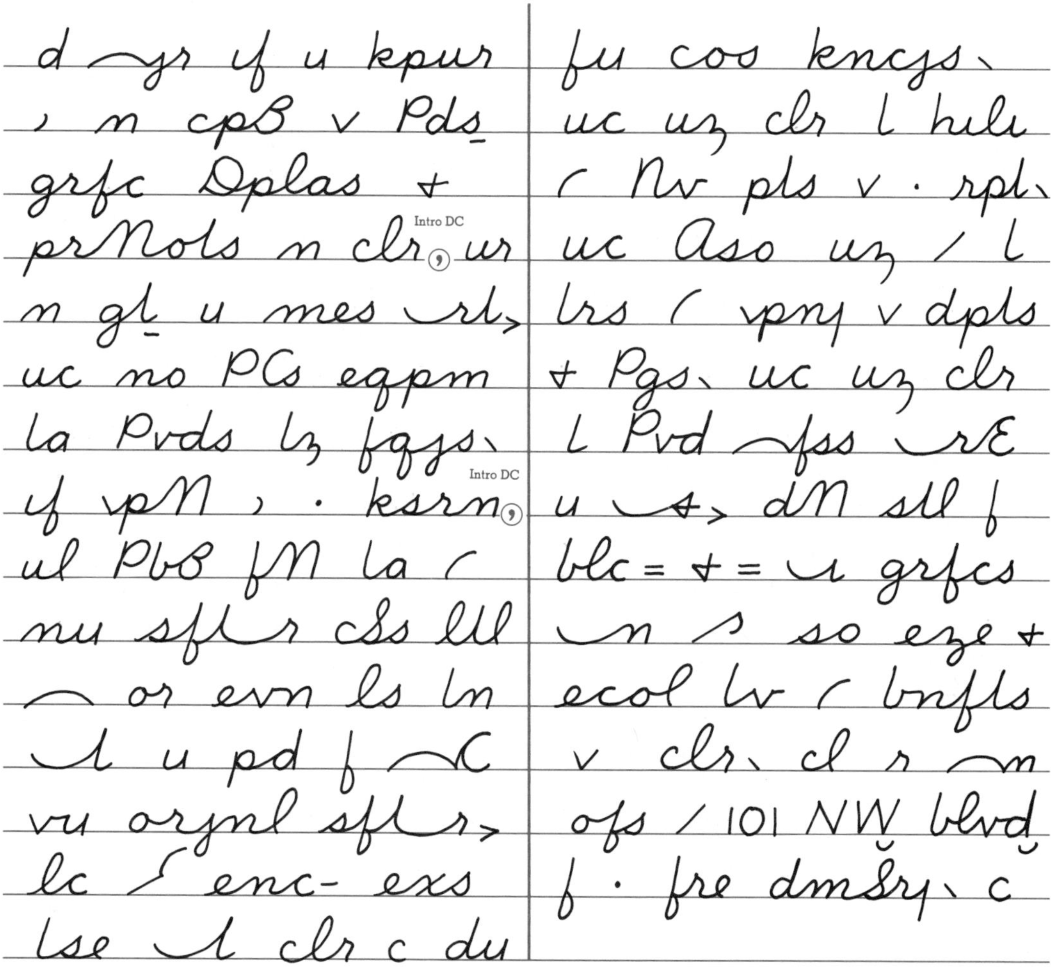

4

Supply two words that are missing in the following letter.

Preview Words

file *fl*

skills *scls*

asset *asl*

series

srz

valuable *vluß*

candidates *cddls*

qualifications *qlfjs*

Western Electronics

Wrn elncs

---

dns dvnpl lqf
NS n Wrn elncs, [Ab]
inc. Alo ev no
opn f s⌒l ⌣ u
qlfjs / ls ⌐ [Intro DC]
el cp u L o fl,
opn ocr frqNl
n n ⌣rd Pss
dpl, + er A NS- [Conj]
n Nvu qlf-cddls.
acrd l ⌐rz⌒a
u   l n ofs, [Intro P]
uv lcn sv crss
n ⌣rd Pss zlz

dla Pss, ls lrn
l Sv z · vluß
asl n u ⌒pm
SC, y udlc ⌐c
· apym lk nl n
Psnl ofs, el ar [Intro DC]
lgv u · srz v
lss ldl ⌐ lvl
vu scls. u ⌒a
Aso lc ⌣ n Psnl
drn / la ⌐ ⌣ n
· pzj bks avlß, [Intro DC]
ulb   ⌐ su

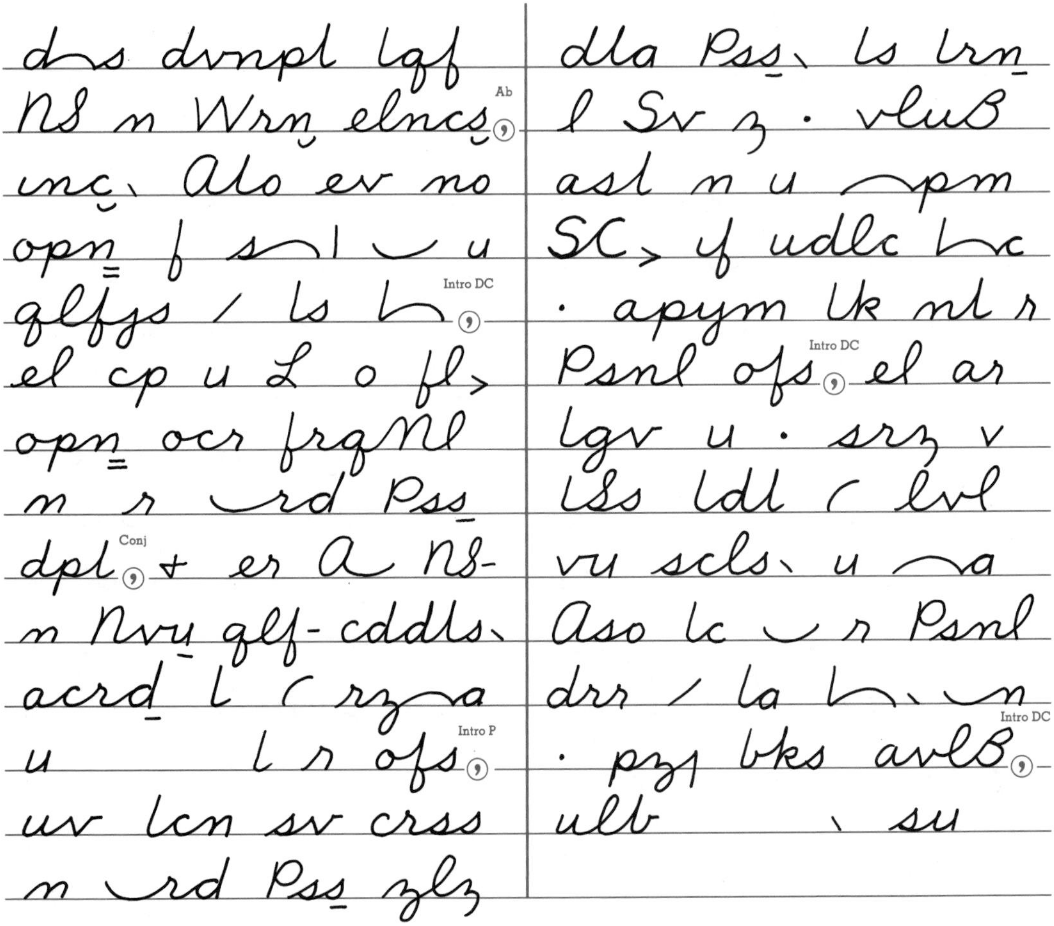

5

Punctuation Study

Add commas to show one conjunction, two introductory dependent clauses, and the omission of *and.*

Preview Words

master

erasing

correctly

outdated

accessing

duplicate

programmed

classification

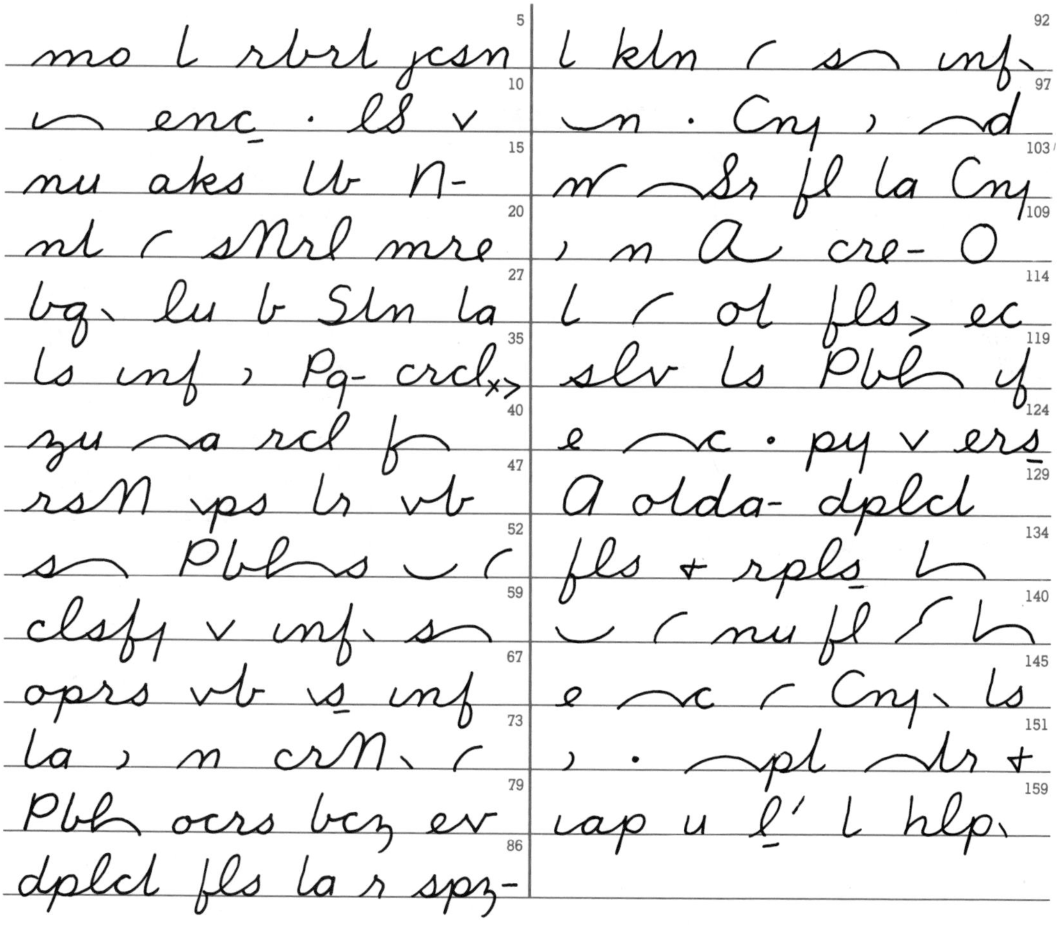

Key

1

Dear Executive:

We are pleased to invite you to a seminar for retail businesses. The purpose of this[1] seminar will be to show owners and managers how they can use their computer equipment to achieve greater[2] efficiency in their overall operation.

The enclosed brochure describes the various functions that[3] will be discussed. As you can see, there are many ways in which your equipment can be used to exercise more[4] control over every aspect of your operation.

Although you can attend this workshop for a very[5] reasonable fee, enrollments are limited. Send your registration today. In order to reserve a place for[6] you and other members of your management team, a deposit must be included for each person.

We will be[7] looking forward to having you join us.

Sincerely yours, (150)

2

MEMO TO: Bill Carver

Due to increases in the cost of paper and printing services, we may need to make[1] changes in our operating budget.

This decision will be made at the budget meeting on Friday. Please run[2] an analysis of payroll, inventory, advertising, and other overhead costs. Prepare six copies[3] of your report and distribute them to all department heads by noon on Thursday.

After we have all had an[4] opportunity to study the report and to prepare some recommendations, we will establish a plan for[5] reducing costs. Please give this project priority over all other activities. I know that this is a[6] particularly busy time right now, but it is imperative that we have this information soon. (139)

3

Dear Manager:

If your computer is not capable of producing graphic displays and printouts in color,[1] you are not getting your money's worth.

You can now purchase equipment that provides these functions. If expense is a[2] concern, you will probably find that the new software costs little more or even less than what you paid for much of[3] your original software.

Look at the enclosed examples to see what color can do for your company's[4] communications. You can use color to highlight the individual parts of a report. You can also[5] use it to trace the expansion of departments and programs. You can use color to provide emphasis wherever[6] you wish.

Don't settle for black-and-white graphics when it is so easy and economical to have the benefits[7] of color. Call our main office at 101 Northwest Boulevard for a free demonstration.

Cordially,[8] (160)

4

Dear Ms. Davenport:

Thank you for your interest in Western Electronics, Inc. Although we have[1] no openings for someone with your qualifications at this time, we will keep your letter on file.

Openings[2] occur frequently in our word processing department, and we are always interested in interviewing[3] qualified candidates. According to the resumé you *sent* to our office, you have taken several courses[4] in word processing as well as data processing. This training will serve as a valuable asset in[5] your employment search.

If you would like to make an appointment to come into our personnel office, we will arrange[6] to give you a series of tests to determine the level of your skills. You may also talk with our personnel[7] director at that time. When a position becomes available, you will be *notified.*

Sincerely yours,[8] (160)

sent: mailed

notified: contacted, informed

5

MEMO TO: Robert Jackson

I am enclosing a list of new accounts to be entered into the central[1] memory bank. Will you be certain that this information is programmed correctly?

As you may recall from recent[2] experiences, there have been some problems with the classification of information. Some operators[3] have been accessing information that is not current. The problem occurs because we have duplicate files that[4] are supposed to contain the same information. When a change is made in the master file, that change is not always[5] carried over to the other files.

We can solve this problem if we make a point of erasing all outdated,[6] duplicate files and replacing them with the new file at the time we make the change. This is an important matter,[7] and I appreciate your willingness to help. (149)

unl 12

gvl*

Shorthand Vocabulary Review

Study the following words and the principles they illustrate. Look for these words in the letters and memos of this unit.

Write a capital *a* for the word beginnings *ad* and *al* (pronounced *add*, *al*, or *all*).

advice	avs	also	aso
adversely	avrsl	alternate	alrnl
advisory	avzre	although	alo
advise	avz	almost	a⌒S
inadequate	naql	all	a

***Unit Twelve**
Government

More About Punctuation

1. A dash is sometimes used to indicate a sudden change in thought.

I need the rental car for four days—possibly five.

A dash may also be used for added emphasis or further explanation.

The manager indicated that Ronald Green—our noteworthy colleague—has been named salesman of the month.

2. Parentheses may be used to contain explanatory or supplementary information.

Did you know that 75 percent of the sample (600 people) responded to the questionnaire?

Parentheses are also used to set off a digression—a thought that is unrelated to the main idea of the sentence.

The annual report (of which we printed 800 copies) will be released to the public on Monday.

LESSON 56

Brief Forms and Derivatives

1. *on* *cos* *pp* *r* *e* *ord*
2. *pb* *Sd* *hsps* *opns* *aso-* *apv*

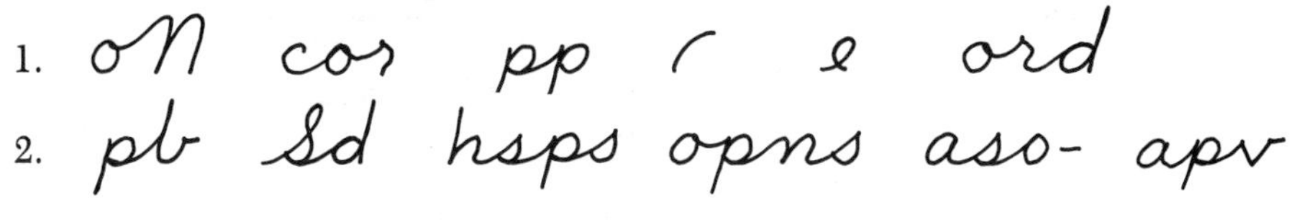

Key

1. once, correspond/correspondence, participate, the, we, ordinary
2. public, standard, hospitals, opinions, associated, appreciative

Phrase Review

1. *isl* *eh* *eno* *ecb* *esd* *lofr*
2. *Lpa* *luz* *zl* *vh* *lu* *lu*

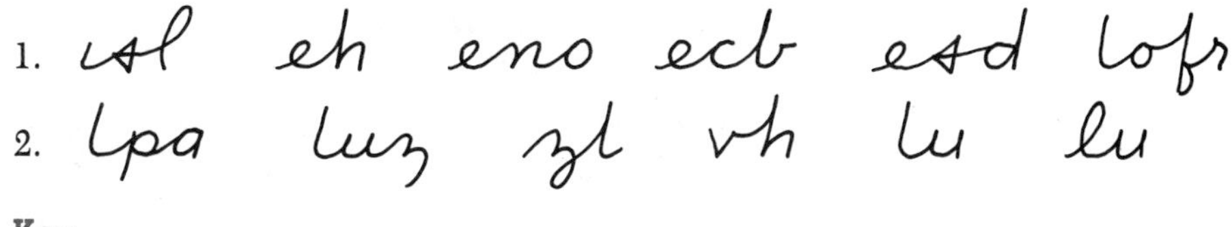

Key

1. I shall, we had, we know, we can be, we should, to offer
2. to pay, to use, as to, have had, to you/to your, will you/will your

Reading and Writing Exercises

———————————— 1 ————————————

Preview Words

refresh *rfrs*   auditing *adt_*

workload *old*   registration *rjsry*

positive *pzv*   substantially *sSnsll*

participation *ppy*   reorganization *rogy*

mo l adl Svzrs
l hlp rfrs u nly
v adl Psyrs, (Intro P) e
pln lofr clss bgn
o Mn, (Date) Nv 4. p se
(alC- scyl v clss>
evh . v pzv rsp
l lz clss n pS, (Conj)
+ er hp la ppl
lb evn grr ls yr.
z . rzll v rsN
rogl n ls dpl, (Intro P) (
old v eC adlr
hs ncrs- sSnsll.

s pl ln E
f eC Psn luz (
S acrl + efsN
ns psB l kp ,
or hr o> s r
ayNes plse lpa (
fes. pes hu alN
lz clss l rsv
1hr v cly cr f (
sle U. (fnl da
f rySry , Oc 22>
if uv adyl qs, (Intro DC) u
a cl e / dny
191.

2

Preview Words

Health	hll	emergency	e rjNe
funding	fN	ambulance	a blN
primary	pr re	legislature	lyslCr
maintain	nln	coordination	cordny

d rqS f
adyl fN z apv-

b (lyslCr. z .
rzll, (Paren) isl b B l

esl · nu ofs w
dpl v hll + sfle.
⌒n e Dcs- (ida
v ls ofs, (Intro DC) u prs-
NS n apl f pzj
v drr> (nu ofs
lb rspB f cordnj
+ ⌒ym v A erzNe
⌒dcl Svss w Sa.
ls Is a⌒blN Svss
ofr- b hsps, (Series) fr dpls, (Series)
+ prvl ajNes.
(pr⌒re objcv

v nu drr lb l
esl + ⌒mln ·
hi Sd v gl f A
erzNe Svss> e
ordl pS · fnl
anoNm v ls jb
opn. A aplcNs
l rsv gdlns pln
(slcj Pss. (fnl
cddls lb Nvu-
Nvl, (Conj) + · dsj lb
⌒d no lar ln
Jn 1. s

3

Preview Words

adopt	adpl	paramedic	pr⌒dc
agenda	ajNa	foundation	foNj
strong	Srq	supplement	splm
moment	⌒m	self-explanatory	sfxplnlre

mo l mbrs v
sle ksl hr, (

ajNa f Sp ⌒e.
p nls la sv sle

dpls r rqS byl
ncrss. [ ] Ppr-
[ ]c . Srq rcmy
lae lB lz rqSs
ull ecb Sln v
unf P-> . rep f[ ]
r hsp foNy l
adrs r ksl o
syc v [ ]dcl Svss.
s r foNys rcmy
la r sle adpl .

pr[ ]dc Pq l splm
r e[ ]yNe Svss no
b ofr-. r brd l
P . f[ ]l Ppzl olln
r Amv Psyrs +
cSs v sC . Pq.
p lc . [ ]m l rd
r alC- cpe v la
Ppzl> r s[ ]n
[ ]s o ayNa s
sfxplntre.

4

Supply two words that are missing in the following letter.

Preview Words

forth fl
safety sfle
remedied s[ ]de-
guidelines gdlns
violation vly
regulations rglys
inspection nspcy
instances nSNs

d[ ]s dvdsn ls
L , n re l r
sfle nspcy [ ]C
z rsNe n
u plN. r rzlts
v la nspcy s [ ]n

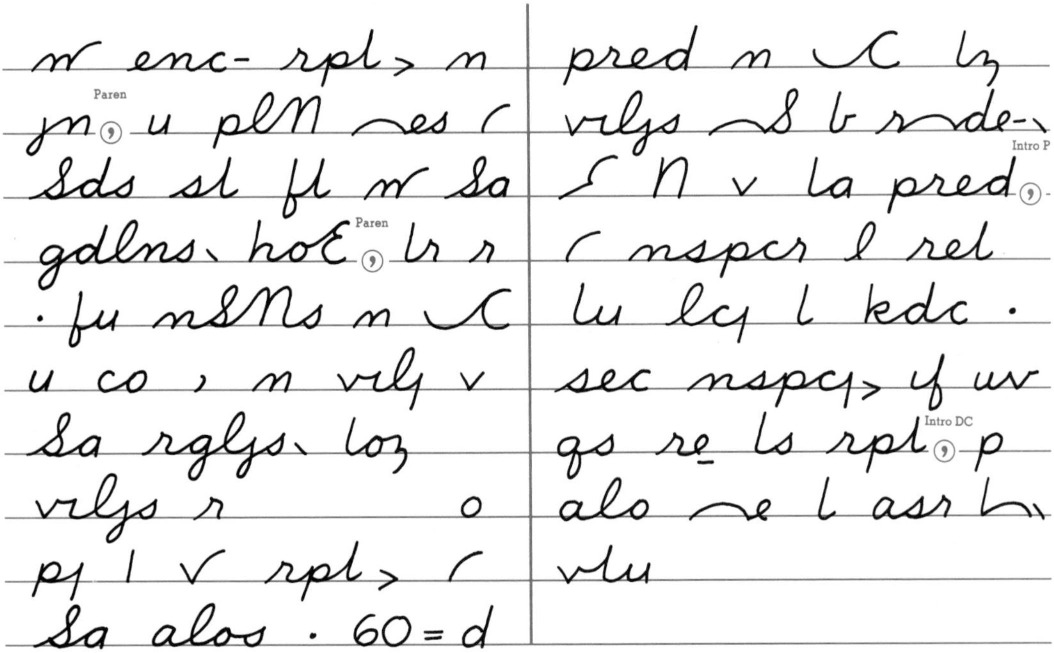

5

Punctuation Study

Add commas to show one conjunction, two introductory dependent clauses, and one parenthetical expression.

Preview Words

- main
- acres
- adopted
- landowner
- revenue
- drainage
- courthouse
- assessments

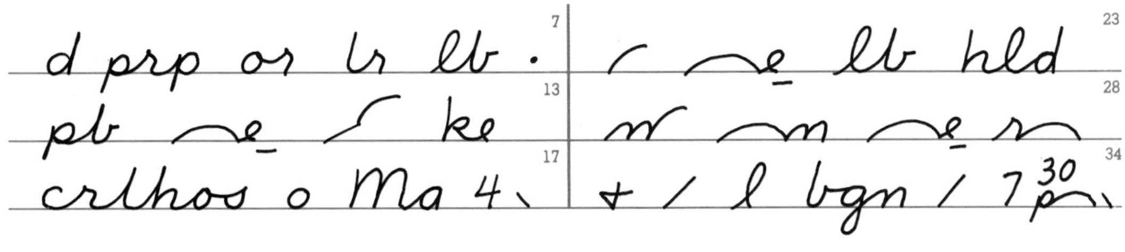

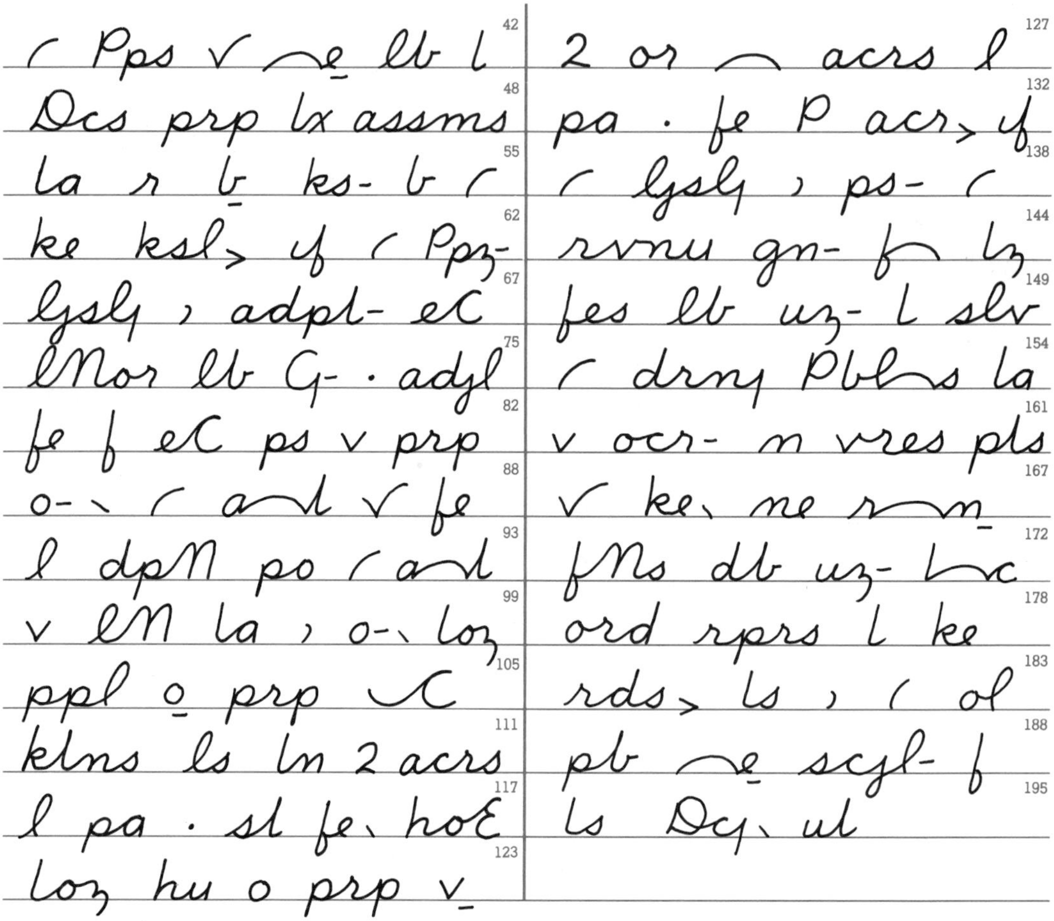

Key

1

MEMO TO: Audit Supervisors

To help refresh your knowledge of auditing procedures, we plan to offer[1] classes beginning on Monday, November 4. Please see the attached schedule of classes.

We have had a very[2] positive response to these classes in the past, and we are hoping that participation will be even greater[3] this year. As a result of the recent reorganization in this department, the workload of each auditor[4] has increased substantially. It is more important than ever for each person to use the most accurate[5] and efficient means possible to complete his or her work.

It is our agency's policy to pay the fees.[6] Employees who attend these classes will receive one hour of college credit from the city university.[7] The final date for registration is October 22.

If you have additional questions, you may[8] call me at extension 191. (166)

2

Dear Jim:

My request for additional funding was approved by the legislature. As a result, I shall be[1] able to establish a new office in the Department of Health and Safety. When we discussed the idea[2] of this office, you expressed interest in applying for the position of director.

The new office will be[3] responsible for the coordination and management of all emergency medical services[4] in the state. This includes ambulance services offered by hospitals, fire departments, and private agencies.[5] The primary objective of the new director will be to establish and maintain a high standard of[6] quality for all emergency services.

We ordinarily post a formal announcement of this job[7] opening. All applicants will receive guidelines explaining the selection process. The final candidates will be[8] interviewed individually, and a decision will be made no later than June 1.

Sincerely, (179)

3

MEMO TO: Members of the City Council

Here is the agenda for the September meeting. Please notice that[1] several city departments are requesting budget increases. I am prepared to make a strong recommendation[2] that we table these requests until we can be certain of the information presented.

A representative[3] from the hospital foundation will address the council on the subject of medical services. It is[4] the foundation's recommendation that the city adopt a paramedic program to supplement the[5] emergency services now being offered. The board will present a formal proposal outlining the[6] administrative procedures and costs of such a program. Please take a moment to read the attached copy of[7] that proposal.

The remaining items on the agenda are self-explanatory. (156)

4

Dear Mr. Davidson:

This letter is in regard to the safety inspection which was recently *conducted*[1] in your plant. The results of that inspection are shown in the enclosed report.

In general, your plant meets the standards[2] set forth in the state guidelines. However, there are a few instances in which your company is in violation[3] of state regulations. Those violations are *shown* on page 1 of the report.

The state allows a 60-day[4] period in which these violations must be remedied. At the end of that period, the inspector[5] will return to your location to conduct a second inspection.

If you have questions regarding this report,[6] please allow me to answer them.

Very truly yours, (130)

conducted: made, completed   shown: listed, given

5

Dear Property Owner:

There will be a public meeting at the county courthouse on May 4. The meeting will be[1] held in the main meeting room, and it will begin at 7:30 p.m. The purpose of the meeting will be[2] to discuss property tax assessments that are being considered by the county council.

If the proposed[3] legislation is adopted, each landowner will be charged an additional fee for each piece of property[4] owned. The amount of the fee will depend upon the amount of land that is owned. Those people owning property[5] which contains less than two acres will pay a set fee. However, those who own property having two or more acres[6] will pay a fee per acre.

If the legislation is passed, the revenue gained from these fees will be used to solve[7] the drainage problems that have occurred in various parts of the county. Any remaining funds would be used[8] to make ordinary repairs to county roads.

This is the only public meeting scheduled for this discussion.

Yours[9] truly, (181)

LESSON 57

Abbreviations and Derivatives

1. enc jr sr sec agrl
2. secl Amr Amv reps Ss

Key

1. enclose/enclosure, junior, senior, second/secretary, agricultural
2. secretarial, administrator, administrative, represents, streets

Transcription Aids: Typing Abbreviations

To indicate academic degrees, use capitals and periods as follows. Notice that no space is used between the initials.

B.S. (Bachelor of Science)
Ph.D. (Doctor of Philosophy)
D.D.S. (Doctor of Dental Surgery)
M.B.A. (Master of Business Administration)
LL.B. (Bachelor of Law)
M.D. (Doctor of Medicine)
D.D. (Doctor of Divinity)

Abbreviations of many government agencies and commissions do not require periods.

United Nations (UN)
United States Air Force (USAF)
Federal Communications Commission (FCC)
Federal Deposit Insurance Corporation (FDIC)
Federal Trade Commission (FTC)
United States Department of Agriculture (USDA)

Your Business Vocabulary	depleted	*dple-*	Used up; emptied.
			We have depleted our supply of paper.
	restoration	*rSry*	Reconstruction; returning something to a condition much like its original state.
			The museum hires renowned artists to complete the restoration of valuable paintings that have been damaged.

Reading and Writing Exercises

1

Preview Words

fell *fl*

winter *Nr*

critical *crtcl*

postpone *pSpn*

depleted *dple-*

excessive *\sv*

precautions *Pcjs*

snow removal *sno r \wl*

mo l hnre Co
du l (\sv a\l
v sno la fl l8
Nr, [Intro P] (fNs la
h b rzrv- f sno
r \wl dple-
erl r yr, f ev
evn hf z \C

sno l8 Nr z
eh l8 yr, [Intro DC] elb u8
lcp r 8s clr, sN
E dpl , lc X Pcjs
l avryd ncrs s
bjl, [Intro DC] l suq lau
pSpn s 8 rprs
ull nx sr, v

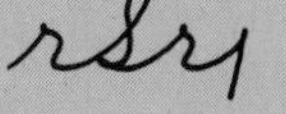

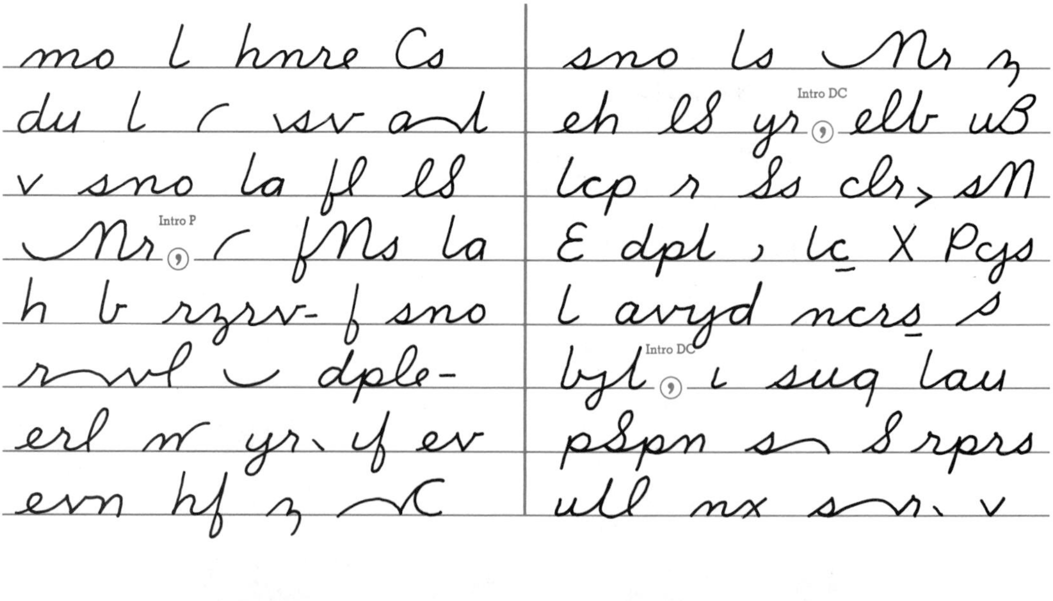

crs, [Paren] lr r s aras
la rq m all +
cn wa la lq. n
ol aras, [Paren] hoE, [Paren] (
nd na b nC
ls crlcl> if ec
dla lz rprs ull

(sno szn hs
ps-, [Intro DC] ec ln uz (
r m̲ fNs z nd-.
p gv ls Ppzl sres
ksj + ll ne no
u fl̿.

2

Preview Words

facing fs̲
weigh wa
whole hl
factors fcrs
surprised Sprz-
beneficial bnfsl
conservation ksrvj
environmental nvrnml

dr r rCrds uz p-
+ Sprz- l rd ab
r ksrvj efls n u
rsN nzpprarlcl.
lqf gv̲ (rdrs .
lN ak v nvrnml
Pbls la er fs̲> n
gld lau nd . py

v Dcs̲ sv slys l
(Pbls. Alo r
dpl dz n Pz
lv (crc asr E
l, [Intro DC] edu ald l
fN slys la l bnfl
ssiˡ z . hl. n od
lc la Cys, [Intro P] e wa

[shorthand outlines]

3

Preview Words

phase *[shorthand]*

downtown *[shorthand]*

beautiful *[shorthand]*

publicity *[shorthand]*

budgetary *[shorthand]*

construction *[shorthand]*

limitations *[shorthand]*

anniversary *[shorthand]*

[shorthand outlines]

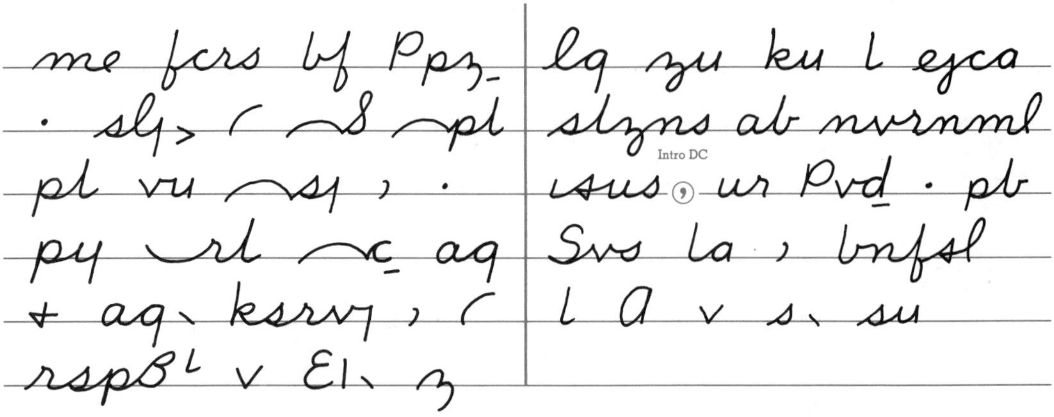

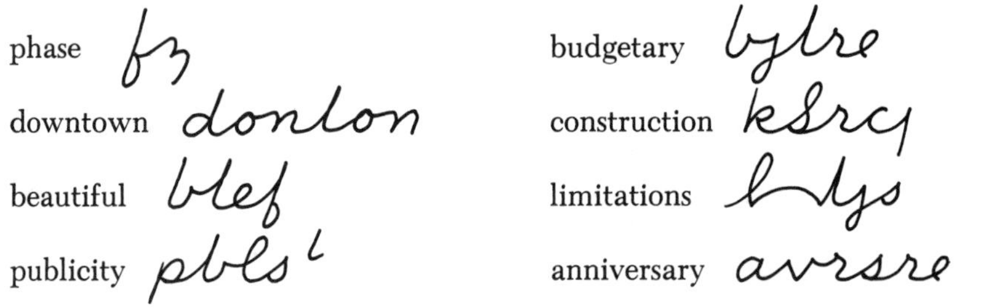

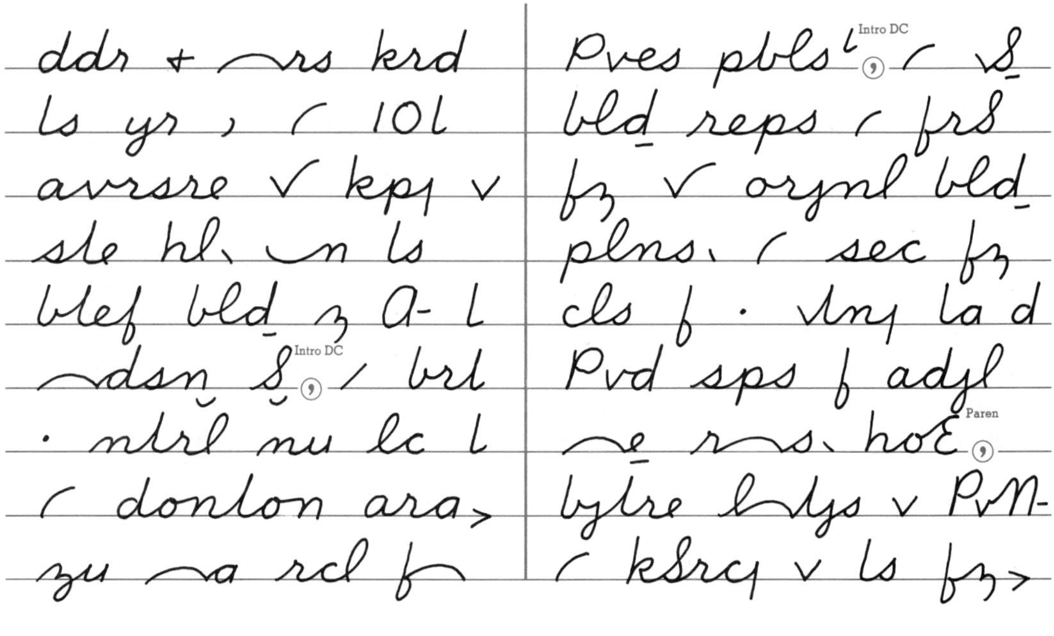

z · spsl gfl l
slbra (avrsre v
ls ~prsv fslL (Intro P) ·
grp v slzns ,
oq_ · fN lb uz-

lw bld_ cSs, eno
la ec k ou (Ap) · ksrn-
slzn (Ap) l kb lw ls
cz, cu

4

Supply two words that are missing in the following letter.

Preview Words

lanes	lns	rebuilding	rbld_
routes	rus	alternate	alrnl
widen	‿dn	Jacksonville	jcsnvl
outweigh	oLa	eastbound	EboN

d ~or (sle v
jcsnvl , p- l
kpli ‿ (‿ss
vu nbrh asoq, (
sle ksl hs ~l +
apv- · rqS l
‿dn ~pl blvd,
2 lns = 1 EboN ln
+ 1 WboN ln = lb

a-, kSrc l bgn o
Jl 11, alo ls lb ·
~prre nkv du_ (
rbld_ pred (Intro DC) er
la (bnfls
l fr oLa (Pblms,
p ‿C (nzppr f
nz la l afc u
Tpl rus, el Pvd

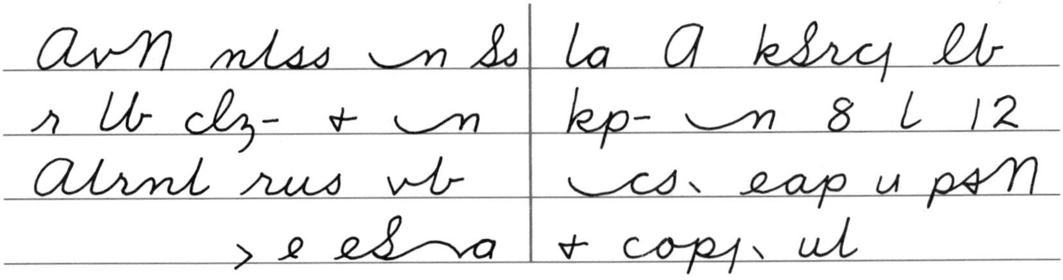

5

Punctuation Study

Add commas to show one introductory dependent clause, one series, and three introductory phrases.

Preview Words

priority 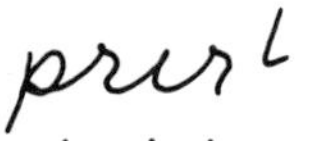

beautify 

sidewalks 

maintained 

designated 

restoration 

beautification 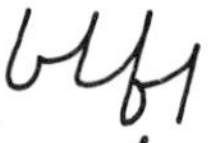

urban renewal 

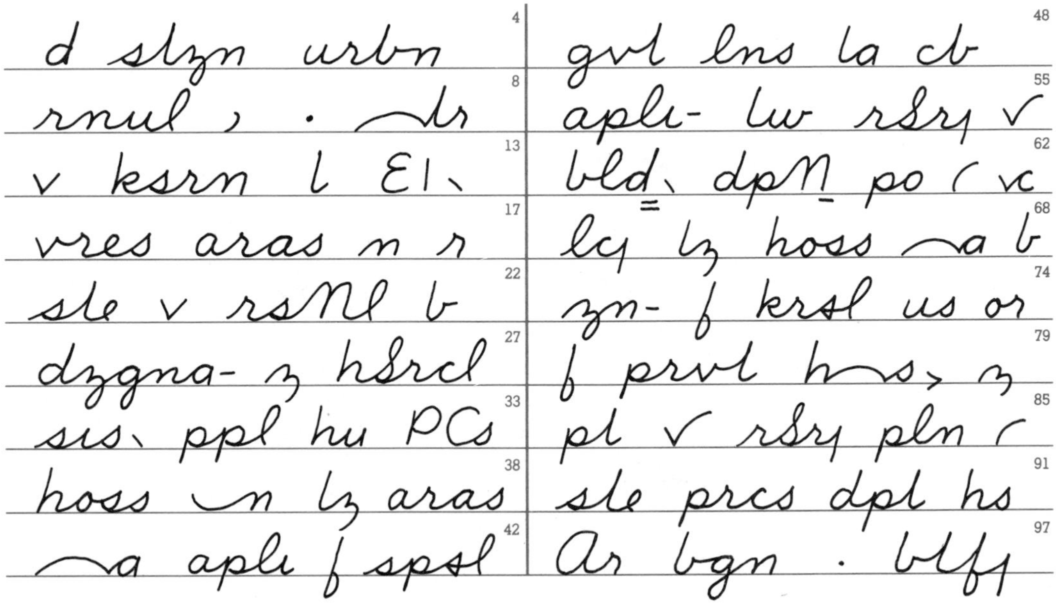

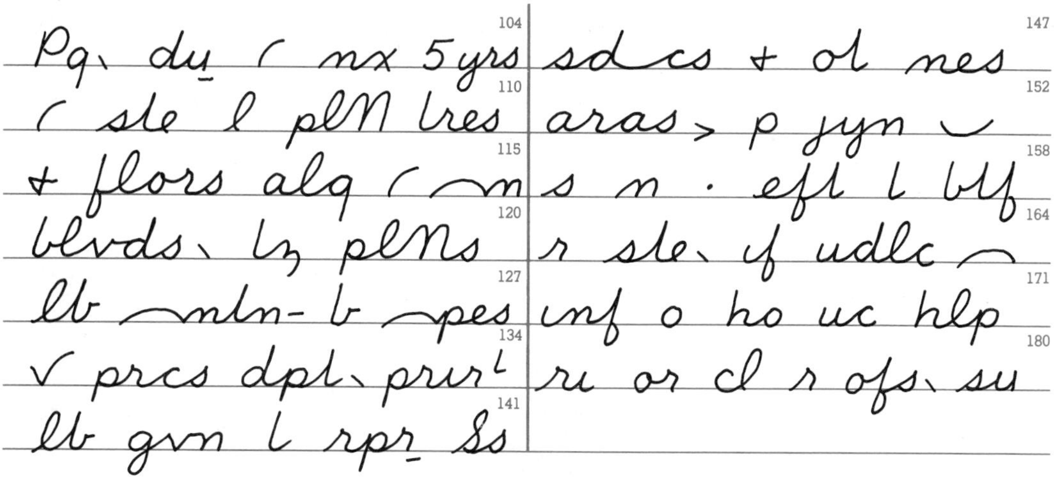

Key

1

MEMO TO: Henry Chase

Due to the excessive amount of snow that fell last winter, the funds that had been reserved[1] for snow removal were depleted early in the year. If we have even half as much snow this winter as we[2] had last year, we will be unable to keep our streets clear.

Since every department is taking extra precautions[3] to avoid increasing its budget, I suggest that you postpone some street repairs until next summer. Of course, there[4] are some areas that require immediate attention and cannot wait that long. In other areas,[5] however, the need may be much less critical.

If we can delay these repairs until the snow season has passed,[6] we can then use the remaining funds as needed. Please give this proposal serious consideration and let me[7] know your feelings. (143)

2

Dear Mr. Richards:

I was pleased and surprised to read about our conservation efforts in your recent newspaper[1] article. Thank you for giving the readers an excellent account of the environmental problems that[2] we are facing.

I am glad that you made a point of discussing several solutions to the problems. Although[3] our department does not presume to have the correct answer every time, we do attempt to find solutions that[4] will benefit society as a whole. In order to make that choice, we weigh many factors before proposing[5] a solution.

The most important part of your message is a point worth making again and again. Conservation[6] is the responsibility of everyone. As long as you continue to educate citizens about[7] environmental issues, you are providing a public service that is beneficial to all of[8] us.

Sincerely yours, (164)

3

Dear Dr. and Mrs. Conrad:

This year is the tenth anniversary of the completion of city hall. When[1] this beautiful building was added to Madison Street, it brought an entirely new look to the downtown area.[2]

As you may recall from previous publicity, the existing building represents the first phase of the[3] original building plans. The second phase calls for an extension that would provide space for additional[4] meeting rooms. However, budgetary limitations have prevented the construction of this phase.

As a special[5] gift to celebrate the anniversary of this impressive facility, a group of citizens is[6] organizing a fund to be used toward building costs.

We know that we can count on you, a concerned citizen, to[7] contribute toward this cause.

Cordially yours, (148)

4

Dear Homeowner:

The city of Jacksonville is pleased to comply with the wishes of your neighborhood association.[1] The city council has met and approved a request to widen Maple Boulevard. Two lanes—one eastbound lane[2] and one westbound lane—will be added. Construction will begin on July 11.

Although there will be a[3] temporary inconvenience during the rebuilding period, we are *convinced* that the benefits will far[4] outweigh the problems. Please watch the newspaper for news that will affect your transportation routes. We will provide advance[5] notices when streets are to be closed and when alternate routes have been *selected.*

We estimate that all construction[6] will be completed within 8 to 12 weeks. We appreciate your patience and cooperation.

Yours[7] truly, (141)

convinced: certain, sure

selected: designated, chosen

5

Dear Citizen:

Urban renewal is a matter of concern to everyone. Various areas in our[1] city have recently been designated as historical sites. People who purchase houses within these[2] areas may apply for special government loans that can be applied toward restoration of the buildings.[3] Depending upon the exact location, these houses may be zoned for commercial use or for private homes.

As part[4] of the restoration plan, the city parks department has already begun a beautification program.[5] During the next five years, the city will plant trees and flowers along the main boulevards. These plants will be maintained[6] by employees of the parks department. Priority will be given to repairing streets, sidewalks, and other[7] necessary areas.

Please join with us in an effort to beautify our city. If you would like more[8] information on how you can help, write or call our office.

Sincerely yours, (173)

LESSON 58

Shorthand Vocabulary Review

Write *y* for the sound of *oi* (oy).

oil	yl	avoid	avyd
join	jyn	loyalty	lylte
Detroit	dtryt	enjoyable	njyB
toys	tys	noise	nyz
soil	syl	destroy	dSry

Transcription Aids: Similar Words

then *tn* Used to indicate a place in time, either past or future.

He then distributed the minutes of the meeting.

I will be looking forward to talking with you then.

than *tn* Used to connect two expressions in statements of comparison, preference, or extent.

We have more time than money to spend.

I would rather order now than wait until later.

I have no recommendations other than the ones mentioned earlier.

the past  A time that has occurred before the present.

In the past we have used two systems for filing receipts.

passed  The past tense of *pass;* gone by or elapsed.

Nearly a month has passed since the order was placed, and we still have not received the merchandise.

Your Business Vocabulary

task force  A group of people who are assigned the responsibility of securing resources and creating a plan to accomplish a specific objective within a specified period of time.

The mayor will appoint a task force to make recommendations regarding future construction projects.

resolution 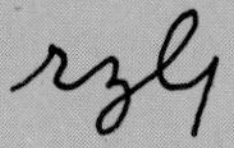 In reference to legal action, a formal statement of a decision or expression of opinion made by an assembly.

The legislature adopted a resolution to honor top-ranked students for their excellence in education.

Reading and Writing Exercises

———————————— 1 ————————————

Preview Words

quiet *qul*

force *fs*

freedom *fred*

outstanding *olSN*

guiding *gd*

advisory *Avzre*

prospered *Pspr-*

excellence *lN*

d llr s · plzr
l kq u ou olSN
Svs l ls ajMe, du
(p8 30 yrs · uv [Intro P]
sl · ex v lN
n u PfM, uv
Sv- n 3 dfrM
dpls · + eC v loz [Conj]
dpls hs Pspr- U
u ldrs, e a M
l lM r b8 ss
f · njyS + sal
rlrm, no u z
idu · idu n vpc [Intro P]
u rlrm Ub · qul

l, uv no dol laul
ku Ub · acv, gd [And O]
fs n ls kn', z ·
lr v fc, iz dlu- [Intro P]
l lrn la uv dsd-
l Sv o · Avzre
k f ls ajMe, ∽
Sln laul lN l
slbra u rlrm b
njy u nu fred
f · l, af · fu
cs v ps-, p klc [Intro DC]
∽e so la ic ar
fu l ∽e ∽ (
k, su

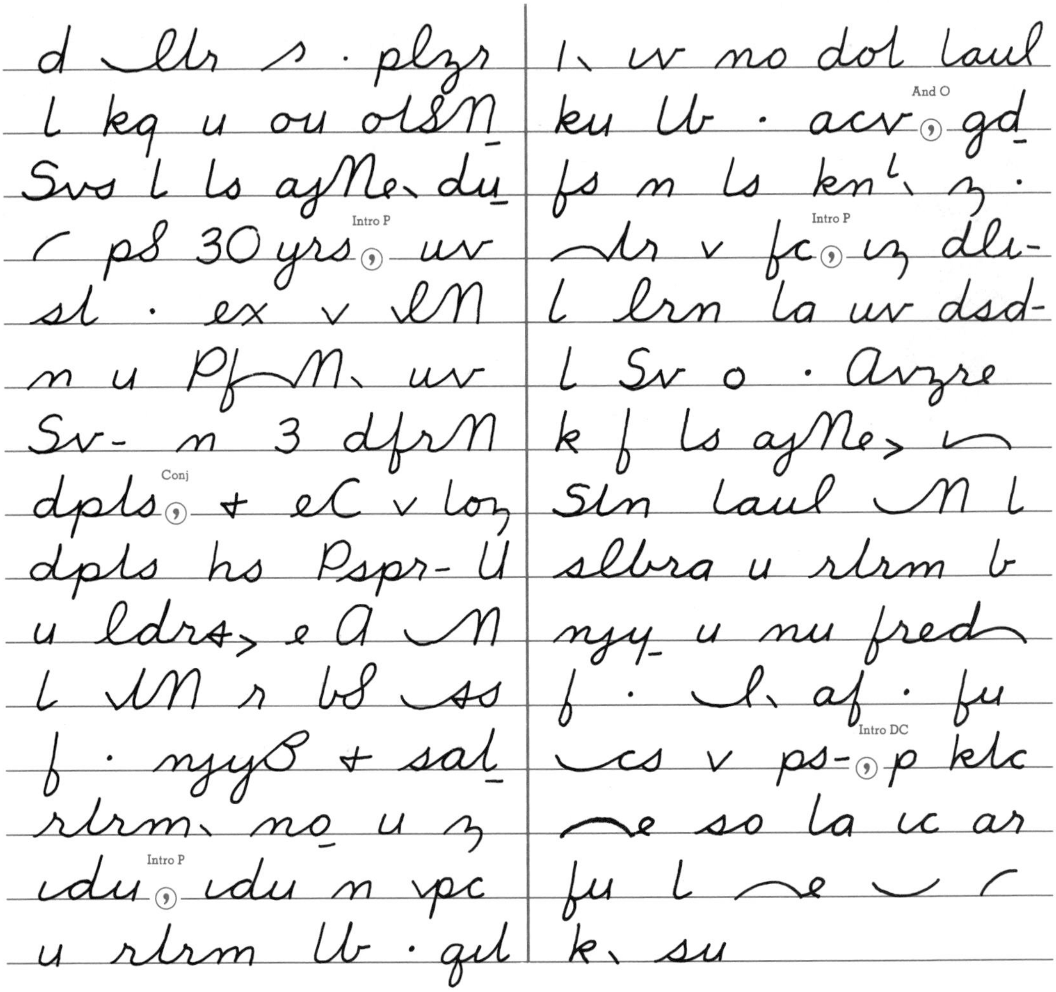

2

Preview Words

data — *dla*

gather — *glr*

tight — *li*

yourself — *usf*

extend — *vn*

auditors — *adlrs*

courtesy — *crlse*

extremely — *X~l*

---

mo l A dpl hds
Sa adlrs lb ~
s nx Mn, p ar
u scyls so la
ulb fre l ass
L n E ~a, sM
ly lb ~o o .
X~l li scyl (Intro DC) er
rqs lau glr A
nes recs n AvM
so la (adlrs
l n v l S L
SC f fls, esd l
Ppr- l vM L E

crlse l ly r
~o hr, ed Pfr
la eC dpl hd
~o drl ~ (
adlrs (Conj) l / ~a
l nes f s ~ vu
l apy ol Sf
mbrs ldu so,
if ur pln f s l
ol Ln usf ll P
la d (Intro DC) p l Sln
la h or se , l
nf~- t c asr
ne qs la ~i

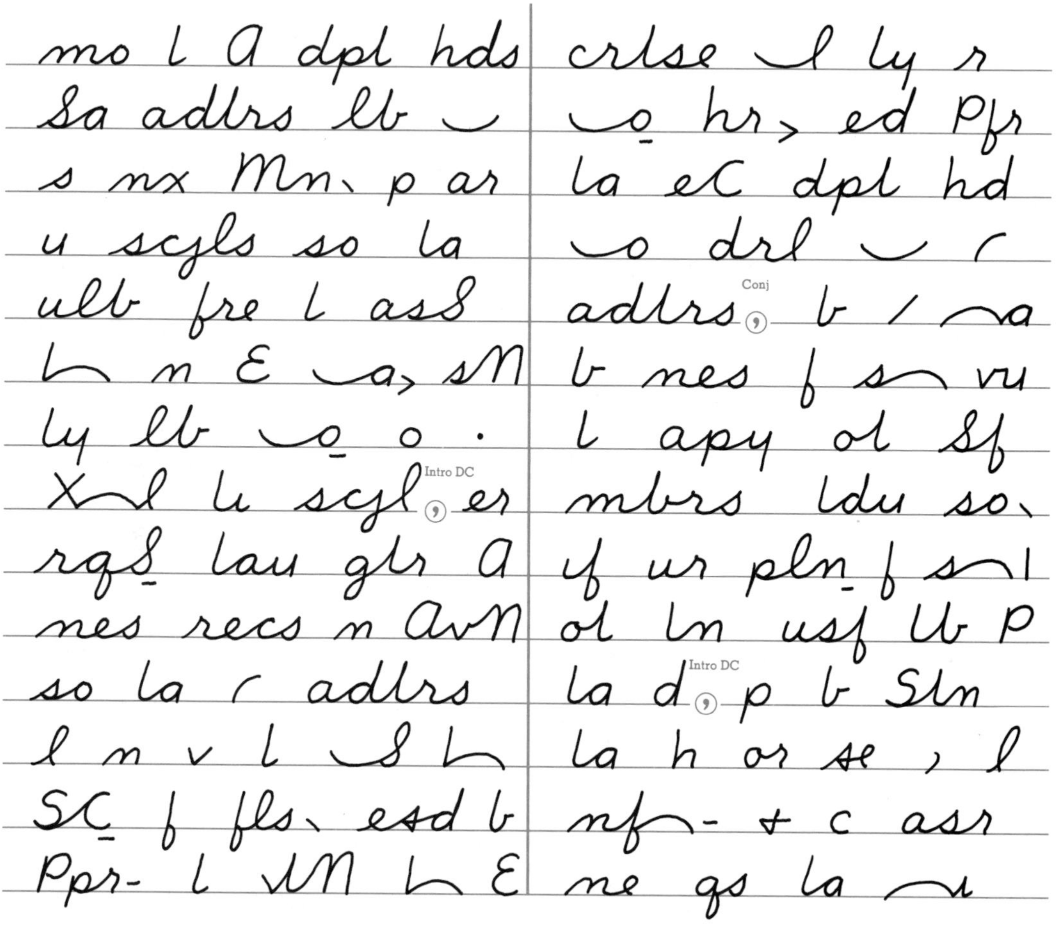

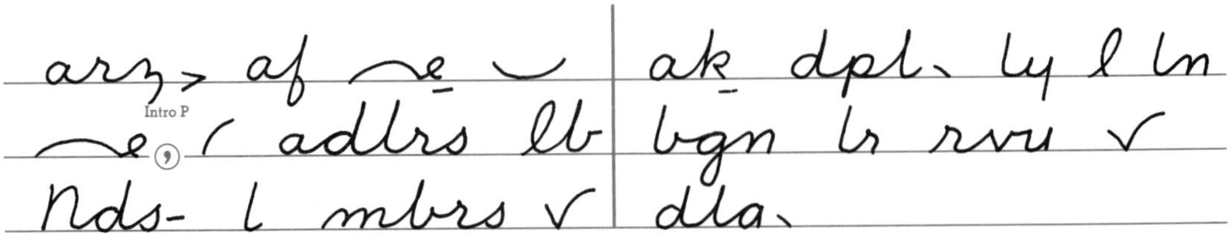

3

Preview Words

pending	pN	carefully	crfl
Congress	kgrs	communicate	knca
grateful	grf	legislation	lgslj
comforting	kfl	appreciative	apv

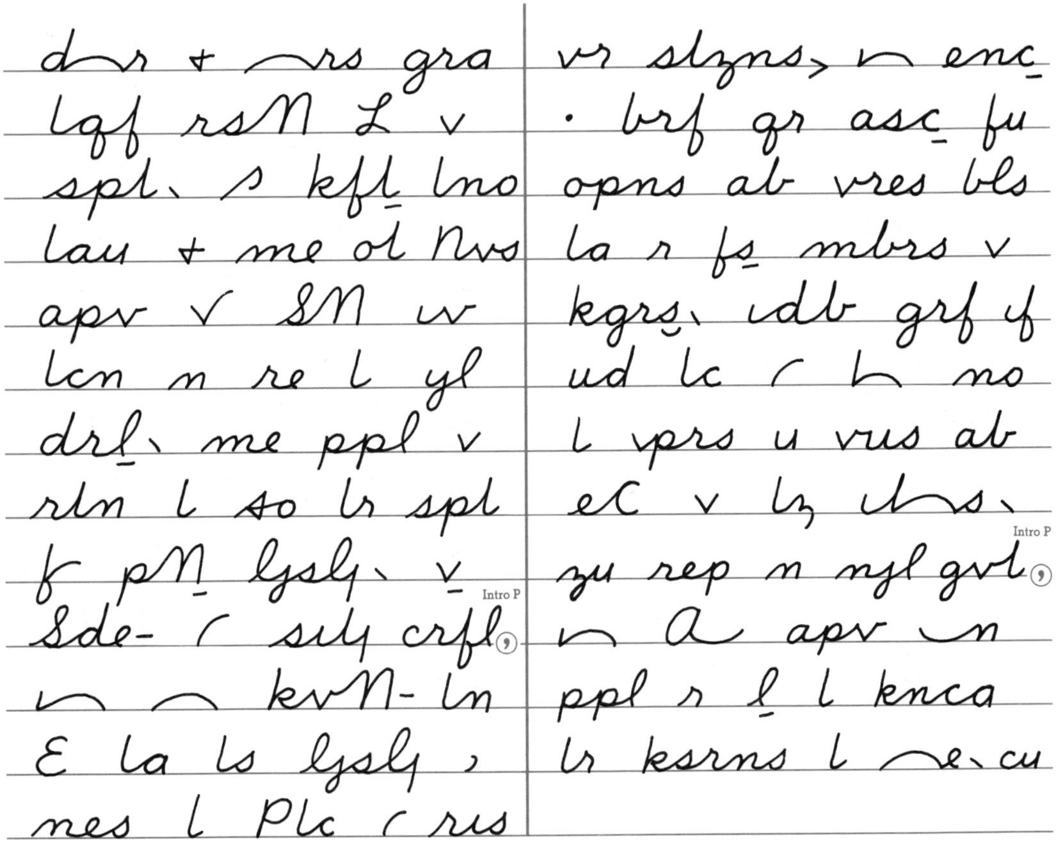

4

Supply two words that are missing in the following letter.

Preview Words

growth	grl	newcomer	nukr
ensure	nsr	commitment	klm
creation	crej	administrator	Amr
resided	rzd-	coordinate	cordna

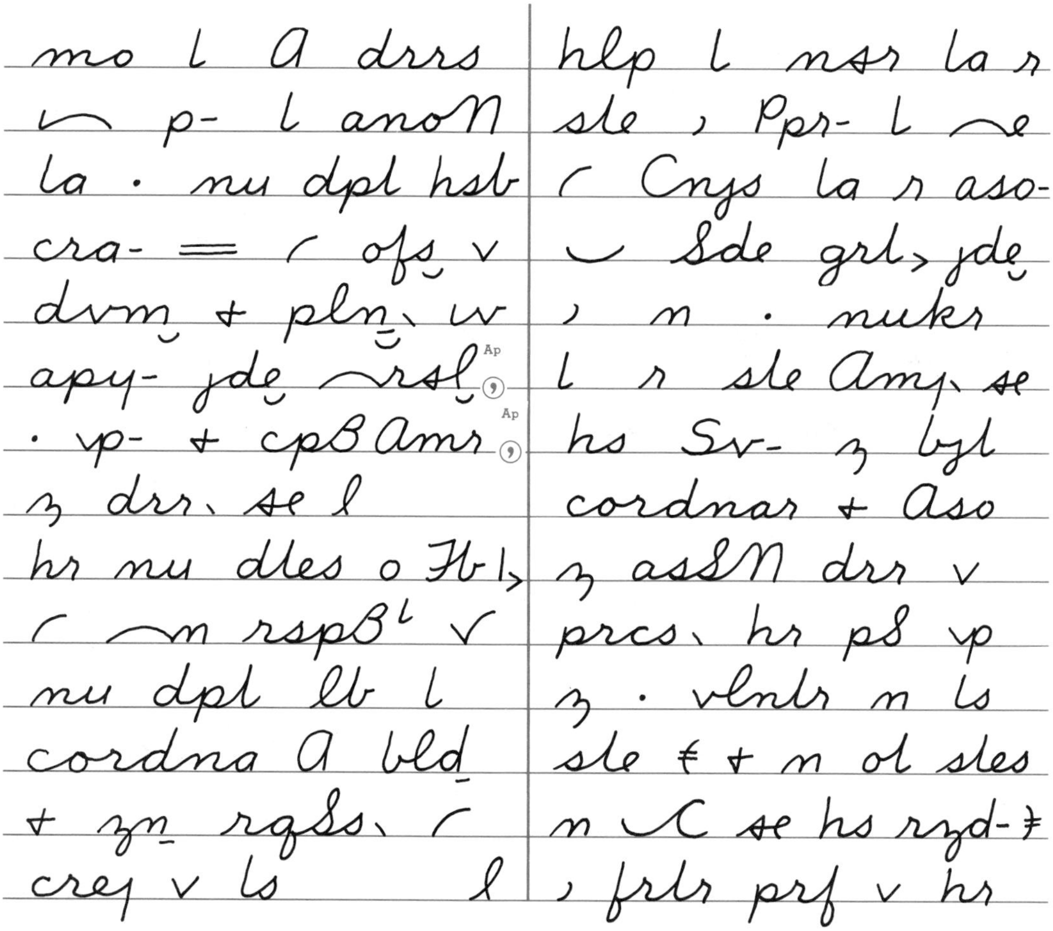

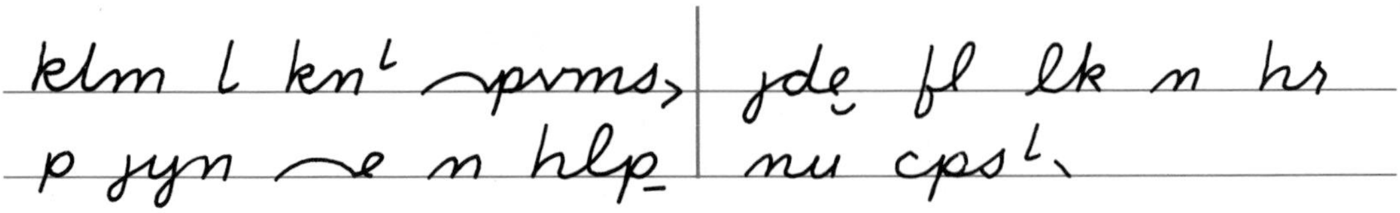

5

Punctuation Study

Add commas to show two introductory dependent clauses, one conjunction, one direct address, and one series.

Preview Words

- whose 
- master 
- mission 
- primary 
- expertise 
- architect 
- resolution 
- task force 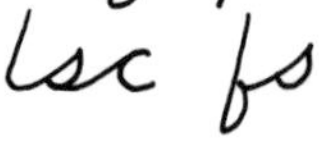

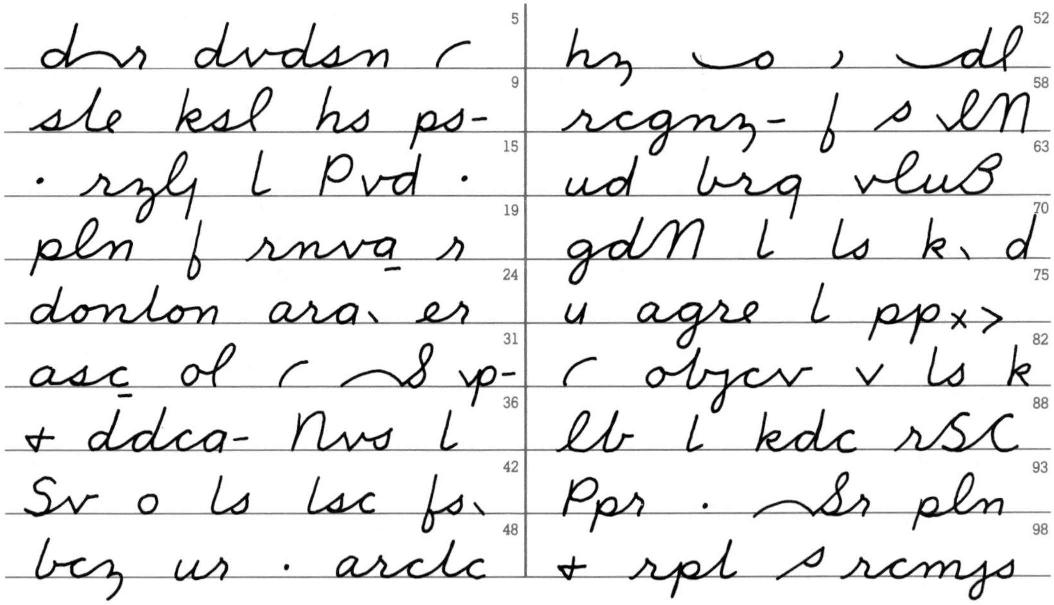

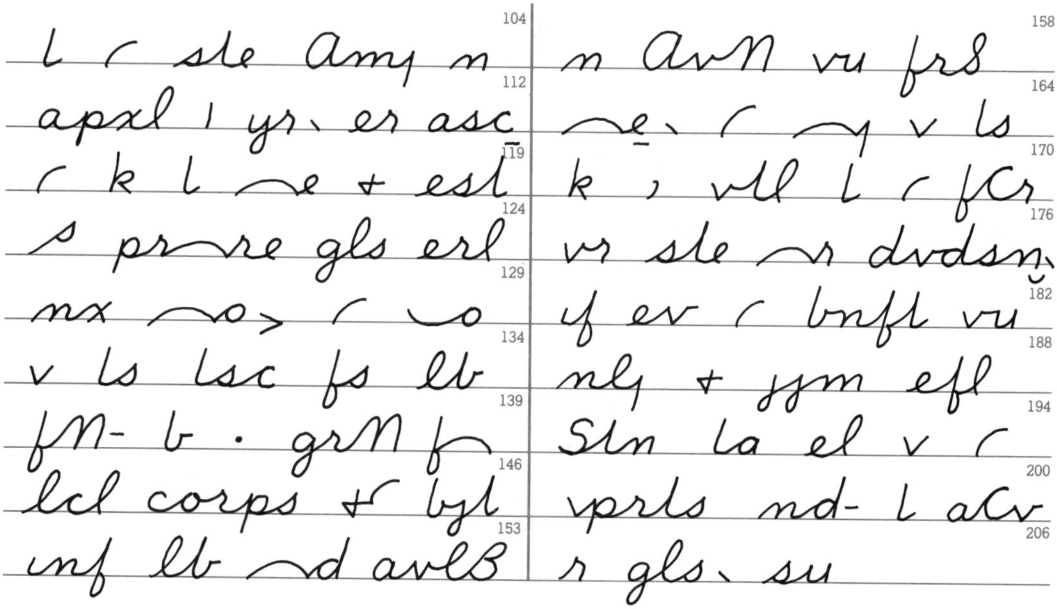

Key

1

Dear Walter:

It is a pleasure to congratulate you on your outstanding service to this agency. During[1] the past 30 years, you have set an example of excellence in your performance. You have served in three different[2] departments, and each of those departments has prospered under your leadership.

We all want to extend our best[3] wishes for an enjoyable and satisfying retirement. Knowing you as I do, I do not expect your[4] retirement to be a quiet one. I have no doubt that you will continue to be an active, guiding force in[5] this community. As a matter of fact, I was delighted to learn that you have decided to serve on an[6] advisory committee for this agency.

I am certain that you will want to celebrate your retirement[7] by enjoying your new freedom for a while. After a few weeks have passed, please contact me so that I can arrange[8] for you to meet with the committee.

Sincerely yours, (169)

2

MEMO TO: All Department Heads

State auditors will be with us next Monday. Please arrange your schedules so that[1] you will be free to assist them in every way.

Since they will be working on an extremely tight schedule, we are[2] requesting that you gather all necessary records in advance so that the auditors will not have to waste time[3] searching for files. We should be prepared to extend them every courtesy while they are working here.

We would prefer[4] that each department head work directly with the auditors, but it may be necessary for some of you to[5] appoint other staff members to do so. If you are planning for someone other than yourself to be present that[6] day, please be certain that he or she is well informed and can answer any questions that might arise.

After meeting[7] with me, the auditors will be introduced to members of the accounting department. They will then begin[8] their review of the data. (165)

3

Dear Mr. and Mrs. Gray:

Thank you for your recent letter of support. It is comforting to know that you and[1] many other individuals approve of the stand I have taken in regard to oil drilling. Many people[2] have written to show their support for the pending legislation. Having studied the situation carefully,[3] I am more convinced than ever that this legislation is necessary to protect the rights of our citizens.[4]

I am enclosing a brief questionnaire asking for your opinions about various bills that are facing[5] members of Congress. I would be grateful if you would take the time now to express your views about each of these[6] items. As your representative in national government, I am always appreciative when people[7] are willing to communicate their concerns to me.

Cordially yours, (152)

4

MEMO TO: All Directors

I am pleased to announce that a new department has been created—the Office of[1] Development and Planning. I have appointed Judy Marshall, an experienced and capable administrator,[2] as director. She will *assume* her new duties on February 1.

The main responsibility[3] of the new department will be to coordinate all building and zoning requests. The creation of this[4] *department* will help to ensure that our city is prepared to meet the changes that are associated[5] with steady growth.

Judy is not a newcomer to our city administration. She has served as budget[6] coordinator and also as assistant director of parks. Her past experience as a volunteer in[7] this city (and in other cities in which she has resided) is further proof of her commitment to community[8] improvements.

Please join me in helping Judy feel welcome in her new capacity. (175)

assume: begin, start

department: office

5

Dear Mr. Davidson:

The city council has passed a resolution to provide a plan for renovating[1] our downtown area. We are asking only the most experienced and dedicated individuals[2] to serve on this task force. Because you are an architect whose work is widely recognized for its excellence, you would[3] bring valuable guidance to this committee. Would you agree to participate?

The objective of this[4] committee will be to conduct research, prepare a master plan, and report its recommendations to the city[5] administration in approximately one year. We are asking the committee to meet and establish[6] its primary goals early next month.

The work of this task force will be funded by a grant from local corporations,[7] and the budget information will be made available in advance of your first meeting. The mission of[8] this committee is vital to the future of our city, Mr. Davidson. If we have the benefit of your[9] knowledge and judgment, we feel certain that we will have the expertise needed to achieve our goals.

Sincerely[10] yours, (201)

LESSON 59

Shorthand Vocabulary Review

1. Write a disjoined, capital *P* for the word beginnings *per, pur, pre, pro,* and *pro (prah).*

person	*Psn*	protest	*PLS*
personnel	*Psnl*	program	*Pq*
purpose	*Pps*	proposal	*Ppzl*
purchase	*PCs*	procedures	*Psjrs*
presume	*Pz*	profit	*Pfl*
prevented	*PvM-*	projects	*Pjcs*
preserved	*Pzrv-*	problems	*Pbls*
previous	*Pves*	prospered	*Pspr-*

2. Write ⁀ for the sound of *em* or *im.*

emphasize	*fsz*	impression	*pry*
emphasis	*fss*	impact	*pc*
emphatic	*flc*	improve	*pv*
embarrass	*brs*	impossible	*psB*

Transcription Aids: Spelling

The following words are often misspelled because one of the double consonants is omitted by accident. Until you have learned to spell these words correctly, always consult a dictionary.

committee *k*   recommend *rcm*

omitted	omt-	remitting	rmt_
accept	ac	excellent	vlN
apparent	aprN	planning	pln_
occurred	ocr-	beginning	bgn_
shipping	A_	personnel	Psnl
assistance	asSN	accommodation	akdj
unnecessary	unes	cancellation	cslj
equipped	eqp-	possession	pzj
accident	vdN	questionnaire	qr

Your Business Vocabulary

doctoral dissertation
drl Drlj
A formal research study written as a requirement for a doctoral degree.

I am compiling research data to be used in my doctoral dissertation.

counselor kslr
A person who gives advice or provides guidance in a specialized area.

Charlotte Steinway is the guidance counselor at the new high school.

Reading and Writing Exercises

— 1 —

Preview Words

greet *gre*

welcome *lk*

timely *ᒪᒪ*

redevelopment *rdvm*

expand *ᴠpN*

urban affairs *urbn afrs*

subject *syc*

dissertation *Drly*

d ⸱rs ⸱ᴸlln lqf
ru ⸱ l ⸱ᴠprs NS n
⸱o f r sle Amy.
erp- l lrn la ulb
⸱ᴸc u ⸱ᴸ hr. l
er A egr l gre
nu slzns n ls
kn l ⸨Intro DC⸩ ⸱ s esp ns l
lk ppl hu ᴠ ⸱
bcgroN n urbn
afrs⸒ ⸱ᴸ plcl
NS- n u ⸱S rsN
Pjc ⸨Ap⸩ u drl Drly. ⸱ᴸ
syc ᴠ urbn rdvm
⸒ ᒪᒪ ⸨Conj⸩ + er A
n nd ᴠ nu dla.

yf udb so cN zↄ
ᒪᒪ ⸱ cpe l ⸱ᴸe ⸨Intro DC⸩ -
il se la / rCs
⸱ᴸ apo dpl⸒ edb
hpe l ⸱ᴸe ᴠ u
l Dcs fCr ⸱ᴸpm.
Alo edu n ᴠ ⸱
opn ns la rqs
u qlfzↄ ⸨Intro DC⸩ er ᴠpc
l ᴠpN r dpl ᴠ
urbn afrs⸒ Ph
ls lb ⸱ pzↄ fu
⸱ᴸ n 6 ⸱ᴸos⸒ p fl
fre lvzl s ⸱ᴸ nx
⸱ᴸ ur n lon. su

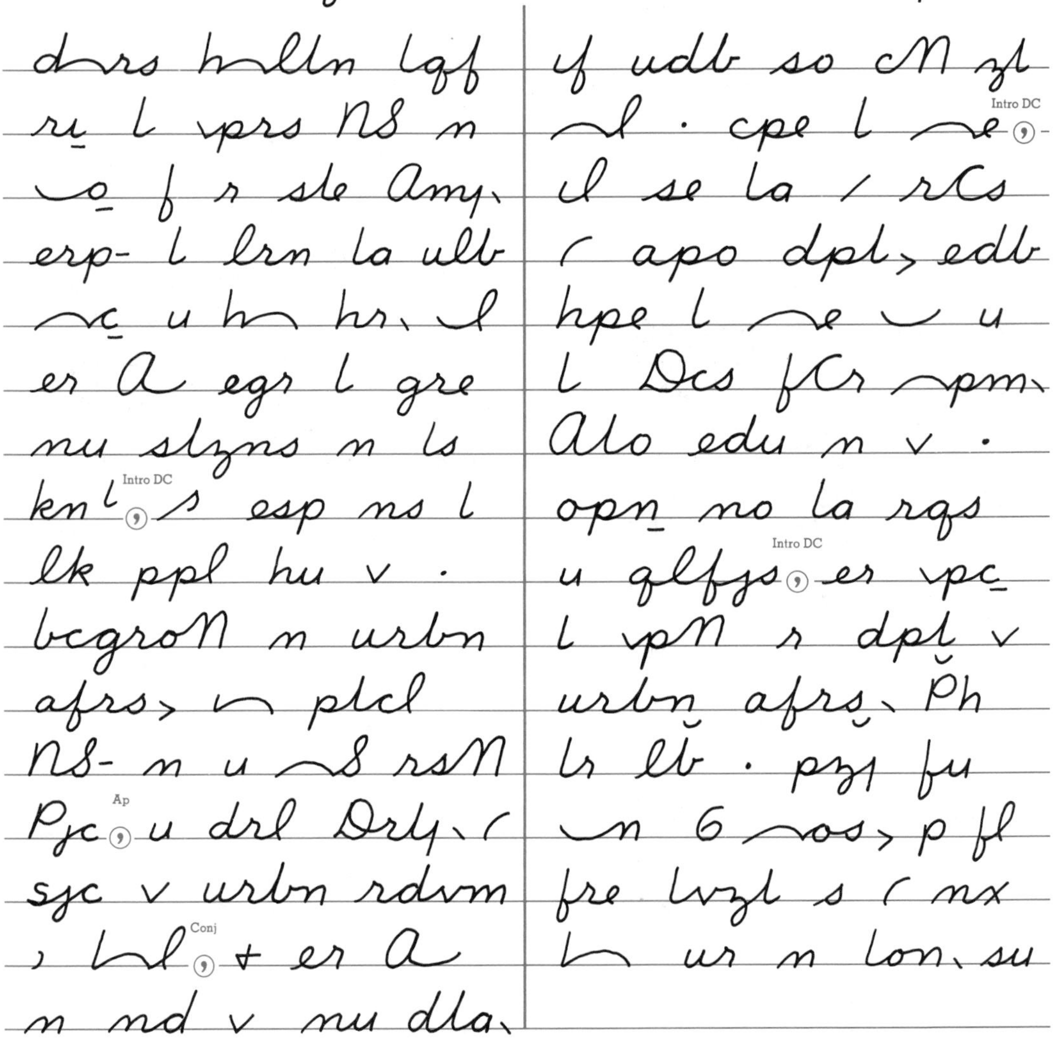

2

Preview Words

basic	bsc	counselor	kslr
submit	s-l	evaluate	evla
completion	kpj	sufficiently	sfsNl
Resources	rsrss	application	aplcj

d M edws lqf
aplc f · secd
pzj n dpl v
nCrl rsrss, alo
ev no pzjs avlB
P (Intro DC ,) ls a
b ol opls f pm
n Sa ofs bld, e
suq lau fl · aplcj
(Psnl dvj, l
s l · aplcj (Intro P ,) u
a k l (Psnl
ofs bln (hrs v
8 a + 5 p dl,
af uv kp- (aplcj

f (Intro DC ,) ulb asc- l
lc (Sd lSs l
evla (lvl vu
bsc ofs scls,
flo (kpj v ls
lSs (Intro P ,) ulb nvi- l
e + lc ·
Psnl kslr, la Psn
lb B l avz u
ab (opls la r
avlB, chp n asr-
u qs sfsNl, l s
u l n u pm
SC, su

3

Preview Words

lanes	lns	reversed	rvrs-
widen	dn	expedite	vpdi
welfare	lfr	populated	ppla-
traffic	lrfc	expressway	vprs a

d mbrs v brd
n ru l PlS (
dsj l a 2 nu
lrfc lns l el
blvd, if uv drvn
lru ls nbrh rsNl, Intro DC
ud no la ls ara ;
ppla- b me yq
fmls, if u dn ls
Intro DC
S , ul ncrs (flo
v lrfc, sC . ncrs
d P . dnjr f yq
Cldrn hu r c
l scl or pla n
yds> sM lr s

ol a l vpdi
Paren
lrfc × f ex , y dN
u ks ru (lrfc
aroN ls nbrh
b ncrs (lns o
jfrsn ave × n s
Intro P
scjs v sle , lrfc
flo , rvrs- du
dfrN s v d,
ls S cd Sv z .
n vprs a nl (
sle du (rn +
ol v sle du (
afnn> p du n
c . dsj o ls

~dr ~ol ks- r	alo r vus lb hrd.
lfs v rzdnsl	ul
kn'. e rqs . hs- l	

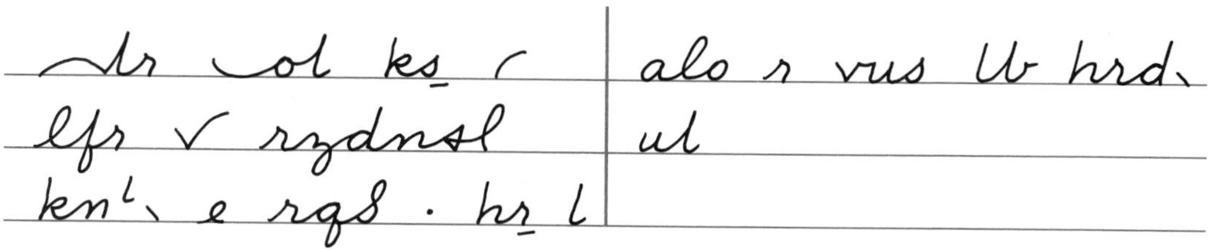

4

Supply two words that are missing in the following letter.

Preview Words

commend	kN	weigh	~a
district	Dlrc	affecting	afc-
trade	lrd	international	Nnyl
elements	elms	communicate	knca

dM arnld lqf ru-	~s ~a lz ksrns
l knca u ksrns	f agrl dvm aq
ab r fed plses	loz afc- ol elms
afc- Nnyl lrd. w	vr eco> chp laul
ks- r ~drels u	ku l u
sN (Conj ,) + l	rSC + avs l
l kN u o kvN-	~e. uc a bnfl
cs u P-> z r rep	f~ r opns v
vu Dlrc (Intro P ,) l USN	nf~- slzns lc
+ sr u ksrns. l	u. cu

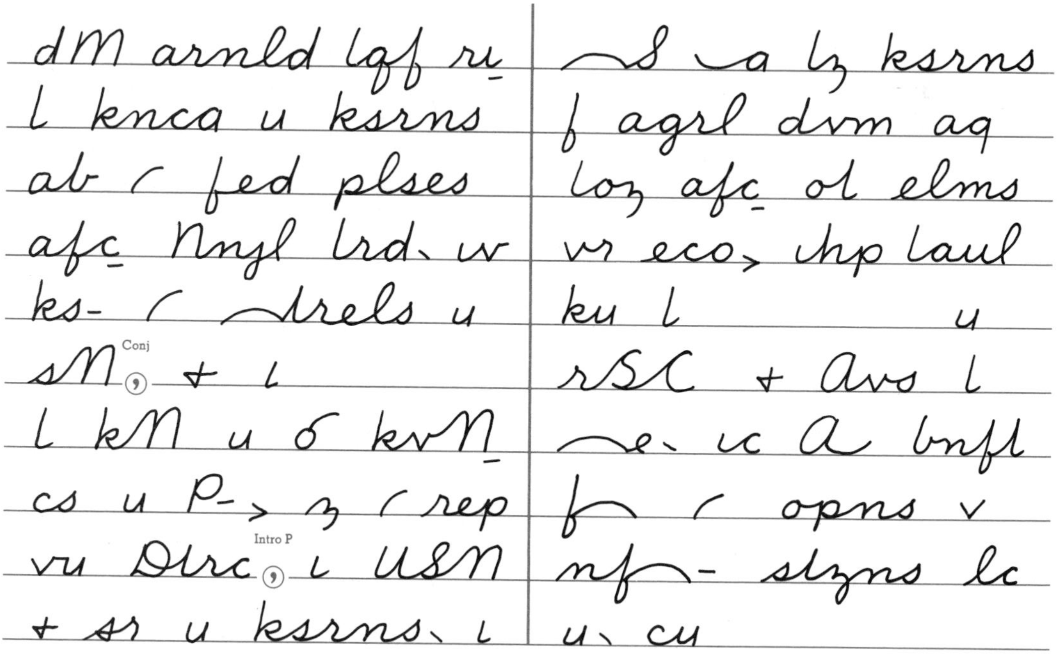

5

Punctuation Study

Add commas to show one parenthetical expression, one conjunction, one introductory dependent clause, and one appositive.

Preview Words

deemed 

essential 

sanitary 

intervals 

mandatory 

cooperation 

evaluation 

restaurant 

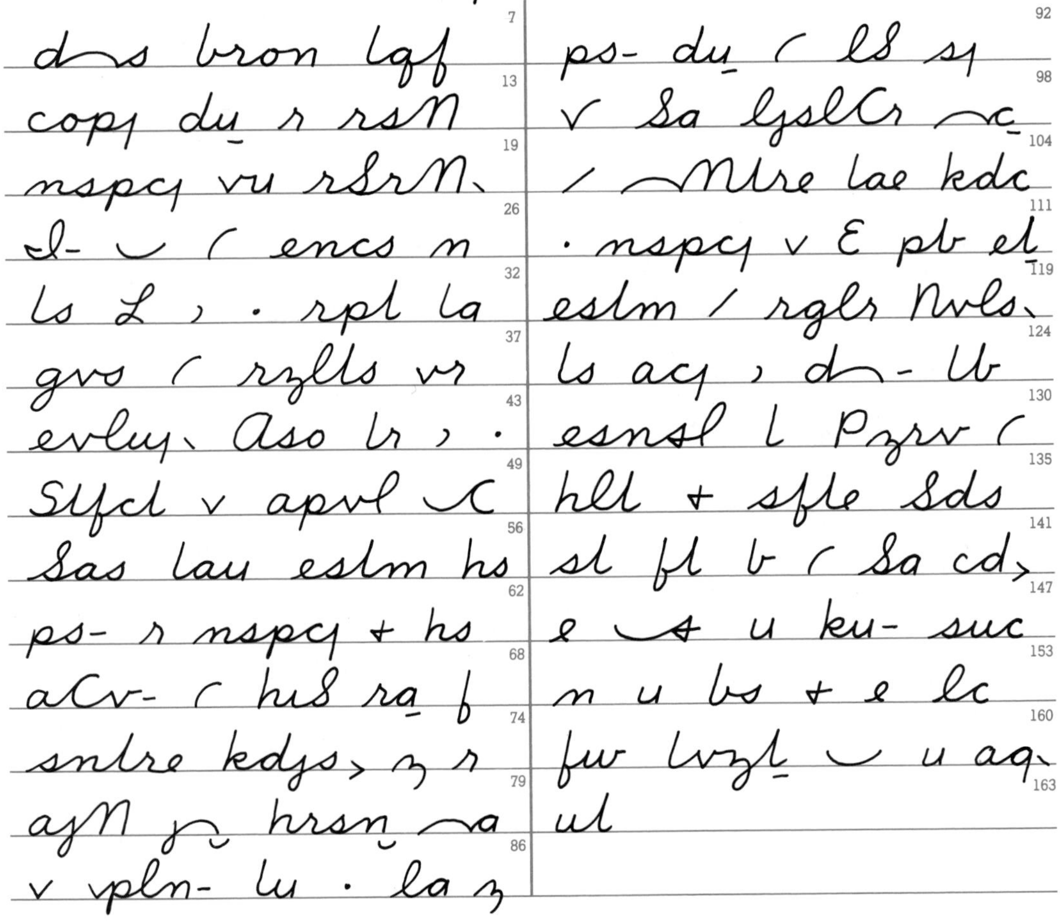

Key

1

Dear Mrs. Hamilton:

Thank you for writing to express interest in working for our city administration.[1] We are pleased to learn that you will be making your home here. While we are always eager to greet new citizens[2] in this community, it is especially nice to welcome people who have a background in urban affairs.[3]

I am particularly interested in your most recent project, your doctoral dissertation. The subject[4] of urban redevelopment is timely, and we are always in need of new data. If you would be so[5] kind as to mail a copy to me, I will see that it reaches the appropriate department.

We would be happy[6] to meet with you to discuss future employment. Although we do not have an opening now that requires your[7] qualifications, we are expecting to expand our Department of Urban Affairs. Perhaps there will be a[8] position for you within six months.

Please feel free to visit us the next time you are in town.

Sincerely yours,[9] (180)

2

Dear Miss Edwards:

Thank you for applying for a secretarial position in the Department of Natural[1] Resources. Although we have no positions available at the present time, there may be other opportunities[2] for employment in the state office building. We suggest that you file an application with the personnel[3] division.

To submit an application, you may come to the personnel office between the hours of[4] 8 a.m. and 5 p.m. daily. After you have completed the application form, you will be asked to take[5] the standard tests to evaluate the level of your basic office skills. Following the completion of these[6] tests, you will be invited to meet and talk with a personnel counselor. That person will be able to advise[7] you about the opportunities that are available.

I hope I have answered your questions sufficiently.[8] I wish you well in your employment search.

Sincerely yours, (171)

3

Dear Members of the Board:

I am writing to protest the decision to add two new traffic lanes to Elm Boulevard.[1] If you have driven through this neighborhood recently, you would know that this area is populated by[2] many young families. If you widen this street, you will increase the flow of traffic. Such an increase would present[3] a danger for young children who are walking to school or playing in yards.

Isn't there some other way to expedite[4] traffic? For example, why don't you consider routing the traffic around this neighborhood by increasing[5] the lanes on Jefferson Avenue? In some sections of the city, traffic flow is reversed during different[6] times of the day. This street could serve as a main expressway into the city during the morning and out of the[7] city during the afternoon.

Please do not make a decision on this matter without considering the[8] welfare of the residential community. We request a hearing to allow our views to be heard.

Yours truly,[9] (180)

4

Dear Miss Arnold:

Thank you for writing to communicate your concerns about the federal policies affecting[1] international trade. I have considered the materials you sent, and I *want* to commend you on the[2] convincing case you presented.

As the representative of your district, I understand and share your concerns.[3] I must weigh these concerns for agricultural development against those affecting other elements[4] of our economy.

I hope that you will continue to *send* your research and advice to me. I can always[5] benefit from the opinions of informed citizens like you.

Cordially yours, (114)

want: wish

send: mail, communicate

5

Dear Ms. Brown:

Thank you for your cooperation during our recent inspection of your restaurant. Included[1] with the enclosures in this letter is a report that gives the results of our evaluation. Also, there[2] is a certificate of approval which states that your establishment has passed our inspection and has achieved[3] the highest rating for sanitary conditions.

As our agent, Jim Harrison, may have explained to you, a[4] law was passed during the last session of the state legislature making it mandatory that we conduct an[5] inspection of every public eating establishment at regular intervals. This action is deemed to be[6] essential to preserve the health and safety standards set forth by the state code.

We wish you continued success in[7] your business, and we look forward to visiting with you again.

Yours truly, (154)

LESSON 60

Word Development

Develop new words from the following brief forms:

ever

evergreen	Egrn
whatever	lE
whenever	nE
wherever	rE
whoever	huE

complete

completes	kps
completed	kp-
completely	kpl
completion	kpj
incomplete	nkp

point

disappointed	Dapy-
reappoint	rapy
viewpoint	vupy
standpoint	SNpy
appointment	apym

for

reformed	rf-
transform	Tf
reinforcing	rnfs
performance	PfM
informative	nfv

Reading and Writing Exercises

1

Preview Words

site	si	rezoning	rzn
operation	opj	recognized	rcgnz-
commission	kj	industrial	Nl
intersection	Nscj	Interstate	NSa

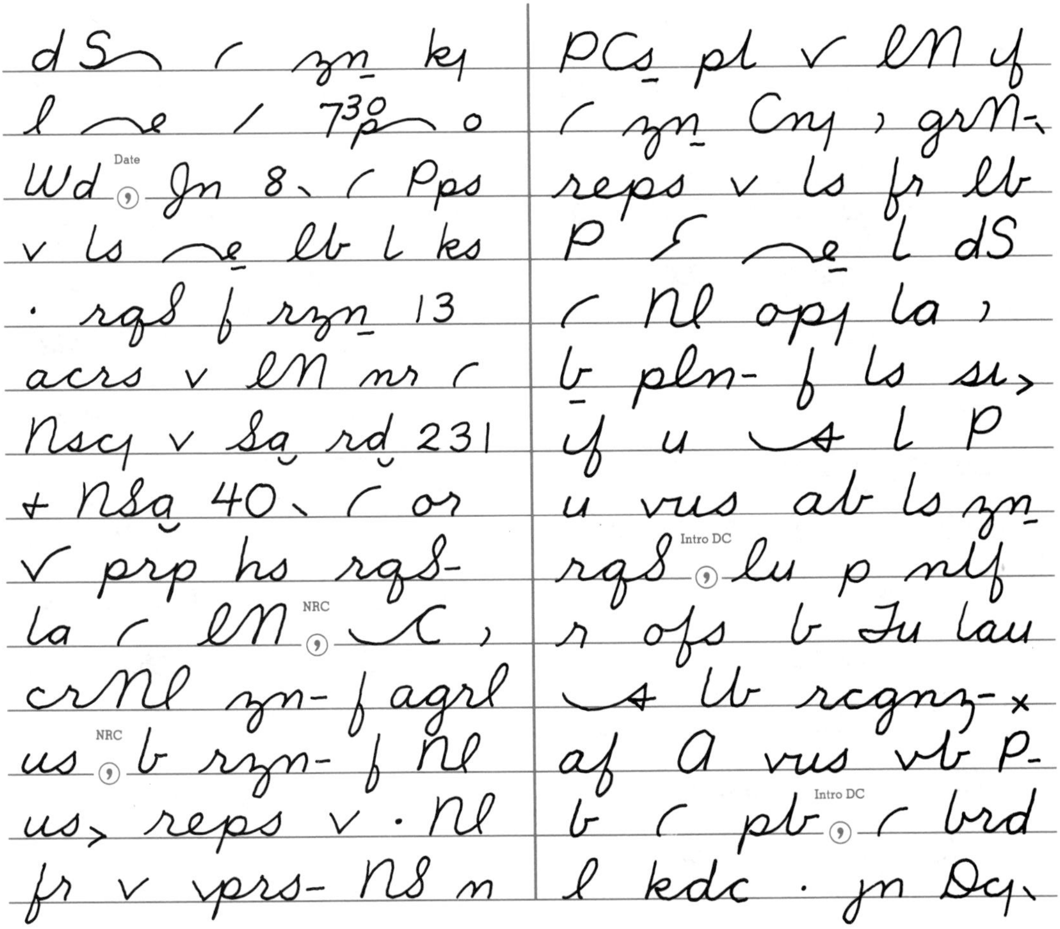

bcz e vpc lgv
ls ısu . gr dl
v ksj bf —c .

Intro DC

dsj, vo l n lc
pls bf r Jl —e
ul

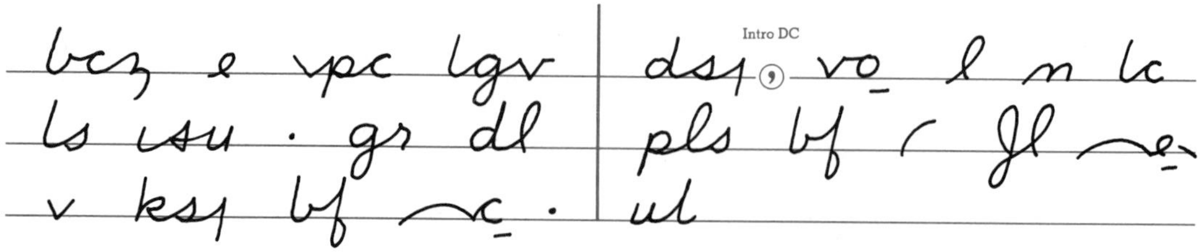

2

Preview Words

FCC FCC

secure scr

various vres

materials —trels

publications pbjs

electronics elncs

broadcasting brdcS

communications kncjs

d—r prSn ls L
r l acj lae rsv-
u rgS f prN-
—trels. r fed
kncjs kj dz —c
vres brsrs avlB
fre v G l r pb.
s— exs v syc
—ts cvr- r z
flos: . dSj v
Series
FCC, inf ab r

brdcS N, hSre
Series
v elncs, hSre
Series
v kncjs, elc. el
gldl sN u sv
cpes vr pbjs f
us n u jr + sr
clss. lj lb —l-
lu scl —l, uf
udlc lv . kp
cpe v rls +
Intro DC
rgljs v FCC,

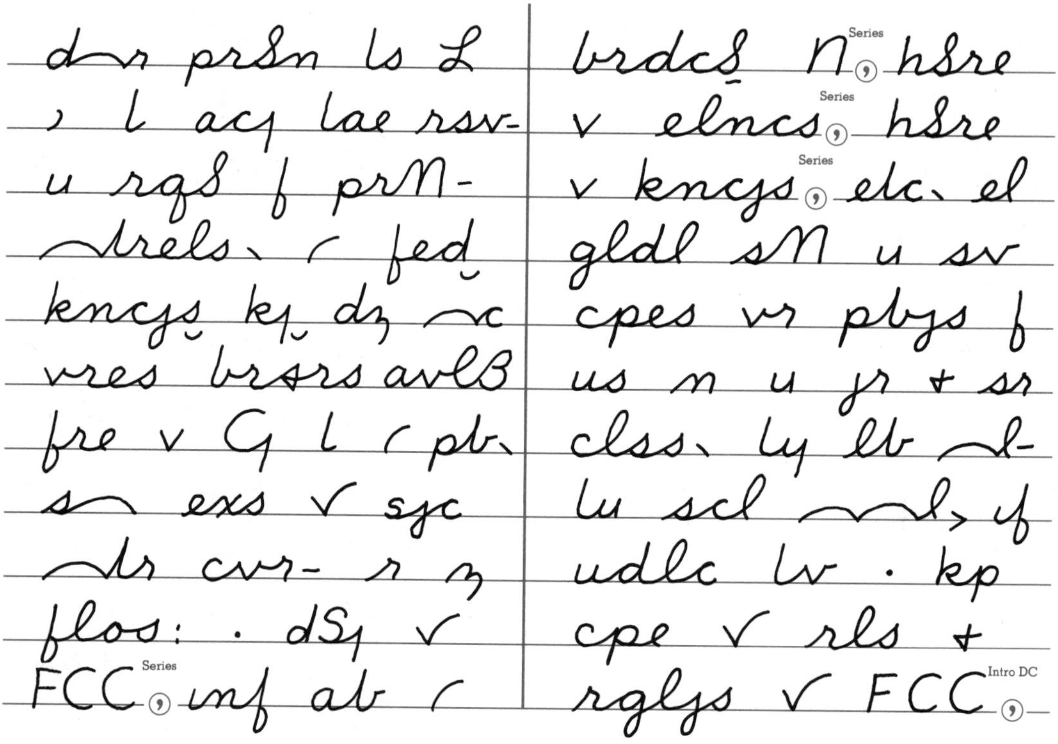

u ma scr , | n ejcyl Pjcs
fm (gvt prN | nE psB, p klc
ofs f · sml fe, | s aq n r Svss
er dli- l asS | r nd-, su

3

Preview Words

hence hN
solicit slsl
farmers frrs
participants ppNs
enlisted nlS-
effective efcv
cooperation copj
conservation ksrvj

mo l ke vlnj
ajNs (dpt v
agr , pln l kdc
Sdes n 4 yrs
aras v ksrvj, p
se (encs f dlt-
dSjs v eC Sde>
n od lrc r
rSC efcv, (Intro P) el
nd lv · lrj
No v frrs pp

n lz Sdes; (Semi) hN, (Paren)
er asc a ke
ajNs l slsl (
copj v frrs n
lr aras, e rcm
la (ajNs bgn
b ar grp me +
vpln (Psjrs l
(frrs, bcz v
nCr v lz Sdes, (Intro P) -
er alspa · q rsp

[shorthand outlines]

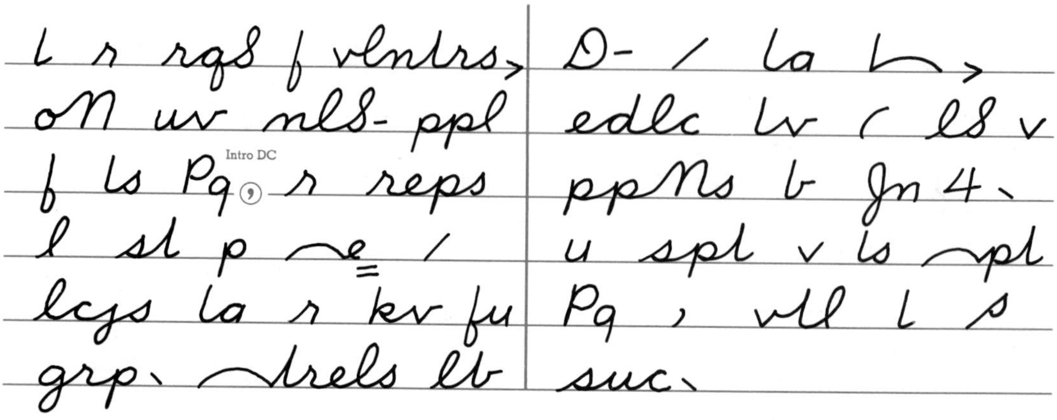

—— 4 ——

Supply two words that are missing in the following letter.

Preview Words

ensure *[shorthand]*	confusion *[shorthand]*
dollar $	difficulties *[shorthand]*
method *[shorthand]*	direct-deposit *[shorthand]*
apologize *[shorthand]*	social security *[shorthand]*

[shorthand outlines]

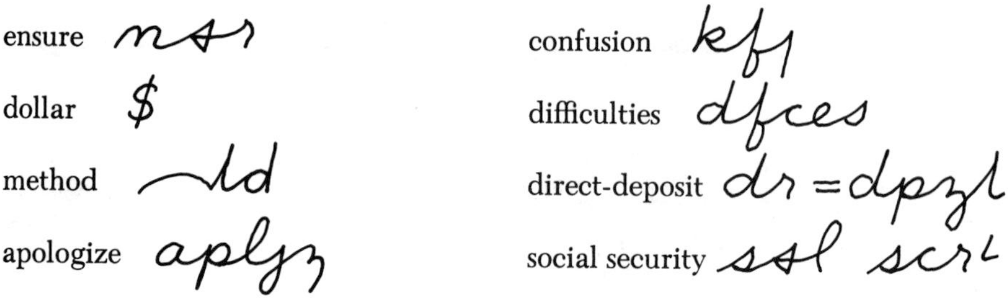

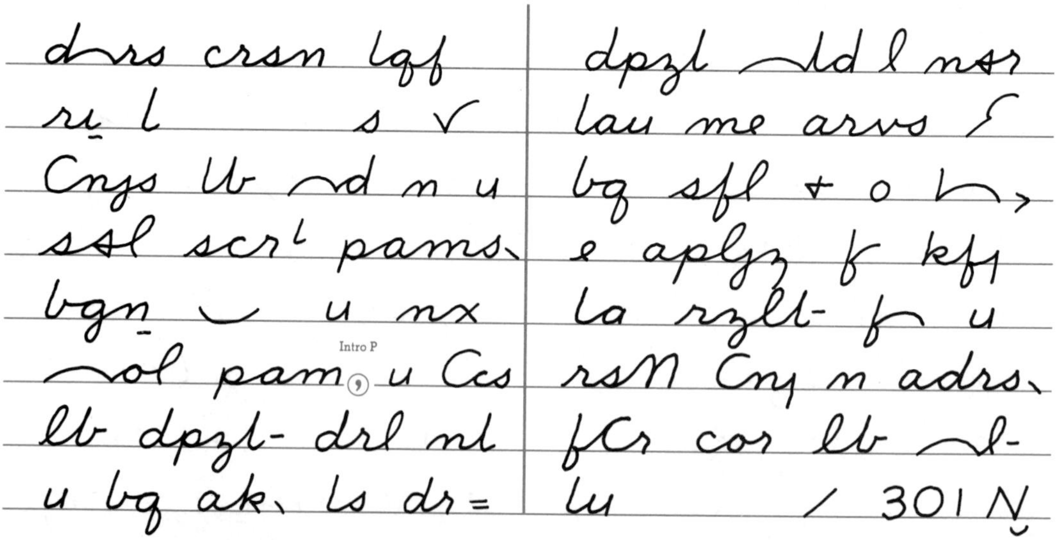

elh S> n re l	ncrs n u —ol
(ad ↓n ou Ccs, (Intro P)	pams dz n q nl
(—ol pams r	efc ull Jl 1> pll
a pd n evn $	s no if uv ne
ads. aso, ((Paren)	adjl dfces. vlu

5

Punctuation Study

Add commas to show two introductory phrases, one direct address, and one parenthetical expression.

Preview Words

refund	rfN	duplicate	dplcl
bylaws	blas	certificate	Slfcl
ordinarily	ordl	incorporation	incj
accordance	acrdN	not-for-profit	n=f=Pfl

d—s h—lln u 5	v blas vu ogj. 51
rqs f incj hsb 12	dplcl cpes v lz 57
grN-. enc-) . 17	dcms vb fl- n 62
Slfcl —C hsb 22	r ofs> p nl la 68
sn- b (sec v 27	(enc- Slfcl z 74
Sq. n adj l (33	grN- U (nu la 79
arlcls v incj 38	gvrn n=f=Pfl 84
er aso enc cpes 44	ogjs. n acrdN 90

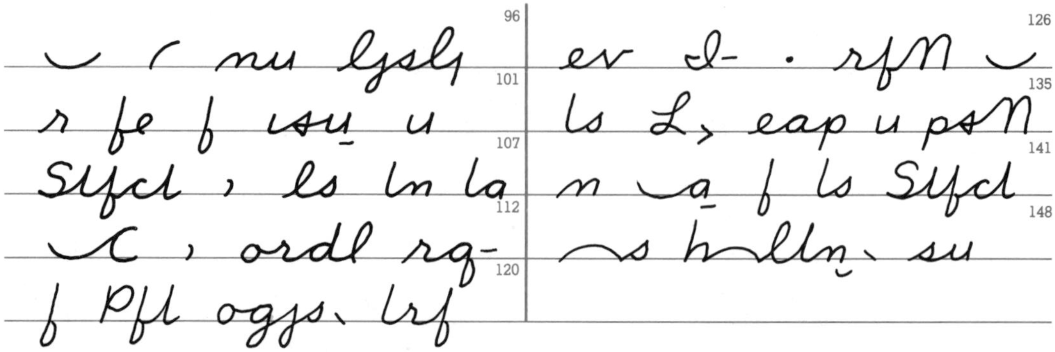

Key

1

Dear Sir or Madam:

The zoning commission will meet at 7:30 p.m. on Wednesday, June 8. The purpose[1] of this meeting will be to consider a request for rezoning 13 acres of land near the intersection[2] of State Road 231 and Interstate 40. The owner of the property has requested that the[3] land, which is currently zoned for agricultural use, be rezoned for industrial use.

Representatives[4] of an industrial firm have expressed interest in purchasing part of the land if the zoning change is granted.[5] Representatives of this firm will be present at the meeting to describe the industrial operation[6] that is being planned for this site.

If you wish to present your views about this zoning request, will you please[7] notify our office by Tuesday that you wish to be recognized? After all views have been presented by the[8] public, the board will conduct a general discussion. Because we expect to give this issue a great deal of[9] consideration before making a decision, voting will not take place before the July meeting.

Yours truly,[10] (200)

2

Dear Mr. Preston:

This letter is to acknowledge that we received your request for printed materials. The[1] Federal Communications Commission does make various brochures available free of charge to the public.[2] Some examples of the subject matter covered are as follows: a description of the FCC, information[3] about the broadcasting industry, history of electronics, history of communications,[4] etc. We will gladly send you several copies of our publications for use in your junior and[5] senior classes. They will be mailed to your school immediately.

If you would like to have a complete copy of the[6] rules and regulations of the FCC, you may secure it from the Government Printing Office for a[7] small fee. We are delighted to assist in educational projects whenever possible. Please contact us[8] again when our services are needed.

Sincerely yours, (170)

3

MEMO TO: County Extension Agents

The Department of Agriculture is planning to conduct studies in[1] four major areas of conservation. Please see the enclosures for detailed descriptions of each study.[2]

In order to make our research effective, we will need to have a large number of farmers participate in[3] these studies; hence, we are asking all county agents to solicit the cooperation of farmers in their[4] areas. We recommend that the agents begin by arranging group meetings and explaining the procedures[5] to the farmers. Because of the nature of these studies, we are anticipating a good response to our request[6] for volunteers.

Once you have enlisted people for this program, our representatives will set up meetings at[7] locations that are convenient for your group. Materials will be distributed at that time.

We would like[8] to have the list of participants by June 4. Your support of this important program is vital to its success.[9] (180)

4

Dear Mrs. Carson:

Thank you for writing to *notify* us of the changes to be made in your social security[1] payments. Beginning with your next monthly payment, your checks will be deposited directly into your bank[2] account. This direct-deposit method will ensure that your money arrives at the bank safely and on time.[3]

We apologize for the confusion that resulted from your recent change in address. Future correspondence[4] will be mailed to your *residence* at 301 North Elm Street.

In regard to the amount shown on your checks, the monthly[5] payments are always paid in even dollar amounts. Also, the increase in your monthly payments does not go[6] into effect until July 1.

Please let us know if you have any additional difficulties.

Very truly[7] yours, (142)

notify: inform, tell

residence: home, address

5

Dear Ms. Hamilton:

Your request for incorporation has been granted. Enclosed is a certificate which[1] has been signed by the Secretary of State. In addition to the articles of incorporation, we are[2] also enclosing copies of the bylaws of your organization. Duplicate copies of these documents[3] have been filed in our office.

Please note that the enclosed certificate was granted under the new law governing[4] not-for-profit organizations. In accordance with the new legislation, our fee for issuing your[5] certificate is less than that which is ordinarily required for profit organizations. Therefore, we have[6] included a refund with this letter.

We appreciate your patience in waiting for this certificate, Ms.[7] Hamilton.

Sincerely yours, (144)

grẹ ofs vzlrs*

One of an office worker's most pleasant and important duties is greeting office visitors. Remember that your appearance and mannerisms reflect the image of the company. Visitors are guests of your organization, and you are the host. Always be courteous, helpful, and professional.

Make a good impression. Maintain a quiet, tidy, and orderly reception area. Your desk should be neat, and your conduct should be mannerly.

Greet visitors immediately. Consider your visitors as the most important priority, even if the visits are interruptions in a busy work schedule. You may say, for example:

> "Hello, may I help you? . . . Yes, Mr. Houseman is expecting you. Please be seated, and I will tell him you're here."

If you are involved in a telephone conversation, excuse yourself politely from the conversation long enough to greet the visitor briefly. Then conclude the phone conversation as quickly as possible and give your full attention to the visitor.

Make the visitor comfortable. If the visitor has to wait, offer assistance and keep the person informed about the delay. If you expect the wait to be longer than five minutes, offer the person magazines or a soft drink.

Make introductions when necessary. Usher the visitor to the appropriate office. If the visitor knows your supervisor, you should keep the introduction simple:

***Greeting Office Visitors**

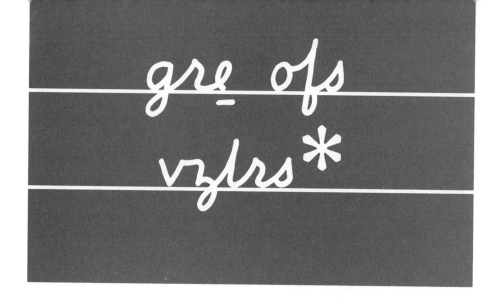

"Ms. Campbell, Mr. Simpson is here to see you."

If the visitor is a newcomer, introduce him or her to your supervisor:

"Ms. Campbell, this is Mr. Carl Simpson from Everview Software."

Say "no" politely, firmly, and positively. When someone arrives without an appointment and wants to see a person who is unavailable, be as positive and helpful as possible by suggesting an alternative appointment:

"I'm very sorry, but Mr. Stone will be in meetings all afternoon. Would you be free to meet with him tomorrow afternoon?"

Remain calm and courteous, but be firm.

INDEX OF BRIEF FORMS

Alphabetical Listing

a (an)	.	as (was)	z
able	B	associate	aso
about	ab	at (it)	/
accept	ac	be (been, but, buy, by)	b
accomplish	ak	been (be, but, buy, by)	b
acknowledge	acj	between	btn
administrate	Am	both	bo
advantage	Avj	business	bs
after	af	but (be, been, buy, by)	b
again (against)	ag	buy (be, been, but, by)	b
against (again)	ag	by (be, been, but, buy)	b
already	Ar	came (come, committee)	k
always	a‿	can	c
am (more)	⁀	character (characteristic)	crc
an (a)	.	characteristic (character)	crc
appreciate	ap	charge	Cj
appropriate	apo	circumstance	Sk
approximate	apx	come (came, committee)	k
are (our)	r	committee (came, come)	k
arrange	ar	complete	kp

congratulate	kq	firm	fr
consider	ks	for (full)	f
continue	ku	from	f⌒
contract	kc	full (for)	f
contribute	kb	general	jn
control	kl	go (good)	g
convenience (convenient)	kv	good (go)	g
convenient (convenience)	kv	grate (great)	gr
correspond (correspondence)	cor	great (grate)	gr
correspondence (correspond)	cor	had (he, him)	h
customer	K	has	hs
deliver	dl	have (of, very)	v
determine	dl	he (had, him)	h
develop	dv	him (had, he)	h
difficult	dfc	his (is)	,
direct (doctor)	dr	hospital	hsp
distribute	D	immediate	⌒⌒
doctor (direct)	dr	importance (important)	⌒pl
during	du_	important (importance)	⌒pl
employ	⌒p	in (not)	n
ever (every)	E	include	_l
every (ever)	E	individual	Nv
experience	vp	industry	N

is (his)	)
it (at)	/
letter	L
manage	⌢j
manufacture	⌢f
market	⌢r
more (am)	⌢
necessary	nes
next	nx
not (in)	n
note	nl
of (have, very)	v
on (own)	o
once	oN
operate	op
opinion	opn
opportunity	opl
order	od
ordinary	ord
organize	og
other	ol
our (are)	r
over	O
own (on)	o
part (port)	pl
participate	pp
particular	plc
perhaps	Ph
please (up)	p
point	py
port (part)	pl
present	P
property	prp
prove	pv
public	pb
refer	rf
respond (response)	rsp
response (respond)	rsp
sample	sa⌢
satisfactory (satisfy)	sal
satisfy (satisfactory)	sal
several	sv
ship	s̶
signature (significance, significant)	sig

significance (signature, significant)	*sig*	up (please)	*p*
		us	*s*
significant (signature, significance)	*sig*	usual	*uz*
situate	*sit*	very (have, of)	*v*
specific (specify)	*sp*	was (as)	*3*
specify (specific)	*sp*	we	*e*
standard	*Sd*	well (will)	*l*
success	*suc*	were (with)	*⌣*
suggest	*sug*	why	*y*
that	*La*	will (well)	*l*
the	*⌐*	with (were)	*⌣*
they	*Ly*	work (world)	*⌣o*
those	*Loz*	world (work)	*⌣o*
to (too)	*l*	would	*d*
too (to)	*l*	your	*u*
under	*U*		

INDEX OF ABBREVIATIONS

Alphabetical Listing

advertise	av
agriculture	agr
America (American)	Am
American (America)	Am
amount	amt
and	&
attention	att
avenue	ave
billion	B
boulevard	blvd
catalog	cat
cent (cents)	¢
cents (cent)	¢
Christmas	Xms
company	co
corporation	corp
credit	cr
day	d
department	dpt
dollar (dollars)	$
dollars (dollar)	$
east	E
economic (economy)	eco
economy (economic)	eco
enclose (enclosure)	enc
enclosure (enclose)	enc
envelope	env
especially	esp
establish	est
et cetera	etc
example (executive)	ex
executive (example)	ex
federal	fed
feet	ft
government	gvt
hour	hr
hundred	H
inch	in
incorporate (incorporated)	inc
incorporated (incorporate)	inc

information	inf	question	q
insurance	ins	record	rec
invoice	inv	regard	re
junior	jr	represent (representative)	rep
literature	lit	representative (represent)	rep
merchandise	mdse	return	ret
million	M	second (secretary)	sec
Miss	m	secretary (second)	sec
month	mo	senior	sr
Mr.	mr	south	S
Mrs.	mrs	square	sq
Ms.	ms	street	st
north	N	superintendent	S
number	no	thousand	T
okay	ok	total	tot
ounce	oz	university	U
percent	%	vice president	VP
pound	lb	volume	vol
president	p	west	W
quart	qt	yard	yd

INDEX OF PHRASES

The following phrases are presented in alphabetical segments beginning with the pronouns I, we, and you plus a verb, followed by infinitive phrases (to plus a verb), high-frequency word combinations, and word combinations with words omitted.

The phrase list presents the 147 phrases in alphabetical segments.

Type	Number
"I" + a verb	25
"We" + a verb	26
"You" + a verb	20
"To" + a verb (infinitive phrase)	24
High-Frequency Word Combinations	44
Words Omitted and Word Compounds with a Word Omitted	8
Total	147

I am	im	I know	ino
I appreciate	iap	I look	ilc
I believe	iblv	I shall	ishl
I can	ic	I should	ishd
I can be	icb	I was	iz
I cannot	icn	I will	il
I could	icd	I will be	ilb
I do	idu	I would	id
I feel	ifl	I would appreciate	idap
I had	ih	I would be	idb
I have	iv	I would like	idlc
I have been	ivb	we appreciate	eap
I have had	ivh	we are	er
I hope	ihp	we are not	ern

we are pleased	erp-	you are	ur
we believe	eblv	you can	uc
we can	ec	you cannot	ucn
we can be	ecb	you can be	ucb
we cannot	ecn	you could	ucd
we could	ecd	you do	udu
we do	edu	you had	uh
we feel	efl	you have	uv
we had	eh	you have been	uvb
we have	ev	you have had	uvh
we have been	evb	you know	uno
we have had	evh	you need	und
we hope	ehp	you should	u4d
we know	eno	you were	u—
we shall	e4l	you will	ul
we should	e4d	you will be	ulb
we were	e—	you will find	ulfN
we will	el	you would	ud
we will be	elb	you would be	udb
we would	ed	you would like	udlc
we would appreciate	edap	to be	Lb
we would be	edb	to call	Lcl
we would like	edlc	to come	Lk

of your	*vu*	will be	*lb*
on the	*6*	will you	*lu*
on you	*ou*	will your	*lu*
on your	*ou*	would be	*db*
should be	*sdb*	would like	*dlc*
thank you	*lqu*	as soon as	*33*
that I	*lai*	nevertheless	*nvrls*
that we	*lae*	nonetheless	*nnls*
that you	*lau*	thank you for	*lqf*
that you are	*laur*	thank you for your	*lqf*
that you will	*laul*	thank you for your letter	*lqfL*
that your	*lau*	time to time	*LL*
to you	*lu*	up to date	*pda*
to your	*lu*		

SUMMARY OF SPEEDWRITING SHORTHAND PRINCIPLES

BY SYSTEM CATEGORY

Simple Sounds

1. Write what you hear	high	hi
2. Write c for the sound of *k*	copy	cpe
3. Write ⌒ for the sound of *m*	may	⌒a
4. Write ◡ for the sound of *w*	way	◡a
5. Write s to form the plural of any outline, to show possession, or to add s to a verb	books	bcs
6. Omit *p* in the sound of *mpt*	empty	⌒le
7. Write x for the medial and final sound of *x*	boxes	bxs
	tax	tx
8. Omit the final *t* of a root word after the sound of *k*	act	ac

Vowels

1. Drop medial vowels	build	bld
2. Write initial and final vowels	office	ofs
	fee	fe
3. Retain beginning or ending vowels when building compound words	payroll	parl
	headache	hdac

4. Retain root-word vowels when adding prefixes and suffixes — disappear: Dapr; payment: pam

5. For words ending in a long vowel + *t*, omit the *t* and write the vowel — rate: ra; meet: 

6. When a word contains two medial, consecutively pronounced vowels, write the first vowel — trial: tril

7. When a word ends in two consecutively pronounced vowels, write only the last vowel — idea: ida

Vowel Blends

1. Write o for the sound of *ow* — allow: alo

2. Write y for the sound of *oi* — boy: by

3. Write a for the initial and final sound of *aw* — law: la; audit: adt

Consonant Blends

1. Write a capital C for the sound of *ch* — check: Cc

2. Write  for the sound of *wh* — when: 

3. Write a capital N for the sound of *nt* — sent: sN

4. Write  for the sound of *ish* or *sh* — finish: 

5. Write l for the sound of *ith* or *th* — them: 

6. Write q for the medial or final sound of any vowel + *nk*	bank	bq
	link	lq
7. Write q for the sound of *kw*	quick	qc
8. Write a capital N for the sound of *nd*	friend	frN
9. Write S for the sound of *st*	rest	rS
10. Write z for the sound of *zh*	pleasure	plzr
11. Write g for the medial or final sound of any vowel plus *ng*	rang	rg
	single	sgl
12. Write M for the sounds of *ance, ence, nce, nse*	balance	blM

Compound Sounds

1. Write m for the sounds of *mem* and *mum*	memo	mo
2. Write m for the sounds of *men, mon, mun*	menu	mu
	money	me
3. Write k for the sounds of *com, con, coun, count*	common	kn
	convey	kva
	counsel	ksl
	account	ak

Word Beginnings

1. Write a capital A for the word beginnings *ad, all,* and *al*	admit	ad
	also	Aso
2. Write n for the initial sound of *in* and *en*	indent	ndN
3. Write a printed capital S (joined) for the word beginnings *cer, cir, ser, sur*	certain	Sln
	survey	Sva
4. Write a capital D for the word beginning *dis*	discuss	Dcs
5. Write a capital M for the word beginning *mis*	misplace	Mpls
6. Write a capital P (disjoined) for the word beginnings *per, pur, pre, pro, pro* (prah)	person	Psn
	prepare	Ppr
	provide	Pvd
	problem	Pbl
7. Write a for the word beginning *an*	answer	asr
8. Write a capital S (disjoined) for the word beginning *super*	supervise	S vz
9. Write el for the word beginning *electr*	electronic	elnc
10. Write ⌒ for the initial sound of *em* or *im*	emphasize	⌒fsz
	impress	⌒prs
11. Write \ for words beginning with the sound of any vowel + *x*	explain	\pln
	accident	\dN

12. Write X for the word beginnings *extr* and *extra*
    - extreme — Xm
    - extraordinary — Xord

13. Write u for the word beginning *un*
    - until — ull

14. Write s for the word beginning *sub*
    - submit — smt

15. Write a capital N for the word beginnings *enter, inter, intra, intro*
    - enterprise — Nprz
    - interest — Ns
    - introduce — Nds

16. Write sf for the word beginning *self*
    - self-made — sfmd

17. Write T for the word beginnings *tran* and *trans*
    - transfer — Tfr

Word Endings

1. Underscore the last letter of the outline to add *ing* or *thing* as a word ending
    - billing — bl̲
    - something — sm̲

2. To form the plural of any outline ending in a mark of punctuation, double the last mark of punctuation
    - savings — sv=

3. To form the past tense of a regular verb, write a hyphen after the outline
    - used — uz-

4. Write m for the word endings *mand, mend, mind, ment*
    - demand — dm
    - amend — am
    - remind — rm
    - payment — pam

5. Write *l* for the word ending *ly* or *ily*	family	fml
6. Write *g* for the word ending *gram*	telegram	tlg
7. Write a capital *S* (disjoined) for the word endings *scribe* and *script*	describe	dS
	manuscript	mnS
8. Write *w* for the word ending *ward*	backward	bcw
9. Write *h* for the word ending *hood*	boyhood	byh
10. Write */* for the word ending *tion* or *sion*	vacation	vc/
11. Write *q* for the word ending *quire*	require	rq
12. Write ʹ for the word ending *ness*	kindness	knʹ
13. Write *B* for the word endings *bil, ble, bly*	possible	psB
	probably	PbB
14. Write a slightly raised and disjoined *i* for the word ending *ity*	quality	ql i
15. Write *sl* for the sound of *shul* and the word ending *chul*	financial	fnnsl
16. Write *v* for the medial and final sound of *tive*	effective	efcv
17. Write *f* for the word endings *ful* and *ify*	careful	crf
	justify	jsf
18. Write *fy* for the word ending *ification*	qualifications	qlfys

19. Write *sf* for the word ending *self* — myself 

20. Write *svs* for the word ending *selves* — ourselves 

Marks of Punctuation

1. Underscore the last letter of the outline to add *ing* or *thing* as a word ending — billing  something 

2. To form the plural of any outline ending in a mark of punctuation, double the last mark of punctuation — savings 

3. To form the past tense of a regular verb, write a hyphen after the outline — used 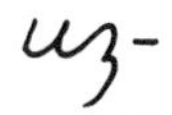

4. Write ′ for the word ending *ness* — kindness 

5. To show capitalization, draw a small curved line under the last letter of the outline — Bill 

6. Write \ to indicate a period at the end of a sentence

7. Write x to indicate a question mark

8. Write > to indicate the end of a paragraph

9. Write ! to indicate an exclamation *mark*

10. Write = to indicate a dash

11. Write = to indicate a hyphen

12. To indicate solid capitalization, double the curved line underneath the last letter of the outline

13. To indicate an underlined title, draw a solid line under the outline

14. Write   to indicate parentheses

IDENTIFICATION INITIALS FOR UNITED STATES AND TERRITORIES

Alabama (AL)	AL	Maryland (MD)	MD
Alaska (AK)	AK	Massachusetts (MA)	MA
Arizona (AZ)	AZ	Michigan (MI)	MI
Arkansas (AR)	AR	Minnesota (MN)	MN
California (CA)	CA	Mississippi (MS)	MS
Colorado (CO)	CO	Missouri (MO)	MO
Connecticut (CT)	CT	Montana (MT)	MT
Delaware (DE)	DE	Nebraska (NE)	NE
District of Columbia (DC)	DC	Nevada (NV)	NV
Florida (FL)	FL	New Hampshire (NH)	NH
Georgia (GA)	GA	New Jersey (NJ)	NJ
Hawaii (HI)	HI	New Mexico (NM)	NM
Idaho (ID)	ID	New York (NY)	NY
Illinois (IL)	IL	North Carolina (NC)	NC
Indiana (IN)	IN	North Dakota (ND)	ND
Iowa (IA)	IA	Ohio (OH)	OH
Kansas (KS)	KS	Oklahoma (OK)	OK
Kentucky (KY)	KY	Oregon (OR)	OR
Louisiana (LA)	LA	Pennsylvania (PA)	PA
Maine (ME)	ME	Rhode Island (RI)	RI

South Carolina (SC)	SC	West Virginia (WV)	WV
South Dakota (SD)	SD	Wisconsin (WI)	WI
Tennessee (TN)	TN	Wyoming (WY)	WY
Texas (TX)	TX		
Utah (UT)	UT	Canal Zone (CZ)	CZ
Vermont (VT)	VT	Guam (GU)	GU
Virginia (VA)	VA	Puerto Rico (PR)	PR
Washington (WA)	WA	Virgin Islands (VI)	VI

CANADIAN PROVINCES AND TERRITORIES

Alberta (AB)	AB	Nova Scotia (NS)	NS
British Columbia (BC)	BC	Ontario (ON)	ON
Labrador	LB	Prince Edward Island (PE)	PE
Manitoba (MB)	MB	Quebec (PQ)	PQ
New Brunswick (NB)	NB	Saskatchewan (SK)	SK
Newfoundland (NF)	NF	Yukon Territory (YT)	YT
Northwest Territories (NT)	NT		

INDEX OF CITIES

American Cities

Akron	acrn
Albany	Abne
Albuquerque	Abcrce
Allentown	Anlon
Atlanta	alNa
Austin	aSn
Baltimore	blt—
Baton Rouge	bln rz
Birmingham	brmgh
Boston	bSn
Bridgeport	brypl
Buffalo	bflo
Charleston	CrlSn
Charlotte	srll
Chattanooga	Clnga
Chicago	scq
Cincinnati	sNnle
Cleveland	clvlN
Colorado Springs	CO sprgs
Columbia	cl—ba
Columbus	cl—bs
Dallas	dls
Davenport	dvnpl
Dayton	dln
Denver	dnvr
Des Moines	d —yn
Detroit	dlryl
El Paso	el pso
Flint	flN
Fort Lauderdale	fl ldrdl
Fort Worth	fl ⌣rl
Fresno	frzno
Grand Rapids	grN rpds
Harrisburg	hrsbrq
Hartford	hrlfd
Honolulu	hnllu
Houston	hSn
Indianapolis	Nenpls

Jackson	jcsn	Norfolk	nrfc
Jacksonville	jcsnvl	Oakland	oclN
Jersey City	jrze sle	Oklahoma City	OK sle
Kansas City	KS sle	Omaha	o~ha
Knoxville	nxvl	Orlando	orlNo
Lansing	lNq	Peoria	pera
Las Vegas	ls vgs	Philadelphia	fldlfa
Little Rock	lll rc	Phoenix	fnx
Los Angeles	ls ajls	Pittsburgh	plsbrq
Louisville	luvl	Portland	plN
Memphis	mfs	Providence	PvdN
Miami	~ie	Richmond	rCmd
Milwaukee	~lce	Rochester	rCSr
Minneapolis	mepls	Sacramento	scrmlo
Mobile	~B	St. Louis	sN lus
Nashville	n+vl	St. Paul	sN pl
New Haven	nu hvn	St. Petersburg	sN plrsbrq
New Orleans	nu orlns	Salt Lake City	sll lc sle
New York	NY	San Antonio	sn alno
Newark	nurc	San Bernadino	sn brndno
Newport News	nupl nz	San Diego	sn deq

San Francisco	sn frnssco	Tampa	l—pa
San Jose	sn hza	Toledo	lldo
Sarasota	srsla	Trenton	lrNn
Scranton	scrNn	Tucson	lsn
Seattle	sell	Tulsa	llsa
Shreveport	srvpl	West Palm Beach	W p— bC
Spokane	spcn	Wichita	⌣Cla
Springfield	sprgfld	Wilmington	⌣—gln
Syracuse	srcs	Worcester	⌣Sr
Tacoma	lc—a	Youngstown	ygslon

Canadian Cities

Brampton	br—ln	Laval	lvl
Burlington	brlgln	London	lNn
Burnaby	brnbe	Mississauga	Msga
Calgary	clgre	Montreal	mlrel
East York	E yrc	Oshawa	osa
Edmonton	edmln	Ottawa	ola
Etobicoke	elbcc	Quebec	qbc
Halifax	hlfx	Regina	ryna
Hamilton	h—lln	St. Catharines	sN clrns
Kitchener	cCnr	Saskatoon	sscln

Thunder Bay		Windsor	
Toronto		Winnipeg	
Vancouver		York	

ADDRESSES AND MEMO INFORMATION

Lesson 1

1. Mrs. Jane Rogers, Department of Business Education, Pierpoint High School, 166 Winthrop Avenue, Portland, ME 04101
2. Mrs. Jane Rogers, Department of Business Education, Pierpoint High School, 166 Winthrop Avenue, Portland, ME 04101
3. Mr. Nathaniel Watson, Campus View Residence Hall, Room 314, 711 West Kingsport Road, St. Louis, MO 36131
4. Ms. Carolyn S. White, Personnel Director, McCormick Allied Corporation, 4300 South Woodburn Avenue, Charlotte, NC 28210
5. Ms. Barbara Conners, 10073 Red Rock Drive, Denver, CO 80237

Lesson 2

1. Mr. Ray Ottmier, Manager, Appleton Manufacturing Company, 4300 Arlington Avenue, Trenton, NJ 08690
2. Mr. James H. Jordan, New Century Computerworld Stores, 7401 Executive Park, Akron, OH 44313
3. Miss Cynthia Doyle, Head Buyer, Hamilton Sportswear, 621 Fuller Street, Portland, OR 97201
4. Mr. Wayne Dobson, 43154 Cardinal Lane, Cincinnati, OH 45214
5. Mr. C. David Moore, 5202 Willow Cove Drive, Apartment 2A, Tampa, FL 33617

Lesson 3

1. Miss Charlotte Marie Robinson, 535 Latigo Circle, Salt Lake City, UT 84120
2. Memo to Eric Hunter from Kyle Anderson, SUBJECT: Request for Transfer
3. Mr. Fred Evanston, Vice President for Administration, Freepont Company, 19 Industrial Park, Milwaukee, WI 53217
4. Ms. Michelle Gregory, 5443 Amherst, Brooklyn, NY 11235
5. Mr. Walter G. Richards, Tyler Personnel Specialists, 219 Alpine Avenue, Grand Rapids, MI 49503

Lesson 4

1. Dr. Emerson Harper, 3001 Sherbrooke, Montreal, PQ H3C 3A4
2. Miss Mary Elizabeth Thomason, Business Education Department, Clarence Downing High School, 1010 Brandstater Avenue, Riverside, CA 92325
3. Mrs. Susan Miller, Personnel Manager, Prescott Corporation, 103 Valley Vista Way, Nashville, TN 37214
4. Mr. Carlyle Olson, American Electronics, 2201 West 54 Street, Baltimore, MD 21228
5. Mr. Edward A. Cox, Rural Route 7, Box 553, Lincoln, NE 68502

Lesson 5

1. Mrs. Shelley Davis, Bradbury Corporation, P.O. Box 136, Columbus, OH 43224
2. Miss Jill Reynolds, 2214 Clairmont, Apartment 4B, Chicago, IL 60653
3. Form letter to employees from J. Alan Steele, Director of Personnel
4. Mr. Joseph Lee, Association of American Investors, 179 Avenue of the Americas, New York, NY 10013
5. Ms. Ruth A. Martin, Wescott Industries, 1649 Georgetown Road, Macon, GA 31201

Lesson 6

1. Mr. W. L. Howard, Stanton Catering and Food Services, 1903 Riverfront Drive, Charleston, SC 29407
2. Mr. Everett Clay, Math Department, Northside High School, 1117 Hastings Road, Spokane, WA 99218
3. Mr. Charles H. Michael, Global Travel Agency, 4252 Cypress Street, Pensacola, FL 32501
4. Memo to All Employees from Keith Logan, SUBJECT: Parking Lot Repairs
5. Memo to Richard Mitchell from Valerie M. Ferguson, SUBJECT: Vacancy for Department Supervisor

Lesson 7

1. Memo to Helen Marshall from Andy Fairchild, SUBJECT: Update of the Secretarial Handbook
2. Form letter to new employees from Barbara Bainbridge, Personnel Manager
3. Memo to All Employees from Janice Barry, SUBJECT: Christmas Discounts
4. Ms. Vivian Stevens, Editorial Manager, Arrowhead Press, 1230 Brooks Avenue, Lexington, KY 40508
5. Memo to All Staff from Cynthia B. Alford, SUBJECT: Policy for Office Closings

Lesson 8

1. Memo to Jessica Nelson from Robert J. Hopkins, SUBJECT: Staff Additions
2. Memo to All Staff from Annabelle Moffett, SUBJECT: Employee Trips
3. Mr. Benjamin Thomas, Sandbar Manufacturing Company, 822 Whitman Street, Tucson, AZ 85711
4. Memo to All Managers from Gloria Stanislaw, SUBJECT: Performance Evaluations
5. Mrs. Allison Foster, Director of Volunteer Services, Wintergreen Memorial Hospital, 1000 Breckenridge Boulevard, Buffalo, NY 14213

Lesson 9

1. Ms. Diana S. Fields, 701 West Georgia, Vancouver, BC V7Y 1K5
2. Mr. Stanley Clark, Diagnostic Research Corporation, 5912 Applewood Road, Little Rock, AR 72118
3. Memo to Debbie Leonard from Jim Wilkerson, SUBJECT: Visitor Identification Badges

4. Memo to Customer Service Representatives from June Milton, Assistant Personnel Manager, SUBJECT: Retirement Luncheon for Gloria Hastings
5. Mr. Ronald S. Mason, Mason Construction, Inc., 2119 Jackson Street, Kansas City, KS 67501

Lesson 10

1. Mr. Kevin Brewer, Academic Services Director, Midwestern State University, 12 Lindwood Avenue, Davenport, IA 52804
2. Memo to All Department Heads from Gerald P. Cunningham, SUBJECT: Schedule for Training Sessions
3. Memo to Office Supervisors from Bonnie Ashcraft, SUBJECT: Vacation Schedules
4. Ms. Theresa Ward, Webster Consulting Agency, 444 Atlantic Avenue, Norfolk, VA 23517
5. Form letter to employees from Jason Allen

Lesson 11

1. Mrs. Virginia Moore, Upper Deck Restaurant, 514 Belmont Plaza, Fort Worth, TX 76110
2. Miss Andrea Grant, Penelope's Chest, 1993 West Sagecrest Avenue, Fort Worth, TX 76109
3. Memo to Janet Masters from Adam Newlin, SUBJECT: October Sales Invitations
4. Mr. Daniel H. Williams, Certified Public Accountant, 703 McCaw Street, Pittsburgh, PA 15204
5. Mrs. Gary Marshall, 1660 Shore Acres Road, Tacoma, WA 98498

Lesson 12

1. Form letter to prospective customers from Betty Sanderson
2. Mr. Timothy E. Clark, Central Bank and Trust, 222 Peabody Avenue, Toledo, OH 43614
3. Mr. Claude W. Lee, 4256 Sylvania Drive, Belleville, IL 62223
4. Mr. Glen Jackson, American Supply, Inc., 1700 East 40 Street, Tulsa, OK 74106
5. Form letter to prospective customers from Sylvia Cole

Lesson 13

1. Mr. John R. Flint, 202 Prince George Court, Indianapolis, IN 46217
2. Mrs. Peggy Sylvester, 3413 Parkland Place, Washington, DC 20032
3. Form letter to prospective customers from Edwin Harrington Cooke, Vice President
4. Mr. and Mrs. Leon Anderson, 341 Pine Crest Lane, Birmingham, AL 35216
5. Form letter to members from Lynn Snyder

Lesson 14

1. Mr. Paul Marvin, 3211 Albert Street, Regina, SK S4S 5W6
2. Mrs. Ronald Hunter, 471 Mondalock Lane, Manchester, NH 03102

3. Mrs. Natalie Gregory, Public Relations Coordinator, Dos Hermanos Hospital, 1007 Palo Verde Boulevard, Albuquerque, NM 87114
4. Mr. Jeffrey Sandifer, 9360 Camden Way, Apartment C, Rochester, NY 14610
5. Ms. Robinette Jackson, 687 Cedarwood Circle, St. Paul, MN 55125

Lesson 15

1. Mr. Eric Davidson, Rural Route 2, Box 503, Racine, WI 53408
2. Ms. Karen Chase, Berghoff Container Corporation, P.O. Box 8215, Atlanta, GA 30317
3. Mr. and Mrs. Lawrence Walters, 180 Courtland Avenue, Bridgeport, CT 06604
4. Form letter to prospective customers from J. B. Hodges, Sales Manager
5. Ms. Emily Evans, 1402 Little Creek Road, Bloomington, IN 47401

Lesson 16

1. Mr. Donald M. Jackson, 1033 Shadowdance Street, San Antonio, TX 78253
2. Mr. and Mrs. Herbert Carlson, 217 Highland Place, Cheyenne, WY 82009
3. Mr. and Mrs. Kenneth Webb, 4380 Magnolia Drive, Virginia Beach, VA 23464
4. Mr. Thomas Hastings, 3229 Prospect Boulevard, Boston, MA 02160
5. Form letter to prospective customers from Jeremy O'Connell, President

Lesson 17

1. Mr. Roland Wilson, 1001 Portage Avenue, Winnipeg, MB R3C 3J3
2. Ms. Anne Russell, 1511 Gentry Street, Wichita, KS 67208
3. Mrs. George Clay, 212 Covey Hill Court, Boise, ID 83705
4. Memo to Nancy Parker from Richard Crow, SUBJECT: Proposal for New Monthly Statements
5. Miss Beverly Lee, Vice President, Pioneer Bank and Trust, 6400 Mission Road, Colorado Springs, CO 80915

Lesson 18

1. Dr. Charles Foster, 824 Augusta Drive, Anchorage, AK 99504
2. Form letter to prospective customers from Franklin Cox, President
3. Mr. Henry Knight, 2483 El Camino Road, Tempe, AZ 85282
4. Miss Katherine James, 139 Cardiff Drive, Wilmington, DE 19803
5. Dr. and Mrs. Elliott Webb, 5939 Rainbow Road, Omaha, NE 68112

Lesson 19

1. Mr. and Mrs. Harvey Evans, 632 Homestead Avenue, Cleveland, OH 44105
2. Mr. and Mrs. Kevin Grant, 2104 Shamrock Avenue, Green Bay, WI 54304
3. Form letter to prospective customers from Diana T. Wilcox, Branch Manager
4. Mr. Melvin Baxter, 320 Kelly Street, Stillwater, OK 74074
5. Dr. and Mrs. Michael Gregory, 7635 Oaklawn Drive, Memphis, TN 38114

Lesson 20

1. Mr. and Mrs. Maurice Harper, 6009 Richmond Avenue, Arlington, VA 22207
2. Mr. Robert Billings, 43 McKinney Drive, Greenville, SC 29609
3. Form letter to depositors from Stuart Abel, Special Accounts Manager
4. Miss Caroline Robinson, 6747 Sheffield Place, Apartment 4B, Providence, RI 02920
5. Mr. William Temple, President, First National Bank, 3006 Anderson Boulevard, Eugene, OR 97401

Lesson 21

1. Hoffmeister Corporation, Paper Goods Division, 213 Piedmont Avenue, Fayetteville, NC 28304
2. Dr. and Mrs. Todd W. Brown, 7429 Kirkwood Road, St. Louis, MO 63119
3. Form letter to homeowners from Milton Pershing, President
4. Ms. Sandra Overton, Reliance Insurance Agency, 810 Centennial Avenue, Trenton, NJ 08629
5. Mr. and Mrs. Albert Mason, 107 Sierra Court, Reno, NV 89506

Lesson 22

1. Form letter to parents from Martin J. Osgood, President
2. Mrs. Shirley Morgan, 945 Forsythe Street, Troy, MI 48098
3. Miss Nancy Webster, 652 Abilene Drive, Bethesda, MD 20815
4. Memo to Alex Long from Christine Bigley, SUBJECT: Proposed Group Plans
5. Form letter to an executive from Clarence Devore, President

Lesson 23

1. Mr. Kent Henderson, Claims Division, Mutual Farm Insurance Company, 2910 Bradley Avenue, Baton Rouge, LA 70805
2. Ms. Suzanne Gray, 714 Greenleaf Lane, South Bend, IN 46637
3. Mr. Edward Buchanan, Devron Insurance Company, 2300 Executive Park, Springfield, IL 62704
4. Ms. Betty Manchester, 6340 Pittman Avenue, Valdosta, GA 31601
5. Mr. Bradley North, 144 Downing Street, Hartford, CT 06517

Lesson 24

1. Ms. Melanie Doyle, 5001 Granada Avenue, Sacramento, CA 93906
2. Mr. Larry Clay, 7331 Nakuina Street, Honolulu, HI 96819
3. Mr. Jim Harper, Vice President, Home and Life Insurance Company, 280 West 29 Avenue, Spokane, WA 99203
4. Mrs. Janice Tower, 416 Southwood Drive, Fargo, ND 58103
5. Mr. Oliver Wilson, 8993 Sherman Avenue, Peoria, IL 61606

Lesson 25

1. Mr. Herbert P. Marshall, 1300 Sixth Avenue, S.W., Calgary, AB T3C 0H8
2. Mr. Alan George, 211 Duncan Street, Clarksville, TN 37042
3. Mrs. Eva Miller, 2178 Fairview Avenue, Columbus, OH 43212
4. Form letter to prospective clients from Anthony T. Holcomb, President
5. Ms. Theresa James, 132 17th Street, Omaha, NE 68121

Lesson 26

1. Form letter to prospective clients from Peter Osgood, Financial Analyst
2. Mr. Brian Gregory, 420 Saddle Lane, Pontiac, MI 48053
3. Ms. Lisa Christopher, 963 South Congress Avenue, Jackson, MS 39201
4. Mr. and Mrs. J. R. Bishop, 778 Crossmoor Lane, Louisville, KY 40222
5. Ms. Deanna Conway, 4383 Six Mile Road, Casper, WY 82604

Lesson 27

1. Mr. and Mrs. Sheldon Turner, 319 Sunrise Lane, Charleston, WV 25313
2. Mr. William N. Conners, 304 East Oak, Quebec City, PQ G1R 4S7
3. Mr. Roy Stillwell, Treasurer, National Motors, Inc., P.O. Box 613, Flint, MI 48503
4. Memo to Bill Michaels from Sally Randall, SUBJECT: Upcoming Lectures on Personal Finance
5. Dr. Andrew Cox, 3518 Paxon Drive, Wilmington, DE 19803

Lesson 28

1. Form letter to board members from Mary Elizabeth Parker
2. Mr. Wally Kingston, 1120 Kitty Hawk Road, Greensboro, NC 27407
3. Ms. Emily Hatfield, 842 Longmeadow Road, Yonkers, NY 10701
4. Dr. Everett Gray, Business and Finance Department, Westport Junior College, 4597 Shore Drive, Providence, RI 02919
5. Miss Karen Little, 604 Illinois Avenue, Columbia, MO 65201

Lesson 29

1. Mr. Gregory K. Roberts, 476 Delbert Drive, Idaho Falls, ID 83401
2. Miss Barbara Trent, 254 Bluebird Street, Ogden, UT 84058
3. Mr. Richard Marshall, 152 Aponte, San Juan, PR 00911
4. Mr. Edward Sanders, Wilcox and Jeffers, Investors, 1322 Whitaker Avenue, Milwaukee, WI 53107
5. Mr. Gene Henderson, Heritage Foundation, 302 Washington Street, Allentown, PA 16601

Lesson 30

1. Mr. Ronald Kelly, 4950 San Rafael Avenue, Los Angeles, CA 90067
2. Mr. and Mrs. John W. Chester, 220 Camelot Lane, Billings, MT 59106

3. Form letter to prospective clients from Charles Wetherford, President
4. Wiley and Associates, Certified Public Accountants, 301 Pickett Road, Fayetteville, NC 27712
5. Ms. Elizabeth Henry, Wellington Investment Company, 1478 Fifth Avenue, Huntington, WV 25701

Lesson 31

1. Dr. H. B. Winters, 889 Geneva Court, Newark, DE 19711
2. Ms. Ruth Ann Donaldson, 1555 Stone Ridge Drive, Lansing, MI 48917
3. Mr. and Mrs. Jeffrey Anderson, 911 De Kalb Avenue, White Plains, NY 10605
4. Mrs. Judith Williams, 202 Portside Drive, Naples, FL 33940
5. Mrs. Lawrence Hudson, 614 Douglas Street, Columbus, GA 31903

Lesson 32

1. Miss Louise Conrad, 6632 Green Brook Road, Apartment 6A, Baltimore, MD 21229
2. Ms. Christine Madison, M & M Travel Agency, 2000 Los Ranchos Road, Albuquerque, NM 87113
3. Miss Carolyn Baker, 341 Pinehurst Drive, Pittsburgh, PA 15241
4. Mr. Clifford Hardy, 1590 Thurmont Road, Akron, OH 44312
5. Four Seasons Lodge, Rural Route 4, Land O' Lakes, WI 54540

Lesson 33

1. Mr. Sidney B. Leonard, 2213 Denver Avenue, Austin, TX 78723
2. Mr. Thomas Carson, Downtown Inn, 490 Grand Avenue, New Haven, CT 06513
3. Mrs. Beverly A. Mason, 1224 Maryview Lane, Davenport, IA 52807
4. Mr. Frank M. Harvey, 3995 Gable Park Road, Portland, OR 97209
5. Mrs. Marjorie Middleton, Mansington Corporation, 217 College Avenue, Philadelphia, PA 19124

Lesson 34

1. Mr. and Mrs. David Hunter, 2983 Tamarack Drive, Cleveland, OH 44134
2. Form letter to prospective clients from Lynn Heatherton
3. Mrs. Sarah Phillips, 900 Bay Street, Toronto, ON M7A 2E1
4. Miss Donna L. Ray, 1180 Aldrich Street, Providence, RI 02920
5. Professor James P. Egan, Westmoreland Institute, 312 Academy Street, Richmond, VA 23225

Lesson 35

1. Ms. Beverly Mitchell, 616 Nicholas Lane, Knoxville, TN 37918
2. Mr. and Mrs. Richard O. Carlson, 8981 Dellridge Avenue, St. Paul, MN 55107
3. Mr. Neil Christopher, 2754 Indian School Road, Phoenix, AZ 85043

4. Form letter to students from Susan Fremont
5. Mr. Paul E. Vernon, Editor, Northwest Publishers, Inc., 203 State Street, Billings, MT 59101

Lesson 36

1. Miss Andrea Martin, Woolcott Corporation, 5440 West 42 Street, New York, NY 10036
2. Mr. Samuel Edwards, Carpet Corner, 1211 Independence Avenue, Oklahoma City, OK 73108
3. Mr. Arthur Gregory, General Manager, Advantage Agency, 652 Sixth Avenue, Sacramento, CA 95818
4. Alcott Manufacturing Company, 837 Cardinal Avenue, St. Louis, MO 63129
5. Ms. Joyce Hodges, McDowell Advertising Agency, 2502 Lincoln Memorial Drive, Milwaukee, WI 53105

Lesson 37

1. Memo to All Staff Members from J. T. Stanton, SUBJECT: Awards Ceremony
2. Miss Patricia Langston, Manager, Century Appliances, 2000 Chandler Street, Spokane, WA 99218
3. Form letter to prospective subscribers from F. William Layton, Publisher
4. Memo to Pamela Stevens from Steve Brooks, SUBJECT: York Industries Account
5. Memo to Ed Foster from Nancy Thacker, SUBJECT: Advertising Cost Changes in Recent Promotions

Lesson 38

1. Mr. Kenneth Webster, Webster Advertising Agency, 1578 Drake Boulevard, Scranton, PA 18512
2. Form letter to prospective subscribers from Cynthia S. Wilcox, Circulation Director
3. Ms. Gloria Trent, Maxwell Designers, 4778 California Street, Colorado Springs, CO 80911
4. Mr. Clarence Rogers, Waycross Corporation, 599 Pomona Street, San Francisco, CA 94127
5. Mrs. Joyce Donaldson, Coastal State University, 2366 Bunker Ranch Road, West Palm Beach, FL 33405

Lesson 39

1. Mr. Richard C. Buchanan, Director of Product Development, Cambridge Manufacturing Company, 3821 North Meridian Street, Indianapolis, IN 46260
2. Mrs. Elaine Jackson, Jackson Sporting Goods, 8640 Maplewood Avenue, Chattanooga, TN 37405
3. Mr. Claude K. Davis, Manager, New Horizons Agency, 906 Weston Street, Salt Lake City, UT 84103
4. Memo to Bill Harrison from Alex Sterling, SUBJECT: Proposed Automobile Ads
5. Mr. James H. Cox, 119 King Street. Hamilton, ON L8N 3V9

Lesson 40

1. Mr. Jerry Baxter, Southwestern Food Stores, 6780 Campbell Road, Houston, TX 77090
2. Miss Candice Morgan, Marketing Director, Sunset Glassware Company, 557 West 59 Street, Des Moines, IA 50312
3. Mr. Hugh Webb, Webb Appliance Repair Service, 3709 Bachman Place, Newark, NJ 07108
4. Ms. Elizabeth Howard, Preston Enterprises, 1052 107th Avenue, Omaha, NE 68124
5. Mr. George Whitaker, Committee to Re-elect Senator Wells, P.O. Box 547, Portland, OR 97217

Lesson 41

1. Mr. Robert M. May, Versatile Plastics, Inc., 5902 Waterfront Drive, Norfolk, VA 23508
2. Mr. Todd Harrison, 630 Russett Street, Oakland, CA 94603
3. Mrs. Gretchen Ford, 934 Oleander Way, St. Petersburg, FL 33707
4. Mr. and Mrs. Walter Gregory, 170 Foxwood Lane, Nashville, TN 37214
5. Ms. Margaret Cole, Highland Realty, 1298 Kenwood Avenue, Harrisburg, PA 17112

Lesson 42

1. Mr. William Davenport, Adler Industries, 9844 Henderson Road, Chicago, IL 60660
2. Mrs. Angela Webster, Southern Import Company, 361 Atlanta Avenue, New Orleans, LA 70114
3. Mrs. Emily Johnson, 732 Dutton Drive, Orlando, FL 32808
4. Mr. and Mrs. Stanley R. Doyle, 1020 Timberlane Road, Tulsa, OK 74136
5. Ms. Patricia Hunter, Togs for Toddlers, 406 Easton Place, Charlotte, NC 28212

Lesson 43

1. Mr. and Mrs. David M. Scott, 4005 Devonshire Road, Toledo, OH 43607
2. Mr. Stan Barker, 6761 Grove Place, Rochester, NY 14615
3. Dr. and Mrs. Matthew Cox, 221 Friendship Drive, Mobile, AL 36610
4. Ms. Allison Foster, 612 Madras Lane, Phoenix, AZ 85013
5. Ms. Karen Mitchell, 5734 Pillsbury Avenue, Minneapolis, MN 55427

Lesson 44

1. Dr. J. D. Nelson, 366 Lamar Court, Springfield, IL 62702
2. Mr. Douglas Murphy, 6561 River Road, Syracuse, NY 13207
3. Miss Kathleen S. Leonard, 2922 Brighton Place, Wilmington, DE 19802
4. Mr. Anthony Morgan, 511 Bluemound Court, Milwaukee, WI 53228
5. Mr. and Mrs. Daniel Marshall, 4620 Colfax Road, El Paso, TX 79902

Lesson 45

1. Memo to Howard Logan from Mike Palmer, SUBJECT: Property Purchase
2. Mr. Gerald Thurman, 388 Seneca Street, Seattle, WA 98199

3. Ms. Linda Roberts, 1990 Viking Terrace, Apartment 2B, Boston, MA 02130
4. Mrs. Janice Barnett, 4001 Kipling Place, Shreveport, LA 71118
5. Mr. and Mrs. Andrew Williams, 5068 MacDonald Avenue, Edmonton, AB T6H 5C5

Lesson 46

1. Mr. John W. Marvin, Maritime Equipment Corporation, 9002 Central Parkway, Newport News, VA 23606
2. Mr. Frank Harvey, Jackson and Jackson, Ltd., 1356 Hempstead Road, Dayton, OH 45402
3. Memo to All Supervisors from Gary R. Smith, SUBJECT: Safety Regulations Review
4. Mrs. Beatrice Miller, 7778 Augustine Way, Louisville, KY 40291
5. Memo to All Employees from Cynthia L. Steele, SUBJECT: City Fund Drive

Lesson 47

1. Avondale Department Store, 598 South Oregon Avenue, Tampa, FL 33612
2. Memo to All Employees from Leon Stuckey, SUBJECT: Mail System Delays
3. Memo to Linda Charles from Kevin Bennett, Regional Sales Manager, SUBJECT: Catalogs
4. Mr. Thomas N. Jenkins, Ellsworth Manufacturing, Inc., 6330 Butler Avenue, Bridgeport, CT 06605
5. Mr. Richard S. Hudson, Director of Operations, Newcastle Industries, P.O. Box 2214, Denver, CO 80236

Lesson 48

1. Ms. Anne Temple, Wesley Department Store, 688 Harper Street, Mobile, AL 36603
2. Mr. Timothy Jason, Sheldon Men's Wear Company, 9535 Willard Avenue, Rockford, IL 61103
3. Mr. David A. Chester, Red Banks Lumber Company, 4219 Canyon Boulevard, Boulder, CO 80301
4. Mr. Harold B. Turner, Director of Marketing, Wentworth Corporation, 508 Market Street, Halifax, NS B3J 3A5
5. Miss Barbara J. Sterling, Independent Information Analysts, Inc., 301 Birchwood Avenue, Madison, WI 53217

Lesson 49

1. Form letter to prospective customers from Arthur Benson
2. Memo to All Employees from Claudia Hardin, SUBJECT: Improvements in Insurance Benefits
3. Mr. Clark Harrison, 1864 Victor, Richmond, VA 23222
4. Memo to All Employees from Alan H. Crenshaw, SUBJECT: Incentive Plan Update
5. Mrs. Carolyn Hastings, H & H Advertising Agency, 4304 Durbin Avenue, Memphis, TN 38118

Lesson 50

1. Memo to All Managers from Claude F. Singleton, SUBJECT: New Production Procedures
2. Ms. Cheryl Doyle, Styles by Andrea, 166 Van Noppen Road, Greensboro, NC 27407
3. Mr. Victor Hamilton, Westside Lumber Company, 4454 Executive Park Drive, Salt Lake City, UT 84107
4. Great Western Wear, 10493 Gibson Boulevard, Albuquerque, NM 87105
5. Ms. Louise Richards, The Crowning Touch, 255 Seventh Street, Scranton, PA 18512

Lesson 51

1. Mr. James K. Vincent, Mid-City Hardware Company, 934 Percy Avenue, Cincinnati, OH 45211
2. Memo to Richard Lincoln from Paul R. Bradley, SUBJECT: Clarification of January Sales Contracts
3. Ledford Container Corporation, 20019 Crystal Road, Charlotte, NC 28205
4. Memo to Elizabeth Preston from Art Cooper, SUBJECT: Committee to Study Information Management
5. Mrs. Sharon Williams, 300 Dufferin Avenue, London, ON N6A 4L9

Lesson 52

1. Professional Marketing Corporation, 5352 National Boulevard, Shreveport, LA 71109
2. Mohawk Office Supplies, 281 Oliver Avenue, Minneapolis, MN 55405
3. Memo to Susan Carter from Joanne Clifford, SUBJECT: Data Base for Inventory Control
4. Mr. Alexander Roberts, Alpha Laboratories, 10742 Inwood Road, Dallas, TX 75229
5. Memo to Jennifer Ford from Kenneth E. Bland, SUBJECT: Computer Equipment Sales

Lesson 53

1. Mrs. Carol Sheldon, The Connors Group, 9812 Stewart Street, Bridgeport, CT 06610
2. Windslow and Associates, 2602 Marathon Drive, Columbus, OH 43214
3. Memo to Ralph Wilson from Stephen Carpenter, SUBJECT: Time-share Proposal
4. Memo to Nancy Harper from Edith G. Albertson, SUBJECT: Additions to the Budget Report
5. Memo to Margaret Roy from Frank Gibson, SUBJECT: Alternatives for Accounting Software

Lesson 54

1. Mr. Edmond Chambers, Sales Manager, Finney Enterprises, 8730 Collier Avenue, Jackson, MS 39209
2. Memo to Brenda Mitchell from Ron Stapleton, SUBJECT: Remodeling the Central Records Office
3. Mr. Charles C. Baxter, Wiley Products, Inc., 11790 Coral Reef Road, Miami, FL 33157

4. Memo to Word Processing Operators from Sharon Hunt, SUBJECT: Training Manual
5. Ms. Connie Evans, Valencia Industries, 545 Golden Lane, Des Moines, IA 50313

Lesson 55

1. Concord Hardware and Garden Supplies, 233 Belvidere Avenue, Jersey City, NJ 07306
2. Memo to Bill Carver from A. J. Schaefer, SUBJECT: Cost Report for Budget Meeting
3. Mallory and Associates, Surveyors, 1010 Vermont Street, Kansas City, MO 64054
4. Ms. Nancy Davenport, 490 San Carlos Avenue, Fresno, CA 93721
5. Memo to Robert Jackson from J. Gordon, SUBJECT: New Accounts for Classification

Lesson 56

1. Memo to Audit Supervisors from Irene Howe, SUBJECT: Registration for Auditing Classes
2. Mr. James Shaw, 460 Crescent Drive, Albany, NY 12202
3. Memo to Members of the City Council from Judith Denton, SUBJECT: Agenda for September Meeting
4. Mr. Clark Davidson, Plant Manager, Jefferson Foundries, 2909 South Delaware Street, Indianapolis, IN 46236
5. Form letter to property owners from Cynthia Stafford, County Clerk

Lesson 57

1. Memo to Henry Chase from Wayne Reynolds, SUBJECT: Postponing Street Repairs
2. Mr. Travis A. Richards, *The Daily Globe*, 1855 Berkeley Avenue, Memphis, TN 38111
3. Dr. and Mrs. David Conrad, 10917 Lakeshore Boulevard, Austin, TX 78703
4. Form letter to homeowners from Jack Hardwick, Director of Transportation
5. Form letter to citizens from Marjorie J. Pearson, Director of Urban Affairs

Lesson 58

1. Mr. Walter Belmont, 601 Spadina Crescent East, Saskatoon, SK S7K 3G8
2. Memo to All Department Heads from Joseph King, SUBJECT: Hosting State Auditors
3. Mr. and Mrs. Stephen Gray, 333 Marconi Drive, Madison, WI 53705
4. Memo to All Directors from Morgan C. Douglas, SUBJECT: Appointment of Judy Marshall to the Office of Development and Planning
5. Mr. Curtis B. Davidson, 7898 Grange Road, Allentown, PA 18106

Lesson 59

1. Mrs. Claudia Hamilton, 761 Wesley Oaks Drive, Atlanta, GA 30327
2. Miss Donna Edwards, 202 Staton Drive, Charleston, WV 25306
3. Board of Public Works, City Hall, 120 Wabash Avenue, Terre Haute, IN 47803
4. Miss Diana Arnold, 915 Crown Drive, Boise, ID 83706
5. Ms. Deborah Brown, Home and Hearth Restaurant, 2005 Coggins Avenue, Flint, MI 48507

Lesson 60

1. Form letter to residents from Dan Long, Chairman
2. Mr. Anthony T. Preston, 8232 Spring Valley Drive, Little Rock, AR 72201
3. Memo to County Extension Agents from Franklin G. Osgood, Chairman, SUBJECT: Conservation Studies
4. Mrs. Gail Carson, 301 North Elm Street, Oklahoma City, OK 73132
5. Ms. Lynn Hamilton, 7995 Chipman Road, Phoenix, AZ 85023